Kiruna

LAPPLAND

NORR-
BOTTEN

NORTHERN
NORRLAND

WITHDRAWN
By
Guthrie Memorial Library
Hanover's Public Library

Luleå

VÄSTER-
BOTTEN

Umeå

ÅNGERMAN-
LAND · Örnsköldsvik

sund

~~T~~HERN
~~R~~LAND

MEDELPAD
· Sundsvall

Gulf of
Bothnia

~~H~~ÄLSING-
LAND · Hudiksvall

GÄSTRIKLAND

Falun · Gävle

UPPLAND

MAN- · Uppsala
~~N~~D · EASTERN SVEALAND
Västerås

SÖDER-
MANLAND STOCKHOLM

· Nyköping

Linköping
~~Ö~~GÖTLAND

~~R~~N Visby
~~A~~ND GOTLAND

ÖLAND

almar Baltic Sea

~~G~~E
· Karlskrona

N GÖTALAND

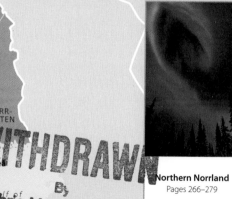

Northern Norrland
Pages 266–279

Gotland
Pages 162–173

Southern Norrland
Pages 250–265

Stockholm
Pages 50–123

Eastern Svealand
Pages 128–143

EYEWITNESS TRAVEL

SWEDEN

EYEWITNESS TRAVEL

SWEDEN

Main Contributors **Ulf Johansson,
Mona Neppenstrom, Kaj Sandell**

DK

Penguin
Random
House

Produced for Dorling Kindersley by Streiffert Förlag AB, Stockholm

Senior Editor Bo Streiffert

Project and Picture Editor Guy Engström

Assistant Picture Editor Ebba Mörner

Main Contributors Ulf Johansson, Mona Neppenström, Kaj Sandell

Photographers Peter Hanneberg, Erik Svensson, Jeppe Wikström

Cartographer Stig Söderlind

Illustrators
Stephen Conlin, Gary Cross, Urban Frank, Claire Littlejohn, Jan Rojmar, John Woodcock

English Translation Kate Lambert, Stuart Tudball

Editor of English Edition Jane Hutching

Printed and bound in China

First American edition 1995

16 17 18 19 10 9 8 7 6 5 4 3 2 1

Published in the United States by DK Publishing,
345 Hudson Street, New York, NY 10014

Reprinted with revisions 2008, 2011, 2014, 2017

Copyright 2005, 2017 © Dorling Kindersley Limited, London
A Penguin Random House Company

Published in the UK by Dorling Kindersley Limited.

A catalog record for this book is available from
the Library of Congress.

ISSN 1542-1554
ISBN 978-1-4654-5713-4

Floors are referred to throughout in accordance
with European usage; ie the "first floor" is the floor above ground level

MIX
Paper from
responsible sources
FSC
www.fsc.org   FSC™ C018179

**The information in this
DK Eyewitness Travel Guide is checked regularly.**
Every effort has been made to ensure that this book is as
up-to-date as possible at the time of going to press. Some details, however, such as
telephone numbers, opening hours, prices, gallery hanging arrangements and
travel information, are liable to change. The publishers cannot accept responsibility
for any consequences arising from the use of this book, nor for any material on third
party websites, and cannot guarantee that any website address in this book will be
a suitable source of travel information. We value the views and suggestions of our
readers very highly. Please write to:
Publisher, DK Eyewitness Travel Guides,
Dorling Kindersley, 80 Strand, London WC2R 0RL, UK,
or email: travelguides@dk.com.

Front cover main image: A typical Swedish boathouse in the Stockholm archipelago

◀ Traditional colorful fishing huts and boathouses along the wooden pier at Smögen

Summer-flowering cottongrass in the
mountains of Sylarna

Contents

Erik XIV's crown in the Treasury at
Stockholm's Royal Palace

Travellers' Needs

Cross-country skiers resting on Åreskutan mountain *(see p263)*

Lingonberries, a much-loved Swedish fruit

Survival Guide

Inner courtyard of Läckö Slott, Västergötland *(see p224)*

Sweden Area by Area

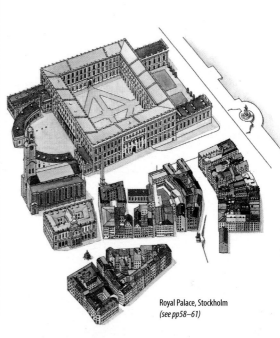

Royal Palace, Stockholm
(see pp58–61)

HOW TO USE THIS GUIDE

This guide helps you to get the most from your visit to Sweden. It provides both expert recommendations and detailed practical information. *Introducing Sweden* maps the country and sets it in its historical and cultural context. The ten regional chapters, including *Stockholm*, describe important sights using maps, photographs and illustrations. Suggestions on restaurants, hotels, shopping and entertainment are in *Travellers' Needs*. The *Survival Guide* has tips on everything from making a local telephone call to using local transportation, as well as information on money, etiquette and safety.

Stockholm

The centre of the capital and its surrounding area has been divided into four sightseeing areas. Each has its own chapter, which opens with a list of the sights to be covered. All sights are numbered and plotted on an area map. The detailed information for each sight follows the map's numerical order, making sights easy to locate within the chapter.

All pages relating to Stockholm have red thumb tabs.

Sights at a Glance lists the chapter's sights by category: Churches, Palaces and Museums, Historic Buildings, Streets and Squares.

A locator map shows where you are in relation to other areas of the city centre.

1 Area Map For easy reference, the sights are numbered and located on a map. Sights in the city centre are also shown on the Stockholm Street Finder on pages 118–23.

A suggested route for a walk is shown in red.

Stars indicate the sights that no visitor should miss.

2 Street-by-Street Map This gives a bird's eye view of the key areas in each chapter.

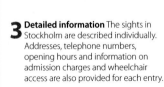

3 Detailed information The sights in Stockholm are described individually. Addresses, telephone numbers, opening hours and information on admission charges and wheelchair access are also provided for each entry.

Sweden Area by Area

Apart from Stockholm, Sweden has been divided into nine regions, each of which has a separate chapter. The most interesting towns and places to visit have been numbered on a *Regional Map*.

1 Introduction The landscape, history and character of each region is described here, showing how the area has developed over the centuries and what it offers to the visitor today.

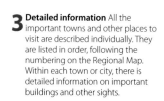

Each area of Sweden can be quickly identified by its colour coding, shown on the inside front cover.

2 Regional Map This shows the road network and gives an illustrated overview of the whole region. All interesting places to visit are numbered and there are also useful tips on getting around the region by car and train.

3 Detailed information All the important towns and other places to visit are described individually. They are listed in order, following the numbering on the Regional Map. Within each town or city, there is detailed information on important buildings and other sights.

For all the top sights, a Visitors' Checklist provides the practical information you will need to plan your visit.

Story boxes highlight noteworthy features of the top sights.

4 Sweden's top sights These are given two or more full pages. Historic buildings are dissected to reveal their interiors. The most interesting towns or city centres are shown in a bird's eye view, with sights picked out and described.

INTRODUCING
SWEDEN

DISCOVERING SWEDEN

The following tours have been created to take in a number of Sweden's highlights. In a country the size of Sweden, some long distance journeys are inevitable in order to reach more far-flung locations such as Lapland; however, the itineraries endeavour to keep travel distances realistic. To begin with, there are three two-day city tours, covering the capital Stockholm, Gothenburg and Malmö. These tours can be done individually or combined to form a seven- or ten-day tour, the latter with added suggestions. The city tours are followed by two seven-day tours taking in some of the most scenic parts of the country: the West Coast and Southern Sweden. Finally, there is a 14-day countrywide tour from south to north. Pick, choose and combine at your leisure.

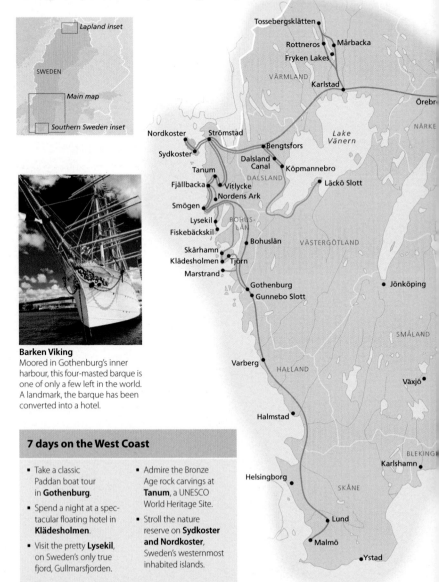

Barken Viking
Moored in Gothenburg's inner harbour, this four-masted barque is one of only a few left in the world. A landmark, the barque has been converted into a hotel.

7 days on the West Coast

- Take a classic Paddan boat tour in **Gothenburg**.

- Spend a night at a spectacular floating hotel in **Klädesholmen**.

- Visit the pretty **Lysekil**, on Sweden's only true fjord, Gullmarsfjorden.

- Admire the Bronze Age rock carvings at **Tanum**, a UNESCO World Heritage Site.

- Stroll the nature reserve on **Sydkoster and Nordkoster**, Sweden's westernmost inhabited islands.

◄ *Queen Christina of Sweden, surrounded by her court* by Louis-Michel Dumesnil the Younger

14 days in Sweden

- Take a dip at the Moorish-style bath house in **Varberg**, a famous sea-bathing resort.
- Hit the slopes at Midsummer at Europe's northernmost ski resort, **Riksgränsen**.
- See the scenic lakes in rural **Värmland** province.
- Admire the impressive towers of **Örebro Slott**.

- Stroll the narrow cobbled streets of Stockholm's **Gamla Stan**.
- Discover the unique 17th-century warship *Vasa* at **Vasamuseet**.
- Spend a night at **ICEHOTEL** in Lapland (in winter).
- Learn about Sami culture and reindeer herding in **Jukkasjärvi**.
- Explore the fishing communities of **Bohuslän**, on the West Coast.

Key

— Sweden tour
— West Coast tour
— Southern Sweden Tour

Örebro Slott
This castle, on an island in Svartån, is one of Örebro's most popular attractions.

7 days in Southern Sweden

- Admire the Turning Torso building in **Malmö's** Västra Hamnen (Western Harbour).
- Visit the stately home and former Benedictine convent of **Bosjökloster**.
- Enjoy a guided walk through the leafy forests of **Söderåsen National Park**.
- Take a boat tour in **Kristianstad** and explore the wetland centre and eco-museum Vattenriket.
- Marvel at the megalithic monument of **Ales Stenar**.

2 days in Stockholm

Sweden's capital Stockholm, spread across more than a dozen islands, has many must-see sights, including the medieval Old Town (Gamla Stan) and the impressive warship museum Vasamuseet.

- **Arriving** Arlanda, Stockholm's main airport, is located 37 km (23 miles) north of the city. The Arlanda Express train runs non-stop from the main railway station. The city also has three smaller airports.

- **Moving on** The journey from Stockholm to Gothenburg takes around 3 hours by express train. Hiring a car or taking a domestic flight are other options.

Day 1
Morning A couple of days in the Swedish capital give you enough time to take in the main sights. Spend a morning in medieval **Gamla Stan** (*pp54–67*), Stockholm's pedestrian-friendly Old Town. Don't miss viewing some of the 600-plus rooms at the **Royal Palace** (*pp58–61*), and pay a visit to **Livrustkammaren** (*p62*), Sweden's oldest museum. Around midday, be sure to catch the changing of the guard, in the Outer Courtyard. Gamla Stan is replete with cosy eateries, perfect for a lunchtime break.

Afternoon After lunch, amble across **Stortorget** square (*p64*), past the impressive 700-year-old late-Gothic cathedral **Storkyrkan** (*p63*), before entering **Riddarholmskyrkan** (*p66*), site of the royal burial vaults. Next, cross the waters of Riddarfjärden and head to **Stadshuset** (*pp106–7*), where the Nobel Prize dinners are held. End the day with drinks at the **Grand Hôtel** (*p83*), where you can enjoy fabulous city views.

Day 2
Morning Take time to discover the treasures of **Vasamuseet** (*pp96–7*) on the Djurgården

Splendidly frescoed ceiling in Stockholm's Baroque-style Royal Palace

island. The museum, the city's most popular, displays the *Vasa*, the only preserved 17th-century warship in the world, which capsized in Stockholm's harbour in 1628.

Afternoon Wander around the picturesque open-air museum and zoo at **Skansen** (*p98*), also on Djurgården, exploring historic buildings from across Sweden, as well as local folklore. Get a ferry across to Nybroplan and relax in the bar at **Berns** (*p85*), a Stockholm drinking and dining institution.

To extend your trip…
Spend a day trip combining **Drottningholm** palace (*pp112–15*) and the Viking settlement of **Birka** (*pp136–7*), and another exploring the **Stockholm Archipelago** (*pp116–17*) by boat.

---

2 days in Gothenburg

Gothenburg, Sweden's second biggest city, has an interesting mix of Dutch-style canals, pleasant gardens and excellent restaurants.

- **Arriving** Landvetter, Gothenburg's airport, is located 20 km (13 miles) southeast of the city. There is an airport bus service from the city's main coach and rail terminal. The airport is not open to commercial traffic.

- **Moving on** The journey from Gothenburg to Malmö takes just over 3 hours by train. Alternatively, it is possible to hire a car.

Day 1
Morning Start the day at **Trädgårdsföreningen** (*p202*), a beautiful park where you can admire the flora of five continents, including 1,900 varieties of rose. Next, take a **Paddan Boat Tour** (*p209*) along the 17th-century canals.

Afternoon After lunch, walk up Kungsportsavenyn, the city's main avenue, viewing Stora Teatern on the way to **Götaplatsen** (*pp204–5*), which has a bronze statue of Poseidon at its centre. Admire the collection of Nordic art at **Konstmuseet** (*pp204–5*) or catch an exhibition at nearby **Konsthallen** (*p205*).

Resident wolves at Skansen zoo, in Stockholm

Malmöhus fortress, built in the 1500s and surrounded by a deep moat

Continue to **Liseberg** musement park (p204) for family fun and impressive rides, including the biggest roller-coaster in the Nordic countries. The park offers plenty of dining and entertainment options.

Day 2
Morning Spend a morning shopping in **Nordstan** (p303), one of the busiest malls; those who prefer independent stores can head to the quirky designer boutiques near **Kronhuset** (p201) and the craft shops in **Kronhusbodarna** sheds (p201), Gothenburg's oldest buildings. Make a lunchtime visit to the bustling fish market, **Feskekôrka** (p205), where you can sample delicious West Coast fish and seafood.

Afternoon Venture into peaceful **Slottsskogen** (p208) for an exploratory wander. The park has some interesting old cottages, and the azalea valley is a must in springtime. Stop at **Naturhistoriska museum** (p208), Gothenburg's oldest museum, inside the park, to see some of the 10 million exhibits.

To extend your trip...
Take a boat to **Nya Älvsborgs Fästning** (p209), a mid-17th-century fortress at the mouth of the Göta Älv.

2 days in Malmö

Malmö, Sweden's third city and its most ethnically diverse, is located just across the strait from Denmark. It is a vibrant, cosmopolitan centre.

- **Arriving** Malmö is served by Sturup airport, located 28 km (17 miles) to the east; airport buses run from downtown Malmö around 30 times a day. Malmö is also easily reached from Copenhagen's airport, Kasturp, which is half an hour away by train.

Day 1
Morning Head for the historic centre, encircled by canals. The main square, **Stortorget** (p182), is surrounded by fine buildings, several of which are open to the public. Take in the impressive façades of **Rådhuset** (p182) and **Jörgen Kocks Hus** (p182), both of which date back to the 16th century, and **Residenset** (p182). Venture into Malmö's 12th-century cathedral **St Petri Kyrka** (p182) to admire the Renaissance altar, before stopping for coffee in **Lilla Torg** (p184), one of the city's most charming squares.

Afternoon Spend the afternoon discovering the art collections at **Moderna Museet** (p182), which is housed inside an old power station.

Day 2
Morning Wander through the pleasant parks of central Malmö, **Slottsparken** (p184) and Kungsparken, strolling along their quaint canals. Make a special stop at **Malmöhus** (p184). An enormous 15th-century structure surrounded by a deep moat, this is the oldest Renaissance castle in Scandinavia and now houses **Malmö Museum** (p184). Don't miss the 18th-century tower with original cannons.

Afternoon A short walk from Malmöhus stands **Kommendanthuset** (p184), a former storage building now used for temporary art shows. Sneak a peek inside for the latest exhibition, then continue to **Västra Hamnen** (Western Harbour) (p185), one of the city's most recent architectural developments. This area is located right by the sea, in the city's former shipyard, and it is home to the impressive **Turning Torso** tower (p185), completed in 2005. The building is mainly residential and therefore not open to the public, but it can be admired from the outside. Complete the afternoon with a leisurely stop at one of the seaside promenade bars or restaurants.

To extend your trip...
Spend a day in quaint **Ystad** (p186), enjoying its medieval architecture.

Malmö's stunning Turning Torso lit up in colour

7 days on the West Coast

- **Airports** Arrive and depart from Gothenburg's Landvetter airport.
- **Transport** The West Coast is best explored by car, although many coastal communities can be reached by train and bus. There are regular ferries from the mainland to many of the islands, including Sydkoster and Nordkoster. The train journey from Gothenburg to Strömstad takes 3 hours.
- **Booking ahead** Day 2: Salt & Sill floating hotel; Day 5: Nordens Ark. To extend your trip: Gunnebo Slott, Dalsland Canal boat trip.

Day 1: Gothenburg
Pick a day from the city itinerary on pages 12–13.

> **To extend your trip...**
> Take a day trip to the Neo-Classical **Gunnebo Slott** *(p229)*, with its beautiful park and garden.

Day 2: Gothenburg to Klädesholmen
Spend the morning exploring Gothenburg further, strolling through the old workers' quarter of **Haga** *(p205)*, now one of the city's trendiest neighbourhoods. Peek into the old wood-and-stone houses, home to interesting craft and design shops, then enjoy a coffee in one of the pretty cafés.
After lunchtime, travel to **Marstrand** *(pp220–21)*, only 45 minutes away by car (1 hour by bus), and pay a visit to Carlstens Fästning, a 17th-century fortress that served as a prison in the 1700s. A guided tour offers a fascinating glimpse into life behind its walls. Spend the night at Salt & Sill, Sweden's first floating hotel; it is located on Klädesholmen, a tiny outcrop on **Tjörn** *(p220)*, one of the West Coast's main islands.

Day 3: Skärhamn to Lysekil
Start the day in **Skärhamn** *(p220)*, the main town on Tjörn. A lively, vibrant community with a scenic location, it is best known for the Nordiska Akvarellmuseet (Nordic Watercolour Museum), housed in an attractive building jutting out into the water. Catch one of the exhibitions, before visiting Pilane nearby. It is an Iron Age burial site with impressive stone circles, sculptures and standing stones on the northwest side of Tjörn. Follow the coastal road north to **Lysekil** *(p218)*. Located in Gullmarsfjorden, Sweden's only real fjord, Lysekil is a charming, long-established seaside resort. Wander through 200-year-old Gamlestaden and admire the quaint architecture of the restored 19th-century sea-bathing area.

Day 4: Lysekil to Fjällbacka
Take a short ferry ride across to **Fiskebäckskil** *(p219)*. This seafaring community, dating back to the late 19th century, is home to many picturesque wooden cottages and plenty of local colour. Spend the morning strolling around the village, before returning to Lysekil by ferry. Continue on to **Smögen** *(p217)*, one of Sweden's largest fishing communities, for some delicious seafood, then aim to reach **Fjällbacka** *(pp216–17)* in the afternoon. Use this village as your base over the next two nights.

Day 5: Fjällbacka and Nordens Ark
A former herring fishing port, Fjällbacka has retained its

Sea-kayaking in the waters of Fjällbacka

seafaring heritage and village atmosphere, despite increasing numbers of visitors. The low-rise wooden houses are painted in bright pastel colours and the harbour area buzzes with restaurants and bars. Try sea-kayaking, or visit some of the outlying islands by ferry. Then take the 3-km (2-mile) trail at nearby nature park **Nordens Ark** *(p217)*, home to several endangered species.

Day 6: Tanum and Vitlycke
Visit **Tanum** *(p216)*, a UNESCO World Heritage Site renowned for its Bronze Age rock carvings. To view the largest of the rock carvings (200 sq m/2,150 sq ft), visit **Vitlycke Museum** *(p216)*, which also has interesting Bronze Age displays. Further carvings can be viewed at Fossum, Tegneby and Asberget, all in the surrounding area.

Day 7: Koster Islands
Take a morning ferry from **Strömstad** *(p215)* and explore Sweden's most westerly inhabited islands,

Panoramic view of Marstrand, a fashionable seaside resort

Sydkoster and **Nordkoster** (p215), part of a nature reserve and marine national park. Sydkoster is best explored by bike, while its smaller neighbour, Nordkoster, is easy to walk around. Both islands are well known for their varied flora, peaceful atmosphere and quaint fishing huts.

> **To extend your trip...**
> Take a boat trip along the scenic **Dalsland Canal** (p214) down to Lake Vänern, or visit the splendid **Läckö Slott** (p224) on the lake's southern side.

7 days in Southern Sweden

- **Airports** Arrive and depart from Malmö Airport.
- **Transport** Southern Sweden is best explored by car, although trains and buses connect towns and villages with the main hubs.
- **Booking ahead** Day 3: Höör Stone Age village; Day 4: Söderåsen National Park; Day 5: Vattenriket river tour.

Day 1: Malmö
Pick a day from the city itinerary on page 13.

Day 2: Lund
Explore the historic university town of **Lund** (p181). Start with a visit to Lund Domkyrka, the 12th-century cathedral, home to a 14th-century astronomical clock, then continue on to the university grounds, which feature some of the oldest university buildings in the country. Next, enjoy Kulturen, an open-air museum with many well-preserved cottages and town houses. If there's time, head to Historiska Museet, which has one of Sweden's largest archaeological collections.

Day 3: Bosjökloster, Höör and Frostavallen
Start the morning at **Bosjökloster** (p180), scenically

An attractive medieval church in the Swedish coastal town of Åhus

situated on the shore of the Ringsjön lakes. This remarkable set of buildings was originally a Benedictine convent dating back to 1080. Today it's Skåne's most popular stately home, with extensive grounds, a restaurant, café and boat hire. Nearby **Höör** (p180) has a Stone Age village where visitors can sample life as it was back then. Continue to the area of **Frostavallen** (p180), one of the most scenic in Skåne, for some late-afternoon canoeing or swimming in Lake Vaxsjön. There are also hiking trails, leisure facilities and plenty of overnight options.

Day 4: Söderåsen National Park and Kristianstad
Take a stroll in **Söderåsen National Park** (p179), which covers a wide variety of landscapes; 1- or 2-hour guided tours give a good overview. Aim to reach the 17th-century town of **Kristianstad** (p190) in the afternoon, in time to visit the main attraction there, the Renaissance Heliga Trefaldighetskyrkan church.

A pretty half-timbered house in one of the idyllic alleys in Ystad

Day 5: Kristianstad and Åhus
Kristianstad's wetland centre and eco-museum **Vattenriket** (p190) can be explored on a guided river tour. Next, head to **Åhus** (p190), a picturesque coastal community surrounded by sandy beaches. Follow the coastal route south, taking in the rolling, fertile landscape of **Österlen** (p187), in the southeast.

Day 6: Ystad with Ales Stenar and Marsvinsholm Slott
Spend the morning discovering the Hanseatic and Danish influences in **Ystad** (p186). Note the medieval buildings, some dating from the 11th century, and the traditional half-timbered houses found in the old parts of the centre. In the afternoon, visit **Ales Stenar** (p186), a megalithic monument in the shape of a ship, before going on to **Marsvinsholms Slott** (p186), an imposing 14th-century castle with beautiful grounds.

Day 7: Östarp, Övedskloster and Malmö
Pay a visit to **Östarp** (pp180–81), a living open-air museum complete with a charming old-world inn. Next, visit another monastery turned stately home, **Övedskloster** (pp180–81), built in Rococo style and surrounded by an elegant park. In the afternoon, return to Malmö.

> **To extend your trip...**
> Relax in the twin towns of **Skanör** and **Falsterbo** (p181). Visit **Helsingborg** (p178–9), **Sofiero Castle** (p179) and **Bjärehalvön** (p178), on Skåne's west coast.

14 days in Sweden

- **Airports** Arrive at Malmö Airport or Kastrup in Copenhagen *(see p326)* and return from Kiruna airport via Stockholm.

- **Transport** Due to the size of Sweden, the country is best explored by car, particularly to reach some of the more remote areas. Trains and buses connect smaller towns and villages with the main hubs, while ferries ply the West Coast, Stockholm Archipelago and some of the larger lakes. To reach Lapland, take a domestic flight to Kiruna or the overnight train from Stockholm.

- **Booking ahead** Day 3: Tour of Gunnebo Slott; Day 7: Dalsland Canal Tour; Day 8: Tour of Mårbacka and Rottneros; Day 9: Gripsholms Slott; Days 11–12: Overnight train or domestic flight; Days 12–14: Kungsleden Trail.

Day 1: Malmö
Pick a day from the city itinerary on page 13.

Day 2: Lund
Spend a day exploring medieval **Lund** *(p181)*. This former capital of Denmark is now a thriving university town. Don't miss Kulturen, the open-air museum in the medieval centre, which

The Neo-Classical southern façade of Gunnebo Slott

has well-preserved old town houses and cottages. The university – the second largest in Sweden – boasts some of the oldest university buildings in the country. Make time to visit the cathedral, Lund Domkyrka, where the Gothic altarpiece and astronomical clock are well worth a look.

Day 3: Southern coastal road Lund–Gothenburg
Follow the southern coastal highway north from Lund and make a stop at **Varberg** *(p230)*. A 19th-century spa and sea-bathing resort, Varberg has plenty of seaside charm. Visit the Moorish-style cold bath house and the impressive fortress, Varbergs Fästning. Continue on to **Gunnebo Slott** *(p229)*, a magnificent mansion built in Neo-Classical Swedish style just outside Gothenburg. Tour the mansion, as well as its park and gardens, before ending the day in Gothenburg.

Day 4: Gothenburg
Pick a day from the city itinerary on pages 12–13.

Day 5: Northern coastal road Gothenburg–Strömstad
Continue along the northern coastal route through **Bohuslän** *(pp215–21)*, one of the most picturesque provinces in Sweden, replete with tiny fishing communities and seaside resorts. Pass two of the largest islands along the coast, **Tjörn** *(p220)* and **Orust** *(p220)*, then stretch your legs at **Smögen** *(p217)*, a lively

Ivy-covered building on the campus of Lund University

summer resort. Wander along the wooden quayside and sample the catch of the day – shrimps are truly a delight here. Next, head further north to **Fjällbacka** *(pp216–17)*, another charming seaside village. Admire the quaint wooden houses and amble the narrow streets, soaking up the atmosphere. Take a short drive inland and stop at **Tanum** *(p216)* to view the extraordinary **Vitlycke** Bronze Age rock carvings, a UNESCO World Heritage Site *(p216)*. End the day in **Strömstad** *(p215)*, the northernmost resort on the Swedish West Coast.

Carl Milles' statue of *Poseidon* on Götaplatsen, Gothenburg

Day 6: Koster Islands
Spend a leisurely day on **Sydkoster** and **Nordkoster** *(p215)*. These two islands, easily reached from Strömstad, form a nature reserve that is renowned for its flora, and they're also part of Sweden's first marine

national park, **Kosterhavets** *(p215)*. In the morning, hire a bike to get around Sydkoster, the larger of the two, and take a picnic lunch to enjoy alfresco. Then take the inter-island ferry link to quieter Nordkoster, which is best explored on foot. Return by ferry to Strömstad in the late afternoon.

Day 7: Dalsland Canal

Arrive at Bengtsfors, and start the day with a quick walk around Gammelgården open-air museum before joining the **Dalsland Canal Tour** *(p214)*. The 5½-hour boat trip from Bengtsfors to Köpmannebro, on Lake Vänern, passes some stunning scenery, as well as rock carvings, manor houses and the spectacular Håverud Aqueduct, on its journey through 19 locks. Return to Bengtsfors by bus or train (1 hour), then drive to **Karlstad** *(p238)* or, if using public transport, continue north along Lake Vänern, ending the day in Karlstad.

Day 8: Exploring Värmland

Use Karlstad as a two-night base. Take a day trip around scenic parts of the province of Värmland, home to many artists, writers and poets. Drive north to the **Fryken Lakes** *(p236)*, three striking lakes in the heart of the province. Follow their east side and stop at **Mårbacka** *(p236)*, the family estate of Selma Lagerlöf, the first woman to be awarded the Nobel Prize for Literature. Take a guided tour of the beautiful manor house and gardens. Head north, then

Gripsholms Slott, home of the National Portrait Gallery

cross over to the west side of the lakes at Sunne to reach **Tossebergsklätten** *(p236)*, a hill near the northernmost lake, Övre Fryken, for splendid views of the surrounding landscape. Next, follow the west side of the lakes south to **Rottneros** *(p236)*, another superb manor house with a unique sculpture park and gardens. Return to Karlstad in the evening.

Day 9: Örebro and Gripsholms Slott

Örebro *(pp242–3)*, on Svartån River near Lake Hjälmaren, has a long-standing history and some impressive sights, including the massive 13th-century castle, Örebro Slott, now seat of the county governor. Take a tour around the Northwest Tower, then admire the façades of the Neo-Gothic-style town hall and St Nicolai Kyrka.

Spend the afternoon taking in the splendours of **Gripsholms Slott** *(pp138–9)*, one of Sweden's most stunning castles, surrounded by Lake Mälaren. The 16th-century castle has a vast collection of portraits in its National Portrait Gallery and some particularly fine pieces of furniture. End the day in Stockholm.

Days 10–11: Stockholm

Follow the city itineraries on page 12.

Days 12–14: Lapland

Sweden's remote frontier, Lapland offers the visitor the opportunity to get up close and personal with nature and experience the great outdoors.

If visiting in winter, spend a night at ICEHOTEL in **Jukkasjärvi** *(p276)*, sampling Arctic cuisine, experiencing Sami culture and taking in a Northern Lights, snow-mobile or husky-sled tour. Next, move on to one of three ski resorts in the area, **Björkliden**, **Abisko** or **Riksgränsen** *(p279)* for some quality cross-country or downhill skiing.

In summer, spend a couple of days hiking amid the stunning scenery. Take the train (or drive) from **Kiruna** *(p276)*, northern Lapland's main hub, to Abisko, part of the scenic **Kungsleden Trail** *(pp278–9)*, and follow the trail through Abisko National Park to Abiskojaure. Alternatively, continue by train to **Riksgränsen**, where skiing on the high slopes is still possible as late as Midsummer.

Opening one of the 19 locks on the Dalsland Canal

Putting Sweden on the Map

The kingdom of Sweden is one of the largest countries in Europe, covering 449,964 sq km (173,732 sq miles). The most southerly point, Smygehuk, lies at about the same latitude as Edinburgh in Scotland, and the northernmost tip, Treriksröset, is nearly 300 km (186 miles) north of the Arctic Circle. As the crow flies, Sweden is 1,572 km (977 miles) from south to north – the same distance as from Smygehuk to Rome. Sweden shares land borders with Norway to the west and Finland to the east, and water borders with Germany, Poland, Estonia, Latvia, Lithuania, Russia and Denmark, which lies across the Kattegat.

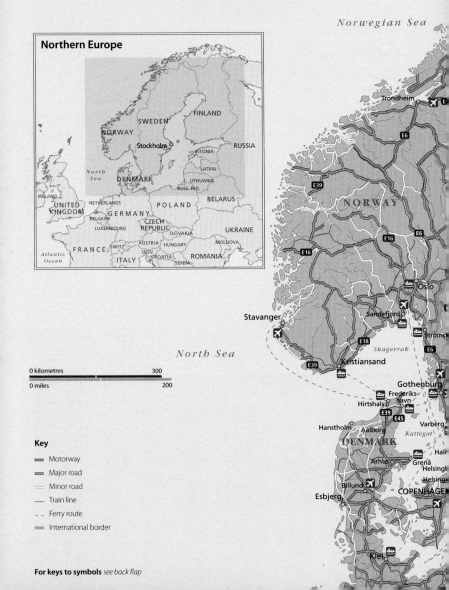

Northern Europe

0 kilometres 300

0 miles 200

Key

▬▬ Motorway

▬▬ Major road

····· Minor road

— Train line

– – Ferry route

▬▬ International border

For keys to symbols see back flap

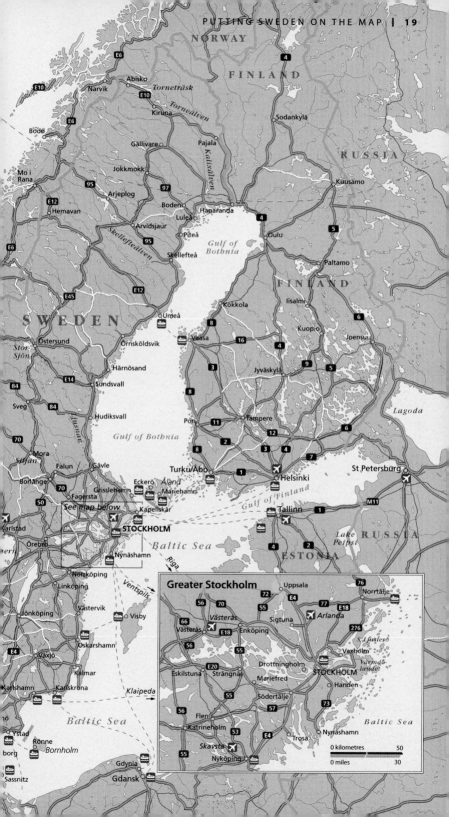

A PORTRAIT OF SWEDEN

Swedes are passionate about nature and the great outdoors, and justly so since their country contains large swathes of Europe's last surviving areas of wilderness. As a nation, Sweden has built its wealth on its natural resources and the ingenuity of its engineers. It has a heritage rich in music, literature and folk traditions, and its people have a deep-rooted sense of peace and democracy.

Few nations in Europe offer such an exceptionally diverse landscape, rich in flora and fauna, as Sweden. From north of the Arctic Circle the country stretches a lengthy 1,572 km (977 miles) south, a distance equal to almost half the length of Europe.

The extreme north is the land of the midnight sun, where daylight lasts for 24 hours in high summer, but is almost non-existent in mid-winter. Moving southwards, the forests and wetlands of Norrland provide habitats for large numbers of elk and a thriving birdlife. In the far south, the rolling plains of Skåne and the area around the great lakes make good arable land.

To the east, the green islands of the Stockholm archipelago contrast with the bare rocky outline of the west coast.

A Country Shaped by Ice

The mountain chain which runs along part of Sweden's border with northern Norway has several peaks more than 2,000 m (6,500 ft) high. It was formed when the ice which covered the country until 10,000 years ago retreated northwards. Several glaciers from this time still linger in the north.

The Climate

Sweden has a relatively mild climate for its northerly location. However, because of the length of the country, the temperature in autumn and spring can vary by more than 20° C (68° F) from one end to the other. Northern Sweden holds the record for the coldest temperature of -53° C (-63° F), while Ultuna, near Uppsala, has recorded the highest temperature of 38° C (100° F).

Start of the annual Vasaloppet race, which attracts some 16,000 skiers

◀ A knight parading during Gotland Medieval Week in Visby

Lars Magnus Ericsson, setting Sweden on the path to industrialization by founding Ericsson in 1876

There are occasional green winters in southern Sweden, but the heaviest snow fell in 1998, with 150 cm (5 ft) accumulating on 4–5 December in Gävle in central Sweden.

Space for All

Sweden covers an area of 449,964 sq km (173,732 sq miles) and with a population of around 10 million inhabitants, Swedes have plenty of space. In the forested areas, towns can be few and far between.

Towards the end of the 19th century and thanks largely to the coming of the railways, Sweden began to exploit its rich natural resources. Forestry and copper industries were established and the rivers were harnessed to produce hydro-electricity. Large manufacturing companies began to develop, such as Ericsson, Volvo and Scania, all of which are still in operation today. The needs of industry led to a massive shift in population. Today 85 per cent of the population lives in the cities and less than 2 per cent is employed in agriculture.

In the postwar period the need for labour led to immigration. The flow of immigrants became even greater at the end of the 20th century and the beginning of the 21st century with the arrival of refugees from the world's trouble spots.

Government and Politics

Sweden is both a parliamentary democracy and a hereditary monarchy. As the head of state, the king has no political power, but he is considered to be an important representative of Sweden to the rest of the world. Carl XVI Gustaf is the descendant of one of Napoleon's marshals, Jean-Baptiste Bernadotte, who was chosen as the heir to the throne of the last of the Vasa kings, the childless Karl XIII. The Frenchman was crowned in 1818 as Carl XIV Johan, King of Sweden and Norway. Carl XVI Gustaf came to the throne in 1973 and married the German Silvia Sommerlath. Despite doubt over the king's choice of a commoner for his bride, Swedes soon took Queen Silvia to their hearts. The couple's eldest daughter, Crown Princess Victoria, is the heir to the throne.

Sweden's parliament, the Riksdag, has 349 members and is Sweden's legislative assembly. Elections are held every four years.

Since World War II, a balance has prevailed between the socialist and non-socialist parties in parliament. With a few exceptions, the Social Democrats, as the largest group, have governed, either alone or with smaller supporting parties, though in recent years, coalition governments have run the country.

Emblem of state

Taxation remains high, but the majority of Swedes tend to believe that they get value for money. However, an economic crisis in the 1990s led to cuts in health, education and social care. The environment is a key issue. Swedes have a deep-rooted love of nature, enshrined in the Right of Public Access, which guarantees free access to the forests and countryside and the right to pick berries and mushrooms. There is widespread support for combating pollution.

Languages and Dialects

While Swedish is the dominant language, Finnish, Tornedalsfinska (the dialect of Finnish spoken in the Torne Valley) and Sami are all official minority languages. The largest of these is Finnish with around 20,000 speakers, while Sami languages are spoken by about 10,000 people.

Sweden players celebrate after scoring a goal against Moldova during a qualifying match for the UEFA Women's Euro 2017

Despite the general use of standard Swedish, dialects also flourish. The majority is multilingual and Swedes in general are often fluent in English.

Rich Culture

Besides the many specialist museums in the cities, there are more than 1,000 rural museums. Great interest is shown in art and handicrafts which can be seen in the galleries and shops.

Swedes are keen musicians, and the country is now one of the biggest exporters of pop music. Folk music and dancing enjoy a natural high season from Midsummer to the end of August. Sweden has won the Eurovision Song Contest six times, with its victory in 2015.

The story of film culture also has a Swedish chapter, thanks to stars such as Greta Garbo, Ingrid Bergman, Max von Sydow and Stellan Skarsgård.

A Sporting Nation

Sweden's abundance of clean, unpolluted waters makes fishing a popular hobby, and the long coastline, glorious archipelagos and numerous waterways have made it a nation of sailors.

Sweden has proud traditions, especially in winter sports. Skiing and ice hockey as well as football, handball, bandy (Russian hockey), tennis and golf, all set Swedish pulses racing, while swimming, athletics, boxing, water sports and motorsports also number several stars at international level.

Sweden on the World Stage

The neutrality which protected Sweden from two world wars is still officially observed, though in reality Sweden is more closely aligned with the US and NATO than ever before.

Sweden has been a member of the EU since 1995 and elections to the European Parliament are held every five years. The attitude towards the EU is divided and in 2003, the Swedes voted "no" to adopting the euro by a considerable majority.

Sweden is an enthusiastic advocate for the work of the UN. Its own Dag Hammarskjöld was a celebrated Secretary-General (1953–61), and Swedish troops have been involved in operations worldwide.

Sheltered archipelagos provide ideal conditions for Sweden's sailing enthusiasts

Landscape and Wildlife

Sweden has a remarkably varied landscape. The flat arable land of Skåne in the south gives way to lakes and forests, rugged mountains, fast-flowing rivers and wild open moorland further north, leading to the Arctic tundra. Plant and animal species from both continental Europe and the Arctic thrive. Large areas of wilderness have become enclaves where endangered species such as bears and wolves, snakes and owls have been able to survive the increased pressure from civilization. The coastline, too, is immensely varied. Marine life is unique, as North Sea fish make their way into the brackish water of the Baltic and mix with species normally only found in fresh water.

Wolves are a threatened species and, despite migration from neighbouring countries, there are only around 350 in Sweden.

Coasts and Islands

Smooth rocks and sandy beaches dominate the west coast, where marine life includes saltwater fish such as cod and haddock. Freshwater pike and whitefish can be found off the northerly stretches of the east coast. On the limestone islands of Öland and Gotland orchid meadows flourish.

Seals declined in number as a result of hunting, pollution and disease. But now populations of grey seals, ringed seals and harbour seals (pictured) are increasing, thanks to their protected status.

Sea eagles, with a wing span of up to 250 cm (8 ft), are Sweden's largest birds of prey. They nest along the east coast and also on lakes in Lappland.

The Arable South

The flat lands of Skåne with their fields of crops, willow windbreaks and half-timbered houses topped by storks' nests are a familiar image of Sweden. But just as typical are the stony pastures and juniper slopes of Småland surrounding red cottages, and the meadows and pasture lands of Mälardalen.

Roe deer were almost extinct in the early 19th century. Now they are so common in southern and central Sweden that they are known to raid local gardens in search of food.

Hedgehogs rely on their 5,000 spines for protection and curl into a ball at the approach of danger. But this is of little effect against cars, and the popular doorstep guest is in decline.

Sweden's Flora

Considering Sweden's unusually rich flora, it is not surprising that the father of botany, Carl von Linné *(see p134)*, was born here. There are more than 2,000 species of flowers alone. After a long cold winter, nature explodes into life with a profusion of blooms, as in the orchid meadows of Öland. Swedes' love of wild flowers is illustrated by the maypoles and garlands used to celebrate Midsummer.

Wood anemones carpeting the forests signal the arrival of spring.

The red water lily can only be found in some lakes in Tiveden National Park.

King Karl's Spire can grow 1 m (3 ft) tall – an impressive height for an orchid. It is most common in swampy mountain areas.

Forests

More than half of Sweden's land area is covered by forests, with deciduous trees in the south, coniferous forests with pines and spruce further north. Here lingonberries, blueberries and chanterelles grow. This is the home of elk and beaver, and forest birds such as capercaillies and black grouse.

The elk is the big game of the forest. Around 100,000 elk are killed in the annual hunting season and, despite the road warning signs, others die in accidents involving cars.

The brown bear is the largest of Sweden's predators and can weigh up to 300 kg (660 lb). It may look slow, but it moves quickly and is dangerous if disturbed.

The Far North

The mountains and moorlands are characterized by their proximity to the Arctic. With late spring come the migratory birds such as hooper swans and the lesser white-fronted goose, and the mountain flora bursts into flower. Wolves, bears, wolverine and lynx inhabit the national parks.

Reindeer live as domesticated animals in northern Sweden, farmed by Sami in the mountains and forests. In winter the herds move further south to graze.

The ptarmigan lives above the tree line and is often encountered, as it is unafraid of mountain hikers. It follows the changing seasons with up to four changes of plumage.

Sweden's Wooden Houses

The quintessential image of Sweden is the red-and-white painted wooden cottage. Originally, wooden houses were not considered attractive so they were painted red to make them look as though they were built of brick, or yellow to represent stone, and this tradition has continued. Every building from the humblest hut to the most majestic mansion was made of timber from the large tracts of forest. Wood triumphs in the grandiose manor houses of Hälsingland and the decoratively carved merchants' homes of the Stockholm Archipelago. Even today, architects are developing innovative ways of using this classic material.

Bell Tower
Many 18th-century churches had wooden bell towers: Delsbo's, with its elegant onion cupola, dates from 1742.

Hut in Härjedalen
This simple log-built hut in the mountain pasture of Ruändan incorporates the centuries-old tradition of a grass roof.

Interlocking posts bind together the external and interior walls, while the façades are often boarded.

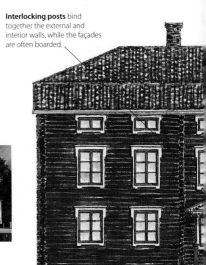

Skogaholm Manor
Built in the 1680s, this Carolean timber house from Närke was originally painted red. In the 1790s, it was given a yellow plaster façade and large windows in line with Gustavian style. It has now been moved to the museum at Skansen.

The façade is clad in pine and painted with a copper-vitriol paint, known as Falun Red, to prevent rotting.

Halsingland's Manor Houses

Reaping the benefits from the lucrative 19th-century timber industry, the forest-owning farmers of Hälsingland built themselves extravagant manor houses. The size of house and magnificence of the painted portico reflected the owner's wealth and status. The interiors were often decorated with wall paintings.

Societetshuset
Decorative wooden buildings, such as this club house for wealthy visitors to the seaside town of Marstrand *(see p220)*, were a feature of the fashionable west coast bathing resorts in the late 19th century.

Swedenborg's Pavilion
The miniature manor house of philosopher Emanuel Swedenborg (1688–1772). It is now at Skansen *(see p98)*.

Modern Wooden Architecture
The Nordic Watercolour Museum *(see p220)* in Skärhamn on the west coast opened in 2000. The Danish architects Bruun/Corfitsen have clad the building's steel and concrete shell with vertical wooden panels in red, using this traditional material in a public setting.

Wooden Lighthouse
Dating from 1840, the wooden lighthouse at Bönan also served as a pilot station. It marked the shipping route into Gävle. The building is now a museum.

Two-storey houses are common in Hälsingland. The finest have an attic floor with half-windows.

Merchant's House in the Archipelago
In the late 19th century Stockholm's upper middle classes spent their summers in the archipelago, where they built magnificent wooden villas with verandas, summer houses, bathing huts and boat houses.

Foundations are a course of cobblestones.

Porticoes and outer doors are particularly richly ornamented and painted. Other details include turned pillars, intricate woodcarving and elegant roofs. The designs vary from parish to parish.

Fishing Cottages at Kungshamn
In fishing villages on the rocky islands of Bohuslän, where space is tight, timber-clad houses in pastel shades crowd in higgledy-piggledy fashion around the harbours.

Decorative Woodwork
More expensive wooden houses dating from around 1900 were often a riot of fretwork and rich ornamentation, known as "carpenter's joy", on verandas, entrances and gables.

Traditions, Customs and Folklore

Since the late 20th century, globalization and the gradual erosion of regional identity have had a major impact on Swedish traditions and lifestyle. Much of the formerly rigid etiquette has been relaxed and today Swedes are more informal when it comes to dress and manners. However, despite this culture shift, Swedes still hold onto their roots, local customs, history and traditions. They are passionate about their little red cottages, the countryside, eating herring at Midsummer and enjoying the first fresh strawberries.

Sami in traditional costume for a celebratory occasion

Feasts and Festivities

Celebrating the high points of the year within the family has again become increasingly important, after a dismissive attitude towards tradition in the 1960s and 70s.

Many traditions have pagan origins, most of them related to the coming and going of seasons, and are an excuse to eat special treats and play games. The most important is Midsummer, the summer solstice feast. Along with dancing and games around the maypole, the light, short night (when all sorts of magic is in the air) can be marked by watching the sun set and rise a few hours apart (or hardly at all in the north). For those who go to bed it is the custom to pick seven different flowers in silence and place them under their pillow; their future partner will appear in their dreams. Walpurgis night, 30 April, is when the last day of winter is chased away with huge bonfires, and songs and speeches welcome spring. Lucia Day, in December, is an intricate mix of pagan and Christian, a festival of light at the onslaught of darkness, which has adopted a Christian martyr as its symbol of hope and bringer of light. Every school, office and church has a Lucia, a girl dressed in white with a red ribbon around her waist symbolizing the martyr's blood, and a crown of candles on her head *(see p35)*.

Easter also has elements of old folk beliefs. Maundy Thursday is the day witches fly to Blåkulla *(see p158)* to dance with the devil. Today, children dress up, broomsticks and all, and give handmade Easter greetings cards in exchange for sweets. Christmas is preceded by the hectic run-up of Advent, when Swedes go partying and consume vast quantities of *glögg* (mulled wine usually mixed with cognac or vodka), *lussebullar* (saffron buns) and *pepparkakor* (ginger snaps).

Dress and Etiquette

Those who own a folk costume take it out for Midsummer, folk dances, weddings and other formal occasions. Each region has its own historic style and there is also a national dress *(see p20)*. The Sami have their own elaborate costumes.

At weddings people are expected to dress up, as specified on the invitation (white tie, black tie or suit). In everyday life, style is more casual, especially in summer.

Although Swedes are more easy-going these days, they are still fond of etiquette. It is important to know how to *"skål"*. Swedes first raise their glass to their female partner at the table, and then to the hostess. People look each other in the eye while raising their glass and saying *"skål"*, looking down as they drink and then re-establishing eye contact before putting down their glass. If the *skål* is communal, everyone has to look each person around the table in the eye before drinking.

Despite this interest in etiquette, Swedes tend not to observe minor courtesies such as holding open doors or apologizing when they bump into someone. They are very informal when addressing one another; everyone is on first name terms from the start, even when doing business.

Singers and Musicians

More than half a million Swedes sing in a choir, and their passion for song is reflected not just in

Midsummer celebrations with games and dancing round the maypole

singing at parties and the ever-increasing repertoire of drinking songs, but also in the popularity of singing together. There are few 50th birthday parties where each plate doesn't come with a songbook or where friends don't perform songs they have written themselves. Everyone is expected to know works by troubadour Carl Bellman and ballads by Evert Taube (see p66).

Folk music is played at clubs and there are festivals dedicated to folk instruments such as the accordion and hurdy-gurdy. Pageants and history plays have also seen a huge upturn in popularity.

Close to Nature

The Swedes' love of nature is deeply rooted. Many feel, subconsciously, an almost spiritual affinity with the forest, mountains or the sea. Legends and folklore are often linked to nature and many mythical beings are part of country lore. Trolls dwell in the forest, as does the Skogsrå or Huldra (siren), a beautiful young woman who lures men deeper and deeper into the woods and then, once they are lost, she turns around and all there is to be seen is a hollow tree. Women who stroll too far might hear a lovely tune drifting among the trees – that is Näcken, a handsome naked man, playing his fiddle in the middle of gushing streams and, needless to say, it is best to stay away from him. Giants and dwarfs roam the

A traditional red cottage, an iconic sight in Sweden

mountains while elves dance in the meadows and marsh-lands. Some beings have adopted modern guises. The Tomte, who traditionally is a stern, grey little man guarding farmers' barns and livestock, has been transformed into a kindly distributor of Christmas gifts. In the countryside, however, a plate of Christmas porridge is left for him on the doorstep, just to be safe.

There is a strong awareness of the changing seasons, linked to how deeply Swedes long for the bright summer. Spring is a slow affair, building up with the blossoming of one flower at a time, each one eagerly awaited. People know when each bloom is due, hence expressions like "between bird cherry and lilac" (ie "at the end of May").

On a more practical note, it is easy to be physically close to nature thanks to the Right of Public Access. This grants everyone access to all land, apart from the immediate surroundings of a house or farm (see p312). Many make the most of this resource, walking, camping, or going mushroom- or berry-picking.

Strawberry cream cake

A Country Cottage

The little red cottage is the symbol of paradise. Maybe it is the Swedes' farming roots combined with the brief summer which makes having

a holiday house in the country-side or out on an island such a major ambition.

When spring comes, people head out to tend their cottage gardens, and as the autumn nights draw in they are still at their cottages, curled up by the fire. Almost half the population have access to a summer cottage and 20 per cent own one of their own.

Culinary Traditions

People are rediscovering old Swedish dishes and there has been something of a revival in husmanskost ("home-cooking"). Few, however, have time to prepare these at home on a daily basis, so childhood favourites such as kalops (a slow-cooked meat stew), köttbullar (meatballs) and freshly cleaned and fried herring fillets are now often enjoyed in restaurants.

Swedes drink lots of coffee, and at work the fika paus (coffee break) is strictly observed. In fact, fika is some-thing everyone does, as proven by the large number of cafés even in small towns. To accompany coffee there is a great variety of bullar (buns), cakes, gateaux and biscuits. Home-made sponge cake layered with lots of whipped cream and strawberries is a summer favourite, especially for birthdays.

Painting depicting mythical beings in the forest

Swedish Design

Swedish design first attracted international attention at the 1925 World Exhibition in Paris, when glassware in particular took the world by storm and the concept of "Swedish Grace" was launched. The nation's design tradition is characterized by simplicity and functionality, with a major emphasis on natural materials. Swedish designers and architects are renowned for creating simple, attractive, "human" objects for everyday use. The 20th century marked the beginning of a new golden age, in which Swedish design has won worldwide acclaim.

Stoneware, Hans Hedberg
Swedish ceramics from the 1940s, 50s and 60s, such as this stoneware egg, are popular with collectors around the world.

Armchair (1969), Bruno Mathsson
Bruno Mathsson, one of Sweden's most famous 20th-century furniture designers, is one of the creators of the style that became known as "Swedish Modern". He designed the first version of the Pernilla armchair in 1942.

Pale wood and simplicity is the concept most closely associated with Swedish style.

Rag rugs are an old Swedish weaving tradition adopted by Karin Larsson, whose skill as a textile designer is widely recognized.

Cabinet (1952), Josef Frank
Frank was born in Austria, but worked in Sweden, and was another disciple of the "Swedish Modern" style. He is best known for his printed textiles, but he also designed furniture.

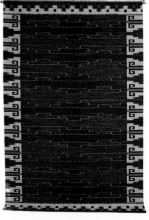

Carpet (1931), Märta Måås-Fjetterström
From 1919, Märta Måås-Fjetterström wove her famous rugs at her studio in Skåne. Her work was inspired by folklore and nature, and she created a design concept that was new but still firmly rooted in tradition.

Silver jug (1953) Sigurd Persson
Persson has an unrivalled ability to handle metal. He made his mark on the history of design with his everyday industrial pieces and exclusive artworks.

Chair (1981), Jonas Bohlin
The *Concrete* chair was the most talked about piece of Swedish furniture in the 1980s. A graduation project, it represented an entirely new approach to furniture design.

Flowers on a Windowsill, by Carl Larrson, typifies the Larssons' ideas on interior decoration, such as the absence of curtains.

Bookshelf (1989), John Kandell
The *Pilaster* bookshelf stores books horizontally instead of vertically. The lines are simple and typically Scandinavian. The maker, Källemo, is one of Sweden's most unconventional furniture companies.

Gustavian late 18th-century style elements have remained a strong feature in Swedish design through the centuries, but made an international comeback in the 1990s.

Vase, Ann Wåhlström
Wahlström is one of Kosta Boda's new generation of glass designers. Organic, warm and beautiful, *Cyklon* (1998) is an excellent example of contemporary Swedish glass.

Where to See Swedish Design

Asplund
Sibyllegatan 31, Stockholm. **Map** 2 E3.

Nationalmuseum
Södra Blasieholmshamnen, Stockholm. **Map** 4 D2.

Nordiska museet
Djurgårdsvågen 6–16, Stockholm. **Map** 4 F1.

Svenskt Tenn
Strandvägen 5, Stockholm. **Map** 2 E4.

Designtorget
Various major towns and cities, including Vallgatan 14, Gothenburg.

Röhsska Museet
Vasagatan 37–39, Gothenburg.

Malmö Modern
Skeppsbron 3, Malmö.

Glassworks shops
Various, Småland.
(See pp156–7).

SWEDEN THROUGH THE YEAR

Thanks to Sweden's geographical location, it experiences wide variations in seasons and climate. Winter retains its icy hold on the north until May, when in the south Skåne is often already basking in sunshine. Once spring gets going in the north and the days lengthen, nature soon catches up. Summers can be pleasantly warm throughout Sweden and that is when Swedes head off into the countryside to swim and enjoy the outdoor life, often staying in a summer cottage. The holiday period from late June to August is the height of the tourist season, with the widest range of attractions on offer. In winter, Swedes make for the mountains, which see the first snowfall as early as November. They value festivals, and events such as Christmas, New Year, Easter, Midsummer's Eve and Walpurgis are celebrated with enthusiasm.

An April start for the salmon fly-fishing season in Mörrum

Spring

After the long, dark Swedish winter, spring makes a welcome appearance. In Skåne the migratory birds return and spring flowers bloom in March, while in the north it's mid-May before winter releases its hold. Traditionally eaten before Lent, the *semla* cream bun is a tempting treat. Walpurgis Night, on the last day of April, marks a farewell to winter with folk dancing, torchlight processions, student choirs, bonfires and fireworks.

March

Vasaloppet Ski Race (early Mar). World famous long-distance ski race (see p249).

Stockholm International Boat Show (early Mar). The spring's major boat exhibition at Stockholm International Fairs in Älvsjö.

Åselenappet (end of Mar). Ice-fishing competition, which is the high point of the winter market in Åsele, Lapland.

The "crane dance", Hornborgasjön (Mar/Apr). Several thousand cranes gather on the fields around this lake in Västergötland for their spectacular annual mating dance. Quite a sight to behold.

April

Start of Salmon Fishing Season, Mörrumsån (1 Apr), Sweden's main salmon river (see p191).

Walpurgis Night (30 Apr). Around the country bonfires welcome in the new season, with students donning their white caps and making merry. In the student town of Uppsala, Walpurgis Night also includes fine student choirs, a fun river-rafting carnival and lots of other events.

May

May Day (1 May). Workers' processions countrywide.

Linné's birthday, Stenbrohult (23 May). The father of botany is commemorated at his childhood home in Småland.

Elite Race (last weekend in May). International trotting competition at Solvalla.

Trollhättan waterfalls (Sat in May, Jun & Sep; daily Jul & Aug). Magnificent falls, usually tamed by the power station, burst into life (3pm).

Stockholm Photography Week (late Mar/early Apr). An event for professionals, amateurs and lovers of the photographic arts. Held at the Swedish Museum of Photography (Fotografiska), at Stadsgårdshamnen 22.

Summer

The school year finishes in early June and summer comes into its own with Midsummer celebrations and dancing

Walpurgis Night bonfire, at Riddarholmen, Stockholm

Spectators cheering runners at the Stockholm Marathon

round the maypole. Evenings are often warm and the nights light, encouraging parties round the clock. In the far north the sun doesn't even set. July is traditionally the main holiday month and favourite spots can become crowded. But Sweden is big and there's room for everyone. The start of the school term at the end of August coincides with two popular culinary festivals celebrating crayfish and fermented Baltic herring.

June
Stockholm Marathon (early Jun). One of the world's ten biggest marathons with up to 21,500 runners.
Archipelago Boat Day, Stockholm (Jun). Classic steamboats assemble at Strömkajen for a round trip to Vaxholm.
National Day (6 Jun). A public holiday since 2005, National Day is celebrated around the country as Swedish Flag Day. The Royal Family attend the celebrations at Skansen in Stockholm.
Postrodden Mail Boat Race, Grisslehamn (mid-Jun). Rowing race to the Åland islands following the old mail route.
"Vätternrundan" (mid-Jun). Classic cycling race 300 km (190 miles) round Lake Vättern with around 20,000 participants, starting and finishing in Motala.
Midsummer's Eve (penultimate Fri in Jun). A major Swedish festival celebrated by dancing around a flower-bedecked maypole. Midsummer in Dalarna,

Rättvik, Leksand and Mora is especially rich in tradition with folk music and the wearing of colourful national costumes.
Peace and Love Festival (end of Jun). Large music festival, held in Borlänge.
ÅF Offshore Race (end of Jun/ early Jul). Major international sailing race around Gotland, starting in Stockholm and finishing in Sandhamn, in the Stockholm Archipelago.

July
Skule Song Festival (first weekend in Jul). One of Sweden's largest singing festivals, held at the foot of the Skule mountain on the High Coast.
Vansbro Swim (early Jul). Up to 8,700 people take part in the 3-km (2-mile) swim in the Vanån and Västerdal rivers, starting in Vansbro.
Stånga Games, Gotland (mid-Jul). Events featuring Gotland sports such as Square-and-border-ball, The Stone, Gotlandic Pole Throwing and "Hook the Bottom".
Gammelvala Brunskog, Värmland (end of Jul). Week-long festival celebrating the domestic skills of the past. Music, exhibitions, drama and local food.
Storsjöyran Festival (end of Jul). This week-long festival of pop and rock music in "the Republic of Jämtland" also offers drama, exhibitions and street artists.

Music in the Kingdom of Crystal, Småland's Glassworks (end of Jul). Folk music, choral singing, opera, wind bands and jazz in a charming setting.
Kukkolaforsen Whitefish Festival (last weekend in Jul). Celebrations in Sweden and Finland to mark the whitefish reaching the Torneälven river, which forms the border between the two countries. The fish are caught in large nets and eaten grilled or smoked.

August
Skänninge Market, Östergötland (first Wed & Thu in Aug). One of Sweden's most traditional markets, attracting 120,000 visitors to this medieval city.
Gotland Medieval Week (early Aug). Visby is turned into a 14th-century Hanseatic city with tournaments, plays and music and participants in colourful medieval costumes.
Royal Philharmonic Orchestra Outdoor Concert, Stockholm (mid-Aug). This concert on the lawn outside Sjöhistoriska Museet is one of the highlights of the season.
Way Out West, Gothenburg (mid-Aug). Held in a city park, the west coast's biggest music festival draws famous artists from around the world.
Gothenburg Jazz Festival (end of Aug). This three-day festival of swing, jazz, gospel and blues takes place at seven locations around the city.
Crayfish and Fermented Herring (end of Aug). Although there is no longer a statutory start date for eating these delicacies – accompanied by ice-cold snaps and cheese – this is when Swedes party the most.

Sailors in vintage clothes at Postrodden Race, Grisslehamn

Beech forest in autumn at Söderåsen, Skåne

Autumn

The nights may be drawing in, but the mornings are light and the days often crisp and clear. In late autumn deciduous trees provide a stunning display of colours. It's harvest time in the forests and countryside, and a wide variety of delicious edible mushrooms, as well as blueberries, lingonberries and the red-gold cloudberries of the northern marshes are all ripe for the picking.

September
Oxhälja Market, Filipstad *(early Sep)*. This traditional market takes place in eastern Värmland.
Tjejmilen, Stockholm *(early Sep)*. In a lively atmosphere at Djurgården, Stockholm's royal park, 33,000 women take part in a 10 km run.
Swedish Trotting Derby, Jägersro *(Sep)*. Sweden's top four-year-old horses compete

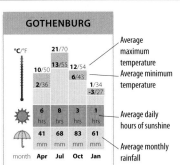
Chanterelles

for the derby title on the trotting track in Malmö.
Kivik Apple Market *(end Sep)*. Apples are the focus of this two-day festival, which attracts around 20,000 visitors. Giant art installations created with tons of apples are a particular highlight.
Harvest Festival, Öland *(end Sep/early Oct)*. Sweden's biggest harvest festival takes place over four days around Michaelmas, with around 900 events attracting 200,000 visitors to enjoy local food, concerts and exhibitions.

October
Lidingöloppet *(first weekend in Oct)*. The world's largest cross-country race, with tens of thousands of competitors, including elite runners, senior citizens and children.
Umeå International Jazz Festival *(end Oct)*. This leading jazz festival was first staged in the 1960s.

STOCKHOLM

°C/°F				
		22/76		
	9/48	13/55	10/50	
	1/34		5/41	
				-1/30
				-5/23
hrs	6	8	3	1
mm	30	72	50	39
month	Apr	Jul	Oct	Jan

GOTHENBURG

°C/°F				
		21/70		
	10/50	13/55	12/54	
	2/36		6/43	
				1/34
				-3/27
hrs	6	8	3	1
mm	41	68	83	61
month	Apr	Jul	Oct	Jan

— Average maximum temperature
— Average minimum temperature
— Average daily hours of sunshine
— Average monthly rainfall

Climate
Considerable variations in climate from north to south sometimes result in southern Sweden having no snow and temperatures above freezing in winter, while the north is blanketed in thick snow. The differences are less extreme in summer. The effect of the North Atlantic and the Gulf Stream is felt on the west coast in mild damp winds and the highest rainfall.

MALMÖ

°C/°F				
		21/70		
	10/50	13/55	12/54	
	2/36		7/45	
				2/36
				-3/27
hrs	6	7	3	1
mm	38	61	57	49
month	Apr	Jul	Oct	Jan

ÖSTERSUND

°C/°F				
		19/66		
	5/41		10/50	6/43
	-3/27		1/34	-6/21
				-13/9
hrs	6	7	2	1
mm	32	86	45	36
month	Apr	Jul	Oct	Jan

LULEÅ

°C/°F				
		20/68		
	4/39		11/52	6/43
	-4/25		0/32	-7/19
				-16/3
hrs	7	10	7	0.6
mm	29	50	50	40
month	Apr	Jul	Oct	Jan

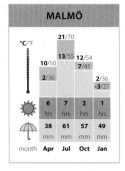
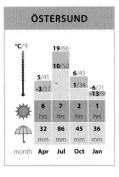

Winter

While Christmas does not always go hand in hand with snow in southern Sweden, there are plenty of opportunities for ice-skating and there's always a chance of a white January. The mountains become a paradise for skiers, while snow cannons help out elsewhere if nature isn't up to the job. From the first day of Advent, the Christmas season is in full swing, culminating in present-giving on Christmas Eve. Restaurants enjoy their busiest time and Lucia processions brighten the winter darkness.

November
Gustav Adolf Day *(6 Nov).* Gothenburg celebrates the royal founder of the city on the anniversary of his death *(see p199).*
St Martin's Day *(10–11 Nov).* Roast goose and "black soup" containing goose blood are served at parties for St Martin of Tours and Martin Luther.

December
Nobel Day *(10 Dec).* The year's Nobel Prize laureates are honoured in a ceremony at Konserthuset (Concert Hall) and a banquet in Stadshuset (City Hall) attended by the King and Queen.
Lucia Celebrations *(13 Dec).* Sweden's chosen Lucia, with her girl attendants and "star boys", serves the Nobel laureates morning coffee with saffron buns and performs traditional songs. In the evening a Lucia procession winds through the

Lucia, the "Queen of Light", with her attendants at Skansen

capital to celebrations and fireworks at Skansen. Similar Lucia processions take place throughout Sweden and, on a smaller scale, in many homes and schools.
Christmas Markets throughout Sweden *(from early Dec).* The markets at Skansen and Stortorget in Stockholm are particularly atmospheric.
Christmas *(24–26 Dec).* Filled with traditions, Christmas is the most important Swedish holiday. The main event is Christmas Eve when an abundant *smörgåsbord* is followed by gifts. Christmas Day often begins with a church service.
New Year *(31 Dec–1 Jan).* People go out on the town. Celebrations are televised from Skansen, including a traditional midnight reading of Tennyson's *"Ring out wild bells…"* Church bells peal and there are spectacular fireworks displays.

January
Hindersmässan *(end Jan).* Market in Örebro dating back to medieval times.
Kiruna Snow Festival, *(last week in Jan).* Renowned festival, especially for its reindeer racing.

February
Jokkmokks Winter Market *(first weekend in Feb).* Colourful festival with market, reindeer sledding and races.
Gothenburg Boat Show *(early Feb).* New boats on show at the Swedish Exhibition Centre in Gothenburg.
Vikingarännet *(as soon as the ice holds).* Long-distance ice-skating race between Stockholm and Uppsala.
Globen Gala *(2nd half of Feb).* Athletes compete at this top indoor competition.
Spring Salon *(Feb–Mar).* Annual art exhibition of new talent at Liljevalchs, Stockholm.

Man in traditional Sami outfit at the Jokkmokks Winter Market in Lapland

Public Holidays
New Year's Day (1 Jan)
Epiphany (6 Jan)
Good Friday (Mar/Apr)
Easter Monday (Mar/Apr)
Ascension Day (6th Thu after Easter)
Labour Day (1 May)
National Day (6 Jun)
Midsummer (Jun)
Christmas Day (25 Dec)
Boxing Day (26 Dec)

Frozen Riddarfjärden in Stockholm as a winter park

THE HISTORY OF SWEDEN

Described in the 4th century BC as a land of frozen seas and midnight sun, this northerly nation of reindeer herders also produced the fearsome Viking traders of the 9th century. By the 17th century, Sweden, in its Age of Greatness, ruled supreme over the Baltic region. Vanquished by Russia in 1809, the country adopted a more peaceful role and today is heavily engaged in world affairs.

In the last 100,000 years, Sweden has been covered by thick inland ice on at least three occasions. As the ice retreated northwards for the last time in approximately 12,000 BC, nomadic reindeer hunters moved in to use the newly revealed land, but it was not until 6500 BC that Sweden was entirely free of ice.

Farming was gradually adopted in southern Sweden from 4000 BC, while hunting continued to remain prevalent in the inland areas of Norrland for a long time to come. The first examples of domestic pottery date from this period and burial mounds appeared in the southern provinces.

Finds from the Bronze Age (1800–500 BC) bear witness to increased contact with the outside world. A chieftain society based on power and social alliances began to develop. Magnificent bronze objects, huge burial mounds and cairns with grave goods as well as rock carvings date from this period (see p216).

The transition to the Iron Age in 500 BC saw the first written accounts about Scandinavia. In the 4th century BC the Greek explorer and trader, Phytheas of Massilia, described the journey to "Thule", with its frozen seas and midnight sun. In his *Germania* (AD 98), the Roman Tacitus refers to the *"sviones"* as a powerful people with strong men, weapons and fleets.

With the growth of the Roman Empire, links with the Continent increased and numerous finds show evidence of trade with Rome via the many German tribes in the area north of the Rhine. The fall of Rome and the subsequent period of population migrations saw the rise of small kingdoms across Europe. In Sweden there was a kingdom centred on Uppsala where large *kungshögar* (King's Mounds) can still be seen today (see p135).

From 800 until Christianity reached Sweden in the mid-11th century, the Vikings took the world by storm. As traders, settlers and plunderers, they set sail in search of land, slaves and treasure. They carried out raids throughout Europe, sailed as far as Baghdad and even reached America. Christian monks wrote of attacks on rich monasteries and towns. But the Vikings were more than wild barbarians. They were also hard-working farmers, traders, experienced sailors, craftsmen and shipbuilders.

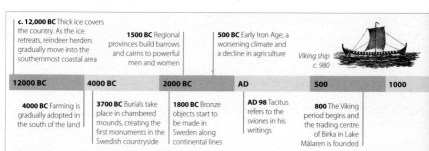

c. 12,000 BC Thick ice covers the country. As the ice retreats, reindeer herders gradually move into the southernmost coastal area

1500 BC Regional provinces build barrows and cairns to powerful men and women

500 BC Early Iron Age; a worsening climate and a decline in agriculture

Viking ship c. 980

12000 BC	4000 BC	2000 BC	AD	500	1000

4000 BC Farming is gradually adopted in the south of the land

3700 BC Burials take place in chambered mounds, creating the first monuments in the Swedish countryside

1800 BC Bronze objects start to be made in Sweden along continental lines

AD 98 Tacitus refers to the *sviones* in his writings

800 The Viking period begins and the trading centre of Birka in Lake Mälaren is founded

◀ Gustav Vasa (1523–60), painting by Cornelius Arendtz

Christianity and the Birth of a Kingdom

During the 11th and 12th centuries several families from different provinces battled for power over the central part of what is known today as Sweden. The country was more like a federation of self-governing provinces, a number of which, for a limited time, had influence over those around them.

Little is known of the kings and chieftains in the early Middle Ages other than brief mentions in sagas. In the 11th century, King Olof Skötkonung (d. 1020) was converted to Christianity and was baptized in 1008, along with his sons Anund Jakob (d. 1050) and Edmund the Old (d. 1060). Thereafter power passed to the Stenkil family, which had strong links with Västergötland where the Christian church had gained the most influence.

The church and the gradual transition to Christianity underway in the 12th century were vital to the growing power of the king. The priests brought with them an administrative tradition, a civil service and a rational system for regulating property. The church also reinforced the strength of the king ideologically through the idea that his power was derived from God.

King Olof Skötkonung's baptism at Husaby well in Västergötland, 1008

Once the Stenkil dynasty came to an end around 1120, the royal houses of Västergötland (Erik) and Östergötland (Sverker) battled for supremacy. Both families died out in the first half of the 13th century at the time when the power of the *riksjarl* (earl) was at its height. The *riksjarl* was the king's most important statesman and the position gained greater influence through Birger Magnusson, known as Birger Jarl, who became *riksjarl* in 1248 under King Erik Eriksson. Until his death in 1266, Birger Jarl was the de facto wielder of power in Sweden, which by then had developed into a medieval kingdom similar to those elsewhere in Europe.

The Hanseatic League and the Bjälbo Dynasty's Power Struggle

The 13th century saw the founding of many of the medieval towns still standing today. Documents show that Stockholm existed as a town in 1252, four years after Birger Jarl became *riksjarl*. In 1289 it was described as the largest town in Sweden, but it was not yet a capital city. Its importance lay in its role as a trading centre, particularly for the German Hanseatic League, during the 14th century. The Hanseatic League had previously established a base in Visby on Gotland, which was one of its most important centres. In some places, the Hansa influence was so great that the king had to prevent Germans from holding more than half of the leading positions in the town.

Through Birger Jarl's son, Valdemar, elected king in 1250, power passed to the Bjälbo dynasty. Valdemar was replaced after

---

1080 Pagan revolt replaces the Christian, Inge the Elder, by the Svea family, who choose Blot-Sven as king

1143 Alvastra monastery in Östergötland is founded by Cistercians

Birger Jarl

1248 Birger Jarl is *riksjarl*, the king's foremost statesman

1100　　　　　**1150**　　　　　**1200**　　　　　**1250**

1008 Olof Skötkonung is baptized a Christian in Västergötland

1101 The meeting of the three kings in Kungahälla sets the borders of the Nordic countries

1130 Östergötland chief Sverker the Elder elected king

1222 The last of the Sverker dynasty, Johan Sverkersson, dies and is succeeded by Erik Eriksson

1250 Erik Eriksson is succeeded by Valdemar Birgersson, son of Birger Jarl and first of the Folkung dynasty

a revolt by his brother Magnus Ladulås who was elected king in 1275. During Magnus's reign, Swedish legislation was reformed and the Ordinance of Alsnö of 1280 granted the nobility and church far-reaching privileges and freedom from taxation.

The king's nickname, Ladulås (literally "lock barn"), is said to derive from his ban on nobles from helping themselves to sustenance from peasants' barns when travelling.

On Magnus' death in 1290, his son Birger was still a minor and Sweden was ruled by a regency. Once the king reached his majority in 1303, a power struggle broke out between Birger and his brothers, Dukes Erik and Valdemar. Sweden was divided between the brothers until in 1317 Birger invited Erik and Valdemar to a banquet at Nyköping Castle and had them both imprisoned and left to die. Soon, Birger himself was forced to flee the country after a revolt and Magnus Eriksson, the three-year-old son of Duke Erik, was elected king of Sweden in 1319.

Magnus's rule was characterized by severe domestic opposition and financial problems. Sweden also suffered the Black Death in 1350 in which one third of the population died. The crisis led to the Swedish nobles in 1363 appealing to the Duke of Mecklenburg, whose son Albrecht was hailed king of Sweden the following year.

The Kalmar Union

Albrecht of Mecklenburg came to the throne with the support of the nobility, who reacted with a revolt when he subsequently sought to wield his own power. The nobles were backed by Queen Margareta of Denmark-Norway and Albrecht

Beheading of 100 members of the Swedish nobility in the Stockholm Bloodbath, 1520

was defeated at Fallköping in 1389, after which Denmark, Norway and Sweden came under the rule of Denmark. At a meeting in Kalmar in 1397, Margareta's nephew, Erik of Pomerania, was crowned king of Denmark, Norway and Sweden, thus establishing the Kalmar Union, which lasted until 1523.

The unification period was characterized by conflict in Sweden. Under Erik of Pomerania there was great dissatisfaction with newly-introduced taxes. A peasant revolt, known as the Engelbrekt revolt after its legendary leader, led to Erik being deposed in 1439. The Kalmar Union was unable to control the Council of State or the castles, and Sweden lacked a recognized supreme authority. Subsequent Danish kings were recognized as rulers in Sweden only for a few years and in between the country was controlled by representatives of the nobility.

At the Battle of Brunkeberg in Stockholm in 1471, the Danish King Christian I sought to enforce his power in Sweden, but was defeated by the viceroy, Sten Sture the Elder. A new Danish crusade under Christian II in 1520 culminated in the notorious Stockholm Bloodbath in which 100 Swedish nobles were executed.

1275 Magnus Ladulås elected king of Sweden at Mora Stones

1349–50 Black Death rampages through Sweden

1364 Albrecht of Mecklenburg elected king of Sweden

Queen Margareta

1434 Engelbrekt leads revolt over the taxes and burdens imposed by the Kalmar Union

1520 Swedish nobles executed in the Stockholm Bloodbath

1300 | **1350** | **1400** | **1450**

1280 Ordinance of Alsnö grants freedom from taxation to the nobility

1350 Magnus Eriksson's law applies throughout the land, although cities have their own laws

1397 The Kalmar Union unites the Nordic countries under Queen Margareta

1471 Sten Sture the Elder defeats Danish King Christian I at Brunkeberg

Gustav Vasa making his ceremonial entry into Stockholm, Midsummer Day, 1523

The Vasa Era

Among the nobles fortunate to avoid execution in the Stockholm Bloodbath was the young Gustav Eriksson. At the end of 1520 Gustav organized an army to oust the Danish King Christian from Sweden. Gustav was successful and on 6 June 1523 – later to become Sweden's National Day – he was named king. On Midsummer Day the new monarch, Gustav Vasa, made his ceremonial entry into war-torn Stockholm.

When Gustav Vasa took the throne, he discovered a nation in financial crisis. He called on parliament to pass a controversial law transferring the property of the church to the state, which then became the country's most important source of economic power. Another important result of this policy was the gradual separation from Catholicism and the adoption of the Lutheran State Church, which was to remain tied to the state until 2000.

During his reign, Gustav Vasa implemented tough economic policies in order to

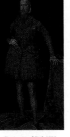

Portrait of Erik XIV (1561)

concentrate central power in Stockholm. This effective dictatorship also resulted in the Swedish parliament's decision in 1544 to make the monarchy hereditary.

Descendants of Gustav Vasa oversaw the rise of Sweden into one of Europe's great powers. During the reign of Gustav's eldest son Erik XIV (r. 1561– 69), there were wars against Denmark, Lübeck and Poland. His brothers dethroned him. Erik died in prison, possibly by eating pea soup poisoned by his brother Johan III. During the reign of Karl IX, the third son, Sweden waged war against Denmark and Russia.

Gustav II Adolf and Kristina

When the next king, Gustav II Adolf, came to power in 1611, Sweden was involved in wars against Russia, Poland and Denmark. This reign came to be as remarkable as that of his grandfather and under his rule Sweden steadily increased its influence over the Baltic region. It was also in the 17th century that Stockholm started to develop into the country's political and

Vasa coat of arms

1523 Gustav Vasa is chosen as king and marches into Stockholm	**1542** Nils Dacke leads a peasants revolt in Småland	**1560** Gustav Vasa dies	**1568** Erik XIV imprisoned by his brothers at Gripsholms Slott	**1611** Gustav II Adolf becomes king
			1577 Erik XIV dies, probably poisoned	
1525		**1550**	**1575**	**1600**
1527 Reformation parliament confiscates church property	**1544** Hereditary monarchy established for Gustav Vasa's descendants	**1561** Eric XIV is crowned king and his brothers' powers curbed	**1570** Nordic Seven Years War ends **1569** Johan III crowned in Stockholm	**1587** Johan III's son Sigismund chosen as king of Poland **1612** Axel Oxenstierna made State Chancellor

administrative centre. In 1630 Gustav II Adolf, with his influential chancellor Axel Oxenstierna, decided to intervene in the Thirty Years War *(see p42)*, first on the side of the Protestants, then in an alliance with France. Sweden had some military successes during the war, but paid a heavy price for winning the bloody battle at Lützen in 1632, as the king was killed in action.

Gustav II Adolf's only child, Kristina, came to the throne at the age of six. During her reign (1633–54), life at court was influenced by the world of science and philosophy. Kristina's reluctance to marry resulted in her cousin, Karl Gustav, becoming Crown Prince. Kristina abdicated and left for Rome, where she converted to Catholicism, a sensation at the time.

The Carolian Era

Karl X Gustav (1654–60) was the first of three Karls to reign. At the height of Sweden's era as a great power, he defeated Denmark by leading his army across the frozen waters of the Great Belt *(see p42)*, thus gaining Sweden's southernmost provinces. Karl XI (1660–97) secured the

Queen Kristina corresponding with leading scientists and philosophers of the time

Young Karl XII with the widowed queen on his arm leaving the burning Tre Kronor Palace, 1697

border and divided the land more evenly between crown, nobility and peasants.

While the body of Karl XI lay in state at Tre Kronor in 1697, a fire broke out which destroyed most of the building. The new monarch was the teenage Karl XII (1697–1718). He faced awesome problems when Denmark, Poland and Russia formed an alliance in 1700 with the aim of crushing the power of Sweden. Karl XII set off to battle.

Denmark and Poland were soon forced to plead for peace, but Russia was a harder nut to crack. A bold push towards Moscow was unsuccessful and the Swedish army suffered a devastating defeat at Poltava in Ukraine in 1709. This marked the beginning of the end of Sweden's Age of Greatness.

Karl XII, possibly the most written about and controversial Swedish monarch, returned to Sweden in 1715 after an absence of 15 years. His plans to regain Sweden's position of dominance never came to fruition and he was killed in Norway in 1718. Sweden was in crisis. Crop failures and epidemics had wiped out one third of the population and the state's finances were drained.

1617 Death penalty introduced for conversion to Catholicism

1632 Gustav II Adolf killed at Battle of Lützen

1633 Six-year-old Kristina becomes queen

1654 Kristina abdicates; Karl X Gustav is crowned

1655 Kristina converts to Catholicism and is ceremonially greeted in Rome

1697 Tre Kronor castle destroyed by fire; 15-year-old Karl XII crowned

1709 Swedish army defeated by Peter the Great at Poltava

1625 **1650** **1675** **1700**

1618 Thirty Years War starts in Germany

1648 Peace of Westphalia gives Sweden new territories

Gustav II Adolf

1658 Sweden acquires new territory, including Skåne, under Peace of Roskilde

1680 Karl XI starts the era of Carolian autocracy and limits powers of the nobility

1718 Karl XII dies during siege of Fredriksten, Norway

Sweden's Age of Greatness

For more than a century (1611–1721) Sweden was the dominant power in northern Europe, and the Baltic was effectively a Swedish inland sea. The country was at its most powerful after the Peace of Roskilde in 1658, when Sweden acquired seven new provinces. Outside today's frontiers, the Swedish Empire covered Finland, large parts of the Baltic states, and important areas of northern Germany. Over 111 years as a great power Sweden spent 72 of them at war, but the period also marked great cultural development and more efficient state administration. Treasures were brought back as trophies and grand palaces were built.

Swedish Empire

Sweden's empire after the Peace of Roskilde, 1658

The Tre Kronor Castle
Built as a defensive tower in the 1180s, the Tre Kronor castle was the seat of Swedish monarchs from the 1520s and became the administrative centre of the Swedish Empire. Named after the three crowns on the spire, it burned down in 1697.

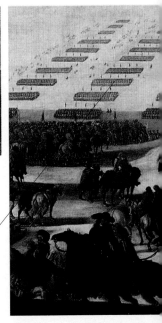

The columns of troops ride out over the shifting ice towards Danish Lolland.

The Thirty Years War

A major European war raged from 1618–48, largely on German soil. Sweden entered the fray in 1630 and joined forces with France in 1631 against the Austrian Habsburgs. The Swedish army had been reorganized and rearmed by Gustav II Adolf and immediately had successes at the battles of Breitenfeld (1630) and Lützen (1632), where the king was killed in action. Later the Swedes pressed into southern Germany and also captured Prague (1648). Rich cultural treasures were brought home from the war. In 1648 the Peace of Westphalia gave Sweden several important possessions in northern Germany.

The death of Gustav II Adolf at the Battle of Lützen in 1632

Stockholm in 1640
The city's transformation from a small medieval town into a capital city can be seen in the network of straight streets, similar to the present layout.

Karl XI's Triumphs

The ceiling painting in Karl XI's gallery at the Royal Palace *(see p60)* by the French artist Jacques Foucquet (1693) shows in allegoric form the king's victories at Halmstad, Lund and Landskrona.

The Powerful Nobility

The nobility were very influential in the Empire era and many successful soldiers were ennobled. The Banér family coat of arms from 1651 is adorned by three helmets and barons' crowns.

Field Marshal Count Carl Gustav Wrangel *(see p133)*

Karl X Gustav himself leads the Swedish army of 17,000 men.

Karl X Gustav

Portrait of Karl X Gustav (r. 1654–60) as a general. It was in this role that he became known throughout Europe during the final phase of the Thirty Years War.

Crossing the Great Belt

When Denmark declared war on Sweden in autumn 1657, the Swedish army was in Poland. Marching west, it captured the Danish mainland, but without the navy was unable to continue to Copenhagen. However, unusually severe weather froze the sea, making it possible for the soldiers to cross the ice of the Great Belt, and the Danes had to surrender.

Karl XII's Pocket Watch

The warrior king's watch-case dates from 1700. It shows the state coat of arms, as well as those of the 49 provinces that belonged to Sweden at that time.

Karl XII's Last Journey

After he was hit by a fatal bullet at Fredrikshald in Norway (1718), the king's body was taken first to Swedish territory then on to Uddevalla for embalming. Painting by Gustav Cederström (1878).

Gustav III with the white armband he wore when mounting his *coup d'etat* in 1772

The Age of Liberty and the Gustavian Era

A new constitution came into force in 1719 which transferred power from the monarch to parliament. As a result, Sweden developed a system of parliamentary democracy similar to that of Britain at the time.

The "Age of Liberty" coincided with the Enlightenment, with dramatic advances in culture, science and industry. The botanist Carl von Linné became one of the most famous Swedes of his time. Another was the scientist, philosopher and author Emanuel Swedenborg, who is thought to have influenced both Balzac and Baudelaire. The production of textiles expanded in Stockholm, and Sweden's first hospital was constructed on Kungsholmen.

Changes in the balance of power around 1770 gave the new king, Gustav III, an opportunity to strike in an attempt to regain his monarchical powers.

On 19 August 1772 Gustav accompanied the guards' parade to the Royal Palace where, in front of his lifeguards, he declared his intention to mount a *coup d'etat*. The guards and other military units in Stockholm swore allegiance to the king, who tied a white handkerchief round his arm as a badge and rode out into the city to be acclaimed by his people. Absolute power had been restored.

Gustav III was influenced by the Age of Enlightenment and by French culture, which had a great effect on Swedish life (*see pp46–7*). Over the years opposition grew to the king's powers, largely because of his costly war against Russia. In 1792 he was murdered by a nobleman during a masked ball at the Opera House.

Gustav III was succeeded by his son, Gustav IV Adolf. During his reign Sweden was dragged into the Napoleonic wars. After a war against Russia in 1808–9, Sweden lost Finland, which at the time accounted for one-third of Swedish territory. The king was deposed and went into exile.

Napoleon's former marshal, Jean-Baptiste Bernadotte, as King Karl XIV Johan surrounded by his family

---

1719 New constitution transfers power from the king to parliament

1741 Carl von Linné appointed professor at Uppsala

1754 Royal Family moves into Royal Palace

1780s Immigrants given religious freedom

1790 Sweden defeats Russia at the Battle of Svenskund

1792 Gustav III is murdered

1809 Swed loses Finla Gustav IV Ac depos

| 1720 | 1740 | 1760 | 1780 | 1800 |

1738 Parliamentary power is established in the Age of Liberty as the "Hat" party wins elections

Carl von Linné

1772 Gustav III crowned and mounts coup d'etat, giving the king absolute power

1778 National costume decreed. Death penalty removed for some crimes

1786 Swedish Academy founded

Newspaper readers outside the *Aftonbladet* office in 1841

The Era of Karl Johan and Bourgeois Liberalism

By the early 19th century the absolute powers of the monarch had been removed for all time, and the privileges of the aristocracy were undermined even more in 1809 with a new constitution that divided power between the king, the government and parliament. With a new class structure and the effect of the French Revolution, a new middle class emerged which also wanted to be more influential. Altercations between middle-class liberals and the conservatives prevailed. One of the best-known newspapers founded at this time was the liberal mouthpiece, *Aftonbladet*.

Difficulties in finding a suitable new monarch led to the choice of one of Napoleon's marshals, Jean-Baptiste Bernadotte, who took on the Swedish name of Karl Johan. Founder of the present royal dynasty, Karl XIV Johan continued to speak French and never fully learned Swedish. His French wife, Desirée, found Stockholm a cultural backwater after Paris. In 1813 a Swedish army, with Karl XIV Johan at its head, became involved in the final battle against

Swedes heading for a new life in North America

Napoleon. The Battle of Leipzig ended in defeat for France, but more significantly for Sweden, Denmark had to hand over Norway to Sweden. The Norwegians were reluctant to unite with Sweden, but after a display of military power in Norway, a union between the two countries was agreed which lasted from 1814 to 1905.

A long era of peace began, and with it came a dramatic increase in population, which grew by 1 million to 3.5 million by 1850. Many Swedes were driven into poverty because of the shortage of work. Mass emigration followed. From the 1850s to the 1930s about 1.5 million people left Sweden, mostly for North America.

Social Movements and Industrialization

As Sweden was transformed from an agricultural society into an industrialized country, the problems posed by the population surplus were gradually tackled. Its industrial revolution started around 1850, gathering momentum in the late 19th century, and the textile, timber and iron industries provided the main sources of employment. Here the early and fast development of a coherent railway network played an important role.

Social movements sprang up in the 19th century which still play an important role in Swedish life. One of the first was the temperance movement, which emerged from a background of alcohol abuse – in the 1820s annual consumption of spirits was 46 litres (80 pints) per person.

10 Parliament chooses n-Baptiste Bernadotte Crown Prince	**1842** Elementary schools established	**1869** Emigration to North America increases due to crop failures	**1876** L M Ericsson starts manufacture of telephones *August Strindberg*	**1905** Parliament dissolves union with Norway
1820	**1840**	**1860**	**1880**	**1900**
1818 Karl XIV Johan is crowned King of Sweden and Norway		**1856** Sweden's first railway opens	**1879** August Strindberg's novel *The Red Room* is published	**1908** Royal Dramatic Theatre opens in Stockholm
1814 Sweden gains Norway in peace treaty with Denmark		**1850** Sweden has 3.5 million inhabitants; 93,000 live in Stockholm		

The Era of Gustav III

Gustav III (r. 1771–92) is one of the most colourful figures in Swedish history. The king's great interest in art, literature and the theatre made the late 18th century a golden age for Swedish culture, and several academies were founded at this time. After a bloodless revolution in 1772, Gustav III ruled with absolute power and initiated a wide-ranging programme of reform. But his attacks on the privileges of the nobility and his adventurous and costly foreign policy made him powerful enemies. In 1792 he was murdered during a masked ball at Stockholm's Opera House.

The Swedish Academy
The academy was founded by Gustav III in 1786 to preserve the Swedish language. Members received a token depicting the king's head at every meeting.

Gustav III's Coronation 1772
The coronation of the all-powerful monarch in Stockholm's cathedral was a magnificent ceremony, portrayed here by C G Pilo (1782). Every detail was overseen by Gustav himself, who used his flair for the dramatic in politics as well.

A courtier entertains by reading aloud.

Gustav III studies architectural designs.

Court Life at Drottningholm

Hilleström's painting (1779) gives an insight into court life at Drottningholm, where the king resided between June and November. In what is now the Blue Salon, Gustav III and Queen Sofia Magdalena socialized with their inner circle. Behaviour was modelled on the French court and etiquette was even stricter at Drottningholm than at Versailles.

The Battle of Svensksund
Gustav III was not known as a successful warrior king, but in 1790 he led the Swedish fleet to its greatest victory ever, when it defeated Russia in a major maritime battle in the Gulf of Finland.

Life in the Inns
Stockholm abounded with inns, frequently visited by the city's 70,000 inhabitants. J T Sergel's sketch shows a convivial dinner party.

Murder at the Masked Ball

In 1792 Gustav III fell victim to a conspiracy at the Opera House. He was surrounded by masked men and shot by Captain Anckarström on the crowded stage. He died of his wounds 14 days later.

Gustav III's Mask and Cocked Hat

Despite his mask, Gustav III was easy to recognize since he was wearing the badges of two orders of chivalry. The drama intrigued the whole of Europe and inspired Verdi's opera *Un Ballo in Maschera*.

Flogging of the King's Murderer

Among the conspirators, only Anckarström was condemned to death. Before he was taken to his execution in Södermalm, he was flogged on three successive days on the square in front of Riddarhuset.

Queen Sofia Magdalena does her needlework.

Bust of Catherine the Great of Russia, the king's cousin

Gustavian Style

The mid-18th century saw the emergence of Neo- Classicism, with the focus on antiquities and Greek ideals. Gustav III embraced this trend with great enthusiasm and supported the country's talented artists and authors. He established his own Museum of Antiquities *(see p61)* with marble sculptures which he brought home from Italy. In handicrafts, the sweeping lines of Rococo elegance were replaced by the stricter forms of what has become known as Gustavian Style. Rooms at the Royal Palace were renovated with decoration and furnishings adapted to suit this style.

Chair designed in Gustavian style

Swedish Court Costume

In 1778, Gustav III introduced a court costume, based on French lines, for daily wear at court, in order to restrain fashion excesses.

Universal Suffrage

Sweden's population reached 5 million around 1900, despite mass emigration to America. Many people moved to the towns to work in industry, and by the early 20th century Stockholm's population was about 300,000, a fourfold increase since the year 1800.

Increasing social awareness and the rise of the Social Democrat and Liberal parties in the early 20th century gave impetus to the demands for universal suffrage. Authors such as August Strindberg became involved. A political battle ensued which was not resolved until 1921, when universal suffrage was introduced for both sexes.

Branting and Gustav V in conversation, 1909

Another question which was hotly debated in the 19th century was the role of the king and the extent of his powers. In his "courtyard speech" at the Royal Palace in 1914, King Gustav V called for military rearmament. This led to a constitutional crisis and the resignation of the Liberal government. After the 1917 election, the king had to accept a government which contained republican-friendly Social Democrats, including the future prime minister, Hjalmar Branting. By then it was parliament, not the king, that decided what sort of government Sweden should have.

The Growth of the Welfare State

In 1936 the Social Democrats and Farmers' Party formed a coalition which developed what was to become known as the welfare state. The Social Democrat prime minister, Per Albin Hansson (1885–1946), defined the welfare state as a socially conscious society with financial security for all. Reforms introduced under this policy included unemployment benefit, paid holidays and childcare. As a result, poverty in Sweden virtually disappeared during the 1930s and 1940s.

The right of everyone to good housing was also part of welfare state policy. Under the principle of "work-home-centre" a new Stockholm suburb, Vällingby, was built in the early 1950s. The idea was to transform the dormitory suburbs into thriving communities where people would both live and work. The concept was unsuccessful. It soon became apparent that the people who lived there still worked somewhere else, and vice versa. The great shortage of housing in the 1960s led to the "million" programme, which involved the building of a million homes in a very short time.

Calls for democratic reforms in June 1917 led to riots like this one outside the parliament building in Stockholm

	1921 Universal suffrage for men and women	**1930** Rise of Functionalist style in architecture, stimulated by the Stockholm Exhibition	**1940** Swedish-German agreement on transit of German military personnel	**1955** Obligatory national health insurance	**1958** Women can be ordained as priests	**1967** Driving on the right introduced

1920		**1940**		**1960**	

Selma Lagerlöf, winner of the Nobel Prize for Literature, 1909

1939 Sweden's coalition government declares neutrality in World War II

1952 Stockholm's first underground railway is inaugurated

1950 First public TV broadcast in Sweden

1964 Art exhibition Moderna Museet sh works by Andy Warh Roy Lichtenstein and Claes Oldenburg

The War Years

Sweden declared its neutrality during both World Wars I and II. Its policy of continuing to trade with nations involved in the conflict during World War I provoked a number of countries into imposing a trade blockade on Sweden. The situation became so serious that hunger riots broke out in some towns.

World War II proved an even more difficult balancing exercise for Swedish neutrality, largely because its Nordic neighbours were at war. Through a combination of luck and skill, Sweden remained outside the conflict, but the concessions it had to make were strongly criticized both nationally and internationally.

Neutrality stamp issued in 1942

The policy of non-alignment has not proved an obstacle to Swedish involvement on the international scene, including the United Nations. The country has offered asylum to hundreds of thousands of refugees from wars and political oppression. Prime Minister Olof Palme (1927–86), probably the best-known Swedish politician abroad, was deeply involved in questions of democracy and disarmament, as well as the problems of the Third World. He was renowned for condemning undemocratic acts by right-wing and left-wing dictators. Palme's assassination on the streets of Stockholm in 1986 sent shock waves across the world. The murder has still not been solved.

These areas soon became known as the "new slums" despite high standards of construction.

The Postwar Era

Although the Social Democrats dominated government from the 1930s to the 1970s, the socialist and non-socialist power blocs in Swedish politics have remained fairly evenly matched since World War II.

Important changes took place during the closing decades of the 20th century. These included a new constitution in 1974 which removed the monarch's political powers. In 1995 Sweden joined the European Union after a referendum approved entry by a narrow majority. The start of the new millennium marked a change in the role of the church in Sweden, which severed its ties with the state after more than 400 years.

Sweden weathered the global financial crisis, which began in 2007, relatively well, with most nationals continuing to lead a good, socially secure life. Rapid technical developments and globalization have given Sweden new job opportunities and new inhabitants, as well as a leading international role in technology and innovation.

The centre of Vällingby, which attracted attention among city planners worldwide in the 1950s

1974 The monarch loses all political powers

1980 New constitution gives women the right of succession to the throne

2000 Öresund Bridge opens between Denmark and Sweden

2003 Sweden rejects the euro

2009 Swedish becomes the official language

2013 King Carl XVI Gustaf celebrates 40 years as reigning monarch

Crown Princess Victoria

1980		2000		2020

1986 Prime Minister Olof Palme murdered in Stockholm

1995 Sweden joins European Union

2003 Foreign Minister Anna Lindh murdered in Stockholm

2016 Crown Princess Victoria gives birth to her second child, Prince Oscar

1973 Gustav VI Adolf dies and is succeeded by his grandson, Carl XVI Gustaf

2000 Swedish church separates from the state

2012 Crown Princess Victoria gives birth to Princess Estelle, who becomes second in line to the throne

STOCKHOLM AREA BY AREA

Stockholm at a Glance

Stockholm has around 100 museums covering every conceivable subject, as well as buildings of historic and architectural interest, such as Stadshuset (City Hall). The museum collections range from the treasures and antiquities of Kungliga Slottet (the Royal Palace) to the latest in contemporary art at Moderna museet and the spectacular *Vasa* warship at Vasamuseet. Open spaces abound, and it is even possible to swim in the heart of the city.

Hallwylska museet
Thanks to a methodical countess and her impeccable taste, this lavish 1890s' palace has become a magnificent museum with 67,000 exhibits displayed in their original setting.

Vasastaden

City

Kungs-
holmen

Gamla St

Stadshuset
This stunning building opened in 1923 is the seat of the capital's government and a symbol of Stockholm. It is also the venue for the annual Nobel Prize festivities.

0 metres	500
0 yards	500

Swimming in the City
In the summer, swimmers bathe in the clean, warm water (about 20 °C/68 °F) in the city centre. Långholmen *(see p108)* has sandy beaches and smooth rocks – an ideal setting for a dip.

Kungliga Slottet
In addition to its own attractions, the Royal Palace has four specialist museums: the Treasury, featuring Erik XIV's orb (1561), the Royal Armoury, Gustav III's Museum of Antiquities, and the Tre Kronor Museum.

◀ An aerial view of downtown Stockholm

Nationalmuseum
This museum is Sweden's largest art gallery, and has collections of 18th- and 19th-century Swedish paintings, applied arts and design, 18th-century French and 17th-century Dutch art. Rubens's *Bacchanal on Andros* dates from the 1630s. The museum is closed until 2018.

Nordiska museet
A statue of Karl X Gustav greets visitors arriving at this enormous building. Opened in 1907, it houses many different artifacts illustrating Swedish life and customs.

Östermalm

Skansen
The world's first open-air museum, founded in 1891, shows the Sweden of bygone days with farms and manor houses, urban scenes and craftspeople at work. Nordic fauna and flora are also on display.

Djurgården

Skepps-
holmen

öder-
malm

Moderna museet
Paradise (1966) by Tinguely/de Saint Phalle marks the way to Moderna museet, which houses remarkable collections of international and Swedish modern art.

Vasamuseet
A fatal capsizal in 1628 and a successful salvage operation 333 years later gave Stockholm its most popular museum. The warship *Vasa* is 95 per cent intact after painstaking renovation.

GAMLA STAN

Relics of Stockholm's early history as a town in the 13th century can still be found on Stadsholmen, the largest island in Gamla Stan (Old Town). The island is a huge area of historical heritage, with the many sights just a few metres apart.

The Royal Palace is the symbol of Sweden's era as a great power in the 17th and early 18th centuries (see pp42–3), and its magnificent state rooms, apartments and artifacts are well matched to the Roman Baroque-style exterior. The historic buildings standing majestically around Slottsbacken underline Stockholm's role as a capital city.

This area has a special atmosphere with much to offer: from the bustling streets of souvenir shops, bookstores and antique shops to elegant palaces, churches and museums. Many medieval cellars are now restaurants and cafés, while the narrow cobbled streets recall a bygone era.

Bridges lead to Riddarholmen, with its 17th-century palaces and royal crypt, and to Helgeandsholmen for the newer splendours of Riksdagshuset (the Parliament building).

Sights at a Glance

Palaces and Museums

1 The Royal Palace (Kungliga Slottet) pp58–61
2 Livrustkammaren
3 Kungliga Myntkabinettet
10 Postmuseum
16 Medeltidsmuseet

Public Buildings

14 Riddarhuset
15 Riksdagshuset

Historic Buildings

4 Tessinska Palatset
12 Wrangelska Palatset

Streets and Squares

6 Stortorget
8 Mårten Trotzigs Gränd
9 Västerlånggatan
13 Evert Taubes Terrass

Churches

5 Storkyrkan
7 Tyska Kyrkan
11 Riddarholmskyrkan

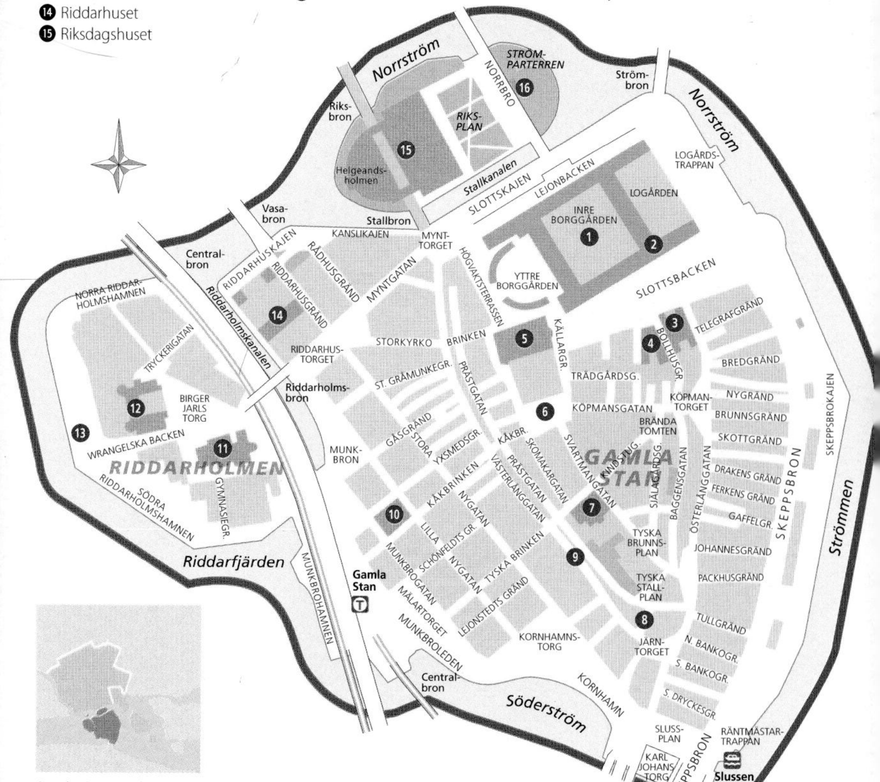

0 metres   250
0 yards   250

See also Street Finder map 3

◄ Bernt Notke's sculpture of *St George and the Dragon* in Storkyrkan

For keys to symbols *see back flap*

Street-by-Street: Slottsbacken

Slottsbacken is much more than just a steep hill linking Skeppsbron and the highest part of Gamla Stan (Old Town). It also provides the background for ceremonial processions and the daily changing-of-the-guard, and is the route for visiting heads of state and foreign ambassadors when they have an audience with the king at the Royal Palace. Alongside Slottsbacken the palace displays its most attractive façade, with the entrance to the Treasury (Skattkammaren), State Room (Rikssalen) and Palace Church (Slottskyrkan). Architect Nicodemus Tessin the Younger's ambition to make Stockholm a leading European city in architectural terms was realized in 1799 with the addition of the Obelisk.

The Olaus Petri statue by Storkyrkan stands in front of a tablet telling the cathedral's history since 1264.

Outer Courtyard

Axel Oxenstiernas Palats (1653) is, for Stockholm, an unusual example of the style known as Roman Mannerism. For 30 years, Axel Oxenstierna (1583–1654) himself was a dominant figure in Swedish politics (see p41).

TRANGSUND

The Obelisk by Louis Jean Desprez was erected in 1799 to thank the citizens for supporting Gustav III's Russian war in 1788–90.

Stock Exchange
(see p64)

STORTORGET

❺ ★ Storkyrkan
An impressive cathedral with a late Gothic interior, it is full of treasures from many different eras.

0 metres		100
0 yards		100

❻ Stortorget
This square is the heart of the "city between the bridges", with a well dating from 1778. It was the scene of the Stockholm Bloodbath in 1520.

For hotels and restaurants in this area see pp284–5 and pp294–5

2 ★ Livrustkammaren
Sweden's oldest museum displays royal weaponry, clothing and carriages from over five centuries. The picture shows Gustav II Adolf's stallion Streiff, from the battle of Lützen in 1632.

Kungsträdgården

Locator Map
See Street Finder map 3

1 ★ The Royal Palace
The southern façade has a triumphal central arch with four niches for statues, created by French artists in the 18th century.

Gustav III's statue was sculpted by J T Sergel in 1799 in memory of the "gallant king" who was murdered in 1792.

↓ Slussen

Köpmantorget with statue of St George Slaying the Dragon (1912).

3 Kungliga Myntkabinettet
In a 16th-century setting, the Royal Coin Cabinet has the world's largest stamped coin, from 1644.

Key
— Suggested route

Finska Kyrkan, Slottsbacken's oldest building, dates from the 1640s. Originally a royal ball-games court for the palace, since 1725 it has been the religious centre for the Finnish community.

4 Tessinska Palatset
Built by and for Nicodemus Tessin the Younger, architect of the Royal Palace, in 1694–7, this palace has been the residence of the Governor of Stockholm County since 1968

❶ The Royal Palace (Kungliga Slottet)

Defensive installations or castles have stood on the island of Stadsholmen ever since the 11th century. The Tre Kronor (Three Crowns) fortress was completed in the mid-13th century, but became a royal residence only during the following century. The Vasa kings turned the fortress into a Renaissance palace which burned to the ground in 1697. In its place the architect Nicodemus Tessin the Younger created a new palace in Baroque style with an Italianate exterior and a French interior toned down to suit Swedish tastes. The palace's 608 rooms were decorated by Europe's foremost artists and craftsmen. Adolf Fredrik was the first king to move into the palace, in 1754. It is no longer the king's private residence, but remains one of the city's leading sights.

★ Changing of the Guard
Stockholm's most popular tourist event is the daily changing of the guard at midday in the Outer Courtyard.

Entrance to the Royal Apartments

The Western Staircase
Tessin was especially proud of the two staircases, made from Swedish marble and porphyry. On the western staircase stands a bust of the gifted architect.

★ The Hall of State
This opulent hall has an atmosphere of ceremonial splendour and forms an ideal setting for Queen Kristina's silver throne, probably the palace's most famous treasure.

Entrance to Treasury and Royal Chapel

KEY

① **The Guest Apartments**

② **The Bernadotte Apartments** are situated on the floor below Karl XI's Gallery.

③ **Tre Kronor Museum** entrance from Lejonbacken (see p61).

④ **Carl Hårleman** played an important role in the design of the palace. His bust adorns this niche.

⑤ **Logården** is the terrace between the palace's east wings.

⑥ **Livrustkammaren** (see p62)

The Royal Chapel
This delightful little church has a rich interior decorated by many different artists. The pulpit is the work of J P Bouchardon.

Official Royal Residence

The king and queen have their offices at the palace, where they hold audiences with visiting dignitaries, and official ceremonies, although they spend most of their time at Drottningholm (see pp112–15). They travel around the country attending special events, official openings and anniversaries, and they make regular State visits abroad. The king is well known for his interest in the environment while the queen is heavily involved with her work for children.

King Carl XVI Gustaf and Queen Silvia

VISITORS' CHECKLIST

Practical Information
Gamla Stan. **Map** 3 B2. **Tel** 08-402 61 30. **W** **kungahuset.se**
Royal Apartments, Treasury, Tre Kronor Museum: **Open** mid-May–mid-Sep: 10am–5pm daily; mid-Sep–mid-May: 10am–4pm Tue–Sun. **Closed** for official functions of Court. 🅿 📷 for tours in Eng, call 08-402 61 30.
📷 ♿ ✎ Gustav III's Museum of Antiquities: **Open** mid-May–mid-Sep: 10am–5pm daily.
Royal Chapel: **Open** mid-Jun–mid-Sep: noon–3pm Wed & Fri.
✝ 11am Sun. ♿ ✎

Transport
🅣 Gamla Stan, Kungsträdgården.
🚌 2, 55.

Gustav III's State Bedchamber
Sergel's bust of Gustav III (1779) stands in the room where the king died after being shot at the Opera House. The 1770s decor is by J E Rehn.

★ Karl XI's Gallery
One of the most magnificent rooms in the palace, this fine example of Swedish Late Baroque is used for banquets hosted by the king and queen. In the cabinet is this priceless salt-cellar dating from 1627–8.

Gustav III's Museum of Antiquities
The museum's collection includes antique statues brought home by Gustav III from his journey to Rome.

Exploring the Royal Palace

The public areas of the Royal Palace allow visitors to walk through grand rooms of sumptuous furnishings and priceless works of art and craftsmanship. The Hall of State and the Royal Chapel are both characterized by their magnificent lavish decor and Gustav III's Museum of Antiquities contains ancient marble sculptures from the king's journey to Italy. The palace also houses the Treasury with the State regalia; the Tre Kronor Museum, which depicts the palace before the 1697 fire; and the Livrustkammaren *(see p62)*.

The Pillar Hall in the Bernadotte Apartments with original decor

Karl XI's Gallery, the finest example of the Late Baroque period in Sweden

The State Apartments

The Royal Family has lived at Drottningholm Palace (*see pp112–15*) since 1982, but official functions still take place in the State Apartments, including banquets hosted by the king during visits by foreign heads of state. Other official dinners are held here, as well as the annual festivities in December to honour the Nobel laureates.

The dinners are served in Karl XI's Gallery, the finest example of Swedish Late Baroque, modelled on the Hall of Mirrors at Versailles. Each window is matched with a niche on the inner wall where some of the palace's priceless works of arts and crafts are exhibited. Most remarkable is the salt-cellar made from ivory and gilded silver designed by the Flemish painter Rubens (1577–1640). The room known as "The White Sea"

King Karl XIV Johan's egg cup

serves as a drawing room. Gustav III's State Bedchamber, where the king died after being shot at the Opera House in 1792 (*see pp46–7*), is the height of Gustavian elegance. Along with Queen Sofia Magdalena's State Bedchamber, it was designed by the architect Jean Eric Rehn. The lintels on the doors to the Don Quixote Room, named after the theme of its tapestries, were made by François Boucher and are among the most treasured pieces.

The Guest Apartments

An imposing part of the palace, these apartments are where visiting heads of state stay. The beautiful rooms include the Meleager Salon, where official gifts and decorations are exchanged, and a large bedroom with a sculpted and gilded bed. Other impressive rooms are the Inner Salon, whose decor was inspired by the excavations in Pompeii, and the Margareta Room, named after the present king's grandmother, which displays some pictures painted by her.

The apartments contain remarkable works of craftsmanship by such 18th-century masters as Georg Haupt, Ephraim Ståhle and Jean-Baptiste Masreliez.

The Bernadotte Apartments

This magnificent suite has earned its name from the gallery displaying portraits of the Bernadotte dynasty. The apartments have some notable ceiling paintings and mid-18th-century chandeliers, and are used for many a ceremonial occasion. The elegant Pillar Hall is the venue for investitures, and the East Octagonal Cabinet with probably the palace's best Rococo decor, is where the king receives foreign ambassadors. Along with the western cabinet, its interior has remained just as it was planned by Carl Hårleman more than 250 years ago.

Oscar II's very masculine Writing Room, dating from the 1870s, also looks much as it did in his day. However, the palace was kept up to date with the latest technical advances: electricity was installed in 1883, and the telephone only one year later.

The Hall of State

Rococo and Classicism were brought together in perfect harmony by the architects Nicodemus Tessin the Younger and Carl Hårleman when they designed the two-storey Hall of State.

The Hall provides a worthy framework for Queen Kristina's silver throne, a gift for the coronation in 1650 and one of the most valuable treasures in the palace. The throne was given to the queen by Magnus Gabriel de la Gardie and was made in Augsburg by the goldsmith Abraham Drentwett.

The canopy was added 100 years later for the coronation of King Adolf Fredrik and was designed by Jean Eric Rehn.

The room is lavishly decorated. The throne is flanked by colossal sculptures of Karl XIV Johan and Gustav II Adolf, while those on the cornice symbolize Peace, Strength, Religion and Justice.

Until 1975 the Hall of State was the scene of the ceremonial opening of the Swedish Parliament (Riksdagen), which included a march past of the royal bodyguard in full regalia. It is now used for official occasions and, like the Royal Chapel, is a venue for summer concerts.

The Hall of State, the most important ceremonial room in the palace

The Royal Chapel

It took 50 years to build the Royal Palace, and a lot of effort went into the interior decoration of the Royal Chapel. The work was carried out largely by Carl Hårleman under the supervision of Tessin. As with the Hall of State, the co-operation between the two produced a magnificent result, enhanced by the contributions of several foreign artists.

A number of remarkable artifacts have been added over the centuries. The most recent was a group of six 17th-century-style bronze crowns, as well as two crystal crowns, given by the Court to King Carl XVI Gustaf and Queen Silvia to mark their marriage in 1976.

It also has some rare relics of the original Tre Kronor fortress: new benches that had been ordered by Tessin. They had been rescued during the palace fire in 1697 and preserved, but not put in the chapel until the 19th century. The benches were made by Georg Haupt, grandfather of the Georg Haupt who was to create some of the palace's most prized furnishings *(see p86)*.

Gustav III's Museum of Antiquities

Opened in 1794 in memory of the murdered king, the Museum of Antiquities initially housed more than 200 exhibits, mainly acquired during Gustav's Italian journey in 1783–4 and then supplemented with more purchases at a later date.

In 1866 the museum's collection was moved to the city's National Museum *(see pp86–7)*. During the 1950s the main gallery was renovated, followed by the smaller galleries 30 years later, which enabled the collection to be returned to its original setting.

The most prized exhibits are in the main gallery, the best known being the sculpture of Endymion, the eternally sleeping young shepherd and lover of the Moon Goddess Selene. The 18th-century sculptor Johan Tobias Sergel is represented by *The Priestess*, ranked as the collection's second most important piece. She is flanked by two large candelabras.

The Treasury

At the bottom of 56 well-worn steps, below the Hall of State on the south side of the palace, is the entrance to the Treasury (Skattkammaren) where the State regalia, the most potent symbols of the monarchy, are kept. Occasionally, for an important event, King Erik XIV's crown, sceptre, orb and the keys of the kingdom are taken out of their showcase and placed beside the uncrowned King Carl XVI Gustaf. The 1-m (3 ft) high silver baptismal font, which took

Erik XIV's crown, made by Cornelis ver Weiden in Stockholm in 1561

the French silversmith Jean François Cousinet 11 years to make, is over 200 years old and is still used for royal baptisms. Hanging in the Treasury is the only undamaged tapestry among six dating from the 1560s, salvaged from the 1697 fire.

Tre Kronor Museum

A fascinating attraction at the Royal Palace is the Tre Kronor (Three Crowns) Museum, which is housed in the oldest parts of the ruined Tre Kronor fortress, preserved under the north side of the palace. About half of a massive 12th-century defensive wall and brick vaults from the 16th and 17th centuries provide a dramatic setting for the museum which illustrates the palace's history over almost 1,000 years.

Two models of the Tre Kronor fortress show changes made during the second half of the 17th century and how it looked by the time of the fire. Among items rescued from the ashes are a snaps glass, amber pots and bowls made from mountain crystal.

A glass bowl in the Tre Kronor Museum, saved from the 1697 fire

❷ Livrust-kammaren

Slottsbacken 3. **Map** 3 C2.
Tel 08-402 30 30. Ⓣ Gamla Stan.
🚌 2, 55. **Open** May: 11am–5pm
daily; Jun: 10am–5pm daily;
Jul–Aug: 10am–6pm daily;
Sep–Apr: 11am–5pm Tue–Sun
(to 8pm Thu). 🅿 🏛 ♿ 📷
Ⓦ **livrustkammaren.se**

Sweden's oldest museum,
Livrustkammaren (the Royal
Armoury) was founded in 1628
and is full of *objets d'art* and
everyday items used by the
Royal Family over the past five
centuries. The oldest exhibit is
Gustav Vasa's crested helmet
dating from 1542. The museum
also houses a variety of royal
items which illustrate events
in Swedish history. Among
them are Gustav II Adolf's
stuffed stallion, Streiff,
which he rode at the
Battle of Lützen in
1632; Gustav III's
costume from the
notorious masked
ball at which he
was murdered in
1792; and Karl XII's
blue uniform with
the still muddy
boots he was
wearing when he
died at the siege of Fredrikshald
in Norway in 1718.

Coronation ceremonies are
illustrated by costumes such
as those worn by King Gustav III
and Queen Sofia Magdalena
in 1766. The king's attire alone
was adorned with some 2 kg
(4 lb) of silver. The coronation
carriage, originally built in the
17th century, was modernized

The coronation carriage of King Adolf Fredrik and Queen
Lovisa Ulrika in Livrustkammaren

for this event. Its renovation
in the 1970s took eight years
and cost 700,000 kronor.
The cellar vault, once used
for firewood, is skilfully lit,
providing an imaginative
setting for the exhibits.

❸ Kungliga Myntkabinettet

Slottsbacken 6. **Map** 3 C3.
Tel 08-519 553 00. Ⓣ Gamla Stan.
🚌 2, 43, 55, 76. **Open** 11am–5pm
daily. **Closed** public hols. ♿ by
appointment. 🅿 🖥 ✏ 🏛 ♿
Ⓦ **myntkabinettet.se**

The Royal Coin Cabinet is a
fabulous museum holding a
priceless collection of currency
and highlighting the history of
money from the 10th century
to the present day – from the
little cowrie shell via
the drachma and
denarius to the
current cash card.
The museum also
gives an insight
into the art of
medal design over
the past 600 years
and shows both
traditional portrait
medals and modern
examples such as
those that have been awarded
to Nobel laureates. Visitors can
also see the first Swedish coin,
struck in the late 10th century
by King Olof Skötkonung.
Other rarities include Queen
Kristina's coin from 1644,
weighing 19.7 kg (43 lb) and
reckoned to be the world's
heaviest coin. From the island of
Yap, in Micronesia, the museum
has acquired what
is thought to be
the world's largest
means of payment,
a so-called "rai-
stone" which greets
visitors in the foyer.

Sweden's first coin, struck
in about AD 995

The kids'
playroom is great
fun. Among its
highlights are a
pirate ship with a
treasure chest of
gold coins and a
kitsch collection
of piggy banks.

The elegant Baroque garden in Tessinska
Palatset's courtyard

❹ Tessinska Palatset

Slottsbacken 4. **Map** 3 C3.
Ⓣ Gamla Stan. 🚌 2, 55.
Closed to the public.

The Tessin Palace at
Slottsbacken is considered to
be the most beautiful private
residence north of Paris. It is
the best-preserved palace
from Sweden's era as a great
power in the 17th century
and was designed by and for
Tessin the Younger (1654–
1728), the nation's most
renowned architect.

Completed in 1697, the
building is located on a narrow
site which widens out towards a
courtyard with a delightful
Baroque garden. The relatively
discreet façade with its beautiful
porch was inspired by the
exterior design of Roman
palaces. The decor and garden
were influenced by Tessin's time
in Paris and Versailles.

Tessin, who became a count
and state councillor, spent large
sums on the building's
ornamentation. Sculptures and
paintings were provided by the
same French masters whose
work had graced the Royal
Palace. Later, however, his son,
Carl Gustaf, had to sell the palace
for financial reasons.

The building was acquired
by the City of Stockholm as a
residence for its governor in
1773. In 1968 it became the
residence of the governor of
the County of Stockholm.

For hotels and restaurants in this area see pp284–5 and pp294–5

❺ Storkyrkan

Trångsund 1. **Map** 3 B3. **Tel** 08-723 30 00. 🚇 Gamla Stan. 🚌 2, 55. **Open** 9am–4pm daily (extended hours in summer). ✝ 11am Sun. ♿ 📷 🏛 ♿ 🌐 **storkyrkan.nu**

Stockholm's 700-year-old cathedral is of great national religious importance. It was from here that the Swedish reformer Olaus Petri (1493–1552) spread his Lutheran message around the kingdom. It is also used for royal ceremonies.

Originally, a small village church was built on this site in the 13th century, probably by the city's founder Birger Jarl. It was replaced in 1306 by a much bigger basilica, St Nicholas, which was altered over the centuries.

The Gothic character of the interior, acquired in the 15th century, was revealed in 1908 when, during restoration work, plaster was removed from the pillars, exposing the characteristic red tiling. The Late Baroque period provided the so-called "royal chairs" and the pulpit, while the façade was adapted to bring it into keeping with the rest of the area around the Royal Palace. The 66-m (216-ft) high tower, added in 1743, has four bells, the largest of which weighs about 6 tons.

Storkyrkan's façade in Italian Baroque style, seen from Slottsbacken

The cathedral houses some priceless artistic treasures, including *St George and the Dragon*, regarded as one of the finest late Gothic works of art in Northern Europe. The sculpture, situated to the left of the altar, was carved from oak and moose horn by Lübeck sculptor Bernt Notke. Unveiled in 1489, it commemorates Sten Sture the Elder's victory over the Danes in 1471 *(see p39)*.

The Last Judgment (1696) is a massive Baroque painting by David Klöcker von Ehrenstrahl. The 3.7-m (12-ft) high bronze candelabra before the altar has adorned the cathedral for some 600 years. One of the cathedral's most prized treasures

is the silver altar, which was a gift from the diplomat Johan Adler Salvius in the 1650s.

The pews nearest to the chancel, the "royal chairs", were designed by Nicodemus Tessin the Younger in 1684 to be used by royalty on special occasions. In 1705, the pulpit was installed above the grave of Olaus Petri.

On 20 April 1535, a light phenomenon was observed over Stockholm – six rings with sparkling solar halos. *The Parhelion Painting*, recalling the event, hangs in Storkyrkan and is thought to be the oldest portrayal of the capital. It shows the modest skyline dominated by the cathedral, at that time still the basilica of St Nicholas.

In 2010, the cathedral underwent a large-scale renovation ahead of the wedding of Crown Princess Victoria.

Storkyrkan's silver altar (detail)

The sculpture *St George and the Dragon* by Bernt Notke (1489) in Storkyrkan

The former Stock Exchange, now home to Nobelmuseet

❻ Stortorget

Map 3 B3. ⓣ Gamla Stan. 🚌 2, 43, 55. Nobelmuseet: **Tel** 08-534 818 00. **Open** Jun–Aug: 10am–8pm daily; Sep–May: 11am–5pm Tue–Sun (to 8pm Tue). **Closed** Midsummer's Eve. ▨ ◩ daily (English). ▣ ◪ ◩ ⓓ ◼ nobelmuseum.se

It was not until 1778, when the Stock Exchange (Börsen) was completed, that Stortorget ("the big square") in the heart of the Old Town, acquired a more uniform appearance. Its northern side had previously been taken up by several buildings that served as a town hall. Since the early Middle Ages the square had been a natural meeting point with a well and market-place, lined with wooden stalls on market days.

A pillory belonging to the jail, which was once on nearby Kåkbrinken, used to stand on the square. It is now in the town hall on Kungsholmen.

The medieval layout is clear on Stortorget's west side, where the red Schantzska Huset (No. 20) and the narrow Seyfridtska Huset were built around 1650. The Schantzska Huset remains unchanged and has a lovely limestone porch adorned with figures of recumbent Roman warriors. The artist Johan Wendelstam was responsible for most of the notable porches in the Old Town. The 17th-century gable on Grilska Huset (No. 3) is also worth a closer study. Today there are cafés and restaurants in some of the vaulted cellars.

The decision to construct the Stock Exchange was taken in 1667, but the many wars delayed the start of the building by 100 years. The architect was the young and talented Erik Palmstedt (1741–1803), who also created the decorative cover for the old well. Trading on the floor of the Stock Exchange ceased in 1990. In 2001 the Nobelmuseet was opened here to mark the centenary of the Prize (see p75). The exhibition explores the work and ideas of more than 700

creative minds by means of short films and original artifacts. On the upper floor, the Swedish Academy holds its ceremonial gatherings, a tradition maintained since Gustav III gave his inauguration speech here in 1786.

❼ Tyska Kyrkan

Svartmangatan 16. **Map** 3 B3. **Tel** 08-411 11 88. ⓣ Gamla Stan. 🚌 2, 3, 43, 53, 55, 71, 76. **Open** May–mid-Sep: 11am–3pm daily (mid-Jul–mid-Aug: to 4:30 pm); mid-Sep–Apr: 11am–3pm Wed, Fri & Sat, 12:30–3pm Sun. **Closed** during services. ⓣ 11am Sun, German. ◩ by arrangement (Swedish & German). ⓓ

The German Church is an impressive reminder of the almost total influence that Germany had over Stockholm during the 18th century. The Hanseatic League trading organization was in control of the Baltic and its ports, which explains why the basic layout of Gamla Stan resembled that of Lübeck. Germany's political influence was only broken after the Stockholm Bloodbath and Gustav Vasa's accession to the throne in 1523 (see p40), but its cultural and mercantile influence remained strong as German merchants and craftsmen settled in the city.

The church's congregation, which today has some 2,000 members, was founded in 1571. The present twin-aisle church was built in 1638–42, as an extension of a smaller church which the parish had used since 1576.

The Stockholm Bloodbath

Stortorget is intimately linked with the Stockholm Bloodbath of November 1520. The Danish king, Christian II, besieged the Swedish Regent, Sten Sture the Younger, until he capitulated and the Swedes chose Christian as their king. The Dane promised an amnesty and ordered a three-day feast at Tre Kronor Fortress. Near the end of the festivities, the revellers were suddenly shut in and arrested for heresy. The next day more than 80 noblemen and Stockholm citizens were beheaded in the square.

Detail of a painting of the Bloodbath (1524)

The royal gallery in the 17th-century Tyska Kyrkan

In German Late Renaissance and Baroque style, the interior has a royal gallery, added in 1672 for German members of the royal household. The pulpit (1660) in ebony and alabaster is unique in Sweden and the altar, from the 1640s, is covered with paintings surrounded by sculptures of the apostles and evangelists.

The sculptures on the south porch by Jobst Hennen date from 1643 and show Jesus, Moses and three figures portraying Faith, Hope and Love.

Mårten Trotzigs Gränd, the narrowest street in the city

❽ Mårten Trotzigs Gränd

Map 3 C4. Ⓣ Gamla Stan. 🚌 2, 53, 55, 76.

At only 90 cm (3 ft) wide, Mårten Trotzigs Gränd is the city's narrowest street. Climbing up the 36 steps gives a good impression of how the various parts of the Old Town differ in height and how tightly the houses are packed together.

Mårten Trotzigs Gränd is named after a German merchant called Traubzich who owned two houses here at the end of the 16th century. After being fenced off at both ends for 100 years, the street was reopened in 1945.

❾ Västerlånggatan

Map 3 B3. Ⓣ Gamla Stan. 🚌 2, 53, 55, 76.

Once a main road outside the city proper, built along parts of the original town wall, Västerlånggatan now runs through the heart of the Old

Town, and is usually thronging with people – tourists and locals – shopping or strolling. Starting at Mynttorget in the north, by the Chancery Office (Kanslihuset) and Lejonbacken, the lively and atmospheric street finishes at Järntorget in the south, where the export of iron was once controlled. On Järntorget is Bancohuset, which served as the headquarters of the State Bank from 1680 to 1906.

The building at No. 7 has been used by the Swedish Parliament since the mid-1990s. Its late 19th-century façade has a distinctive southern European influence.

No. 27 was built by and for Erik Palmstedt, who also designed the Stock Exchange and the well at Stortorget. No. 29 is a truly venerable building, dating from the early 15th century. The original pointed Gothic arches were revealed during restoration in the 1940s.

No. 33 is a good example of how new materials and techniques in the late 19th century made it possible to fit large shop windows into old houses. The cast-iron columns which can be seen in many other places also date from this period.

No. 68, Von der Lindeska House, has a majestic 17th-century façade and a beautiful porch with sculptures of Neptune and Mercury.

❿ Postmuseum

Lilla Nygatan 6. **Map** 3 B3. **Tel** 010-436 44 39. Ⓣ Gamla Stan. 🚌 3, 53. **Open** 11am–4pm Tue–Sun (Sep–Apr: to 7pm Wed). 🅿 by arrangement. 🏠 📷 ✏ 📷 ♿ 🌐 postmuseum.posten.se

An attraction in itself, the Postmuseum building takes up a whole area bought by the Swedish Post Office in 1720.

Västerlånggatan, Gamla Stan's most popular shopping street

About 100 years later the majestic-looking Post Office was built, incorporating parts of the 17th-century buildings. Stockholm's only Post Office until 1869, it was turned into a museum in 1906.

Letters have been sent in Sweden, in an organized way, since 1636, and the museum's permanent exhibits include a portrayal of early "peasant postmen" fighting the Åland Sea in their boat *Simpan*. Also on display is the first post bus which ran in northern Sweden in the early 1920s and a stagecoach used in eastern Sweden.

Mauritian stamp in the Postmuseum

The collection includes Sweden's first stamp-printing press and no less than four million stamps among which are the first Swedish stamps, produced in 1855. Also on show is "Penny Black", the world's first stamp dating from 1840, and some stamps issued by Mauritius in 1847.

There is a philatelic library holding 51,000 volumes and stamp collections, as well as computers and multimedia equipment for research. A special exhibition for children is on display in the basement.

⓫ Riddarholms-kyrkan

Birger Jarls Torg. **Map** 3 A3.
Tel 08-402 61 30. Ⓣ Gamla Stan.
🚌 3, 59. **Open** mid-May–mid-Sep:
10am–5pm daily; mid-Sep–Nov:
10am–4pm Sat & Sun. 🅿️ 📷 mid-
May–mid-Sep: noon daily (English).
♿ 🚻

This church on the island of
Riddarholmen is best known as a
place for royal burials. Its interior
is full of ornate sarcophagi and
worn gravestones, and in front
of the altar are the tombs of the
medieval kings Karl Knutsson
and Magnus Ladulås.

Built on the site of the late
13th-century Greyfriars abbey,
founded by Magnus Ladulås,
the majestic brick church was
gradually enlarged over the
centuries. After a serious fire in
1835, it acquired its present
lattice-work cast-iron tower.

Inside, burial vaults, dating
back to the 17th century, surround the church. The coffins
rest on a lower level with space
for a memorial above. The most
recent was built in 1858–60
for the Bernadotte dynasty.

The vaults contain the remains
of all the Swedish sovereigns
from Gustav II Adolf in the 17th
century to the present day with
two exceptions: Queen Kristina
was buried at St Peter's in Rome
in 1689 and Gustav VI Adolf,
who was interred at Haga in
1973 (see p102). The most
magnificent sarcophagus is
that of the 19th-century king,
Karl XIV Johan, which was
towed here by sledge from
his porphyry workshops
in northern Sweden.
Particularly moving

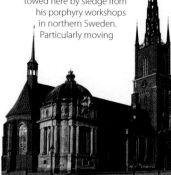

Riddarholmskyrkan and the external burial vault by
Tessin and Hårleman

Wrangelska Palatset, a royal residence after the Tre Kronor fire of 1697

are the graves of royal children,
including the many small tin
coffins that surround the last
resting place of Gustav II Adolf
and his queen, Maria Eleonora.

⓬ Wrangelska Palatset

Birger Jarls Torg 16. **Map** 3 A3.
Ⓣ Gamla Stan. 🚌 3, 59. **Closed** to
the public.

Only two parts of Gustav Vasa's
fortifications from 1530 remain
– Birger Jarl's Tower and the
southernmost tower of what
became the Wrangel Palace.
Built as a residence for
the nobleman
Lars Sparre in
1652–70, it was
remodelled a few
decades later by Carl
Gustaf Wrangel. A field
marshal in the Thirty
Years War, Wrangel
chose Nicodemus Tessin
the Elder as his architect.
The result was
Stockholm's largest
privately owned palace.
In 1697 the Royal Family
moved into the palace
after the Tre Kronor
fortress (see p58) was
ravaged by fire. It became
known as the King's House,
and it was here in the
same year that the
15-year-old Karl XII took
the oath of office after
the death of his father.
Gustav III was born here
in 1746 and in 1792 his
assassin was incarcerated
in the dungeons.
The Court of Appeal

Evert Taube
(1890–1976)

now uses this building, as
well as Rosenhane Palace
(Birger Jarls Torg 10) and
Hessenstein House (Birger Jarls
Torg 2), built in 1630 by Bengt
Bengtsson Oxenstierna.

⓭ Evert Taubes Terrass

Norra Riddarholmshamnen. **Map** 3 A3.
Ⓣ Gamla Stan. 🚌 3, 59.

A statue of Evert Taube, the
much-loved troubadour and
ballad writer, stands on the
terrace below Wrangelska
Palatset looking out
over the waters of
Riddarfjärden.
In an ideal position,
given the poet's
close links to the sea,
the bronze sculpture
was created by Willy
Gordon in 1990. Close
by stands Christer Berg's
granite sculpture *Solbåten*
(Sun Boat), unveiled
in 1966. Inspired by
the shape of a shell,
from some angles it also
resembles a sail.

⓮ Riddarhuset

Riddarhustorget 10. **Map** 3 A3.
Tel 08-723 39 90. Ⓣ Gamla Stan.
🚌 3, 59. **Open** 11am–noon Mon–Fri.
Closed public hols. 🅿️ 📷 by
appointment. 🌐 **riddarhuset.se**

Often regarded as one of
Stockholm's most beautiful
buildings, Riddarhuset
(House of Knights) stands on
Riddarhustorget, the city's
centre until the 19th century.

Built in 1641–7 on the initiative of the State Chancellor, Riddarhuset provided the knights with a base for meetings and events. The building is a supreme example of Dutch Baroque design by the architects Simon and Jean de la Vallée, Heinrich Wilhelm and Justus Vingboons.

Over the entrance on the northern façade is the knights' motto *Arte et Marte* (Art and War) with Minerva, Goddess of Art and Science, and Mars, God of War.

The sculptures on the vaulted roof symbolize the knightly virtues. On the south side is *Nobilitas* (Nobility) holding a small Minerva and spear. She is flanked by *Studium* (Diligence) and *Valor* (Bravery). Facing the north is the male equivalent, *Honor*, flanked by *Prudentia* (Prudence) and *Fortitudo* (Strength).

Inside, a magnificent double staircase leads up to the Knights' Room. This has a painted ceiling by David Klöcker Ehrenstrahl (1628– 98) and Riddarhuset's foremost treasure, a sculpted ebony chair, 1623. The walls are covered with coats of arms.

Riddarhuset, built in the 17th century in imposing Dutch Baroque style

⑮ Riksdagshuset

Riksgatan 3 A. **Map** 3 B2. **Tel** 08- 786 40 00. Ⓣ Kungsträdgården. 🚍 3, 53, 65. **Open** tours & meetings in the Chamber. 📷 daily in summer; weekends in winter; ring for details. 📅 ♿ ⓦ **riksdagen.se**

The Parliament building (Riksdagshuset) and Bank of Sweden (Riksbank) on Helgeandsholmen were inaugurated in 1905 and 1906 respectively. In the 1970s and

1980s the two buildings were combined and restored and a modern extension built to house a new, single debating chamber. The chamber is truly Nordic in its decoration with benches of Swedish birch and wall-panelling in Finnish birch. A large tapestry, *Memory of a Landscape* (1983), by Elisabeth Hasselberg-Olsson, covers 54 sq m (581 sq ft) of wall and took 3,500 hours to make. Parliamentary debates can be watched from the public gallery.

The original two-chamber Parliament is used for meetings of the majority party. The former First Chamber has three paintings by Otte Sköld (1894–1958); the other chamber contains works by Axel Törneman and Georg Pauli. Between the chambers is a 45 m (148 ft) long hall with an elegant display of coats of arms. The Finance Committee meets in the oak-panelled library surrounded by old prints and *Jugendstil* (Art Nouveau-style) lamps. Facing the Norrbro entrance is the original 1905 stairwell with columns, floor,

steps and balusters in various marbles. The present entrance was the Bank of Sweden's main hall until 1976.

⑯ Medeltidsmuseet

Strömparterren, Norrbro. **Map** 3 B2. **Tel** 08-508 316 20. Ⓣ Kungsträdgården. 🚍 53, 65. **Open** noon–5pm Tue–Sun (to 8pm Wed). 📷 📎 ♿ 🖼 ⓦ **medeltidsmuseet. stockholm.se**

This fascinating museum of medieval Stockholm is built around some of the capital's archaeological remains, mainly parts of the city wall that date from the 1530s. They were discovered in 1978–80. Completely underground, the dimly lit, atmospheric museum includes finds evoking Stockholm's early

Medieval stone head of Birger Jarl at Medeltidsmuseet

history. Among them is the 22 m (72 ft) long Riddarholm ship, dating from the 1520s, which was found off Riddarholmen in 1930.

The museum provides a good picture of Stockholm's early days. From the entrance, a 350-year-old tunnel leads into a reconstructed medieval world. There is a pillory in the square and gallows with the tools of the executioner's trade. The city has been recreated with a church, harbour and a square. Visitors can also see a 55 m (180 ft) long section of the original city wall, complete with a skeleton which had been concealed there.

The new Parliament building, with the older building behind

CITY

The area known as City today was where, in the mid-18th century, the first stone-built houses and palaces outside Gamla Stan started to appear for the burghers and nobility. After World War II, the run-down buildings around Hötorget were demolished to form what is now Sergels Torg; many homes were replaced by rather dreary office blocks.

In the 21st century, though, the area has livened up and become the true heart and commercial centre of Stockholm.

A hub for public transport and banking, City is the place for the best department stores and shopping malls, exclusive boutiques and nightspots. The centre also has some beautiful parks and pleasant squares which serve as popular meeting places. The unique landscape surrounding Stockholm permeates even City, offering sudden unexpected glimpses of water complete with bustling boat life and a string of anglers along the embankments.

Sights at a Glance

Museums
- ⑤ Dansmuseet
- ⑥ Medelhavsmuseet
- ⑪ Strindbergsmuseet
- ⑭ Armémuseum
- ⑮ Scenkonstmuseet
- ⑱ Hallwylska museet

Churches
- ③ Jacobs Kyrka
- ⑧ Klara Kyrka
- ⑫ Adolf Fredriks Kyrka

Squares
- ② Kungsträdgården

Public Buildings
- ① Nordiska Kompaniet (NK)
- ⑦ Arvfurstens Palats
- ⑬ Kungliga Biblioteket
- ⑯ Hovstallet

Theatres and Concert Halls
- ④ Kungliga Operan
- ⑨ Kulturhuset and Stadsteatern
- ⑩ Konserthuset
- ⑰ Kungliga Dramatiska Teatern

See also Street Finder maps 1, 2 & 3

◀ Statue of Gustav II Adolf in the middle of Gustav Adolfs Torg

For keys to symbols *see back flap*

Street-by-Street: Around Kungsträdgården

With a history going back to the 15th century, the King's
Garden (Kungsträdgården) has long been the city's most
popular meeting place and recreational centre. Both
visitors and Stockholmers gather here for summer
concerts and festivals, or just to enjoy a stroll under
the lime trees. Around the park is a wealth of shops,
including the upmarket department store Nordiska
Kompaniet, boutiques, churches, museums and
restaurants. A short walk takes you to Gustav Adolfs
Torg, flanked by the Royal Opera House and other
stately buildings, including the Swedish Foreign Office.

❹ ★ Kungliga Operan
Built in 1898 with a magnificently
ornate auditorium, the Royal Opera
House replaced an earlier one
from the time of Gustav III.

❻ ★ Medelhavsmuseet
This museum near Gustav Adolfs Torg
has vast collections from prehistoric
cultures around the Mediterranean.

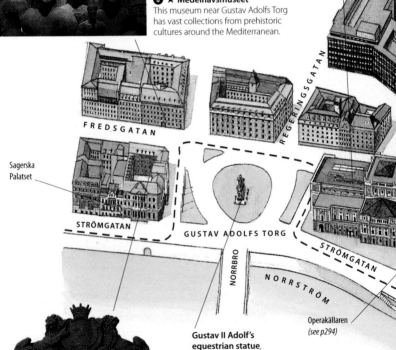

Sagerska
Palatset

FREDSGATAN

REGERINGSGATAN

STRÖMGATAN

GUSTAV ADOLFS TORG

NORRBRO

STRÖMGATAN

NORRSTRÖM

Operakällaren
(see p294)

**Gustav II Adolf's
equestrian statue,**
designed by
L'Archevêques, was
unveiled in 1796.

SOPHIA·ALBERTINA
ÆDIFICAVIT·

❼ Arvfurstens Palats
The Swedish Foreign Office is based in
this palace, built for Gustav III's sister
Sofia Albertina in 1794.

Key
— Suggested route

For hotels and restaurants in this area see pp284–5 and pp294–5

Queen Kristina's summer house by the cobble-stoned Lantmäteri-backen.

The NK clock, part of the city skyline.

Locator Map
See Street Finder maps 2 & 3

VASASTAN

CITY

Riddarfjärden   GAMLA STAN

Stockholm

Sergels Torg

HAMNGATAN

VÄSTRA TRÄDGÅRDSGATAN

KUNGSTRÄDGÅRDSGATAN

❶ **Nordiska Kompaniet (NK)**
Designed by Ferdinand Boberg in 1915, the granite palace houses Sweden's most exclusive department store.

Statue of Karl XIII

Molin's fountain

❷ **Kungsträdgården**
The king's kitchen garden was sited here in the 15th century. Today it is one of the most popular recreation centres in the city, both in summer and winter.

❸ **Jacobs Kyrka**
Started in 1580, the church was consecrated in 1643. Its stone porches are beautifully crafted.

0 metres   100
0 yards   100

Karl XII's statue by Molin was built in 1868 to mark the 150th anniversary of the king's death.

❶ Nordiska Kompaniet (NK)

Hamngatan 18–20. **Map** 2 D4.
Tel 08-762 80 00. T T-centralen.
🚌 7. **Open** 10am–8pm Mon–
Fri, 10am–6pm Sat, 11am–5pm Sun.

Designed by Ferdinand Boberg, the granite palace on Hamngatan houses the department store Nordiska Kompaniet (NK). Opened in 1915, NK was – and still is – aimed at an exclusive clientele. It made its name as a showcase for Swedish arts and crafts, writing design history when the textiles department, Textilkammaren, opened in 1937. The manager was the textile artist Astrid Sampe who commissioned leading contemporary artists and designers to supply work. Olle Baertling, Arne Jacobsen, Alvar Aalto and Viola Gråsten all contributed patterns. Sampe also introduced new fabric printing techniques.

Today at NK you can find almost everything from perfume, clothing and sporting equipment to glass, silver and porcelain, but above all, the store is, as its founder Josef Sachs once described it, a commercial and cultural theatre.

❷ Kungsträdgården

Map 3 B1. T Kungsträdgården.
🚌 47, 69.

The "King's Garden" is a popular meeting place for Stockholmers where there is something for everyone going on all year round. This open urban space

is bordered by treelined promenades, with a modern fountain in the middle. At the Strömgatan end there is a square named after Karl XII with J P Molin's statue of the warrior king, unveiled in 1868, at its centre. In Kungsträdgården itself there is a statue of Karl XIII (1809–18) by Erik Göthe. During the summer, the park is the venue for food festivals, concerts, dancing and street theatre. In winter, the skating rink attracts children and grown-ups alike. Also to be seen is Molin's fountain, made from gypsum in 1866 and cast in bronze.

Molin's fountain

It is the city's oldest park, starting as the royal kitchen garden in the 15th century. During Erik XIV's reign in the 16th century, it was transformed into a formal Renaissance garden. Queen Kristina built a stone summer house here in the 17th century, which stands at Västra Trädgårdsgatan 2, by the cobblestoned Lantmäteribacken.

❸ Jacobs Kyrka

Jakobs Torg 5. **Map** 3 B1. **Tel** 08-723 30 38. T Kungsträdgården. 🚌 53, 65. **Open** 11am–5pm Mon–Wed & Sat–Sun, 11am–6pm Thu & Fri.
📷 In Eng 6pm Sun. ♿

In medieval times there was a small chapel where Kungsträdgården now lies. Dedicated to St Jacob, the patron saint of wayfarers, the chapel and another modest-sized church were pulled down by King Gustav Vasa in the 16th century. His son, Johan III,

wanted to provide two new churches in Norra Malmen, as the area was then called, and work to build the churches of St Jacob and St Klara (see p74) started in 1580. St Jacob's was consecrated first, in 1643. It has been restored several times since then, in some cases rather clumsily. However, several valuable items have been preserved, including a baptismal font from 1634 and some church silver, as well as porches by the stonemasons Henrik Blom and Hans Hebel.

The organ's façade was created by the architect Carl Hårleman and the large painting on the west wall of the southern nave is by Fredrik Westin, Sweden's most distinguished historical painter of the early 19th century.

Altar in Jacobs Kyrka, dating in part from the 17th century

❹ Kungliga Operan

Gustav Adolfs Torg. **Map** 3 B1.
Tel 08-791 44 00. T Kungsträdgården. 🚌 53, 65. Ticket Office:
Open noon–5pm Mon–Fri, noon–
3pm Sat (open Sun for performances).
📷 In Eng 1pm Sat. 🅿 🚫 📷 ♿
🆆 operan.se

Opera has been staged in Sweden since 18 January 1773, when a performance took place at Bollhuset at Slottsbacken. Kungliga Operan (The Royal Opera House) on Gustav Adolfs Torg was inaugurated on 30 September 1782, but by the late 19th century it had become a fire hazard. The architect Axel Anderberg was commissioned to design a new opera house

View of Kungsträdgården, towards Hamngatan

For hotels and restaurants in this area see pp284–5 and pp294–5

The splendid golden foyer at Kungliga Operan

which was given to the State in 1898 by a consortium founded by the financier K A Wallenberg.

The colouring of the building in Late Renaissance style is in keeping with the Royal Palace and Parliament building, and some details of the architecture are common to all three. The beautiful staircase with ceiling paintings by Axel Jungstedt was inspired by the Paris Opera. The same artist's portrait of Oscar II hangs in the 28 m (92 ft) long golden foyer, where Carl Larsson was responsible for the decorative paintings. The wings at either side of the stage have been retained, as has the width of the proscenium arch (11.4 m/37 ft). Also saved was J T Sergel's group of angels above the stage. An angel in Vicke Andrén's ceiling painting is holding a sketch of the Opera House.

Gold ceiling in Kungliga Operan

❺ Dansmuseet

Drottninggatan 17. **Map** 3 A1. **Tel** 08-441 76 50. Ⓣ Kungsträdgården. 🚌 53, 65. **Open** 11am–5pm Tue–Fri, noon–4pm Sat & Sun. 🌐 dansmuseet.se

Located in the heart of Stockholm, the Dance Museum is housed in a former bank building on Drottninggatan. The museum was originally

established in Paris in 1953 by the Swedish aristocrat Rolf de Maré (1888–1964). He was a noted art collector and founder of the renowned avant-garde company Les Ballets Suédois. The collection features all aspects of dance – costumes and masks, scenery sketches, art and posters, books and documents – and includes an archive on popular dance. Apart from the exhibition hall, there is also a data bank – the Rolf de Maré Study Centre – which contains video/DVD facilities, a library and archives. The museum shop stocks Sweden's largest collection of dance DVDs for sale.

❻ Medelhavs-museet

Fredsgatan 2. **Map** 3 B1. **Tel** 010-456 12 00. Ⓣ Kungsträdgården. 🚌 53, 65. **Open** noon–8pm Tue–Thu, noon–5pm Fri–Sun. 🌐 medelhavsmuseet.se

Gods and people from prehistoric cultures around the Mediterranean rub shoulders in Medelhavsmuseet (the Museum of Mediterranean and Near East Antiquities). Its many treasures include a large group of terracotta figures discovered by archaeologists on Cyprus in the 1930s. There is an extensive display covering ancient Egypt, with bronze

weapons, tools and some remarkable mummies. Greek and Islamic culture, Roman and Etruscan art are all represented and complemented by temporary exhibitions.

Medelhavsmuseet is housed in a former bank, built in the 17th century for Gustav Horn, a general in the Thirty Years War. The stairwell, dating from 1905, and the peristyles and colonnade around the upper part of the hall are worth a visit in themselves.

❼ Arvfurstens Palats

Gustav Adolfs Torg 1. **Map** 3 B1. Ⓣ Kungsträdgården. 🚌 53, 65. **Closed** to the public.

Opposite the Royal Opera House, on the other side of Gustav Adolfs Torg, stands Arvfurstens Palats (Prince's Palace), built for Gustav III's sister Sofia Albertina and completed in 1794. She commissioned the architect Erik Palmstedt to carry out the work. He was a pupil of Carl Fredrik Adelcrantz, designer of the original opera house.

The palace and its decor are shining examples of the Gustavian style, thanks to the contributions of artists and craftsmen such as Louis Masreliez and Georg Haupt and their pupils Gustaf Adolf Ditzinger, J T Sergel and Gottlieb Iwersson. In 1906 the building was taken over by the Swedish Foreign Office.

Nearby is the elegant Sagerska Palatset (1894) in French Renaissance style, which is used by the prime minister as an official residence.

Arvfurstens Palats (1794), now the Swedish Foreign Office

Edvin Öhrström's obelisk in Sergels Torg, with Kulturhuset to the left

❽ Klara Kyrka

Klara Östra Kyrkogata. **Map** 1 C4.
Tel 08-411 73 24. Ⓣ T-centralen.
🚌 53. **Open** 10am–5pm Sun–Fri,
5–7:30pm Sat. ✝ 8pm & 3:45pm
Mon–Fri. 🖼 ♿

The convent of St Klara stood
on the site of the present
church and cemetery until
1527, when it was pulled
down on the orders of Gustav
Vasa. Later, his son Johan III
commissioned a new church,
completed in 1590.

The church was ravaged by
fire in 1751. Its reconstruction
was planned by two of the
period's most outstanding
architects, Carl Hårleman and
Carl Fredrik Adelcrantz. The
pulpit was made in 1753 to
Hårleman's design, and
J T Sergel created the angelic
figures in the northern gallery.
A pair of identical angels adorn
the chancel, based on the
gypsum originals.

In the 1880s, the 116 m
(380 ft) tower was added. The
20th-century church artist,
Olle Hjortzberg, created the
paintings in the vault in 1904.

Interior of Klara Kyrka with decoration by
Olle Hjortzberg

❾ Kulturhuset and Stadsteatern

Sergels Torg 3. **Map** 1 C4.
Tel 08-506 202 00. Ⓣ T-centralen.
🚌 54, 57, 69. **Open** 9am–7:30pm
Mon–Fri, 11am–5pm Sat & Sun.
♿ some areas. 🖼 🎧 📷 ♿
🖥 **kulturhusetstadsteatern.se**

The distinctive glass façade of
Kulturhuset (Cultural Centre)
fronts the southern side of
Sergels Torg. The winning entry
in a Nordic architectural competition, Kulturhuset has become a
symbol of Swedish Modernism.
It was designed by Peter Celsing
and opened in 1974.

Refurbished to meet the
needs of the new millennium,
the complex contains several
galleries which mount regularly
changing exhibitions. In the
auditorium, a varied programme
of music, dance, drama and
lectures is presented.

In the Children's Room,
youngsters can read books,
draw pictures, listen to
stories or watch films. "Lava"
focuses on youth culture
nationwide. There is a library
for fans of strip cartoons
and reading rooms providing
computers, newspapers
and magazines.

Among the shops here
is Designtorget, selling
items of Swedish design.
There are two cafés: the
top-floor Café Panorama
offers diners fantastic city
views, while Café Ekoteket
serves organic and locally
produced food and also
hosts tasting sessions.

Kulturhuset also houses
Stadsteatern (City Theatre),
whose main auditorium
opened in 1990. This part of
the building was formerly
occupied by Parliament while
its chamber on Helgeands-
holmen was being rebuilt
(*see p67*). The theatre was
designed by architects Lars
Fahlsten and Per Ahrbom and
contains six stages of varying
size and style under one roof.

❿ Konserthuset

Hötorget. **Map** 1 C4. **Tel** 08-786 02 00.
Ⓣ Hötorget. 🚌 1, 56, 59. Ticket
Office: **Open** 11am–6pm Mon–Fri,
11am–3pm Sat, and an hour before
a concert. 🎧 🖼 📷 ♿
🖥 **konserthuset.se**

A Nordic version of a Greek
temple, Konserthuset (the
Concert Hall) is a masterpiece
of the architect Ivar Tengbom
(1878–1968) and is an
outstanding example of the

City's Transformation

During the 20th century Stockholm's population grew from 250,000
to more than 1.6 million. By the 1920s it was obvious that the old
heart of the city would not meet
the future needs of business, public
administration and the growth in
traffic. In 1951 a controversial
30-year ongoing programme to
transform the lower Norrmalm city
centre was launched. Slums on
335 of the 600 sites were pulled
down and 78 new buildings were
built. Two-thirds of the area's
buildings were added during
this period.

The first steps towards a new Hötorg
City, 1958

The *Orpheus* sculpture group by Carl Milles at Konserthuset

Neo-Classical style of the 1920s. Tengbom's tradition has been carried on by his son Anders (b. 1911), who was in charge of its renovation in 1970–71, and his grandson Svante (b. 1942), who had a similar task in 1993–6.

Constructed in 1923–6, the main hall has undergone major reconstruction and modernization to overcome acoustical problems. Its interior is very simple in contrast to the Grünewald Hall, by the artist Isaac Grünewald (1889–1946), which is in the more lavish style of an Italian Renaissance palace. The four marble statues in the main foyer are by Carl Milles, creator of the *Orpheus* sculpture group outside.

The Concert Hall is the home of the Swedish Royal Philharmonic Orchestra, which gives some 70 concerts every year, and international star soloists perform regularly. It is also the venue for the Nobel Prize presentations.

⓫ Strindbergs-museet

Drottninggatan 85. **Map** 1 C3. **Tel** 08-411 53 54. Ⓣ Rådmansgatan. 🚌 57. **Open** Jul–Aug: 10am–4pm Tue–Sun; Sep–Jun: noon–4pm Tue–Sun. 🖼 🏛 ♿ 🅦 strindbergsmuseet.se

The world-famous dramatist August Strindberg (1849–1912) lived at 24 different addresses in Stockholm over the years. He moved to the last of these in 1908, and gave it the name Blå Tornet (the Blue Tower). By then he had gained international recognition.

The apartment, now Strindbergsmuseet, was newly built with central heating, toilet and lift, but lacked a kitchen. Instead he relied on Falkner's Pension, in the same building, for food and other services. On his last few birthdays the great man would stand on his balcony and watch his admirers stage a torchlight procession in his honour.

Opened in 1973, the museum shows the author's home with his bedroom and dining room and his study as it was on his death, as well as 3,000 books, photographic archives, press cuttings and posters. In the adjoining premises, a permanent exhibition portrays Strindberg as author, theatrical director, artist and photographer. Temporary exhibitions and other activities are often held here.

Strindberg's desk and writing materials in his study

⓬ Adolf Fredriks Kyrka

Holländargatan 16. **Map** 1 C3. **Tel** 08-20 70 76. Ⓣ Hötorget. 🚌 52. **Open** 1–7pm Mon, 10am–4pm Tue–Sun. 🕯 7pm Thu, 11am Sun. 🎟 by appointment. 🖼 🏛 ♿

King Adolf Fredrik laid the foundation stone of this church in 1768 on the site of an earlier chapel dedicated to St Olof. Designed by Carl Fredrik Adelcrantz, in Neo-Classical style with traces of Rococo, the church has been built in the shape of a Greek cross and has a central dome.

The interior has undergone a number of changes, but both the altar and pulpit have remained intact. The sculptor Johan Tobias Sergel created the altarpiece and the memorial to the French philosopher Descartes who died in Stockholm in 1650. The paintings in the dome were added in 1899–1900 by Julius Kronberg. More recent acquisitions include altar silverware by Sigurd Persson.

Memorial to Descartes

The cemetery is the resting place of the assassinated Prime Minister Olof Palme (1927–86). J T Sergel is also buried here.

Armémuseum, with the dome of Hedvig Eleonora Kyrka in the background

⓭ Kungliga Biblioteket

Humlegården. **Map** 2 D3. **Tel** 010-709 30 00. Ⓣ Östermalmstorg. 🚌 1, 55. **Open** 9am–6pm Mon–Thu, 9am–5pm Fri, 11am–3pm Sat (except Jul). 📷 by appointment. 🖥 ♿ Ⓦ **kb.se**

This is Sweden's national library and an autonomous Government department in its own right. Ever since 1661, when there were only nine printing presses in Sweden, copies of every piece of printed matter have had to be lodged with Kungliga Biblioteket (Royal Library). Since 1993 this requirement has also applied to electronic documents. As there are now some 3,000 printers and publishers in Sweden the volume of material is expanding rapidly. The stock of books is increasing at the rate of 35,000 volumes a year.

The imposing original building, dating from 1865–78, had to be expanded in the 1920s, and again in the 1990s.

The library is in a beautiful setting in Humlegården, created by Gustav II Adolf in 1619 to grow hops for the royal household. Ever since the 18th century, the park has been a favourite recreation area for Stockholmers.

The 13th-century "Devil's Bible" in Kungliga Biblioteket

⓮ Armémuseum

Riddargatan 13. **Map** 2 E4. **Tel** 08-519 563 00. Ⓣ Östermalmstorg. 🚌 54, 69. **Open** 11am–8pm Tue, 11am–5pm Wed–Sun. 📷 🍴 🏠 ♿ Ⓦ **armemuseum.se**

The old armoury on Artillerigården has been the home of the Armémuseum (Royal Army Museum) since 1879. During the 1990s, the 250-year-old building and its displays underwent extensive renovation to create one of the capital's best-planned and most interesting museums.

Exhibits are arranged over three floors. Dramatic life-size settings have been made to portray Sweden's history of war and defence, showing not only what happened in battle but how the lives of the women and children at home were affected. Diaries, intelligence manuals, rifles, flags, banners and even cutlery add a note of reality.

During the summer, guardsmen march from here to the Royal Palace at 11:45am daily for the changing of the guard.

⓯ Scenkonstmuseet

Sibyllegatan 2. **Map** 2 E4. **Tel** 08-519 554 00. Ⓣ Östermalmstorg, Kungsträdgården. 🚌 47, 62, 69, 76. **Open** check website for details. 📷 Ⓦ **musikverket.se/scenkonstmuseet**

In 2017, following an extensive renovation project, Stockholm's Museum of Music will re-open as Scenkonstmuseet – the national performing arts museum. Housed in a 300-year-old building, the museum's collection of instruments will be displayed across three floors

and will celebrate music and performing arts, in all art forms. There will be interactive exhibits to engage visitors and inspire the next generation of performers. The museum will also have a concert venue.

The State Coach, built for Oscar II in 1897 by Adolf Freyschuss Hofvagnfabrik

⓰ Hovstallet

Väpnargatan 1. **Map** 2 E4. **Tel** 08-402 61 05. Ⓣ Östermalmstorg. 🚌 54, 69. **Open** for guided tours. 📷 🍴 1pm Sat (Eng); Jul–Aug: Mon–Fri. Ⓦ **kungahuset.se**

The Royal Stables looks after transport for the Royal Family and Royal Household. It maintains about 40 carriages, a dozen cars, carriage horses, and a few horses used for riding. The royal horses are Swedish half-breeds.

There are many treasures among the carriages, such as the glass-panelled State Coach known as a "Berliner". It was built in Sweden at the Adolf Freyschuss carriage works and made its debut at Oscar II's silver jubilee in 1897. It is still used today on ceremonial occasions.

Incoming foreign ambassadors travel to the Royal Palace for their formal audience with the monarch in Karl XV's coupé. Open horse-drawn carriages from the mid-19th century are normally used for processions.

Ingmar Bergman

The playwright and producer Ingmar Bergman was born at
Östermalm in 1918. His long series of
masterly films have made him world-
famous, but he started his career in the
theatre. From 1963 to 1966 he was
Director of Kungliga Dramatiska Teatern.
His breakthrough as a film producer
came with *Smiles of the Summer Night*
(1955), and *The Seventh Seal* (1957) was a
cinematic milestone. *Fanny and
Alexander* (1982) was his last major film,
after which he wrote screenplays and
published his autobiography, *Magic
Lantern*. Ingmar Bergman died in 2007.

Ingmar Bergman at a press
conference, 1998

The Hallwylska museet courtyard, seen
through the gateway arch

⑰ Kungliga Drama-
tiska Teatern

Nybroplan. **Map** 2 E4. **Tel** 08-667 06
80. Ⓣ Östermalmstorg. 🚌 54, 69.
🚋 7. Ticket Office: **Open** noon–1pm
& 5–7pm Tue–Fri, noon–7pm Sat,
noon–4pm Sun. 🎭 🚫 ♿ 📷
🆆 dramaten.se

When plans were drawn up in
the early 20th century to build
the present Kungliga Dramatiska
Teatern (Royal Dramatic Theatre)
at Nybroplan, the State refused
to give financial aid, so it was
funded by lotteries instead. The
results exceeded all expectations,
giving the architect Fredrik
Lilljekvist generous resources
which he used to the full.

The new theatre, known as
Dramaten, took six years to
build and opened in 1908. The
design was lavish, both in
the choice of materials and in
the contributions by leading
Swedish artists.

The Jugendstil façade,
inspired by Viennese

architecture, is in expensive
white marble. Christian Ericsson
created the powerful relief
frieze, Carl Milles the centre
section and John Börjesson the
bronze statues *Poetry* and
Drama. These are complemented in the foyer by *Tragedy*
and *Comedy* by Börjesson and
Theodor Lundberg respectively.

The ceiling in the foyer is by
Carl Larsson, while the upper
lobby's back wall was painted by
Oscar Björk, and the auditorium's
ceiling and stage lintel by Julius
Kronberg. Gustav Cederström
provided the central painting in
the marble foyer.

When Gustav III founded the
Royal Dramatic Theatre in 1788
it performed in a building on
Slottsbacken. The colour
scheme there – blue, white and
gold – was chosen for the new
venue, but was changed to
"theatre red" in the 1930s. The
original colours were
reinstated in 1988.

Kungliga Dramatiska Teatern's Jugendstil façade in white marble

⑱ Hallwylska
museet

Hamngatan 4. **Map** 2 D4. **Tel** 08-402
30 99. Ⓣ Östermalmstorg. 🚌 2, 55.
Open Jan–May: noon–4pm Tue–Sun
(to 7pm Wed); Jun: 10am–4pm Tue–
Sun; Jul–Aug: 10am–7pm Tue–Sun;
Sep–Dec: noon–4pm Tue–Sun (to
7pm Wed). 🎭 🏠 📷
🆆 hallwylskamuseet.se

The impressive façade of
Hamngatan 4 is nothing in
comparison with what is
concealed behind the heavy
gates. The Hallwyl Palace was
built from 1892–7 as a residence
for the immensely wealthy Count
and Countess Walther and
Wilhelmina von Hallwyl. When
the Countess died in 1930, the
State was left a fantastic gift:
an unbelievably ornate palace
whose chatelaine had amassed
a priceless collection of *objets
d'art* over many decades. Eight
years later the doors opened
on a new museum with 67,000
catalogued items.

Wilhelmina left nothing to
chance, often visiting the
building site. The architect Isak
Gustav Clason (1856–1930) had
no worries about cost and nor
did the decorative painter and
artistic adviser Julius Kronberg.
Every detail had to be perfect.
A typical example is the billiards
room which has gilt-leather
wallpaper and walnut panelling,
with billiard balls sculpted into
the marble fireplace.

The paintings in the gallery,
mostly 16th- and 17th-century
Flemish, were bought over a
period of only two years.

BLASIEHOLMEN & SKEPPSHOLMEN

Opposite the Royal Palace on the eastern side of the Norrström channel lies Blasieholmen, a natural springboard to the islands of Skeppsholmen and Kastellholmen.

Several elegant palaces were built at Blasieholmen during Sweden's era as a great power in the 17th and early 18th centuries. But the area's present appearance was acquired in the period between the mid-19th century, when buildings such as Nationalmuseum were erected, and just before World War I. In the early 1900s, stately residences such as Bååtska Palatset became overshadowed by smart hotels, opulent bank buildings and

entertainment venues. Blasieholmen is also the place for auction houses, art galleries, antiques shops and second-hand bookshops. And the quayside is the departure point for sightseeing and archipelago boats.

Skeppsholmen is reached by a wrought-iron bridge with old wooden boats moored next to it. In the middle of the 17th century the island became the base for the Swedish Navy and many of its old buildings were designed as barracks and stores. Today they house some of the city's major museums and cultural institutions, juxtaposed with the avant-garde construction of Moderna museet.

Sights at a Glance

Museums
1 Östasiatiska museet
2 Moderna museet pp84–5
3 Arkitektur och designcentrum
7 Nationalmuseum pp86–7

Islands and Squares
6 Kastellholmen
9 Blasieholmstorg
12 Raoul Wallenbergs Torg

Synagogues
10 Synagogan

Hotels and Restaurants
4 af Chapman
8 Grand Hôtel
11 Berns

Concert Halls
13 Musikaliska

Public Buildings
5 Kungliga Konsthögskolan

0 metres 250
0 yards 250

See also Street Finder maps 2, 3 & 4

◀ *af Chapman*, Stockholm's most unusual youth hostel

Street-by-Street: Skeppsholmen

Skeppsholmen has long since lost its importance as a naval base and has been transformed into a centre for culture. Many of the naval buildings have been restored and traditional wooden boats are moored here, but pride of place now goes to the exciting Moderna museet. The island is ideal for a full-day visit, with its location between the waters of Strömmen and Nybroviken acting as a breathing space in the centre of Stockholm. The attractive buildings, the richly wooded English-style park and the view towards Skeppsbron and Strandvägen also make Skeppsholmen a pleasant place for those who would just prefer to have a quiet stroll.

Teater Galeasen is Stockholm's avant-garde theatre for new Swedish and international drama.

Blasieholmen

Skeppsholmsbron (bridge)

S V E N S K S U N D V Ä G E N

Ö S T R A B R O B Ä N K E N

❶ ★Östasiatiska museet
This yellow-enamel dish with a blue dragon is part of a collection of arts and crafts from China, Japan, Korea and India covering the period from the Stone Age to the 1800s.

Skeppsholmen Church
(1824–42) in well-preserved Empire style.

Salute battery
(see p82)

Admiralty House

Paradise (1963), a sculpture group by Jean Tinguely and Niki de Saint Phalle for Montreal's World Exposition, has stood outside the site of the Moderna museet since 1972.

Youth Hostel

Swedish Society of Crafts & Design

❹ af Chapman
Built in 1888, the full-rigged former freighter and school ship has served as a popular youth hostel since 1949. Skeppsholmen Church *(left)* and the Admiralty House (1647–50, rebuilt 1844–6) are in the background.

❺ Kungliga Konsthögskolan
The first part of the Royal College of Fine Arts was completed in the 1770s, but it acquired its present appearance in the mid-1990s. This cast-iron boar stands at the entrance.

For hotels and restaurants in this area see pp284–5 and pp294–5

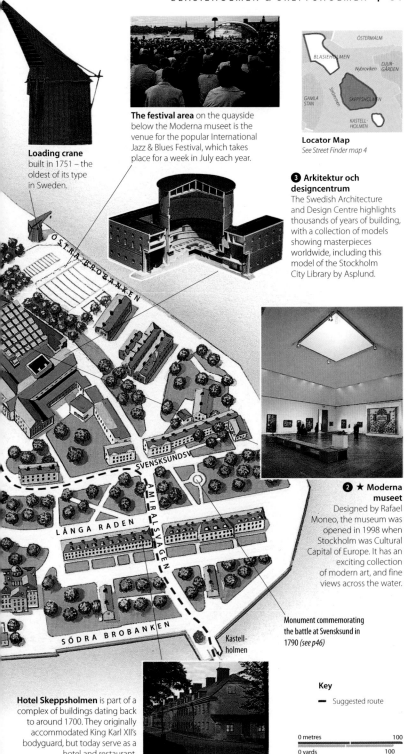

Loading crane
built in 1751 – the
oldest of its type
in Sweden.

The festival area on the quayside
below the Moderna museet is the
venue for the popular International
Jazz & Blues Festival, which takes
place for a week in July each year.

Locator Map
See Street Finder map 4

❸ **Arkitektur och
designcentrum**
The Swedish Architecture
and Design Centre highlights
thousands of years of building,
with a collection of models
showing masterpieces
worldwide, including this
model of the Stockholm
City Library by Asplund.

❷ ★ **Moderna
museet**
Designed by Rafael
Moneo, the museum was
opened in 1998 when
Stockholm was Cultural
Capital of Europe. It has an
exciting collection
of modern art, and fine
views across the water.

Monument commemorating
the battle at Svensksund in
1790 *(see p46)*

Hotel Skeppsholmen is part of a
complex of buildings dating back
to around 1700. They originally
accommodated King Karl XII's
bodyguard, but today serve as a
hotel and restaurant.

Key

━ Suggested route

0 metres   100
0 yards   100

Arkitektur och designcentrum, housed in the Neo-Classical former naval drill hall

❶ Östasiatiska museet

Tyghusplan. **Map** 4 D2. **Tel** 010-456 12 00. ⓣ Kungsträdgården. 🚌 65. 🚢 Djurgårdsfärja. **Open** 11am–7pm Tue–Sun. 🎧 by appointment only. 🏠 ♿ 🆆 **ostasiatiskamuseet.se**

It is not unusual for Western capitals to have a museum devoted to art and archaeology from China, Japan, Korea and India. But it is not every Museum of Far Eastern Antiquities that, like Östasiatiska museet, can claim one of the world's foremost collections of Chinese art outside Asia.

On a visit to the Yellow River valley in China in the early 1920s, the Swedish geologist Johan Gunnar Andersson discovered hitherto unknown dwellings and graves containing objects dating from the New Stone Age.

He was allowed to take a selection of items back to Sweden, and these formed the basis for the museum, founded in 1926. A key figure in its development was the then Crown Prince, later to

become King Gustav VI Adolf, who was both interested in and knowledgeable about archaeology. Later, he bequeathed to the museum his own large collection of ancient Chinese arts and crafts.

The museum has been on Skeppsholmen since 1963, when it was moved into a restored house which had been built in 1699–1700 as a depot for Karl XII's bodyguard.

❷ Moderna museet

See pp84–5.

❸ Arkitektur och designcentrum

Exercisplan 4. **Map** 4 E3. **Tel** 08-587 270 00. ⓣ Kungsträdgården. 🚌 65. 🚢 Djurgårdsfärja. **Open** 10am–8pm Tue & Fri, 10am–6pm Wed – Thu & Sat – Sun. 🎫 (free up to age 19; free for everyone 6–8pm Fri; combined ticket with Moderna museet.) 🎧 in English, by appointment only. 🏠 🍴 ✏ 📷 ♿ 📷 🆆 **arkdes.se**

The Swedish Architecture and Design Centre shares an entrance hall and restaurant

with Moderna museet. It has also reclaimed its earlier Neo-Classical home, a one-time naval drill hall.

In the permanent exhibition, more than 100 architectural models guide visitors through the history of Swedish building. They include the oldest and simplest of wooden houses to the highly sophisticated construction techniques and innovative styles of the present day.

It is fascinating to move from an almost 2,000-year-old long-house to a modern supermarket, interspersed with examples of architecture in Gothenburg from the 17th century to the 1930s.

Models of historic architectural works worldwide, from 2000 BC up to the present day, are also on show.

The museum offers an ambitious programme – albeit only in Swedish – alongside the permanent and temporary exhibitions, including lectures, study days, city walks, guided tours, school visits and family events on Sunday afternoons, which involve model-building.

Chinese Bodhisattva in limestone (c.530), Östasiatiska museet

The Skeppsholmen Cannons

A salute battery of four 57-mm rapid-fire cannons is sited on Skeppsholmen and is still in use. Salutes are fired to mark national and royal special occasions at 12 noon on week-days and 1pm at weekends: 28 January – the King's name day; 30 April – the King's birthday; 6 June – Sweden's National Day; 14 July – Crown Princess Victoria's birthday; 8 August – the Queen's name day; 23 December – the Queen's birthday.

The salute battery on Skeppsholmen

❹ af Chapman

Västra Brobänken. **Map** 4 D3.
Tel 08-463 22 66. Ⓣ Kunsträdgården.
🚌 65. ⛴ Djurgårdsfärja. 🖥 ✍ *See
Where to Stay p284.*

The sailing ship *af Chapman* is
one of Sweden's most attractive
and unusual youth hostels.
The ship has 125 beds, and
there are a further 155 beds
in the hostel building facing
the gangway.

Visitors staying in more
conventional accommodation
can still admire the boat from
a café nearby. The three-masted
ship was built in 1888 at the
English port of Whitehaven
and used as a freight vessel.
She came to Sweden in 1915
and saw service as a sail
training ship until 1934. The
City of Stockholm bought the
vessel after World War II and
she has been berthed here
since 1949. She is named after
Fredrik Henrik af Chapman, a
master shipbuilder who was
born in Gothenburg in 1721.

❺ Kungliga Konst-högskolan

Flaggmansvägen 1. **Map** 4 E3.
Tel 08-614 40 00. Ⓣ Kungsträdgården.
🚌 65. ⛴ Djurgårdsfärja. **Open** to the
public for special events. 🖥 🛗 ♿

A stroll around Skeppsholmen
provides an opportunity to have
a closer look at the beautifully
restored 18th-century naval
barracks which now houses
Kungliga Konsthögskolan (the
Royal Institute of Arts). At the
entrance there are two statues
depicting a lion and a boar.
"In like a lion and out like a
pig" is an old saying among
the lecturers and the 200 or
so students at this college, still
rich in tradition.

The college started out in
1735 as an academy for painting
and sculpture for the decorators
working on Tessin's new Royal
Palace. Gustav III granted it a
royal charter in 1773. Before it
moved here in 1995, the college
was located on Fredsgatan as
part of Konstakademien,
although since 1978 it had

been run independently with
departments for painting,
sculpture, graphics, computing
and video, as well as offering
courses for architects.

The college is not normally
open to the public, apart from
an "open house" once a year.
Then visitors can enjoy the
beautiful interiors, especially the
vaulted 18th-century cellars.

The medieval-style castle on
Kastellholmen, built in 1846–8

❻ Kastellholmen

Map 4 F4. Ⓣ Kungsträdgården.
🚌 65. ⛴ Djurgårdsfärja.

Right in the middle of
Stockholm, Kastellholmen is
a typical archipelago island
with granite rocks and steep
cliffs. From Skeppsholmen it is
reached by a bridge built in
1880. Every morning since
1640 a sailor has hoisted the
three-tailed Swedish war flag
at the castle. Whenever a
visiting naval vessel arrives,

the battery's four cannons fire
a welcoming salute from the
castle terrace.

The charming brick pavilion
by the bridge was built in 1882
for the Royal Skating Club,
which used the water between
the two islands when it froze.

❼ Nationalmuseum

See pp86–7.

❽ Grand Hôtel

Södra Blasieholmshamnen 8.
Map 3 C1. **Tel** 08-679 35 00.
Ⓣ Kungsträdgården. 🚌 2, 55, 65.
🖥 ✍ *See Where to Stay p284 and
Where to Eat p294.* 🌐 **grandhotel.se**

Oscar II's head chef, Régis Cadier,
founded the Grand Hôtel, one
of Stockholm's leading five-star
hotels, in 1874. Since 1901, the
hotel has accommodated the
Nobel Prize winners each year.

Traditional Swedish delicacies
are served in an abundant
smörgåsbord in the elegant
Veranda. The hotel also has two
Michelin-starred restaurants
and the Cadier Bar, named
after its founder.

The hotel has 24 banqueting
and conference suites, the best
known of which is the lofty
Vinterträdgården (Winter Garden)
which can accommodate 800
people. The *Spegelsalen* (Hall of
Mirrors) is a copy of the hall at
Versailles and was where the
Nobel Prize banquet was held
until 1929, when it became
too big and was moved to City
Hall *(see p106).*

The exclusive Grand Hôtel on Blasieholmen

❷ Moderna museet

The Museum of Modern Art is an airy building, designed by the Catalan architect Rafael Moneo in 1998. The museum has a top-class collection of international and Swedish modern art, as well as photography and film. Built partly underground, the complex includes a cinema and auditorium; the photographic library is the most comprehensive collection of its type in northern Europe and there is also a collection of video art and art documentaries. A wide choice of books on art, photography, film and architecture can be found in the bookshop and the restaurant has attractive views over the water.

Breakfast Outdoors (1962)
This sculpture group by Picasso, executed in sandblasted concrete by Carl Nesjar, stands in the museum garden near the entrance.

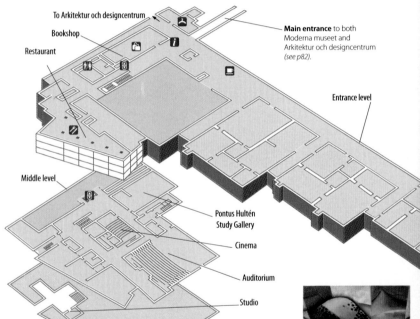

To Arkitektur och designcentrum

Bookshop

Restaurant

Main entrance to both Moderna museet and Arkitektur och designcentrum (see p82).

Entrance level

Middle level

Pontus Hultén Study Gallery

Cinema

Auditorium

Studio

★ **Marzella** (1909–10)
This boldly coloured portrait by Ernst Ludwig Kirchner (1880–1938) highlights his desire to bring fresh ideas to art by refuting traditional artistic conventions.

Rafael Moneo

Rafael Moneo (b. 1937) is one of the leading contemporary architects. As a young architect, Moneo took part in the project to build the Sydney Opera House. His flair for adapting building design to sensitive surroundings was recognized in 1989 when his was chosen out of 211 entries as the winner of the competition to design the new Moderna museet.

Moderna museet's northern façade

★ **Landscape from Céret** (1913)
Inspired by Braque and Picasso, Spanish Cubist artist Juan Gris (1887–1927) developed his own unique take on the discipline, as seen in this vivid, geometric landscape painting.

Gallery Guide

*The large room on the entrance
level is used for temporary
exhibitions. Three rooms on the
same level have an alternating
selection of collections from the
eras 1900–45, 1946–70 and
1971 to the present day. The
middle level has an auditorium,
cinema and study gallery.
Another entrance is at the
lowest level.*

Key

⬜ Museum's own collections

⬜ Temporary exhibitions

⬜ Non-exhibition space

★ **The Child's Brain** *(1914)*
The surrealist Giorgio de Chirico
gave his work the title *The Ghost*,
but in the irrational spirit of the
movement Louis Aragon renamed
it in a pamphlet about the artist's
1927 retrospective.

❾ Blasieholmstorg

Map 3 C1. 🚇 Kungsträdgården.
🚌 2, 55, 65, 76.

Two of the city's oldest palaces
are located in this square,
flanked by two bronze horses.
The palace at No. 8 was built in
the mid-17th century by Field
Marshal Gustaf Horn. It was
rebuilt 100 years later, when it
acquired the character of an
18th-century French palace.
Foreign ambassadors and
ministers lodged here when
they visited the capital, so it
became known as the Ministers'
Palace. Later it became a base
for overseas administration and
soon earned its present name
of Utrikesministerhotellet
(Foreign Ministry Hotel). Parts of
the building
are now used
as offices by
the Musical
Academy and the
Swedish Institute.
  Bååtska Palatset
stands nearby at
No. 6. Its exterior
dates from 1669
and was designed
by Tessin the Elder.
In 1876–7 it was partly rebuilt
by F W Scholander for the
Freemasons, who still have
their lodge here.
  Another interesting
complex of buildings can
be found on the square at
No. 10. The façade which
faces on to Nybrokajen,
along the water's edge, is an
attractive example of the
Neo-Renaissance style of the
1870s and 1880s.

**Bronze horse on
Blasieholmstorg**

❿ Synagogan

Wahrendoffsgatan 3B. **Map** 3 C1.
Tel 08-587 858 24. 🚇 Kungsträdgården. 🚌 2, 55, 65, 76.
⭐ all year 9.15am Sat; Sep–May:
5:30pm Fri; Hebrew and partly English.
🖊 summer and by appointment. ♿

It took most of the 1860s to
build the Conservative Jewish
community's synagogue on
land reclaimed from the sea.
When it was inaugurated in
1870, the building was
standing on 1,300 piles which

**Monument to the victims of the Holocaust
during World War II**

had been driven down to a
depth of 15 m (50 ft). It is
built in what the architect,
F W Scholander, called
"ancient Eastern style". The
synagogue can be visited
on guided tours during the
summer. Alongside is the
congregation's assembly
room and library. Outside
is a monument erected in
1998 in memory of
8,000 victims of the
Holocaust whose
relations had been
rescued and taken
to Sweden during
World War II.
  There is also an
Orthodox synagogue
in Södermalm. Its entrance is
just around the corner from
Ragvaldsgatan 14C.

⓫ Berns

Berzelii Park. **Map** 2 D4. **Tel** 08-566
322 00. 🚇 Kungsträdgården,
Östermalmstorg. 🚌 2, 55, 65, 76. ♿
Where to Stay p284.

This has been one of Stockholm's
most legendary restaurants and
entertainment venues since
1863. Both salons, with their
stately galleries, magnificent
crystal chandeliers and elegant
mirrors, were restored to their
original splendour by the British
designer and restaurateur
Terence Conran to mark the
new millennium.
  Berns is one of Stockholm's
biggest restaurants with seating
for 400 diners. The gallery level,
with its beautifully decorated
dining rooms, was made
famous by August Strindberg's
novel *The Red Room* (1879). The
building also has a luxury hotel.

❼ Nationalmuseum

The Nationalmuseum is a landmark on the southern side of Blasieholmen. The location by the Strömmen channel inspired the 19th-century German architect August Stüler to design a building in the Venetian and Florentine Renaissance styles.

Completed in 1866, the museum houses Sweden's largest art collection, with some 16,000 classic paintings and sculptures. Drawings and graphics from the 15th century up to the early 20th century bring the total to 500,000. Other exhibits include a 500-year-old tapestry and examples of work by master furniture-makers, such as Georg Haupt. Space is also devoted to the development of modern Swedish design *(see pp30–31)*. Note the museum is undergoing renovations and expected to stay closed until 2018.

The Love Lesson *(1716–17)*
Antoine Watteau's speciality was the so-called *fêtes galantes*, depicting young couples in playful mood.

★ **The Conspiracy of the Batavians under Claudius Civilis** *(1661–2)*
Originally intended for Amsterdam, Rembrandt depicts the Batavians' conspiracy against the Romans, symbolizing the Dutch liberation campaign against Spain.

Level 2

Cupid and Psyche *(1787)*
Johan Tobias Sergel is considered the foremost sculptor of the Gustavian era. This piece is regarded as one of his most triumphant works. The sculpture refers to the victory of love over weakness.

Atrium through levels 1 and 2

Gravure gallery

Alhambra Vase
Discover the roots of European design development in furniture, embroidery, gold, glass and porcelain, featuring this late-14th Century Alhambra Vase, from Granada in Spain, on show in the permanent Design in Sweden *(1500–1740)* exhibition.

Entrance

Entry for wheelchairs

★ The Lady with the Veil
Alexander Roslin's elegant portrait (1769) is often considered to be a glamorized symbol of 18th-century Sweden.

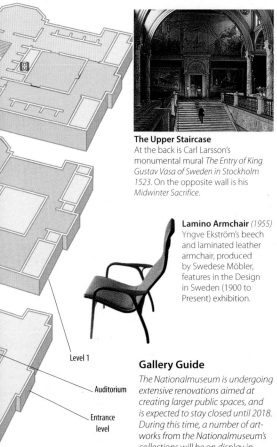

The Upper Staircase
At the back is Carl Larsson's monumental mural *The Entry of King Gustav Vasa of Sweden in Stockholm 1523*. On the opposite wall is his *Midwinter Sacrifice*.

Lamino Armchair *(1955)*
Yngve Ekström's beech and laminated leather armchair, produced by Swedese Möbler, features in the Design in Sweden (1900 to Present) exhibition.

Level 1

Auditorium

Entrance level

Key

⬜ Painting and sculpture
⬜ Applied art and design
⬜ Temporary exhibitions
⬜ Non-exhibition space
⬜ No admission

Gallery Guide
The Nationalmuseum is undergoing extensive renovations aimed at creating larger public spaces, and is expected to stay closed until 2018. During this time, a number of artworks from the Nationalmuseum's collections will be on display in rotating temporary exhibitions at the Royal Academy of Fine Arts (Konstakademien) at Fredsgatan 12. In addition, some other works from the collection will appear at other museums in the city. Check the website for more details.

⓬ Raoul Wallenbergs Torg

Map 2 E4. Östermalmstorg.
2, 54, 69, 76. 7.

This square is dedicated to Raoul Wallenberg (1912–unknown), who during World War II worked as a diplomat at the Swedish Embassy in Budapest. By using Swedish "protective passports" and safe houses throughout the city he helped a large number of Hungarian Jews to escape deportation to the Nazi concentration camps.

In 1945, when Budapest was liberated, Wallenberg was imprisoned by the Soviet Union and according to Russian sources he died in Moscow's Lubianka prison in 1947. His fate has never been satisfactorily explained despite strenuous efforts by the Swedes to seek the truth.

The small square adjoins Berzelii Park and Nybroplan and faces the Nybrokajen waterfront. The definitive design of the square has been hotly debated because it is set in an architecturally sensitive area, but great efforts have been made to ensure that it remains a worthy memorial to Raoul Wallenberg.

⓭ Musikaliska

Nybrokajen 11. **Map** 3 C1.
Tel 08-545 703 00.
Kungsträdgården,
Östermalmstorg. 54, 69, 76.
Djurgårdsfärja. **Open** for concerts (see website for details).
W **musikaliska.com**

Constructed in the 1870s, this building facing the waters of Nybroviken once housed the Musical Academy. Its concert hall, opened in 1878, was the first in the country, and was used to present the inaugural Nobel Prize in 1901. Designed in Neo-Renaissance style with cast-iron pillars, the hall has a royal box and galleries, and can seat up to 600 people.

Musikaliska is a popular venue for chamber and choral concerts, jazz and folk music.

MALMARNA & FURTHER AFIELD

As Stockholm grew, the heart of the city, Gamla Stan, became cramped and building spread out to the surrounding areas, known as "Malmarna" (the "ore hills"). Parts of these now make up present-day Stockholm.

Södermalm came into the ownership of the city in 1436. Much of Stockholm's old charm can still be found in the areas around Fjällgatan, Mosebacke and Mariaberget. To the north, the Norrmalm area expanded rapidly and became known as Stockholm's northern suburb in the 17th century. The once-rural Östermalm was transformed in the late 19th century into an affluent residential area with grand, wide boulevards, contrasting with the 1930s Functionalist style of the adjoining Gärdet district.

To the west is Kungsholmen, the centre for local government, with distinguished buildings such as Stadshuset (the City Hall) and Rådhuset (the Law Court). Djurgården, a green area of ecological and cultural interest immediately east of the city centre, offers lovely walking routes and many of the city's foremost museums.

Sights at a Glance

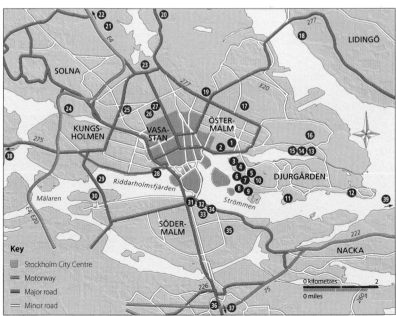

Key

- Stockholm City Centre
- Motorway
- Major road
- Minor road

◄ An old-fashioned ride at Gröna Lund, Sweden's oldest amusement park

For keys to symbols *see back flap*

❶ Historiska museet

The Swedish History Museum, Historiska museet, was opened in 1943. It was designed by Bengt Romare and Georg Sherman. Bror Marklund (1907–77) was responsible for the decoration around the entrance and the richly detailed bronze gateways depicting events in early Swedish history. The museum originally made its name with its exhibits from the Viking era, as well as its outstanding collections from the early Middle Ages. Contemporary church textiles are also on show. Many of Historiska museet's gold treasures have been gathered together to form one of Stockholm's most remarkable sights, Guldrummet (the Gold Room).

Upper floor

Courtyard

Ground floor

Bronze Age Find
This Bronze Age artifact, thought to be a percussion instrument, was discovered in a bog in southern Sweden in 1847.

The Bäckaskog Woman
The 155 cm (5 ft) tall Bäckaskog woman lived around 5000 BC. She died at the age of 40–50 and was buried sitting in a cramped pit.

Rosen-gården

★ The Alunda Elk
This 21 cm (8 inch) stone axe, discovered in 1920 at Alunda in central Sweden, resembles an elk's head. It is a ceremonial axe, probably made in Finland or Karelia in around 2000 BC.

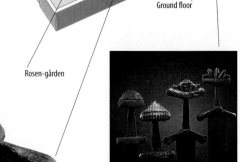

The Viking Era
This is the world's largest permanent Viking exhibition, with more than 4,000 artifacts. The Vikings were most famous as warriors, but they were also keen traders.

The Skog Tapestry
This once hung in the wooden church at Skog in northern Sweden. It is one of the museum's oldest textile treasures.

Textile Chamber

Baroque Hall

Stairs descending to the Gold Room

Main entrance

★ Maria from Viklau
This gilded wooden Madonna figure is the best-preserved example from Sweden's early medieval period. It is found in the medieval exhibition on the upper floor.

VISITORS' CHECKLIST

Practical Information
Narvavägen 13–17.
Map 2 F4.
Tel 08-519 556 00.
Open Sep–May: 11am–5pm Tue–Sun (to 8pm Wed); Jun–Aug: 10am–6pm daily. **Closed** 24, 25 & 31 Dec and some holidays.
🌐 historiska.se

Transport
🚌 67. Ⓣ Karlaplan.

Gallery Guide

The exhibitions are divided chronologically on two floors with the prehistoric section on the ground floor and the Middle Ages on the upper floor, where there is also a Baroque Hall. In the basement, reached by a staircase from the entrance hall, is the Gold Room with stunning gold and silver objects.

Key

- Prehistoric Era
- Middle Ages and Baroque
- Temporary exhibitions
- Vikings
- History of Sweden
- Non-exhibition space

★ The Gold Room

Since the early 1990s the museum's many priceless gold artifacts have been on show in Guldrummet (the Gold Room), a 700 sq m (7,500 sq ft) underground vault built with 250 tons of reinforced concrete to ensure security. The room is in two circular sections. The inner section houses the main collection, with 50 kg (110 lb) of gold treasures and 250 kg (550 lb) of silver from the Bronze Age to the Middle Ages.

The Elisabeth Reliquary was originally a drinking goblet which was mounted with gold and precious stones in the 11th century. In about 1230 a silver cover was added to enclose the skull of St Elisabeth. Sweden seized it in Wurzburg in 1631, as a trophy in the Thirty Years War.

The Gold Collars were found between 1827 and 1864; the three-ringed collar in a stone quarry in eastern Sweden, the five-ringed in a ditch on the island of Öland, and the seven-ringed hanging on a spike in a barn.

The underground Gold Room in Historiska Museet

Strandvägen with its stately houses and boats along the quayside

❷ Strandvägen

Map 4 E1. 🚌 69, 76. 🚇
Östermalmstorg, Karlaplan. 🚋 7.

In the early 1900s Stockholm's ten richest citizens – seven of whom were wholesale merchants – lived in palatial new houses along Strandvägen. Before 1897, when a major exhibition was held just across the water on Djurgården, this muddy, hilly stretch known as Ladugårdslands Strandgata aspired to becoming "a street, the like of which will not be found anywhere else in Europe". It was a long process. Even after all the grand buildings had been completed, the wooden quay erected in the 1860s was something of an eyesore. It was still used up to the 1940s by boats bringing firewood from the archipelago islands.

Nevertheless, the renamed Strandvägen, with its three rows of lime trees, soon became the elegant boulevard envisaged and, then as now, it was a popular place for a stroll, to admire the elegant façades, watch the boats and to see and be seen.

The financiers behind this and other housing projects in the early 1900s were wealthy and could call on the best architects, including I G Clason (1856–1930). Clason was influenced by Italian and French Renaissance styles for his work on No. 19–21 (Thaveniuska Huset) and No. 29–35 (Bünszowska Huset), where he designed gateways made of ships' timbers. No. 55 (Von Rosenska Palatset) is also by Clason.

❸ Junibacken

Galärvarvsvägen 8. **Map** 4 F1.
Tel 08-587230 00. 🚌 67. 🚋 7.
🚢 Djurgårdsfärja. **Open** Jan–Apr & Sep: 10am–5pm Tue–Sun; May–Dec: 10am–5pm daily (July–early Aug: to 6pm). 🚼 🖥 🚺 🏛 🚻
W junibacken.se

They are all here – Pippi Longstocking, Mardie, Karlsson on the Roof, Emil, Nils Karlsson Pyssling, Ronja the robber's daughter, the Lionheart Brothers and many more favourite characters from Astrid Lindgren's children's books. In accordance with the novelist's wishes, visitors can also meet the creations of other Swedish children's authors. When she heard about Staffan Götesam's project for a children's cultural centre, she was adamant it should not be just an Astrid Lindgren museum.

Nevertheless Junibacken is still something of a tribute to the much-loved author. It was officially opened by the Royal Family in 1996 and has become one of the city's most popular tourist attractions. A mini-train takes visitors from a mock-up of the station at Vimmerby (the author's home town) to meet some of her characters, finishing with a visit to Pippi's home in Villekulla Cottage, where children can play in the different rooms.

There is also a well-stocked children's bookshop and a restaurant.

❹ Nordiska museet

See pp94–5.

❺ Biologiska museet

Lejonslätten. **Tel** 08-442 82 15. 🚌 67. 🚋 7. **Open** Apr–Sep: 11am–4pm daily; Oct–Mar: noon–3pm Tue–Fri, 11am–3pm Sat–Sun. 🏛 🚻 by appt. 🚼 **W** skansen.se

The National Romantic influences of the late 19th century inspired the architect

Wooden Boats Along Strandvagen

Until the 1940s sailing vessels used to carry firewood from Roslagen on the Baltic coast to the quayside at Strandvägen. This trade had lost its importance by the 1950s, and boating enthusiasts started buying up these old vessels. Some were renovated and sailed to the Caribbean, others became illegal drinking or gambling clubs on Strandvägen. New harbour regulations led to the formation of two associations to administer the boats. The wooden boats moored along Strandvägen today are owned by people who want to preserve a piece of the area's cultural heritage.

Old wooden boats along the Strandvägen quay

Astrid Lindgren and Pippi Longstocking

Astrid Lindgren wrote around 100 children's books which have been translated into 74 languages, making her one of the world's most-read children's authors. Publishers turned down her first book about Pippi Longstocking, but she went on to win a children's book competition two years later, in 1945. Her headstrong and tough character Pippi soon won the hearts of children worldwide.

Born on 14 November 1907 in Vimmerby in southern Sweden, Astrid stopped writing books at 85, but her characters live on at Junibacken.

Astrid Lindgren (1907–2002)

Agi Lindegren when he was commissioned to design Biologiska museet (Museum of Biology) in the 1890s. He based his plans on the simple lines of the medieval Norwegian stave churches.

The man behind the museum was the zoologist, hunter and conservationist Gustaf Kolthoff (1845–1913). In 1892, he persuaded the industrialist C F Liljevalch – who later financed the nearby art gallery – to form a company with the aim "to develop and maintain a biological museum to include all the Scandinavian mammals and birds as stuffed specimens in natural surroundings". Within a few months of opening in autumn 1893, Gustaf Kolthoff had delivered a couple of thousand stuffed animals, as well as birds' nests, young and eggs, to the museum. Many of the creatures are shown against a diorama background, with about 250 species of Scandinavian birds and land mammals in their respective biotypes. Kolthoff's friend, the artist Bruno Liljefors, was responsible for the paintings.

Since 1970 the Museum of Biology has belonged to the Skansen Foundation. During the 1990s it underwent extensive renovation and was reopened on 13 November 1993 – exactly 100 years after its original inauguration.

Snaps label, Spritmuseum

❻ Vasamuseet

See pp96–7.

❼ Spritmuseum

Djurgårdsvägen 38. **Tel** 08-121 313 00.
🚇 Karlaplan. 🚌 67. 🚋 7.
⛴ Djurgårdsfärja. **Open** Sep–May: 10am–5pm daily (to 8pm Tue); Jun–Aug: 10am–6pm daily (to 8pm Tue).
🅿 🅫 🄰 🅘 🄰 ♿
🌐 spritmuseum.se

The Spritmuseum (Spirits Museum) is located in Stockholm's two remaining 18th-century naval buildings on the island of Djurgården, close to the Vasamuseet. The exhibits explore the Swedish people's relationship with alcohol. Visitors follow a through-the-year itinerary, discovering the pleasure that can be derived from sipping a chilled beer on a park bench on a summer's evening, as well as the warming effects of a glass of red wine during the winter months. The visit also illustrates the processes linked to alcohol production,

attitudes towards drinking and the art of the traditional Swedish drinking song.

The museum hosts temporary exhibitions, too. Past successes include the Absolut Art Collection, a compilation of the images used in Absolut Vodka's advertising campaigns. Such artworks were commissioned from the likes of Andy Warhol, Keith Haring, Ralph Steadman and Pierre et Gilles.

Another highlight of the Spritmuseum is the elegant restaurant, with its enviable location right on the water.

❽ ABBA Museum

Djurgårdsvägen 68. **Tel** 08-121 328 60.
🚌 67. 🚋 7. ⛴ Djurgårdsfärja.
Open 10am–6pm daily. 🅿 🅫 🌀
🄰 ♿ 🌐 abbathemuseum.com

This museum is dedicated to ABBA, Sweden's best-known and loved pop band, which enjoyed enormous success all over the world during the 1970s.

In addition to stage costumes, gold records, an audio guide with fascinating insights into life as a band and original press cuttings (many sourced from the private scrapbook of band member Björn Ulvaeus's father), the ABBA Museum delivers a delightfully interactive experience. Visitors can sit at a piano that is connected to Benny Andersson's own piano in his music studio; when the composer tinkles the ivories, the museum piano also starts playing. Other fun experiences include auditioning to be ABBA's fifth member at a perfect replica of the band's Polar Studio and recording a music video.

Biologiska museet's wooden façade, inspired by Nordic medieval design

❹ Nordiska museet

Resembling an extravagant Renaissance castle, Nordiska museet portrays everyday life in Sweden from the 1520s to the present day. It was created by Artur Hazelius (1833–1901), who was also the founder of Skansen (see p98). In 1872, he started to collect objects which would remind future generations of the old Nordic farming culture.

The present museum, designed by Isak Gustav Clason, was opened in 1907. Today it has more than 1.5 million exhibits, with everything from luxury clothing and priceless jewellery to everyday items, furniture and children's toys, and replicas of period homes.

Doll's Houses
The doll's houses show typical homes from the 17th century to modern times. This example illustrates one from 1860.

Level 3

Corridor to staircase

Level 2 (Main Hall)

Level 1 (Ground Floor)

State Bedchamber from Ulvsunda Castle
At the end of the 17th century, the lord of the manor at Ulvsunda would accommodate prominent guests in this prestigious bedchamber.

Obelisk with the inscription: "The day may dawn when not even all our gold is enough to form a picture of a bygone era."

Equestrian statue of Karl X Gustav

Main entrance

Gallery Guide

The museum is arranged over four floors. From the entrance, stairs lead up to the temporary exhibitions in the Main Hall on Level 2. Floor 3 houses the Strindberg Collection, Doll's Houses, Table Settings, Traditions and the Fashion and Textile Galleries. On the fourth floor are sections dealing with Folk Art, Interiors, Swedish Homes, Small Objects and a section covering the Sami People and Culture.

★ Table Settings
In the mid-17th century, table settings were a feast for the eyes. A swan is the centrepiece at this meal.

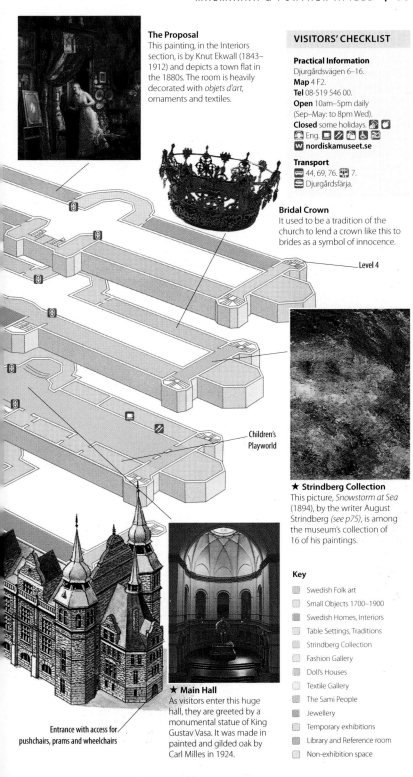

The Proposal
This painting, in the Interiors section, is by Knut Ekwall (1843–1912) and depicts a town flat in the 1880s. The room is heavily decorated with *objets d'art*, ornaments and textiles.

VISITORS' CHECKLIST

Practical Information
Djurgårdsvägen 6–16.
Map 4 F2.
Tel 08-519 546 00.
Open 10am–5pm daily
(Sep–May: to 8pm Wed).
Closed some holidays.
Eng.
w nordiskamuseet.se

Transport
44, 69, 76. 7.
Djurgårdsfärja.

Bridal Crown
It used to be a tradition of the church to lend a crown like this to brides as a symbol of innocence.

Level 4

Children's Playworld

★ **Strindberg Collection**
This picture, *Snowstorm at Sea* (1894), by the writer August Strindberg *(see p75)*, is among the museum's collection of 16 of his paintings.

Key

- Swedish Folk art
- Small Objects 1700–1900
- Swedish Homes, Interiors
- Table Settings, Traditions
- Strindberg Collection
- Fashion Gallery
- Doll's Houses
- Textile Gallery
- The Sami People
- Jewellery
- Temporary exhibitions
- Library and Reference room
- Non-exhibition space

★ **Main Hall**
As visitors enter this huge hall, they are greeted by a monumental statue of King Gustav Vasa. It was made in painted and gilded oak by Carl Milles in 1924.

Entrance with access for pushchairs, prams and wheelchairs

❻ Vasamuseet

After a maiden voyage of just 1,300 m (1,422 yd) in calm weather, the warship *Vasa* capsized in Stockholm's harbour on 10 August 1628. About 30 people went down with what was supposed to be the pride of the navy, only 100 m (109 yd) off the southern tip of Djurgården. Almost all the guns were salvaged from the vessel in the 17th century and it was not until 1956 that a private researcher's persistent search led to the rediscovery of *Vasa*. A complex operation began to salvage the wreck, followed by a 17-year conservation programme. The city's most popular museum opened in 1990, less than a nautical mile from the scene of the disaster. The museum has undergone reconstruction, and its plan may differ from the illustration shown.

Gun-port Lion
More than 200 carved ornaments and 500 sculpted figures decorate *Vasa*.

★ Lion Figurehead
King Gustav II Adolf, who commissioned *Vasa*, was known as the Lion of the North. So a springing lion was the obvious choice for the figurehead. It is 4 m (13 ft) long and weighs 450 kg (990 lb).

Emperor Titus
Carvings of 20 Roman emperors stand on parade on *Vasa*.

Entrance

KEY

① Information desk

② To the restaurant

③ **The main mast** was originally 52 m (170 ft) high.

④ **Exit to Museifartygen**

⑤ **Reconstruction of the upper gun deck**

⑥ **Main film auditorium**

Bronze Cannon
More than 50 of *Vasa's* 64 original cannons were salvaged in the 17th century. Three bronze cannons are on display in the museum.

★ **Stern**
Vasa's stern was badly damaged, but has been painstakingly restored to reveal the ship's magnificent ornamentation.

Gun Ports
Vasa carried more heavy cannons on its two gun-decks than earlier ships of the same size. This contributed to its capsizing.

The Salvage Operation

The marine archaeologist Anders Franzén had been looking for *Vasa* for many years. On 25 August 1956 his patience was rewarded when he brought up a piece of blackened oak on his plumb line. From the autumn of 1957, it took divers two years to clear space beneath the hull for the lifting cables. The first lift using six cables was a success, after which *Vasa* was raised in 16 stages into shallow water. Plugs were inserted into holes left by rusted iron bolts, then the final lift began and on 4 May 1961 *Vasa* was towed into dry dock.

Vasa in dry dock after being salvaged in 1961

Gun Deck
Although visitors cannot board the ship, there is a full-size replica of a part of the upper gun deck, which gives a good idea of what conditions on board were like.

Hornborgastugan, a 19th-century timber cottage at Skansen

❾ Gröna Lund

Lilla Allmänna Gränd 9. **Tel** 010-708 91 00. 🚌 67. 🚋 7. 🚢 Djurgårdsfärja. **Open** late Apr–mid-Sep: opening hours vary. 🚼 ♿ 🅿 📷 ♿ ♿ **W gronalund.com**

A tavern called Gröna Lund (Green Grove) existed on this site in the 18th century, and it was one of the haunts of the renowned troubadour Carl Michael Bellman *(see p99)*.

Jakob Schultheis used the tavern's name for the modest-sized funfair which he opened here in 1883 with a two-level horse-drawn roundabout as the main attraction. Today Gröna Lund is Sweden's oldest amusement park.

The 130-day season, starting around the end of April, is short but hectic. Gröna Lund draws up to 18,000 visitors a day to its attractions, which include a thrilling roller-coaster and haunted house. Popular attraction "Insane", is a vertical roller-coaster that can reach speeds of 60 km per hour (47 miles per hour), and it is

Gröna Lund funfair seen from Kastellholmen

considered to be one of the highest and longest of its kind in the world.

The park also has restaurants and cafés, two stages, a cabaret restaurant, a theatre and beautiful gardens.

Nearby is Liljevalchs Konsthall, a gallery featuring collections of Swedish, Nordic and international art. It also holds temporary exhibitions, including the annual Spring Salon.

❿ Skansen

Djurgårdsslätten 49. **Tel** 08-442 80 00. 🚌 44. 🚋 7. 🚢 Djurgårdsfärja. **Open** Oct–Mar: 10am–3pm Mon–Fri (to 4pm Sat & Sun); Apr: 10am–3pm daily; May–late Jun & Sep: 10am–6pm daily; late-Jun–Aug: 10am–8pm daily. **Closed** 24 Dec. 🚼 ♿ 📷 Jun–Aug. 🅿 📷 ♿ Seglora Kyrka 🛈 call for details. **W skansen.se**

The world's first open-air museum, Skansen was established in 1891 to show an increasingly industrialized society how people once lived. It comprises around 150 houses and farm buildings from all over Sweden. But it is not just a museum, Skansen also plays an important role in nurturing the country's folklore and traditions. Sweden's National Day, Walpurgis Night, Midsummer, Christmas and New Year's Eve celebrations take place here *(see pp32–5)*.

In the Town Quarter, complete with 19th-century wooden town houses, glass-blowers, bookbinders and other craftspeople demonstrate their skills. The 300-year-old Älvros farmhouse, from the Härjedalen region, represents rural life with

an intriguing collection of everyday tools. At the other end of the scale, Skogaholm Manor *(see p26)*, a Carolean manor from 1680, shows how the wealthy lived. The shingle-roofed Seglora Church (1729) is popular for weddings.

Nordic animals such as elk and wolves can be seen in the zoo, and exotic snakes in the aquarium.

⓫ Waldemarsudde

Prins Eugens Väg 6. **Tel** 08-545 837 00. 🚋 7. **Open** 11am–5pm Tue–Sun (to 8pm Thu). 🚼 📷 🅿 📷 📷 ♿ **W waldemarsudde.se**

Prince Eugen's Waldemarsudde, which passed into State ownership after his death in 1947, is one of Sweden's most visited art galleries. The prince was trained as a military officer, but became a successful artist and was one of the leading landscape painters of his generation. He produced monumental paintings for several of the city's important buildings, including Kungliga Operan and Stadshuset. Among his own works hanging in Waldemarsudde, his former palace, are three of his most prized paintings: *Spring* (1891), *The Old Castle* (1893) and *The Cloud* (1896).

Together with works by his contemporaries, the gallery holds an impressive collection of early 20th-century Swedish art. Oscar Björck, Carl Fredrik Hill, Richard Bergh, Nils Kreuger, Eugène Jansson, Bruno Liljefors and Anders Zorn are all featured.

Prince Eugen was a generous patron to the next generation – the group known as "The Young Ones" – so works by younger artists, including Isaac Grünewald, Einar Jolin, Sigrid Hjertén and Leander Engström are also in the collection. Sculptors of the same era are well represented, particularly Per Hasselberg, whose works can be seen in both the gallery and the park.

Prince Eugen and his architect, Ferdinand Boberg, drew up the sketches for the palace, completed in 1905.

Hornsgatan (1902) by Eugène Jansson, in Thielska Galleriet

The same architect was called in later to design the gallery, which was finished in 1913. This now includes parts of the collection of some 2,000 works, as well as the Prince's own paintings.

The guest apartments remain largely unchanged, and the two upper floors with the Prince's studio at the top are used for temporary exhibitions. The buildings are surrounded by beautiful gardens.

⑫ Thielska Galleriet

Sjötullsbacken 6–8. **Tel** 08-662 58 84.
🚌 69. **Open** noon–5pm Tue–Sun (to 8pm Thu). 🎭 🖼 by appointment.
📧 🌐 **thielska-galleriet.se**

When the magnificent apartments of the banker Ernest Thiel (1860–1947) on Strandvägen started to overflow with his comprehensive collection of Nordic art from the late 19th and early 20th centuries, he commissioned the architect Ferdinand Boberg to design a dignified villa on Djurgården.

However, during World War I Thiel lost most of his fortune. His collection was bought by the State, which opened Thielska Galleriet in his villa in 1926.

Thiel was regarded as something of a rebel in the banking world. He was particularly fond of works by painters belonging to the Artists' Union, which had been formed in 1886 to counter the influence of the traditionalist Konstakademien (Royal Academy of the Arts).

There are paintings by all the major Swedish artists who formed an artists' colony at Grèz-sur-Loing, south of Paris, including Carl Larsson, Bruno Liljefors, Karl Nordström and August Strindberg.

In additon, the gallery features works by Eugène Jansson, Anders Zorn and Prince Eugen, as well as wooden figures by Axel Petersson and sculptures by Christian Eriksson. Thiel also acquired pieces by foreign artists, not least his good friend Edvard Munch.

⑬ Etnografiska museet

Djurgårdsbrunnsvägen 34. **Tel** 010-456 12 00. 🚌 69. **Open** 11am–5pm Tue–Sun. 🎭 🖼 🍴 📷 ♿
🌐 **etnografiska.se**

The National Museum of Ethnography is a showcase for the collections brought home to Sweden by enterprising travellers and scientists from the 18th century to the present day. All are arranged in imaginative displays designed to provide a better understanding of the unknown or unfamiliar from around the world.

Another aspect of the museum's work is to reflect the multicultural influences on Sweden brought about by the large-scale immigration into the country during the late 20th century.

The explorer Sven Hedin (1865–1952), who was the last Swede to be ennobled (in 1902), contributed many exhibits to the museum, including Buddha figures and Chinese costumes, as well as Mongolian temple tents donated by leaders of the Kalmuck people in western China to King Gustav V. Another section of interest shows masks and totem poles from western Canada.

A Japanese tea house was opened in 1990, which is a work of art in itself. Here, visitors to the museum can take part in traditional tea ceremonies during the summer.

The museum runs an educational programme with lectures, courses and workshops. In addition to the permanent exhibitions, the museum also displays themed temporary exhibits.

The MatMekka restaurant, located in the museum, offers a menu of Swedish and international dishes made with organic and locally produced ingredients.

An Immortal Troubadour

Carl Michael Bellman (1740–95) was a much-loved troubadour. Gustav III gave him a job as secretary of a lottery, but he was best known around Stockholm's many taverns – particularly on Djurgården. His works about the drunken watchmaker Jean Fredman and his contemporaries (*Fredman's Epistles* and *Fredman's Songs*) have never lost their popularity and form part of Sweden's musical heritage. A bust of Bellman was unveiled on Djurgården in 1829 in the presence of Queen Desideria.

Bust of Bellman by J N Byström (1829)

Kaknästornet with the buildings of Sjöhistoriska museet, Tekniska museet and Folkens museum Etnografiska in the foreground

⓮ Tekniska museet

Museivägen 7. **Tel** 08-450 56 00.
🚌 69. **Open** 10am–5pm daily
(to 8pm Thu). **Closed** 1 Jan,
Midsummer, 24, 25 & 31 Dec.
🅿 🖸 by appointment. 🖸 ✏
🖼 🔊 🖳 tekniskamuseet.se

The Museum of Science and Technology contains a wealth of exhibits connected with Sweden's technical and industrial history. It also houses the science centre, Teknorama, with hands-on experiments designed for children and young people.

The machinery hall features the country's oldest preserved steam engine. Built in 1832, it was used in a coal mine in southern Sweden. The classic Model T Ford and early Swedish cars from Volvo, Scania and Saab are also on display. Swinging from above is Sweden's first commercial aircraft, built in 1924. There is another rarity – the scientist Emanuel Swedenborg's model of a "flying machine" (1716).

The museum also has sections on electric power, computing, technology in the home, and the Swedish forestry, mining, iron and steel industries.

Tekniska museet's machinery hall with historic aircraft

⓯ Sjöhistoriska museet

Djurgårdsbrunnsvägen 24.
Tel 08-519 549 00. 🚌 69.
Open 10am–5pm Tue–Sun. 🖸
🖸 🖼 🔊 🖳 sjohistoriska.se

The National Maritime Museum focuses on shipping, shipbuilding and naval defence. It is housed in an attractive building, designed by the architect Ragnar Östberg in 1938, in a beautiful location by the calm waters of Djurgårdsbrunnsviken.

There are some 100,000 exhibits, including more than 1,500 model ships. The oldest Swedish model is a reproduction of the "Cathedral ship" from the early 1600s. The model collection comprises every conceivable type of ship from small coasters to oil tankers, coal vessels, dinghies, full-riggers and submarines. A series of models on a scale of 1:200 shows the development of ships in Scandinavia since the Iron Age.

Life-size settings provide a good idea of life on board the various ships. Among them are the exquisite original cabin and elegant stern from the royal schooner *Amphion*. Designed by the leading shipbuilder F H af Chapman and built at the Djurgården shipyard, *Amphion* was

Figurehead, about 1850

Gustav III's flagship in the 1788–90 war with Russia.

The museum has some notable examples of ship decoration from the late 17th century. They include part of the national coat of arms recovered by divers in the 1920s from the stern of the *Riksäpplet*, which sank at Dalarö in 1676. A large relief portrayal of Karl XI on horseback from the stern of *Carolus XI* – an 82-cannon ship launched from the shipyard in 1678 – is also on show. It is thought that the relief was removed some years later when the ship was renamed *Sverige*. There are many fine figureheads in the collection, including one depicting Amphion, the son of Zeus, playing his lyre, which adorned the schooner of the same name.

The museum often hosts temporary exhibitions focusing on themes such as piracy, shipping and treasure recovered from shipwrecks.

Linked to the museum is the Swedish Marine Archaeology Archive, containing an extensive collection of maritime documents and photographs. There is a special children's section with a workshop which is open on Saturdays and in school holidays. On the gable facing Djurgårdsbrunnsviken is *The Sailor*, a monument to the victims of naval warfare by Nils Sjögren.

⓰ Kaknästornet

Ladugårdsgärdet. **Tel** 08-667 21 80.
🚌 69. **Open** 10am–9pm Mon–Sat;
10am–6pm Sun. 🅿 🖸 by
appointment. 🖸 ✏ 🖼 🔊
🖳 kaknastornet.se

Anchored by 72 steel poles, driven 8 m (26 ft) into the rock, the 34-storey Kaknästornet soars to a height of 155 m (508 ft). The tower, designed by the architects Bengt Lindroos and Hans Borgström, was opened in 1967. It was erected as a centre for the country's television and radio broadcasting and also contains technical equipment to conduct conferences by satellite between European cities. Five dishes to the left of the tower – the largest of which has a diameter of 13 m (43 ft) – relay signals to and from satellites. The main hall containing the transmitters and receivers has been blasted out of the rock below the dishes.

The observation points on levels 30 and 31 provide a spectacular view of the city, and the restaurant on the 28th floor has panoramic windows. It is reached by two lifts, travelling at 18 km/h (11 mph). There is a tourist information office at the entrance, selling souvenirs and maps. Decorative features include a wall relief by Walter Bengtsson, which was inspired by the tower's daunting technology.

⓱ Tessinparken & Nedre Gärdet

Map 2 F2. ⓣ Karlaplan, Gärdet. 🚌 1, 54, 91.

Three generations of the Tessin family of architects have given their name to this park which opened at Lower Gärdet in 1931. Tessinparken runs from north to south and is attractively designed with lawns, play areas, paths and ponds. The adjoining houses, built between 1932 and

Millesgården, home of the sculptor Carl Milles in the early 20th century

1937, have their own gardens and blend in such a way that they give the impression of being part of the park itself.

The earliest houses, nearest to Valhallavägen, still show signs of 1920s Classicism, although Gärdet's real hallmark is Functionalism. The lower white houses along Askrikegatan, marking the northern boundary of the park, are Functionalist in style and noticeably different from other buildings in Gärdet. Some 60 different architects were involved in designing the Gärdet development, including Sture Frölén.

A granite statue of a woman with a suitcase, *Housewife's Holiday*, stands in the part of Tessin Park adjoining Valhallavägen. It was made by Olof Thorwald Ohlsson in the 1970s. At the other end of the park is a colourful concrete statue, *The Egg*, by Egon Möller-Nielsen.

⓲ Millesgården

Herserudsvägen 32, Lidingö. ⓣ Ropsten, then bus 201, 202, 204, 206, 208, 212 to Torsvik. **Tel** 08-446 75 90. **Open** May–Sep: 11am–5pm daily; Oct–Apr: 11am–5pm Tue–Sun. 🅿 🅰 by appointment. 🔲 🚫 ♿ 🅦 **millesgarden.se**

Carl Milles (1875–1955) was one of the 20th century's greatest Swedish sculptors and the best known internationally. From 1931 he lived for 20 years in the USA, where he became a prolific monumental sculptor with works such as the *Meeting of the Waters* fountain in St Louis and the *Resurrection* fountain in the National Memorial Park outside Washington DC. In Stockholm visitors can see 15 of his public works, including the *Orpheus* fountain in front of Konserthuset (*see p75*).

In 1906 Milles purchased land on the island of Lidingö on which he built a house, completed in 1908. He lived here with his wife until 1931, and also after his return from the USA. In 1936 he and his wife donated the property to the people of Sweden. Millesgården extends over a series of terraces filled with sculptures and includes Milles' studios with originals and replicas of his work. There is a magnificent garden – a work of art in itself – and a fine view over the water.

Tessinparken, surrounded by Functionalist-style housing dating from the late 1930s

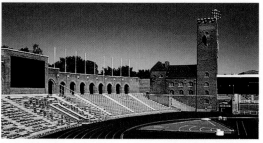

Running track at Stadion, built in 1912

⓳ Stadion

Lidingövägen 1–3. **Map** 2 E2.
Tel 07-392 190 07. Ⓣ Stadion.
🚌 4, 55, 72, 73. **Open** 7am–9pm
Mon–Fri, 8am–8pm Sat & Sun. 🎽
during events. ♿

A new main arena was built for
the 1912 Olympic Games in
Stockholm, the towers of which
have become a familiar landmark
on the capital's skyline. The
architect of Stadion, Torben
Grut (1871–1945), followed the
National Romantic influences of
the day. The complex is richly
decorated. The clock tower has
two figures by Carl
Fagerberg, *Ask and
Embla*, the
counterparts of
Adam and Eve in
Nordic mythology.
There are also busts
of Victor Balck, the
man behind the 1912
Olympics, and P H
Ling, the father
of Swedish
gymnastics.

Polar bear, Naturhistoriska
Riksmuseet

Four notable
sculptures were added in the
1930s. The painter and gymnast
Bruno Liljefors created *Play* at
the main entrance, Carl Eldh
made *The Runners*, and Carl
Fagerberg provided *Relay
Runners* and *The Shot-Putter*.

Stadion is an important venue
for athletics events and can
hold up to 35,000 spectators.
The European Athletics
Championships were held here
in 1958, and an international
athletics gala is staged every
summer. In 1990 it hosted the
World Equestrian Championships.

The arena is also used as a
venue for concerts by internationally renowned bands.

⓴ Naturhistoriska Riksmuseet

5 km (3 miles) N of city centre
along road 264. **Tel** 08-519 540 00.
Ⓣ Universitetet. 🚌 50, 540.
Open 10am–6pm Tue–Fri,
11am–6pm Sat & Sun. 📷 by
appointment. 🔲🖥️🖊️📷♿
🌐 **nrm.se**

Completed in 1916, the vast
Naturhistoriska Riksmuseet
(Swedish Museum of Natural
History) was designed by Axel
Anderberg and decorated by
Carl Fagerberg. The museum is a
venerable institution, founded in
1739 by Carl von Linné *(see p134)*
as part of Vetenskaps-
akademien (the
Academy of
Science). It is one
of the 10 largest
museums of its
kind in the world.
Over the centuries,
the number of
exhibits has risen
to 17 million.
During the 1990s
it was modernized
and there are both permanent
and temporary exhibitions on a
wide range of themes from
dinosaurs and sea creatures
to the human body. The
hugely popular Cosmonova
opened at the same time.

Both a planetarium and an
IMAX cinema, its screen is 25
times the size of a conventional
one. The *Vega Monument* was
erected in front of the museum
in 1930 to mark the 50th
anniversary of explorer Adolf
Erik Nordenskiöld's return from
the first voyage through the
Northeast Passage in his ship
Vega. Designed by Ivar Johnsson,
it is an obelisk in granite topped
with a copper ship.

㉑ Hagaparken

4 km (2.5 miles) N of city centre,
along E4. 🚌 515. Haga Parkmuseum:
Tel 08-27 42 52. **Open** Oct–mid–May:
10am–3pm Fri–Sun; mid–May–Sep:
11am–5pm daily. Gustav III's Paviljong:
Tel 08-402 61 30. 📷 every 30 mins
mid-Jun–mid-Aug: noon–3:30pm
daily. Fjärilshuset Haga Ocean: **Tel**
08-730 39 81. **Open** 10am–4pm
Mon–Fri, 10am–5pm Sat & Sun.
Closed Midsummer's Eve. 🎽🖥️🖊️
in Koppartälten and Fjärilshuset Haga
Ocean and Café Vasaslätten.

King Gustav Vasa decided to
create a royal park in the
popular Haga area in the mid-
18th century. The king's vision
was realized by the architect of
the moment, Fredrik Magnus
Piper. The result was an English-
style park with some very
unusual buildings, including the
Chinese Pagoda and the Roman
battle tent, Koppartälten. A
royal palace inspired by
Versailles in France was also
planned, but construction came
to a halt after the king's death
and it remained unfinished.

Gustav III's Pavilion, a Gustavian
masterpiece designed by Olof
Tempelman, with an interior by
Louis Masreliéz, is the park's
greatest architectural attraction,
while Fjärilshuset Haga Ocean
has colourful, exotic butterflies

Hagaparken's Roman battle tent, designed by Louis Jean Desprez (1790)

and birds flying freely around a tropical greenhouse, plus a shark tank.

Haga Slott, built in 1802–04 for Gustav IV Adolf, was the childhood home of the present monarch, Carl XVI Gustaf, and his sisters. Now it is used for official receptions and to accommodate visiting heads of state.

Hagaparken is very popular with Stockholmers. The park is part of the Royal National City Park (Ekoparken), an oasis of nature and culture close to the city centre *(see box)*.

Ulriksdal with its magnificent 18th-century Baroque exterior

Exotic butterflies in the greenhouses at Hagaparken

🏛 Ulriksdal

7 km (4 miles) N of Stockholm.
Tel 08-402 62 80. 🚌 503. Palace:
Open May–mid-Jun & mid-Aug–Oct:
noon–4pm Sat & Sun; mid-Jun–mid-Aug: noon–4pm daily. 🕐 noon, 1pm, 2pm & 3pm. Orangery: **Open** May–mid-Jun & mid-Aug–Oct: Sat & Sun for guided tours only; mid-Jun–mid-Aug: noon–4pm daily. 🕐 1pm.
📷🔲♿🏠♿✉
🌐 **kungahuset.se/royalpalaces**

Situated on a headland in the bay of Edsviken, Ulriksdal's attractive buildings and leafy surroundings are well worth a visit. At the entrance to the grounds is one of Stockholm's best-known restaurants, Ulriksdals Wärdshus.

The original palace was built in the 1640s and designed by Hans Jakob Kristler in German/Dutch Renaissance style. The owner, Marshal of the Realm Jakob de la Gardie, named the palace Jakobsdal. It was bought in 1669 by the Dowager Queen Hedvig Eleonora. Fifteen years later, she donated the palace to her grandson Ulrik as a christening gift, and it was renamed Ulriksdal.

Around this time the architect Tessin the Elder suggested

some rebuilding work, but only a few of his proposals saw the light of day. In the 18th century the palace acquired its Baroque exterior.

After being a popular place for festivities in the time of Gustav III (1746–92), it began to lose its glamour. Interest was revived under Karl XV (1826–72), and furnishings and handicrafts many hundreds of years old are on show in his rooms.

The park was laid out in the mid-17th century. It has 300-year-old lime trees, as well as one of Europe's most northerly beechwoods. Carl Milles' two sculptures of wild boars stand by the pool in front

of the palace. A stream is crossed by a footbridge, which is supported by Per Lundgren's *Moors Dragging the Nets*.

More art can be seen in the Orangery, designed by Tessin the Elder in the 1660s for Queen Hedvig Eleonora. It now houses a sculpture museum.

The palace chapel, a popular place for weddings, was designed by F W Scholander and built in 1865 in Dutch Neo-Renaissance style. The riding school, built in 1671, was converted into a theatre by Carl Hårleman and C F Adelcrantz in the 1750s, and performances continue to be staged in the theatre every summer.

The Royal National City Park (Ekoparken)

Ekoparken – the world's first National City Park – was established by the Swedish Parliament in 1995. Its creation has enabled the capital to safeguard the ecology of its "green lung", a 27 sq km (10.5 sq miles) area for recreation and outdoor activities.

The park threads through Stockholm's central districts, including Skeppsholmen and the southern part of Djurgården, and continues northwest to northern Djurgården, Hagaparken, Brunnsviken and Ulriksdal. It also encompasses the tiny islands of Fjäderholmarna *(see p116)*. Much of the park was a royal hunting ground as early as the 16th century, scattered with beautiful palaces and other sights.

Today visitors can encounter all sorts of animals here – deer, and even moose, plus a plethora of rare wildlife. There are also boat tours on Brunnsviken, with stops at some of the sights. For further details, visit www. nationalstadsparken.se.

Breeding herons at Isbladskärret, part of Ekoparken's rich bird-life

Karlbergs Slott, a palace dating from the 1630s – now one of Sweden's military academies

㉓ Bellevueparken

South of Brunnsviken Lake, Ekoparken.
690, 691. Carl Eldhs Ateljémuseum:
Lögbodavägen 10, Bellevueparken.
Tel 08-612 65 60. **Open** May & Sep:
noon–4pm Thu–Sun; Jun–Aug: noon–
4pm Tue–Sun; Apr & Oct: noon–4pm
Sun. 🅿 🏠 🛗 ✉ 1:30pm in English.
☐ 🏠 🛗 ✉

This park is part of Ekoparken
(see p103), Stockholm's Royal
National City Park. Built by
architect Fredrik Magnus Piper,
Bellevue offers winding paths,
groves, tree-lined avenues and
open green areas. It also boasts
200-year-old lime trees and rare
medicinal plants. The name
(French for "beautiful view") came
from Baron Carl Sparre who
purchased a villa on Bellevue
Hill in 1782. Today the villa is
used as a conference centre.

On Bellevue Hill is the
Lögbodavägen viewpoint, which
looks out over the Brunnsviken
inlet and is close to the monument *The Young Strindberg in
the Archipelago* by Carl Eldh
(1873–1954). This sculptor's
studio, in an unusual wooden
building dating from 1919, is
now preserved as the Carl Eldhs
Ateljémuseum and is located
nearby. Eldh was one of Sweden's
most prolific sculptors, and his
works can be seen at 30 public
sites around Stockholm. The
plaster casts of these sculptures
are on show in his studio and
include the *Branting Monument*
at Norra Bantorget, the statue

of Strindberg in Tegnérparken
and *The Runners* at Stadion *(see
p102)*. Also here are drawings,
tools and other personal
belongings of the artist.

㉔ Karlbergs Slott

Karlsbergs Slottsväg. 🅃 St Eriksplan.
72 to Karlberg station, then
15-min walk. Park **Closed** to
the public.

Admiral Karl Karlsson
Gyllenhielm started to build
Karlbergs Slott in the 1630s,
during the Thirty Years War. From
1670 the palace was extended
and rebuilt by Magnus Gabriel
de la Gardie, an important
political and military figure at
the time, with Jean de la Vallée
as his architect. When Karlberg
became royal property in 1688,
it was one of Sweden's most
majestic palaces. It was where
the "hero King" Karl XII (1682–
1718) grew up, and it was here
that he lay in state after his death
at the Battle of Fredrikshald.
In 1792 the architect
C C Gjörwell converted the
property into the Royal War
Academy, which later
became the Karlberg Military
School, and since 1999 it has
been the site for one of the
country's military academies.

The interior decorations
include Carl Carove's
magnificent stucco-work
which can be seen in the
grand hall. The palace

church has been renovated
several times, but the
17th-century lanterns are
original. De la Gardie's wood-
panelled "rarities room" is now
the sacristy, but once it housed
his collection of valuables.

㉕ Judiska museet

Hälsingegatan 2. **Map** 1 A2.
Tel 08-557 735 60. 🅃 Odenplan.
67, 69, 72. **Open** noon–4pm
Sun–Fri. 🅿 🏠 🛗 in English by
appointment. ☐ 🏠 🛗
🆆 **judiska-museet.se**

In 1774 Aaron Isaac became the
first Jewish immigrant to settle
in Stockholm and practise his
religion. Today, half of Sweden's
Jewish population of around
18,000 live in the Stockholm
area. Judiska museet depicts
the history of the Swedish
Jews from Isaac's time to the
present. It focuses on Judaism
as a religion, its integration
into Swedish society and the
Holocaust. A comprehensive
collection of pictures and

An eight-stemmed *chanuki* (candlestick) at
Judiska museet

other items provide an insight into Jewish life in Sweden with its traditions and customs. The beautiful *Torah* (the five books of Moses), the bridal canopy, and the collection of eight-stemmed *chanukis* (candlesticks) are just some of the museum's treasured spiritual artifacts.

The old observatory (1748–53) at the top of the Observatory hill

❷❻ Observatorie-museet

Drottninggatan 120. **Map** 1 B2.
🚇 Odenplan. 🚌 40, 42, 65, 72.
Closed to the public. 🖥 🚫 📷
🌐 observatoriet.kva.se

A number of institutions connected with science and education can be found on and around the hill of Brunkeberg. The oldest is the former observatory designed by Carl Hårleman for the Royal Swedish Academy of Sciences and opened in 1753. In 1931, astronomical research was moved to Saltsjöbaden in the Stockholm archipelago and replaced by Observatoriemuseet (the Observatory Museum). Until recently, visitors could see the observation room with its instruments, the two median rooms and the weather room. The observatory has been closed since 2014. Although there are plans to re-open, it is not clear when they will go ahead.

The grove which surrounds the old observatory began to take shape in the 18th century. It is an idyllic enclosed area, first opened to the public in the 20th century. On top of Brunkeberg is Sigrid Fridman's statue *The Centaur*.

Gunnar Asplund

Gunnar Asplund (1885–1940) was a dominant figure among Swedish and internationally renowned architects in the 1930s. His first major commission was the chapel at the Skogskyrkogården Cemetery, designed in National Romantic style. His last work was Heliga Korsets Kapell, the cemetery's crematorium (1935–40). Regarded as a masterpiece in the Functionalist style, it has earned a place on the UNESCO World Heritage list *(see p111)*. Asplund designed Stadsbiblioteket (City Library, 1920–28). He pioneered the Functionalist style as chief architect for the Stockholm Exhibition in 1930.

Stockholm Exhibition, by Gunnar Asplund, 1930

A park stretches down to Sveavägen, where a pond is fed by a hillside stream. The statue *Dancing Youth* is by Ivar Johnsson. At the southern entrance of the park is Nils Möllerberg's sculpture *Youth*.

❷❼ Stadsbiblioteket

Sveavägen 73. **Map** 1 B2. **Tel** 08-508 310 60. 🚇 Odenplan, Rådmansgatan. 🚌 2, 4, 50, 57. **Open** 9am–9pm Mon–Thu, 9am–7pm Fri, noon–4pm Sat & Sun (mid-Jun–mid-Aug: 9am–7pm Mon–Fri, noon–4pm Sat). ♿
🌐 biblioteket.stockholm.se

Gunnar Asplund's masterpiece, Stadsbiblioteket (City Library), is one of the capital's most architecturally important buildings. Asplund, the champion of the Functionalist style prevalent in the 1930s, designed a public library which was dominated by Classical ideals. It was opened in 1928.

Internally, the furnishings and many of the light fittings were designed by Asplund himself. The work of Swedish artists is well represented: in the entrance hall are Ivar Johnsson's stucco reliefs with themes from Homer's *Iliad*; the sparkling mural in the children's section, *John Blund*, is by Nils Dardel; and the depiction of the stars in the heavens by Ulf Munthe. The door lintels, door handles and drinking fountains are by Nils Sjögren. Hilding Linnquist was responsible for the giant-sized tapestry, and also for four mural paintings using ancient fresco techniques.

The library lends more than a million books every year and also organizes author sessions and other events.

Stadsbiblioteket, in Neo-Classical style, designed by Gunnar Asplund

⓯ Stadshuset

Probably Sweden's biggest architectural project of the 20th century, the City Hall was completed in 1923 and has become a symbol of Stockholm. It was designed by Ragnar Östberg (1866–1945), the leading architect of the Swedish National Romantic style, and displays influences of both the Nordic Gothic and Northern Italian schools. Several leading Swedish artists contributed to the rich interior design. The building contains the Council Chamber and 250 offices for city administrative staff. The annual Nobel Prize festivities take place in the Blue Hall.

★ **The Golden Hall**
The Byzantine-inspired wall mosaics by Einar Forseth (1892–1988) are made up of 18.6 million pieces of glass and gold. The northern wall's theme is *Queen of Lake Mälaren*.

KEY

① Stairway to the gallery

② **Norra Trapptornet**, crowned by a sun.

③ **Courtyard**

④ **Marriage room**

⑤ **Engelbrekt the Freedom Fighter** by Christian Eriksson (1858–1935).

★ **The Blue Hall**
The banqueting room is made from handmade bricks. The name is from the initial plan to paint the bricks blue, but the architect changed his mind.

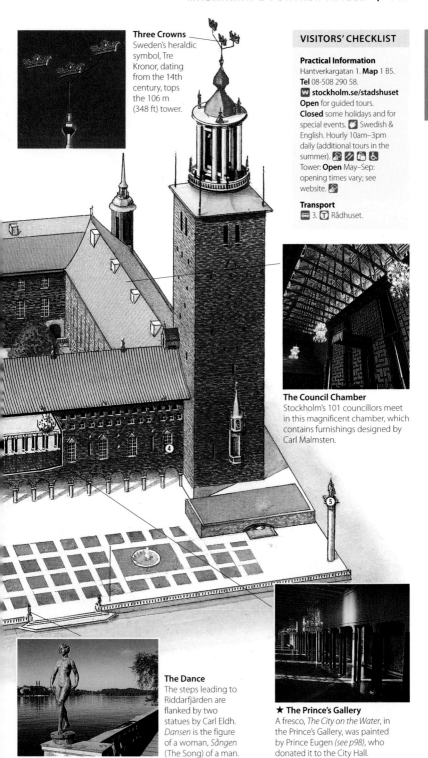

Three Crowns
Sweden's heraldic symbol, Tre Kronor, dating from the 14th century, tops the 106 m (348 ft) tower.

The Council Chamber
Stockholm's 101 councillors meet in this magnificent chamber, which contains furnishings designed by Carl Malmsten.

The Dance
The steps leading to Riddarfjärden are flanked by two statues by Carl Eldh. *Dansen* is the figure of a woman, *Sången* (The Song) of a man.

★ The Prince's Gallery
A fresco, *The City on the Water*, in the Prince's Gallery, was painted by Prince Eugen *(see p98)*, who donated it to the City Hall.

Västerbron bridge, opened in 1935, linking Kungsholmen with Södermalm across Lake Mälaren

㉙ Västerbron

 4, 77.

As Stockholm expanded and car-use increased in the 1920s, it became necessary to build an additional bridge between the northern and southern shores of Lake Mälaren. German experts dominated the architectural competition launched in 1930, but their plans were implemented by Swedish architects and engineers and Västerbron bridge was completed in 1935. Twenty years later it was broadened to increase its capacity.

The attractive design blends well with the landscape. The bridge is built in two spans of 168 m (551 ft) and 204 m (669 ft) with a vertical clearance of 26 m (85 ft). There are footpaths and cycle lanes on each side and a walk to the centre of Västerbron is rewarded with a magnificent view of central Stockholm.

Exercise yard in the former royal prison on Långholmen

㉚ Långholmen

ⓣ Hornstull, then 10 min walk.
🚌 4, 77. 🚢 🏊

Below the majestic Västerbron bridge is the island of Långholmen, which is linked

to Södermalm by two bridges. Långholmen is best known for the various prisons which have been located here since 1724. During the 20th century it was the site of the largest prison in Sweden, housing 620 inmates. The prison closed in 1975.

The island has now become a popular recreational area. The prison buildings have all been demolished, but the former royal jail, dating from 1835, remains. The one-time cells now form both a hotel and a prison museum. There is also a youth hostel and an excellent restaurant, as well as a museum to the poet C M Bellman (see p99) with a café in the gardens, which run down towards Riddarfjärden.

Långholmen's park has an open-air theatre, and offers excellent swimming both from the beaches and the rocks.

㉛ Stockholms Stadsmuseum

Ryssgården. **Map** 3 B5. **Tel** 08-508 316 00. ⓣ Slussen. 🚌 2, 3, 43, 53, 55, 76. **Closed** for renovations until 2017.
📷🏛🎥♿🅿
🌐 **stadsmuseum.stockholm.se**

Hemmed in between the traffic roundabouts of Slussen and the steep hill up to Mosebacke Torg is Stockholms Stadsmuseum (City Museum). It is housed in a late-17th-century building originally designed by Tessin the Elder as Södra Stadshuset (Southern City Hall). After a fire, it was completed by Tessin the

Younger in 1685. It has been used for various purposes over the centuries, including law courts and dungeons, schools and city-hall cellars, theatres and churches, until in the 1930s it became the city museum.

The museum documents the history of Stockholm. The city's main stages of development are described in a slideshow and a series of four permanent exhibitions. The first starts with the Stockholm Bloodbath of 1520 (see p64) and continues through the 17th century. The eventful 18th century is illustrated with exhibits that include the Lohe Treasure – 20 kg (44 lb) of silver discovered in Gamla Stan in 1937. The other sections depict industrialization in the 19th century and the tremendous growth in the 20th century with the emergence of a new city centre and new suburbs.

The museum is scheduled to reopen in autumn 2017 with a new exhibition focusing on the stories of Stockholm. In the meantime, visitors can go on

The 18th-century Lohe Treasure at Stockholms Stadsmuseum

guided city-walks organized by the museum. There are also tours that take in the locations mentioned in writer Stieg Larsson's popular *Millennium* trilogy.

❷ Katarinahissen

Stadsgården. **Map** 3 C5. Ⓣ Slussen. 2, 3, 53, 55, 59. **Closed** to the public.

Katarinahissen is the oldest of Stockholm's "high-rise" attractions. The 38 m (125 ft) high lift was opened to the public in March 1883 and is still a prominent silhouette on the Söder skyline. The first Swedish neon sign was erected here in 1909 – a legendary advertisement for Stomatol toothpaste. Since the 1930s, the sign has been placed on a nearby rooftop.

The original lift was driven by steam, but it switched to electricity in 1915. In the 1930s it was replaced by a new lift. In its first year of operation, the lift was used by more than a million passengers, but its record year was 1945, when it carried a total of 1.8 million people between Slussen and Mosebacke Torg.

Although the original lift is no longer in use, there is another less iconic lift that takes diners up to a gourmet restaurant, Gondolen *(see p295)*. The views from here are spectacular.

Katarina Kyrka (1695) after its extensive restoration due to a devastating fire in 1990

❸ Katarina Kyrka

Högbergsgatan 13. **Tel** 08-743 68 00. Ⓣ Slussen, Medborgarplatsen. 2, 3, 53. **Open** 11am–5pm Mon, Tue & Thu–Sat, 10am–7pm Wed & Sun. by appointment. 11am Sun. **svenskakyrkan.se**

The buildings surrounding the hilltop on Katarinaberget date partly from the 18th century, although there have been churches on the site since the late 14th century. The most impressive of all the buildings is the 17th-century Katarina Kyrka, designed by one of the era's greatest architects, Jean de la Vallée (1620–96). King Karl X Gustaf was also deeply involved in the project, and specified that the church should have a central nave with the altar and pulpit positioned right in the middle. Construction began in 1656 and the church was finally completed in 1695. In 1723 it was badly damaged by fire, along with large parts of the surrounding area, but it was restored over the next couple of decades. The architect Göran Josua Adelcranz designed a larger, octagonal tower.

Major restoration was carried out in the 20th century, and a new copper roof was added in 1988. Then two years later, on the night of 16 May 1990, there was another fire and the interior and virtually all its fittings were destroyed. Only the outer walls survived.

The architectural practice of Ove Hidemark was commissioned to design a new church which, as far as possible, was to be a faithful reconstruction of the original.

In order to carry out such a detailed reconstruction, the architects resorted to the use of 17th-century building techniques. Experts and craftsmen skilfully joined heavy timbering on to the central dome in the traditional way, and the church's central arch was rebuilt with bricks specially made in 17th-century style.

In 1995, Katarina Kyrka was reconsecrated and, in the eyes of many people, looked more beautiful than ever. The altar was sited exactly where it was originally planned.

The reconstruction cost 270 million kronor, of which 145 million kronor was covered by insurance. The remainder was raised through public donations.

Katarinahissen with Stockholms Stadsmuseum in the background

❷ Fjällgatan

Per Anders Fogelström (1917–98), probably Söder's best-known author, wrote: "Fjällgatan must be the city's most beautiful street. It's an old-fashioned narrow street which runs along the hilltop with well-maintained cobblestones … and with street lights jutting out from the houses. Then the street opens up and gives a fantastic view of the city and the water…" This area offers an experience of the authentic Söder and its unique atmosphere.

The Heights of Söder
With its 300-year-old houses and terraced gardens, the Söder hilltop stands like a giant stage-set behind Stadsgården harbour.

| 0 meters | | 100 |
| 0 yards | | 100 |

Viewpoint with magnificent vista across the city.

Café

Fjällgatan
Most of the houses were built along this picturesque street after a devastating fire in 1723. No. 34 is said to be the area's oldest.

Katarina Vägen

FJÄLLGATAN

STIGBERGSGATAN

Norwegian Church

Stigberget

Mamsell Josabeth's Steps were named after Josabeth Sjöbert (1812–82), a local painter.

Tjärhovsplan

Sista Styverns Trappor
This alley of steps was once known as Mikaelsgränd after a 17th-century executioner. Later it was named after the inn on the harbour, Sista Styver ("The Last Penny").

Söder Cottages
Typical well-preserved cottages can be found along Stigbergsgatan. One of them is No. 17, the house of the blockmaker Olof Krok during the 1730s.

Key
— Suggested route

㉟ Vita Bergen

Södermalm. ☷ 3, 57, 66, 76.

Famous today for its popular open-air theatre performances, this park is also an opportunity to see houses originally built for workers at Söder's harbours and factories. They were simple homes, often with a small garden and surrounded by a fence. In 1736 the building of new wooden houses was forbidden because of the fire risk, but slum districts, as this was then, were exempted.

Around 1900, when Sofia Kyrka was built, the area was turned into a leafy hillside park with allotment-garden cottages to the east. The park has a bronze statue, *Elsa Borg*, by Astri Bergman Taube (1972), wife of the great troubadour Evert Taube *(see p66)*.

㊱ Ericsson Globen

3 km (2 miles) S of Stockholm. ⓣ Globen. ☷ 168, 195. **Tel** 08-600 91 00. **Open** during events. 🚡 gondola ride. ⏲ by appt. ▢ ∥ 🏠 ☖ ⓦ **globen.se**

In 1989 Stockholm acquired a new symbol in the shape of the indoor arena Ericsson Globen, which has a circumference of 690 m (2,260 ft) and a height of 85 m (279 ft). The arena offers a wide programme of events, from international sports to performances by musicians and bands from around the world.

The spectacular Skyview ride enables visitors to travel up the outside wall of the arena in glass gondolas.

Skyview's glass gondolas taking visitors to the top of the Ericsson Globen

Chapel of the Holy Cross by Gunnar Asplund at Skogskyrkogården

㊲ Skogskyrkogården

6 km (3.5 miles) S of Stockholm. **Tel** 08-508 317 30. ⓣ Skogskyrkogården. 📷 Jul–Sep: 10:30am Sun (call 08-508 316 20). ▢ ☖ ⓦ **skogskyrkogarden.se**

Nature and architecture have combined to give the Skogskyrkogården Cemetery a place on the UNESCO World Heritage list. The cemetery is the creation of architects Gunnar Asplund *(see p105)* and Sigurd Lewerentz, winners of a design competition for the site in 1915. It is set amid pinewoods which provide a framework for the various chapels and crematorium, all of which are examples of Sweden's National Romantic and Functionalist styles.

Asplund's first work, Skogskapellet (Woodland

Epitaph to Gunnar Asplund

Chapel), featuring a steep shingled roof, was opened at the same time as the cemetery in 1920, and was decorated by Carl Milles. This was followed five years later by Uppståndelsekapellet (the Resurrection Chapel), designed by Lewerentz.

In 1940 Asplund's last masterpiece, Skogskrematoriet (Woodland Crematorium), was completed, along with its three chapels representing Faith, Hope and the Holy Cross. John Lundqvist's *The Resurrection* stands in the pillared hall of Heliga Korsets Kapell, the largest of the chapels, where there is also a mural painted by Sven Erixson. Adjoining the chapel is Asplund's black granite cross. The Hill of Meditation lies to the west. Skogskyrkogården is the final resting place of Greta Garbo.

Greta Garbo

The legendary Greta Garbo, one of the 20th century's outstanding film stars, was born in 1905 in a humble part of Södermalm. At the age of 17 she joined the theatre academy of Dramaten and made her film debut in *Peter the Tramp*. Her breakthrough came in 1924 in Mauritz Stiller's film of Selma Lagerlöf's book *The Atonement of Gösta Berling*. The following year she moved to Hollywood, where she soon became the reigning star. Garbo appeared in 24 films, including *Anna Karenina* (1935) and *Camille* (1936). She never married and lived a solitary life until her death in 1990. Her ashes were interred at the Skogskyrkogården Cemetery in 1999.

Garbo in *As You Desire Me* (1932)

❸ Drottningholm

The unique Baroque and Rococo environment of Drottningholm – its palace, theatre, park and Chinese Pavilion – have been perfectly preserved. This royal palace emerged in its present form towards the end of the 17th century, and was one of the most lavish buildings of its era. Contemporary Italian and French architecture inspired Tessin the Elder (1615–81) in his design, which was also intended to glorify royal power. The project was completed by Tessin the Younger, while architects such as Carl Hårleman and Jean Eric Rehn finished the interiors. The Royal Family uses parts of the palace as their private residence. Drottningholm was designated a UNESCO World Heritage Site in 1991.

Baroque Garden
The bronze statue of *Hercules* (1680s) by the Dutch Renaissance sculptor Adrian de Vries adorns the parterre in the palace's Baroque Gardens.

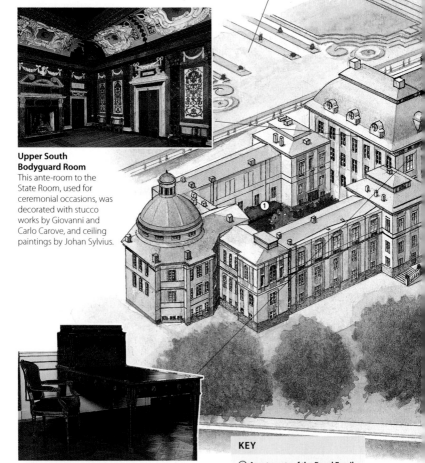

Upper South Bodyguard Room
This ante-room to the State Room, used for ceremonial occasions, was decorated with stucco works by Giovanni and Carlo Carove, and ceiling paintings by Johan Sylvius.

Writing Table by Georg Haupt
Standing in the Queen's Room is this masterpiece (1770) commissioned by King Adolf Fredrik as a gift to Queen Lovisa Ulrika. Textiles for the walls and furnishings date from the 1970s.

KEY

① **Apartments of the Royal Family**

② **The Palace Church** in the northern cupola was completed by Hårleman in the 1720s.

★ Queen Lovisa Ulrika's Library
The Queen commissioned Jean Eric Rehn (1717–93) to decorate this splendid library, which illustrates her influence on art and science in Sweden in the 18th century.

VISITORS' CHECKLIST

Practical Information
10 km (6 miles) W of Stockholm.
Palace: **Tel** 08-402 62 80.
Open Apr: 11am–3:30pm daily;
May–Sep: 10am–4:30pm daily;
Oct: 11am–3:30pm Fri–Sun; Nov–
Mar: noon–3:30pm Sat & Sun.
Closed 14–30 Dec. 🌐 📷 📹 ♿
Chinese Pavilion: **Open** May–Aug:
11am–4:30pm daily; Sep: noon–
3:30pm daily. 📷 📹 ♿
Ⓦ royalcourt.se

Transport
Ⓣ Brommaplan, then bus 301 or
302. 🚢 late Mar–Oct.

Entrance

★ Queen Hedvig Eleonora's State Bedroom
Morning receptions (*"levées"*) were held in this lavish Baroque room designed by Tessin the Elder. It took about 15 years for Sweden's foremost artists and craftsmen to decorate the room, which was completed in 1683.

★ Staircase
Trompe-l'oeil paintings by Johan Sylvius adorn the walls, giving the impression that the already spacious interior stretches further into the palace.

Exploring Drottningholm

The Palace of Drottningholm, a UNESCO World Heritage Site, is complemented by the Court Theatre (Slottsteatern), the world's oldest theatre still in active use, and the elegant Chinese Pavilion (Kina Slott), which has one of the finest European Rococo interiors with chinoiserie. The complex is situated on the shores of Lake Mälaren, surrounded by Baroque and Rococo gardens, and lush English-style parkland. In summer the theatre stages opera and ballet.

Karl XI's gallery at Drottningholm, featuring the victory at Lund, 1667

Drottningholm Palace Area

Stockholm

Sights
① Palace
② Chinese Pavilion
③ Palace Park
④ Court Theatre

0 metres 250
0 yards 250

The Palace Apartments

The first thing that meets the eye on entering the apartments is a Baroque corridor with a view that frames part of the gardens in all their splendour. The central part of the palace is dominated by the staircase, crowned by a lantern with ceiling paintings by Ehrenstrahl. There are examples of Baroque stucco work by Giovanni and Carlo Carove. Marble statues of the nine muses and their protector, Apollo, are placed at the corners of the balustrades.

The Green Salon is reached from the lower vestibule via the Lower Northern Bodyguard Room. This is the beginning of the main ceremonial suite, which continues with Karl X's Gallery where paintings illustrate his major military exploit, the crossing of the iced-over Store Bælt (Great Belt) by the Swedish army in 1658. Queen Hedvig Eleonora (1636–1715) held

Medallion symbolizing life and death

audiences in the Ehrenstrahl Salon, named after the artist whose paintings dominate the walls. More prominent guests were received in the State Bedroom which later in Queen Lovisa Ulrika's time was in fact used for sleeping. Her Meissen porcelain can be seen in the Blue Cabinet; the Library has her collection of more than 2,000 books. Behind the Upper Northern Bodyguard Room, with a ceiling by Johan Sylvius, is a Gustavian drawing room with a bureau by Johan Niklas Eckstein. In 1777, following Gustav III's assumption of power, the Blue Salon was decorated in the Neo-Classical style.

The Chinese Salon was used as a private bedroom by King Adolf Fredrik. It is directly above the Queen's State Bedroom and there is a hidden staircase linking the two floors. The "bureau" opposite

the tiled stove is also a sofa bed. The Oscar Room was refurbished by Oscar I (1799–1859) and is adorned by a tapestry dating from the 1630s. After the General's Room, Karl XI's Gallery commemorating the victory at Lund (1667), and the Golden Salon, comes the Queen's Salon. Just as the adjoining State Room has portraits of all the European monarchs, the portraits in the Queen's Salon are of European queens. This floor finishes with the Upper South Bodyguard Room, an ante-room to the State Room and lavishly decorated by the Carove stucco artists and the ceiling painter Johan Sylvius.

The Chinese Pavilion

On her 33rd birthday in 1753 Queen Lovisa Ulrika was given a Chinese pavilion by her husband, King Adolf Fredrik. It had been manufactured in Stockholm and the previous night it was shipped to Drottningholm and assembled a short distance from the palace. It had to be taken down after 10 years because rot had set in, and was replaced by the

The Chinese Pavilion, an extravaganza in blue and gold

Chinese Pavilion (Kina Slott) which is still one of the major attractions at Drottningholm. The polished-tile building was designed by D F Adelcrantz (1716–96).

At this time there was great European interest in all things Chinese. In 1733 the newly formed East India Company made its first journey to China. After Lovisa Ulrika's death in 1782 this interest waned, but it was rekindled in the 1840s. The Chinese Pavilion is a mixture of what was considered 250 years ago to be typical Chinese style along with artifacts from China and Japan. Efforts have been made to restore the interior to its original state with the help of a 1777 inventory.

Four smaller pavilions belong to the building. In the northeastern pavilion the king had his lathe and a carpenter's bench. Alongside is the Confidencen pavilion, where meals were taken if he wished to be left undisturbed. The food was prepared in the basement, the floor opened and the dining table hauled up. The adjoining Turkish-style "watch tent" was built as a barracks for Gustav III's dragoons. It now houses a museum about the estate.

Tiled stove in a cabinet in the Chinese Pavilion

The Palace Park

The palace's three gardens are each of a completely different character but still combine to provide a unified whole. The symmetrical formal garden started to take shape in 1640. The garden was designed to stimulate all senses with sights, sounds and smells. It starts by the palace terrace with its "embroidery" parterre and continues as far as the Hercules statue. The water parterre is situated on slightly higher ground and is broken up with waterfalls and topiaries. The sculptures, mainly carved by

the Flemish sculptor Adrian de Vries (1560–1626) were war trophies from Prague in 1648 and from Fredriksborg Castle in Denmark in 1659.

The avenues of chestnut trees were laid out when the Chinese Pavilion was completed, as well as the Rococo-inspired garden area – a cross between the formal main garden and the freer composition of the English park.

The English park has natural paths and a stream with small islands, along with trees and bushes at "natural" irregular intervals. Gustav III is reputed to have been responsible for its design and also planned several buildings. Not all his plans were realized, but he added four statues which he had bought during his travels in Italy.

The first 300 of a total of 846 lime trees were planted in the avenues flanking the Baroque garden as early as 1684.

The Court Theatre

The designer of the Chinese Pavilion, Carl Fredrik Adelcrantz, was also responsible for the Drottningholm Court Theatre (Slottsteatern), which dates from 1766. The theatre was commissioned by Queen Lovisa Ulrika, but Adelcrantz did not

Court Theatre stage machinery dating from 1766

The magnificent 18th-century stage in the Drottningholm Court Theatre

have the same resources as the architects of the palace itself. This simple wooden building with a plaster façade is now the world's oldest theatre still preserved in its original condition. The interior and fittings are masterpieces of simple functionality. The pilasters, for example, are made from gypsum and the supports from papier mâché. The scenery, with its wooden hand-driven machinery, is still in working order.

After Gustav III's death in 1792 the theatre fell into disuse until the 1920s, when the machinery ropes were replaced, electric lighting was installed, and the original wings were refurbished.

The scenery is adapted to 18th-century plays. It can be changed in just a few seconds with the help of up to 30 scene-shifters. The sound effects are simple but authentic: a wooden box filled with stones creates realistic thunder, a wooden cylinder covered in tent cloth produces a howling wind. Every summer there are about 30 performances, mainly opera and ballet from the 18th century. The theatre is open daily for visitors to the palace. There are also guided tours, which conclude at Déjeuner Salon Bar. The bar serves champagne and has beautiful views of the English garden. Pre-performance tours lasting around 45 minutes are also offered.

Other sites on the palace grounds include a royal chapel, which was inaugurated in 1746, and a visitors' centre with a gift shop.

☉ The Stockholm Archipelago

Extending 80 km (50 miles) east from the sheltered waters of Stockholm to the open sea, the archipelago encompasses tens of thousands of islands of all shapes and sizes, some inhabited, others not. Many of the inner archipelago's larger islands, such as Värmdö, Ingarö and Ljusterö, are linked to the mainland by bridges and car ferries, making them in parts little more than city suburbs. But the majority of the archipelago islands, with their traditional wooden houses, cosy hotels and youth hostels, and summer sailing regattas, can be reached by an extensive network of scheduled ferries departing from Stockholm, Vaxholm, Stavsnäs and Dalarö.

Passengers boarding steamships on a Stockholm wharf on Archipelago Boat Day

Archipelago Highlights

① Fjäderholmarna
② Vaxholm
③ Grinda
④ Finnhamn
⑤ Möja
⑥ Sandhamn
⑦ Utö

🦞 Fjäderholmarna

6 km (4 miles) E of Stockholm.
Tel 08-718 01 00. May–Sep from Nybrokajen and Slussen.

With the inclusion of the Fjäderholmarna islands in the Royal National City Park *(see p103)*, the city's "green lung" has acquired a small part of the archipelago. The main island, Stora Fjäderholmen, is only 25 minutes by boat from Nybrokajen or Slussen.

There was an inn here as long ago as the 1600s, conveniently sited for islanders on their way to the city to sell their wares. Today there is an attractive harbour, restaurants, an art gallery and museums devoted to boating and angling as well as the Baltic Sea Museum, home to virtually every type of aquatic creature from Stockholm to Landsort. Local handicrafts include metalwork, weaving, wood-carving and glass-making. The other three islands have a rich birdlife and one, Libertas, has Sweden's last remaining gas-powered lighthouse.

🏰 Vaxholm

25 km (16 miles) NE of Stockholm.
Tel 08-541 314 80. 670. from Strömkajen and Nybrokajen. Vaxholm Fortress and Vaxholm Fortress Museum: **Tel** 08-541 718 90. **Open** mid-Jun–Sep: 11:30am–5:30pm daily.

The archipelago's main community, Vaxholm, is easily reached by boat from Stockholm on a delightful one-hour journey through the archipelago. Vaxholm Fortress, on the nearby island of Vaxholmen, guards this busy port. First fortified in 1548 by Gustav Vasa, the more recent 19th-century citadel houses a military museum.

Two of Stockholm's best-known architects have left their mark on Vaxholm. The law courts were given their present appearance in 1925 by

The Fjäderholmarna islands, a popular summer excursion just 25 minutes by boat from the city

Vaxholm Fortress, strategically sited on the approach to Vaxholm

Cyrillus Johansson, and the hotel on the headland, by Erik Lallerstedt (1899), has Jugendstil ornamentation.

The wooden buildings and shops around the square and along Hamngatan provide a pleasant stroll.

🏖 Grinda

30 km (19 miles) E of Stockholm.
Tel 08-542 490 72. 670 from Östra station to Vaxholm, then boat. from Strömkajen and Nybrokajen. (summer only).

Grinda is a leafy island, typical of the inner archipelago, about one and a half hours by boat from the city. It has some excellent beaches and rocks for swimming, as well as good fishing. The architect Ernst Stenhammar, who designed the Grand Hôtel in Stockholm *(see p83)*, built a large Jugendstil

For hotels and restaurants in this area see pp284–5 and pp294–5

Sandhamn, the yachting centre in Stockholm's outer archipelago

villa here, which is now a pub and restaurant with guest rooms. There are chalets to rent, a camp site and a youth hostel in a former barracks. Boats can be hired.

🏝 Finnhamn
40 km (25 miles) NE of Stockholm.
Tel 08-542 462 12. from Strömkajen and Nybrokajen. 📷 📷 📷

Finnish ships used to moor at Finnhamn on their way to and from Stockholm. This attractive group of islands lies two and a half hours by boat from Stockholm at the point where the softer scenery of the inner archipelago gives way to the harsher landscape of the outer islands. As on Grinda, the main island has a wooden villa designed by Ernst Stenhammar (1912). Today it is the largest youth hostel in the archipelago. There is a restaurant, chalets to rent and a camp site. Smaller islands nearby are accessible by rowing boat.

🏝 Möja
50 km (31 miles) E of Stockholm.
Tel 08-571 640 53. 670 to Vaxholm, then boat. from Strömkajen and Nybrokajen. 📷 📷 📷

Fishing and strawberry-growing were the mainstays of this idyllic corner of the archipelago. Now there are few Möja strawberry growers and only one profess-ional fisherman among the island's 300 inhabitants. Instead, picturesque harbours attract the sailing fraternity in particular. Nature reserves on and around Möja shelter a rich abundance of wildlife. Services on the island are good in the summer, with cottages, boats and kayaks for hire, and guest houses.

🏝 Sandhamn
50 km (31 miles) E of Stockholm.
Tel 08-571 530 00. 433, 434 from Slussen to Stavsnäs, then boat. from Nybrokajen. 📷 📷 📷
W **destinationsandhamn.se**

Over the past 200 years the village of Sandhamn has been a favourite meeting point for sailors. The Royal Swedish Yacht Club is based in Seglarrestaurangen (Sailors' Restaurant), and every summer the world's yachting elite arrive to take part in the Round Gotland Race.

A pretty village with narrow alleys and houses adorned with decorative carvings, Sandhamn has shops, crafts centres and a swimming pool. About 100 people live here permanently. The Customs House, built in 1752, is a listed heritage building and the former home of poet and artist Elias Sehlstedt (1808–74).

Although camping is not permitted, there is no shortage of hotel, bed-and-breakfast and chalet accommodation. There are also great sandy beaches.

🏝 Utö
50 km (31 miles) SE of Stockholm.
Tel 08-501 574 10. in summer, from Strömkajen. 📷 📷
W **utoturistbyra.se**

No other island in the archipelago has as rich a history as Utö, which was inhabited before the Viking era. In the 12th century the islanders started to mine iron ore; this activity continued until 1879. Their story is told in the Mining Museum adjoining the hotel. Today's holiday homes along Lurgatan were built as miners' cottages in the 18th century. A windmill, built in 1791, provides an unrivalled view of the island.

Utö is one of the best seaside resorts in the Stockholm area, and is ideal for a weekend or full-day excursion.

A range of accommodation options is available. Bicycles, rowing boats and canoes can be hired. The bakery is renowned for its delicious "Utölimpa" bread.

Excursions by Steamboat

Traditional steamboats are a familiar feature on the waters around Stockholm. Both in the archipelago and on Lake Mälaren visitors can still enjoy the tranquil atmosphere of a steamboat voyage. One of the veterans, *SS Blidösund*, built in 1911, is operated by voluntary organizations and serves mostly the northern archipelago. Some routes, for example Stockholm–Mariefred, are operated partly or completely by steamers. Most of the other passenger boats from the early 20th century have been fitted with oil-fired engines, but still provide a nostalgic journey back in time.

SS Blidösund, one of the oldest in Stockholm's fleet of steamboats

STOCKHOLM STREET FINDER

Key to Street Finder

- Major sight
- Place of interest
- Other building
- Train station
- Tunnelbana station
- Ferry boarding point
- Tram stop
- Bus station

- Tourist information office
- Hospital
- Police station
- Church
- Synagogue
- Viewpoint
- Railway line
- Pedestrian street

Scale of Map Pages 1–2

0 metres   200
0 yards   200

Scale of Map Pages 3–4

0 metres   200
0 yards   200

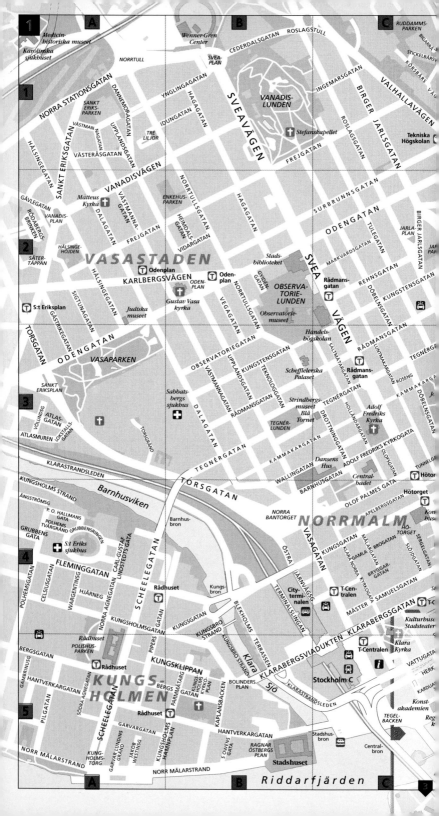

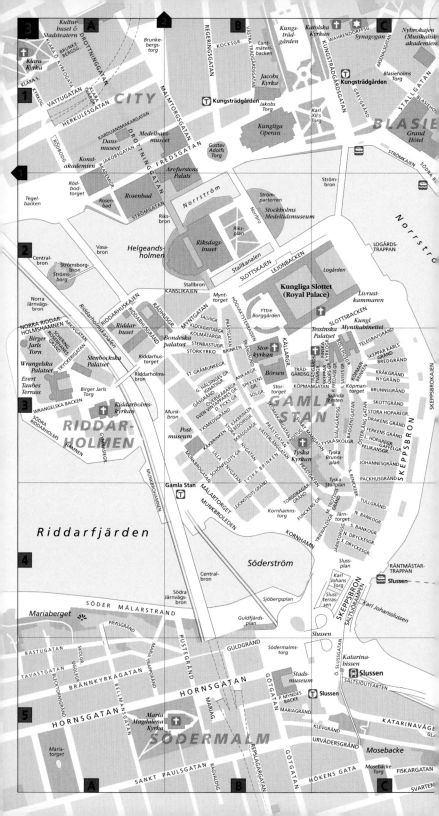

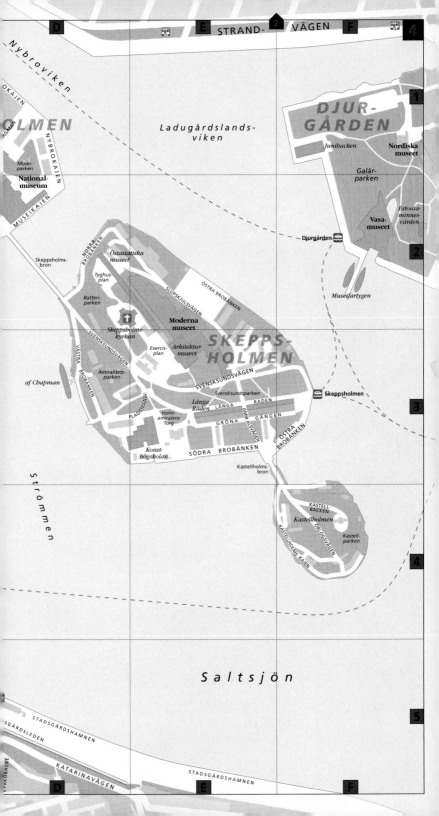

SWEDEN
AREA BY AREA

Sweden at a Glance

Sweden is a long country, traditionally divided into Norrland, Svealand and Götaland. In Norrland the landscape is characterized by its proximity to the Arctic, with mountains in the west, rivers running east towards the coast, and an interior of forest or marshland. With the exception of the larger towns along the coast, the area is sparsely populated. In Svealand the countryside is hilly, with lakes and rivers interspersed with farmland. Island archipelagos lie offshore. The population is concentrated in Mälardalen, centring on Stockholm. Götaland, comprising the southern part of the country, offers the most variation with differing landscapes and a high urban and rural population.

The Mountains of Härjedalen are a haven for outdoor activities in both summer and winter (see pp264–5).

The Fryken Lakes in Värmland are edged by superb manor houses such as Rottneros, whose park overlooking Mellanfryken contains an outstanding collection of statues, including works by Carl Milles.

Götaplatsen, Gothenburg's finest square, features Carl Milles' statue *Poseidon* with Konstmuseet in the background (see p204).

Fiskebäckskil, with its red fishermen's huts and white wooden houses, is typical of the coastal villages of Bohuslän (see p219).

Österlen, on the southeastern coast of Skåne, is characterized by rolling agricultural land and the half-timbered farmhouses typical of the area (see p187).

Gä

Öste

Stc
Sjö

Sve

Mo
Silj

Karlstad

Vänern

Skagerrak

Vättern

Jönköping

Gothenburg   Borås

Varberg

Kattegat   Vä

Halmstad

Karlsha

Helsingborg

Malmö

◄ Aerial view of the fortified citadel in Landskrona

The ICEHOTEL in Jukkasjärvi is an extraordinary creation built entirely of ice and snow. It melts in the spring each year and is recreated in November *(see p276)*.

Uppsala, the seat of Sweden's archbishop, has a High Gothic cathedral consecrated in 1435 – although parts of it date from the 13th century – and the oldest university in the Nordic countries, established in 1477 *(see pp134–5)*.

Visby, "the town of roses and ruins", with its medieval perimeter wall and half-timbered houses, is a UNESCO World Heritage Site *(see pp168–71)*.

The Kingdom of Crystal is the part of Småland known for its glassware, both artistic and practical. The plate, *Amber*, was designed by Göran Wärff at Kosta Glasbruk in 2003 *(see pp156–7)*.

0 kilometres 200
0 miles 100

EASTERN SVEALAND

The waterways of Lake Mälaren and the vast archipelago extending to the Baltic both divide and unite the provinces of Uppland, Södermanland and Västmanland. This is a land of verdant islands and glittering bays, splendid castles and little wooden towns, and a cultural heritage that predates the Vikings. With Stockholm at the centre, the region is home to one third of Sweden's population.

This area was the cradle of ancient Svea, as can be seen in the rock carvings, burial mounds and standing stones in the shapes of ships that dot the landscape. It was from the town of Birka on Lake Mälaren and from Roslagen in Uppland that the Vikings headed east on plundering raids and trading missions around Europe and beyond *(see p37)*. The centre of the ancient pagan Æsir cult in Uppsala held out against Christianity until the 12th century. Many beautiful, small medieval churches testify to the fact that Christianity finally dominated. They are richly decorated with paintings depicting biblical scenes for the benefit of the local congregations. Uppsala itself became a cathedral city and the seat of the archbishop in 1273.

The many castles and fortresses which guard the waterways are an eye-catching sight. Several of these date back to the Middle Ages, but the most important, such as Skokloster, are the result of the great wealth which flooded into the country after Sweden's victories in the various European wars of the 17th century *(see pp41–3)*. Shipping brought further prosperity to the region, with centres such as Arboga lying on the iron route between Bergslagen, Stockholm and the Uppland harbours. There are well-preserved ironworks in all three provinces, including Engelsbergs Bruk, a UNESCO World Heritage Site.

The extensive archipelago straddles the coasts of Uppland and Södermanland, and Lake Mälaren itself is so full of islands that the archipelago appears to continue uninterrupted.

All the architectural sights and natural attractions of Eastern Svealand are best enjoyed at a slow pace by bicycle or boat, or on foot.

The flat skerries of the outer archipelago

◄ Traditional houses and church in Mariefred, on Lake Malaren

Exploring Eastern Svealand

This, the heartland of Sweden, offers as many tempting treats as the most well-stocked Swedish *smörgåsbord*. Whether travelling by car, bus, train, bicycle or on foot, visitors will enjoy frequent glimpses of lakes and bays, as water is a constant presence. This makes travelling by boat an unbeatable way of discovering Eastern Svealand's history and culture and enjoying the area's natural beauty. There are hundreds of canoe trails, and canoes and boats can be hired all over the region. For walkers, Sörmlandsleden, Upplandsleden and Bruksleden in Västmanland offer more than 1,500 km (940 miles) of stunning trails.

Botanist Carl von Linné's Hammarby, outside Uppsala *(see p135)*

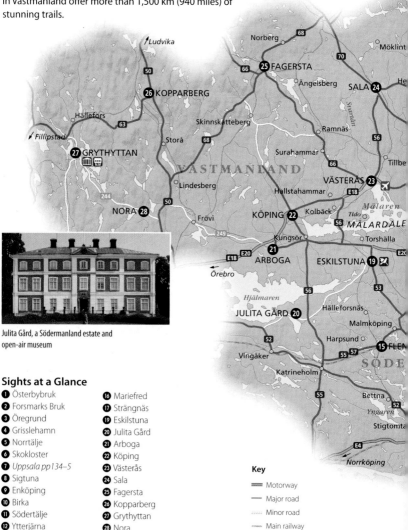

Julita Gård, a Södermanland estate and open-air museum

Sights at a Glance

Key

- ▭ Motorway
- — Major road
- ⋯ Minor road
- ∿ Main railway
- — Minor railway

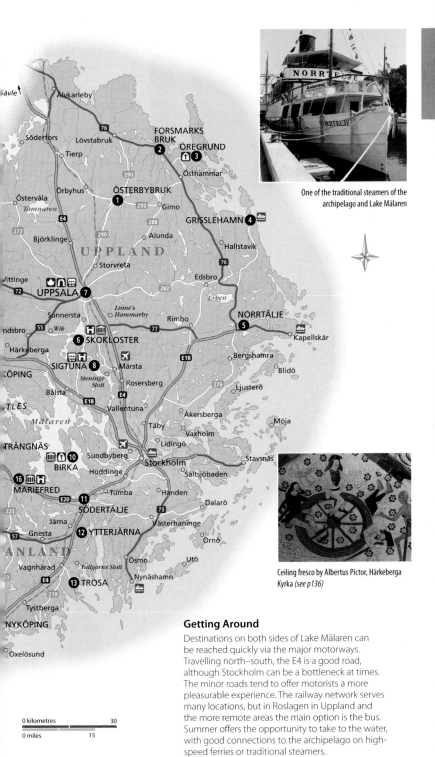

One of the traditional steamers of the archipelago and Lake Mälaren

Ceiling fresco by Albertus Pictor, Härkeberga Kyrka (see p136)

0 kilometres 30

0 miles 15

Getting Around

Destinations on both sides of Lake Mälaren can be reached quickly via the major motorways. Travelling north–south, the E4 is a good road, although Stockholm can be a bottleneck at times. The minor roads tend to offer motorists a more pleasurable experience. The railway network serves many locations, but in Roslagen in Uppland and the more remote areas the main option is the bus. Summer offers the opportunity to take to the water, with good connections to the archipelago on high-speed ferries or traditional steamers.

Österbybruk's English gardens with estate offices and clock tower

❶ Österbybruk

Uppland. 🏔 2,200. 🚹 1 Jun–31 Aug: Ånghammaren 0295-214 92. 🚌 823 from Uppsala. 🎭 🖼 ∅ Vallonsmedjan: **Open** Jun–Aug: daily. 🎫 by appointment, 0295-200 72. Liljeforsateljén: **Open** May–mid-Jun, mid-Aug–Sep: noon–4pm Sat & Sun; mid-Jun–mid-Aug: noon–5pm daily. 🎪 Fire Festival (2nd weekend Aug).

Iron played a key role in the region and nowhere is this more apparent than at Österbybruk. It is the area's oldest ironworks, dating back to the 15th century, but things only really took off when Dutchman Louis de Geer bought the foundry in 1643. With the help of migrant Walloon blacksmiths, he developed the iron industry so crucial to Sweden's position as a great power.

As the world's only fully preserved Walloon forge, the 15th-century **Vallonsmedjan** uses puppets, sound and light to recreate life in the hammer mills. Around it are charming 18th- and 19th-century streets.

The 18th-century manor house was home to wildlife painter Bruno Liljefors in the early 20th century. In summer, his popular animal paintings are exhibited in **Liljeforsateljén** in the gardens.

Dannemora Gruva was the mine on which local iron-working was built. Gaping opencast pits such as Storrymningen are relics of an industry that has gone on here since the Middle Ages. Above the mine is the building in which Mårten Triewald built

Sweden's first steam engine in 1726.

🏛 Dannemora Gruva
2 km (1 mile) west of Österbybruk. **Tel** 0295-214 92. **Open** Jun–Sep: daily. 🎫 🖼

❷ Forsmarks Bruk

Uppland. 🚌 751 from Uppsala. 🚹 next to Brukscaféet, Jun–Aug: 0173-500 15. **Open** mid-Jun–mid-Aug: 10:45am–4pm daily. 🎫 mid-Jun–mid-Aug: 10am (call to book). 🖼 ∅ 🎫 ♿

The historic ironworks of Forsmarks Bruk retains its well-preserved streets with their beautiful, whitewashed rows of houses and a manor house built in 1767–74. The manor is set in English-style gardens.

The nuclear power station of **Forsmarks Kärnkraftverk** lies on the coast, 3 km (2 miles) from the ironworks. It provides one seventh of Sweden's electricity. Guided tours include such features as the vast biotest lake where the environmental impact of the cooling water is studied.

Louis de Geer's Walloon ironworks empire also included the impressively preserved **Lövstabruk**.

🏭 Forsmarks Kärnkraftverk
3 km (2 miles) north of Forsmark. 🚹 0173-810 00. **Open** Mon–Fri. 🎫 mid-Jun–mid-Aug: tours from Forsmarks Bruk; other times by appointment. ♿

🏘 Lövstabruk
16 km (10 miles) north from Forsmark. 🚹 summer: 0294-310 70. **Open** summer: daily (manor). 🖼 🖼 ∅ ♿

❸ Öregrund

Uppland. 🏔 1,600. 🚌 639 from Stockholm. 🚹 Jun–Aug: Harbour Office, 0767–650 660; all year round: Östhammar Tourist Office, Rådhusgatan 6, Östhammar, 0767–650 660. 🚤 🎪 Östhammar Music Festival (late Jun or early Jul), Roslagsloppet speedboat race (late Jul/early Aug). 🌐 **roslagen.se**

The twin towns of Öregrund and Östhammar are closely linked geographically and historically. At the end of the 15th century, the citizens of Östhammar founded Öregrund in order to obtain a better harbour. Seafaring and iron-exporting became vital to the town. In 1719, Öregrund was burned by the Russians, but the wooden buildings were rebuilt according to a town plan from 1744. The town hall is from 1829. At the end of the 19th century, the sleepy area became a seaside resort and continues to attract visitors to this day.

The Öregrund and Östhammar region is home to many well-preserved old ironworking communities, including **Harg** and **Gimo**. Built in 1763–70, Gimo Manor was the first in Sweden to be designed in Gustavian style by Jean Eric Rehn.

Outside Gimo lies **Skäfthammars Kyrka**, a medieval church particularly renowned for its lectern, which was built for the Gimo smiths.

⛪ Skäfthammars Kyrka
Gimo, 16 km (10 miles) southeast of Östhammar. **Tel** 0173-400 77. **Open** call for info.

Öregrund Church's shingle-clad, free-standing bell tower (1719)

Albert Engström's studio on the granite cliffs outside Grisslehamn

❹ Grisslehamn

Uppland. 🄰 250. 🚌 637 from Norrtälje. 🚢 🎿 Postrodden boat race to Åland (Jun).

The choppy Åland Sea constantly batters the red granite cliffs of northern Väddö at Grisslehamn. This is the closest point in Sweden to Finland and the reason for the town's existence. Today's ferry crossing to Eckerö takes only two hours, but things were much tougher in the 17th and 18th centuries when this was the main link with the eastern outposts of the Swedish empire. Until 1876, the post was rowed across the water by local fishermen in open boats. To commemorate the "post rowers", a race is held across the Åland Sea every year in similar boats.

Today, apart from those making the ferry crossing, the sleepy fishing port of Grisslehamn attracts Väddö's many holidaymakers. Delicious fresh fish can be bought from the red sheds on the harbourside.

In 1902, painter and writer Albert Engström (d. 1940) moved to Grisslehamn. He became much loved for his priceless characters such as the tramp, Kolingen, and the Roslagen figure, Österman. The **Albert Engströmsmuseet**, a reconstruction of his home containing Engström's art and memorabilia, was moved to Augustberg in 2006.

🏛 **Albert Engströmsmuseet**
Augustberg. **Tel** 0175-308 90.
Open late Jun–Aug; rest of year by appointment only. 🗎 🗀 🖵

❺ Norrtälje

Uppland. 🄰 18,000. 🚌 676 from Stockholm. 🛈 Lilla Brogatan 3, 0767-650 660. 🚢 🎿 Norrtälje Blues & Rock Festival (late Jul).
🆆 **norrtalje.se**

An idyllic town, built of wood, Norrtälje is the natural hub of Roslagen, the area which covers large parts of the Uppland coast. Norrtälje received its town charter from Gustav II Adolf in 1622, when an important armaments factory was established here. In the second half of the 19th century, the town became a seaside resort, not least due to the health-giving properties of the mud found in Norrtälje Bay.

Thousands of summer residents from Stockholm still head for Norrtälje. The town centre and the buildings along the Norrtäljeån river retain their 18th-century features. The church was built in 1726 and the town hall dates from 1792. Attractions include **Roslagsmuseet** in the old armaments factory, focusing on seafaring and coastal life. **Pythagoras** is an unusual museum in a former diesel engine factory and one of Sweden's best preserved industrial relics.

Viking ship in Norrtälje

🏛 **Roslagsmuseet**
Hantverkargatan 23. **Tel** 0176-576 30. 🚾

🏛 **Pythagoras**
Verkstadsgatan 6. **Tel** 0176-100 50.
Open mid-Jan–mid-Dec: noon–4pm Tue–Sun. 🗎 🗀 🖵

❻ Skokloster

Uppland. **Tel** 08-402 30 70. 🚆 SL train from Stockholm to Bålsta, then bus 311. 🚌 from Uppsala. **Open** May & Sep: 11am–4pm Sat & Sun; Jun–Aug: 11am–5pm daily. 🗎 🗀 🖵 🏛

One of the best preserved Baroque castles in Europe, Skokloster, on Lake Mälaren, contains a unique collection of furniture, art, weapons, textiles and books. Construction was started in 1654 for army commander Carl Gustav Wrangel, who accumulated incredible treasures during the Thirty Years War (1618–48). This magnificent building was a way for Wrangel to show off his success, but he only ever lived here for a few weeks. Time seems to have stood still at the castle: the Banquet Hall, for example, remains incomplete, with all the tools lying where the craftsmen left them. The most sumptuous rooms are the armoury and library.

Next to the castle is Sweden's second oldest brick church. Built in the 13th century for nuns of the Cistercian order, it still contains a 13th-century triumphal cross. In the 17th century, it became the Wrangel family church. The churchyard contains several runestones, some of which are signed by the Viking runemaster, Fot, who was active in the mid-11th century.

The Baroque Skokloster Castle, beautifully situated on Lake Mälaren

❼ Uppsala

The city of learning on the idyllic Fyrisån river long remained a small town despite becoming the seat of the archbishop in 1273, having the first university in Scandinavia in 1477 and being the venue for parliaments and coronations. Scientists such as Carl von Linné and Anders Celsius gained the university worldwide glory, but as late as 1800 the town had only 4,000 inhabitants. It wasn't until 20th-century industrialization and the expansion in education that Uppsala grew into Sweden's fourth largest city. The Gothic cathedral, castle, historic university buildings, botanical gardens and ancient Gamla (Old) Uppsala make this one of Sweden's foremost sights.

The cathedral's twin spires, restored in the 19th century

🏛 Domkyrkan

Domkyrkoplan 2. **Tel** 018-430 35 00. **Open** 8am–6pm daily. 🎫 🚫 📷 📹 daily. ♿ ✝ Skattkammaren: **Open** 10am–4pm Mon–Sat, 12:30–4pm Sun. 🎫

The first sight on approaching Uppsala is the 119 m (390 ft) high twin spires of the largest cathedral in the Nordic region. The building, with its impressive, Gothic nave, was consecrated in 1435. Many monarchs have been crowned here and kings Gustav Vasa and Johan III, as well as botanist Carl von Linné and theosophist Emanuel Swedenborg (1688–1772), are buried here. The chapel contains the remains of St Erik, patron saint of Sweden, in a golden shrine.

The cathedral treasury, Skattkammaren, has a superb collection of textiles and silver.

🏛 Gustavianum

Akademigatan 3. **Tel** 018-471 75 71. **Open** 11am–6pm Tue–Sun. **Closed** public holidays. 🎫 🚫 Sat & Sun (also Eng; book ahead). 🏠 ♿ ✉

Named after King Gustav II Adolf, who donated both funds and land, this is the oldest preserved building of Uppsala University. The unusual dome was built in 1662 for Olof Rudbeck's Theatrum Anatomicum. This is an amphitheatre with standing room for 200 spectators – students and paying members of the public – who would gather here to watch dissections of executed criminals. The room which visitors see today is largely a faithful reconstruction.

The Gustavianum mounts exhibitions connected with the work of the university since its foundation in 1477. One of the gems on show is the Augsburg Art Cabinet from the early 17th century. It is a kind of universal museum showing the world view of the time in miniature. Various archaeological collections from Egypt and the Classical world are also on display.

🏛 Universitetshuset

St Olofsgatan/Övre Slottsgatan. **Tel** 018-471 17 15. **Open** Mon–Fri and for events. ♿

The university's imposing main building was constructed in 1887 in Neo-Renaissance style. It contains an attractive auditorium.

🏛 Carolina Rediviva

Dag Hammarskjölds Väg 1. **Tel** 018-471 39 09. **Open** 8:30am–9pm Mon–Fri, 9am–6pm Sat & Sun). **Closed** public holidays. 🎫 mid-May–mid-Sep. ♿

In 1841, the 200-year-old university library moved into this specially designed building which houses 5 million printed books and 4 km (2 miles) of shelving holding handwritten manuscripts. Rarities include the Silver Bible from the 6th century and Olaus Magnus's *Carta Marina* (1539).

🏛 Uppsala Slott

Slottsbacken. **Tel** 018-727 24 82. 🚫 phone for info. Konstmuseet: **Open** Tue–Sun. House of Peace (museum): **Tel** 018-50 00 08. 🎫 🚫 ✏ 📷

Standing on a glacial ridge, this Vasa castle competes with the cathedral for domination of the city. Established as a fortress in 1549, it was added to several times, but never finished. A disastrous city fire in 1702 destroyed much of the castle and restoration work was started by Carl Hårleman. The castle now houses Uppsala's art

---

Carl Von Linné

Bust of Carl von Linné, 1707–78

"God created, Linné organized," goes the saying about the Swedish king of plants. It is thanks to Linné's ground-breaking *Systema Naturae*, first published in 1735, that the world has the familiar system of binomial nomenclature, giving all plants and animals two Latin names. In 1741, Linné, also known as Linnaeus, became professor of medicine at Uppsala and his spirit has suffused the city ever since. At his country house in Hammarby, Linné tutored students. It was not unknown for him to greet them dressed only in his nightshirt, for the morning's nature walk. According to Linné "nature does not wait for powder and wigs".

Burial mounds next to Gamla Uppsala church

VISITORS' CHECKLIST

Practical Information
Uppsala. ⊞ 207,000.
ⓘ Kungsgatan 59, 018-727 48 00.
⊠ Vaksala market (Sat).
⊡ Walpurgis Night celebrations
(30 Apr), Culture Night (mid-Sep).
ⓦ **destinationuppsala.se**

Transport
⊠ 25 km (16 miles) south of the
centre. 🚇 🚌 Kungsgatan.

museum, the governor's residence and the House of Peace, a museum that explores world conflicts and Sweden's long history of neutrality.

🌿 Botaniska Trädgården
Villavägen 8. **Tel** 018-471 28 38.
Open daily. **Closed** public holidays.
🌱 greenhouse.

The botanical gardens have had an educational function since the end of the 18th century. They hold more than 130,000 plants, many exotic, in a beautiful setting that includes several greenhouses, one of which is tropical. The first garden was established on the banks of the Fyrisån river by Olof Rudbeck in 1655. In 1741, Carl von Linné took it over and made it one of the leading gardens of its time. Lovingly restored, it is now known as the Linné garden. After a donation from Gustav III in the late 18th century, teaching was switched to the castle garden,

where the Linneanum, housing the orangery, opened in 1807.

🏛 Gamla Uppsala
Route 290 or E4, 5 km north of the centre. Disagården: **Tel** 018-16 91 80.
Gamla Uppsala Museum: **Tel** 018-23 93 12. **Open** mid-May–Aug: daily.
🌱 🔲 Sun.

Gamla Uppsala and its museum are like a time capsule. Royal burial mounds rise up from the plain as they have done for 1,500 years. This was a centre for worshipping the Norse gods long into the 11th century, with a temple which, according to Adam of Bremen's description from 1070, was clad entirely in gold and contained images of Odin, Thor and Frey. Every nine years, a bloody festival was celebrated with men, stallions and dogs sacrificed around the temple. In the early 12th century, the heathen temple gave way to a Christian church, then a cathedral. But in 1273,

the seat of the diocese moved to Uppsala and the cathedral became a parish church of which only small parts remain. Nearby is Disagården, an open-air museum about the life of local farmers in the 19th century.

🏛 Linné's Hammarby
13 km (8 miles) southeast of Uppsala.
Tel 018-471 28 38. **Open** May–Sep:
Gardens: daily. Museum: Jun–Aug:
Tue–Sun; May & Sep: Sat & Sun.
Closed Whitsun, Midsummer's Eve.
🌱 🔲

Linné bought Hammarby farm in 1758, because he thought the air in Uppsala was bad for his health. The estate was his rural retreat, where he was able to cultivate plants that could not tolerate the moist soil in the botanical gardens. The farm is now owned by the state and run by Uppsala University.

Uppsala City Centre

① Domkyrkan
② Gustavianum
③ Universitetshuset
④ Carolina Rediviva
⑤ Uppsala Slott/Konstmuseet
⑥ Botaniska Trädgården

0 metres 300
0 yards 300

For keys to symbols see back flap

Steninge Slott near Sigtuna, one of the best examples of a 17th-century Carolian country house

❽ Sigtuna

Uppland. 🖼 44,000. 🚊 🚃 to Märsta C, then bus. 🚌 🛥 ℹ Stora Gatan 33, 08-594 806 50.
🖥 sigtuna.se

Sweden's second oldest town after Birka was founded in 980 and soon became a centre of Christianity. Ruins of three of the original seven churches in medieval Sigtuna, St Per, St Lars and St Olof, still remain. The attractive main street, Stora Gatan, is lined with colourful wooden buildings and follows the original route. Still in use today is the 13th-century church of St Maria, with its medieval paintings. It is the oldest brick-built church in Mälardalen.

Sigtuna has Sweden's smallest town hall, built in 1744, and Lundströmska Gården, an early 20th-century home furnished in the style of the period. There are around 150 11th-century rune stones in the surrounding region.

The area is well-endowed with stately homes. These include Skokloster (see p133) and the royal palace of **Rosersberg**, with some of Europe's best-kept interiors from the period 1795–1825.

East of Sigtuna is Steninge Slott, architect Tessin the Younger's Italianate Baroque masterpiece built in the 1690s. The attractive house and gardens were a popular tourist spot, but the site is now being transformed into a residential area with more than 600 homes.

🏠 Rosersbergs Slott
15 km (9 miles) from Sigtuna.
Tel 08-590 350 39. **Open** for guided tours only. 🚫 🎥 May–Sep: 11am–3pm (Jun–Aug: to 4pm).
📷 🎥

🏠 Steninge Slott
7 km (4 miles) east of Sigtuna.
Tel 08-592 595 00. Palace:
Open Jun–Aug daily. 🚫 🎥 🎥 🏠

❾ Enköping

Uppland. 🖼 40,000. 🚊 🚃 🚌
ℹ Rådhusgatan 3, 0171-625 040.
🖥 enkoping.se

This centrally located town on Lake Mälaren calls itself Sweden's "nearest town". Another name is "Horseradish Town" from the vegetable production which made the town known in the 19th century. And Enköping remains a city of greenery with its inviting parks.

Enköping was granted a town charter in 1300. It was a spiritual centre with three churches and a monastery. Of these, only the largely remodelled Vårfrukyrkan remains.

Northeast of the town, the medieval church of **Härkeberga** is a real gem. At the end of the 15th century, its star chamber was decorated by the master painter Albertus Pictor with colourful representations of biblical stories (see p131).

🏠 Härkeberga Kyrka
10 km (6 miles) northeast of Enköping. **Open** Mar–Oct: daily.

Triumphal cross, Härkeberga Kyrka

❿ Birka

Uppland. 🚢 from Stockholm during summer season only. Birkamuseet:
Tel 08-560 515 40. **Open** times vary; check website. 🚫 🎥 📷 🎥 🏠
🖥 stromma.se/sv/Birka

The trading post of Birka on the island of Björkö in Lake Mälaren was established in the 8th century and is thought to be the oldest town in Scandinavia. The founder was the Svea king, who had his royal residence on nearby Adelsö. About 100 years later, Birka is described by a writer as having "many rich merchants and an abundance of all types of goods and a great deal of money and valuables". It was thought to have had 1,000 inhabitants, including craftsmen of every kind, whose products attracted merchants from distant countries. The town was planned on uncomplicated lines. People lived in modest houses which stood in rows overlooking the long jetties. At these lay the ships which took the Vikings out on trading missions and war expeditions. In 830 the arrival of a monk named Ansgar marked the start of Sweden's conversion to Christianity. But Birka's moment of greatness soon passed.

Iron Age burial ground at Birka on the island of Björkö in Lake Mälaren

In the 10th century, the town was abandoned in favour of Sigtuna, on the nearby mainland.

Today, Björkö is a green island with meadows and juniper-covered slopes. It has a fascinating museum and ongoing archaeological digs. The museum shows how Birka would have looked in its heyday, along with some of the finds. Visitors can also share in the day's discoveries when digs are in progress.

In summer, services are held in the Ansgar Chapel. There is a harbour, restaurant, and good places to swim.

Testing the laws of nature at Tom Tits Experiment, Södertälje

⓫ Södertälje

Stockholms län. 🚗 92,000. ✈ 🚌 ⛴
ℹ Saltsjögatan 1, 08-523 010 00.
🔳 **sodertalje.nu**

Good communications are the key to the economic success of Södertälje, one of Sweden's oldest cities. In the 9th century, a rise in land levels rendered the sound between the Baltic Sea and Lake Mälaren unnavigable and so Tälje became a reloading point. The small town flourished in the Middle Ages but fires, war and plague almost eradicated it in the 17th and 18th centuries. Fortunes improved with the construction of the canal in 1819, and with the arrival of the railway in 1860 industrialization took off. The town grew quickly. Today, major companies such as vehicle-maker Scania and pharmaceuticals giant Astra Zeneca form the basis of a booming commercial life.

Södertälje's history is the focus of **Torekällbergets museet**, an open-air museum with animals, historic buildings and a craft quarter. **Marcus Wallenberg-hallen** contains a large collection

of veteran vehicles from Scania's 100-year production history.

Tom Tits Experiment is a science centre with many fun activities, both indoors and outdoors, for kids of all ages.

🏛 **Torekällbergets museet**
Tel 08-523 014 22. **Open** daily. 🖥 ⬛

🏛 **Marcus Wallenberg-hallen**
Tel 08-553 825 00.
Open call ahead for details.

🏛 **Tom Tits Experiment**
Storgatan 33. **Tel** 08-550 225 00.
Open 10am–5pm Wed–Fri (to 6pm Sat & Sun). **Closed** 1 Jan, 23–26 Dec & 31 Dec. 🖼 🖥 ⬛ 🏠 ♿
🔳 **tomtit.se**

⓬ Ytterjärna

Stockholms län. 🚌 to Järna, then bus. ℹ Kulturhuset, 08-554 302 00.
Open 10am–5pm daily. **Closed** public holidays. 🖼 🖥 ⬛ ♿

Since the 1960s, Ytterjärna has become the centre for Swedish anthroposophists, followers of the teachings of Austrian philosopher Rudolf Steiner (1861–1925). Anthroposophists focus on the development of the whole human being, particularly in the fields of art, music, farming and medicine. There are a number of Steiner organizations here, including schools, the Vidarkliniken hospital, biodynamic farms and market gardens. Kulturhuset is renowned as a centre for art, music and theatre, and for the building's audacious design by architect Erik Asmussen, with its intertwined dialogue of colour and shape.

Neat wooden houses lining the harbour canal in Trosa

⓭ Trosa

Södermanland. 🚗 5,500. 🚌 to Vagnhärad or Södertälje, then bus.
ℹ Rådstugan Torget, 0156-522 22.
⛴ 🛒 Trosa Market (2nd Sat in Jun).
🔳 **trosa.com**

Known as the end of the World, idyllic Trosa is something of a geographical dead end if you are not venturing into the wonderful Trosa archipelago beyond. It was burned to the ground by the Russians in 1719, although the church dating from 1711 was spared. Pretty groups of red wooden buildings can be found mainly in Kåkstan, where Garvaregården is an arts and crafts museum. The main square, with its miniature town hall and market, is a focal point for the town.

Nearby, **Tullgarns Slott** was the favourite summer residence of Gustav V (1858–1950). The beautiful 18th-century palace has magnificent interiors and English-style gardens.

🏰 **Tullgarns Slott**
On E4, 10 km (6 miles) north of Trosa.
Tel 08-551 720 11. **Open** May: 11am–3:30pm Sat; Jun–Aug: 11am–4:30pm Tue–Sun; Sep: 11am–3:30pm Sat & Sun. 🖼 🖼

Kulturhuset by Erik Asmussen, in the anthroposophists' Ytterjärna

Nyköpingshus, site of the fatal Nyköping Banquet in 1317

⓮ Nyköping

Södermanland. 33,000.
Rådhuset, Stora Torget, 0155-24 80 00. Nyköping Banquet (Jul).
nykoping.se

Södermanland's county town is probably best known for the notorious Nyköping Banquet in 1317. King Birger invited the Dukes Erik and Valdemar to a banquet at which the disputes between the brothers were to be resolved. Instead, Birger had the dukes thrown into Nyköpinghus's dungeon, where they were left to die. The story is retold in summer in a colourful pageant at the castle. A fire in 1665 destroyed the original castle and only the tower remains. In the adjoining county governor's residence, the **Sörmlands Museum** contains a lively mix of historical exhibitions.

A pleasant way to see the sights in the summer is to take the Tuffis tourist train which departs from Stora Torget. On the coast north of the town, Nynäs Slott nature reserve is also worth a visit.

Sörmlands Museum
Nyköpingshus. **Tel** 0155-24 57 00.
Open Jun–Aug: daily; other times: 10am–4pm Sun.

⓯ Flen

Södermanland. 7,000.
Södra Järnvägsgatan 2, 0157-43 09 96; Malmköping (summer) 0157-202 04. Malma Market (last Sat & Sun in Jul).

One of the youngest towns in Sweden, Flen only gained its town charter in 1949. Although the town itself has little to offer, it is a good starting point for the attractions in the area.

Environs

On Lake Valdemaren, just east of the town, lies Stenhammar's beautiful castle, renowned as the residence of Prince Vilhelm in the early 1900s. The castle is now used by Carl XVI Gustav and is not open to the public. Northeast of Flen is the prime minister's summer residence, **Harpsund**, where the gardens are open to visitors. The old regimental town of Malmköping has **Malmahed**, a former military site, now a museum and nature centre. There are several military museums, as well as **Museispårvägen**, displaying veteran trams and other public transport vehicles. Visitors can enjoy a short tram ride through the countryside.

Volvo taxi (1950), Museispårvägen

Museispårvägen
Malmköping, 17 km (11 miles) north of Flen, road 55. **Tel** 0157-204 30.
Open late May–end Jun: weekends only; end Jun–Aug: daily (call for opening hours).

⓰ Mariefred

Södermanland. 4,000.
Rådhuset, 0159-297 90.
Steam Day (1st Sat in Jun).
mariefred.se

This town should ideally be approached from the water to get the best view of the splendid **Gripsholms Slott**. The first fortress on this site was built in the 1380s by the Lord High Chancellor, Bo Jonsson Grip, who gave the castle its name. Work on the present building, initiated by Gustav Vasa, started in 1537, but extensive alterations were made by Gustav III in the late 18th century. It was during this period that the National Portrait Gallery was set up. It now contains 4,000 portraits, representing the celebrities of the past 500 years.

Gripsholms Slott has a number of well-preserved interiors from various periods, with highlights including Gustav III's theatre and the White Salon. The town of Mariefred, which grew up in the shadow of the castle, derives its name from a medieval Carthusian monastery. An inn has stood on the site of the monastery since the early 17th century.

The peaceful old streets of Mariefred with their delightful wooden buildings are a pleasure to stroll around. Art enthusiasts should head for Grafikens Hus on a hill leading up to the former royal farm, where stables and haylofts have been converted into attractive galleries.

Mariefred Town Hall (1784), site of the town's tourist office

For hotels and restaurants in this area see p285 and pp295–6

One of the best ways to visit Mariefred is by boat. The 1903 steamer *S/S Mariefred* plies the three-and-a-half-hour voyage from Stockholm. There is a Railway Museum in the town and **ÖSLJ** (Östra Södermanlands Järnväg museum society) operates narrow-gauge steam trains from the harbour on a 20-minute trip to Läggesta and, on certain days, on to Taxinge.

Red-painted, 18th-century wooden buildings in central Strängnäs

⛪ Gripsholms Slott
500 m (546 yd) southwest of the centre. **Tel** 0159-101 94. **Open** early May–Sep: daily; Apr, Oct & Nov (see website for details).
 gripsholmsslott.se

🏛 ÖSLJ
500 m (546 yd) west of the centre. **Tel** 0159-210 00. **Open** See website for departure times.
oslj.nu

Bedchamber of Duke Karl (Karl IX, 1550–1611), Gripsholms Slott

⑰ Strängnäs
Södermanland.  12,000. 🚉 🚌
🛈 Eskilstunavägen 2, 0152-296 94. **Open** Jun–Aug. 🗓 Strängnäs market (2nd Sat in Oct). 🌐 strangnas.se

As keeper of the keys of the Kingdom, Strängnäs was an important centre in the Middle Ages. It was mentioned as an episcopal see as early as 1120 and is dominated by the imposing tower of its Gothic cathedral, **Domkyrkan**, completed in 1280. It was here that Gustav Vasa was chosen as king on 6 June 1523, the date which was to become Sweden's National Day. Quaint wooden buildings surround the cathedral. To its east is Roggeborgen, the bishop's palace from the 1480s.

Gyllenjelmsgatan, the street that runs from the city centre to the mighty gates of the cathedral, was described by the poet Bo Setterlind as the most beautiful in Sweden.

Strängnäs Municipality includes the largest island in Lake Mälaren, **Selaön**. There are more rune stones here than in any other part of Södermanland, indicating that this was a major cultural centre in ancient times. Nowadays the island has no connections to the mainland.

The renovated Mälsåkers Palace dating from the 17th century is another of Selaön's attractions.

⛪ Domkyrkan
Biskopsgränd 2. **Tel** 0152-245 00. **Open** daily. 🗓 by appointment. ⛪ Wed & Sun.

⑱ Mälardalen's Castles
See pp140–41.

⑲ Eskilstuna
Södermanland.  100,000. 🚉 🚌
🛈 Tullgatan 4, 016-710 70 00.
🌐 eskilstuna.se

The town is named after St Eskil, the Englishman who became Svealand's first Christian bishop and built his church on the riverbank along Eskilstunaån at

A Sumatran tiger, one of the many exotic animals at Eskilstuna's Parken Zoo

the end of the 10th century. During Sweden's Age of Greatness in the 17th century, Eskilstuna flourished after Karl X Gustav gave master smith Reinhold Rademacher a 20-year monopoly on the manufacture of items such as cannons, knives and scissors. Rademachergatan still has a few forges kept as they were in the 1650s, where visitors can try their hand at being a blacksmith.

Today's modern industrial town and centre of learning features more than 200 items of public art, including Carl Milles' *Hand of God* (see p101) in Stadsparken.

Parken Zoo is one of Sweden's leading zoos, with animals from all around the world, including some endangered species. There is also a heated outdoor pool and an amusement park, which is popular with young children.

Environs
North of Eskilstuna is **Torshälla**, a small town of cobbled streets and well-kept wooden houses. The magnificent 12th-century church dominates the old quarter. Northeast of Torshälla is **Sunbyholms Slott** *(see p140)* from where a 10-minute walk leads to **Sigurdsristningen**, Sweden's finest rock carving, which is thought to date back to 1040.

🐾 Parken Zoo
1 km (half a mile) west of the centre. **Tel** 016-100 100. Zoo: **Open** early May–mid-Sep: 10am–5pm daily; mid-Jun–mid-Aug: 10am–7pm daily; Oct: 10am–4pm Sat. Amusement Park: **Open** May & late Sep: Sat & Sun; Jun–mid-Aug: daily; mid-Aug–mid-Sep: Sat–Sun.

⑱ A Tour of Mälardalen's Castles

There are more than 100 sturdy castles, opulent palaces and ravishing country houses around Lake Mälaren. Often strategically located near Iron Age and Viking settlements, they highlight the significance of this extensive waterway. Wik's 15th-century castle and the Vasa kings' solid, 16th-century fortress of Gripsholm show how long the need for defences lasted. From the mid-17th century, the grand palaces of Sweden's Age of Greatness, such as Skokloster, predominated, as manifestations of their owners' wealth and power. Many have excellent museums.

⑤ Engsö
The medieval castle was reworked in French Rococo style in the 1740s. It has many beautiful interiors from various periods and a major art collection. The castle grounds are a nature reserve full of wildlife.

⑥ Tidö
Lord Chancellor Axel Oxenstierna's country house, built in 1642, is a fine example of a Baroque manor. It is noted for its handsome state apartment and 43 inlaid wooden doors. A museum displays 30,000 antique toys.

④ Grönsöö
The grand manor from the early 17th century stands guard high above Lake Mälaren. It is still occupied by the von Ehrenheim family, and its grounds represent 400 years of garden history.

⑦ Strömsholm
Equestrianism dates from the 16th century at Strömsholm, with its beautiful pastureland and bridle paths. The palace was built in the 1670s in Carolian Baroque style.

Key

- ▬ Suggested route
- ═ Other roads
- 🏰 Other castles open to the public

⑧ Gripsholm
Gustav Vasa's brick Renaissance castle *(see p138)*, started in 1540, is a symbol of Swedish independence. Visitors have access to 60 rooms from various periods, the highlight of which is Gustav III's theatre, and the National Portrait Gallery.

Tips for Drivers

This tour, taking in the ten suggested palaces, involves a trip of more than 500 km (300 miles), lasting three days, despite the generally good roads. An option is to select a group of palaces close to each other.
For more information, see www.malarslott.nu

| 0 kilometres | 15 |
| 0 miles | 10 |

For hotels and restaurants in this area see p285 and pp295–6

③ Wik

This 15th-century castle is Svealand's best-preserved late-medieval fortress. With its solid walls and moat, Wik was considered impregnable. It was remodelled in 1656–60. Today, Wik is a hotel and conference centre.

② Skokloster

Field Marshal Carl Gustaf Wrangel's 17th-century showpiece contains treasures from his campaigns, as well as exceptional collections of art, furniture, textiles, weapons and books (see p133).

① Steninge

Built in the 1690s, the palace was designed by Nicodemus Tessin the Younger in the style of an Italian villa (see p136).

⑩ Drottningholm

This royal palace, built in the 17th century, was one of the most lavish undertakings in Sweden. With its theatre, gardens and Chinese Pavilion, Drottningholm is a UNESCO World Heritage Site (see pp112–15).

⑨ Sturehof

This stylish 18th-century country house in Botkyrka was designed by C F Adelcrantz for Gustav III's finance minister, Johan Liljekrantz, who owned the renowned Marieberg porcelain factory. The building houses a collection of the factory's famously stunning tiled stoves.

⑳ Julita Gård

Södermanland. **Tel** 0150-48 75 00. Train to Katrineholm, then bus 405. **Open** May–Sep daily.

This extensive Södermanland estate on Lake Öljaren is said to be the world's largest open-air museum. It was created in the first half of the 20th century by the romantic Lieutenant Arthur Bäckström and in 1941 was donated to Stockholm's Nordiska museet. Julita is a working estate farm with parks and gardens, and an 18th-century manor house built on the site of a medieval Cistercian monastery.

The estate has a collection of buildings reflecting rural life in Södermanland. Threatened national species of cow, pig, sheep, hen and duck are cared for at the Swedish agricultural museum. There is also a dairy museum. Children are welcome to pop into the house of the much-loved children's literary character, Pettson, and his cat Findus.

Julita Gård's buildings representing rural life in Södermanland

㉑ Arboga

Västmanland. 14,000. Medieval Festival (Aug).

Red-painted iron warehouses, Ladbron quay and the railway line recall Arboga's great age as the chief shipping port for iron from Bergslagen. Fahlströmska Gården is a typical 16th-century warehouse with a huge loft.

Arboga was an important town in medieval times and the site of Sweden's first parliament in 1435. Churches from the period include the hospital chapel on Stortorget, which has been preserved as a town hall. The 14th-century **Heliga Trefaldighets Kyrka** on Järntorget has a splendid Baroque pulpit by Burchardt Precht.

Anundshögen, the 7th-century burial mound of King Bröt-Anund, with a stone ship in the foreground

㉒ Köping

Västmanland. 🚊 24,000. 🚌 🚢
ℹ️ Barnhemsgatan 2, 0221-256 55.
🎭 Köpingsfesten Festival (28–30 May).

The port of Köping on Lake
Mälaren has been a vital link for
transporting products to and
from the mines and forests of
Bergslagen since medieval
times. The city burned down in
1889, but buildings to the west
of the river were saved, including
the 17th-century **Nyströmska
Gården**, a joiner's yard where
visitors can see how the town's
special tilt-top table was made.
Other attractions include the
motor museum, **Bil och
Teknikhistoriska Samlingarna**.
East of Köping is the 11th-
century church of Munktorp.

🏛 Bil och Teknikhistoriska Samlingarna
Glasgatan 19. **Tel** 0221-206 00.
Open May–Sep: 10am–6pm Tue–Sun.
Pre-booked groups all year round.
Closed Midsummer. 🚻 🖥 🏠

㉓ Västerås

Västmanland. 🚊 144,000. 🚌 🚢 ✈️
ℹ️ Kopporbergvägen 1, 021-39 01 00.
🎭 City Festival (1st week Jul), Power
meet (Jul).

Strategically situated at the point
where the Svartån river runs into
Lake Mälaren, the county town
of Västerås has been an important trading centre since Viking
times. Construction of the castle
and cathedral began in the 13th
century and in 1527 Parliament
was convened here. The cathedral, **Domkyrkan**, contains the
sarcophagus of Erik XIV
(r. 1561–69), the unfortunate
king who was allegedly poisoned
by his brother Johan III, by pea
soup laced with arsenic.

Around the cathedral lies the
town's old centre of learning,
where Johannes Rudbeckius
opened Sweden's first upper
secondary school in 1623.
In the 17th and 18th centuries
Västerås became a major port
for the Bergslagen region. Today
it is an industrial centre and
headquarters of the engineering
giant Asea-Brown-Boveri (ABB).
To the east of the town lies
the 7th-century Anundshögen
mound where Bröt-Anund, the
king who settled Bergslagen,
is said to be buried. Standing
stones in the shapes of ships
50 m (164 ft) long can be seen
around the mound. The area was
a major Viking meeting place.
Northwest of the town is
Skultuna Messingsbruk,
Europe's oldest active
brassworks, founded in 1607
and renowned for its cannons
and stylish candlesticks.

🏠 Domkyrkan
Västra Kyrkogatan 6. **Tel** 021-81 46 00.
Open daily. 🎦

🏛 Skultuna Messingsbruk
16 km (10 miles) NW of Västerås.
Tel 021-783 00. **Open** daily.
🎦 tel for info. 🖥 🏠

㉔ Sala

Västmanland. 🚊 22,000. 🚌 🚢
ℹ️ Stora Torget, 0224-74 78 02.
🎭 Autumn market (last Fri & Sat in
Sep). 🌐 **sala.se/turism**

During the 16th century, the
silver mine in Sala was one of the
richest in the world; 200,000 kg
(440,000 lb) were mined up to
1570, providing valuable funds
for the state coffers. The former
Silvergruvan mine is open to
the public down to levels of 60 m
(200 ft) and 155 m (508 ft). There
is a 'mine suite' at this level,

where visitors can spend the
night below ground. There are
beautiful walks around the old
pits and canals, and treasure
hunts are organized for children.
Aguélimuseet showcases
the work of Sala's own artist,
Orientalist Ivan Aguéli (1869–
1917), and other Modernists.

🏛 Silvergruvan
Drottning Christinas Väg. **Tel** 0224-677
260. **Open** Jan–mid-Jun & mid-Aug–
Dec: 11am–4pm daily; mid-Jun–mid-
Aug: 10am–5pm daily. **Closed** Mid-
summer Eve. 🚻 🎦 🖥 🚻 🏠

🏛 Aguélimuseet
Vasagatan 17. **Tel** 0224-138 20.
Open 11am–4pm Wed–Sat. 🎦 🖥 🏠

Hauling plant at the Sala silver mine, in use
until 1908

㉕ Fagersta

Västmanland. 🚊 12,000. 🚌
ℹ️ Norbergsvägen 19, 0223-440 00.

Iron-working has shaped
Fagersta since the outset.
In Dunshammar, just south of
the town, Iron Age blast furnaces
show how iron used to be
extracted from bog ore. Today
Fagersta is home to metal-
manufacturing and stainless-
steel industries.
At the privately owned
UNESCO World Heritage Site of
Engelsbergs Bruk, the historic
blast furnace and ironworks
have been preserved in full
working order and give a
remarkable impression of how
the site, which consists of about

50 buildings, operated between the 17th and 19th centuries.

Oljeön, the world's oldest preserved oil refinery (1875–1902), lies 1.5 km (1 mile) from the ironworks.

Running through Fagersta is the 200-year-old Strömsholm canal from Lake Mälaren to Smedjebacken in Dalarna. Completed in 1795, it was a vital transport link for the Bergslagen foundries. Twenty-six locks, six of them in Fagersta, raise boats a total of 100 m (330 ft). Passenger ferries operate on the canal.

🏛 Engelsbergs Bruk
15 km (10 miles) E of Fagersta. **Tel** 08-788 50 00. **Open** for guided tours only (call to book).

The Engelsberg Bruk ironworks, founded in 1681 and now a UNESCO World Heritage Site

㉖ Kopparberg

Västmanland. 🚶 3,300. 🛈 Gruvstugutorget, 0580-805 55. 🗓 Gold panning competitions (end Jun). 🌐 bergslagen.se

The discovery of copper in the early 17th century attracted miners from Falun, who brought with them the name of their old mine and called the place Nya Kopparberget (New Copper Hill). Today, the town shares its name with the famous brand of pear cider, which is produced locally. The 2.5 km (2 mile)

Kopparstigen (Copper Trail) takes in 28 places of interest. Along the way is **Kopparbergs Miljömuseer**, a complex including a goldsmiths' museum, postal museum and 1880s photography studio. The 17th-century courthouse and a wooden church from 1635 are also worth looking at.

🏛 Kopparbergs Miljömuseer
Gruvstugutorget. **Tel** 0580-805 55. **Open** Jun–Aug: daily. 🖼

㉗ Grythyttan

Västmanland. 🚶 900. 🚌 to Örebro, then bus.

A local vein of silver brought prosperity and town status to Grythyttan in 1649, but when the silver ran out 33 years later, the town charter was withdrawn. Today, Grythyttan has awakened from its long slumber and is now a gastronomic centre.

It all started when the inn, built in 1640, was given a new lease of life in the 1970s, thanks to inspired innkeeper Carl Jan Granqvist. Now, in addition to Grythyttan's wooden houses and red-painted church, there is a catering college centred on **Måltidens Hus i Norden**. It occupies Sweden's spectacular pavilion built for EXPO 1992 in Seville. A varied range of activities offers something for everyone interested in food and cooking, alongside exhibitions and a cookery book museum.

South of Grythyttan lies **Loka Brunn**, a classic Swedish

Grythyttan's inn with its beautifully renovated 17th-century interior

spa founded in the 1720s. The site has state-of-the-art facilities, but the old spa, with its gardens and spring, has been preserved in the Swedish spa museum. You can sample the spring water and view the restored bathhouse, pharmacy, clinic and royal kitchen built in 1761.

🏛 Måltidens Hus i Norden
Sörälgsvägen 4. **Tel** 0591-340 60. 🖼 🖼 end of Jun–mid-Aug: daily; other times: Mon–Fri. 🖼 daily.

🏛 Loka Brunn
15 km (9 miles) S of Grythyttan. **Tel** 0591-631 00. Pool: **Open** daily. Museum: **Open** summer only. 🖼 🖼 museum. 🖼 🖼 🖼 🖼

㉘ Nora

Västmanland. 🚶 6,500. 🚌 to Örebro, then bus. 🛈 Stationshuset on Norasjön side, 0587-811 20. 🗓 Nora Festival (Jul), Noramarken fair (4th weekend in Aug). 🌐 nora.se

This idyllic wooden town is an ideal place to stroll around, with its cobbled streets and charming shops, many in 18th-century buildings. **Göthlinska Gården** (1793) is an interesting museum furnished in the style of a middle-class family home from around 1900.

The highlight of the Nora mining area's monuments is **Pershyttan**, 3 km (2 miles) west of the centre, where the charcoal blast furnace dates from 1856. In summer, a steam train operates from Nora on the Nora Bergslags Veteranjärnväg, Sweden's first normal-gauge railway. Nora's train sheds house historic steam trains, diesel engines and carriages.

Kopparberg's old mining community, now an idyllic wooden village

EASTERN GÖTALAND

The three provinces of Östergötland, Småland and Öland, which make up Eastern Götaland, each retain their own distinctive character. Östergötland is the agricultural heart of Sweden, Småland is the centre of glassmaking and Öland attracts sun-seekers and nature lovers. They are all popular tourist areas typified by their little red cottages and historical sights, quiet lakes and great coastlines.

In north Östergötland, the major towns of Norrköping and Linköping are almost part of Greater Stockholm. Once beyond the steep hills of Kolmården, which form the northern border, flat agricultural land extends as far as the eye can see. Besides being the granary of Sweden, this is historical soil – it was here that the royal Folkung dynasty had its roots and it was here that Birgitta Gudmarsson (St Bridget) advised the political and religious leaders of the 14th century.

The hills north of Gränna and the ruins of Brahehus castle mark the beginning of Småland. For a long time Småland formed the border with Denmark and it was from this region that Nils Dacke led a peasants' revolt in the 16th century. The land is poorer and stonier than Östergötland with small farms and crofters. Mass emigration drained the area of thousands of people during the famine of the 19th century. However, Småland has had its success stories: it is the ideal location for one of its major industries, glassworking, which relies on timber and water. The landscape has also been immortalized in the books of Astrid Lindgren, who was born in the province and turned the place where she grew up into a playground for her popular children's characters, Emil and Pippi Longstocking.

The region's archipelago is a favourite with boat-lovers, stretching south from the Sankta Annas islands in Östergötland through the Kalmarsund between Småland and Öland. Thanks to Ölandsbron bridge, the long narrow island of Öland is easily accessible. Holiday-makers are drawn to its sandy beaches, while botanists head for the Alvar plain and ornithologists for Ottenby bird station.

The peaceful Göta Canal at Borensberg

◄ Sailing boats in Västervik harbour, Småland

Exploring Eastern Götaland

This is too big an area to explore in just a few days, but by leaving the major roads and heading cross-country it is possible to have a taste of the different provinces. The Royal Route, or Eriksgatan, created in 2005, has a historical theme and is marked on maps of the region available in any service station or tourist office. Cycling is also an excellent way to see the region, and cruising in comfort on the Göta Canal (see pp150–51) offers an unforgettable experience. For a tour of the Kingdom of Crystal (see p156) a car is almost essential, but otherwise Småland has countless canoeing routes, lakes for swimming and sights along small forested roads ideally explored by bike.

The calm waters of Lake Vättern and surrounding forest, seen from Omberg

Key

▬▬ Motorway

— Major road

····· Minor road

--- Main railway

— Minor railway

▲ Summit

Getting Around

The main artery for traffic in this part of the country is the E4 which passes west of Växjö, via the cities of Norrköping, Linköping and Jönköping, on its way south towards Helsingborg. The E22 runs along the coast, leaving the E4 at Norrköping and continuing via Västervik and Kalmar to Malmö. The larger towns, both on the coast and inland, can be reached by train, but local buses or a car will be needed to visit places in the countryside. There are domestic flights to all major cities.

For keys to symbols see back flap

Örebro

MEDEVI BRUNN **5**

Övralid

Motala

VADSTENA **6**

Mjölby

OMBERG **7**

Ödeshög

Boxholm

Vättern

Tranås

Visingsö

8 GRÄNNA

Sonn

Gothenburg

Bankeryd

Aneby

JÖNKÖPING **9**

Huskvarna

Taberg
343m

Forserum

EKSJÖ **10**

Nässjö

Stensjön

Vaggeryd

Vetlanda

Skillingaryd

Gnosjö

Sävsjö

Gislaved

Anderstorp

Vrigstad

SMÅLAND

Smålandsstenar

Värnamo

Lammhult

Vidöstern

Bor

Nissan

Rydaholm

Helgasjön

Bolmen

Lagan

Alvesta

VÄXJÖ **11**

Ljungby

Hovmantorp

Vislanda

Röjt

Halmstad

Äsnen

Tingsr

Traryd

Strömsnäsbruk

Älmhult

Mien

Helsingborg

Karlshamn

| 0 kilometres | | 50 |
| 0 miles | 30 | |

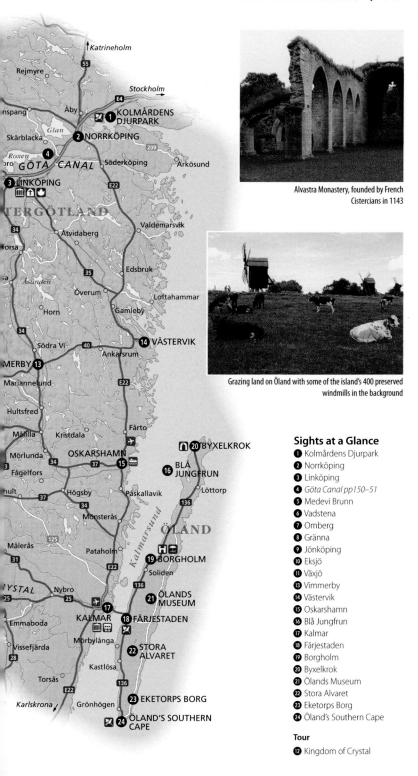

Alvastra Monastery, founded by French
Cistercians in 1143

Grazing land on Öland with some of the island's 400 preserved
windmills in the background

Sights at a Glance

1. Kolmårdens Djurpark
2. Norrköping
3. Linköping
4. *Göta Canal pp150–51*
5. Medevi Brunn
6. Vadstena
7. Omberg
8. Gränna
9. Jönköping
10. Eksjö
11. Växjö
13. Vimmerby
14. Västervik
15. Oskarshamn
16. Blå Jungfrun
17. Kalmar
18. Färjestaden
19. Borgholm
20. Byxelkrok
21. Ölands Museum
22. Stora Alvaret
23. Eketorps Borg
24. Öland's Southern Cape

Tour

12. Kingdom of Crystal

A red panda at Kolmårdens Djurpark

❶ Kolmårdens Djurpark

Östergötland. Junction from E4, 12 km
(7 miles) N of Norrköping. 🚗 🚌
ℹ 010-708 70 00. **Open** May: 10am–
5pm daily; Jun–Aug: 10am–6pm daily;
Sep: 10am–5pm Sat–Sun. 🐾 🎫 💻
🖊 🍴 ♿ **W** kolmarden.com

Kolmårdens Djurpark is no
ordinary animal park – the
enclosures are large and
attractively landscaped.
Creatures of the savannah
live here alongside Nordic
species such as brown bears
and wolves.

Snakes and crocodiles inhabit
the outdoor Tropicarium, while
the Aparium is designed so
that the apes can be viewed
indoors and out. Tiger World,
offers a unique walk-through
experience in close proximity
to the big cats. A cable-car ride
provides a bird's eye view of
the grounds.

There are a variety of
accommodation options
available for visitors, including
African tents on the savannah
and a youth hostel with a
mixture of shared dorms, which
offer nice views. There's also a
themed spa on-site.

❷ Norrköping

Östergötland. E4. 🚶 137,000. 🚗 🚌
ℹ Källvindsgatan 1, 011-15 50 00.
📷 Norrköping International Horse
Show (4th week in May), National
Day Festival (first week in Jun).
W destination.norrkoping.se

In the 17th century the skills
of entrepreneur Louis de Geer,
combined with water power
from the Motala Ström river
system, transformed Norrköping

into Sweden's first industrial town.
Norrköping and neighbouring
Linköping make up Sweden's
fourth largest urban region.

Although Norrköping is an
industrial town, the mix of old
and new buildings, parks and
trams make it an attractive place
to visit. On a small island in
Motala Ström sits **Arbetets
museet** (Museum of Labour),
in an old spinning mill known
as Strykjärnet (the Iron).

Environs
The area has a long history
of habitation - around 1,650
carvings, some dating back
to 1000 BC, can be seen at
Himmelstalund on the edge of
town. About 10 km (6 miles)
south of Norrköping on the E4 is
the 17th-century **Löfstad Slott**
with its beautiful English-style
park. The castle remains as it
was in 1926 on the death of
the owner, Emelie Piper.

🏛 Arbetets museet
Laxholmen. **Tel** 011-18 98 00.
Open daily. **Closed** public hols.
🎫 💻 🖊 📷

🏛 Löfstad Slott
10 km (6 miles) S of Norrköping.
Tel 011-33 50 67. **Open** Jun–Aug:
daily; Apr–May: Sat & Sun; Sep–Oct:
Sun; Nov–Mar: phone for info.
🎫 💻 🖊 📷

Strykjärnet (the Iron) in Norrköping,
housing Arbetets museet

❸ Linköping

Östergötland. E4. 🚶 150,000. 🚗 🚌
📷 **ℹ** Storgatan 15, 013-190 00 70.
📷 Ekenäs Castle Tournament
(Whitsun), Folk Music Festival (Oct).
W visitlinkoping.se

The county capital and
cathedral city of Linköping lies
in the middle of the Östgöta
plain. First populated 3,000 years
ago, it is now Sweden's fifth
largest city, and is known for its
university and high-tech industry.

Construction of the
Domkyrkan (Cathedral) started
in the mid-13th century. The
interior contains superb
medieval stone carvings.
The Renaissance altarpiece is
by the Dutch painter M J Van
Heemskerck (1498–1574).

The old town open-air
museum, **Gamla Linköping**,
is a collection of 80 buildings
from the city and surrounding
area. This charming setting,
complete with picturesque
wooden buildings, cobbled
streets and gardens, is a
window on a past way of life.

Malmen, site of Sweden's
first military flying school
(1911), is now home to the
Flygvapenmuseum (Swedish
Air Force Museum). Exhibits
include examples of Swedish
military aircraft.

Environs
Kaga Kyrka, one of the
region's best-preserved
medieval churches, is located
on the Svartån river south of
Linköping. Dating from the
12th century, its walls are
decorated with frescoes.

On Erlången lake, 10 km
(6 miles) southeast of the
centre, lies the castle of
Sturefors, which is renowned
for its 18th-century interiors
and beautiful grounds. The
castle is a private residence,
but parts of the grounds are
open to the public.

🏛 Domkyrkan
St Persgatan. **Tel** 013-20 50 50.
Open daily. 📷 phone for info. ♿ 🍴

🏛 Gamla Linköping
2 km (3 miles) west of the centre.
Tel 013-12 11 10. **Open** daily. 💻
🖊 📷

Ⅲ Flygvapenmuseum
4 km (3 miles) west of the centre.
Tel 013-28 35 67. **Open** Sep–May:
Tue–Sun; Jun–Aug: daily.
phone for details.

❹ Göta Canal

See pp150–51.

❺ Medevi Brunn

Östergötland. Road 50.
0141-911 00. Grötlunken marching
band processions (Jun/Jul).

In the 17th-century the scientist
and doctor Urban Hjärne
analyzed water from the Medevi
spring and declared it to be
"superior to other medication".
Thus began the transformation
of Medevi Brunn into a health
spa. Today, the season at Medevi
starts at Midsummer and lasts
for seven weeks, during which
time the traditional brass
sextet Brunnsorkester
performs daily concerts.

South of Medevi, on the edge
of Lake Vättern, lies **Övralid**, the
former home of poet and Nobel
laureate Verner von Heidenstam
(1859–1940). Designed by Heidenstam himself, the house has
stunning views across the lake.

Ⅲ Övralid
10 km (6 miles) N of Motala, Road 50.
Tel 0141-22 05 56, 22 00 36. **Open** 15
May–31 Aug: daily. 10am–5pm
on the hour.

Vadstena Slott, built in 1545 for protection against the Danes

❻ Vadstena

Östergötland. Road 50. 5,500.
Castle, 0143-31571.
St Bridget Festival (3rd week in
May), Vadstena Academy Opera
performances (Jul). **W vadstena.com**

Situated on Lake Vättern,
Vadstena is dominated by the
abbey, which dates back to
the 14th century and St Bridget,
and the mid-16th-century castle
of the Vasa kings. Cobbled
streets, wooden buildings and
glorious gardens add to the
town's character.

The stately **Vadstena Slott**
was built in 1545 as a fortress
against the Danes and is
surrounded by a moat. As well
as being a museum, the castle
also hosts opera, theatre
performances and concerts.

The abbey area encompasses
the original abbey, Vadstena
Kloster, established in 1384 and
dissolved after the Reformation

in 1595, and **Vadstena
Klosterkyrka** (1430). This abbey
church houses the relics of
St Bridget and a life-like wooden
sculpture of the saint. It is also
the site of the Pax Mariae
convent, which was founded
in the 1980s and is home to
around ten nuns.

Environs
Less than 20 km (12 miles)
south of Vadstena towards
Skänninge is **Bjälbo Kyrka**,
a late-12th-century church.
Bjälbo is said to be the birth-
place of the founder of
Stockholm, Birger Jarl.

Ⅲ Vadstena Slott
100 m (110 yd) SW of the centre.
Tel 0143-62 16 00. **Open** Sep–May:
Mon–Fri; Jun–Aug: daily.
Jun–Aug.

ⓘ Vadstena Klosterkyrka
Open daily. **Tel** 0143-31570, 0143-
298 50. Sun. Jun–Aug.

St Bridget, Sweden's Patron Saint

At the age of only 13, Bridget (c.1303–73) was married to local
dignitary Ulf Gudmarsson. She became lady of the manor of Ulvåsa in
Östergötland and the mother of eight children. Even as a child, she
had religious visions and as an adult
made pilgrimages to Santiago de
Compostela in Spain in 1341–2, Rome
in 1349 and Jerusalem in 1372–3.
Some of her visions also had political
themes and Bridget became
influential in the political arena.
In 1370 she gained the Pope's
permission to found a monastic order,
the Brigittine Order. The first nuns
were ordained in 1384. Bridget died
on returning to Rome following her
pilgrimage to Jerusalem. Her remains
were taken to Vadstena in 1374.
Canonized in 1391, Bridget is the
patron saint of Sweden, and in 1999
became the patron saint of Europe.

Sculpture of St Bridget in Vadstena
Klosterkyrka

Medevi Brunn, the first health spa in the
Nordic countries

➍ Göta Canal

Opened in 1832, the Göta Canal provided a vital link for transporting timber and iron between Stockholm and Gothenburg. But it was another 100 years before leisure traffic took off on the waterway. Today in summer, the canal bustles with small craft and passenger boats and it is possible to cruise the entire length on the classic *M/S Diana* (1931), *Wilhelm Tham* (1912) and *Juno* (1874). Other boats take passengers along shorter stretches and there are numerous special packages available, such as combining cycling holidays with canal trips. There are guest marinas offering services along the entire length of the canal. Motala is regarded as the "capital" of the canal, and the man behind its construction, Baltzar von Platen (1766–1829), is buried here.

Building the Canal
Karl XIV Johan inspects construction near Berg in Östergötland with Crown Prince Oscar. Baltzar von Platen is standing bare-headed to the left of the king.

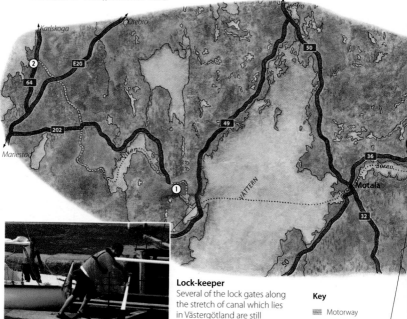

Lock-keeper
Several of the lock gates along the stretch of canal which lies in Västergötland are still worked by hand by friendly and patient lock-keepers.

Key

- ▬ Motorway
- ▬ Other road
- ⁘ Canal

KEY

① **Karlsborgs Fästning** *(see p225)*, towers above the canal.

② **Sjötorp** on Lake Vänern marks the end point of the canal in Västergötland.

③ **The lake of Roxen** is home to some 260 species of birds, including wetland species, as well as some rarer varieties.

④ **Mem** is the first lock in the canal system on the journey west.

Borensberg
The long-established Göta Hotell is an idyllic summer spot on the canal. Built in 1894, it offers food and accommodation to passers-by.

Bergs Slussar
The staircase of seven locks at Berg raises boats a total of 18 m (59 ft). The spectacle of opening the lock gates always attracts an audience.

VISITORS' CHECKLIST

Practical Information
Östergötland and Västergötland.
i AB Göta Kanalbolag in Motala, 0141-20 20 50.
w gotakanal.se

Transport

Canal Boats
From May to August traditional white boats such as *M/S Juno* ply the canal. Built in 1874, *Juno* is one of the oldest boats afloat with sleeping accommodation still in use.

Climbing from the Baltic to Lake Vanern

"The Blue Band of Sweden" as the Göta Canal is known, is the high point of Swedish engineering history. It took 58,000 men, mainly soldiers, and 22 years to build a waterway across Sweden from the Baltic Sea to join the already completed Trollhättan Canal *(see p221)*, and provide a route through to the Kattegatt. The problem was not simply digging the canal, but coping with a difference in height of around 92 m (301 ft). Completing this mammoth project took more than just spades and advantage was taken of the latest technological innovations – dredgers, hoists, cranes, pile drivers, mortar mills and optical instruments. Most of the machinery was imported from England, but as the project grew, and with it the need for mechanical equipment, Baltzar von Platen eventually took the initiative to set up a factory in Motala where the mechanical equipment could be made or modified. The canal has 58 locks between Mem on the Baltic and Sjötorp on Lake Vänern.

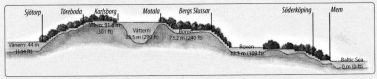

From Mem the canal begins its climb to reach the highest point between Lakes Vättern and Vänern

View over Lake Vättern from Hjässan, the highest point of Omberg

❼ Omberg

Östergötland. 20 km (12 miles)
S of Vadstena. 🚌
🌐 visitostergotland.info

Rising mountain-like from the wide Östgöta plains is Omberg. Its highest point is 175 m (574 ft) above Lake Vättern. It is the legendary home of Queen Omma, whose name means "steam" and indeed the fog that often surrounds the hill gives it a mythical quality. Orchid marshes, beech woodlands and ancient forest flourish on the limestone-rich rock. Walking trails cross the area. To the south lies author Ellen Key's home, **Strand**, and the nature reserves of Bokskogen and Stora Lund. On the plains southeast of Omberg is the ruin of **Alvastra Kloster** where St Bridget *(see p149)* once stayed.

To the east, Omberg slopes down to Lake **Tåkern**, barely 1 m (3 ft) deep and favoured by flocks of geese and cranes in spring and autumn. The **Rökstenen** at Röks Kyrka is a large 9th-century runestone.

🏠 Strand

10 km (6 miles) N of Ödeshög.
Tel 0144-330 30. **Open** mid-May–
Aug: Tue–Sun; early May & Sep: Sat
& Sun. 🖼️

❽ Gränna

Småland. E4. 🔼 2,600. 🚌
ℹ️ Brahegatan 38, 0771-21 13 00.
🎭 Andrée Festival (2nd week in Jul),
County Festival (3rd week in Jul).
🌐 jkpg.com

Gränna was at its height in the 17th century in the days of Count Per Brahe, who founded the town and whose plan is still evident today. On the square in the centre of town, **Grenna Museum** has fascinating tales to tell of the tragic expedition to the North Pole headed by the town's famous son Salomon August Andrée in the hot-air balloon *Örnen*. Inspired by Andrée, Gränna has become a centre for balloon flights. The town is also known for its *polkagris* (peppermint rock), an ideal souvenir. The red and white sweet originated in 1859 when widow Amalia Eriksson started a rock factory in the town.

Polkagris

Along the beautiful stretch of the E4 beside Lake Vättern, just north of Gränna, lies the ruined **Brahehus** castle, built for Count Per Brahe in the 1640s. On a clear day Brahehus offers magnificent views over Vättern towards Västergötland on the other side of the lake and **Visingsö**. This flat island can be reached by boat from Gränna. It is the largest island in Lake Vättern, 14 km (9 miles) long and 3 km (2 miles) wide with a

population of 800. In the 12th and 13th centuries the island was the seat of Sweden's first kings, including Magnus Ladulås. Per Brahe built the castle, Visingsborgs Slott, now a ruin, and a church on the island in the 17th century. The boat trip from Gränna takes about 25 minutes and the service is frequent in the summer months.

🏛️ Grenna Museum

Brahegatan 38–40. **Tel** 0390-410 15.
Open daily. **Closed** 1 Jan, 24, 25, 31
Dec. 🖼️ 🖼️ 🖼️ 🖼️

❾ Jönköping

Småland. E4. 🔼 132,000. 🚗 🚌 ✈️
ℹ️ Södra Strandgatan 13, 0771-21 13
00. 🎭 Jönköping Market (dates vary,
but usually between May and Jul).
🌐 jonkoping.se

King Magnus Ladulås granted Jönköping its charter in 1284, by which time the town was already an important trading centre. For a long time Småland formed Sweden's southern border with Denmark, but when the Danes invaded in 1612 the people set fire to their town and fled to Visingsö.

In the 19th century Jönköping became synonymous with matchstick production; the Lundström brothers opened their first factory here in the 1840s. In the old part of town, **Tändsticksmuseet** (the Match Museum) is set in a former match factory (1848). The historic Västra Storgatan 37 houses **Viktor Rydbergs**

The ruins of Brahehus Castle on Lake Vättern looking towards Visingsö

Museum. Local history comes under the spotlight at **Jönköpings Läns Museum**. The museum also has a display of work by the local artist John Bauer, as well as contemporary art.

Environs
Just outside Jönköping, **Hakarps Kyrka** is famous for its paintings by Edvard Orm. **Taberg**, south of Jönköping, is known as "the Alps of Småland" and is 343 m (1,125 ft) above sea level. The countryside is stunning, with extensive views over Lake Vättern. Sights include a mine and an industrial museum and there are hiking trails and overnight accommodation.

🏛 **Tändsticksmuseet**
Tändsticksgränd 27. **Tel** 036-10 55 43. **Open** daily (Sep–May: Tue–Sat). **Closed** public hols & eves of public hols. 🖼 🎫 🏛

🏛 **Jönköpings Läns Museum**
Dag Hammarskjölds Plats 2. **Tel** 036-30 18 00. **Open** Tue–Sun. 🖼 🎫 🖥 🏛

❿ Eksjö
Småland. Road 32/40. 🚗 16,000. 🚉 🚌 🛈 Norra Storgatan 29b, 0381-361 70. 🎪 Guard-mounting Parade (summer), Ränneslättsloppet Motocross Race (end Sep), Christmas Market (Dec). 🌐 visiteksjo.se

The small town of Eksjö, in the highlands of southern Sweden, is the country's most genuine wooden town. This was border country until the 17th century and Eksjö was burned down by its own people in conjunction with a Danish retreat. In the 1560s Erik XIV drew up a new town plan for Eksjö, which largely remains today. Gamla Stan (the Old Town) escaped the fire and its buildings remain intact and have been sympathetically renovated.

Environs
About 13 km (8 miles) east of Eksjö, the **Skurugata** nature reserve encompasses an impressive canyon in porphyritic rock, 800 m (2,625 ft) long and 35 m (115 ft) deep. From Eksjö to the neighbouring town of

Nässjö is just over 20 km (12 miles). Nässjö owes its existence to the coming of the railway in the 1860s. At that time the village had 57 inhabitants; today it has nearly 30,000 and the railway companies Statens Järnvägar and Banverket are still the main employers. Sights in Nässjö include **Järnvägs-museum** (the Railway Museum) and Hembygdsparken with its woodlands and collection of 18th- and 19th-century buildings.

🏛 **Järnvägsmuseum**
Brogatan 10, Nässjö. **Tel** 0380-132 00. **Open** 11am–3pm Wed, Fri & Sun; Jun–Aug: 11am–3pm Tue–Sun. 🖼

⓫ Växjö
Småland. Road 23/25/27/30. 🚗 87,000. 🚉 🚌 ✈ 🛈 Residenset, Stortorget, 0470-73 32 80. 🌐 vaxjo.se

A bishopric as early as the 12th century, Växjö was granted its town charter by King Magnus Erikson in 1342. For some time the town lay on the border with Denmark and it was from here that Nils Dacke led his peasant revolt against the King of Sweden in the 16th century. Devastating fires, the most recent in 1843, destroyed the town, which has since been rebuilt. The cathedral dates originally from the end of the

The twin steeples of Växjö's 12th-century cathedral

12th century, but has been remodelled over the centuries. It contains an altarpiece in glass and wood made in 2002 by the glass artist Bertil Vallien.

Smålands Museum, with Sveriges Glasmuseum (Glass Museum), depicts the history of the county of Kronoberg and the development of the glassworks. Next to it is **Utvandrarnas Hus**, which focuses on the mass emigration in the 19th century.

🏛 **Smålands Museum**
Södra Järnvägsgatan 2. **Tel** 0470-70 42 00. **Open** 10am–5pm Tue–Fri, 11am–4pm Sat & Sun. **Closed** public holidays. 🖼 🎫 🖥 🏛 ♿

🏛 **Utvandrarnas Hus**
Vilhelm Mobergs Gata 4. **Tel** 0470-70 42 00. **Open** 10am–5pm Tue–Fri, 11am–4pm Sat & Sun. 🖼 🎫 🖥 🏛 ♿

Emigration to America
Disillusioned by poverty, religious intolerance and political discontent, many Swedes in the late 1860s dreamed of a better life in North America. Famine in Sweden, combined with the end of the Civil War in the fast expanding USA, prompted around 100,000 Swedes to emigrate in 1868–71, the majority from southern Sweden, particularly the barren lands of Småland. Another major wave followed in the 1880s when 350,000 people left Sweden.

Nobel Prize-winner Vilhelm Moberg's epic trilogy The Emigrants describes the tough life Swedish emigrants faced in their new land.

Emigration to the USA tailed off with the Depression of the 1930s, but by then 1.2 million Swedes had already left their homeland.

Emigrants on the Way to Gothenburg, Geskel Saloman (1821–1902)

⑫ A Tour through the Kingdom of Crystal

Växjö, home to the Swedish Glass Museum, is an ideal starting point for a tour of at least nine of the famous glassworks set in the beautiful countryside between Växjö and Nybro. Access to timber and water accounts for the concentration of glassworks in this area of Småland, where forest, lakes and waterways dominate the landscape. The glassworks are mostly only 20–30 km (12–20 miles) apart, and many have shops offering discounted items and displays of the designers' latest creations.

① **Bergdala**
Bergdala's signature is blue-edged glass, but designers are pushing the boundaries when it comes to colour and shape. The temperature of the smelting oven is a constant 1,150° C (2,102° F).

③ **Kosta**
The oldest glassworks, Kosta (1742), like Boda and Åfors, has attracted some of Sweden's foremost contemporary designers. Shown here is the entrance to the original office.

[Map showing the tour route between Växjö and Nybro, with locations including Vetlanda, Herråkra, Ljungby E4, Växjö, Furuby, Hovmantorp, Ingelstad, Bergdala, Strömbergshyttan, Lessebo, Kosta, Åfors, Skruv. Roads marked 23, 25, 30, 31, 28.]

② **Strömbergshyttan**
Studioglas was established in 1987 by three master glassblowers, who work with young designers to create ground-breaking works of art.

Key
■ Suggested route
= Other roads

Tips for Drivers

Tour length: Växjö–Nybro, road 25, approx. 85 km (53 miles). Well signposted.
Places to eat: Many glassworks have a café/restaurant and some of the larger ones hold herring evenings. Check opening times.

④ **Åfors**
Bertil Vallien, Ulrica Hydman-Vallien and upcoming artist Ludvig Löfgren work for the glassworks in Fina Stugan, one of the area's most exciting galleries. Glass eggs are by Ulrica Hydman-Vallien.

0 kilometres   10
0 miles   5

⑧ Orrefors

The glassworks was founded in 1898 and has become the flagship of Swedish glassmaking, producing functional, decorative items and *objets d'art*. The work of Orrefors over the years is on show in its museum.

Crystal bowl by Simon Gate (1883–1945)

⑨ Måleräs

The employees bought this glassworks from Kosta in 1981. It is famous for its crystal animal reliefs by glass artist and master etcher Mats Jonasson.

⑦ Pukeberg

The glassworks was founded in 1871. Extensive production in this beautiful old setting has mainly been focused on lighting and domestic glassware using traditional methods.

⑤ Johansfors

This glassworks is known as the Eden of the Kingdom of Crystal, symbolized by Christopher Ramsey's *Astrakhan Apple*. Glassblowing is demonstrated daily and there is a museum.

⑥ Boda

The traditional Boda glassworks has been converted into a Kosta Boda factory shop, museum and exhibition area with a special focus on local artist Erik Höglund.

⑬ Vimmerby

Småland. Road 33/34. ⯍ 8,000.
🚆 🚌 ⓘ Rådhuset 1, 0492-310 10.
🎭 Holiday Race (2nd week in Jul).

The small town of Vimmerby began as a marketplace on the "King's Road" between Stockholm and Kalmar. It was strategically important and constantly fought over by the Danes, who burned it to the ground on many occasions. Few old buildings remain, but along Storgatan there is the austere Neo-Classical-style Rådhuset (town hall) from the 1820s. Like the houses of Tenngjutar-gården and Grankvistgården, it is one of Vimmerby's historical monuments.

For many years Vimmerby has been associated with Astrid Lindgren *(see p93)*, who was born in Näs and set many of her popular children's books in this area. All her beloved characters can be encountered in **Astrid Lindgrens Värld** (Astrid Lindgren's World). The park also includes the Astrid Lindgren Centre with an exhibition about the author's life and work.

Environs

Norra Kvill National Park, 20 km (12 miles) northwest of Vimmerby, is an area of virgin forest in the highlands of Småland containing pine trees over 350 years old. The park slopes down to a small lake, Stora Idegölen, with waterlilies and bogbean.

🏰 **Astrid Lindgrens Värld**
Fabriksgatan. **Tel** 0492-798 00.
Open 15 May–end of Aug: daily.
🎭 🎫 🖵 ✏ 🏛 👤 ⌨ **alv.se**

Miniature house in Astrid Lindgrens Värld, Vimmerby

Picturesque red cottages on Båtsmansgränd in Västervik

🕲 Västervik

Småland. E22. 🖼 36,000. 🚗 🚌 ✈
🄸 Rådhuset, Stora Torget, 0490-875
20. 🎨 Song Festival (Jul).
🅦 vastervik.com

Strategically sited at the mouth
of Gamlebyviken Bay, Västervik
was the subject of frequent
Danish attacks, despite
protection from the once
mighty fortress of Stegeholm.
The last attack in 1677 destroyed
the town. Rebuilt, it became a
major seafaring centre. The area
known as Gamla Norr contains
the oldest preserved houses in
Västervik, including Aspagården
and the former poor-house,
Cederflychtska Huset.
Västerviks Museum outlines
the history of the town. Part of
the museum is in the open air
with a nature exhibition and
traditional buildings. The railway
line was closed in 1984, but
train enthusiasts have reopened
the 70-km (43-mile) stretch
from Västervik to Hultfred, to
preserve it as part of Sweden's
industrial heritage.

The annual Folk Festival first
took place in 1966 and has
since grown to become a
major event. It is held in the
ruins of Stegeholm fortress.

Lunds By, just outside
Västervik, is the region's oldest
and best preserved village,
comprising eight small red
cottages around a square.
It was chosen as a location
to film Astrid Lindgren's book
The Bullerby Children.

🏛 **Västerviks Museum**
Kulbacken. **Tel** 0490-211 77.
Open Jun–Aug: daily; Sep–May:
Mon–Fri, Sun. 🎨 🗐 🎨

🕲 Oskarshamn

Småland. E22. 🖼 26,000. 🚗 🚌
🄸 Hantverksgatan 3, 0491-770 72.
🎨 Oskarshamn Harbour Festival
(end Jul). 🅦 oskarshamn.com

King Oskar I gave his name
to this town, previously
known as Döderhultsvik,
which gained its charter in
1856. Oskarshamn grew up
around the harbour and today
is still an important place with
a lively seafaring industry.
The old areas of Besväret and
Fnyket have wooden 19th-
century houses and are ideal
for a leisurely exploration on
foot. There are great views over
the water and the island Blå
Jungfrun from Långa Soffan,
an extraordinarily long 72-m
(79-yd) bench built close to
the harbour in 1867.

Oskarshamn has several
museums. On display at
Döderhultarmuseet are the
original wooden figures by
sculptor Axel Petersson, also
known as "Döderhultarn",
together with a description of
his life in late-19th-century
Småland. **Oskarshamns
Sjöfartsmuseum** (Maritime

An expressive carved wooden figure by "Döderhultarn"
Axel Petersson (1865–1925)

Museum) has a superb collection of local maritime history.
Biologiska museet has a
botanical collection that focuses
mainly on Swedish plants.

Environs
Stensjö By is a cultural
museum showing how a village
looked in the 18th century.
Just under 40 km (25 miles)
west of Oskarshamn at Högsby
there is the **Bråbygden** nature
reserve and a permanent
exhibition about film star Greta
Garbo, whose mother came
from here.

🏛 **Döderhultarmuseet**
Hantverksgatan 18. **Tel** 0491-880 40.
Open daily. 🎨 🗐 🎨 🎨 🕭

🏛 **Oskarshamns
Sjöfartsmuseum**
Hantverksgatan 18. **Tel** 0491-880 40.
Open Mon–Sat (Jun–Aug: daily).
🎨 🗐 🎨 🎨 🕭

🏛 **Biologiska museet**
Gyllings väg 9. **Tel** 0491-771 61.
Open Tue–Fri. 🅦 bimon.se

🕲 Blå Jungfrun

Småland. 20 km (12 miles) E of
Oskarshamn. 🚢 from Oskarshamn &
Byxelkrok. 🄸 Oskarshamn Tourist
Office, 0491-770 72.

In the northern part of
Kalmarsund, the sound separa-
ting the mainland from the
island of Öland, the national
park Blå Jungfrun (the Blue
Maiden) encompasses an
island about 800 m (875 yd)
in diameter and the waters
surrounding it. Blå Jungfrun's
highest point is 86 m (282 ft)
above sea level, making it easily
visible from the mainland and
from Öland.

According to legend, the
island is the site of Blåkulla,
home of the witches, and is the
subject of many a dark tale.
Carl von Linné *(see p134)*
described it as "horrible".
Others have found it
romantic, including the poet
Verner von Heidenstam, who
was married here in
1896. The island is
mainly bare pink
granite, polished
smooth by ice and

Medieval Kalmar Slott, a beautifully preserved castle rebuilt in Renaissance style in the 16th century

water, with deciduous forest in the south and a population of black guillemots. It is unlikely that it was inhabited, although a stone labyrinth was built here and there are caves. Boats run from Oskarshamn or Byxelkrok (see p160) to Blå Jungfrun, once a day, weather permitting. The journey takes 90 minutes from Oskarshamn with a three-and-a-half-hour stay on the island.

⑰ Kalmar

Småland. E22. 🚗 36,000. 🚌 🚆 ✈
ℹ Ölandskajen 9, 0480-41 77 00.
🎪 Kalmar Market (Jul), Kalmar City Festival (2nd weekend in Aug).
🌐 kalmar.com

Founded in the 12th century, Kalmar's key position on Kalmarsund made it a flourishing trading post as well as a target for Danish attack. To prevent the latter, **Kalmar Slott** was built in 1200 and it was here in the castle that the Kalmar Union was formed in 1397, binding the Scandinavian kingdoms for 130 years (see p39). In 1523 Gustav Vasa gained control of Kalmar and fortified the town.

Today, the magnificent Renaissance castle has been restored and contains furnished apartments and exhibitions. With its twisting streets and 17th and 18th-century buildings, the area around the castle, Gamla Stan (Old Town), is made for walking. Next to the castle is **Kalmar Konstmuseum** (Art Museum) showing Swedish art.

The Italian Baroque **Domkyrkan** (cathedral) on the island of Kvarnholmen dates from the second half of the 17th century and was designed by Tessin the Elder. In front of it is the square Stortorget, restored to its original austere appearance. Kvarnholmen is also home to **Kalmar Läns Museum** with the man-of-war *Kronan* and out on "Kattrumpan" **Kalmar Sjöfartsmuseum**, featuring 5,000 maritime exhibits.

Environs
Ölandsbron, the bridge across Kalmarsund, opened in 1972 and provided a major boost for tourism to Öland. The bridge is 6,072 m (19,921 ft) long, 13 m (43 ft) wide and a sight in its own right. Nearly 35 km (22 miles) north of Kalmar on the coast is the idyllic village of **Pataholm**, a shipbuilding and seafaring community dating from the Middle Ages, with well-preserved historic buildings and cobbled streets.

🏰 **Kalmar Slott**
Kungsgatan 1. **Tel** 0480-45 14 90
Open May–Sep: daily; other times: weekends. 🚻 🎫 ♿ 📷

🏛 **Kalmar Konstmuseum**
Stadsparken. **Tel** 0480-42 62 82.
Open Tue–Sun. **Closed** some public hols. 🚻 🎫 pre-book. 📷

🏛 **Kalmar Läns Museum**
Skeppsbrogatan 51. **Tel** 0480-45 13 00. **Open** daily. **Closed** some public hols. 🚻 🎫 pre-book. 🖥 📷

⑱ Färjestaden

Öland. Road 136. 🚗 5,000. 🚌
🎪 Victoria Day (14 Jul).

The Ölandsbron Bridge connects Färjestaden on Öland with the mainland. Since the bridge's arrival in the 1970s, Färjestaden has more or less become a suburb of Kalmar. The first turning to the north

in Färjestaden leads to **Ölands Djurpark**, a popular destination for families. The zoo has 200 species of animals, a water world and amusement park, circus and theatre performances.

Beijershamn, south of Färjestaden, is an interesting reed-covered birdwatching area with wetland and archipelago species. Not far from here is **Karlevistenen**, a remarkable 11th-century runestone dedicated to a hero named Sibbe the Wise.

Vickleby village street, on road 136 to the south, is the epitome of idyllic Öland. Next to the church is Capellagården School of Craft and Design, founded by furniture designer Carl Malmsten in the 1950s and currently a centre for various design-related courses. The school exhibits and sells students' work.

East of Färjestaden, in the forest, is the Iron Age fort of **Gråborg** with the medieval ruins of St Knut's chapel just outside it.

🦁 **Ölands Djurpark**
3 km (2 miles) N of Färjestaden.
Tel 0485-392 22.
Open Easter–Sep: 10am–4pm daily. 🚻 🎫 🖥 ♿ 📷

A gigantic clown at the entrance to Ölands Djurpark

Solliden, the king's summer residence, whose park is open to the public

⑲ Borgholm

Öland. Road 136. 🚂 3,200. 🚌
🏛 Victoria Day 14 Jul.

In summer Borgholm town centre bustles with shoppers and boats fill the guest harbour. Borgholm became a seaside resort at the end of the 19th century and some of the older buildings still have their ornamented wooden verandas where gentlemen enjoyed their coffee and punsch at the beginning of the last century.

Dominating the town is **Borgholms Slottsruin**, a vast ruined medieval castle with an eventful historical past. There is a museum inside. Guides recount the history of the ruins and offer special tours for children in summer. Also in summer, the castle stage is a popular venue for concerts.

Environs
Just south of the centre lies **Sollidens Slott**, the summer residence of the Swedish Royal Family, completed in 1906. On 14 July each year, the birthday of Crown Princess Victoria is celebrated here with various events. Exhibitions are held in the pavilion and there is a palace gift shop.

Störlinge Kvarnrad, a row of seven windmills on the eastern coast road, is just a sample of the 400 windmills still standing on the island. There are around 150 km (93 miles) of beaches around Borgholm, two of the best being Köpingsvik and Böda.

🏰 **Borgholms Slottsruin**
1 km (half a mile) S of Borgholm.
Tel 0485-123 33. **Open** Apr–Sep: daily; Oct–Mar: by appointment. 🅿 🍴 💻 🔲 🏠 ♿

🍴 **Solliden**
1.5 km (1 mile) S of Borgholm.
Tel 0485-153 56. **Open** mid-May–mid-Sep: daily. 🅿 🍴 💻 🏠 ♿

⑳ Byxelkrok

Öland. Road 136. 🚂 200. 🚌

Almost at the northernmost end of Öland's west coast on Kalmarsund is the popular old fishing village of Byxelkrok. Boats to Blå Jungfrun (see p158) depart from here.

About 5 km (3 miles) to the north is **Neptuni Åkrar**, an area of ridged stones resembling ploughed fields with several ancient monuments, including the Iron Age stone ship Forgallaskeppet.

Löttorp, the largest town in northern Öland, is home to a paradise for car-mad children – **Lådbilslandet** (Boxcar Country), Glabo Gocart. Here youngsters

Byxelkrok from across the water, a popular fishing village at the northernmost end of Öland's west coast

can race round the 6-km (4-mile) course in motorized vehicles, attend driving school or enjoy the playground.

Böda, 10 km (6 miles) north of Löttorp, has wonderful sandy beaches. It is also the site of **Skäftekärr Järnåldersby**, a reconstructed Iron Age village. Complete with goods, animals, houses and people, it provides a fascinating insight into Iron Age life.

The village also has an arboretum featuring a collection of *Thuja occidentalis* planted in the late 19th century.

🚗 **Lådbilslandet**
40 km (25 miles) N of Borgholm.
Tel 0485-203 35. **Open** mid-Jun–mid-Aug: daily. 🅿 🍴 💻 🏠

🏰 **Skäftekärr Järnåldersby**
50 km (31 miles) N of Borgholm.
Tel 070-634 19 50. **Open** end Jun–Aug: daily; other times: call to check.
🅿 🍴 💻 🏠

㉑ Ölands Museum

Öland. 20 km (12 miles) NE of Färjestaden. 🚌 ℹ 0485-56 10 22.
Open Jun–Aug: 11am–5:30pm daily; Sep: 11am–5:30pm weekends.
🅿 🍴 💻 🏠

Himmelsberga, in the centre of the island, is home to Ölands Museum, an open-air museum of art and cultural history. It centres around a well-preserved linear village with 18th- and 19th-century farms. The interiors of the houses show how life was once lived, and pigs, chickens and sheep are kept in the grounds. A shop sells crafts and books about Öland. Next to the museum is a gallery showing work by local artists. North of Himmelsberga, **Gärdslösa Kyrka** is one of the most interesting churches on Öland. It dates from the mid-13th century and has excellent limestone murals, a beautiful votive ship and a 17th-century pulpit.

The fort of **Ismantorps Borg** in Långlöt has been dated to the 5th century. Archaeological finds show that it was probably an important marketplace and cult site. It is encircled by a wall up to 6 m (19 ft) thick and 3 m (10 ft) high with nine gates.

Öland's best preserved row of windmills can be seen in Lerkaka, just to the south of Himmelsberga. Situated along a road, the mills are widely considered to be among the country's most beautiful. One of the mills is always open, allowing visitors to go inside and look around.

❷ Stora Alvaret

Öland. 🚌

The extraordinary limestone plain of Stora Alvaret dominates southern Öland. Here, the bedrock is around 400 million years old and is covered in a thin layer of soil that was used from prehistoric times as grazing land. In the year 2000 the area was declared a UNESCO World Heritage Site.

In spring the ground is covered in pasque flowers (*Pulsatilla pratensis*). The dominant species include meadow oat-grass (*Helictotrichon pratense*), sheep's fescue (*Festuca ovina*) and a moss species, *kalkbackmossa* (*Homalothecium lutescens*). Juniper bushes are common and lichen inches over bare rock.

The extreme climate has created almost desert-like conditions to which the flora and fauna have had to adapt. Mountain and Mediterranean plants grow here as well as a unique species of rock-rose (*Helianthemum oelandicum*). The island is a resting place for cranes, but conditions on the plain are so harsh that only a few birds, such as the skylark and wheatear, have succeeded in adapting to the environment.

❷ Eketorps Borg

Öland. 🚌 🚹 0485-66 20 00. **Open** May–Aug; see website for hours. **Closed** Midsummer's Eve. 🅿 🆆 **eketorp.se**

The only one of Öland's ancient forts to have been completely excavated, Eketorps Borg was built in three stages. It originated in the 4th century to protect the population and was later converted into a fortified farming village with military functions, but was abandoned in the 7th century. It was thrust into use again at the end of the 12th century in the war between the royal houses of Erik and Sverker.

The fort has been partly reconstructed to show how people lived and worked in the Iron Age. In the museum the numerous artifacts uncovered on the site are on display, including jewellery and weapons.

Around 10 km (6 miles) north of Eketorp lies **Seby Gravfält** with no fewer than 285 visible ancient monuments in the form of different kinds of burial sites, mainly dating from the Iron Age.

Långe Jan at Öland's Southern Cape, Sweden's tallest lighthouse

❷ Öland's Southern Cape

Öland. 🚌 🚹 Ottenby Naturum, 0485-66 12 00 (Jun–Aug: daily). 🅿

In the mid-16th century the area around Öland's southern cape became a royal hunting ground and even today descendants of the fallow deer introduced by Johan III in 1569 can be spotted. The northern boundary of his land is marked by Karl X's wall, built in the 1650s to prevent local people and their animals from entering the grounds. To the south, Sweden's oldest and tallest lighthouse, **Långe Jan**, stands to attention, 41.6 m (136 ft) high, and offers amazing views.

Look out for hedgehogs, a threatened species

At the southernmost tip of the island is a nature reserve, Ottenby Naturum, and **Ottenby Fågelstation** (the bird station). Ornithologists come here to study migratory birds close up and conduct research. The station has several bird-related exhibitions and offers guided tours around the nature reserve.

🔲 **Ottenby Fågelstation**
Öland's Southern Cape. **Tel** 0485-66 10 93. **Open** Mar–Oct: daily. 🅿 🗺 Set guided bird tours mid-Mar– mid-Nov. 🖥

The mighty walls of Eketorps Borg, a partly reconstructed Iron Age fort

GOTLAND

Sweden's largest island, Gotland is a popular holiday destination, favoured for its mild climate, sandy beaches, distinctive landscape and beautiful walled town of Visby. It is known as the "Pearl of the Baltic". The island's strategic position made it an important trading centre especially in the Middle Ages. Gotland celebrates its heritage with enthusiasm in the annual Visby Medieval Week.

In geological terms, Gotland is fairly old. It consists of layers of rocks which were deposited in a tropical sea during the Silurian period around 400 million years ago. Fossils can still be found washed up along the shore. At the northern and southernmost tips of the island, the limestone comes to the surface and plant life is sparse. In the centre of the island forest dominates. The high limestone cliffs with their large bird population are broken by sandy beaches beloved by sun-worshippers, and standing offshore are numerous extraordinary sea stacks, known as *raukar*.

The long, warm autumns and mild winters allow trees such as walnut and apricot to survive in sheltered spots. No less than 35 different orchids can be found on the island and the flower meadows which blossom at Midsummer are typical of Gotland. The island's fauna lacks the large mammals of the mainland. The odd fallow deer is probably an escapee from an enclosure, but there is a herd of *russ*, Gotland's little wild ponies, as well as foxes and wild rabbits.

A wealth of archaeological finds have been uncovered on the island, from the ship burials of the Bronze Age to the silver treasure of the Viking period. More than 90 medieval churches dot the landscape and the museums have numerous artifacts from the Hanseatic period and the Danish King Valdemar Atterdag's capture of Visby in 1361. Visby itself is a UNESCO World Heritage Site.

Gotlanders have their own dialect, *Gutamål*, and their own traditions. These are especially reflected in the games of the annual Gotland Olympics and in the Medieval Week in Visby *(see p33)*, a 21st-century re-creation of the Middle Ages with tournaments, jesters and fair maidens.

Hoburgen in southern Gotland, a 35-m (115-ft) high limestone cliff containing red "Hoburg" marble

◄ Almedalen Park and the spires of Domkyrkan Sta Maria, Visby

Exploring Gotland

A visit to Gotland naturally begins in Visby, where the ferry terminal and airport are located. To experience this unusual part of Sweden it is best to strike out into the countryside and discover the exceptional landscape with its distinctive flora, long sandy beaches, curious limestone sea stacks and multitude of medieval churches. Hiring a bike and cycling round Gotland is a popular way of seeing the island. There are almost no hills and car-free country lanes constantly lead to new hideaways. There is plenty of bed-and-breakfast accommodation and the island has many good camp sites for those with tents or caravans. Bookings should be made well in advance for the month of July.

A ruined medieval church towering above the Visby rooftops

Sights at a Glance

1. Fårö
2. Bunge
3. Slite
4. Tingstäde
5. Lummelundagrottan
6. Bro Kyrka
7. *Visby pp168–71*
8. Roma
9. Ljugarn
10. Lojsta
11. Fröjel Kyrka
12. Karlsöarna
13. Petes
14. Hoburgen
15. Gotska Sandön

0 kilometres 20

0 miles 10

Key

— Motorway

— Major road

··· Minor road

For keys to symbols *see back flap*

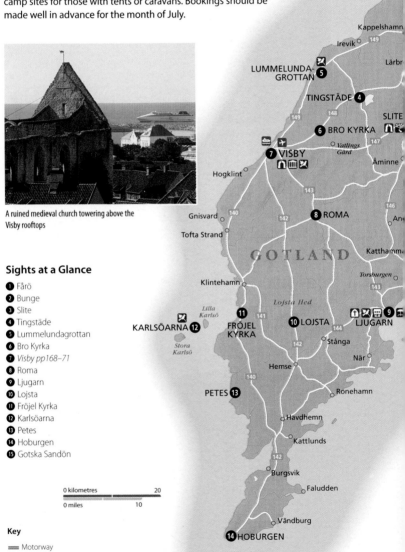

Kappelshamn

Irevik ○ 149

Lärbr

LUMMELUNDA-GROTTAN 5

TINGSTÄDE 4

148

SLITE

149

6 BRO KYRKA

147

○ *Vatlings Gård*

7 VISBY

Åminne

Hogklint ○

143

Gnisvard ○ 140

8 ROMA

146

Tofta Strand ○

An

GOTLAND

Katthamm

Torsburgen ○

Klintehamn ○

143

Lojsta Hed

Lilla Karlsö

11

KARLSÖARNA 12

FRÖJEL KYRKA

141

10 LOJSTA

144

9

LJUGARN

Stora Karlsö

142

○ Stånga

När ○

Hemse ○

140

PETES 13

○ Rönehamn

○ Havdhemn

○ Kattlunds

142

○ Burgsvik

○ Faludden

○ Vändburg

14 HOBURGEN

Sheep in front of a typical Gotland farmhouse, today a tempting renovation project for incomers from the mainland

Getting Around

The most common way to get to Gotland is by ferry or fast catamaran, either from Nynäshamn or Oskarshamn. In summer there are several crossings a day to Visby. Another option is to arrive by air on one of the daily flights from Stockholm, Norrköping or Nyköping. On Gotland, the only means of public transport is the bus. Services outside Visby are infrequent with perhaps just one morning and one afternoon bus, making a car or a bike a necessity for getting around. Bicycles can be hired at the ferry terminal and elsewhere around the island.

One of Gotland's many long sandy beaches attracting hundreds of thousands of visitors to the island every summer

❶ Fårö

Gotland. 500. Mar–Sep: at Fårö church 0498-22 40 22; Oct–Feb: Visby Tourist Office, 0498-20 17 00. **gotland.com**

A summer paradise for visitors from the mainland and further afield, Fårö appears exotic even to a Gotlander from the main island. Lying at the northern tip of Gotland, the little island of Fårö has a language and traditions all of its own. During the summer car ferries shuttle back and forth on the 15-minute trip from Fårösund to Broa. At other times of year the service is more limited.

Sparse, low pine forest and moorland with swamp and marshland cover the island. There are sheep everywhere. Off the main road between Broa and Fårö lighthouse there are plenty of cattle grids, which prevent the sheep from straying.

Off the northwest coast are the spectacular limestone stacks, known as *raukar*, of Langham-mars and Digerhuvud. The sand dune of Ullahau is at the northern end of the island, and Sudersand's long sandy beach is popular with holiday-makers. The easternmost cape of Holmudden is topped by the 30-m (98-ft) high lighthouse, Fårö Fyr. Roughly in the centre of the island, **Fårö Kyrka** offers views over the inlet of Kyrkviken. The church contains votive paintings dating from 1618 and 1767, depicting seal hunters being rescued from the sea.

🏠 Fårö Kyrka
5 km (3 miles) N of Broa. **Tel** 0498-22 10 74. **Open** Jun–Aug: daily; Sep–May: Sat & Sun. 🏠 📷 by appointment.

"The coffee pot", an eroded limestone stack on Fårö's coast

❷ Bunge

Gotland. Road 148. 🚗 950. 🚌
🎭 Tournament (2nd week in Jul).

The village of Bunge is
renowned for its 14th-century
church **Bunge Kyrka**, built in
Gothic style. Its tower was
constructed in the 13th century
to defend an earlier church –
holes from pikes and arrows
in the north wall bear
witness to past battles.

Inside are beautiful
limestone paintings
dating from around
1400, which are
thought to depict
the Teutonic Knights
fighting the Vitalien
brothers, pirates of
Mecklenburg who
occupied Gotland
in the 1390s. In the
chancel is a poor
box in limestone
signed by stone-
mason Lafrans
Botvidarson. Like
the font, it dates
from the 13th century.

8th-century picture stone,
Bungemuseet

Next to the church is
Bungemuseet, one of Sweden's
largest rural museums. It was
created in 1917 by Bunge
schoolteacher Theodor
Erlandsson, who wanted to
show how the people of
Gotland used to live. In the
fields next to the school he
gathered together cottages,
buildings and cultural objects
from different parts of Gotland
covering the 17th, 18th and
19th centuries as well as four
carved stones from the 8th
century. The museum hosts
many events in the summer,
including medieval tournaments,
markets and handicraft festivals.
In Snäckersstugan cottage, with
the date 1700 carved into the
gable, visitors can enjoy a cup
of coffee and attempt to make
out the Gotland proverbs
painted on the ceiling.

Just north of Bunge is
the busy **Fårösund**, one of
the larger towns in northern
Gotland with around 1,000
inhabitants. For many years
the area was dominated
by the military and
countless young men
were drilled here in
defence of the island.
Since the coastal
artillery unit was
disbanded in 2000
with the loss of many
jobs, the area risks
going into decline.

🏛 **Bunge Kyrka**
60 km (37 miles) N of
Visby. **Tel** 0498-22 27 00.
Open mid-May–
mid-Sep: daily.

🏛 **Bungemuseet**
2 km (1 mile) E of Bunge. **Tel** 0498-22
10 18. **Open** Jun–Sep: daily. 📷 ring
for appointment. 🈺 🖥 🏠

❸ Slite

Gotland. Road 147 🚗 1,500. 🚌 ⛴
ℹ️ Visby Tourist Information Centre,
0498-20 17 00. 🎭 Golf round Gotland
(2nd week in May).

Occupying a stunning setting in
a bay facing its own archipelago
is the town of Slite. It is the
second largest community in
Gotland. Slite had a long and
troubled history from the

Majestic limestone stack at Kyllaj, Slite Bay

Viking period onwards, and
development only really took
off in the late 19th century with
an upturn in seafaring. Today
the town is dominated by a
cement factory.

In summer, the fine sandy
beaches, harbour, tennis courts,
stunning stone stacks and lime
kiln attract holiday-makers. The
islands offshore are perfect for
short trips, including Enholmen
with Karlsvärd fortress, which
dates from 1853–6.

Environs
On the opposite side of the
bay is Hellvi, with the delightful
old harbour of **Kyllaj**. The quiet
beach is in a beautiful setting
overlooking weathered sea
stacks. Strandridaregården, the
18th-century coastguard's house,
now belongs to Bungemuseet.

Northwest of Slite is **Lärbro
Kyrka**, a mid-13th century
church with an 11th-century
watch tower next to it. In the
churchyard are buried 44 of
the former prisoners of war
who came from the German
concentration camps to the
hospital at Lärbro in 1945.

St Olofsholm, nearby, is
dedicated to Olav the Holy
who visited Gotland in 1029
to convert the island to
Christianity. In medieval times
it was a place of pilgrimage.
This is also the site of
Ytterholmen's large group
of limestone stacks and a
glorious pebble beach.

🏛 **Lärbro Kyrka**
10 km (6 miles) N of Slite. **Tel** 0498-22
27 00. **Open** mid-May–mid-Sep: daily.
🈺 🖥 🏠 ♿

Buildings at Bungemuseet with thatched roofs of Gotland sedge

For hotels and restaurants in this area see p286 and p297

❶ Tingstäde

23 km (14 miles) N of Visby. 🚗 280.
🚌 ℹ Visby Tourist Information
Centre, 0498-20 17 00. 🌳 Nature trail
with lady's slipper in flower (early Jun).

Halfway between Visby and
Fårösund on road 148 lies
Tingstäde, a community best
known for its sea rescue radio
station and its marsh. The
church dating from the
13th and 14th centuries has
one of the highest towers on
the island.

Tingstäde marsh is, in fact, a
shallow lake and popular, child-
friendly bathing spot. Submerged in the centre of the
lake is Bulverket, a 10th–11th-
century fortress surrounded
by a palisade of 1,500 stakes.

❺ Lummelunda-grottan

Road 149, 13 km (8 miles) N of Visby.
🚌 ℹ 1 May–Sep, plus some
weekends: 0498-27 30 50, ring
ahead to book. 📷 obligatory. Cave
adventure must be pre-booked.
📷 🖥 🏠 ♿

In 1948 two local school boys
discovered an opening in the
ground in Martebo marsh and
crawled in. They had chanced
upon the entrance to a network
of caves and passageways,
now Gotland's main tourist
attraction. Today the entrance
is at Lummelundas Bruk.
Exploration of the caves continues, but the part which is open
for viewing provides a fantastic
show of stalactites and stalag-
mites, magic mirrors of water
and spine-tinglingly tight
openings. Hour-long tours are
organized for young children

aged 4 to 6 years.
Immediately to the
south of the caves is
Krusmyntagården, a
herb garden designed
in traditional monastic
style with wonderful
views over the sea.

🎋 Krusmyntagården
Road 149, 10 km (6 miles)
N of Visby. **Tel** 0498-29 69 00.
Open May–Sep: daily.
📷 🖥 🖊 🏠

❻ Bro Kyrka

Road 148, 11 km (7 miles) NE of Visby.
🚌 **Tel** 08-584 808 80. **Open** mid-
May–mid-Sep: 9am–5pm daily.

Tradition has it that Bro Kyrka
is built over a votive well and
in medieval times it was a
famous votive church,
particularly among sailors.
The building dates from the
13th and 14th centuries. Inside,
the prayer chamber contains
5th-century picture stones.

About 1 km (half a mile)
north of Bro Kyrka, on road
148, are two picture stones
known as "Bro Stajnkällingar".
According to legend, two
elderly women were turned
to stone for arguing on the
way to the Christmas Mass.
From Bro, a turning leads
to Fole church on road 147,
and a short detour takes
you to **Vatlings Gård**. The
estate has Gotland's best-
preserved medieval stone
house outside Visby and
is well worth a visit.

🚌 Vatlings Gård
Road 147, 18 km 18 km (11 miles) E of
Visby. **Open** daily. **Tel** 0498-29 27 00.

Roma Kungsgård, built in 1733 using materials
from Roma Kloster

❼ Visby
See pp168–71.

❽ Roma

18 km (11 miles) SE of Visby. 🚌
ℹ Roma Kungsgård: 070-543 33 34.
Open May–Aug: 10am–6pm daily.

Cistercian monks from Nydala
monastery in Småland founded
Roma Kloster in 1164. The
monastery was built on the
pattern of the French mother
monastery and became a
religious centre for the entire
Baltic region. The three-aisle
church in the Fontenay style
was completed in the 13th
century. The monastery was
abandoned during the
Reformation in 1530 and
ended up in the ownership
of the Danish crown as a royal
manor under Visborg Castle.

When Gotland came under
Swedish rule in 1645, the
monastery was practically in
ruins. The county governor
used materials from the site
to build his residence, **Roma
Kungsgård**, in 1733. Only the
church remained intact, and
that was used as a stable. In
1822, Roma Kungsgård was
rented to the crown and
served as an army store.

The ruins of Roma
monastery are a popular
tourist attraction. Even today
they bear witness to the
monks' skill in construction
techniques. The beautiful
vaulted ceilings are reminiscent
of Roman aqueducts.

In the summer, Romateatern
performs Shakespearian plays
on an open-air stage set among
the ruins.

A painting on wood in Bro Kyrka showing Adam and Eve in paradise

❼ Street-by-Street: Visby

A town of roses and ruins, the walled city of Visby is a
UNESCO World Heritage Site as well as a popular party
town in summer, when it fills up with holiday-makers from
the mainland. Its cobbled streets are lined with picturesque
cottages, haunting medieval ruins and a multitude of cafés
and bars. Away from the busy, more touristy parts of
Strandgatan, Stora Torget and around the pleasure boat
harbour, the evocative ambience recalls the town's
medieval history *(see p171)*. This is also evident from the
imposing town wall and its many towers, including
Kruttornet (the Gunpowder Tower).

Konstmuseet
Visby Town Wall by Hanna Pauli
(1864–1940) is on display in the
Museum of Art.

★ Gotlands Museum
The museum is devoted to Gotland's past from
ancient times to modern day. The art museum is
part of the same complex.

Burmeisterska Huset
Hans Burmeister, a wealthy merchant
from Lübeck, built this house in the
17th century. It is one of the best-
preserved examples of its kind in Visby.

**Visby town
wall** has 19
towers and
gates, including
Kruttornet
(Gunpowder
Tower).

Krut-
tornet

RIGAGRÄND

LYBSKA GR.

STRANDGATAN

BIRGERS GRÄND

MELLANGATAN

Alme-
dalen

PACKHUS
PLAN

DUBBGR.

Almedalen

DONNERS
PLATS

Key

— Suggested route

For hotels and restaurants in this area see p286 and p297

Kapitelhusgården
In this leafy medieval courtyard setting, the public can try their hand at medieval crafts. During the summer, it can become busy, especially during Medieval Week.

Botaniska trädgården

St Drotten, the sister church to St Lars.

S:T DROTTENS GATA
SKOLGATAN
V. KYRKOGATAN
KYRKOGATAN

STORA TORGET

Söderport

★ **Domkyrkan Sta Maria**
Completed in 1225, the cathedral was the church of the German merchants. It is the only one of Visby's 17 medieval churches which is not in ruins.

St Lars, also known as the church of Sta Anna after the mother of the Virgin Mary.

Around Stora Torget
Entertainment focuses on the main square, Stora Torget. Munkkällaren, with a terrace on the square, is one of the many restaurants and bars here.

Ruins of Sta Karin (St Catherine's) Church
Franciscan monks built the church and monastery of Sta Karin in 1233. Dominicans rebuilt it in the 14th century. But in 1525 was destroyed by an army from Lübeck.

Exploring Visby

Within the walls, Visby is relatively small and all the sights are within easy walking distance. The main streets run north to south: Strandgatan with historic sights and nightlife spots, St Hansgatan with its many churches, and Adelsgatan, the shopping street leading from Söderport (South Gate) to Stora Torget, the main square. North of here are quieter residential streets and alleyways, making for a lovely stroll. Near Norderport (North Gate) it is possible to climb up on the ramparts and admire the magnificent wall.

Visby Town Centre
Street-by-Street: Visby, see pp168–9

Medieval vaulted street in Visby, a UNESCO World Heritage Site

The Heart of the Town

The medieval inner town of Visby is shaped by its mighty town wall, almost 3.5 km (2 miles) in length. Construction of the wall began at the end of the 13th century. It was originally 5.5 m (18 ft) high and designed to protect against attack from the sea. On the inland side, the wall was surrounded by a deep moat. Within the ramparts, narrow cobbled streets are lined with tightly packed houses, wealthy merchants' homes and the ruins of historic churches. UNESCO described the town as the "best fortified commercial city in northern Europe" and declared it a World Heritage Site in 1995.

Just outside the wall is Almedalen, the former site of the Hanseatic harbour. Today the area is a park. South of Almedalen is Visby marina, which throngs with boats, especially during Medieval Week in August.

Around Stora Torget

At the heart of Visby lies Stora Torget (Big Square) from which the roads to the town gates

radiate. This is still a focal point for visitors to Visby, despite the development of a modern town centre outside Österport, and there is a lively market here in summer. Several medieval houses surround the square, including the restaurants of Gutekällaren, with its characteristic stepped gable, and Munkkällaren, with its deep vaulted cellars and inner courtyard.

The ruins of the church of Sta Karin (St Catherine), dating from the 1230s, form a dramatic backdrop on the southern side of Stora Torget. In the shadow of the ruins is Rosengård, a café where generations have ordered coffee and delicious pastries.

Gotlands Museum

Strandgatan 14. **Tel** 0498-29 27 00.
Open May–Sep: daily; Oct–Apr: Tue–Sun.
W gotlandsmuseum.se

Gotland's long history going back to prehistoric times has made this collection one of Sweden's richest regional museums. It is housed in a former royal distillery, built in the 1770s.

The Hall of Picture Stones contains an impressive array of carved stones from the 5th–11th centuries, some of which feature runic inscriptions. Next door, the Gravkammaren (Grave Room) shows burial customs from ancient times to the Vikings. Several skeletons are on display, including the 8,000-year-old Stenkyrkamannen (Stenkyrka Man). One of the most remarkable sights is the collection of Viking silver treasure – no fewer than 700 items have been recovered from sites around the island.

Church art is well represented. The museum holds the original, Gothic Öja Madonna (Öja church in southern Gotland has to make do with a copy). A large gallery displays medieval furniture, as well as collections from later periods. The museum is close to Fenomenalen, a hands-on science centre.

Picture stones from the 5th–11th centuries in Gotlands Museum

Visby's medieval town wall, approximately 3.5 km (2 miles) long and up to 5.5 m (18 ft) high

 Ruins of St Nicolai

St Nicolaigatan. **Tel** Visby Tourist Office, 0498-20 17 00.

The ruins of St Nicolai are all that remains of a Dominican monastery founded in Visby in 1228. The Black Friars expanded it and built a Gothic cathedral which they dedicated to the patron saint of sailors and merchants, St Nicholas. When the people of Lübeck stormed Visby in 1525 much of the cathedral was destroyed.

Between 1929 and 1990 a pageant, *Petrus de Dacia*, was performed here every summer. This Gotlander was a famous mystic and author, and prior of the Dominican monastery at the end of the 13th century. Today, musical and theatrical events are staged in the ruins and the Gotland Chamber Music Festival is usually held here each summer. The audience sit protected from wind and weather by the remaining part of the roof.

Ruins of Helge And

Helge Ands Plan. **Tel** Gotlands Museum, 0498-29 27 00.

Helgeandstiftelserna was a religious order founded during the early 13th century to take care of the poor and the sick. The ruin of Helge And (Church of the Holy Spirit) is one of Visby's most remarkable church ruins and dates from this period. The octagonal building has two floors opening onto a choir. Two large staircases lead up to the first floor. It was designed in this way to allow patients from the hospital to reach the church via a passage from the upper floor. Today the ruins are used for cultural events and are open to visitors during the summer.

Botaniska Trädgården

Visby. **Tel** 0498-26 94 77.
Open 24 hrs daily.

Gotland's Botanical Garden was founded in 1856 by the Badande Wännerna (Society of the Bathing Friends), a gentlemen's club formed in 1814 to work for the benefit of the public. The society also established Gotland's first school and set up its first bank. To reach the garden, follow the promenade along the shore from the harbour and go through Kärleksporten (Gate of Love) in the northwest corner of the town wall.

Inside the gate, the lush park offers a spice-scented herb garden and a pretty rose garden (at its peak Jul–Aug). There are over 16,000 species including many plants and trees that are exotic to the Nordic countries, such as walnut, mulberry and ginkgo. In its midst stand the ivy-clad ruins of St Olof's church and there is a water-lily pond and a small pavilion making an ideal resting place.

Visby's Early History

Archaeological finds, including Roman, Arabic and Russian coins, show that Gotland had a lively foreign trade already in Viking times. At the end of the 12th century, trade with Germany took off and the Hanseatic League was formed – a mercantile and political association between German merchants and towns around the North Sea and the Baltic. The League was centred on Visby and the town enjoyed a boom in the 13th century with people coming from all around to settle here. Towards the end of the century a trading-political power struggle on Gotland led to internal strife and the gradual decline of Visby. Poor harvests and the Black Death contributed to the decline, as did the introduction of large ships capable of travelling longer distances. In 1361 Visby was captured by Valdemar Atterdag and Gotland succumbed to Danish rule. Then in 1525 Visby was plundered by its rival Hanseatic town, Lübeck, and buildings were destroyed or abandoned.

Valdemar Atterdag pillaging Visby in 1361

The small community of Ljugarn with typical Gotland limestone houses close to the sea

flourishing port and limeworks. In the early 1800s lime baron Axel Hägg bought Katthamra manor, which he had rebuilt and decorated in Empire style. Today there is a hotel and youth hostel here, but the manor house itself is a private home.

⑨ Ljugarn

40 km (25 miles) SW of Visby. 🚌 300. 🚍 ℹ️ Visby Tourist Office, 0498-20 17 00.

This cheerful resort was Gotland's first and makes a good centre for touring the southeast of the island. There was a harbour here long before Russian forces raided Ljugarn on their way to laying waste to the east coast of Sweden in 1714–18. By 1900, the small community, with its long sandy beach, limestone sea stacks and guesthouse, had become a popular bathing spot.

South of Ljugarn is the 13th–14th century **Lau Kyrka**. One of Gotland's largest churches, it has a triumphal crucifix from the 13th century and excellent acoustics for the concerts held there.

Northwest of Ljugarn, **Torsburgen** fortress was built in the 3rd or 4th century and is one of the largest of its kind in Scandinavia. It is protected by naturally steep slopes and a wall 7 m (23 ft) high and up to 24 m (79 ft) wide. To reach it, take the forest road from the 146 towards Östergarn, 2 km (1 mile) east of Kräklingbo church.

About 6 km (4 miles) south of Ljugarn, at **Guffride**, are seven Bronze Age stone-settings, in the form of ships, and are the largest on Gotland. Open to tourists is the 11th Century Church of Garde, southwest of Ljugarn. The Church features paintings in the Byzantine style.

The idyllic **Katthammarsvik**, north of Ljugarn, was once a

⑩ Lojsta

15 km (9 miles) S of Visby. 🚌 120. 🚍 ℹ️ Visby Tourist Office, 0498-20 17 00. 🐎 Gotland pony judging (4th week in Jul).

Like so many of Gotland's churches, **Lojsta Kyrka** dates from the mid-13th century. The choir and the nave have ornamental paintings and the figures above the triumphal arch are by the master known as "Egypticus" in the mid-14th century.

On **Lojsta Hed**, an area of forest and heath north of the church, lives a herd of semi-wild Gotland ponies (russ), the stubborn little horse native to the island. The animals are owned by local farmers and by Gotlands Läns Hushållnings-sällskap. Several annual events are organized, such as the release of the stallion in early June, and the high point of the year, the Gotland pony judging at the end of July.

About 2.5 km (2 miles) from Lojsta towards Etelhem is a large building with a sedge roof, **Lojstahallen**. This is an excellent reconstruction of a late-Iron Age hall building. Next to it is a medieval fortress, Lojsta Slott.

⑪ Fröjel Kyrka

40 km (25 miles) S of Visby. 🚌 **Tel** 0498-24 00 05. **Open** daily. 🏠 call for details. 🚻 ♿

In a stunning location, high up overlooking the sea, is the saddle-roof church of Fröjel Kyrka, built in the 12th and 13th centuries. Inside is an impressive triumphal crucifix by the craftsman who created the rood screen of Öja church. The churchyard has an ancient maze which shows that the site was used long before the arrival of Christianity.

North of the church lies the magnificent **Gannarve Skeppssättning** (Gannarve Ship Barrow), which is considered to be one of the best in Gotland. This has been dated to the late Bronze Age (1000–300 BC) and is 30 m (98 ft) long and 5 m (16 ft) wide.

The splendid Gannarve Bronze Age stone ship barrow

⑫ Karlsöarna

Gotland. Stora Karlsö 🚢 from Klintehamn during summer season only. ℹ️ Visby Tourist Office, 0498-20 17 00. 🚻 🅿️ ♿ Lilla Karlsö 🚢 from Klintehamn. ℹ️ 0498-24 05 00. 🚻

Many myths have been spun around Stora and Lilla Karlsö, the rocky islands 6.5 km (4 miles) off the west coast of Gotland.

Stora Karlsö covers 2.5 sq km (1 sq mile) and is a nature

Thin-billed (or common) murres at Stora Karlso, Gotland

reserve with steep cliffs, caves such as "Stora Förvar", moorland, leafy groves, and rare flowers and birds. Here, between the bare rocks in May and June, the orchids *Adam och Eva (Dactylorhiza sambucina)* and *Sankt Pers nycklar (Orchis mascula)* form carpets of blooms. Sea birds such as auks, gulls and eider duck can be seen. Razorbills lay their eggs among the stones on the beach, while guillemots prefer the shelves of the steep cliffs.

A guided tour takes a couple of hours and is included in the price of the boat crossing. There is also a museum in Norderhamn.

Like Stora Karlsö, **Lilla Karlsö** is also a nature reserve. The island has been grazed by sheep since the Bronze Age. It is home to guillemots, razorbills, cormorants and gulls. Eider duck, little terns, Sandwich terns and velvet scoters nest on the flat land. The Swedish Society for Nature Conservation organizes guided tours. There is a youth hostel on the island – book in advance.

Petes Museigård, typical 18th- and 19th-century Gotland houses

⑬ Petes

Gotland. 🚌 🛈 Gotlands Museum, 0498-29 21 00. **Open** mid-Jun–mid-Aug: 11:30am–2:30pm daily.

To the southwest of Gotland, just before Hablingbo church on coastal road 140, there is a turning to the seaside community of Petes. Here, the well-preserved houses show Gotland's architecture from the 18th and 19th centuries.

For younger visitors, **Barnens Petes** displays classic toys such as stilts, hobby horses, hoops, wooden rifles and wooden dolls.

The unbroken sandy beaches of Gotska Sandön

⑭ Hoburgen

80 km (50 miles) S of Visby. 🚌

Far to the south lies Hoburgen, a 35-m (115-ft) high steep cliff of fossil-rich limestone with seams of the local red Hoburgen marble. On the clifftop is a lighthouse built in 1846. From here it is 176 km (97 miles) to the northernmost lighthouse on the island of Fårö.

Below the lighthouse is Sweden's most famous sea stack, Hoburgsgubben (the Old Man of Hoburg), guarding the caves of Skattkammaren (the Treasure Chamber) and Sängkammaren (the Bed Chamber).

Hoburgen is a favourite spot for ornithologists who come to study the multitude of birds which swoop over Gotland's southernmost outpost all year round. In summer there is a restaurant nearby.

Profile of Hoburgsgubben, the "Old Man of Hoburg"

⑮ Gotska Sandön

🛈 Visby Tourist Office, 0498-20 17 00; booking: 0498-24 04 50. 🚢 from Nynäshamn and Fårösund.

Just 40 km (25 miles) north of Fårö lies the most isolated island in the Baltic, Gotska Sandön. It is one of Sweden's national parks and features a unique landscape of deserted, constantly changing sandy beaches and dunes, pine forests and a rich flora. There are migratory birds, unusual beetles, but only one mammal, the hare. The island became a national park in 1909.

Gotska Sandön has been inhabited since the dawn of civilization, although the population has never been large. Colonies of grey seals led seal hunters to settle on the island and the dangerous waters offshore attracted wreck plunderers. In the 17th and 18th centuries sheep were grazed here and later crops were grown. As recently as the 1950s a few lighthouse keepers and their families (and one female teacher) lived here, but now the lighthouse is automated and the only permanent resident is a caretaker.

There is no harbour and boat traffic from Fårösund or Nynäshamn is infrequent and dependent on the weather. It is possible to camp or stay in a shared sleeping hut or cottage. Accommodation must be booked before arrival.

SOUTHERN GÖTALAND

Sweden's two southernmost provinces, Skåne and Blekinge, together form Southern Götaland, with the country's third largest city, Malmö, as the region's main town and gateway to Europe. The gentle, undulating landscape retains its Danish atmosphere from times past. Castles and medieval and Viking sites abound, and the historic naval port of Karlskrona is a UNESCO World Heritage Site.

The province of Skåne has an undeserved reputation for being completely flat, but apart from the plain of Söderslätt the countryside is surprisingly hilly with the rocky ridges of Söderåsen, Linderödsåsen and Romeleåsen dividing the region. To the northwest, the area is bounded by the imposing Hallandsåsen ridge.

The province of Blekinge, criss-crossed by rivers and lakes, is known as the Garden of Sweden. It has its own island archipelago with sheltered harbours beloved by sailors. North, towards the border with Småland, the slightly wild forest landscape predominates.

Throughout Southern Götaland the Danish influence prior to 1645 *(see p41)* is still evident, not least in the architecture, which differs greatly from elsewhere in Sweden. A common sight in rural Skåne is the traditional, often half-timbered farmhouse with a thatched roof, built around a cobbled courtyard. Castles and manor houses, in many cases built by the Danish nobility, are a feature of the countryside. In the coastal communities, former fishing huts are today cherished by their summer residents.

Southern Götaland differs from the rest of Sweden in atmosphere, too. The people of Skåne are known for being relaxed and for loving good food – and in large quantities – something which has lent this part of the country its tavern culture, which has its equivalent in the Danish *kroen* just across Öresund.

Having been sparring partners in the long-distant past, Sweden and Denmark are now linked by the Öresund Bridge from Malmö to Copenhagen. Both sides of the sound are now collaborating over the creation of a visionary new Swedish-Danish region, Öresund.

Ales Stenar, a stone ship on Skåne's south coast, thought to be a late Viking grave or cult site

◄ Malmö's West Harbour at dusk, with the spectacular Turning Torso skyscraper in the background

Exploring Southern Götaland

As well as arable fields and willow windbreaks, this
southernmost part of Sweden has its share of gently
rolling hills, forests and lakes. The region is ideal for cycling
through the country from village to village, discovering
manor houses and castles along the way, walking through
nature reserves or along the Skåneleden trail, canoeing,
fishing, swimming in the many small lakes and rivers,
driving, or sailing along the coast and putting into shore at
fishing harbours on tiny islands. Towns such as Lund and
Malmö offer a wealth of history, best discovered on foot,
Karlskrona is renowned for its naval port and maritime
past, and Trelleborg has a reconstructed Viking fortress.

Spiral beech trees in Trollskogen forest,
Torna Hällestad

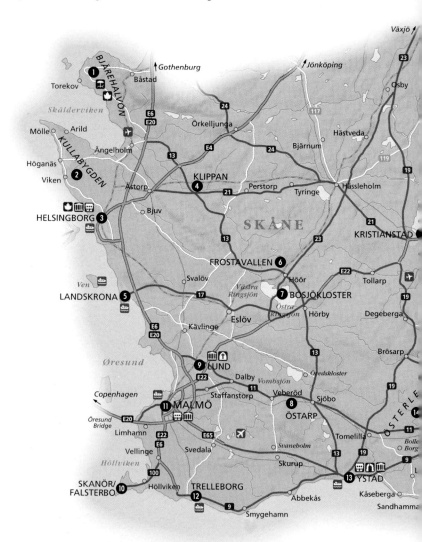

Sights at a Glance

Statue of the founder of Karlskrona, Karl XI, in front of Trefaldighetskyrkan

The 8-km (5-mile) long Öresund Bridge, completed in 2000, links Sweden with Denmark and Continental Europe

Key

▬ Motorway

▬ Major road

⋯⋯ Minor road

⌇⌇ Main railway

— Minor railway

Getting Around

The E20 motorway across the Öresund Bridge from Continental Europe joins the E6, E22 and E65 south of Malmö and continues north to Helsingborg where it meets the E4 to Stockholm. The region has several airports and there are train connections to the large towns. Local commuter trains serve districts around the major cities. Ferries from Germany operate to Trelleborg and Ystad and there are frequent ferries from Denmark to Helsingborg.

```
0 kilometres        30
0 miles          20
```

Hovs Hallar, a nature reserve on the bay of Laholmsbukten

❶ Bjärehalvön

Skåne. Road 105. 🚌 🚍 🚏
ℹ️ Båstad Tourist Office 0431-750 45,
Torekov Tourist Office 0431-36 31 80.
🎵 Båstad Chamber Music Festival
(4th week in Jun), Swedish Open
Tennis Tournament (Jul).
🌐 **bastad.com**

There are several popular resorts
surrounding the peninsula
of Bjärehalvön, between the
bays of Skälderviken and
Laholmsbukten. The medieval
town of **Båstad** is now best
known for hosting the
annual Swedish Open tennis
tournament, but it also has
beautiful old houses and
glorious beaches. Just over
10 km (6 miles) to the west
is the old fishing village of
Torekov. Boat trips run from
Torekov to the nature reserve
Hallands Väderö, a remnant
of the Hallandsåsen ridge
now left 3 km (2 miles) out
to sea. Of special note is the
alder marsh.

On the northern cape of the
peninsula is **Hovs Hallar**, a
geologically interesting area
with dramatic rocks and caves.
The area is a nature reserve
popular with birdwatchers
and walkers. Hovs Hallar is
the westernmost end of the
Hallandsåsen ridge, which
forms the border between the
Bjärehalvön peninsula and
Halland (see p211). With its
meadows and varied flora,
the ridge is ideal for walking.

West of Båstad along the
coast is **Norrvikens Trädgårdar**,
a paradise for garden lovers

Fruit trees in blossom at Norrvikens
Trädgårdar gardens

created by architect Rudolf
Abelin in the early 20th century.
There are several different
gardens, including a Baroque
garden and a Japanese garden.

The town of **Ängelholm**,
nestling between the
Bjärehalvön and Kullahalvön
peninsulas at the end of the bay
of Skälderviken, has a sandy
beach 6 km (4 miles) long.
Historically, Ängelholm was
known for its pottery industry
and today clay cuckoos, the
town's symbol, are made here.

🌷 **Norrvikens Trädgårdar**
5 km (3 miles) W of Båstad.
Open May–Aug: daily. 🎵 🅿️ ♿

❷ Kullabygden

Skåne. Road 111/112. 🚍 🚌
ℹ️ Centralgatan 20, Höganäs,
042-33 77 74. 🎵 Music in
Kullabygden (2nd week in Jul), Kulla
Market in Jonstorp (mid-Jul).

The beautiful Kullen Peninsula
has been inhabited since the
Iron and Bronze Ages. Today, the
pretty medieval fishing villages
of Arild, Mölle, Höganäs and
Viken have become popular
seaside resorts. Höganäs is
best known for its ceramics.

Just outside Arild lies **Brunnby
Kyrka**, parts of which are 12th-
century. The church contains
impressive ceiling paintings.
Krapperups Slott, north of
Höganäs, dates from the mid-
16th century; the castle houses
an art gallery and museum.

🏰 **Krapperups Slott**
7 km (4 miles) N of Höganäs. **Tel** 042-
34 41 90. Castle: **Open** by appointment.
Gallery & museum: **Open** Apr–May:
Sat & Sun; Jun–mid-Aug: daily. 📷 🅿️
♿ 🌐 **krapperup.se**

❸ Helsingborg

Skåne. E4. 🔺 130,000. 🚉 🚌 🚍 ⛴️
ℹ️ Kungsgatan 11, 042-10 43 50
🎵 Helsingborg Festival (late Aug),
Horse Festival (late Oct); Antiques Fair
(end of Jul). 🌐 **helsingborgs
turistbyra.skane.org**

Known as the "Pearl of the
Sound", Helsingborg is a lively
town, spectacularly located on

Tycho Brahe

Astronomer Tycho Brahe was born in Skåne in 1546 into a Danish
noble family. At the age of 13 he was sent to university in
Copenhagen to study philosophy and went on to study at several
German universities. Inspired by an eclipse of the sun in 1560, he
took up astronomy. He believed that the old methods of measure-
ment to determine the position of the planets were not sufficiently
exact and designed a new system. In 1572
he observed a new bright star in the
constellation Cassiopeia. His discoveries
in astronomy paved the way for a new
view of the universe. In recognition, the
Danish king granted Brahe the island of
Ven, where he had an observatory
built (see p179) which became the
finest in Europe. Following a
difference of opinion with the
Danish court, Brahe went into
exile and settled in Prague,
where he died in Prague in 1601.

Statue of Tycho Brahe in St Ibbs
Kyrka on Ven island

the shores of the Öresund within sight of the Danish coast. The town's strategic position at the narrowest point of the sound led to a stormy history, and the 34-m (111-ft) tower **Kärnan** is all that remains of its 12th-century fortress. The brick tower of the town hall (1897) also features on the skyline. It was designed by architect Alfred Hellerström and contains glass paintings by Gustav Cederström.

Jacob Hansen's half-timbered house, built in 1641, is the oldest house in Helsingborg. The **Dunkers Kulturhus**, by Danish architect Kim Utzon, encompasses a museum, art gallery and theatre under one roof.

The open-air **Fredriksdal Friluftsmuseum** displays historical buildings from the region and has a botanical garden containing the wild plants of Skåne.

Environs
Ramlösa Brunn, 5 km (3 miles) southeast of Helsingborg, is known for its spring water, discovered in the late 19th century and now on offer in the Water Pavilion.

The castle of **Sofiero** was bequeathed to Helsingborg municipality by Gustav VI Adolf. The park is particularly famous for its Royal Gardens, containing more than 300 varieties of rhododendron.

Kärnan
Slottshagen. **Tel** 042-10 59 91.
Open daily.

Helsingborg's renovated tower, Kärnan, dating from the 12th century

Tycho Brahe's underground observatory on the island of Ven

Dunkers Kulturhus
Kungsgatan 11. **Tel** 042-10 74 00.
Open Tue–Sun.

Fredriksdals Friluftsmuseum
Gisela Trapps Vag. **Tel** 042-10 45 00.
Open daily.

Sofiero
Sofierovägen, 5 km (3 miles) N of the centre. **Tel** 042-10 25 00.
Parken: **Open** Apr– Sep: daily.
Slottet: **Open** Jun–Aug: guided tours only.

❹ Klippan

Skåne. Road 21. 8,000.
Storgatan 46, 0435-282 00.
Åby Market (3rd Tue–Wed in Jun), Ljungbyhed old-time market (3rd Fri–Sat in Aug).

Located on the Söderåsen ridge, 30 km (19 miles) east of Helsingborg, Klippan is known for having Sweden's oldest operating paper mill, built in the 16th century.

Söderåsen National Park offers leafy forests, dramatic screes, babbling brooks and breathtaking views from Kopparhatten and Hjortspränget. The Skåneleden trail runs through the park.

The 17th-century mansion **Vrams Gunnarstorp**, 10 km (6 miles) west of Klippan, is built in the Dutch Renaissance style. The stunning park with its acclaimed hornbeam avenue is open to the public.

❺ Landskrona

Skåne. 30,000.
Skeppsbron 2, 0418-47 30 00.
Vallå-kraträffen Customized Car Festival (mid-Aug), Gardening Festival (Aug).

The shipbuilding town of Landskrona was granted its charter in the 15th century.

In 1549, the Danish king Christian III built the **Landskrona Slott Citadellet** (Citadel) as protection against the Swedes. This substantial fortress surrounded by a moat dominates the town. Most of the sights can be found in the area around it, including **Landskrona Museum**, with its local history collection, and Konsthallen (Art Gallery) surrounded by a sculpture park.

Environs
In the sound between Sweden and Denmark lies the island of **Ven**, where Tycho Brahe set up his underground observatory, Stjärneborg, in the 1580s. The Tycho Brahe Museum features multimedia shows about the observatory.

There is a ruined castle on Ven, Uraniborg, and at the highest point of the island stands the medieval church of St Ibb. Steep Backafallen is the place for the most spectacular views.

The island can be reached by regular ferries from Landskrona all year round and by fishing boat from Råå during the summer.

Landskrona Slott Citadellet
Slottsgatan. **Tel** 0418-44 82 50.
Open courtyard and exhibition: daily. daily in summer.
 citadellet.com

Landskrona Museum
Slottsgatan. **Tel** 0418-47 31 20.
Open Tue–Sun. **Closed** Easter Saturday, Saturday before Whitsun, Midsummer Eve, 24, 25 & 31 Dec.

Ven
In Öresund 7 km (4 miles) W of Landskrona. from Landskrona.
Tel 0418-47 30 00, 0418-724 20. Tycho Brahe Museum: **Tel** 0418-725 30.
Open May–Sep: daily02. pre-book.

Bosjökloster, originally an 11th-century Benedictine convent

❻ Frostavallen

Skåne. 3 km (2 miles) N of Höör on road 21. 🚌 to Höör. 🚌 ℹ️ Höör Tourist Office, 0413-275 75.
W turisthoor.se

The beautiful countryside around Höör in central Skåne offers something for everyone, from hiking, canoeing and swimming to fishing from the shore or by boat on Vaxsjön lake. With its many restaurants, cafés, hotels and camp sites, Frostavallen is ideal for a day trip or a longer stay. There are playgrounds and all kinds of leisure equipment are available for hire.

Nearby is **Skånes Djurpark**, a zoo specializing in Nordic animals. Popular with children, it has more than 1,000 wild and domesticated Nordic animals. Watch lynx being fed or enjoy a pony ride.

A different kind of experience is offered at **Höörs Stenåldersby**, where visitors can see for themselves what life was like in a Stone Age village. Flint-knapping and bow-making can be tried.

🦌 **Skånes Djurpark**
Frostavallen. **Tel** 0413-55 30 60. **Open** daily. 🐾 📷 🖥️ summertime. 🏠 ♿

🏛️ **Höörs Stenåldersby**
Next to Skånes Djurpark. **Tel** 0413-55 32 70. **Open** Jul by appointment.

❼ Bosjökloster

Skåne. Road 23. **Tel** 0413-250 48. 🚌 **Open** daily. May, Jun & Sep: 11am–5pm; Jul & Aug: 10:30am–5:30pm. 🐾 📷 🖥️ 🖊️ Park: **Open** daily. May–Sep: 8am–7pm; Oct–Apr: 10am–5pm. 🎪 Game Fair (last weekend in Aug). **W** bosjokloster.se

On a peninsula between the lakes of Östra and Västra Ringsjön lies one of Sweden's most remarkable houses. Bosjökloster was built around 1080 as a convent and soon became one of the wealthiest in Skåne. Rich families paid a great deal to secure a place for their daughters, often donating goods and land. This all came to an end with the Danish Reformation in 1536 and its possessions were transferred into private ownership.

In 1875–9 Bosjökloster was reconstructed to a design by architect Helgo Zettervall and became the prime example of his skill for renovating Swedish manors and palaces.

In the early 20th century the property was bought by Count Philip Bonde and today it is owned by his grandson.

The family opened the house to the public in 1962 and now it is one of the most popular stately homes in Skåne with parks and gardens, a restaurant, café, mini-zoo, boats for hire and fishing, too. The park features a 1,000-year-old oak tree. The oldest room in the house, Stensalen, is devoted to exhibitions of arts and crafts.

❽ Östarp

Skåne. Near road 11. 🚌 Kulturens Östarp **Tel** 046-350 400. **Open** 1 May–16 Jun: 11am–5pm Sat, Sun & public hols; 18 Jun–18 Aug: 11am–5pm Tue–Sun; 24 Aug–1 Sep: 11am–5pm Sat & Sun. **W** kulturen.com/ovriga-besoksmal/kulturens-ostarp

In the Middle Ages the town of Östarp was owned by a monastery, but it fell to the crown during the Reformation in the 16th century and was later destroyed. All that remained of the town was Östarps Gamlegård, built in 1812. Bought by Kulturen in Lund in 1923, today this former farmhouse forms the centrepiece of the open-air Kulturens Östarp. It is a living museum using horses rather than machinery to farm the land.

The countryside around Östarp is dotted with castles and stately homes, and Lake Vombsjön is a paradise for birdwatchers and fishermen alike. On the eastern shore of the lake is **Övedskloster**, a beautiful 18th-century manor house set in an elegant park. The main house, "Stora huset", is one of the most stunning Rococo-style houses in Sweden. It was designed by Carl Hårleman and completed in 1776. The park, modelled on Versailles, is open to the public in the summer. Surrounding the estate are woods and meadows, as well as a village of half-timbered houses.

🏛️ **Övedskloster**
Road 11 from Lund towards Sjöbo. **Tel** 046-630 63. **Open** daily (park only). 🐴 Horse trials (early Sep).

The 18th-century windmill at Kulturens Östarp museum

Old buildings of Lund preserved by the open-air museum of Kulturen

❾ Lund

Skåne. E 22. 🏠 85,000. ✈ Sturup. 🚌
🚆 ℹ Botulfsgatan 1a, 046-35 50 40.
🎭 Walpurgis Night (30 Apr), Cultural
Evening (3rd Sat in Sep).
🌐 visitlund.se

Founded by King Sven Tveskägg
more than 1,000 years ago, the
university town of Lund was once
Denmark's capital. In the Middle
Ages it was a religious, political
and cultural centre and site of
a cathedral, **Lund Domkyrka**,
which was consecrated in 1145.
Over the centuries it has been
rebuilt, most recently by Helgo
Zettervall, 1860–80. Look out for
the 14th-century astronomical
clock and a sculpture in the crypt
of the giant Finn supporting the
cathedral's vaulting.

Lund University was
established in 1666, in the
grounds of the bishop's palace,
Lundagård. Now the university
is the second largest seat of
learning in Sweden with
around 47,000 students.

In the heart of the partly
medieval city centre lies
Kulturen, an open-air museum
with perfectly preserved streets,
cottages and town houses.
Kulturen also has extensive
historical collections. The 14th-
century chapel of Laurentii-
kapellet, in central Lund, is
thought to have been the library
of the monastery of St Laurence.

Historiska Museet, containing
Domkyrkomuseet, is one of
Sweden's largest museums of
archaeology, and includes an
exhibition about the history of
the cathedral. **Lunds Konsthall**,

designed by Klas Anshelm,
displays contemporary art, while
the **Museum of Sketches** shows
the development of the creative
process through a series of
original sketches and models.

Environs
The spring flowers are
magnificent at **Dalby
Söderskog**, a national
park 10 km (6 miles)
southeast of Lund, where
there is a forest of elm,
ash and oak trees.

Established as a royal
stud in 1661 by King
Carl X Gustaf, **Flyinge
Kungsgård**, 16 km
(10 miles) northeast of
Lund, combines historic
buildings with cutting-
edge architecture.

🏛 **Lunds Domkyrka**
Kyrkogatan. **Tel** 046-35 87 00.
Open daily. 🎫 🚻 ♿

🏛 **Kulturen**
Tegnerplatsen. **Tel** 046-35 04 00.
Open May–Aug: daily; Sep–Apr:
Tue–Sun. 🎫 🚻 ♿
🌐 kulturen.com

🏛 **Historiska Museet**
Krafts Torg 1. **Tel** 046-222 79 44.
Open Sun–Tue. 🎫 🌐 luhm.lu.se

🏛 **Lunds Konsthall**
Mårtenstorget 3. **Tel** 046-35 52 95.
Open Tue–Sun. 🎫 Thu & Sun.
🚻 ♿ 🌐 lundskonsthall.se

🏛 **Museum of Sketches**
Finngatan 2. **Tel** 046-222 72 83.
Open Tue–Sun. 🎫 🌐 adk.lu.se

🏛 **Flyinge Kungsgård**
Kungsgård, Flyinge. **Tel** 046-64900.
Open daily. 🎫 🌐 flyinge.se

❿ Skanör/Falsterbo

Skåne. Road 100. 🏠 7,000. ✈ Sturup.
🚌 ℹ Videholms allé 1a, Höllviken,
040-42 54 54. 🎭 Foteviken Viking
Week (last week in Jun), Falsterbo Horse
Show (Jul), Sandcastle Competition
(last Sun in Jul), Falsterbo Bird Show
(late summer). 🌐 vellinge.se/turism

Today the twin towns at the far
end of Skåne's southwestern
cape are idyllic seaside resorts,
but they owe their development
to the lucrative herring industry
in the Middle Ages.
Sights include the
ruins of the 14th-cen-
tury fort of **Falsterbohus**,
Falsterbo Museum with
its local history collection,
and **Falsterbo Konsthall**,
an art gallery in the old
railway station. On the
headland is **Falsterbo
Lighthouse**, built in 1793
and still in working order.
It is now a historical monument. Skanör town hall
dates from 1777 and the
church is 13th-century.
Bärnstensmuseet,
the Amber Museum in
Höllviken, near the
Viking earthworks of
Kämpinge Vall, is worth a visit.

Giant Finn in the
cathedral

🏛 **Bärnstensmuseet**
Kämpinge, 10 km (6 miles) E of
Falsterbo. 🚌 **Tel** 040-45 45 04.
Open see website for details.
🎫 🌐 brost.se

The low, single-storey houses in the small town of Skanör

⓫ Malmö

Sweden's gateway to Europe, Malmö is the country's third largest city. It was founded in the mid-13th century. Under Danish rule from 1397 to 1658, Malmö was an important town, but once it was returned to Sweden its position waned until an upturn in its fortunes at the end of the 18th century. Today, thanks largely to the Öresund Bridge and associated development, Malmö is once more in the spotlight. The city has a lively, distinctly European atmosphere and has become a centre for contemporary art and design. The old town is centred on Stortorget with its historic town hall and governor's residence.

Stortorget with Residenset (left) and Rådhuset (right)

🏛 Rådhuset
Stortorget. **Closed** to the public.
The centre of Malmö is the square Stortorget, laid out in the 1530s by the town's mayor Jörgen Kock. Stortorget is dominated by Rådhuset, the town hall, originally built in Renaissance Dutch style in 1546. The cellar remains of the medieval building, which served both as a prison and an inn. In 1860 architect Helgo Zettervall renovated the town hall, giving it a completely new look. A number of changes were made in the cellars, (including the removal of the prisoners). The inn is still standing today and is one of the most popular bars in Malmö.

🏛 Jörgen Kocks Hus
Stortorget. **Closed** to the public.
Stortorget also contains Jörgen Kocks Hus, a large six-storey building with a stepped gable roof, constructed in 1525. Jörgen Kock was appointed mint-master for Denmark in 1518. Four years later he was elected mayor of the city, becoming one of the most powerful men in Malmö. He was involved in the rebellion over the Danish succession and was

captured and sentenced to death, but escaped and was reinstated as mayor of Malmö in 1540.

🏛 Residenset
Stortorget. **Closed** to the public.
In the mid-18th century two buildings Kungshuset and Gyllenpalmska Huset were combined to form the new governor's residence. Around 100 years later the building was given a new façade by architect F W Scholander, to which Helgo Zettervall adapted his extensive redesign of the town hall. Today the building is the home of the county governor.

⛪ St Petri Kyrka
Göran Olsgatan 4. **Tel** 040-27 90 56.
Open daily. 🚻 🔁 🌐 malmo-pastorat.smrt.se
In a street behind Stortorget is Malmö's cathedral, St Petri Kyrka. Built in the 12th century, the church, modelled on St Mary's in Lübeck, is made from red brick. The high tower, constructed in the late 19th century, after two 15th-century towers collapsed, is prominent in Malmö's skyline. The church used to contain limestone

paintings, removed during renovation in the mid-19th century. Only the paintings in Krämarkapellet (the Tradesman's Chapel) are preserved.

The cathedral has treasures from the 16th and 17th centuries when Malmö's prosperity was high. The magnificent 15-m (49-ft) high altar in Renaissance style is beautifully ornamented, painted and gilded. The pulpit dating from 1599 is in sandstone and black limestone. Later additions include the organ front, a masterpiece created to a design approved by Gustav III in 1785. The original medieval organ is said to be one of the oldest working organs in the world and is now in Malmö Museum.

🏛 Moderna Museet Malmö
Ola Billgrens plats 2–4. **Tel** 040-685 79 37. **Open** 11am–6pm Tue–Sun. **Closed** some public holidays. 🅿 🖥 🔁 🌐 modernamuseet.se/sv/malmo

The Moderna Museet in Stockholm is one of Europe's leading museums of modern and contemporary art, and the only one north of Amsterdam with an international collection covering the entire 20th century.

In autumn 2009, the Moderna Museet moved to another location, housed in an old power station that was built in 1900. Architecturally striking in its combination of past and present design styles, this gallery hosts rotating exhibitions that range from the Russian avant-garde to contemporary Swedish art.

Moderna Museet Malmö, occupying an old power station

For hotels and restaurants in this area see pp286–7 and pp297–8

City library Stadsbiblioteket

🏛 Malmö Konsthall

St Johannesgatan 7. **Tel** 040-34 60 00.
Open daily. **Closed** Midsummer Eve,
Midsummer, 24, 25 & 31 Dec.
📅 daily. 🖥 🔲 🏚 ♿
 konsthall.malmo.se

Malmö Konsthall (Art Hall) is
one of Europe's largest spaces
for contemporary art. It arranges
and hosts exhibitions with an
international focus that range
from modern classics to current
artistic experiments.

Past exhibitions have featured
the work of such artists as
Edvard Munch, Paul Klee, Joan
Miró, Alberto Giacometti, Keith
Haring, Andres Serrano, Louise
Bourgeois, Peter Greenaway and
Tony Cragg. Associated special
events organized by the gallery
include theatre performances,
films, poetry readings, lectures
and debates, as well as
extensive educational activities
for both children and adults.

The Konsthall opened in 1975
and was designed by architect
Klas Anshelm with a keen eye for
three main elements: flexibility,
spaciousness and light.

🏛 Stadsbiblioteket

Kung Oscars Väg. **Tel** 040-660 85 00.
Open daily. **Closed** public holidays.
📅 🖥 ♿

The City Library moved into the
"castle" on Kung Oscars Väg in
1946, but by the 1960s there was
talk of expansion. Finally, in 1999,
the new state-of-the-art library
opened. The famous Danish

architect Henning Larsen
renovated and extended the
old edifice, adding the cylindrical
entrance building and the airy
Calendar of Light hall.

The library offers free access
to computer terminals, Wi-Fi
and a media collection. Tools
for digital needs such as
editing, scanning and printing
are available in the Learning
Centre. The library puts on
events for people of all ages
and draws almost one million
visitors a year.

VISITORS' CHECKLIST

Practical Information
Skåne. E6/E22. 🚗 320,000.
ℹ opposite Central Station,
Skeppsbron 2, 040-34 12 00.
🎡 Malmö Festival (Aug), Malmö
City Horse Show (mid-Aug).
Ⓦ malmotown.com

Transport
✈ 30 km (19 miles) E of centre.
🚆 Skeppsbron. 🚌 Skeppsbron 10.

Central Malmö

① Rådhuset
② Jörgen Kocks Hus
③ Residenset
④ St Petri Kyrka
⑤ Humanitetens Hus
⑥ Moderna Museet
   Malmö
⑦ Malmö Konsthall
⑧ Stadsbiblioteket
⑨ Malmöhus/Malmö
   Museum
⑩ Kommendanthuset
⑪ Teknikens och
   Sjöfartens Hus

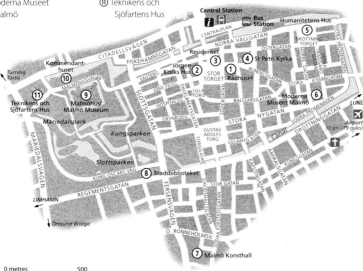

0 metres 500
0 yards 500

For keys to symbols *see back flap*

Exploring Malmö

The centre of Malmö, where most of the sights are located, is compact and easy to explore on foot. Start at Västra Hamnen, near the fortress of Malmöhus, and walk towards the centre, in the direction of the tower of St Petri Kyrka on Stortorget. Lilla Torg and Möllevångstorget are lively squares, and the beautiful parks, such as Slottsparken or Pildammsparken, are a delight to wander through. While the centre retains its old-town atmosphere, futuristic projects are taking shape on the outskirts as part of the visionary new Öresund region.

Malmöhus fortress, built in 1537 and now the home of Malmö Museum

🏛 Malmöhus/Malmö Museum

Malmöhusvägen. **Tel** 040-34 44 00.
Open daily. **Closed** 1 Jan, 1 May, Midsummer Eve, Midsummer, 24, 25 & 31 Dec. 🅿 🎦 by appointment. 🖥 🅿 partly. Ebbas Hus: Snapperupsgatan 10. **Open** Wed.

Originally built by Erik of Pomerania in 1434, the fortress of Malmöhus was largely destroyed as a result of the war. It was rebuilt by Christian III in 1537. Today it is the oldest preserved Scandinavian Renaissance castle in the Nordic region. Originally, it was a fortified royal manor and mint. After the 17th century the fortress was reinforced with bastions, but it fell into disrepair and through most of the 18th and 19th centuries served as a

Calendar of Light hall in Malmö's award-winning library

prison. The solid brick fort is surrounded by a deep moat. Extensive restoration work was carried out in 1932, after which Malmö Museum moved into the building. The museum's collections cover archaeology, ethnography, the history of art and handicrafts, and zoology.

Stadsmuseet (the City Museum) illustrates the history of Malmö and surrounding Skåne with tools, weapons and domestic objects. It contains models, a large textiles collection and an ethnographical collection.

The aquarium housed in the Malmö Museum is a popular destination for families and school groups. They come to observe typical marine life from the waters of southern Sweden, as well as tropical fish such as piranhas and the unusual lungfish, which can live without water and hybernate for several years. There are also a jellyfish aquarium, terrariums with snakes and creepy-crawlies and a Nocturnal Hall filled with bats.

Some of the rooms in the fortress can also be seen. Another popular attraction is the 18th-century tower with its 7.5-m (25-ft) thick walls and original cannons.

Malmö's smallest museum, Ebbas Hus, was donated to the city by its owner Ebba Olsson, and now belongs to Malmö Museum. The museum is a tiny terraced house that has been preserved just as it was in the early 20th century.

Malmö Museer also runs Teknikens och Sjöfartens Hus, Kommendanthuset and Malmö Konstmuseum, which can all be visited on a single ticket.

🏛 Kommendanthuset

Malmöhusvägen. **Tel** 040-34 44 00.
Open daily. **Closed** 1 Jan, 1 May, Midsummer Eve, Midsummer, 24, 25 & 31 Dec. 🅿 🖥 🎦 🅿

In the latter part of the 18th century the storage buildings in the Malmöhus courtyard had fallen into disrepair and Gustav III ordered the construction of a new armoury. It was built outside the fortress in the Bastion Banér and was completed in 1794. By 1814 the fortress's military days were over and it had become a prison. Kommendanthuset (the Governor's House) became the quarters first for the prison's doctor and priest and later the prison governor.

In the 20th century the city of Malmö took over the building and restored it to its original appearance, incorporating it into Malmö Museer. It now houses Fotografins rum, an exhibition hall for photography. It also organizes a number of events and activities aimed at children and young people.

🏛 Teknikens och Sjöfartens Hus

Malmöhusvägen. **Tel** 040-34 44 00.
Open daily. **Closed** 1 Jan, 1 May, Midsummer Eve, Midsummer, 24, 25 & 31 Dec. 🅿 🖥 🎦 🅿

The Museum of Technology and Seafaring is also part of Malmö Museer. Its exhibits cover virtually everything to do with technological development and seafaring, as well as the history of roadbuilding and aviation, engines, and steam engines in particular, just to name a few

The 8-km (5-mile) long Öresund Bridge between Sweden and Denmark, carrying a motorway and railway line

examples on display. Among the exhibits is the delta-winged fighter plane J35 Draken from the 1960s. The technically curious can satisfy their urge to experiment in the *kunskapstivoli* interactive test lab.

The museum also covers the industrial and seafaring history of Skåne. Here, the star exhibits include experiencing the *U3* submarine and the steam launch *Schebo*. For those who have never been in a submarine, it is an opportunity not to be missed. This exhibit is very popular with children.

The shipbuilding and shipping industry and the development of the ports from the 17th century onwards are highlighted, as is ferry traffic, so vital to Skåne. There is also an interactive knowledge park, where you can do your own science experiments.

🚇 Limhamn

5 km (3 miles) SW of the centre.
ℹ️ Malmö Tourist Office,
040-34 12 00. ♿

On the southern edge of Malmö lies Limhamn, a shipping port for lime since the 16th century. Nowadays Limhamn is home to one of southern Sweden's largest marinas, with spectacular views over the Öresund Bridge.

One of Limhamn's sights is the early-19th century small, blue Soldat-torpet (soldier's house), which shows how soldiers used to live. The cottage was inhabited until

1956. The Limhamn Museum Society runs various events at Midsummer and Christmas. Another fascinating sight is the disued limestone quarry, a huge gaping hole that is now a nature reserve.

🌿 The Öresund Bridge

E20. 6 km (3 miles) SW of the centre.
The idea of a bridge between Sweden and Denmark had been discussed for more than 100 years, but it was only in 1991 that both countries agreed on how and where this dream could be realized.

Opened in July 2000, the Öresund Bridge is 8-km (5-mile) long linking Lernacken in

Sweden, southwest of Malmö, and the 4-km (2.5-mile) long Danish artificial island of Peberholm, south of Saltholm. The highest part rests on four pylons, 204 m (670 ft) tall and the roadway is around 30 m (100 ft) wide. The E20 runs along the upper level with a railway along the lower level. It is the longest cable-stayed bridge to carry both a railway and motorway.

On the west side of Peberholm the link plunges into a 4-km (2.5-mile) long tunnel leading to Copenhagen's international airport. The journey by train from Malmö to Copenhagen takes 35 minutes.

The Öresund Region

As part of the EU's vision for a Europe without borders, the Öresund Region project aims to integrate southern Skåne in Sweden with the area around Copenhagen in Denmark, allowing people to cross from one country to another without restrictions. The construction of the Öresund Bridge and tunnel has brought with it enormous benefits for Malmö. It has made the region considerably more attractive to business, cultural exchanges between the two countries are easier and the improved communications have brought more visitors.

Architect Santiago Calatrava's stunning Turning Torso tower, in the Western Harbour, is an expression of the region's faith in the future. Completed in 2005, the 190 m (623 ft) sculptural high rise consists of nine cubes twisting skyward. The Western Harbour waterfront, which has developed into a residential area with offices and services, is internationally recognized as a model for sustainable urban regeneration.

The Turning Torso building soaring 190 m (623 ft) high

Trelleborgen, a reconstructed Viking fortress

⑫ Trelleborg

Skåne. E22. 🚗 43,000. 🚌 🚐 🚤
ℹ Kontinentgatan 2, 0410-733 320.
🎭 Viking Battle (1st weekend in Jul),
Smygehuk Jazz Festival (late Jul),
Palm Festival (last weekend in Aug).
🌐 soderslatt.com

The town of Trelleborg was at its most prosperous in the Middle Ages, when German merchants came to trade salt for herring. Some of the old Skåne houses can be seen in the quarter around Gamla Torg (Old Square) and in Klostergränden, where the ruins of a 13th-century Franciscan monastery still stand. Stadsparken, the town park, boasts a gorgeous rose garden and is worth a visit.

Trelleborgen is a reconstruction of a Viking fortress. It is situated exactly where a fortress thought to have been built by King Harald Blue Tooth in the 10th century, and excavated 1,000 years later, once stood. There is also a Viking museum.

Other sights of interest include **Trelleborgs Museum**, focusing on local history, **Trelleborgs Sjöfartsmuseum** (Seafaring Museum) and **Axel Ebbes Konsthall** (art gallery), with its collection of sculptures by Skåne artist Axel Ebbe.

Environs
A short distance west of Trelleborg lies the village of Skegrie and beside the E6 is **Skegriedösen**, a Stone Age burial mound. The rectangular grave chamber is formed from four stone blocks with a pointed block as a roof, surrounded by 17 foot-stones. This type of Stone Age burial site is only found in southern and western Sweden.

🏛 **Trelleborgen**
Västra Vallgatan 6. **Tel** 0410-73 30 21.
Open times vary; see website.
📷 📷 📷

🏛 **Trelleborgs Museum**
Stortorget 1. **Tel** 0410-733 045.
Open Tue–Sun. 📷 📷 📷 📷 📷

🏛 **Trelleborgs Sjöfartsmuseum**
Gråbrödersgatan 12. **Tel** 0410-195 45.
Open Apr–Nov: Sat & Sun.

🏛 **Axel Ebbes Konsthall**
Hesekillegatan 1. **Tel** 0410-733 056.
Open Jun–Aug: Tue–Sun; Sep–May:
Sat & Sun. 📷 📷 📷

⑬ Ystad

Skåne. E65. 🚗 29,000. 🚌 🚐 🚤
ℹ St Knuts Torg, 0411-57 76 81.
🌐 visitystadosterlen.se

In Ystad the impact of Danish rule and contact with the German Hanseatic League is apparent and the medieval church and monastery communities have also left their mark on the town. Among the many old buildings is the 13th-century **Sta Mariakyrkan**,

Apoteksgården, one of Ystad's many fine half-timbered houses

where every night the watchman in the tower declares that all is well by blowing his horn. In **Karl XII's Hus** on Stora Västergatan the warrior king is said to have spent the night in 1715 following his return from Turkey (see p41).

Ystad has a number of museums, including **Ystads Konstmuseum** (Art Museum), **Charlotta Berlins Museum** (an intact home of a 17th-century nobleman) and a military museum. A fine theatre on the harbourside offers a varied repertoire ranging from opera to stand-up comedy.

Environs
High above the fishing community of Kåseberga lies the stone ship **Ales Stenar**. The 67-m (220-ft) monument comprises 59 stones. This mystical place is well worth a visit.

Bollerups Borg, 20 km (12 miles) east of Ystad, is a 13th-century fortress which has been rebuilt several times. The fort is owned by an agricultural college, but is open to the public.

Sandhammaren is best known for its sandy beaches, but in the past was feared by sailors as new reefs were constantly forming around the cape. The lighthouse dates from 1862.

Marsvinsholms Slott is an estate dating back to the 14th century. The castle is not open to the public, but during the summer visitors can enjoy the park within the castle's grounds or see a play (in Swedish) at the open-air theatre.

Valleberga Kyrka, 17 km (11 miles) east of Ystad, is the only round church in Skåne. It has a 12th-century font by Majestatis.

🏛 **Ystads Konstmuseum**
St Knuts Torg. **Tel** 0411-577 285.
Open Tue–Sun. **Closed** public holidays. 📷 📷 📷
🌐 konstmuseet.ystad.se

🏛 **Ales Stenar**
Kåseberga. Road 9, 20 km (12 miles) E of Ystad. **Tel** 0411-57 76 81. **Open** daily.

🏛 **Marsvinsholms Slott**
On E65, 12 km (8 miles) NW of Ystad.
Tel 0411-577 681. House: **Closed** to the public. Park: **Open** daily. 📷 in summer.

⓮ A Tour of Österlen

The name Österlen means "the land to the east" and refers to the southeast corner of Skåne from Ravlunda south to Ystad and west to the Linderödsåsen ridge. The land is the most fertile in Sweden and across the rolling plains are many of the country's most treasured ancient monuments, grandest castles and forts and oldest churches. Along the coast, idyllic fishing villages are dotted like pearls on a string and the entire region has become a haven for painters and writers.

Apple orchard in spring, Kivik

② Kivik
Kivik is best known for its annual market and apple orchards, but it is also a charming fishing village with winding streets and half-timbered houses.

① Brösarps Backar
This nature reserve is awash with rare flowers. The sight of anemones and cowslips blooming in spring is particularly spectacular. The area has lots of walking trails.

⑤ Tomelilla
Tomelilla is an ideal starting point for a tour of Skåne's rolling countryside. The town is also famous for its art museum, located in an idyllic rural setting.

Key
- ■ Suggested route
- ⸗ Other roads

③ Simrishamn
Old low-rise houses give the town its character. Craftsmen lived around the square, Lilla Torg, and fishermen made their home by the harbour.

Tips for Drivers

Length: around 55 km (34 miles). Major roads are of a good standard, but country roads can be in poorer condition.
Places to eat: cafés and/or restaurants are found in most towns. Hammenhög has a typical Skåne inn, ideal for a lunch break. Äpplets Hus, Kivik, is worth a look.

0 kilometres   10
0 miles   5

④ Glimmingehus
The evocative 16th-century knight's manor offers exciting ghost trails and a taste of medieval cooking.

Heliga Trefaldighetskyrkan, a Renaissance church, Kristianstad

🅑 Kristianstad

Skåne. E22. 🏔 36,000. ✈ 🚇 🚌 ℹ
Stora Torg, 044-13 53 35. 🎭 Sommar i
City (Jul). 🅦 kristianstad.se/turism

The Danish King Christian IV built the town of Kristianstad in the early 17th century and the original street layout with two gates can still be seen today. The town's main sight is **Heliga Trefaldighetskyrkan** (the Church of the Holy Trinity) from the same period, an excellent example of Renaissance architecture. A more recent attraction is the eco-museum **Naturum Vattenriket**, a 35-km (22-mile) stretch of wetlands on the Helgeån river. It is best seen on a guided river tour. Fishing permits can be bought at the tourist office.

Environs

About 15 km (9 miles) to the northeast is **Bäckaskog Slott**, a former monastery dating from the 13th century, which was rented by the Swedish Royal Family during the 19th century. Set in beautiful parkland, the castle is now a hotel with a restaurant. **Rinkaby Kyrka** lies halfway between Kristianstad and Åhus.

The 13th-century church contains paintings from the 15th century depicting the seasons and farming life.

Among the most idiosyncratic objects to be seen at the castle of **Trolle-Ljungby**, 10 km (6 miles) east of Kristianstad, are the Ljungby drinking horn and pipe, which feature in a local legend. On Wednesdays and Saturdays in summer they are exhibited in a window facing the courtyard.

The park of **Wanås Slott**, 20 km (12 miles) northwest of Kristianstad, is a setting for international contemporary art.

Åhus, 18 km (11 miles) southeast of Kristianstad, is a coastal community with half-timbered houses and sandy beaches. It is renowned for its many golf courses, beach handball festival and beach soccer tournament.

🌿 Naturum Vattenriket
Härlövsängaleden 2. **Tel** 044-13 23 30. **Open** daily. **Closed** Mon (winter) and some public hols. 🚻 💻 🚫 🛗 (some parts). 🍴 🅦 **vattenriket. kristianstad.se/naturum**

🏰 Bäckaskog Slott
Fjälkinge, 15 km (9 miles) NE of Kristianstad. Restaurant: **Tel** 044-532 20.

🏰 Trolle-Ljungby
Fjälkinge, 10 km (6 miles) NE of Kristianstad. **Tel** 044-550 43. **Open** (park & courtyard only) Jun–Sep: Wed & Sat.

🅖 Sölvesborg

Blekinge. E22. 🏔 17,000. 🚇 🚌
ℹ Repslagaregatan 1, 0456-100 88. 🎭 Sweden Rock Festival (early Jun). 🅦 **solvesborg.se**

In the Middle Ages, Sölvesborg, on the cape of Listerlandet, was an important trading centre protected by a castle. The town has a Danish feel to it and still retains its medieval charm.

In a former granary and distillery, **Sölvesborgs Museum** traces the history of Lister. The town's oldest building is **St Nicolai Kyrka**, a church with parts dating from the 13th century.

Environs

Southeast of Sölvesborg and at the far end of the cape lies the old fishing village of **Hällevik** with its traditional wooden houses, fishing harbour, smokery and guest harbour. It also has a great little fishing museum and is well worth a visit.

Ferries run from Nogersund to the island of **Hanö** in Hanöbukten bay. It's an attractive place and a popular destination for sailors. The island served as an English naval base in the Napoleonic Wars in the early 19th century and includes a graveyard for British seamen.

🏛 Sölvesborgs Museum
Skeppsbrogatan. **Tel** 0721-58 15 25. **Open** mid-Jun–mid-Aug: Tue–Sun; rest of the year: by appointment.

🅦 Karlshamn

Blekinge. E22. 🏔 19,000. ✈ 🚇 🚌
ℹ Pirgatan 2, 0454-812 03 🎭 Baltic Festival (3rd week in Jul). 🅦 **karlshamn.se/VisitKarlshamn**

Founded in 1664, this town was planned as a naval base, and **Kastellet**, on the island of Frisholmen, was built to defend it. However, the naval port role went to Karlskrona (*see pp192–3*) and Karlshamn became a trading centre with a reputation for the production of punsch. A reconstruction of Punsch-fabriken, the factory which produced the alcoholic drink "Flaggpunsch", forms part of **Karlshamns Museum**. Next to the punsch factory is **Karlshamns Konsthall** (Art Gallery).

Kastellet on the island of Frisholmen, Karlshamn

◀ The stunning interior of St Petri Kyrka, Malmö's cathedral

Other places of interest include **Skottsbergska Gården**, a merchant's house built in 1763 where both the living quarters and tobacco shop can be seen as they were in the 18th century. **Kreativum** is a science centre that will appeal to people of all ages. **Asschierska Huset**, on the square, was Karlshamn's first town hall. The celebrated **Mörrumsån** salmon fishing river runs through the municipality.

Renovated spa pavilions at Brunnsparken in Ronneby

Environs
Around 15 km (9 miles) east of Karlshamn is **Eriksbergs Vilt- och Naturpark**, one of the largest wildlife and nature sanctuaries in Europe and home to golden eagles, sea eagles and deer.

🏛 **Karlshamns Museum**
Vinkelgatan 8. **Tel** 0454-148 68. **Open** mid-Jun–mid-Aug: 1–5pm Tue–Sun; Sep–May: 1–4pm Mon–Fri.
🦽 🖾

🏛 **Kreativum**
Strömmavägen 28. **Tel** 0454-30 33 60. **Open** Fri–Sun; daily during school holidays. 🦽 🖳 **kreativum.se**

⑱ Ronneby

Blekinge. E22. 👥 19,000. 🚄 🚌 🚏
ℹ Västra Torggatan 1, 0457-61 75 70.
🎪 Tosia Bonnadan Market (2nd week in Jul). 🖳 **visitronneby.se**

Founded in the 13th century, Ronneby did not become Swedish until 1658. Prior to that, it was the main town of Blekinge and a busy trading centre. In 1564, during the Seven Years War with the Danes, it was overrun by the army of Erik XIV and burned. About 3,000 inhabitants – the majority of the population – were slaughtered in what became known as the Ronneby Bloodbath. In the early 19th century the town gained a new lease of life thanks to the Kockums foundry and enamel works in Kallinge and the Ronneby Brunn spa.

There are a few old buildings in Bergslagen and around Brunnskällan, and the beautiful 18th-century spa park has been restored.

Environs
Just east of Ronneby is the 13th-century church **Edestads Kyrka**, which once served as a defensive fort. A remarkable 4-m (13-ft) high, 8th-century runestone, **Björketorpsstenen**, lies 7 km (4 miles) east of the town. The text inscribed on the stone is a curse.

Hjortsberga Grave Field on the Johannishus ridge contains 120 ancient burial mounds. About 12 km (7 miles) northeast of Ronneby is **Johannishus Åsar**, a nature reserve set in beautiful pasture land.

⑲ Kristianopel

Blekinge. E22. 👥 1,500. 🚌 🚏
ℹ Stortorget 2, Karlskrona, 0455-30 34 90. 🖳 **kristianopel.se**

Enjoying a beautiful location on a peninsula in Kalmarsund, the little fortified town of Kristianopel has become a popular summer haunt with a guest harbour and tourist facilities. It was built by the Danish King Christian IV and gained its town charter in 1600. At the Peace of Roskilde in 1658 it became Swedish.

Environs
Brömsebro lies 8 km (5 miles) north of Kristianopel, just inland from the coast. Here on the border between Blekinge and Småland is where peace with Denmark was declared in 1645, when Jämtland, Härjedalen and Gotland once more became Swedish provinces. The negotiations were held on an islet in Brömsebäcken river and a commemorative stone was raised here in 1915. At the mouth of the river are the ruins of Brömsehus, a fortress which was captured in 1436 by Swedish rebel hero Engelbrekt (see p39).

Salmon Fishing in Mörrumsån

Every year the salmon fishing in the Mörrumsån river attracts enthusiasts from all over the world. Fishing here dates back to the 13th century when the king held all the rights. The river flows through a beautiful landscape from Lake Vrången in the north to the sea at Elleholm via the lakes of Helgasjön and Åsnen.

A fishing permit is required and these cost between 300 and 1,200 Kr per day. During the 2003 season 1,160 salmon were caught here, the record catch weighing in at 18.36 kg (40.34 lbs).

Laxens Hus (Salmon World) in Mörrum gathers together everything to do with fishing and mounts a variety of exhibitions on, for example, the animal life of the river, and the history of the sport.

Fly-fishing for salmon in Mörrumsån

⑳ Karlskrona

The naval town of Karlskrona is built over several islands in the Blekinge archipelago. Granted a town charter in 1680, it was planned by Erik Dahlbergh and is said to have been inspired by both Versailles and Rome. It centres around the two squares, Stortorget on the island of Trossö, and Amiralitetstorget. The decision to locate Sweden's main naval base in Karlskrona was taken because in winter the fleet was often ice-bound in Stockholm, and an ice-free port was needed further south. Karlskrona has a number of outstanding sights from Sweden's Age of Greatness (see pp42–3). In 1998 the town was declared a UNESCO World Heritage Site on account of its naval architecture.

Fredrikskyrkan on Stortorget, designed by Tessin the Younger in Baroque style, 1744

🏛 Grevagården/Blekinge Museum

Fisktorget 2. **Tel** 0455-30 49 60.
Open Jun–Aug: daily; rest of the year: Tue–Sun. **Closed** some public holidays. 🚬 🖥 🖊 📷 ♿
🌐 blekingemuseum.se

Grevagården on Fisktorget is the main building of Blekinge Museum. The building dates from the early 18th century and was the home of Admiral-General Hans Wachtmeister – the café is set in what was once his kitchen and store room. The museum focuses on the history of Blekinge and Karlskrona's heyday. There is a small Baroque garden reached via a double staircase flanked by two yew trees, believed to date from 1704. Outside on the square stands Erik Höglund's statue of the Fisherwoman.

🏛 Stortorget

The imposing square is said to be the largest in northern Europe. It is flanked, in the Baroque tradition, by two impressive churches, both designed by the architect Nicodemus Tessin the Younger.

Fredrikskyrkan is a large basilica consecrated in 1744, but characterized by the 17th-century taste for Baroque lines. The southern tower has 35 bells which ring three times a day. The other church, Heliga Trefaldighetskyrkan (Holy Trinity), is also known as the German Church after Admiral-General Hans Wachtmeister who inspired it and is buried in the crypt. It was completed in 1709. After a fire in 1790 the church was rebuilt with a lower dome than its predecessor.

The town hall, completed in 1798, has been rebuilt several times. Today it serves as the seat of Karlskrona district court.

Vattenborgen, the now protected water tower, was built in 1863 to supply Trossö with fresh water. It was replaced by a water tower outside the town in 1939.

🏛 Marinmuseum

Stumholmen. **Tel** 0455-359 300.
Open Jan–Apr & Oct–Dec: Tue–Sun; May–Sep: daily. **Closed** some public hols. 🚬 🖥 🖊 📷 ♿
🌐 marinmuseum.se

The fascinating naval museum, opened in 1997, stands on the harbour on Stumholmen, an island which for almost 300 years has been part of the main base of the Swedish navy. The museum was founded originally in 1752 by King Adolf Fredrik to collect and document naval objects in what was known as Modellkammaren (the Model Room).

Marinmuseum covers every imaginable aspect of maritime activity. It holds a particularly impressive collection of figureheads, weapons and uniforms. From an underwater glass corridor it is possible to see the wreck of an 18th-century ship lying on the bottom of the sea.

One of the world's smallest full-rigged ships, *Jarramas*, a training ship for naval ratings, is moored on the quay outside the museum, along with the minesweeper *Bremön* and the torpedo boat *T38*. The Sloop and Long-Boat Shed contains an exhibition of working boats and often allows visitors the opportunity to see how old wooden boats are restored.

Marinmuseum, showcase for Karlskrona's naval heritage

🏛 Gamla Örlogsvarvet

Högvakten, Amiralitetstorget 1.
Tel 0455-30 34 90. **Open** Jun–Aug: daily. 🚬 🖊 compulsory.

The Karlskrona shipyard, founded in 1679, became over time one of the country's foremost military shipyards, a position it still holds today. Fortifications and buildings were constructed to build, equip and repair warships. Additional buildings went

The "Old Man" Rosenbom poor-box outside Amiralitetskyrkan

up on the islands of Lindholmen, Söderstjärna and Stumholmen. The only way to see this vast naval harbour and its many 18th-century buildings and workshops is to take a guided tour. Among the most interesting sights in Gamla Örlogsvarvet are the 300-m (984-ft) long Rope Walk, where the rigging for the fleet was manufactured, the Wasa Shed and Polhem Dock on Lindholmen and Five-finger Dock and the Old Mast Crane in the western part of the shipyard. It is the existence of buildings such as these,

and the fact that Karlskrona is such a well-preserved example of a late-17th-century planned naval base, that has earned the town its World Heritage Site status. Karlskrona was a model for other naval bases throughout Europe in the 18th century.

Close to the entrance to the old shipyard, Högvakten, is Amiralitetskyrkan (the Admiralty church). Consecrated in 1685, it is Sweden's largest wooden church. In front of the church is a replica of the Gubben "Old Man" Rosenbom poor-box.

Today's high-tech shipyard, Karlskronavarvet, run by Kockums, is not open to the public, but new vessels can often be seen along the quay.

Kungsholm Fortress

Tel 0455-30 34 90. book via the tourist office.

Located on a tiny island in the Blekinge archipelago, this remarkable circular fortress has guarded the entrance to Karlskrona from the sea for more than 300 years. It was part of a vast complex of

fortifications that included the Drottningskär citadel, towers and powder magazines.

The magnificent circular harbour at Kungsholm Fortress

Karlskrona Town Centre

① Grevagården/Blekinge Museum
② Stortorget
③ Marinmuseum
④ Gamla Örlogsvarvet
⑤ Karlskronavarvet

GOTHENBURG

The people of Gothenburg have nicknamed their city "the face of Sweden". This maritime metropolis has for centuries been one of Sweden's gateways to the outside world. Historically, the Göta Älv river was the country's only outlet to the west, as can be seen by the remains of fortresses and earthworks that once protected it. Gothenburg is still Sweden's most important port and holds fast to its maritime past.

With its great harbour and seafaring traditions, it is perhaps only natural that Sweden's second largest city is also its most outward looking. Visitors are always welcome and it is not for nothing that the entertainment on offer and the atmosphere have led to Gothenburg being called "Little London".

Today's Gothenburg (Göteborg in Swedish) was preceded by four earlier towns along the Göta Älv river. These were pawns in a period of constant conflict between Sweden and Denmark. The first town was built by Dutch settlers on the island of Hisingen in the early 17th century. It was hardly established before Gustav II Adolf decided in 1619 that it should be moved to the area where the suburbs of Vallgraven and Nordstaden now stand. The inhabitants still came from Holland and the grid of canals is reminiscent of Amsterdam. Gothenburg's 17th-century incarnation was as a fortified town created by the architect and field marshal Erik Dahlbergh. The 18th century saw Gothenburg become even more cosmopolitan thanks to German, English and Scottish immigration. With the advent of steam power, the shipping industry flourished in the mid-19th century, and the city became a prominent shipbuilding centre. The shipyards have mostly gone, but Gothenburg is still a major industrial city and home of the car manufacturer Volvo.

This vibrant little metropolis of 540,000 people (famous for their particular sense of humour) is ideal for sightseeing, and is peppered with green spaces, such as the Botanical Gardens, the Garden Society of Gothenburg and the amusement park, Liseberg. It is a good starting point for excursions to the west coast islands with their pretty fishing villages and smooth rocks for bathing.

Gothenburg's Botanical Gardens, a green oasis not far from the centre of the city

◀ Ships docked at the harbour in Gothenburg, Sweden's most important port

Exploring Gothenburg

A good quick way to get an overview of Gothenburg is to see the city from one of the many excellent observation points such as GötheborgsUtkiken or Sjömanstornet (part of the Maritime Museum). The central parts of the town lie south of the Göta Älv river, but it is easy to cross to the large island of Hisingen by ferry, or by car via the Götaälvbron or Älvsborgsbron bridges, or the Tingstad tunnel. Gothenburg has retained its excellent tram network that provides an ideal way to tour the town, especially on the vintage carriages of the Ringlinjen line. Paddan's white tour boats (see p209) operate trips along the 17th-century canals and out into the lively harbour.

Sights at a Glance
1. GötheborgsUtkiken
2. Barken Viking
3. GöteborgsOperan
4. Maritiman
5. Kronhuset
6. Gustav Adolfs Torg
7. Göteborgs Stadsmuseum
8. Domkyrkan
9. Trädgårdsföreningen
10. Ullevi
11. Röhsska Museet
12. Universeum
13. Världskulturmuseet
14. Liseberg
15. Götaplatsen
16. Skansen Kronan
17. Gamla Haga
18. Feskekôrka
19. Sjöfartsmuseet Akvariet
20. Gathenhielmska huset
21. Slottsskogen and Natur-historiska Museet
22. Botaniska Trädgården
23. The Harbour
24. Nya Älvsborgs Fästning

Feskekôrka fish market reflecting in the water of the Rosenlund Canal

For keys to symbols see back flap

Getting to Gothenburg

The sea has always been the key to Gothenburg and ferries run daily from Norway, Denmark and Germany. Fast trains whisk travellers from Stockholm or Malmö in 3 hours. A well-developed commuter train network and express bus lines ease regional trips. The E6 along the west coast and the E20 from Stockholm meet at the Göta Älv river. Landvetter international airport is Sweden's second largest airport with direct flights to many domestic and international destinations. Gothenburg City Airport is a 20-minute drive from the city centre.

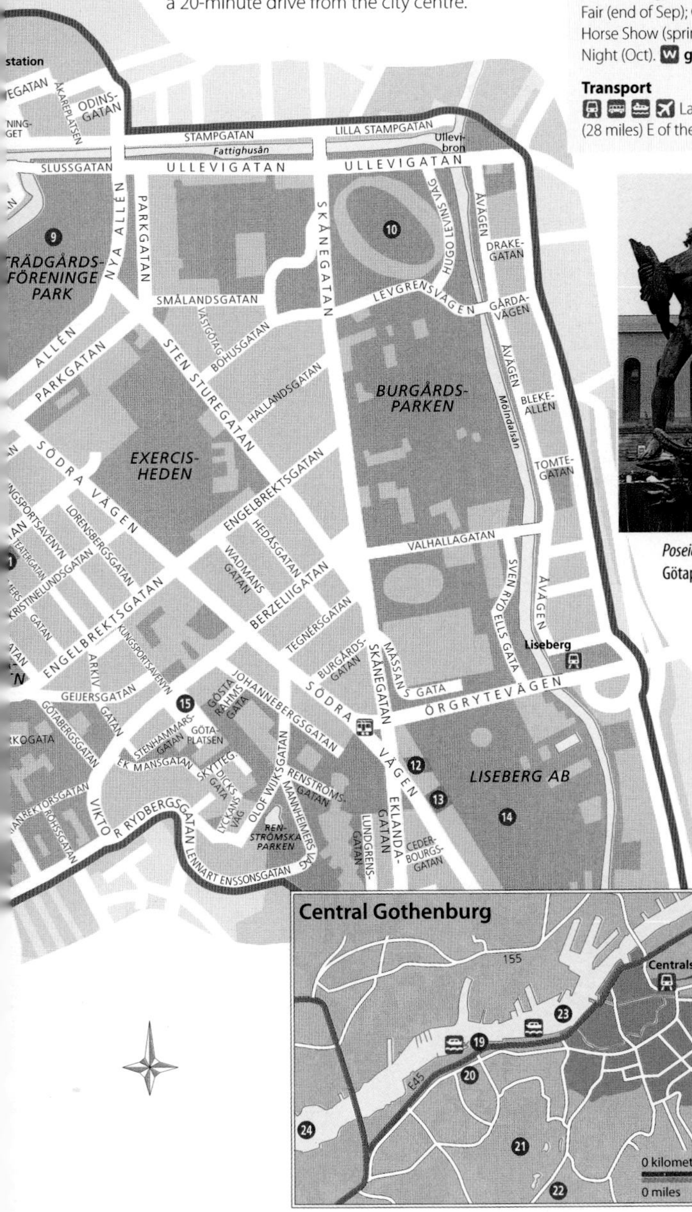

Poseidon by Milles in Götaplatsen

VISITORS' CHECKLIST

Practical Information

540,000. Gothenburg Tourist Information Centre, Kungsportsplatsen 2 & Nordstan, 031-368 4200. Gothenburg Film Festival (Jan/Feb); Science Festival (spring); Gothenburg Cultural Festival (Aug); Jazz Festival (Aug); International Book Fair (end of Sep); Gothenburg Horse Show (spring); Culture Night (Oct). **w** goteborg.com

Transport

Landvetter 45 km (28 miles) E of the centre.

Central Gothenburg

Street-by-Street: Västra Nordstan

This part of Gothenburg is the pulse of the seafaring city, encapsulating almost 400 years of history. On the quayside along the Göta Älv river the maritime world is ever present, with museum ships at anchor and the constant to-ing nd fro-ing of boats and ferries. Spectacular modern buildings, such as GöteborgsOperan and GötheborgsUtkiken, contrast with the city's historic monuments. These include the East India Company building on Stora Hamnkanalen, a reminder of the Dutch influence on Gothenburg's design, and Kronhuset, the city's oldest secular building. Shoppers should head for nearby Nordstan, with its department stores and galleries.

❸ ★ GöteborgsOperan
Generous donations enabled the building of the long-awaited Opera House, which opened in 1994.

❹ ★ Maritiman
In the harbour is one of the world's largest floating ship museums. Both the destroyer *Småland*, launched 1952 (in the background), and the submarine *Nordkaparen*, 1962, can be boarded.

Ture Rinman footbridge

Key

— Suggested route

❼ Göteborgs Stadsmuseum
The former East India Company's classical 18th-century headquarters building is now the setting for Göteborgs Stadsmuseum.

For hotels and restaurants in this area see p287 and pp298–9

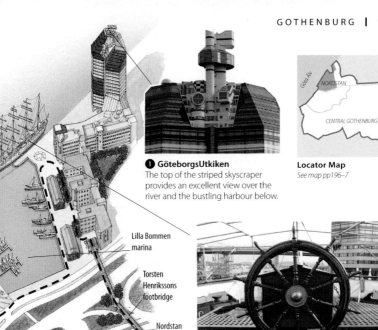

1 GöteborgsUtkiken
The top of the striped skyscraper provides an excellent view over the river and the bustling harbour below.

Locator Map
See map pp196–7

Lilla Bommen marina

Torsten Henrikssons footbridge

Nordstan shopping-mall

2 ★ Barken Viking
After a lifetime on the high seas, the 1906 barque, *Viking*, lies at anchor in the harbour. It now serves as a restaurant and hotel.

6 Gustav Adolfs Torg
"The town shall be here," pointed King Gustav II Adolf, as depicted by Bengt Erland Fogelberg's statue (1854). The anniversary of the king's death at the Battle of Lützen on 6 November 1632 is commemorated in the square every year.

ÖSTRA HAMNGATAN

NEDRE KVARNBERGSG

TORGGATAN

HUS-GATAN

POSTGATAN

GUSTAV ADOLFS TORG

Kungs-torget

NORRA HAMNGATAN

5 Kronhuset
Next to the 17th-century Kronhuset, the Kronhusbodarna sheds are occupied by craft-workers and restaurants.

0 metres		200
0 yards		200

GötheborgsUtkiken (the "Lipstick"), and the sailing ship *Viking*

❶ Götheborgs-Utkiken

Lilla Bommen 2. **Tel** 031-368 42 00. 🚋 5, 10. 🚌 18, 19, 25, 52, 90, 91. **Open** 11am–3pm daily (Jul & Aug: to 4pm). Access by lift every hour. 🅿️ 🖥️

The cheeky red and white GötheborgsUtkiken office building has dominated the Lilla Bommen harbour area since 1989. Architects Ralph Erskine and Heikki Särg's daring design was soon christened the "Lipstick" by Gothenburg wits. Standing 86 m (282 ft) above sea level, it offers incredible views over the harbour and the city centre from the top floor.

❷ Barken Viking

Gullbergskajen. **Tel** 031-63 58 00. 🚋 5, 10. 🚌 40, 42, 52, 99. **Open** daily. **Closed** 22–31 Dec. 🖥️ summer. 🍴 ♿ limited access. 🌐 **barkenviking.com**

One of the world's few preserved four-masted barques from the great age of sail is permanently moored in Gothenburg. The *Viking* was built in 1906 by the Copenhagen shipyard Burmeister & Wain. She sailed the wheat route to Australia and shipped guano from Chile in South America. A fast and beautiful vessel, she logged a record speed of 15.5 knots in 1909. Her days as a merchant ship ended in 1948. In 1950

she became a training centre for sailors and chefs.

Today, the *Viking* is an unusual setting for an hotel and conference centre. In summer the 97 m (318 ft) deck becomes a popular harbourside café, restaurant and bar, with a very lively, bustling atmosphere.

❸ Göteborgs-Operan

Christina Nilssons Gata. **Tel** 031-13 13 00. 🚋 5, 10. 🚌 18, 19, 25, 52, 90, 91, 114. **Open** mid Aug–Jun: in conjunction with performances; other times: phone for info. **Closed** 1 May, Good Friday, 24, 25, Dec. 🎭 🎫 (Swedish and English); book in advance. 🖥️ 🍴 🎁 ♿ 🌐 **opera.se**

The 1994 opening of the impressive Opera House reflected in the water of the Göta Älv river had been eagerly anticipated by western Sweden's music lovers. This is shown by the vast donation wall listing the names of the 6,000 people who helped to fund the new building.

The theatre is designed on a grand scale. The octagonal auditorium seats 1,300 people, all able to enjoy the excellent acoustics. The main stage covering 500 sq m (5,380 sq ft) is complemented by a

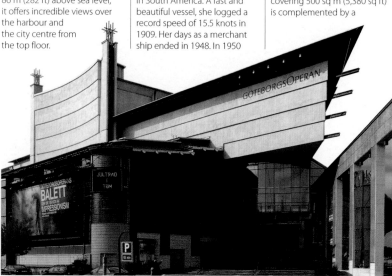

The striking exterior of the riverside GöteborgsOperan, the city's main venue for opera, musicals and ballet

For hotels and restaurants in this area see p287 and pp298–9

further four equally large areas for storing sets. Using advanced technology, it is possible to switch quickly between productions, thus enabling the Opera House to stage a repertoire of opera, musicals and contemporary dance.

Architect Jan Izikowitz was inspired by Gothenburg's harbourside location, the aim of his design being for the "building to be possessed by a lightness which encourages thoughts to soar like seagulls' wings over the mighty river landscape".

The destroyer *Småland*, 1952, in Maritiman

❹ Maritiman

Packhusplatsen 12. **Tel** 031-10 59 50.
🚊 5, 10. 🚌 18, 19, 25, 50, 52, 86, 90, 91, 96, 114, 194, 197. **Open** Apr: Sat & Sun; May & Sep: 11am–5pm daily; Jun–Aug: 10am–6pm daily. 🅿
🆆 maritiman.se

As the city's new port facilities moved further out towards the sea, Gothenburg's inner harbour became denuded of ships. Fortunately, the situation was rectified in 1987 when Göteborgs Maritima Centrum was set up on the harbour. The museum now has 13 vessels at anchor, comprising what is said to be the world's largest floating ship museum.

Vessels include the destroyer *Småland*, built in 1952 at Eriksbergs shipyard on the other side of the river, the submarine *Nordkaparen* (1962), and the monitor *Sölve* (1875), as well as lightships, fireboats and tugs.

Gustav Adolfs Torg flanked on its north side by Börsen, built in 1859

❺ Kronhuset

Postgatan 6–8. 🚊 1, 2, 3, 4, 5, 6, 7, 9, 10, 11, 13. 🚌 16, 42, 50, 52, 58, 60, 86, 90, 91, 99. 🖿 🏠 🅿

A grand brick building in Dutch style, Kronhuset was constructed in 1643–55 and is Gothenburg's oldest preserved secular building. This part of town was originally a storage area for the artillery. The ground floor was converted into a chamber for the parliament of 1660.

Today, the building is used regularly for popular events such as concerts and exhibitions.

Around the square are Kronhusbodarna (the Kronhus sheds), which create a pleasant setting for crafts people whose

Mid-17th-century Kronhuset, one of Gothenburg's oldest buildings

wares include pottery, glass, clocks and homemade sweets. There is also an old-fashioned country store with a café.

❻ Gustav Adolfs Torg

🚊 1, 2, 3, 4, 5, 6, 7, 9, 10, 11, 13.
🚌 16, 42, 50, 52, 58, 60, 86, 90, 91, 99.

Gothenburg's founder, Gustav II Adolf, gave his name to the city's central square. Since 1854 Bengt Erland Fogelberg's statue of the "hero king" has gazed imperiously over the square and Rådhuset (the town hall), Börsen (the Stock Exchange) and Stadshuset (the City Hall).

On 6 November, the date on which the king died at the Battle of Lützen in 1632, a special marzipan cake is made in his honour. It is topped with a piece of chocolate in the shape of the king's head.

Rådhuset, closest to Norra Hamngatan, was designed by Nicodemus Tessin the Elder and completed in 1673. It has a Functionalist extension designed in 1937 by Gunnar Asplund *(see p105)*.

Both the 18th-century **Stadshuset** and Wenngrenska Villa, located on the north side of the square, are used by the city administration. **Börsen**, designed by P J Ekman in 1849, is the city's main venue for receptions and council meetings.

Ostindiska Huset (East India House) housing Göteborgs Stadsmuseum

❼ Göteborgs Stadsmuseum

Norra Hamngatan 12. **Tel** 031-368 36 00. 🚊 1, 3, 4, 5, 6, 7, 9, 10. 🚌 Brunnsparken or Domkyrkan. **Open** 10am–5pm Tue–Sun (to 8pm Wed). **Closed** public holidays. 🅿 pre-book. ♿🅿🅿♿ 🌐 stadsmuseum.goteborg.se

The City Museum is located in the Ostindiska Huset (East India House). The building, designed by Bengt Wilhelm Carlberg and Carl Hårleman, was constructed in 1747–62 as management premises, auction rooms and a warehouse for the East India Company. When trading ceased

Chinese plate in the collection of Göteborgs Stadsmuseum

in the early 19th century the building became a natural history museum, and in 1861 the City Museum was founded.

The permanent exhibitions show the early history of Western Sweden and the importance of the Göta Älv river as a route to Europe from the Viking period onwards. Displays focus on the history of the first inhabitants of Gothenburg and the industrialization and social upheavals of the 20th century. The work of the East India Company and its trade in exotic goods such as Chinese porcelain, silk and lacquer work, is also featured.

❽ Domkyrkan

Västra Hamngatan. **Tel** 031-731 88 00. 🚊 1, 2, 6, 9, 11, 13. 🚌 16, 40, 60. **Open** daily. 🅿 pre-book. 🅿♿ 🅿 daily.

Gothenburg's cathedral, Gustavi Domkyrka, was designed by C W Carlberg in Neo-Classical style in 1815–25. It stands on the ruins of its two predecessors, which were both destroyed by fire.

The East India Company

Attracted by goods such as tea, silk and porcelain, Sweden was one of the countries which invested in trade with China in the 18th century and Gothenburg became a natural centre for this highly lucrative industry. The Swedish East India Company received its charter in 1731 and operated for 82 years, based in Ostindiska Huset

The East Indiaman *Wasa* at Nya Älvsborgs Fästning

(see above). In total, 132 expeditions were made to China in 38 different ships. In recent years interest in the work of the Company has resulted in the building of the East Indiaman *Götheborg*. This exact replica of the ship, which sank off Nya Älvsborgs Fästning *(see p209)* on its homeward voyage 250 years ago, set out to sail the traditional trade route to Canton in 2005. Since its return in 2007, the ship has been moored in the harbour.

In front of the cathedral in Domkyrkoplan is one of the city's preserved watering places: from the late 18th century water was transported here in hollowed-out oak logs from the well of Gustafs Källa to the south of the city.

Gustavi Domkyrka's impressive gilded altarpiece

❾ Trädgårds-föreningen

Slussgatan. **Tel** 031-365 58 58. 🚊 1–5, 7, 9–11, 13. 🚌 21, 25, 28, 58, 59, 60, 514. Park: **Open** Oct–Apr: 7am–6pm daily; May–Sep: 7am–8pm daily. 🅿🅿🅿🅿♿ Palm House: **Tel** 031-365 58 58. **Open** Sep–May: 10am–4pm daily; Jun–Aug: 10am–8pm daily. **Closed** 24, 25 & 31 Dec. ♿ 🌐 tradgardsforeningen.se

Gothenburg has many parks, but Trädgårdsföreningen is in a class of its own. In 1842 work began to transform a marshland south of Vallgraven into beautiful parkland for the benefit of the city's residents.

The flora of five continents are represented in the magnificent Palmhuset (Palm House) built in 1878. The building is filled with flowering camellias, giant bamboo, exotic orchids and plenty of palm trees.

Vattenhuset (the Water House) is carpeted by the twisting roots of mangrove trees and the 2-m (6-ft) wide petals of the giant water lily.

The Rosarium is not to be missed, especially by rose lovers. It has become a leading world collection with more than 1,900 varieties.

There are cafés in the park and Trägår'n, a restaurant and nightclub which has been

Trädgårdsföreningen's Palmhuset, containing plants and trees from five continents in various climatic zones

entertaining pleasure-seeking locals since the 19th century. It is now housed in a new building with a large open-air terrace for partying.

⑩ Ullevi

Skånegatan. **Tel** 031-81 10 20.
🚃 1, 3, 6. 🚌 60. **Open** during events. 🍴♿

Sweden's largest arena, Ullevi, opened for the 1958 football World Cup and over the years has hosted numerous international events. Architect Fritz Jaenecke's elegant wave-shaped ellipse has been renovated and modernized several times. The arena seats 43,000 spectators for sporting events and can accommodate an audience of 75,000 for concerts.

In front of the arena, a statue has been erected in honour of the great Swedish boxer Ingemar "Ingo" Johansson (1932–2009).

⑪ Röhsska Museet

Vasagatan 37–39. **Tel** 031-61 38 50.
🚃 3, 4, 5, 7, 10. 🚌 18, 52, 753, 761.
Open noon–8pm Tue, noon–5pm Wed–Fri; 11am–5pm Sat & Sun.
Closed some public hols (check the website). 🍴🎫 pre-book.
📷♿ⓦ **designmuseum.se**

The country's leading museum of applied art and design, Röhsska Museet contains a marvellous collection of 20th-century Nordic domestic and decorative items. Other parts of the museum are devoted to European applied art, and antiquities from the ancient world, Japan and China. A mere fraction of the total of 50,000

objects can be displayed at any one time. Specialist temporary exhibitions are also mounted.

The museum was founded with donations from financiers Wilhelm and August Röhss. It opened in 1916 as the Röhss Museum of Handicrafts in the beautiful brick building designed by architect Carl Westman.

Next to the museum is the University College for Arts and Crafts Design.

Chinese sculpture, Röhsska Museet

⑫ Universeum

Korsvägen. **Tel** 031-335 64
50. 🚃 2, 4, 5, 6, 8. 🚌 50, 52, 100, 330, 513, 753. **Open** 10am–6pm daily.
📷📱💻🍴📷♿
ⓦ **universeum.se**

Along the Mölndalsån river, not far from Kungsportsavenyn, spreads an area containing several of Gothenburg's major sights and venues, including Liseberg (see p204), Ullevi and Universeum, the largest science centre in Scandinavia.

While the aim of Universeum is to stimulate the interest of

Universeum, designed by Gert Wingårdh and built in 2001

children and young people in science and technology, it provides a fun, educational experience for the entire family.

The centre was built largely with recycled or ecologically friendly materials, and solar panels on the roof ensure that the building has a low impact on the environment.

Exhibits are often interactive and include a tropical rainforest populated by snakes, frogs and spiders; a large aquarium with sharks and rays, as well as a Swedish West Coast tank filled with local sea life; and a space station where you can learn about the life of an astronaut in space.

⑬ Världskultur-museet

Södra Vägen 54. **Tel** 010-456 12 00.
🚃 2, 4, 5, 6, 8, 13. 🚌 50, 52, 91, 513, 761. **Open** noon–5pm Tue, Thu & Fri, noon–8pm Wed, 11am–5pm Sat & Sun (Jun–Aug: noon–5pm Tue–Fri, 11am–5pm Sat & Sun). **Closed** some public hols. 📷📱💻🍴📷♿
ⓦ **varldskulturmuseet.se**

Designed by the London-based architects Cécile Brisac and Edgar Gonzalez and completed in 2005, the icecube-like Världskulturmuseet is a museum of world cultures. The exhibitions, like the building, are far from traditional; they are intended to surprise, provoke and question stereotyped attitudes towards culture and subculture, and are comple-mented by a programme of concerts, films, dance and poetry.

Konstmuseet on Götaplatsen, the city's main square, with Carl Milles' statue of Poseidon in the foreground

⑭ Liseberg

Örgrytevägen 5. 🚋 2, 4, 5, 6, 8, 13. 🚌 50, 52, 91, 513, 761. **Tel** 031-400 100. **Open** last week in Apr–mid-Oct: opening times vary. Christmas opening: mid-Nov–30 Dec. **Closed** Mon & public holidays. 🏊 💻 ⚲ 🏠 ♿ 🅆 liseberg.se

The people of Gothenburg are rightly proud of their amusement park which attracts huge numbers of visitors. Apart from the latest rides, this is the place for dancing and entertainment, shows and theatre performances. It is also a beautiful green park where garden design has always played a major role.

The park's history began in the 18th century when financier Johan Anders Lamberg bought the land and built the first magnificent house,

Flower Girl by Gerhard Henning in Liseberg park

Landeriet, in 1753. He had two passions in life – gardening and his wife Lisa, after whom the new house on the hill was named, Liseberg.

The City of Gothenburg bought the site for the Gothenburg Exhibition in 1923 and founded the amusement park with the installation of a wooden roller-coaster. Other rides followed, attracting 140 million visitors over the past 80 years. "Balder" is said to be the best wooden roller-coaster in the world. It reaches a speed of 90 km/h (56 mph) from a top height of 36 m (118 ft). This roller-coaster is reminiscent of the park's first one. "Kanonen" offers another extreme experience, with its rapid acceleration, sharp loops and turns and 360-degree rotation.

⑮ Götaplatsen

🚋 4, 5. 🚌 18, 52. Konstmuseet: **Tel** 031-368 35 00. **Open** 11am–6pm Tue, Thu; 11am–8pm Wed; 11am–5pm Fri–Sun. **Closed** 1 Jan, Good Friday, 1 May, Midsummer, 6 Jun, 24, 25 & 31 Dec. 🏊 💻 🏠 ♿ 🅆 **konst museum.goteborg.se** Konsthallen: **Tel** 031-368 34 50. **Open** 11am–6pm Tue, Thu; 11am–8pm Wed; 11am–5pm Fri–Sun. 💻 🏠 ♿ 🅆 **konst hallen.goteborg.se** Konserthuset: **Open** for concerts. **Tel** 031-726 53 10. Stadsteatern: **Tel** 031-708 71 00. **Open** for performances. ⚲ 🅆 **stadsteatern.goteborg.se**

The focal point of the city is Götaplatsen, the square at the southwestern end of Kungs-portsavenyn. Here Gothenburg's bastions of culture, Konstmuseet (the Art Museum), Konsthallen (the Art Hall), Konserthuset (the Concert Hall), Stadsteatern (the City Theatre) and Stadsbiblioteket (the City Library) sit in state. In the centre of this grand square, the water plays around Carl Milles' giant statue *Poseidon*, which has become the symbol of Gothenburg.

Götaplatsen was built for the city's 300th anniversary and the Gothenburg Exhibition in 1923, which is why many of the buildings were exhibition premises from the start. Wide steps lead up from the south-eastern side of the square to **Konstmuseet**, designed by Sigfrid Ericson. It contains a rich collection of Nordic art, with key works by Carl Larsson, Ernst

Liseberg's main stage and venue for shows, bands, acrobats and more

Josephson and the Gothenburg Colourists. The Danish golden age, Dutch and Flemish painting and French Modernists are also represented. Pride of place is taken by Furstenbergska Galleriet, a copy of the gallery which the great patron of the arts had in his private palace in the late 19th century. The neighbouring **Konsthallen** shows temporary exhibitions. The bronze lion on the façade is by Palle Pernevi.

Konserthuset on the south-western side of the square was designed by Nils Einar Eriksson and opened in 1935. The foyer is decorated with murals by Prince Eugen (*Grove of Memories*) and Otte Sköld (*Folk Song*) as well as a large tapestry by Sven X-et Erixson (*Melodies in the Square*).

Stadsteatern, built in 1934, reopened in 2002 after extensive renovation to highlight the best of Carl Bergsten's elegant 1930s architecture.

Skansen Kronan fortress (1687) on guard high above Gothenburg

⑯ Skansen Kronan

Skansberget. 🚊 1, 6. 🚌 60.
Tel 031-711 30 33. **Open** 10am–3pm Tue–Fri. **Closed** public holidays. 🅿
🎟 pre-book. ♿ limited access.
🌐 skansenkronan.se

Topped by a golden crown, the octagonal Skansen Kronan fortress dates from Sweden's Age of Greatness (*see pp42–3*). It sits enthroned on the peak of Skansberget. Like its counterpart Skansen Lejonet, near the station area, Kronan is one of the most striking survivors of Erik Dahlbergh's fortifications. It was built in 1687 to protect the city from attack from the south. During the 1850s it was used as a shelter for homeless citizens and has also been a prison.

The fortress is surrounded by Skansberget, a leafy park

Walkers and shoppers in Haga with its pleasant wooden houses

offering excellent views from the top, up steep steps.

⑰ Gamla Haga

🚊 1, 3, 6, 9, 11. 🚌 60, 80, 760, 764, 765.

The former working-class area of the city south of Vallgraven is one of the few places to experience old Gothenburg. The cobbled streets, courtyards and wood-and-stone houses of Gamla Haga are home to crafts-people and lined with small shops, cafés and restaurants.

Haga was Gothenburg's first suburb as early as the 17th century and was mainly populated by harbour workers. During the industrialization of the 19th century a shanty town grew up here and tene-ments filled with people thronging in from the country-side to seek work.

In the 1960s and 70s Haga was fast becoming a slum and threatened with demolition. Widespread public opposition to the plans ensured that important parts were saved and the houses renovated. Some of the *landshövdingehusen* ("county governor's houses") typical of the area can be seen. These were built in the 1880s,

when rules set in 1854 banning wooden houses in the centre more than two storeys high were circumvented – with the governor's approval. Providing the building had a ground floor in brick, as these do, it could have two wooden floors above and not constitute a fire risk.

⑱ Feskekôrka

Rosenlundsvägen. 🚊 1, 3, 6, 9, 11.
🚌 50, 60, 91. **Open** 10am–6pm Tue–Fri, 10am–3pm Sat. **Closed** public holidays. 📷 🚫 ♿

It is easy to see why the wits of Gothenburg nicknamed the fish market Feskekôrka (the fish church). Victor von Gegerfelt borrowed from Gothic church architecture when he designed this market hall in 1874, incorporating a steeply pitched roof and large oriel windows.

The catch from the North Sea is brought here directly, guaranteeing the freshest mackerel and the most delicious shellfish. These days there is more to the market than simply selling fish over the counter – the hall provides a colourful setting for restaurant tables at which seafood specialities can be sampled.

Feskekôrka fish market, a paradise for lovers of fish and seafood

⓳ Sjöfartsmuseet Akvariet

Karl Johansgatan 1–3. **Tel** 031-368 35 50. 🚋 3, 9 and 11. **Open** 10am–5pm Tue–Sun (10am–8pm Wed). **Closed** some public holidays. 🅿 🎧 phone for info. 🖥 🎁 ♿ 🌐 sjofartsmuseum.goteborg.se

The maritime history of Gothenburg and Bohuslän is one of the subjects of Sjöfarts-museet (the Maritime Museum). Set up in 1933, it was funded by the Broström shipping family and is situated on Stigberget, high above the Göta Älv river. The fascinating displays also explore the some-times complex relationship between man and sea, and show how the port has adapted to a changing world.

Those who wish to find out more about marine life can head to **Akvariet** (the Aquarium), which has 25 tanks covering both Nordic and tropical waters. Here, it is possible to see how crabs, starfish and sea anemones live 40 m (130 ft) below the surface. A touch-pool allows visitors to come into close contact with some creatures.

Gamla Varvsparken contains various busts including one of the shipbuilder F H af Chapman (1721–1808) *(see p83).*

Sjömanstornet tower outside the museum is topped by Ivar Johansson's bronze sculpture *Woman by the Sea,*

The sculpture *Woman by the Sea* topping the "sailors' tower"

Gathenhielmska huset, once the home of Privateer Captain Lars Gathenhielm

1933, in memory of the sailors from western Sweden who died in World War I.

⓴ Gathenhielmska huset

Allmänna Vägen. 🚋 3, 9, 11. **Closed** to the public.

The western side of the Stigberget hill was formerly the site of the Amiralitetsvarvet shipyard and it was here in the early 1700s that Privateer Captain Lars Gathenhielm was granted land by Karl XII. His widow built a two-storey manor house here in 1740. It is one of Sweden's best examples of a Carolian wooden house designed to imitate stone.

Next to the house is an open-air museum of small wooden houses showing what a suburb looked like in 1800.

㉑ Slottsskogen and Naturhistoriska Museet

Linnéplatsen. 🚌 49, 52. 🚋 1, 2, 6. Naturhistoriska museet: **Tel** 010-441 44 00. **Open** 11am–5pm Tue–Sun. **Closed** some public holidays. 🅿 🎧 phone to book. 🖥 🎁 ♿ 🌐 gnm.se

Since the 1870s, Slottsskogen has been one of the city's finest green spaces. Criss-crossed by paths, it features dazzling planting, ponds, a zoo and various activities. In spring the azalea valley is ablaze with colour. In 1999, what was then the world's longest border, with over 90,000 flowering bulbs,

was created. There are a number of old cottages from western Sweden to be seen in the park. Areas for sport and outdoor activities include Slottsskogsvallen. The park has several cafés and a restaurant.

Gothenburg's oldest museum, **Naturhistoriska Museet** (the Museum of Natural History), lies in the northern part of the park. Dating from 1833, it moved to Slottsskogen in 1923. Its vast collection of more than 10 million exhibits incorporates animals of all sizes from all around the world, including brightly coloured insects and an African elephant.

The most famous of its stuffed animals is Malmska Valen, a blue whale measuring more than 16 m (52 ft) long, which was beached in Askimviken in 1865. It was stuffed and mounted on a treetrunk. The upper jaw opens, and inside the whale there is a room with benches and wall hangings where it is said coffee used to be served. Now the whale is only open for visits on special occasions.

㉒ Botaniska Trädgården

Carl Skottsbergs Gata 22 A. **Tel** 031-741 11 00. 🚌 58. 🚋 1, 2, 7, 8, 13. **Open** 9am–sunset daily. 🅿 voluntary. 🖥 🎁 ♿ 🌐 gotbot.se

Covering 1,750,000 sq m (432 acres) and containing 16,000 species, Gothenburg's Botanical Garden is one of the largest of its kind in Europe. Just under a fifth of the area has been developed into gardens, while the remainder forms a nature reserve partly consisting of primeval forest.

The gardens began to be designed in 1916 and have been expanded continually ever since. The Rhododendron Valley offers a rich tapestry of

◀ The beautiful *Götheborg*, a replica of an 18th-century sailing ship

dazzling flowers in late spring each year.

The Rock Garden, in a former quarry, contains 5,000 alpine plants from around the world. In early summer the Japanese Glade with its scented magnolias is a delight while autumn sees an oriental riot of colour.

Large greenhouses shelter the plants from the sometimes bitter climate. The controlled environments within recreate a variety of conditions from desert to steaming rain forest. In the tropical house, bamboo and banana plants stretch more than 10 m (33 ft) up to the ceiling and there are 1,500 orchids in the most amazing colours and shapes.

Eriksbergs shipyard with Sjömanstornet and Älvsborgsbron bridge

Botaniska Trädgården, a blossoming oasis in the city

㉓ The Harbour

N of the centre between Götaälvbron and Älvsborgsbron bridges. **Tel** 031-60 96 60. 🚌 to Lilla Bommen. 🚢 from Lilla Bommen or Paddan sightseeing boat from Kungsports-platsen bridge, up to 3 times an hour. **W** stromma.se/en/Gothenburg

Seafaring has been of immense importance to Gothenburg and the harbour and shipyard have long dominated the area along the Göta Älv river. Now the shipbuilding industry is a shadow of its former self and

apart from ferry traffic, the major shipping activities have moved down to the mouth of the river. Yet, although there is little loading and unloading to be seen in the centre of the city these days, three times more goods are shipped today than in the 1960s.

The inner harbour and shipyard area bordered by the imposing **Älvsborgsbron** bridge have been transformed to provide housing, offices and centres for research and education. Nevertheless, the pulse of seafaring can still be experienced either on a regular ferry from Lilla Bommen to **Eriksbergsvarvet** shipyard, or on the white, flat-bottomed **Paddan Boats** which run from Kungsportsplatsen bridge (about a 10-minute walk away) via 17th-century Vallgraven down the river to the inner harbour. The round trip takes about 50 minutes.

GöteborgsOperan is best viewed from the water (see p200), as are **Barken Viking** (see p200) and **Maritiman** (see p201). Eriksbergs shipyard on Hisingen is the home port of the

spectacular East Indiaman *Götheborg* (see p202), which is often out on voyages all around the world. Tours also operate around the island of Hisingen and the outer harbour, and to the Gothenburg archipelago. The **Fishing Harbour** holds an auction Tuesdays to Fridays at 6:30am.

㉔ Nya Älvsborgs Fästning

8 km (3 miles) W of the centre. **Tel** 031-15 81 51. 🚢 from Lilla Bommen. **Open** Jul–mid-Aug. 🎫 🏛 ♿

In 1660 a new fortress on Kyrkogårdsholmen, at the mouth of the Göta Älv river, replaced the dilapidated, centrally located Älvsborg castle to defend Sweden's precious gateway to the North Sea. It was besieged by the Danes in 1717 and 1719, but never captured. In the late 18th century it became a prison which closed in 1869.

Today the fortress is a popular tourist destination in summer; it even has a wedding chapel.

Gothenburg's Inner Harbour

Key
🚢 Ferry and tour-boat boarding
-- Paddan sightseeing route

Frihamnen
Barken Viking
Götaälv-bron
GöteborgsOperan
Eriksbergs-varvet
Goteborgs Maritima Centrum
Fiskhamnen
Sjöfartsmuseet
Göta Älv
Älvsborgsbron

0 metres 1000
0 yards 1000

WESTERN GÖTALAND

Spanning four provinces – Dalsland, Bohuslän, Västergötland and Halland – this attractive and immensely diverse part of Sweden borders Norway to the west, touches on the great forests in the north and reaches to Lake Vättern in the east. Sweden's largest lake, Vänern, lies at its heart. The waters of the Kattegat and Skagerrak wash the rocky shores and sandy beaches along the coast.

Dalsland in the northwest of Western Götaland is one of Sweden's smallest provinces and is relatively unknown even among Swedes. The landscape is hilly and it is often said that the border with Norrland starts here with the mountain area of Kroppefjäll as its southwestern outpost. From the plains of agricultural Dalsland this border can be seen rearing up like a dark forest-clad wall to the west, while the blue expanse of Lake Vänern glistens to the east. The area is sparsely populated, but has a huge variety of wildlife including many species of birds and fish.

In the southwest, Dalsland borders Bohuslän, a coastal province where the smooth bare rocks are dotted with brightly painted little wooden houses. Here fishing and the stone industry have been the backbone of the economy since the Middle Ages, but today tourism is the chief money earner; the population of many coastal communities doubles in summer. Bohuslän's main city is Gothenburg, Sweden's second largest metropolis *(see pp194–209)*.

Västergötland lies between lakes Vänern and Vättern. The area has been inhabited since ancient times and has many prehistoric remains. It was the first region in Sweden to be converted to Christianity and has an abundance of early churches. The country's first Christian king, Olof Skötkonung, is thought to have been baptised at Husaby in 1008 *(see p38)* and two of the medieval royal dynasties had their roots in Västergötland. Some claim that this was indeed the cradle of Sweden.

Halland, the coastal region south of Gothenburg, is also a summer paradise, with its long sandy beaches. There are several towns for shopping and some of southern Sweden's most interesting castles and manor houses.

Gunnebo, a wealthy merchant's 18th-century manor house near Gothenburg, now a museum

◄ Sailing past a typical West Coast settlement in Bohuslän, with fishermen's huts and boats

Exploring Western Götaland

Driving is one of the best ways to explore Western Götaland and experience Dalsand's landscape of lakes, mountain plateaus and rural flatlands, and still have time to spend on the sandy beaches of Halland in the south. Boat trips are a popular way of seeing the small islands and fishing hamlets off the coast of Bohuslän, while the scenery around lakes Vänern and Vättern can be enjoyed from aboard a ferry. Between the lakes, the great forest of Tiveden offers opportunities for hiking. The region as a whole is one in which the ancient past is always present, especially at the UNESCO World Heritage Site of Tanum, where Bronze Age people carved pictures in the rock.

The former lighthouse-keeper's cottage on the approach to Marstrand, now an exclusive summer residence

Getting Around

For drivers, two major roads cross through Western Götaland: the E20, which comes from the northeast via Örebro across the plains to Gothenburg on the west coast, and the E6, which follows the coast northwards towards Norway. Road 45 from Värmland runs south through Dalsland. There are bus and train links between the large towns and populated areas. Regular ferries operate to the majority of inhabited islands along the coast.

Key

▬▬ Motorway

▬ Major road

═ Minor road

— Railway line

— Minor railway

▬▬ International border

▲ Summit

For keys to symbols *see back flap*

Tylösand outside Halmstad, one of the many glorious, long sandy beaches of Halland

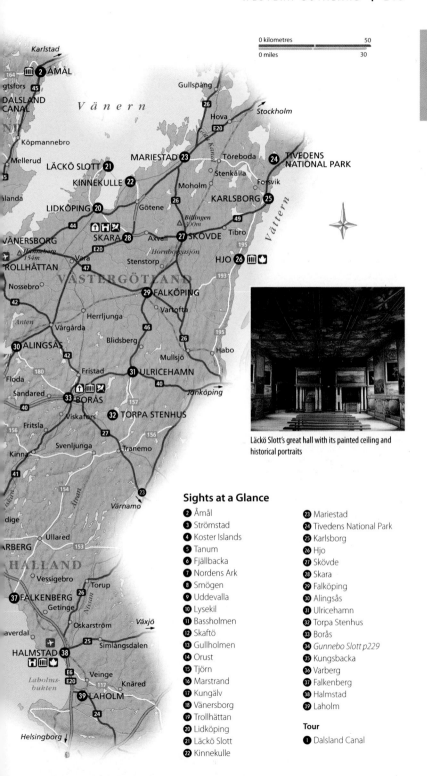

Karlstad

164 **2** ÅMÅL

gtsfors **45**

**DALSLAND
CANAL**

Köpmannebro

Mellerud

LÄCKÖ SLOTT 21

KINNEKULLE 22

LIDKÖPING 20

Götene

44 🏰🏥✈

SKARA 28

E20

VÄNERSBORG

ROLLHÄTTAN

Nossebro

42

VÄSTERGÖTLAND

Herrljunga

Vårgårda

30 ALINGSÅS

42

Floda

Sandared

33 BORÅS

41

Kinna

Fritsla

156

Svenljunga

Tranemo

dige

Ullared

ARBERG

HALLAND

Vessigebro

Torup

37 FALKENBERG

Getinge

Oskarström

averdal

25 Simlångsdalen

HALMSTAD **38**

🏰🏛️

Labolms-
bukten

E6
E20

Veinge

117 Knäred

39 LAHOLM

24

Helsingborg

Vänern

Gullspång

26

Hova

E20

Stockholm

MARIESTAD 23

Töreboda

**24 TIVEDENS
NATIONAL PARK**

Stenkälla

Moholm

Forsvik

KARLSBORG 25

26

Billingen
△ 300m

49

Axvall

27 SKÖVDE

Tibro

195

Hornborgasjön

HJO 26 🏛️📷

Stenstorp

193

29 FALKÖPING

Vartofta

195

46

Blidsberg

Habo

26

Mullsjö

31 ULRICEHAMN

Fristad

180

40

Jönköping

🏰🏛️✈

Viskafors

32 TORPA STENHUS

27

156

Värnamo

23

Läckö Slott's great hall with its painted ceiling and
historical portraits

Sights at a Glance

2 Åmål
3 Strömstad
4 Koster Islands
5 Tanum
6 Fjällbacka
7 Nordens Ark
8 Smögen
9 Uddevalla
10 Lysekil
11 Bassholmen
12 Skaftö
13 Gullholmen
14 Orust
15 Tjörn
16 Marstrand
17 Kungälv
18 Vänersborg
19 Trollhättan
20 Lidköping
21 Läckö Slott
22 Kinnekulle

23 Mariestad
24 Tivedens National Park
25 Karlsborg
26 Hjo
27 Skövde
28 Skara
29 Falköping
30 Alingsås
31 Ulricehamn
32 Torpa Stenhus
33 Borås
34 *Gunnebo Slott p229*
35 Kungsbacka
36 Varberg
37 Falkenberg
38 Halmstad
39 Laholm

Tour

1 Dalsland Canal

● A Tour on the Dalsland Canal

From Bengtsfors the Dalsland Canal carves its way south towards Köpmannebro on Lake Vänern, passing through 19 locks and dropping 45 m (148 ft) to the lake. The scenery varies from beautiful, almost untouched countryside to modern communities, from old ironworks to historic manor houses. The spectacular aqueduct at Häverud is formed from a series of steel plates joined by 33,000 rivets. Both a rail and a road bridge traverse the deep gorge. The canal was designed by Nils Ericsson in the 1860s.

One of the canal's 19 locks making navigation possible

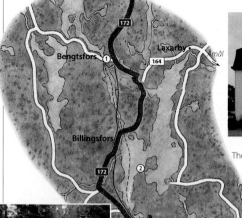

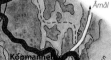

② **Baldersnäs Herrgård**
The manor house stands on a promontory in Lake Laxsjö, on the Dalsland Canal. It is set in a romantic park with paths, caves and artificial islands.

① **Bengtsfors**
The canal trip begins or ends here. Don't miss Gammelgården open-air museum with its wooden cottages and storehouses.

Key

- ▬ Suggested route by car
- – – Route by boat
- ═ Other roads
- ▬ Railway line

③ **Högsbyn Rock Carvings**
Pictures of ships, people and footprints carved in stone 3,000 years ago can be reached by special boat from Häverud, or by car.

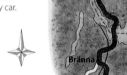

④ **Håverud Aqueduct**
A solution to the problem of crossing a gorge and a 9-m (30-ft) high waterfall was to build four locks and a long steel aqueduct over the waterfall, followed by another lock.

Tips for Drivers

Length: 5½ hours by boat.
Boat route: from Bengtsfors to Köpmannabro or reverse. The boat stops at several points along the way. Return by bus or train in around 1 hour.

0 kilometres 5
0 miles 3

Hotell Skagerack on the harbourfront in Strömstad

❷ Åmål

Dalsland. Road 45. 🔲 12,000.
🚃 🚌 ✈ Karlstad. 🚤 ℹ Marinan,
Hamngatan 3, 0532-170 98. 🎿 Åmål
Blues Festival (2nd week in Jul).
🔲 **dalsland.nu**

Dalsland's only town, Åmål,
was founded in 1643. Thanks to
its strategic location on Lake
Vänern, Åmål soon became
an important market place,
controlling timber exports to
Norway and later acting as a
transit port for timber and iron
to Gothenburg. After several
fires in the 17th century and a
major fire in 1901, a new town
was built on the north side of
the Åmålsån river. Little remains
of the original buildings apart
from a few 18th-century
houses around the town park,
Plantaget. The local history
museum, **Åmåls
Hembygdsmuseum**, whose
three floors house a dentist's
clinic and a flat furnished in
1920s style, can be found in
Snarhögsgården. The Railway
Museum is located in former
engine sheds at Åmål Östra.

At **Forsbacka** on the Åmålsån
river, 7 km (4 miles) from Åmål
towards Bengtsfors, a
mechanical hammer for
producing iron bars was built
at the end of the 17th century.
It was used until the end of the
19th century. Today the 18th-
century house at Forsbacka
ironworks is a hotel and the
old buildings are protected.
A golf course is on the land.

🏛 **Åmåls Hembygdsmuseum**
Hamngatan 7. **Tel** 0532-158 20.
Open mid-Jun–Aug: daily; Sep–mid-
Jun: Mon–Fri. 🖼 🚹 partly.

❸ Strömstad

Bohuslän. E6. 🔲 12,000. 🚃 🚌
🚢 from Sandefjord, Norway. ✈ from
Rygge, Norway. 🎿 ℹ Norra Hamnen,
0526-623 30. 🎿 Winter World Festival
(1st weekend in Mar), Strömstad
Shrimp Festival (Jul), Summer music
(Jul). 🔲 **vastsverige.com**

When Strömstad became
Swedish in 1658 it was just a
small fishing village, but by 1676
it had become a town, acting
as a strategic counter to the
Norwegian towns of Halden
and Fredrikstad. In the mid-19th
century sea-bathing became
the fashion and ever since,
Strömstad, with its glorious island
archipelago and many hours of
sunshine, has been one of
Sweden's major holiday resorts.

Strömstad is a modern town
and its proximity to Norway is
evident from the number of
Norwegian cars and boats. The
Svinesund bridges between
Sweden and Norway offer
magnificent views.

The **Strömstads Museum**
focuses on local history, while
Friluftsmuseet Fiskartorpet is

an open-air museum featuring
fishermen's cottages.

The harbour with bars and
shops is in the centre of the
town and boats from here
serve the islands, including
Kosteröarna. Seal safaris
operate to waters around the
Ursholmarna islands south of
Sydkoster. The nature reserves
on Rossö and Saltö can be
reached by car.

🏛 **Strömstad Museum**
Södra Hamngatan 26.
Tel 0526-102 75. **Open** Tue–Fri; Jul &
Aug: Sat. **Closed** public holidays.

🏛 **Friluftsmuseet Fiskartorpet**
Karlsgatan 45. **Tel** 0526-617 53.
Open summer: daily. 🖼

❹ Koster Islands

Bohuslän. 🔲 300. 🚢 from Strömstad
(about 45 mins). 🚤 ℹ Norra
Hamnen, Strömstad, 0526-623 30.

The islands of Koster are
renowned for their beauty and
their flora. Together they form
a nature reserve. These are the
westernmost Swedish islands
to be inhabited. Sydkoster is
the largest island in the group.
It is greener than Nordkoster
and is best explored by bike.
In contrast, Nordkoster is
much more barren and can
easily be explored on foot.

The highlights of the Koster
Islands' calendar include the
Koster Chamber Music Festival
in July and the lobster festival
in the autumn, when visitors
can sample the freshest
seasonal shellfish and take part
in thrilling fishing trips.

Made for sunbathing, the polished granite rocks on Nordkoster

For hotels and restaurants in this area see pp287–8 and p299

❺ Tanum

Bohuslän. E6. 🏛 12,000. 🚌 🚂
ℹ️ Tourist Office, Tanumshede, 0525-
611 88. 🆆 **tanumturist.se**

The municipality of Tanum
has an extraordinary 525 km
(326 miles) of coastline indented
with fjords and bays. It stretches
from Gerlesborg in the south
to Resö in the north, and is
sheltered by a mass of islets and
skerries offshore. Inland, farms
nestle between rocky outcrops.

Above all, Tanum is renowned
for its Bronze Age rock carvings,
with the earliest dating from
around 1000 BC. Indeed, the
concentration of these pictorial
images and their contribution
to the understanding of Bronze
Age culture is such that they
were designated a UNESCO
World Heritage Site in 1994.
Subjects include human life,
animals, boats and weapons
carved onto smooth rock.

The largest carving, covering
200 sq m (2,150 sq ft), can be
seen at Vitlycke. **Vitlycke
Museum** is well worth a visit for
a fascinating insight into this
form of rock art. The museum
contains exhibitions and a
reconstructed Bronze Age farm.
Guided tours by night, when
carvings that are not visible by
day emerge in the light of a

Fjällbacka's painted wooden houses in the shadow of Vetteberget

torch, are especially enthralling
for any age group.

Around the region, carvings
featuring hunting scenes can
be seen at **Fossum**, east of
Tanumshede; **Tegneby** has
images of ships; and at
Asberget scenes containing
animals, ploughs and axes
can be found.

🏛 **Vitlycke Museum**
3 km (2 miles) S of Tanumshede.
Tel 0525-209 50. **Open** May–Nov. 🅿️
🚗 by arrangement. 🖼 🖥 ✏️ 🎒 ♿

Bronze Age Rock Carvings

The rock carvings at Tanum represent a high point in the artistic
language of pictures and symbols used by Bronze Age people more
than 3,000 years ago. Images reflect daily life and hardships, battles
won and lost, weapons and hunting scenes. Mating scenes, fertility
symbols and the afterlife are also common. The importance of the
sea is reflected in the proliferation of ships and fishing scenes. It is
thought that the rock paintings were primarily of ritual significance,
but the depiction of animals
could have acted as a calendar
to show when various
creatures could be hunted.
Hands and feet as motifs are
thought to be associated with
a godly being too holy to have
his whole body depicted.

Rock carvings can be found
all over the world, with the
oldest dating from 20,000 BC.
Those in Sweden are younger,
since it wasn't completely free
of ice until 6,500 BC. The
carvings at Tanum date from
1000–500 BC.

Bronze Age warrior in a state of sexual
arousal, Tanum

❻ Fjällbacka

Bohuslän. E6/road 163. 🏛 850. 🚌 to
Tanum, then bus. 🚌 ℹ️ Torget, 0525-
321 20. 🎣 Mackerel Fishing World
Championships (last Sat in Aug).

On the coast between
Strömstad and Uddevalla lies
the picturesque village of
Fjällbacka. There has been a
settlement here since the 17th
century and like many other
villages along this coast the
community made a living from
herring fishing and seafaring.
Today, holidaymakers come for
the swimming and boating.

Attractive low-rise wooden
houses and shops line the
narrow streets, but it is the
harbour which is the heart
of the community. Fjällbacka
has a stunning location with
islands offshore and the 70-m
(230-ft) high mountain,

Bust of actress Ingrid Bergman (1915–82)
in Fjällbacka

Vetteberget, creating a precipitous backdrop to the village centre and square known as Ingrid Bergmans Torg. Actress Ingrid Bergman spent many summers in Fjällbacka and after her death her name was given to the square and a bust made by Gudmar Olovson (1983). Fjällbacka is also known as the location of author Camilla Läckberg's series "The Fjällbacka Murders", which has sold millions of books worldwide.

Vetteberget is divided by a huge gorge, known as Kungsklyfta, named after King Oscar II who visited Fjällbacka in 1887 and had his name carved at the entrance to the chasm. This dramatic setting was also used as a location for the film of Astrid Lindgren's children's book *Ronja Rövardotter* (Ronja the Robber's Daughter).

❼ Nordens Ark

Bohuslän. Road 17, 20 km (12 miles) N of Smögen. ☎ **Tel** 0523-795 90. **Open** daily; check website. 🐾 🖥 📷 **w** nordensark.se

This nature park and zoo caters specifically for endangered species. Located in Åby Säteri, it contains animals from every corner of the world, including ancient Swedish breeds such as Gotland sheep and mountain cows, Nordic wild animals such as wolves and wolverine, and

Red panda, one of the many endangered species at Nordens Ark

exotic species such as the Amur leopard and a variety of parrots. Many of the creatures are part of special programmes to protect them from extinction.

To see the animals up close, follow the 3-km (2-mile) walk around the park – and bring binoculars to spot the wide variety of birds. The route takes you between the enclosures via wooden bridges and along gravel paths. Admission in the summer includes a guided tour. The breeding and quarantine areas are not open to the public.

Nordens Ark is a particularly enjoyable outing for families as there are special children's activities throughout the park. Youngsters can find out how animals adapt in relation to their

food, enemies and the environment by being active themselves, trying things out and playing – even adults find these activities entertaining.

Overnight accommodation is also available.

❽ Smögen

Bohuslän. E6/Road 174. 🏔 1,500. 🚌 from Gothenburg. ⛴ 🚹 Sotenäs Tourist Office, Kungshamn, 0523-66 55 50. 🎣 Herring and Shellfish Festival (last weekend in Sep), Tradjazz (first weekend in Aug). **w** vastsverige.com/sotenas

One of Sweden's largest fishing communities, Smögen today is a delightful holiday resort with shrimp trawlers and the daily fish auction providing popular entertainment. Commerce is particularly lively along the wooden quayside.

Ferries operate to the island of Hållö, a nature reserve south of Smögen where there is a lighthouse, **Hållö Fyr**, which has guided seafarers since 1842.

The **Sotenkanalen** links Smögen and Hunnebostrand. Built in the 1930s, the canal is 6 km (4 miles) long and a popular tourist route. **Hunnebostrand** is a typical west coast holiday destination and home to Svenska Hummerakademien (the Swedish Lobster Academy). The village's development was based on stonemasonry.

Wooden houses lining the quays of Smögen's well-protected harbour

❾ Uddevalla

Bohuslän. E6, road 44. 🚗 36,000. 🚌
🚆 🚕 Trollhättan. 𝒊 Uddevalla,
0522-58 71 78. 🏁 Motocross World
Championships (first weekend in Jul),
West Coast Dance Festival (mid-Jul),
Uddevallakalaset (last weekend in Jul).
🌐 **uddevalla.com**

The town of Uddevalla was
famous for shipbuilding on
a grand scale until the 1980s
when an economic crisis forced
the closure of its shipyard.
Uddevalla's history dates from
1498 when it gained its town
charter. Its strategic location
helped trade to flourish, but
also left it open to attack. It
became Swedish in the Peace
of Roskilde in 1658, as the
statues of Karl X Gustav and
Erik Dahlbergh in front of the
old town hall testify. Among
the town's attractions, the
collections at **Bohusläns
Museum** focus on the cultural
and natural heritage of the
region. The museum is situated
by the harbour, and includes
Konsthallen, a gallery for
contemporary art. **Sveriges
Sjömanshusmuseum**
concentrates on the history
of seafaring. **Bohusläns
Försvarsmuseum** (Defence
Museum) has a soldier's
cottage among its exhibits.
Uddevalla also has a pleasant
seaside promenade.

Environs
Nature lovers will enjoy the
unusual shellbanks and
museum devoted to them,
Skalbanksmuseet, in Kuröd,
outside Uddevalla.
The old church of **Bokenäs**
is originally from the 12th
century. The tower and the

Ornate carving on the façade of Restaurang Havsbadet, Lysekil

church's restored ceiling
paintings date from the
18th century. The church is
on road 161, 23 km (14 miles)
west of Uddevalla.

🏛 Bohusläns Museum
Museigatan 1. **Tel** 0522-65 65 00.
Open daily. **Closed** some public hols.
📷 by arrangement. ⬛ ✏ 📷

🏛 Skalbanksmuseet
5 km (3 miles) E of Uddevalla.
Tel 0522-65 65 00. **Open** Jun–Aug:
Tue–Sun. ⬛

❿ Lysekil

Bohuslän. E6/road 162. 🚗 7,500.
🚌 from Uddevalla. 🚢 from
Fiskebäckskil. 𝒊 Strandvägen 9,
0523-130 50. 🏁 Hot Bulb Engine
Festival (3rd weekend in Aug).
🌐 **lysekil.se**

When Lysekil gained its town
charter in 1903 the town
was already an established
seaside resort. Buildings in the
old part of Lysekil, Gamlestan,
are more than 200 years old.
A walk along Strandgatan
reveals the charm of this
old quarter.
The 19th-century sea-bathing
area has been beautifully
restored. There is a cold
bath house, Oscars
Festsal, and the Nordic-
style Curmanska Villas.
The rest of the town is
dominated by the
large, Neo-Gothic
granite church dating
from 1901.
Lysekil lies at the far
end of the Stångenäset
peninsula, with
Gullmarsfjorden –
Sweden's only real "fjord"

in a Norwegian sense – to
the south and Brofjorden to the
north, and here the sea has
always played a major role.
The town's aquarium, **Havets
Hus**, is devoted to the marine
and plant life found off the
Bohuslän coast. Around 100
different species of fish can
be viewed in their natural
habitats. There is a walk-through
aquarium and a multi-media
centre. The town's fishing
traditions can also be
experienced at the Hot Bulb
Engine Festival.

🏛 Havets Hus
Strandvägen 9. **Tel** 0523-66 81 61.
Open Feb–Nov: daily.
🐟 📷 🏛 ⬛ 📷 ♿

⓫ Bassholmen

Bohuslän. Road 161 towards
Fiskebäckskil. 🚌 to Källeviken, then
2 km (1 mile) walk and boat. 🚢 from
Uddevalla daily. 🚆 𝒊 Uddevalla,
0522-58 71 78.

The nature reserve on the island
of Bassholmen, between Orust
and Skaftö, is one of the highlights of the Bohuslän
archipelago. The landscape is
one of narrow valleys, leafy
meadows and pine forest, with
grazing horses and sheep. It is
a particularly attractive area
for walking. In the centre of
the island an old farm stands
amid parkland and trees.
Bassholmen is also home
to a number of traditional
shipbuilder's yards, which
come under the care of the
Föreningen Allmoge Båtar, a
society which works to preserve
and renovate the traditional

Bohusläns Museum in Uddevalla with a display of old
working boats

wooden boats of Bohuslän. Many of these boats can be seen in the museum.

Every summer boating enthusiasts converge on the island for a nostalgic feast to study the craftsmanship involved in greater detail and experience the life of a boatman at the end of the 19th century.

There is a guest jetty in the former shipyard for visiting craft. In summer boats run to Bassholmen from Uddevalla.

Grundsund harbour, edged with original fishermen's huts

Fiskebäckskil, a summer paradise on Skaftö in Gullmarsfjorden

⑫ Skaftö

Bohuslän. Road 161 towards Fiskebäckskil. 🚌 from Uddevalla. ℹ️ Lysekil Tourist Office, 0523-130 50.

The best way to see the island of Skaftö is to walk or cycle around it. The scenery varies between fertile agricultural land, pine forests and bare hills. Skaftö's potatoes and strawberries are justifiably famous. In the centre of the island is Gunnesbo, a favourite spot for children where pony rides and a mini-zoo can be found.

In the far south on the slopes running down towards the sea lies **Rågårdsvik**, a small community overlooking the wide Ellösefjorden and the village of Ellöse, site of the internationally successful Hallberg Rassy shipyard. Rågårdsvik Pensionat provides excellent west-coast cuisine.

Between Skaftölandet and Orust are the winding, narrow Malö straits, made famous by the songs of troubadour Evert Taube, while the beautiful Snäckedjupet separates

Skaftö from the mainland. **Fiskebäckskil** in Gullmarsfjorden is a seafaring community established at the end of the 19th century, featuring a captain's house, richly decorated wooden cottages and romantic gardens. It is also the site of Kristineberg Marine Research Station.

The village of **Grundsund** dates from the 17th century. A canal runs through it past the closely packed red fishermen's huts on the lively quayside, so typical of the west coast. The small wooden church, built in 1799, is well worth a look. Delicious fresh seafood is served in the harbourside inn.

⑬ Gullholmen

Bohuslän. 🚶 150. 🚌 from Tuvesvik, Orust. ℹ️ Henåns Tourist Office, 0304-33 44 94. 🌐 **sodrabohuslan.com**

Dating from 1585, Gullholmen is one of the oldest fishing communities in Bohuslän. In the mid-19th century one of Sweden's early canning factories was set up here. Line fishing on the Dogger Bank in the North Sea produced good catches

Weathervane, Fiskebäckskil

and in 1910 Gullholmen had a fishing fleet of more than 50 cutters. As the fishing industry declined, so did the population and summer residents have taken over many of the houses. Gullholmen is a typical west-coast summer paradise.

Sights include the church, inaugurated in 1799, and the pilot's lookout which was dismantled in 1916, but is now being rebuilt. **Skepparhuset**, a late 19th-century captain's home with original interiors, is well worth a look. South of Gullhomen, as if thrown out to sea, lies the completely barren **Käringön**. The island is so bare that in the past earth for its small churchyard had to be transported from Orust. The charming tightly packed houses are almost entirely used by summer visitors and in the season the popular guest harbour is bursting with life. A fishing cottage houses a small museum. The island can be reached by boat from Hälleviksstrand or by ferry from Tuvesvik.

🏛️ Skepparhuset
Tel 0304-570 70. **Open** six weeks in summer. Contact the tourist office.

Picturesque houses by the harbour in Gullholmen

Mollösund, a typical fishing village on Orust

⑭ Orust

Bohuslän. 🗺 15,000. 🚌 from Stenungsund. 🛈 Hamntorget 18, 0304-33 44 94. 🛥 Boatyard open days (last weekend in Aug).
🅦 orust.se; 🅦 sodrabohuslan.com

One of Sweden's largest islands, Orust's fortunes over the centuries have been tied to the rise and fall of herring fishing. On the southwest coast, the village of **Mollösund** dates from the 16th century, when herring fishing was at its height. A decline in stocks brought poverty, but with the herring's reappearance in the 1750s the population increased, inns opened and refineries for making fish oil from herring developed. The bare rocks of Bohuslän are a reminder of this time; the fish oil refineries needed lots of wood and the coastline was practically deforested.

Most homes had a fisherman's hut on the harbour and even today the houses and huts are closely packed together. There is a strong smell of stockfish hanging out to dry to produce *Lutfisk* for the Swedish Christmas table.

Today Orust is a centre for the manufacture of superior leisure boats. Half the boats exported from Sweden come from here. The boatyards display their craft in the "Öppna Varv" open days.

Fishing net float

⑮ Tjörn

Bohuslän. 🗺 15,000. 🚌 from Stenungsund. 🛈 Tjörn Tourist Office, 0304-60 10 16. 🛥 Round Tjörn Yacht Race (3rd Sat in Aug). 🅦 tjorn.se; 🅦 sodrabohuslan.com

The municipality of Tjörn comprises six inhabited islands. Fishing, boat-building and small businesses are the cornerstones of the economy and in summer the population doubles with the arrival of holidaymakers.

Opened in 1960, the **Tjörn Bridges** offer fantastic views over land and water. Tjörnbroleden, the road linking the islands of Tjörn and Orust to the mainland at Stenungsund, crosses the bridges of Stenungsöbron, Källosundsbron and Tjörnbron over Askeröfjorden. In 1980 Tjörnbron collapsed when a ship collided with it in thick fog; a new bridge opened the following year. At its northern end is an ideal site for camping with great views.

Skärhamn, on the west side of Tjörn, is the island's main town. It has a guest harbour, restaurants and hotel. Sights include **Sjöfartsmuseum** (the Seafaring Museum) and the popular **Nordiska Akvarellmuseet** (Nordic Watercolour Museum), a stunning building hosting exhibitions and courses for amateur painters.

Tjörn Bridge, 664 m (726 yd) long, and 45 m (147 ft) high

Pilane Gravfält, a burial site with more than 100 Iron Age mounds, stone circles, rings and standing stones, is on northwest Tjörn. In the summer, it hosts an amazing sculpture park. Take the road towards Kyrkesund, turn left to Hällene and after 1 km (half a mile) there is a car park.

🏛 Nordiska Akvarellmuseet
Skärhamn. Södra Hamnen.
Tel 0304-60 00 80. **Open** Tue–Sun.
Closed some public holidays.
🎫 🍴 🖊 📷 ♿

The Watercolour Museum, Tjörn, resting on piles in the water

⑯ Marstrand

Bohuslän. Road 168. 🗺 1,400.
🚌 🚢 ⛴ 🛈 0303-600 87 (summer); 0303 833 27 (winter). 🛥 Swedish Match Cup (one week in early Jul), Marstrand Regatta (last week in Jul).
🅦 kungalv.se 🅦 vastsverige.com

Sun, sailing and the sea are what Marstrand is all about. The little town of pastel-coloured wooden houses has its roots in the herring boom of the mid-16th century, which attracted fortune-hunters. But it really took off in the mid-19th century as a fashionable seaside resort. Marstrand built its baths and society arrived.

The town is crowned by the impressive **Carlstens Fästning**, a fortress built in 1666–73 and redesigned in the 1680s by architect Erik Dahlbergh. At one time it was a notorious prison. Tours provide a glimpse into the life and times of the fortress and its inmates in the 18th century. Plays are staged here and feasts held during the summer.

Northwards into the wide waters of Marstrandsfjorden is the rocky island of **Åstol**, almost entirely covered by characteristic white houses and fishing huts. The island can be reached by a 10-minute ferry ride from Rönnäng on Tjörn.

Carlstens Fästning
Tel 0303-602 65. **Open** daily. 🌐
summer and by appointment. partly.

⓱ Kungälv

Bohuslän. E6. 🔺 21,000. 🚂 to Ytterby then bus. 🚌 🚉 Landvetter. 🛈 0303-189 00. 🎭 Medieval Festival (mid-Jul). 🖥 **kungalv.se**; 🖥 **vastsverige.com**

Strategically located between the Nordre Älv and Göta Älv rivers, Kungälv occupies the site of the 10th-century Viking settlement of Kongahälla. It is dominated by the ruins of **Bohus Fästning**, a fortress built by the Norwegian King Håkon Magnusson in 1308. Constructed first in wood and later in stone, the fortress was at the frontline in the constant wars between Sweden, Norway and Denmark. At the Peace of Roskilde in 1658 it became Swedish, but it went on to be besieged no less than 14 times without being captured.

In 1678, 900 Swedish defenders faced 9,000 Norwegians and 7,000 German mercenaries, but still the castle didn't fall. In the 18th century it became a prison and in 1789 all the towers were destroyed apart from the main one known as "Fars Hatt" (Father's Hat).

Red-roofed Gungälv church, situated in the market square, dates from 1679.

Bohus Fästning
Tel 0303-23 92 03. **Open** May–Sep: daily. **Closed** Midsummer's Eve. 🌐 by arrangement.

⓲ Vänersborg

Västergötland. Road E45. 🔺 4,700. 🚂 🚌 🚉 🛈 Railway Station, 0521-135 09. 🎄 Christmas market (Dec). 🖥 **visittv.se**

Vänersborg is otherwise known as "Little Paris" after the poems of Birger Sjöberg (1885–1929). A statue of the local poet's muse, Frida, can be seen in the beautiful Skräckleparken on the lake shore, and a reconstruction of his home is in **Vänersborgs Museum**. Other museums focus on medical history, dolls and sport. The town was founded in 1644 and its Neo-Classical church completed in 1784.

Environs
Just over 5 km (3 miles) east of the town, the steeply sided hills of Halleberg and Hunneberg rise up over the landscape. The hillside forests are a nature reserve featuring a large elk population, which is the focus of an annual royal hunt.

On top of Hunneberg is **Kungajaktmuseet Älgens Berg** where the "king of the forest" is presented in interactive displays. The intricacies of elk hunting are explained and visitors can try their hand at shooting an elk themselves, virtually of course.

Vänersborgs Museum
Tel 0521-600 62. **Open** Tue, Thu, Sat & Sun (also Wed Jun–Aug). 📷 🛗 🖥 **vanersborgsmuseum.se**

Kungajaktmuseet Älgens Berg
Hunneberg. On road 44. **Tel** 0521-27 00 40. **Open** Dec–Jan: Tue–Fri; Jun–Aug: daily; Sep–Nov & Feb–May: Tue–Sun. **Closed** some public hols. 🌐 by appointment. 🏛 🖥 🖊 📷 🛗 🖥 **algensberg.com**

Staircase of locks on the Trollhättan Canal, rising 32 m (105 ft)

⓳ Trollhättan

Västergötland. Road E45. 🔺 56,000. 🚂 🚌 🚉 ⚓ 🛈 Innovatum, Åkerssjövägen 10, 0520-135 09. 🎭 Fallens Dagar (3rd weekend in Jul). 🖥 **visittv.se**

The opening of the Trollhättan Canal in 1800, linking Lake Vänern and the North Sea, marked the birth of Trollhättan as an industrial town. Today, Trollhättan successfully combines high-tech industries such as GKN with a burgeoning film industry that has earned the town its local nickname, "Trollywood".

The town's main sight is the waterfall area where four locks regulate the once wild 32-m (105-ft) high falls. In summer the sluices are opened several times a week to let the mass of water rush freely down river.

The technology centre **Innovatum Science Center** (ISC) features multi-media exhibits on the history and development of Trollhättan. From the Innovatum area, a cable car transports visitors 30 m (98 ft) above the canal to the opposite bank. A short walk leads to the Canal Museum.

Innovatum Science Center (ISC)
Åkerssjövägen 10. **Tel** 0520-28 94 00. **Open** mid-Jun–mid-Aug: daily; other times: Tue–Sun. 🌐 🖥 🖊 📷 🛗

Bohus Fästning, the impregnable 14th-century fortress at Kungälv

⑳ Lidköping

Västergötland. Road 44. 🚗 25,000.
🚆 🚌 📧 *i* Gamla Rådhuset
på Nya stadens torg, 0510-200 20.
W **lackokinnekulle.se**

The town of Lidköping lies at
the heart of the area of Västergötland that is considered to be
the cradle of the Svea Kingdom.
Like so many of Sweden's
wooden towns, Lidköping
suffered a devastating fire in
1849, though some of the 17th-
century buildings around the
square of Limtorget survived.

The Lidan river divides the
town into old and new, and the
two main squares (1446 and
1671 respectively) face each
other across the water. Nya
Stadens Torg (New Town Square)
is the site of a former hunting
lodge, which the founder of
the new town, Magnus Gabriel
de la Gardie, brought here to
serve as a town hall.

Lidköping is known for the
Rörstrands Porcelain Factory and
Rörstrands Museum attracts
visitors in search of bargain dinner
services or simply to enjoy the
showpieces in the museum.

Vänermuseet with the Paleo
Geology Centre is an interactive
science museum.

Environs
Husaby, 10 km (6 miles) east of
Lidköping, encapsulates

Rörstrand ceramic stove, now in the
porcelain factory museum

Läckö Slott, a splendid castle on the shore of Lake Vänern

Swedish history. It was here at
Husaby well that King Olof
Skötkonung was baptised by
the English monk Sigfrid in
1008. A 12th-century church
now stands at the site.
Gösslunda Kyrka, just west
of the town, also dates from
the 12th century. Outside is a
rune stone that was originally
part of the church wall.

To the northwest of Lidköping
is **Spikens Fiskehamm,
Kållandsö**, the only active
fishing harbour on Lake Vänern,
and a lively tourist destination.

🏛 **Rörstrands Museum**
Fabriksgatan 4. **Tel** 0510-612 10.
Open daily. **Closed** some public
holidays. 📷 ✍ 🏠
W **rorstrandcenter.se**

🏛 **Vänermuseet**
10 min walk from the centre. **Tel** 0510-
77 00 65. **Open** Jun–Aug: daily; Sep–
May: Tue–Sun. **Closed** some public
holidays. 🎨 📷 by arrangement.
📷 ✍ 🏠 **W** **vanermuseet.se**

㉑ Läckö Slott

Västergötland. 25 km (15 miles)
N of Lidköping. 📧 from Lidköping.
Tel 0510-48 46 60. **Open** May–Sep:
times vary; see website. 🎨 📷 📷
📷 🏠 **W** **lackoslott.se**

Jakob de la Gardie was the
first to make his mark on
Läckö Slott after it was assigned
to him in 1615. In 2001 Läckö
was named the most beautiful
castle in Sweden. It is
surrounded by water on three

sides. Originally built in the
13th century by Bishop Brynolf
Algotsson, it became the seat
of the bishops of Skara. Count
Jakob and his son, Magnus de la
Gardie, embarked on
remodelling the castle in the
17th century. But in 1681 Läckö
was claimed by Karl XI in his
recovery of crown lands from
the nobility and its contents
were scattered.

Restoration work in the
20th century has revealed more
than 200 rooms, including the
richly decorated apartment of
Princess Marie Euphrosyne, wife
of Marcus de la Gardie, and the
King's Hall with its paintings
of the Thirty Years' War.

Läckö is the setting for art
exhibitions and summer opera
performances are held in the
courtyard. The garden is also
open to the public.

㉒ Kinnekulle

Västergötland. Road 44. *i* Gamla
Rådhuset på Nya stadens torg,
Lidköping, 0510-200 20.
W **lackokinnekulle.se**

The 306-m (1,000-ft) high
plateau of Kinnekulle, known
as "the flowering mountain",
rises from the Västergötland
landscape, providing habitats
for wild flowers, deciduous
woods, pine forests, meadows
and pastures. It is topped with
bare limestone and a 20-m
(66-ft) high lookout tower.
Those not up to the climb

can enjoy the views from the restaurant at Högkullen. Limestone has been quarried here since the 12th century. In summer demonstrations at the remaining quarry show how the work used to be carried out.

The area is peppered with ancient Stone Age and Bronze Age sites.

Forshems Kyrka, just to the east, dates from the 12th century and is known for its stone reliefs. The churchyard of the 12th-century church at **Kinne-Vedum**, 2 km (1 mile) north of Götene, has several lily stones, typical of this area.

㉓ Mariestad

Västergötland. E20. 🔝 15,000. 🚉 🚌
🚆 Lidköping. ⛴ 🛈 Kyrkogatan 2,
0501-75 58 50. 🏊 Göta Canal Swim
(late Jul/early Aug). 🔳 **mariestad.se**

Duke Karl founded the pretty town of Mariestad in 1583, naming it after his wife, Maria of Pfalz. He built the cathedral and lavishly decorated it in the Baroque style. It is well worth exploring the interesting little streets surrounding the cathedral, as these are lined with buildings from the 18th and 19th centuries.

In 1660 Mariestad became the county town of Skaraborg. The former royal manor of Marieholm, on an island where the River Tidan flows into Lake Vänern, was the governor's residence. It now houses **Vadsmo Museum and Mariestads Industrimuseum** (Industrial Museum).

Mariestad's location on Lake Vänern and the River Tidan makes it an idyllic summer town. The Göta Canal *(see pp150–51)* runs through it and

Kanalmuseet (the Canal Museum) is located in Sjötorp just north of the town.

Those keen on rural life should head for **Klockarbolet** in Odensåker, a reconstructed village dating from the 17th and 18th centuries.

🏛 **Vadsbo Museum and Mariestads Industrimuseum**
Marieholm. **Tel** 0501-75 58 30.
Open Wed; other days: by
appointment. 🖼 🎒 🖥 🗂 🏠 ⛴

🏛 **Kanalmuseet**
Sjötorp, off road Rv 26. **Tel** 0141-20
20 50. **Open** May–Sep: daily. 🖼

㉔ Tivedens National Park

Västergötland. Road 49. 🚌 from
Karlsborg. 🛈 Karlsborgs Tourist
Office, 0505-173 50.

On the border between Närke and Västergötland lies Tiveden National Park, an untouched area of rugged wilderness. It was established in 1983 to protect the remaining primeval forest and lakes, of which Fagertärn is the original habitat of the large red water lily *(see p25)*.

The area is very hilly and demanding for walkers. There is a visitor centre at Stenkälla with information on trails, parking and things to see inside the park.

Giant Ice Age boulders, some up to 10 m (33 ft) high, litter the forest around **Trollkyrka**, the hill east of the road by the visitor centre. The mountain's name is thought to be derived from the fact that the site was used by local people who came here to worship after the ban in 1726 on holding religious services outside churches.

Karlsborgs Fästning, a 19th-century wartime hideaway

㉕ Karlsborg

Västergötland. Road 49. 🔝 7,000.
🚌 ⛴ 🛈 Karlsborgs Tourist Office,
Storgatan 65, 0505-173 50. Fortress:
Tel 0505-173 50. **Open** call for
opening hours. 🖼 🎒 🖥
🔳 **karlsborgsturism.se**

In 1819 King Karl XIV Johan decided that a fortress should be built at Vanäs on the shore of Lake Vättern. It was named Karlsborg and was to act as an emergency capital in the event of war; a place of safety for the Royal Family, the national bank and the government. The 90 years it took to build meant that by the time it was finally finished the fortress was out of date and it never had any real significance. Today, however, it is a major tourist attraction. The "town" enclosed within the 5-km (3-mile) long walls is best viewed on one of the hour-long guided adventure tours that run daily in the summer. Action fans can watch *Fästningsäventyret*, an adventure depicting life in the fortress in the 1860s complete with stunt men and special effects.

Outside the fortress, the Göta Canal wends its way towards Lake Vänern, passing **Forsviks Bruk**, which offers an interesting glimpse into Sweden's industrial heritage, with a blacksmith's forge, sawmill and working flour mill.

🏛 **Forsviks Bruk**
8 km (5 miles) north of the centre.
Tel 010-441 43 65. **Open** Jun–Aug:
daily. 🔳 **forsviksbruk.se**

Marieholm, the former governor's residence in Mariestad

Hjo's wooden buildings, awarded the Europa Nostra medal in 1990

26 Hjo

Västergötland. Road 193/194.
🚗 6,000. 🚌 to Skövde then bus.
⚓ ℹ️ Floragatan 1, 0503-352 55.
🎨 Craft Fair (2nd weekend in Jul),
Round Vättern cycle race (3rd
weekend in Jun). 🌐 hjo.se

Mention Hjo and Swedes
immediately think of the
exquisite little wooden houses
dating from the end of the
19th century with their ornately
carved verandas. Hjo is a delightful town to visit. On the shore of
Lake Vättern is Stadsparken, a
park created when Hjo Spa was
founded in the late 19th
century. Villa Svea, one of the
former spa buildings in the park,
houses **Hjo Stadsmuseum** (the
Town Museum). It is worth a
look for its remarkable calendar
clock *Hjouret*, and recreated
rooms from the heyday of the
spa. The park also contains
Fjärilsmuseum (the Butterfly
Museum) and Vätternakvarium,
an aquarium.

Just like the town, the harbour
has medieval origins, but
the present one was built in the
mid-19th century after the
construction of the Göta Canal.
In summer, the *Lok-Hjo-Motivet*
train takes guided tours (daily
except Monday) through the
town starting from the harbour.
The steamer *S/S Trafik* (1892)
runs Sunday tours to Visingö,
and jazz cruises to Vadstena
across the lake.

The Hjoån river valley,
stretching from Lake Vättern
to Mullsjön lake 4 km (2.5 miles)
west of Hjo has several
spectacular waterfalls.

🏛️ **Hjo Stadsmuseum**
Villa Svea, Stadsparken. **Tel** 0503-352
55. **Open** May–Aug. 🦽 partly.

27 Skövde

Västergötland. Road 48/49. 🚗 33,000.
🚆 🚌 ℹ️ Sandtorget, 0500-44 66 88.
🎨 Food Festival (last weekend in
Aug), Skövde Film Festival (Nov).
🌐 skovde.se

Skövde is situated between the
two largest lakes in Sweden:
Vänern and Vättern. According
to local folklore, it became a
trading centre in the 12th century, when pilgrims came here
to honour Sweden's first female
saint – St Elin, or Helena. Skövde
has been destroyed by fire on
several occasions; the last time
was in 1759. The only building
that survived was a single 17th-
century house, **Helénsstugan**,
which today is part of Skövde
Stadsmuseum (Town Museum).
The museum also holds
exhibitions in the main
museum building in Norrmalm.

Kulturhuset, designed by
Hans-Erland Heineman in
1964, houses the
library, an art gallery,
a cinema and a theatre
that often hosts shows
featuring popular
Swedish musicians
and comedians.

The town has
a bustling city
centre with many
independent shops
and several large malls.

Environs
Rising to the west of
Skövde is the 300-m
(984-ft) high **Billingen**
plateau, with views
stretching as far as Lake
Vättern. The area is a
popular recreation spot,
with everything from
hiking and mountain-
bike trails to canoe

rentals, an outdoor swimming
pool and a small fishing lake.
In winter there is a ski slope
and cross-country ski trails.

West of Skövde, on road
49, is the 12th-century
church **Våmbs Kyrka**. The
church was restored to its
original appearance in the
1940s. On the same road,
slightly nearer to Skövde, is
Varnhems Klosterkyrka, a
13th-century three-aisle basilica.

🏛️ **Helénsstugan**
Helénsparken, Skövde Stadsmuseum.
Tel 0500-49 80 69. **Open** summer. 🚶
🔧 by arrangement.

🏛️ **Kulturhuset**
Trädgårdsgatan. **Tel** 0500-44 66 88
(tourist office). 🚶 📱 🔧

28 Skara

Västergötland. E20. 🚗 11,000. 🚌
ℹ️ Biblioteksgatan 3, 0511-325 80.
🎨 Naturum Crane Dance (end Mar–
Apr). 🌐 skara.se/turism

Traditionally an important seat of
learning and a bishopric, Skara is
one of Sweden's oldest towns.
The 11th-century cathedral lies
at its heart, surrounded by a
network of streets following a
pattern set out in the Middle
Ages. On Stora Torget stands
Krönikebrunnen, a well which
on its exterior chronicles
important events in the history

The nave of Skara's Gothic cathedral, founded in the
12th century

For hotels and restaurants in this area see pp287–8 and p299

of Skara and of Sweden. Stadsparken is the site of **Västergötlands Museum** with its local history collection, and Fornbyn, an open-air museum complete with cottages showing how people lived in the past.

Environs
Axvall, 8 km (5 miles) from Skara on road 49, is the location of **Skara Sommarland**, the largest amusement park in Scandinavia, with a water park, go-kart track, camp site and holiday cottages.

Around 20 km (12 miles) east of Skara, Lake **Hornborgasjön** is a popular resting place for birds; every year, in March and April, dancing cranes gather here in their thousands. There is an observation tower and two information centres.

🏠 Skara Sommarland
Axvall, road 49 towards Skövde.
Tel 010 708 80 00. **Open** Jun–Aug (times vary). 🏞 **W** sommarland.se

🦅 Hornborgasjön
Naturum Hornborgasjön, road 189.
Tel 010-224 50 10. **Open** daily in season. **W** hornborga.com

㉙ Falköping
Västergötland. Road 46. 🏘 15,000. 🚉
ℹ Trädgårdsgatan 27, 0515-88 70 50.
W falkoping.nu

Between the hills of Mösseberget and Ålleberg lies the old town of Falköping. Of particular interest are the 12th-century church, St Olofs Kyrka, the medieval wooden houses and the town square, Stora Torget, with Ivar Tengbom's statue *Venus Rising from the Waves* (1931). **Falbygdens Museum** describes the local history.

Environs
Ekornavallen, 15 km (9 miles) north of Falköping, is an important historic burial site from the Stone, Iron and Bronze Ages.

Dalénmuseet in Stenstorp uses sound-and-light shows to illustrate the life and work of the 1912 Swedish Nobel laureate Gustaf Dalén, who invented the AGA oven and was an innovator

in the the field of lighting technology.

Gökhems Kyrka, west of the town, is a small Romanesque apse church without a tower. It dates from the early 12th century. Inside, limestone paintings depict *The Creation*.

Gudhems Klosterruin and **Klostermuseum** north of the town are the ruins of a convent founded in 1160. Today it is a museum. **Karleby**, to the east, is one of three villages along a road which probably existed in the Stone Age. Each farm had its burial site and there are 13 passage tumuli here, including one with a burial chamber 17 m (56 ft) long.

🏛 Falbygdens Museum
St Olofsgatan 23. **Tel** 0515-88 50 50.
Open Tue–Fri & Sun. **Closed** some public holidays.

🏛 Dalénmuseet
Stenstorp, 10 km (6 miles) N of centre.
Tel 0500-45 71 65. **Open** Mar–Sep: Tue–Sun, Jul also Mon; Oct: Sat & Sun. **Closed** Dec–Feb, Midsummer Eve. 🏞
W dalenmuseet.se

㉚ Alingsås
Västergötland. E20. 🏘 25,000. 🚉 🚌
ℹ Estrad, Bryggaregatan 2, 0322-61 62 00. 🥔 Potato Festival (3rd weekend in Jun), Ljus i Alingsås (Oct).
W alingsas.se

Jonas Alströmer and the textile industry have, between them, left their mark on Alingsås. In the early 18th century,

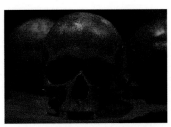
Skulls of Stone Age inhabitants from the Falköping area in Falbygdens Museum

Ahlströmer founded his textile factory and on the proceeds he built **Nolhaga Slott**, a manor which today has a zoo and bird park.

Alingsås Kulturhus contains Alingsås Museum, an art gallery and library, and organizes regular events.

Environs
Gräfsnäs Slottsruin and Park is a ruined castle and park on Lake Anten, 20 km (12 miles) north of Alingsås. An exhibition describes its history. On the road towards Gothenburg lies **Nääs Slott**, a 17th-century castle with an impressive 19th-century interior. Here, the handicraft tradition of western Sweden is cultivated through events and exhibitions. The Midsummer celebrations here are fantastic.

🏛 Alingsås Kulturhus
Södra Ringgatan 3. **Tel** 0322-61 65 98.
Open hours vary. **Closed** some public holidays. 🏞 (free on Fri). ♿

🏰 Nääs Slott
Floda, E20, 30 km (19 miles) N of Gothenburg. **Tel** 0302-318 39.
Open winter: Mon–Fri; summer: daily.
🏞 💼 🖥 ✏ 📷 **W** naas.se

Nolhaga Slott, home of the textile magnate Jonas Ahlströmer, 1727

Ulricehamn Town Hall, 1799, located at the market square

⚠ Ulricehamn

Västergötland. Road 40. ⚠ 9,000.
🚌 🚏 ℹ Järnvägsgatan 2b,
0321-59 59 59. ☑ ulricehamns turistbyra.se

The town of Ulricehamn occupies a beautiful setting on Lake Åsunden in an area rich in historic monuments. Originally known as Bogesund, there has been a settlement here since the 14th century. The old coaching road across Västergötland to Halland ran through the town along Storgatan, the main street.

Textile enterprises dominate the local economy and in Gällstad the knitwear shops south of the town are open daily.

Boat trips on the *M/S Sylvia* leave Ulricehamn and sail to Fästeredssund, or even further south to Hofsnäs, where it is possible to rent a bike for the return trip. There are also themed trips available, including one that takes in several of the mansions around the lake.

Environs

Bystad, a farmstead 30 km (19 miles) south of Ulricehamn, has one of Sweden's oldest wolf traps, a pit measuring about 5 m (16 ft) in diameter and more than 3.5 m (11 ft) deep.

Along the road between Ulricehamn and Mullsjö lies **Näs Gård**. The manor's six historic red-painted buildings date from

the 17th, 18th and 19th centuries and now form a regional cultural centre and art gallery. Concerts and other cultural events are held here.

Södra Vings Kyrka is a medieval gem of a church, dating in part from the 12th century. The artistic decoration is unusually lavish and includes 15th-century limestone paintings in the nave. The stately lectern was carved in Rococo style in 1748.

🚢 M/S Sylvia

For information and bookings, contact the Tourist Office. **Tel** 0321-59 59 59.
☑ rederiasunden.se

⚠ Torpa Stenhus

Västergötland. 30 km (19 miles) SE of Borås. **Tel** 033-28 13 24.
Open May–mid-Sep: Sat–Sun (mid-Jun–mid-Aug: daily). 🅿 🎫 Eng 11am. 🖥 ☑ torpastenhus.se

Standing on a promontory at the southern end of Lake Åsunden is the medieval castle Torpa Stenhus. It belonged

Painting of Saturn at Torpa Stenhus

to the Stenbock family and from the 14th–mid-17th century was an important stronghold for defence against the Danes. In summer, Torpa Slottsteater stages a series of theatrical performances in a splendid outdoor setting.

⚠ Borås

Västergötland. Road 40. ⚠ 105,000.
✈ 🚌 🚏 ℹ Sven Eriksonsplatsen 3, 033-35 70 90. 🎭 Culture Night (first week in May), Harvest Festival (first week in Sep). ☑ boras.com

In 1620 King Gustav II Adolf decided that the textile pedlars of the Knallebygden area should have a town of their own and Borås was founded. Textile factories still line the Viskan river, which winds through the town,

although the industry has lost ground in recent years.

Borås is a green town with beautiful parks: Stadsparken in the centre is popular, as is Ramnaparken where the open-air Borås Museum is located. Also in the town centre is **Borås Djurpark**, a zoo with more than 80 species from all corners of the world. Large enclosures and attractive grounds make this zoo a pleasant family park.

Environs

On the road between Borås and Alingsås lies **Hedareds Kapell**, Sweden's only preserved stave church. Apart from its windows and shingled roof, the little, wooden 16th-century church remains as it was when it was built, complete with original 16th-century paintings.

Textilmuseet (the Textile Museum of Sweden), formerly housed in a late-19th-century spinning shed, has moved into the Textile Fashion Center in Simonsland. Its collection ranges from displays on industrial history to future textiles via art and design.

🦒 Borås Djurpark

Boråsparken, bus line 1.
Tel 033-35 32 70. **Open** May–mid-Sep: daily; Oct & Apr: Sat & Sun; some school holidays: daily. 🅿 🖥 🎫 ☑ boraszoo.se

🏛 Textilmuseet

Kvarteret Simonsland. **Tel** 033-35 89 50. **Open** Tue–Sun. 🅿 🎫 by arrangement. 🖥 🎫
☑ boras.se/textilmuseet

Pink flamingo, one of the many exotic species at Borås Djurpark

❸ Gunnebo Slott

In the 1780s, John Hall, one of the richest men in Sweden at the time, commissioned city architect Carl Wilhelm Carlberg of Gothenburg to design a summer villa and park at Gunnebo. On completion in 1796, Carlberg had created one of the most beautiful and stylistically pure examples of Neo-Classical Swedish architecture. Hall is said to have paid the bill with 38 barrels of gold, but that included everything: the interiors, servants' quarters, orangery, park, kitchen gardens and greenhouse. An adjoining farm made the estate virtually self-sufficient.

The Hall
Three magnificent French windows let in the sunlight, which is reflected on the beautiful parquet floor.

Oval vestibule

Northern Façade
Ionian columns frame the sheltered terrace which opens onto the garden with its neatly clipped trees.

The frieze on the southern gable is made from lead painted to imitate marble.

The staircase leads to the park with its parterres and gravel paths.

The entrance is through the cellar, the starting point for tours.

Ceramic Stoves
The interior design, including exquisite ceramic stoves, is by Carlberg who adopted the light Gustavian style which pervades the entire house.

Park and Gardens
The French-inspired formal garden surrounding the house was also designed by Carlberg, as was the English park, which makes an ideal setting for a walk.

Varbergs Fästning, a fortress on the shores of the Kattegat housing a local history museum

🟥 Kungsbacka

Halland. E6/E20. 🚗 17,000. 🚆 🚌
ℹ️ Storgatan 15, 0300-83 45 95.
🎭 Kungsbacka Chamber Music
Festival (first weekend in Aug).
🌐 **kungsbacka.se**

Although Kungsbacka was
an important trading centre
in the 13th century, almost
nothing remains of the old
wooden town. All but two of
the houses were destroyed in a
devastating fire in 1846. The two
survivors are the red cottage
in Norra Torggatan and the
mayor's house at Östergatan 10.
The pretty pastel-painted
wooden houses that replaced
the old at the end of the 19th
century can be seen around
the square. Today, Kungsbacka
is almost a southern suburb
of Gothenburg.

Environs
Around 10 km (6 miles) outside
Kungsbacka at Rydet is
Mårtagården, a typical 18th-
century sea captain's house.
Tjolöholms Slott, one of
Sweden's more unusual buildings,
lies 15 km (9 miles) south of
Kungsbacka. This magnificent
English Tudor-style mansion was
built for a Scottish merchant
and completed in 1904. It
contained state-of-the-art
features such as vacuum
cleaners, showers and hot-air

heating. The house is
surrounded by lovely parkland.

🏛️ **Tjolöholms Slott**
10 km (6 miles) S of the centre, E6/E20
to Fjärås exit, then road 939. **Tel** 0300-
40 46 00. **Open** Mar–May & Sep–Nov:
Sat & Sun; mid-Jun–Aug: daily. Park:
Open daily. 🎫 🌐 **tjoloholm.se**

🟥 Varberg

Halland. E6/E20. 🚗 25,000. 🚆 🚌
🛳️ from Grenå. ℹ️ Brunnsparken,
0340-868 00. 🌐 **visitvarberg.se**

The coastal town of Varberg
has, since the 19th century,
been famous for its bathing,
whether the cold curative baths
fashionable of the period or
swimming from the rocks and
sandy beaches. The town was
founded in the 13th century,
but little from that time remains
after several fires.
   The harbour area is worth
a look and, in particular,
Kallbadhuset, the renovated
cold bath house in Moorish style
with separate sections for men
and women. The oriental touch
is repeated in **Societetshuset**,
built in the 1880s when the
town's popularity as a spa
was at its height. Today it
houses a restaurant, pub and
disco, playground and mini-
golf. On summer evenings
concerts are held on the stage
in the park.
   Guarding the
approach from the sea
is the mighty Varbergs
Fästning. Most of the
fortress was built in
the 17th century with
parts dating from
the 13th century.
Today it houses a
museum, **Hallands
Kulturhistoriska
Museum**, focusing

on the history of Halland. The
museum's biggest attraction
is the 14th-century Bocksten
Man whose body was
discovered in a bog still dressed
in a complete outfit from the
Middle Ages. The notorious
bullet which killed King Karl XII
in 1718 is also on show. An
outpost of the museum is
Båtmuseet, the boat museum
in Galtabäck, 10 km (6 miles)
south of Varberg, displaying
traditional boats and models.

🏛️ **Hallands Kulturhistoriska
Museum**
Varbergs Fästning. **Tel** 0340-828
30. **Open** Tue–Sun. 🎫 🎫 by
arrangement. 🌐 **hkm.varberg.se**

🟥 Falkenberg

Halland. E6/E20. 🚗 19,000. 🚆 🚌
ℹ️ Holgersgatan 11, 0346-88 61 00.
🎭 Song festival (first week in Jul).
🌐 **visitfalkenberg.se**

A town with medieval roots,
Falkenberg stands at the mouth
of the River Ätran. The oldest
areas of the town still have their
wooden buildings, including
St Laurentii Kyrka (St Laurence's
church), parts of which date
from the 14th century.
   The pottery **Törngrens
Krukmakeri** (1789) is still in
operation, run by the seventh
generation of potters.
   Falkenbergs Museum is
housed in a half-timbered
granary at Söderbron. The
grain dryer is a lofty landmark
in the old town. The museum
features a faithful reproduction
of an apartment from the
1950s and the café has a
working jukebox.
   Falkenberg has several
interesting smaller museums,
including **Falkenbergs
Hembygdsmuseum** (Rural

Tjolöholms Slott, an eccentric English Tudor-style
mansion with Art Nouveau interiors

Museum) in St Lars Kyrkogata, a rural museum with a section on salmon fishing. The **Fotomuseet Olympia** in Sandgatan is housed in the town's first cinema (1912) and displays cameras and photos.

Environs
North of the town is **Morups Tånge**, known for its lighthouse built in the mid-19th century. The beach below is a nature reserve, a wetland area of international interest and a home for waders.

🏛 **Törngrens Krukmakeri**
Krukmakaregatan 4. **Tel** 0346-103 54.
Open daily. 📷 Nygatan 34 (Mon–Sat).

🏛 **Falkenbergs Museum**
Skepparesträtet 2. **Tel** 0346-88 61 25.
Open Sep–May: Tue–Thu & Sat; Jun–Aug: Tue–Sun. 📷

Fly-fishing in the salmon-rich River Ätran in Falkenberg

❸❽ Halmstad

Halland. E6/E20. 🏙 90,000. 🚌 🚢
🚲 🚢 from Grenå. 🛈 Tourist Office, Fattighuset, Köpmansgatan 20, 035-12 02 00. 🎭 Street Theatre Festival (Aug). 🌐 **halmstad.se**

At the point where the River Nissan flows into Laholmsbukten bay lies Halmstad. In the Middle Ages it was the largest town on the west coast. Today, the medieval inner city with its half-timbered architecture is classified as being of national interest. Kirsten Munk's house on Storgatan is a 17th-century building in green-glazed Dutch brick. Craftsmen can be seen at work in **Fattighuset**, Lilla Torg, a former poorhouse dated 1859.

Several modern artists have left their mark on the town and Carl Milles' fountain *Europa and the Bull* in Stora Torg and Picasso's *Woman's Head*, which

The former training ship *Najaden* against a backdrop of Halmstad Slott

stands between the bridges over the river Nissan, are easily encountered on a stroll.

Halmstad Slott, a 17th-century castle, was built by the Danish King Christian IV. The former training ship *Najaden* is moored on the quayside in front of the castle. Visitors have access to the courtyard, however the castle is closed to the public.

Hallands Konstmuseum (the County Museum) has a wide collection of art and cultural history.

Environs
Äventyrslandet, 9 km (5.5 miles) west of Halmstad, is a fun destination for children, with its water park, funfair, dinosaur park and circus show. To the north, the popular summer resorts of Tylösand, Haverdal and Frösakull spread out along the coast.
Simlångsdalen, around 20 km (12 miles) from Halmstad on road 25, has several natural attractions including Danska Fall in the River Assman, a 36-m (118-ft) high waterfall.

🏛 **Fattighuset**
Lilla Torg. **Tel** 035-12 02 00.
Open Mon–Sat. 📷

🏛 **Hallands Konstmuseum**
Tollsgatan. **Tel** 035-16 23 00.
Open Tue–Sun. 🖥 📷
🌐 **hallands konstmuseum.se**

🎡 **Äventyrslandet**
Gamla Tylösandsvägen 1.
🚌 free, from Halmstad.
Tel 035-10 84 60.
Open Jun–Aug: daily.
🚲 🌐 **aventyrs landet.se**

❸❾ Laholm

Halland. Road 24. 🏙 6,000. 🚌 🚢
🛈 Teckningsmuseet, Hästtorget, 0430-154 50. 🎣 Salmon Festival (mid-Sep).

Halland's oldest and smallest town, Laholm is primarily associated with the long sandy beaches around the bay of Laholmsbukten. Mellbystrand, on the bay 6 km (4 miles) to the west of the town, throngs with holidaymakers in summer. The River Lagan also attracts visitors for the salmon fishing.

Laholm itself is characterized by its winding streets and low houses, reminiscent of Danish rule before 1645. Of the buildings around the square, the 200-year-old **Rådhuset** (town hall) is particularly beautiful. On the western gable there is an automaton symbolizing the meeting in Laholm in 1278 between the Swedish King Magnus Ladulås and Danish King Erik Klipping.

The renovated old fire station, with a beautiful view over the Lagan, houses the tourist office, as well as Teckningsmuseet, a museum of drawings with large, airy galleries.

Laholm's tidy rows of houses bearing the hallmarks of the town's Danish past

WESTERN SVEALAND

Värmland, Närke and Dalarna, with their rich rural heritage, colourful folk costumes, red-painted wooden houses and pastoral scenes, attracted visitors long before the onset of tourism. Stretching from the flatlands of Närke to the mountains of Dalarna, this region is known for its annual ski race and Midsummer festivities, as well as its industrial heritage based on mining and forestry.

Large expanses of water dominate all three provinces. Southern Värmland encompasses the huge Lake Vänern, which is also the end of the line for the arterial Klarälven river. The beautiful Fryken lakes provided inspiration for one of the province's well-known authors, Selma Lagerlöf (see p237). Her home, Mårbacka, was in this region where so many of her adventures are set. There is plenty of scope for outdoor activities in Värmland, including boating, canoeing, rafting on the Klarälven river and fishing. The forests have exciting trails where walkers are unlucky if they don't see an elk, and on wildlife safaris there is even the chance of glimpsing one of the big four predators – bear, wolf, lynx or wolverine.

Närke, one of Sweden's smallest provinces, is sandwiched between two large lakes, Hjälmaren and Vättern.

The centre of the province is dominated by the fertile Närke flatlands, encircled by forest, including the once infamous haunt of bandits, Tiveden, in the south. Örebro, Western Svealand's largest metropolis and Närke's county town, has all the charm of a small town.

Dalarna has the beautiful Siljan lake and the Dalälven river with its arms stretching into the mountains. The province offers more contrasts than most – from the gentle farmland around Siljan to the mountainous north. Every year, on the first Sunday of March, these are linked by the Vasaloppet race (see p249), when tens of thousands of skiers head from Sälen down to Mora. Midsummer celebrations on Siljan are emblematic of Dalarna. Villages compete to see who has the most stylish maypole, the most accomplished musicians and the best folk dancers.

Rustic interior of Gammelgården in Mora, Dalarna

◀ Swedes in traditional costume performing a folk dance in the Dalarna region

Exploring Western Svealand

Fertile agricultural land spreads out around the major lakes, Vänern, Vättern, Hjälmaren and Siljan, and along the river valleys, giving way to a predominantly forested landscape. The region provides ample opportunities for nature lovers, with its abundance of wildlife, and for anglers, who will easily find a good catch. The mountains in Dalarna are the setting for some of the country's most popular ski resorts, walking trails and national parks. Motorists have many attractive small roads to choose from, while the Fryksdalsbanan and Inlandsbanan railway lines guarantee spectacular sights from the train window and leisurely boat trips provide glorious views from the water.

Author and Nobel laureate Selma Lagerlöf's Mårbacka, one of Värmland's many stately homes

Getting Around

Passing through Örebro and Karlstad, the E18 motorway crossing from Stockholm to Oslo is the main artery for traffic to this region. Travelling up into Värmland and Dalarna, the roads follow the river valleys, where the local population is also concentrated. Rail links are good to the southern parts of the provinces, but the northern areas can only be reached by car or bus. Between towns and popular tourist areas the bus services are quite frequent, but they can be patchy in rural areas. In summer, boats ply the major lakes of Vänern, Hjälmaren and Siljan.

Key

▬▬	Motorway
▬	Major road
═	Minor road
▬	Main railway
⎯	Minor railway
▬▬	International border
▲	Summit

For keys to symbols see back flap

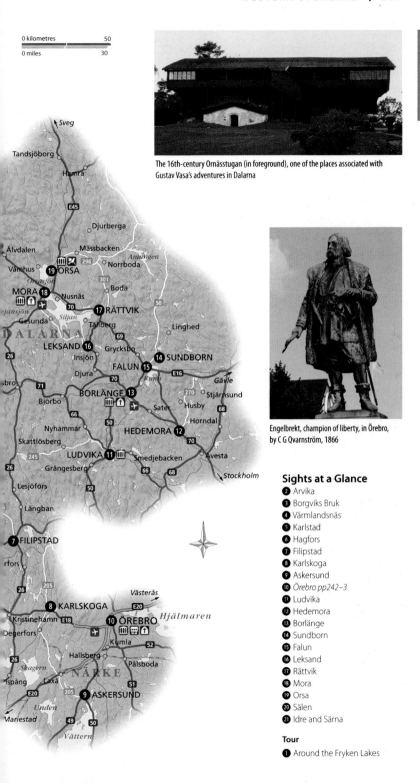

0 kilometres 50

0 miles 30

The 16th-century Ornässtugan (in foreground), one of the places associated with Gustav Vasa's adventures in Dalarna

Engelbrekt, champion of liberty, in Örebro, by C G Qvarnström, 1866

Sights at a Glance

❶ A Tour around the Fryken Lakes

Author Selma Lagerlöf called the Fryken lakes the "smiling leaves", and it is the natural surroundings, the glittering waters, the flowering meadows and the dark forests on the horizon that strike visitors most. The author's spirit is a constant presence, and no more so than at the Rottneros estate, which is Ekeby in *Gösta Berling's Saga*, and the author's home, Mårbacka, across the water. The best ways to experience the lakes are aboard the vintage steamer *Freja af Fryken*, or by bicycle or car from Sunne, the main centre of the area.

View across Övre Fryken from Tossebergsklätten

② Sunne
The regional centre of the Fryksdal valley, Sunne is beautifully situated on the water between Övre Fryken and Mellanfryken. Heritage centres and a host of events in summer, including the Fryksdal Dance, reflect the area's rich folk traditions.

① Sahlströmska Gården
The home of artist siblings Sahlström in Utterbyn features mementos of some of the early 20th century's most colourful Swedish artists.

④ Mårbacka
Nobel laureate Selma Lagerlöf's home has been kept just as it was on her death in 1940. Exhibitions linked to the author's work are held in the summer.

③ Rottneros
The estate has magnificent gardens and a large sculpture collection. For children, there is Nils Holgersson's Adventure Park.

Key
▬ Suggested route
═ Other roads
— Fryksdalsbanan railway line

⑤ S/S Freja av Fryken
In 1896, the queen of the Fryken lakes capsized; 98 years later she was salvaged from the lake bed and now sails from the port of Kil, powered by her original 1868 engine.

Tips for Drivers
Length: 75 km (47 miles) by road.
Stopping-off point: Tosseberg, 20 km (12 miles) north of Sunne on the road to Torsby.
Other routes: train, Kil–Torsby on Fryksdalsbanan, "Sweden's most beautiful railway". Boat trips: S/S Freja av Fryken (Tel: 0567-167 70).

0 kilometres 8
0 miles 5

Malung
Torsby
239
45
Sunne
238
238
45
61
Arvika
Nedre Fryken
Kil
Karlstad
Övre Fryken
Mellan Fryken

❷ Arvika

Värmland. Road 61. 🏔 26,000.
🚌 🚆 ➤ 🚢 ℹ Storgatan 22,
0570-817 90. 🎪 Gammelvala (late
Jul), Arvika Hamnfest (early Aug).
W **visitarvika.se**

The people of Värmland are
known for their wit and ability
to tell funny stories, particularly
in Jösse, where Arvika is the
main town. It is situated on a
hill above the bay of Kyrkviken,
which is linked to the lake of
Glafsfjorden by a narrow strait.

Arvika Fordonsmuseum,
centrally located next to the
fire station, has an exciting
collection of veteran vehicles,
including hundreds of cars,
motorcycles and carriages.

The area has long been
home to craftworkers and
artists, as can be seen in the
Rackstadmuseet in Taserud just
outside the town. This is where
sculptor Christian Eriksson set
up his studio, Oppstuhage,
in the mid-1890s. For many
years it was a magnet for
artists attracted by the pristine
Värmland countryside, such as
the painter Gustaf Fjaestad,
renowned for his winter scenes.

Klässbols Linneväveri, 20 km
(12 miles) south of Arvika, is the
Nordic region's only damask
weaving mill and a rewarding
destination for those who
want to see how the linen
tablecloths for the Nobel Prize
banquets, or fabric for the
Royal Family, are made.

A 1903 Humber in Arvika Fordonsmuseum

🏛 **Arvika Fordonsmuseum**
Thermiavägen 2. **Tel** 0570-803 90.
Open daily. Group bookings: by
appointment. 🅿️ 🎫 📷 🏠 ♿

🏛 **Rackstadmuseet**
Taserud. **Tel** 0570 809 90. **Open** May–
Aug: daily; Sep–Apr: Tue–Sun.
Closed some public hols. 🅿️ 🖥 📷
W **rackstadmuseet.se**

🏭 **Klässbols Linneväveri**
Damastvägen 5. 20 km (16 miles)
S of Arvika. **Tel** 0570-46 01 85.
Open Oct– Apr: Mon–Fri & Sat;
May–Sep: daily. 📷 only pre-booked.
🖥 📷 ♿ W **klassbols.se**

❸ Borgviks Bruk

Värmland. 35 km (22 miles) W of
Karlstad. Road 45. 🏔 400. 🚌 Borgvik
Byggnadsvård: **Tel** 0555-740 81.
Open Jun–Aug.

The ironworks in Borgvik
operated from 1600 to 1925.
The foundry ruins and works
buildings along with the striking
manor and 18th-century

church make Borgvik one
of the leading monuments
to a bygone industrial age in
Värmland. Near Västra Smedbyn
is **von Echstedtska Gården**.
This impressive 1760s' Carolian
manor is known for its murals.
Even the privy has burlesque
and, to say the least, educational paintings.

🏠 **von Echstedtska Gården**
Västra Smedbyn. 20 km (12 miles) NW
of Säffle. **Tel** 0533-630 74. **Open** May–
Sep. 🅿️ 📷 only pre-booked. 🖥 📷

❹ Värmlandsnäs

Värmland. 5 km (2 miles) S of Säffle.

Jutting out into Lake Vänern
is a large peninsula noted for
its excellent agricultural land
and the medieval churches of
Botilsäter and **Millesvik**.

From the southernmost tip
in Ekenäs it is possible to head
out to **Lurö**, Sweden's largest
inland archipelago. This is the
ideal spot to enjoy countryside
well off the beaten track. The
boat trip to the main island of
Lurö takes an hour.

Selma Lagerlöf

In 1909, Selma Lagerlöf (1858–1940) became the first woman to
receive the Nobel prize for literature. And despite the passing of
a century since she wrote her first masterpiece, interest in the

Selma Lagerlöf, sculpture by
Carl Eldh, Rottneros

author's captivating adventures continues
unabated. Numerous film and TV versions
of her works have been produced,
including *The Treasure, Thy Soul Shall Bear
Witness!, The Emperor of Portugallia* and
Jerusalem. When she made her debut in
1891 with the imaginative novel *Gösta
Berling's Saga*, she put the Värmland
countryside around the Fryken lakes and
the family estate of Mårbacka on the
literary map. Even more remarkable was
the success of *The Wonderful Adventures
of Nils*. The tale of the tiny boy's epic
journey with wild geese was translated
around the world.

Perfect bathing spots along the shore
at Värmlandsnäs

For hotels and restaurants in this area see p288 and pp299–300

The Almen quarter, a heritage centre in Karlstad on the Klarälven river

❺ Karlstad

Värmland. E18. 🚗 85,000. ✈ 🚌 🚢
🛈 Västra Torggaton 26, 054-540 24
70. 🎺 Swedish Rally (early Feb),
Putte i Parken music festival (Jul).
🖥 **destinationkarlstad.se**

The phrase *"Sola i Karlsta"* (Enjoy
the sun in Karlstad) has been
used to attract visitors to the
Värmland metropolis. Yet this is
no sunnier a place than any
other in the province. It was, in
fact, a jovial hostess at the town's
inn who brought sunshine into
people's lives in the early 1800s
– her statue now stands outside
the Stadshotell. Karlstad was
built on the delta formed by
the Klarälven river before it
flows into Lake Vänern, and
was a market town in medieval
times. It received its charter in
1584 along with its name from
the then king, Karl IX.

Karlstad has been devastated
by fire on many occasions, most
recently in 1865. The Almen
quarter on Västra Älvgrenen is
a heritage centre comprising
traditional wooden houses which
survived the blaze. The bishop's
palace, built in 1781, survived
as well. The cathedral was less
fortunate, having to have its
exterior rebuilt along with its
tower. Parts of the early 18th-
century interior were preserved.
A well-known feature of the town
is the 12-arched Östra Bron
bridge, built in 1811. Insight
into Värmland's history and
folk culture can be gained at
Värmlands Museum down by
the river. **Sandgrund Lars Lerin**
is an art gallery devoted to Lars
Lerin, one of Sweden's most

famous artists. **Alsters Herrgård**,
east of Karlstad, is the birthplace
of poet Gustaf Fröding in 1860.
The manor is a memorial to him
and other local poets.

The open-air museum in
Mariebergsskogen has several
historic buildings,
including a sauna and
smoking hut built by
Finnish immigrants. In
the grounds lies
Värmlands Naturum,
featuring the flora and
fauna of the province.

🏛 **Värmlands Museum**
Sandgrundsudden. 400 m
(440 yd) N of the centre.
Tel 054-701 19 00.
Open daily. 🎨 🎫 🏪 ♿ 📷
♿ 🖥 **varmlandsmuseum.se**

🏛 **Sandgrund Lars Lerin**
V. Torgg. 28. **Tel** 054-10 07 80.
Open Tue–Sun. 🏪
🖥 **sandgrund.org**

🏛 **Alsters Herrgård**
8 km (5 miles) E of Karlstad. **Tel** 054-
540 23 50. **Open** May–Aug: daily;
Sep: weekends only. 🎨 🎫 🏪 📷

❻ Hagfors

Värmland. Road 62. 🚗 6,500. 🚌
🛈 Folkets Väg 1, 0563-187 50.
🎺 Swedish Rally (early Feb), Klar-Hälja
Festival (early Jul), Klarälvsmässan Fair
(3rd week in Aug).

In the heart of Värmland on the
Klarälven river lies Hagfors, which
has long been a centre for the
steel and forestry industries.
Today, steel is still manufactured
in Uddeholm, just to the west
of the town.

Hagfors is a good starting
point for trips up the Klarälven
valley and out into the forest.
Various places upriver offer raft
and small boat launch areas,
providing the opportunity to
spend a few relaxing days
drifting at 1–2 knots. **Ekshärad**,
20 km (12 miles) north of Hagfors,
has a red shingled church built
in 1686 with superb
views of the river. The
churchyard is known
for around 300 iron
crosses with "leaves"
which play in the wind.
Southwest of the
town is Uddeholm, a
small village with an
original 1940s mill
that now houses a
museum and art
gallery, **Stjärnsfors
Kvarn**. Visitors can enjoy a ride
on an inspection trolley from
the mill to Hagfors, a 6-km
(3.5-mile) round trip.

Gustaf Fröding
(1860–1911)

🏛 **Stjärnsfors Kvarn**
Uddeholm. **Tel** 0563-234 00.
Open Jun–Aug: daily; other
times: by appt. For trolley rides,
call 0563-187 50.

Alsters Herrgård, near Karlstad, birthplace of poet Gustaf Fröding

❼ Filipstad

Värmland. Road 63. ⛰ 6,500. 🚌 🚐
ℹ️ Viktoriagatan 8, 0590-613 54.
🎪 Oxhälja Market (1st Sat in Sep).

Karl IX founded Filipstad in 1611, naming it after his son Karl Filip. Mining, ironworking and blacksmithing were the mainstay of the town, but today it is known for a very different type of industry – it is home to the world's largest crispbread bakery, which bakes the famous Wasabröd. A bread museum is combined with the bakery – both are open from Monday to Saturday.

Two of the town's great sons have contrasting memorials. A life-size sculpture by K G Bejemark of the popular poet and songwriter Nils Ferlin (1898– 1961) in top hat and tails has been placed on a park bench. Next to Daglösen lake stands inventor John Ericsson's imposing mausoleum. He was a locomotive and warship pioneer and inventor of the screw propeller. Two *Monitor*-type cannons stand next to the monument.

John Ericsson grew up along with his equally illustrious brother Nils in the mining community of **Långban**, 20 km (12 miles) north of Filipstad. Here an entire community built around iron has been preserved,

Alfred Nobel's laboratory in the Nobelmuseet, as it was when he died

including a foundry, gaming house and pithead buildings. Mineral hunters investigating the slag heaps of Långban have unearthed an exceptionally diverse collection of no less than 312 minerals.

🏛 Långban
20 km (12 miles) N of Filipstad.
Tel 0590-221 81. **Open** mid-Jun– mid-Aug: daily. 🚫 🎫 📷 🅿️

Statue of the poet Nils Ferlin on his park bench in Filipstad

---

The Inventor John Ericsson

The multi-talented Swedish-American inventor John Ericsson (1803– 89) was born in Långban, Värmland, where his father was mine captain. At the age of 13, he was employed in the construction of the Göta Canal (*see p150*), together with his brother, Nils (1802–70), the father of the Swedish railway. He wrestled with the development of a steam engine and in his early twenties went to England to exploit his invention. He constructed a groundbreaking engine

John Ericsson's mausoleum

(1829) which, in the locomotive *Novelty*, took part in the Manchester–Liverpool race and was narrowly beaten by George Stephenson's *Rocket*. In the USA, Ericsson designed the frigate *Princeton*, and fitted his newly created screw propeller. In competition, the ship claimed victory over the fastest paddle-steamer of the day, the *Great Western*. Ericsson's ultimate triumph came in the American Civil War with the design of the armour-plated warship *Monitor*, with a rotating cannon tower. She overcame the Southern States' *Merrimac* in 1862.

---

❽ Karlskoga

Värmland. E18. ⛰ 29,000. 🚌
ℹ️ Kyrkbacken 9, 0586-614 74.
🎪 Swedish Touring Car Champion-ship (mid-Aug). 🌐 **karlskoga.se**

Iron ore has been mined and processed in this area since the 13th century, but it was not until Alfred Nobel (*see p75*) bought the Bofors ironworks and cannon factory in 1894 that the foundation was laid for Karlskoga's expansion. During the 20th century, Bofors grew to become one of the world's leading arms manufacturers.

The **Nobelmuseet** in Björkborns manor, Nobel's last home, shows developments at Bofors and offers an insight into the life of the inventor. Nobel's laboratory is just as he left it when he died. The stable where he kept his Russian stallions is now an industrial museum displaying the history of the ironworks.

Karlskoga's only preserved blast furnace can be found at **Granbergsdals Hytta**, 10 km (6 miles) north of the town.

At the end of the Ice Age water poured out from a lake at **Sveafallen** near Degerfors, 15 km (9 miles) south of Karlskoga. The landscape it created can be seen in the Domedagsdalen (Doomsday valley) and from walking trails through the nature reserve.

Kristinehamn is an idyllic town 25 km (16 miles) west of Karlskoga. Its claim to fame is Picasso's 15-m (50-ft) high sculpture of a Native American head to the south of the town.

🏛 Nobelmuseet
2 km (1 mile) N of the centre.
Tel 0586-834 94. **Open** Tue–Sun (Jun–Aug: daily). **Closed** some public hols.
🚫 🎫 (Swedish and English). 🅿️

Stjärnsunds Slott, home of Gustaf, the 19th-century "singing prince"

❾ Askersund

Närke. 🗻 4,000. 🚌 🚏 ℹ Rådhuset, 0583-810 88. 🎵 Trad Jazz Festival (2nd week in Jun), Golf Week (2nd week in Jul), All Car and Bike Meet (end of Jul). 🌐 **askersund.se**

On the north shore of Lake Vättern lies Askersund, the main town of southern Närke, offering easy access to the forests of Tiveden and islands on the lake. Askersund received a mention in a Papal letter dated 1314. A devastating fire struck the town in 1776, but many wooden buildings constructed since then have been preserved.

The brick-built church, **Landskyrkan**, designed by Jean de la Vallé in 1670, survived the fire. It is one of the most splendid religious buildings from Sweden's Age of Greatness (see pp42–3), with its magnificent Baroque pulpit and altarpiece. The Oxenstierna-Soopska chapel designed by Erik Dahlbergh contains a tin sarcophagus.

Environs
Lake Vättern's northern archipelago comprises around 50 islands, most of which are a nature reserve. The islands can be reached by boat from Askersund. Plying the route is the S/S Motala Express, which entered service in 1895 and is known as "the prisoner of Vättern" as she is too large to leave the lake via the Göta Canal.

Stjärnsunds Slott 4 km (2 miles) south of Askersund was the home of the "singing prince" Gustaf (1827–52), the song-writing son of Oscar I. It was so lavishly decorated that today

it is considered to contain Sweden's finest mid-19th-century interiors.

🏛 Stjärnsunds Slott
4 km (2 miles) S of Askersund. **Tel** 0583-100 04. House: **Open** 15 May–31 Aug: daily; other times: by appt. 📷 🎫 oblig. 🏞 Park: **Open** daily.

❿ Örebro

See pp242–3.

⓫ Ludvika

Dalarna. Road 50. 🗻 14,000. 🚌 🚏 ✈ ℹ Bergslagsgatan 10, 0771-62 62 62. 🎵 Dan Andersson Week (last week in Jul), Dragon Boat Festival (May/Jun), Ludvika Festival (1st week in Jul). 🌐 **visitsodradalarna.se**

The western part of Bergslagen has foundries, mines and mining magnates' estates around every corner. The industry has also left its mark on the main town, Ludvika. **Ludvika Gammelgård och Gruvmuseum** offers a good impression of mining as it was in bygone times as does the surrounding countryside.

Environs
For many years Grängesberg, 16 km (10 miles) southwest of Ludvika, was central Sweden's largest iron ore mine. It was

closed in 1989. Ore deposits extended beneath the settlement, and in places buildings had to be abandoned to allow mining to continue. The ore was taken by railway to Oxelösund on the Baltic coast.

Grängesbergs Lokmuseum (the Locomotive Museum) contains the world's only operational steam turbine locomotive.

Skattlösberg 35 km (22 miles) northwest of Ludvika, is where Dan Andersson, "poet of the forests", was born in 1888. It is typical of the villages created by immigrant Finns in the 17th and 18th centuries. **Luossa-stugan**, where Andersson used to write, is now a memorial to the much loved poet.

🏛 Ludvika Gammelgård och Gruvmuseum
Ludvika. **Tel** 0240-100 19. **Open** 16 Jun–17 Aug: daily; 1–15 Jun & 18–31 Aug: Mon–Fri. 📷 🎫 🏞

🏛 Grängesbergs Lokmuseum
Grängesberg. **Tel** 0240-207 35. **Open** mid-Jun–mid-Aug: daily. **Closed** Midsummer's Eve. 📷 🎫 🏞 📷

🏛 Luossa-stugan
Skattlösberg. **Open** Jun–Aug: daily. 📷 🎫

⓬ Hedemora

Dalarna. Road 70. 🗻 16,000. 🚌 🚏 ℹ Railway station, 0225-343 48. 🎵 Hedemora Market (mid-May).

This small Dalarna town is the oldest in the province with a charter dating from 1446. The 13th-century church and the pharmacy built in 1779 are among the few buildings which survived a major fire in 1849. Another survivor is **Theaterladan** from the 1820s.

Hedemora, Dalarna's oldest town, granted a town charter in 1459

It was built by a theatre-loving merchant above a granary. Performances take place here in the spirit of the early 19th century and the grain has made way for a museum.

Environs

Husbyringen, north of Hedemora, is the location for a 60-km (37-mile) circular tour, taking in the countryside and local culture. There are mining centres en route and Kloster has the ruins of an abbey. The star feature is Stjärnsund's 18th-century mining settlement, where the father of Swedish mechanics, Christopher Polhem, worked.

Polhemsmuseet exhibits the work of this inventive genius, including the Stjärnsund clock and ingenious Polhem lock.

Christopher Polhem (1661–1751)

🎭 Theaterladan

Gussarvsgatan 10. **Tel** 0225-210 64. **Open** times vary. 📷 phone for tour. 🌐 teaterladanhedemora.se

🏛 Polhemsmuseet

Stjärnsund, 15 km (9 miles) S of Hedemora. **Tel** 0225-803 05. **Open** times vary. 🅿 📷 pre-book. 🖥 📷 ♿

🔴 Borlänge

Dalarna. Road 50/E16. 🚗 49,000. 🚌 ℹ Sveagatan 1, 0771-62 62 62. 🎿 Dalecarlia Cup (early Jul). 🌐 visitsodradalarna.se

Dalarna's second largest town, Borlänge came to prominence in the 1870s when the Domnarvets Jernverk iron-works was established and several railway lines came together here. But it only received its town charter in 1944. In recent years it has gained a university college to add to its iron and paper industries. **Jussi Björlingmuseet** celebrates the town's greatest son, the internationally renowned tenor Jussi Björling (1911–60). All his recordings can be enjoyed here.

Carl Larssongården, a place of pilgrimage for interior designers

Environs

Stora Tuna, 4 km (2 miles) southeast of Borlänge, is the traditional centre of the flatlands. The medieval church was built at the end of the 15th century with the aim of becoming Dalarna's cathedral, but the province never became a diocese. Its treasures include a 15th-century crucifix.

At **Ornässtugan**, it is said that in the 16th century the future king, Gustav Vasa, fled from Danish knights via the privy.

🏛 Jussi Björlingmuseet

Borganäsvägen 25. **Tel** 0243-742 40. **Open** Sep–May: Tue–Fri; Jun–Aug: daily. **Closed** some public holidays. 🅿 📷 🏠 ♿

🏛 Ornässtugan

8 km (5 miles) NE of Borlänge. **Tel** 0243-22 30 72. **Open** May: pre-book; Jun–Aug: daily. 🅿 📷 obligatory. 🖥 📷

🔴 Sundborn

Dalarna. 12 km (7 miles) NE of Falun. 🚗 800. 🚌 ℹ 023-600 53.

In the village of Sundborn is **Carl Larssongården**, Lilla Hyttnäs, home of the artist Carl Larsson (1853–1919). The well-preserved interior contains wooden furniture, traditional Swedish textiles and influences from the Arts and Crafts movement and Art Nouveau. Sundborn's shingled wooden church, built in 1755, features paintings by Larsson (1905) and the graveyard contains the artist's family plot.

Nearby, **Stora Hyttnäs** manor is a complete home from the early 20th century with a textile collection and garden.

🏛 Carl Larssongården

Tel 023-600 53. **Open** Jan–Sep: daily; other times: by appt. **Closed** public holidays. 🅿 📷 obligatory. 🖥 ♿ limited access. 🌐 carllarsson.se

🏛 Stora Hyttnäs

Tel 073-550 62 25. 🌐 storahyttnas.se

Carl and Karin Larsson

Through his book *A Home* (1899), the interior design of artist Carl Larsson and particularly his wife, Karin, as expressed in their house in Sundborn, attracted attention worldwide. The couple had lived around Europe before settling with their children in a wooden farmhouse in Sundborn. Here they were able to develop their ideas for home interiors, producing a decorative scheme in traditional rural Swedish style using rustic furniture, home-woven textiles and colourful country patterns combined with a touch of the Arts and Crafts and Art Nouveau movements. This was in strong contrast to the stifled, bourgeois tastes which prevailed at the end of the 19th century. The joy and happiness in the Larsson home can be traced in every brushstroke and line of his book illustrations, which perhaps explains why Carl and Karin's Swedish idyll continues to inspire interior designers (*see pp30–31*).

Karin and Kersti by Carl Larsson

⑩ Örebro

There has been a town on this site for 750 years, but in 1854 a major fire destroyed the centre of Örebro. This gave scope for a new, more spacious layout on both sides of the Svartån river and elegant buildings coupled with the castle and St Nicolai Kyrka created a particularly fine townscape. A local newspaper described it as "a magnificent 19th-century salon, extravagantly furnished with buildings which proclaim growth and success". But there is also a greener side to Örebro with the promenade that follows the Svartån river to the delights of Wadköping and Karlslund. The river can be explored on foot, by bicycle or in a rowing boat. The free salmon fishing should not be missed.

Örebro Slott on the Svartån river, now the county governor's residence

🏛 Örebro Slott

Kansligatan. **Tel** 019-21 21 21.
Open Mon–Sat (daily in summer).
🎥 obligatory. 🖥 📷 🏰 ♿ limited access. Northwest Tower: **Open** Sat & Sun (daily in the summer). 📷 🎥 obligatory. 🌐 **orebroslott.se**

Örebro Slott has dominated the town since Örebro received its charter in the 13th century. In 1347, King Magnus Eriksson gathered the great and the good at Örebro House, as the castle was then called, to adopt a common law for Sweden. At the end of the 16th century, King Karl IX remodelled the castle to create a Renaissance palace. Today's appearance, however, with its mighty round towers, is the result of major rebuilding in the 1890s.

The castle has been the scene of a number of historical events, including the adoption of the first Swedish Parliament Act in 1617 and the election of the French Marshal Jean-Baptiste Bernadotte as heir to the Swedish throne in 1810. Now it is the official residence of the county governor and has a small tourist information point. An exhibition

in the Northwest Tower highlights the castle's history.

🏛 Örebro Läns Museum

Engelbrektsgatan 3. **Tel** 019-602 87 00. **Open** Tue–Sun. **Closed** public holidays. 🌐 phone to book.
🖥 ♿ 🌐 **olm.se**

With its roots in the 1850s, the county museum is Sweden's oldest, although the main collection of more than 100,000 objects from across the county is on show in a 1960s' building in Slottsparken. A permanent exhibition focuses on farming since the Stone Age. The museum's most valuable artifacts, including the Viking silver from Eketorp *(see p161)*, are housed in the Treasury.

🏛 Rådhuset

Stora Torget. **Closed** to the public.
Built in 1858–63, the magnificent Neo-Gothic town hall was something of a showpiece in its time. King Karl XV didn't think the castle-like building befitted a provincial town, calling it: "… sparkling wine not weak beer!" Today only a fraction of Örebro's

administration fits into the town hall, although it remains the seat of the Municipal Executive Board. When the clock chimes (at 12:03 and 18:03pm, and at 9:03pm in the summer), automatons from Örebro's history appear, such as reformer Olaus Petri *(see p63)*.

⛪ St Nicolai Kyrka

Nikolaigatan 8. **Tel** 019-20 95 30.
Open daily. 🌐 phone for info.
♿ 🌐 Sun.

The church on Stortorget has origins from the 13th century, but has been restyled many times. The north and south entrances are from the original church and were carved from Närke limestone. The rest is an example of English-inspired Neo-Gothic style, with the tower added at the end of the 19th century.

🌳 Stadsparken

Floragatan 1. **Tel** 019-21 10 00.
Open daily.
Voted Sweden's most beautiful city park, this green area boasts a series of themed gardens, including a rose garden, a magnolia garden and a herb garden. There is also a theatre and a children's island featuring its own railway and a petting zoo.

🏛 Wadköping

On the Svartån river, 1 km (half a mile) from the centre. **Tel** Tourist Office, 019-21 21 21. **Open** Tue–Sun. 🖥 🖉 🏰 🌐 **orebro.se/wadkoping**

The beautiful promenade along the Svartån river through Stadsparken leads to the idyllic

Wadköping, an open-air museum with traditional wooden houses

wooden houses of Wadköping. This is a cultural centre to which old buildings have been moved to make way for the modern town. It is a vibrant community with craftworkers and small shops, and many people live here.

The oldest building is the early 16th-century Kungsstugan (King's Cabin), named after its use by the then Duke Karl on his visits to Örebro in the 1580s. His bedchamber has murals painted by his personal artist.

Other buildings include Hamiltonska Huset (1844), moved here from the south of the town, where it was the grandest building of its era, and Cajsa Warg's Hus (17th century), the childhood home of the well-known cookery writer Casja Warg. In summer there are concerts and theatre performances.

🚇 Svampen

Dalbygatan 3. **Tel** 019-611 37 35. **Open** daily. 🚻 🅿 ✏ ♿
🆆 **svampen.nu**

The mushroom-shaped water tower, which offers a superb view of the town, the flatlands of Närke and Lake Hjälmaren, has become a symbol of Örebro. Since its opening in 1958,

8 million visitors have enjoyed the panorama from a height of 55 m (180 ft). Its construction has set something of a trend – there is a copy in Riyadh in Saudi Arabia.

The tower contains the science centre **Aqua Nova**, where the public has the opportunity to conduct practical experiments with water in all its forms.

🚇 Karlslunds Herrgård

5 km (3 miles) W of Örebro. Diedens Allé 11. **Tel** 019-27 07 88. **Closed** to the public.

Owned by Örebro town, the royal estate of Karlslunds Herregård dates from the 16th century and brings together nature and culture in perfect harmony. The Gustavian manor house, built in 1804–09, incorporates wings from the 18th century.

Karlslunds Herrgård's Gustavian manor house dating from 1804–09

The estate was once a self-sufficient community with around 80 buildings, including Carlslunds Kraftstation, built in 1897, which is the country's oldest working power station.

🏊 Gustavsvik

Gustavsviksvägen 11. **Tel** 019-19 69 10. **Open** see website. 🆆 **gustavsvik.se**

A leisure complex with several pools (including a paddling pool for young kids), a golf course and camping facilities, Gustavsvik draws a large number of visitors every year.

Orebro Town Centre

① Örebro Slott
② Örebro Läns Museum
③ Rådhuset
④ St Nicolai Kyrka
⑤ Stadsparken
⑥ Wadköping

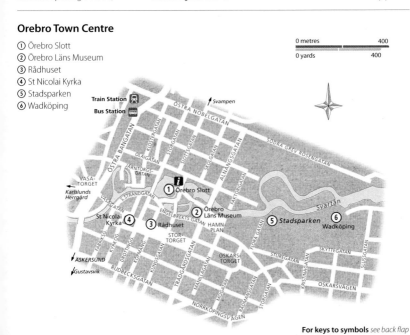

For keys to symbols *see back flap*

The huge Stora Stöten (Great Pit) in the old Falu copper mine outside Falun

⓯ Falun

Dalarna. Road 50/E16. 🚶 37,000. 🚉 🚌 ➤ ℹ Ttotzgatan 10–12, 0771-62 62 62. 🎭 Old World Christmas Market at Falu Gruva (2nd Sun in Dec). 🌐 **visitsodradalarna.se**

It goes without saying that Falun still has a colourful impact on Sweden. Wooden buildings painted in the distinctive Falun Rödfärg (Falun Red) can be seen everywhere. The paint has been made since the 17th century from powdered ore containing ferrous sulphate from the **Falu Gruva** (Falun copper mine), on the back of which the town was founded. Falu Gruva was the country's treasure chest – at its peak, two-thirds of the world's copper was mined here. The entire area, including Stora Stöten (the Great Pit, formed by a collapse in 1687), Falun's historic buildings and industrial remains, and outlying settlements, was designated a UNESCO World Heritage Site in 2001.

Dalarnas Museum gives an insight into the cultural history of Dalarna with extensive collections of folk costumes, local paintings and traditional craftwork.

🏛 **Falu Gruva**
1 km (half a mile) S of the centre.
Tel 023-78 20 30. **Open** daily (hours vary). **Closed** 1 Jan, Good Friday, Mid-summer, 24 & 25 Dec. 🌸 🌿 May–Sep: daily; Oct–Apr: Tue–Sun (Swedish and English). 🚌 🌿 🏠 ♿ above ground only. 🌐 **falugruva.se**

🏛 **Dalarnas Museum**
Tel 023-666 55 00. **Open** daily.
Closed 1 Jan, Good Friday, Midsummer's Eve, Midsummer Day, 24, 25 & 31 Dec. 🌸 🌿 🖥 ♿
🌐 **dalarnasmuseum.se**

⓰ Leksand

Dalarna. Road 70. 🚶 16,000. 🚉 🚌 ℹ Norsgatan 27, 0248-79 72 00. 🎭 Music by Siljan Lake (1st week in Jul), Rowing race in church boats (1st Sun Jul). 🌐 **siljan.se**

The landscape around Siljan lake is especially beautiful, but the Leksand area is the most striking. One of the best times to see the lake is during the annual rowing race in church boats in early July.

Another event worth seeing is Himlaspelet, one of Sweden's oldest rural pageants. First performed in 1941, Rune Lindström's play about a path which leads to heaven depicts the witch trials of the 1670s.

The onion dome of Leksand's 18th-century Baroque church can be seen from far and wide. Parts of the church date from the 13th century.

Environs
Karlfeldtsgården – Sångs i Sjugare was the summer retreat of author and Nobel prize-winner Erik Axel Karlfeldt (1864–1931). It lies on Opplimen lake just north

The folk sculpture *Dalecarlian Couple* in Leksand

of Leksand. Here it is possible to follow in the footsteps of the author's heroine, who came wandering over the meadows of Sjugara. Also worth a visit is the garden on the poet's estate.

Younger visitors to Leksand will be attracted by **Äventyret Sommarland**, comprising three amusement parks on the banks of Siljan lake: Waterland, Motorland and Summerland.

Insjön, 8 km (5 miles) south of Leksand was the birthplace in 1899 of the Swedish mail order business run by Åhlén & Holms. The mail order tradition lives on with Clas Ohlson, whose store attracts so many DIY enthusiasts that Insjön has become Dalarna's most visited tourist destination.

🏛 **Karlfeldtsgården – Sångs i Sjugare**
7 km (4 miles) N of the centre. Road Rv 70. **Tel** 0247-600 28. **Open** mid-Jun–early Aug: Tue, Thu & Sat; other times: by appointment. 🌸

🎢 **Äventyret Sommarland**
Tel 0247-138 00. **Open** mid-Jun–mid-Aug: daily. **Closed** Midsummer's Eve.
🌸 🌿 🖥 🌿 🌐 **sommarland.nu**

⓱ Rättvik

Dalarna. Road 70. 🚶 4,500. 🚉 🚌 ℹ Riksvägen 40, 0248-79 72 00. 🎭 Music on Siljan Lake (Jul), Classic Car Week (late Jul). 🌐 **siljan.se**

No one can fail to notice Rättvik's landmark, Långbryggan pier. After docking at the pier on the *M/S Gustaf Wasa*, passengers have a 628-m (690-yd) walk to reach the mainland. The pier with all its fine carpentry was built in 1895 to allow steam boats to moor near the shallow shore.

Rättvik also has a medieval church, beautifully situated on a promontory surrounded by former church stables – the oldest dating from the 1470s.

Environs

A search for older Dalarna buildings, rural communities and paintings will be rewarded at **Gammelstan** in Norrboda, 35 km (22 miles) north of Rättvik. The village street is lined with old buildings, some of which date back to the 17th century.

Tällberg, 12 km (7 miles) south on the shore of Lake Siljan, has many preserved timber houses in the classic Dalarna style. It is also known for its top-class hotels and guest houses, including the renowned Åkerblads *(see p288)* with its excellent restaurant. At the top of the village, Holens Gammelgård features workshops selling traditional handicrafts.

At **Dalhalla**, 7 km (4 miles) north of Rättvik, a limestone quarry has been converted into an auditorium. The quarry forms an amphitheatre with unique acoustics which have been praised by the world's top opera singers. Concerts are held in summer, and Dalhalla can also be toured in the day. The area was formed 360 million years ago when a meteor landed here, creating a crater which encompasses the whole of the Siljan region.

Bedroom in Zorngården, Anders Zorn's home and studio

of attractions. Mora is particularly associated with King Gustav Vasa (1496–1560) and artist Anders Zorn (1860–1920). Gustav Vasa's travels in Dalarna in 1520 to mobilize local men against the Danish occupation have left many traces. Near Mora, the Utmeland monument (1860) shows several romanticized paintings chronicling Gustav's adventures. It was built over the cellar where he is said to have hidden from Danish scouts. The annual Vasaloppet ski race *(see p249)* is another memorial to the king. At the finishing line in Mora stands Anders Zorn's statue of Gustav Vasa and the nearby **Vasaloppsmuseet** recounts the history of the famous ski race and has a permanent exhibition.

Anders Zorn became known internationally not least for his portraits of plump, naked local women. He was genuinely interested in peasant culture and an ardent collector of local handicrafts. In **Zorngården**, which he built himself, he revelled in a world of National Romanticism. On the estate there are a number of older buildings which have been moved here, such as the 12th-century bakehouse which was used as a studio. The nearby Zornmuseet displays Zorn's own art and private collections.

Environs

Nusnäs, 8 km (5 miles) south of Mora, is where the national symbol of Sweden, the Dala horse, is manufactured. Originally a 19th-century toy,

the horses are carved with a knife and colourfully decorated. It is possible to watch them being made on weekdays.

On the island of **Sollerön** on Lake Siljan is the boatyard where the traditional church boats used on church outings and rowing races between the lakeside villages are made. There is also a pretty church dating from 1785.

Tomteland in Gesunda is the home of Father Christmas and his workshop, which is busy all summer making presents for children. The huge park offers various activities, including the witch's school – for youngsters who want to learn about magic and how to help friends and protect the environment.

🏛 **Vasaloppsmuseet**
Vasaloppets Hus. **Tel** 0250-392 00. **Open** Mon–Fri; mid-Jun–mid-Aug: daily. **Closed** some public holidays. 📷 🎥 by appt. 🏪 ♿ 🌐 vasaloppet.se

🏛 **Zorngården**
Vasagatan 36. **Tel** 0250-59 23 10. **Open** daily. **Closed** Good Friday, 24 & 25 Dec. 📷 🎥 🌐 zorn.se

🏛 **Tomteland**
Gesunda. 12 km (7.5 miles) S of Mora. **Tel** 0250-287 70. **Open** varies, phone for info. 📷 🏪 🌐 santaworld.se

Zorn's statue of Gustav Vasa in Mora

🏛 **Dalhalla**
7 km (4 miles) NW of the centre. Road 70. **Tel** 0248-79 79 50. **Open** for performances and tours. 📷 🎥 🖥 📝 🏪 ♿ 🌐 dalhalla.se

⑱ Mora

Dalarna. Road 70. 🚗 11,000. 🚌 🚲 ➔ ℹ Siljan Tourism Mora, Köpmannagatan 3 A, 0248-79 72 00. 🎿 Winter Festival (Feb), Vasaloppet Ski Race (1st Sun in Mar). 🌐 siljan.se

The municipality of Mora and the town itself – beautifully situated between Orsasjön and Siljan lakes – offers a wide range

A giant-sized Dala horse, manufactured in Nusnäs

Horse-riding in Dalafjällen, one of the many outdoor activities on offer

⓳ Orsa

Dalarna. Road Rv 45. 🏔 5,000. 🚌
ℹ️ Dalagatan 1, 0248-79 72 00. 🎭
Orsayran Music Festival (Weds in Jul).
🌐 siljan.se

The Orsa region extends from the gentle agricultural landscape around Lake Orsasjön to the desolate lands of Finnmark in the north.

In the past many of the local inhabitants made grindstones as a sideline, a skill which can now be studied at **Slipstensmuseet** in Mässbacken, 12 km (7 miles) northeast of Orsa.

In this part of Sweden animals are still taken to the mountains for summer grazing. Around Djurberga, Fryksås and Hallberg it is possible to see how dairymaids used to live, far from their villages, churning butter and making cheese from the milk of hornless mountain cattle and goats.

In **Våmhus**, on the western side of Orsasjön, two crafts are practised which in the past were a major source of income locally: basket weaving and making jewellery out of hair. The women used to walk as far afield as St Petersburg in Russia, and Germany, to sell their work.

Orsa Grönklitt, 14 km (9 miles) north of Orsa, is the main area for outdoor activities. At Orsa Björnpark (Orsa Bear Park) special paths and ramps allow a close-up view of the bears, wolves, lynx and wolverine which live here in large enclosures.

🏛 **Slipstensmuseet**
Mässbacken. **Tel** 0250-55 02 55.
Open summer. 🅿️ 🅲 pre-book.
💻 📄 🌐 orsaslipsten.se

🅼 Orsa Grönklitt
Grönklitt. 15 km (9 miles) NW of Orsa.
ℹ️ 0250-462 00. **Open** daily. 💻 📄
🏠 🅲 🌐 orsagronklitt.se

⓴ Sälen

Dalarna. Road 71. 🏔 1,200. 🚌
ℹ️ Centrumhuset, 0280-187 00.
🎿 Snowboarding World Cup, Speed Skiing World Cup (Mar), Vasaloppet Ski Race (1st Sun in Mar).
🌐 salenfjallen.se

Like the majority of Dalarna's mountains, Transtrandsfjällen, with Sälen at their heart, are rounded and undulating and less dramatic than the those further to the north. The highest peak, Östra Granfjället, is 949 m (3,114 ft) above sea level. However, the terrain is excellent for both downhill and cross-country skiing and this, combined with its relative proximity to Sweden's cities, has made the area one of the country's leading destinations for winter sports enthusiasts.

Whether it's black runs for advanced skiers, velodrome curves, spines or jumps for snowboarders, or family slopes for children, there is plenty to choose from in Sälen. Around 200 km (124 miles) of trails are marked for cross-country skiers and summer hikers alike.

Sälen is the starting point of the 90-km (56-mile) Vasaloppet ski race to Mora.

㉑ Idre and Särna

Dalarna. Road 70. 🏔 1,500. 🚌 ℹ️
Framgårdsvägen 1, Idre; Högenvägen 2, Särna; 0771-99 88 00. 🎿 World Cup Skicross (Feb), Mountain Orienteering (4th week in Jun), Festival Week (3rd week in Jul). 🌐 visitidre.se

Northernmost Dalarna, with the towns of Idre and Särna, belonged to Norway until 1644 and the local dialects still sound Norwegian. This is a mountainous region, with impressive views. In the Nipfjället mountains it is possible to drive up to a height of 1,000 m (3,280 ft) for a good view of Städjan, a peak 1,131 m (3,710 ft) high. The STF mountain station at **Grövelsjön** on Långfjället, to the north, is an ideal starting point for mountain tours.

Idrefjäll is a year-round mountain resort with excellent slopes and lifts. It offers geat skiing in winter and a range of activities in the summer. Särna has a beautiful wooden church dating from the late 17th century and the rural museum of Buskgården.

Fulufjället National Park contains Sweden's highest waterfall, Njupeskär, with a drop of 90 m (295 ft). The effects of a violent storm in August 1997 can still be seen at Göljån, where 400 mm (16 in) of rain fell in 24 hours. Streams became torrents and fallen trees dammed the water, ploughing wide furrows through the forest.

The distinctive peak of Städjan in the Nipfjället mountains

◀ The picturesque town of Mora on a summer's day in early July

The Vasaloppet Ski Race

The world's longest and oldest ski race was first held in 1922 when 122 competitors skied the 90 km (56 miles) from Sälen to Mora. Today more than 15,000 skiers take on the challenge on the first Sunday in March. The race also includes spin-off events such as *TjejVasan* (for women, 30 km/18 miles) and *HalvVasan* (half-course, 45 km/28 miles). A staff of 3,000 support the skiers by providing blueberry soup, ski waxing and blister plasters. And all because in 1520 Gustav Vasa could not get the men of Dalarna to rise up against the Danes. Disheartened, he fled on skis from the Danish troops towards Norway, but when the local men heard about the Stockholm Bloodbath *(see p64)*, they changed their minds and their two best skiers raced to intercept their future king near Sälen.

In summer, a hiking trail follows the course from Berga in Sälen to the finish at Zorn's statue of Gustav Vasa in Mora.

Berga, just south of the village of Sälen, is the starting point for the more than 15,000 skiers who are let loose in the early dawn in several stages, top skiers first.

Evertsberg lies halfway between Sälen and Mora. Here, as in many places along the route, the competitors fortify themselves with blueberry soup. Those only skiing half the race can leave the track at this point.

The first steep hills are succeeded by flat marshland.

Sälen

Smågan
11 km (7 miles)

Berga
Transtrand

Mångsbodarna
24 km (15 miles)

Risberg
35 km (22 miles)

Evertsberg
47 km (29 miles)

Oxberg
61 km (38 miles)

Hökberg
70 km (43 miles)

Eldris
80 km (50 miles)

Mora
90 km
(56 miles)

VÄSTERDALÄLVEN

VANÅN

ÖSTERDALÄLVEN

0 kilometres   20
0 miles   10

The First Vasaloppet

At Christmas 1520 Gustav Vasa fled on skis from Mora towards Norway to escape Danish troops. At Lima, near Sälen, local men caught up with him and persuaded the future king to turn back. Since 1922 almost 750,000 skiers have repeated the achievement, albeit skiing in the opposite direction.

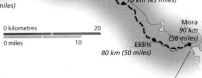

Mora marks the end of the race. The winning time is usually just over four hours, but some entrants can take ten hours. The text on the finishing line reads: "In the footsteps of our forefathers for the victories of tomorrow."

For hotels and restaurants in this area see p288 and pp299–300

SOUTHERN NORRLAND

The six provinces of Southern Norrland cover almost a quarter of the country. The character shifts noticeably from the coast with its industry and fishing to the farming communities up along the river valleys, then westwards through forests to the mountains of Härjedalen and Jämtland. Natural resources such as timber and waterpower have had a visible impact on the region.

In the Middle Ages, the southeasterly province of Gästrikland belonged to Svealand and its gently rolling landscape is more akin to that of neighbouring Uppland than Norrland. An offshoot of the Bergslagen mining district extends into this area and ironworking formed the basis of today's manufacturing industry. The trading port of Gävle has long been a gateway to Norrland.

The pass between Kölberget and Digerberget in the province of Hälsingland is another gateway to the north, beyond which the mountainous Norrland landscape becomes more evident. Huge wooden mansions stand proud with their ornate porches and exquisitely decorated interiors. These houses are evidence of the successful trade in the green gold of the local forests in a landscape of which 80 per cent is covered with productive woodland.

Exploitation of the forests had an even bigger impact on the provinces of Medelpad and Ångermanland. At the end of the 19th century, the timber barons of Sundsvall and Ådalen had made themselves a fortune. Today, processing wood into pulp and paper is still a key industry. The smell of sulphur can be quite striking – as is the herring dish *surströmming* (fermented Baltic herrings), best sampled by those who dare at one of the fishing villages along the High Coast, a UNESCO World Heritage Site *(see p260)*.

The provinces of Jämtland and Härjedalen only became part of Sweden in 1645. There is often talk of the "Republic of Jämtland" among diehard locals who seek self-rule. The mountains stretch out to the west, attracting visitors both to the ski resorts and to the upland areas where the wildlife and countryside can still be enjoyed undisturbed.

A reindeer herd round-up for division according to owner, by use of lassos and ear tags

◀ Spectacular winter landscape, Härjedalen

Exploring Southern Norrland

In this region of immense contrasts, the coastal provinces of
Gästrikland and Hälsingland are home to a colourful rural
culture enlivened with traditional folk music and dancing.
The High Coast, with its dramatic island archipelago
accessible by bridges and ferries, is Ångermanland's
contribution to UNESCO's list of World Heritage Sites.
Inland, the mountainous provinces of Jämtland and
Härjedalen offer wide open spaces for skiing and hiking.

One of the best ways to experience Norrland's varied
landscape is to start from the coast and follow one of
the river valleys which cut across the country. As the
roads wind up-river, they pass through dense
forests and on up into the mountains.

The heather and rushing streams of Helag, with the
mountain of Helagsfjället in the distance

Getting Around

The E4 along the coast and the E14
from Sundsvall across the country to
Trondheim in Norway are the main
arteries for motorists. The inland roads
running north–south are of a generally
good standard. The roads east–west tend
to follow the courses of the rivers. The
main railway line runs north–south. Along
the coast, the railway goes as far north as
Härnösand before heading inland. The
Jämtland mountains can be reached by
train, but in Härjedalen transport is by car
or bus. The Inlandsbanan railway operates
in summer. Air travel is an option and the
range of domestic flights is good.

Key

▬▬▬ Motorway

▬▬ Major road

═══ Minor road

⌁⌁⌁ Main railway

──── Minor railway

▬▬▬ International border

▲ Summit

For keys to symbols *see back flap*

A wooden mansion in Arbro, Hälsingland, typical of the area's
traditional architecture

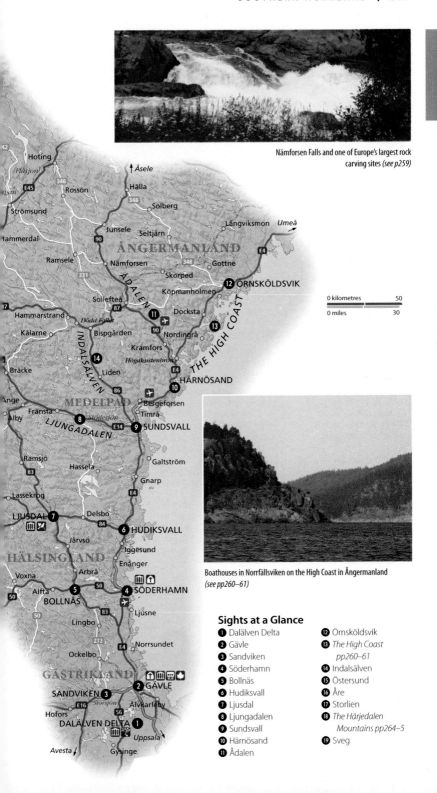

Nämforsen Falls and one of Europe's largest rock carving sites *(see p259)*

0 kilometres 50
0 miles 30

Boathouses in Norrfällsviken on the High Coast in Ångermanland *(see pp260–61)*

Sights at a Glance

1. Dalälven Delta
2. Gävle
3. Sandviken
4. Söderhamn
5. Bollnäs
6. Hudiksvall
7. Ljusdal
8. Ljungadalen
9. Sundsvall
10. Härnösand
11. Ådalen
12. Örnsköldsvik
13. *The High Coast pp260–61*
14. Indalsälven
15. Östersund
16. Åre
17. Storlien
18. *The Härjedalen Mountains pp264–5*
19. Sveg

The Dalälven delta, one of the top ten fishing spots in Sweden

❶ Dalälven Delta

Gästrikland, Uppland. Gysinge Tourist Office, 0291-210 00. Weir Day in Älvkarleby (first Sun before Midsummer).

Before the mighty Dalälven river empties into the bay at Gävle, it forms an expansive delta with hundreds of small islands. The flora and fauna are abundant and the area offers some of the best sport fishing in Sweden.

Least affected by forestry and farming is the area around Färnebofjärden, part of which was declared a national park in 1998. The birdlife is incredibly diverse, with more than 100 breeding species, including several different endangered woodpeckers and owls.

A good place to start exploring the area is Gysinge on road Rv 67, 38 km (24 miles) south of Gävle. The falls between Färnebofjärden and Hedesundafjärden attracted ironworking here at the end of the 17th century. The well-preserved industrial community has a main street dating from the 1770s and a magnificent manor from 1840. Gysinge is also home to **Dalälvarnas Flottnings-museum**, which shows just how important the river once was for timber transportation.

Another important feature of the Dalälven river is hydroelectric power, which manifests itself in **Älvkarleby**, further down-river. The imposing power station, built in 1915, is an attraction in itself, but the most impressive sight is when the water is released at full-flow on Weir Day. Älvkarleby attracts many anglers, who annually land as much as 20 tonnes of salmon and sea trout.

In **Österfärnebo**, Koversta rural heritage centre is an 18th-century village, offering an insight into local rural life.

🏛 Dalälvarnas Flottningsmuseum
Gysinge Bruk. **Tel** 0291-210 00. **Open** mid-May–mid-Aug: daily.

❷ Gävle

Gästrikland. 96,000.
Drottninggatan 22, 026-17 71 17.
w visitgavle.se

Gästrikland's main town has been the gateway to Norrland since the Middle Ages. The mouth of the Gävleån river made an ideal port and traders set up base here to conduct business in the north. The harbourside warehouses along Skeppsbron bear witness to this. Gävle remains one of Sweden's larger ports, although operations have moved further out into the bay. A fire in 1869 destroyed the buildings north of the river, with the exception of the town hall built in 1790 and **Heliga Trefaldighetskyrkan**, a three-aisle Baroque church dating from 1654. As a result, Gävle has attractive 19th-century buildings and tree-lined esplanades as protection against fires. The jewel is the splendid theatre on Rådhusesplanaden, built in 1878. The city park, **Boulognerskogen**, which features Carl Milles' famous sculpture, *Five Playing Geniuses,* is the most popular of Gävle's parks.

South of the Gävleån river lies **Gävle Slott**, Sweden's northernmost royal fortification, dating from the 16th century. This is also the location of the old town, "Gamla Gefle", with fine streets of wooden houses from the 18th century which have attracted many artists and craftsmen. **Joe Hill Gården** on N Bergsgatan, the birthplace of the Swedish-American union agitator, is now a museum. Other museums include **Länsmuseet Gävleborg** with extensive collections relating to the history of Gästrikland.

Sveriges Järnvägsmuseum offers a delightful selection of old locomotives and carriages, from mining titans to neat little narrow-gauge carriages.

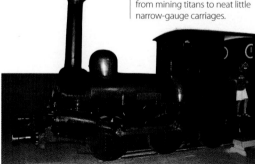

The oldest Swedish locomotive (1855) in Sveriges Järnvägsmuseum

Fängelsemuseet is a small but fascinating museum housed in 17th-century prison cells. It gives an insight into prison life at the time.

Furuviksparken attracts families who come to enjoy its Nordic and exotic animals, and live performances, and to swim in a beautiful setting.

🏛 **Länsmuseet Gävleborg**
S. Strandgatan 20. **Tel** 026-65 56 00. **Open** Tue–Sun. **Closed** public holidays. 🖥 📷
🌐 lansmuseetgavleborg.se

🏛 **Sveriges Järnvägsmuseum**
Rälsgatan 1. **Tel** 010-123 21 00. **Open** Jun–Aug: daily; Sep–May: Tue–Sun. **Closed** public holidays. 🚻 🖥 📷 ♿

🏛 **Fängelsemuseet**
Hamiltongatan 1. **Tel** 026-65 44 30. **Open** Wed–Sun. **Closed** public holidays. 🚻 🌐 fangelsemuseet.se

🎢 **Furuviksparken**
10 km (6 miles) E of the centre. Road Rv 76. 🚌 **Tel** 010-123 21 00. **Open** end May–Aug: daily. 🚻 🖥 ✏ ♿

❸ Sandviken

Gästrikland. 🗺 23,000. 🚉 🚌
ℹ Folkets Hus, Köpmangatan 5–7, 026-24 13 80. 🎷 Bangen Jazz Festival (end Jun), Chamber Music Festival (end Jul). 🌐 gastrikland.com

The town of Sandviken grew up with the establishment of an ironworks on the shore of Storsjön lake in 1860. The new railway line to Gävle was one of the factors in its location. Using the groundbreaking Bessemer production process, Sandviken soon gained a reputation for its steel. In the 1920s it began making stainless steel and by the 1940s it was the world's leading producer of steel for tools and drill bits.

Environs
Evidence of Sandviken's ironworking roots can be seen in Högbo. Today the community is a centre for recreation and adventure sports. Located nearby in Kungsgården is **Rosenlöfs Tryckerimuseum**, which has a still-functioning printing press from the 1890s.

Opposite Sandviken, on the southern shores of Storsjön, lies the medieval church of **Årsunda**, with paintings by the master Eghil. Just south of the church is a Viking burial ground, which inspired the Årsunda Viking centre, offering activities with a Viking slant.

🏛 **Rosenlöfs Tryckerimuseum**
Kungsgården, 10 km (6 miles) W of Sandviken. **Tel** 0290-376 18. **Open** Jul–late Aug: Tue–Fri. **Closed** Midsummer. 🚌 ✏ 📷

❹ Söderhamn

Hälsingland. 🗺 13,000. 🚉 🚌
ℹ Köpmangatan 11, 0270-753 53.
🎪 Family fun evenings at Östra Berget (Thu in Jul), BBQ Battle (mid-Aug).

Sweden's ambitions for power and the need for armaments led to the foundation of Söderhamn in 1620. Hälsingland's weapon makers were brought together from around the region to work in the town. The gun and rifle-making factory, built in 1748, now houses the town museum, **Söderhamns Stadsmuseum**.

Russian attacks in 1721 and four disastrous fires have meant that the only remaining building of significance is **Ulrika Eleonora Kyrka**. The red cruciform church was designed by Tessin the Younger in 1693. The upside of

Oscarsborg lookout tower, offering a superb view of Söderhamn

Part of an old furnace in the town of Sandviken, famous for its steel production

the fires is that a series of parks now creates a green patchwork around the city. Söderhamn's landmark is the **Oscarsborg** tower, which rises proudly on Östra Berget. Anyone braving the 125 steps is rewarded with a breathtaking view of the town and archipelago.

Today Söderhamn is a thriving coastal community that offers great opportunities for swimming, boating and fishing.

Environs
The 10 km (6 miles) of the Söderhamnsfjärden inlet were lined with 11 steam-powered sawmills during the industrial boom of the late 19th century. The industrial museum in Ljusne and **Bergviks Industrimuseum** tell the story. Modern technology is on display at **Söderhamns/F15 Flygmuseum**, which exhibits military aircraft.

The 13th-century church **Tronö Kyrka**, 17 km (11 miles) northwest of Söderhamn, complete with walls, gates and bell tower, is unusually redolent of the Middle Ages. The archbishop and Nobel prize-winner Nathan Söderblom (1866–1931) was born in the rectory, which now houses his memorabilia.

🏛 **Söderhamns Stadsmuseum**
Oxtorgsgatan 5. **Tel** 0270-157 91. **Open** by appt or for exhibitions.

🏛 **Bergviks Industrimuseum**
15 km (9 miles) west of the centre. **Tel** 0270-42 44 65. **Open** by appointment. 🚌 voluntary. 📷

🏛 **Söderhamns/F15 Flygmuseum**
Flygstaden, 4 km (2 miles) east of the centre. **Tel** 0270-142 84. **Open** Jun–Aug: daily; Sep–May: Sun–Tue. 🚻 📷 by appointment. ✏

Kämpen rural heritage centre at a 16th-century farm in Bollnäs

❺ Bollnäs

Hälsingland. 🗺 13,000. 🚉 🚌
ℹ️ Kulturhuset, Odengatan 17b,
0278-258 80. 🎭 Karlslunds Festival
(late Jul). 🌐 **bollnas.se/turism**

Located in the heart of
Hälsingland's rich farming land,
Bollnäs is the gateway to the
valleys of the Voxnan and
Ljusnan rivers. The town itself
has a semi-modern centre, with
some wooden mansions. The
church, built in the 1460s,
contains ornate medieval
sculpture work. The
Classical-style **Bollnäs
Museum** (1929) is worth a
visit, as is the Kulturhuset
next door, which
has a room
devoted to
Onbacken, an Iron
Age settlement just a
stone's throw away.
Also worth visiting is
Kämpen rural heritage centre,
a 16th-century farm displaying
a wealth of local culture.

Environs
Hälsingland was a major flax-
growing area in the 1700s,
and local landowners displayed
their wealth in lavishly
decorated wooden mansions
(see p24). These farmhouses
are now a designated UNESCO
World Heritage Site. Some of
Hälsingland's finest estates
and farms can be seen around
Alfta, about 20 km (12 km)
into the Voxnadalen valley.
Alfta rural heritage centre, **Löka**,
in Gundbo, comprises three
farm buildings, some with
beautiful murals. **Hansers** farm
has wall hangings from the
15th century. In **Arbrå**, 16 km
(10 miles) north of Bollnäs,

there is an 18th-century
wooden mansion (Träslottet)
on the Hans-Andersgården
estate where journalist Willy
Maria Lundberg (b.1909)
created a centre for the preser-
vation of old buildings. As well
as being an attraction in its
own right, the manor also has
exhibitions and specialist
gardens. In summer, the
tourist office runs guided tours
of Hälsingland's farms and
manor houses.

Växbo, east of Bollnäs,
has the only flax-
spinning works
in Sweden, which
produces and sells
items such as tablecloths
and napkins.

Log-floater by Per
Nilsson Öst (1972)

🏛 **Bollnäs Museum**
Odengatan 17. **Tel** 0278-
253 26. **Open** during exhibitions Tue–Sat. 🎨 ♿

❻ Hudiksvall

Hälsingland. 🗺 17,000. 🚉 🚌 ⛴
ℹ️ Trädgårdsgatan 4, 0650-191 00.
🎭 Delsbo Festival (1st Sun Jul).
🌐 **hudiksvall.se**

Fishing, seafaring and trade
have been the mainstay of
Hudiksvall throughout its

400-year history. In the late
19th century the timber
industry boomed and the
town became known for its
high living, giving rise to the
phrase "Happy Hudik".

Despite attacks by Russian
forces in the 18th century and
numerous fires, a number of
older buildings remain, giving
the town charm and character.
The Sundskanal in the centre,
a canal linking Lillfjärden and
Hudiksvallsfjärden inlets, is
lined with red huts and
merchants' warehouses from
the mid-19th century.

East of the inlet is Fiskarstan
(Fishermen's Town), with its
partly preserved warehouse
houses from the early 19th
century. Along Hamngatan
there are several fine old
merchants' yards featuring
the elegant wood-panelled
architecture of the time.
They have terraces on the
waterside and shops on the
parallel street of Storgatan.
An example is the **Bruns Gård**
pharmacy, which has an
ornate pharmacy entrance on
Storgatan and a winged house
on the terraces of Hamngatan.

Dominating the skyline is
St Jakobs Kyrka, a church
built in the 17th and 18th
centuries, although its onion
dome dates from 1888.

Hälsinglands Museum, in
an imposing former bank
building, provides a good
picture of the colourful history
of the area.

Environs
Hudiksvall municipality covers
a large area of northern
Hälsingland, including **Delsbo**
and the beautiful Dellensjö
lakes to the west. South of

Picturesque warehouses and quay on Sundskanalen in Hudiksvall

For hotels and restaurants in this area see pp288–9 and pp300–301

Torpsjön, a typical lake on the mighty Ljungan river, with Fränsta Kyrka on its shore

the town is **Iggesund**, with its 400 years of ironworking history, and **Enånger**, where the 15th-century church contains exquisite medieval ceiling paintings by Andreas Erici and wooden sculptures by master sculptor Håkon Gullesson.

🏛 Hälsinglands Museum
Storgatan 31. **Tel** 0650-196 01. **Open** Mon–Sat. **Closed** public holidays & eves of public holidays. 🎫 by appointment. 🖥 📷 ♿

❼ Ljusdal

Hälsingland. 🚉 🚌 ℹ Stations-gatan 2, Järvsö, 0651-403 06. 🌐 ljusdal.se

In the heart of northwest Hälsingland on the Ljusnan river is Ljusdal. Settlers have long been attracted to this fertile valley and their history is explored at **Ljusdalsbygdens Museum**. Christianity came early to the area; parts of the church of **St Olovs Kyrka** are 12th-century.

Environs
Opportunities for fishing and walking present themselves at every turn around this area. From **Lassekrog**, 40 km (25 miles) upstream from Ljusdal, those who dare can run the rapids on the Ljusnan river. Lassekrog has been an inn since the 17th century. Here, author Albert Viksten's forest camp is a monument to the foresters of old.

South of Ljusdal, at **Järvsö**, wildlife from the north, including predators such as bear, wolf, wolverine and lynx and their prey, can be seen at **Järvzoo Djurpark** and the

adjacent Rovdjurscentret (Predator Centre). Järvsö village itself is known for having Sweden's largest provincial church; when it was completed in 1838 it had space for 2,400 parishioners. Also here is **Järvsö Bergscykel Park**, which offers downhill mountain biking facilities. On the opposite bank lies **Stenegård**, a 19th-century trading post, now a centre for arts and crafts, with a theatre in the wooden barn.

🏛 Ljusdalsbygdens Museum
Museivägen 5, Ljusdal. **Tel** 0651-71 16 65. **Open** Tue–Sat. **Closed** public holidays. 🎫 by appointment. 📷

🐾 Järvzoo Djurpark
1 km (half a mile) south of Järvsö centre. **Tel** 0651-411 25. **Open** daily. 🐾 🎫 by appointment. 📷

🐾 Järvso Bergscykel Park
Anders Persvägen 29, Ljusdal. **Tel** 0651-76 91 92. **Open** Jun–Sep: daily. 🌐 jarvsobergscykelpark.se

Ljusdalsbygdens Museum, in a wooden Hälsingland building

❽ Ljungadalen

Medelpad. E14. ℹ Sundsvalls Tourist Office, 060-658 58 00.

The 350-km (220-mile) Ljungan river rises at Helagsfjällen mountain and flows into the Gulf of Bothnia just south of the town of Sundsvall. In Medelpad, the river forms an often wide valley with a series of lakes. The E14 follows long stretches of the river, offering spectacular views. The great Norrland forests loom on the horizon and the river was an important timber route.

Stöde Kyrkby on Stödesjön lake, 40 km (25 miles) west of Sundsvall, has a long history, which is illustrated at the Huberget rural heritage centre. The church was built in the 1750s, but contains medieval artifacts from an older, now demolished church.

Borgsjö, 40 km (25 miles) further upriver, has a fine Rococo church built in 1768, with a superb wooden bell tower from 1782. Next to the church is Borgsjö rural heritage centre featuring Jämtkrogen Inn, which was relocated here from the Jämtland border.

Ånge, a railway junction 100 km (60 miles) west of Sundsvall, is an ideal starting point for exploring the area. To the west, the countryside of Haverö spreads out around the Havern and Holmsjön lakes, which are good for canoeing. **Haverö Strömmar** is an 8-km (5-mile) stretch of at times wild rapids with three streams where former dams, mills and fishing huts have been preserved. **Alby**, just off route 83, has a restored eel house showing a fishing method used in the 16th century.

The carefully restored Hotell Knaust's marble staircase

❾ Sundsvall

Medelpad. 🕅 50,000. 🚌 🚍 ✈
Midlanda. 🛳 🚹 Stora Torget, 060-
658 58 00. 🎭 Sundsvall Street Festival
(1st or 2nd weekend Jul), Dragonboat
Festival (1st week in Aug), Selånger
market (2nd weekend in Aug).
🅆 visitsundsvall.se

The view from Norra and Södra
Stadsberget hills shows
Sundsvall sandwiched between
the mouths of the Ljungan and
Indalsälven rivers. The sheltered
inlets attracted traders to this
spot in the 6th century, as
can be seen from the Högom
burial ground near Selånger.
Alongside Selånger's
12th-century church lay
St Olofs Hamn, the starting
point for trading missions
and pilgrimages to
Norway's Nidaros
(Trondheim).
  Sundsvall was
founded in 1624.
It took off in the
mid-1800s with
the advent of the
steam-powered
sawmill. Sweden's first such
sawmill was built in 1849 in
Tunadal; when the industry was
at its height there were 19
sawmills on the island of Alnön
alone. In 1888, fire destroyed
large parts of the town centre.
The railway station survived, and
the attractive wooden building
is now a casino. A grand "stone
town" rose from the ashes. In

Stora Torget stands the statue of
the founder King Gustav II Adolf.
The square is flanked by the
town hall and the **Hirschska
Huset** with its extravagant
pinnacles and towers. A notable
building on Storgatan is the
newly renovated **Hotell Knaust**,
built in 1890, with its superb
marble staircase. The cultural
centre, Kulturmagasinet, near
the harbour, contains the town
library and **Sundsvalls Museum**.
On Norra Stadsberget lies
Sundsvalls Stadspark, which
has a collection of buildings
from Medelpad, as well as
animal enclosures and lookout
towers. Södra Stadsberget's
outdoor recreation centre has
adventure trails for children.

Statues on the roof of Sundsvall
town hall

Environs
Linked to
Sundsvall by
the Alnöbron
bridge, **Alnön**
has many
monuments
to the timber
industry. The 13th-
century church is interesting
for its wooden interior and
medieval paintings and
sculptures, and the fishing
village of **Spikarna** is well worth
a visit.
  Around 26 km (16 miles) southeast of Sundsvall lies **Galtström**,
Medelpad's first ironworks,
built in 1695. The works have
been restored.

🏛 **Sundsvalls Museum**
Kulturmagasinet. **Tel** 060-19 18 00.
Open daily. **Closed** Easter Mon,
Whit Mon, Midsummer's Eve.
🎟 by appointment. 🖼 📷 ♿

🏛 **Sundsvalls Stadspark**
Norra Stadsberget. **Tel** 060-15 40 00.
Open daily. **Closed** eves of public
holidays. 🐾 (by Stadsparken). 🎟 by
appointment. 🖼 ⚙ 📷 ♿

❿ Härnösand

Ångermanland. 🕅 18,000. 🚌 🚍
🛳 🚹 Stora Torget, 0611-204 50.
🎭 Midsummer celebrations at
Murberget, Nostalgic Days (Jul),
Park Festival (2nd–3rd week in Jul).

The county town of western
Norrland has a proud history.
It received its town charter
from Johan III in 1585, became
diocesan capital in 1647 and
had an upper secondary
school by 1650.
  Härnösand's rich history,
combined with the fact that,
in contrast to other Norrland
coastal towns, it was spared
major fires for almost 300 years,
makes it an interesting place to
stroll around. The Russians
plundered Härnösand in 1721.
A new wooden town replaced
the old and charming districts
such as Östanbäcken and
Norrstan still remain. Standing
out among the many public
buildings are the town hall from
the 1790s on Stora Torget, the
old upper secondary school and
the county governor's residence.
  At Murbergets Friluftsmuseum,
which is part of **Länsmuseet
Västernorrland**, 18th-century
buildings have been preserved,
including the town hall built
in 1727. This large open-air
museum also reflects farming
culture, with crofts and farms,
a blacksmith's and sawmill,
and a Norrland church village.
  Skeppsbron fills with yachts in
July when the town's maritime
history is celebrated at the
Härnösandskalaset festival.

🏛 **Länsmuseet Västernorrland**
Murberget. **Tel** 0611-886 00.
Open Tue–Sun (mid-Jun–mid-Aug:
daily). **Closed** 1 Jan, Easter, 1 May, 24,
25, 31 Dec. 🎟 by appointment. 🖼
📷 ♿ 🅆 murberget.se

⑪ Ådalen

Ångermanland. Road 90. 🚌 from Örnsköldsvik. ℹ️ Kramfors Tourist Office, 0612-800 00. 🎭 Kramfors Town Festival (weekend before Midsummer).

As the forestry industry flourished, Ådalen, the river valley leading to Junsele, became a hotbed of trade unionism and earned the nickname "Red Ådalen". In 1931, the year of the Great Depression, a most unlikely event occurred: the military shot indiscriminately into a peaceful strikers' march in Lunde, killing five people. Lenny Clarhäll's powerful sculpture depicting the drama stands beside Sandöbron bridge.

Already in the mid-18th century, Livonian Christoffer Kramm set up a water-powered sawmill on the site which in 1947 became the town of Kramfors. Cargo ships were able to navigate 50 km (31 miles) up the river and the lower valley became a magnet for the forestry industry. The line of factories is now almost entirely gone. Further up river, however, there are numerous

One of the many rock carvings in Nämforsen from around 4000 BC

power stations – the Faxälven tributary is home to 36 alone. Particularly worth visiting is **Nämforsen**, where in summer visitors can view the large power station and occasionally see the mighty waterfall burst into life. The islands in the falls are an outstanding site for rock carvings. From 4000–2500 BC, hunters carved out over 2,500 figures.

⑫ Örnsköldsvik

Ångermanland. 🚋 to Sundsvall or Mellansel, then bus/taxi. 🚌 🚕 ⛴️ ℹ️ Lasarettsgatan 5, 0660-881 00. 🎭 Harbour Festival (1st weekend in Jul), Dragonboat Festival (late Aug). 🌐 **ornskoldsvik.se/turism**

Nolaskogs is one of the names by which this part of northern Ångermanland is known. It means "north of the forest" – the wild frontier forest of Skule (*see p260*).

Its main town, Örnsköldsvik, or Ö-vik as it is often called, was founded in 1842. Unusually for the time, it was named after a non-royal figure, the county governor Per Abraham Örnsköld. There are good views of the town from Varvsberget and from the top of the ski-jumping tower on Paradiskullen. Many of the town's older buildings have been lost to modern development. A few exceptions include the delightful town

Arken, designed by architect Per Eddi Byggstam, 1991

hall which, thankfully for Ö-vik's remarkably large artists' colony, was saved as an exhibition space. The beautifully restored junior secondary school houses **Örnsköldsviks Museum**, which displays the history of Nolaskogs.

Attractive new architecture can be seen in the development of the inner harbour, where **Arken** – a centre for offices, university buildings and a library – forms an exciting backdrop. One of its glass-roofed courtyards houses the **Hans Hedbergs Museum** dedicated to the Swedish sculptor (*see p30*).

Environs
Next to an excavation site in **Gene fornby**, 5 km (3 miles) south of the town, a 6th-century farm has been reconstructed, where people come to live and work as they did in the Iron Age.

The most striking medieval church in the area is the octagonal **Själevads Kyrka** from 1880, which was voted Sweden's most beautiful church in a nationwide poll.

🏛️ **Örnsköldsviks Museum**
Läroverksgatan 1. **Tel** 0660-886 01. **Open** Midsummer–Aug: daily; other times: Tue–Sat. **Closed** public holidays. 🖥️ 📷

🏛️ **Arken**
Strandgatan 21. **Tel** 0660-785 00. Public areas: **Open** daily. Hans Hedbergs Museum: **Open** ring Tourist Office 0660-881 00 for info. **Closed** public holidays. 🖥️ 🚫

Surströmming, a Fishy Delicacy

The coast of Southern Norrland has a speciality which many Swedes, not only the people of Norrland, consider to be the ultimate delicacy, although the majority probably detest it. This treat is fermented herring, known as *surströmming*, which, after around eight weeks of fermenting, is canned. When the can is opened it produces what is, to say the least, a characteristic aroma, which aficionados consider absolutely divine. The fishing villages along the High Coast (*see pp260–61*), such as Ulvöhamn, are the centre of production, and a market is now opening up as far afield as Japan. The fermented herring is eaten reverentially, almost ritually, in early autumn, accompanied by small almond-shaped potatoes and chopped onion. It is best washed down with

Can of Surströmming copious amounts of beer and snaps.

⓭ The High Coast

Sweden's spectacular high coast is best experienced on a light summer evening, when the wooded hills are reflected in the calm waters of the bays, or on the quay in Ulvöhamn during the *surströmming* season *(see p259)*, when the peculiar speciality of fermented herring is enjoyed with flat bread, tiny potatoes and snaps. A boat is ideal for getting around, but the Högakustenbron bridge provides easy access and ferries sail regularly from several ports. The dramatic landscape is the main attraction. Declared a UNESCO World Heritage Site in 2000, it is the result of the land rising 300 m (984 ft) since the ice receded around 9,600 years ago. At that time Skuleberget hill, north of Docksta, was a tiny island.

Skuleskogens National Park
Watched over by Skuleberget hill, the park covers 30 sq km (12 sq miles) of wilderness, with walking trails through magical ancient forest and over the clifftops along the coast.

Ullångersfjärden
Motorists on the E4 rejoin the Gulf of Bothnia at Ullångersfjärden bay which, with its high, sheer cliffs, is almost fjord-like.

Nordingrå
"Fair Nordingrå" was a tourist destination long before the term High Coast was coined. Beautiful roads lined with steep hills pass through stunning scenery.

Högakustenbron
Since 1997, the 1,800-m (6,000-ft) bridge, suspended on 180-m (600-ft) high pylons, has offered travellers breathtaking views. There is a tourist information point in the hotel on the north side of the bridge.

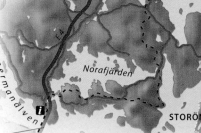

Örnsköldsv
Norrfjä
Docksta
Ullånger
Ullångersfjä
Nordingrå
Gaviksfj
Ångermanälven
Norafjärden
STORÖN
Härnösand

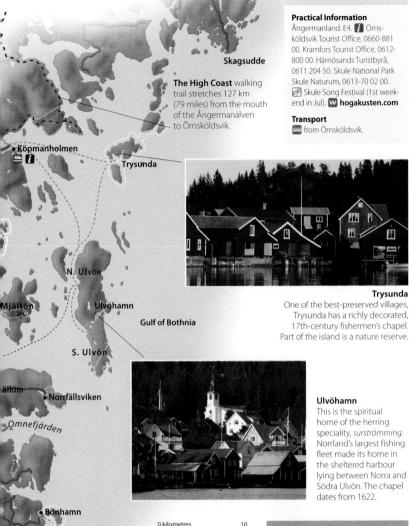

Skagsudde

The High Coast walking
trail stretches 127 km
(79 miles) from the mouth
of the Ångermanälven
to Örnsköldsvik.

Köpmanholmen

Trysunda

N. Ulvön

Mjälton

Ulvöhamn

Gulf of Bothnia

S. Ulvön

ällom

Norrfällsviken

Omnefjärden

Bönhamn

Trysunda
One of the best-preserved villages,
Trysunda has a richly decorated,
17th-century fishermen's chapel.
Part of the island is a nature reserve.

Ulvöhamn
This is the spiritual
home of the herring
speciality, surströmming.
Norrland's largest fishing
fleet made its home in
the sheltered harbour
lying between Norra and
Södra Ulvön. The chapel
dates from 1622.

| 0 kilometres | 10 |
| 0 miles | 5 |

Högbonden
The 100-year-old lighthouse
on the island of Högbonden
warned shipping of the rocky
coastline. Today it is a youth
hostel, reached by boat from
Bönhamn, the most authentic
fishing village on the
mainland, and the place to
savour local specialities such
as fresh river salmon, whitefish
and, of course, surströmming.

Key

▬ Major road
▬ Minor road
-- Ferry route
- - High Coast walking trail
National Park
Nature Reserve

Thai monument in Utanede, commemorating the King of Siam's royal visit in 1897

⑭ Indalsälven

Jämtland/Medelpad. Road 86. 🚌 to Sundsvall, then bus. 🛈 Ragunda Tourist Office, 0696-68 10 90.
🎭 Vildhussen Festival (1st and 2nd weeks in Jul). 🌐 **ragundadalen.se**

The 430-km (270-mile) long Indalsälven river rises in the mountains of Norway and flows into Klingerfjärden, north of Sundsvall. The lower stretch of the river from Ragunda in Jämtland includes **Döda Fallet** (the Dead Falls) caused by a disastrous attempt by Vildhussen (*see box*) to control the river in 1796.

Döda Fallet is now a nature reserve where it is possible to walk around the rocky landscape and see the giant basins carved out by stones in the falls. An extraordinary revolving open-air theatre has been created next to

the falls, with a stand for an audience of 420. A stage in the round is set against breathtaking natural scenery.

Utanede features an exotic Thai pavilion, the **King Chulalongkorn Memorial**, erected in memory of the King of Siam's trip along the river in 1897 as a guest of King Oscar II. The decorative elements of the golden pavilion were built by Thai craftsmen and seven million parts were shipped to Sweden and assembled. The interior holds a life-sized bronze statue of the king.

Among the churches along the river, **Lidens Kyrka**, dating from 1510, has the most attractive location (road 86, 37 km/23 miles northwest of Sundsvall) and contains medieval sculptures, with a Madonna from the 13th century. Vildhussen is buried in the cemetery here.

Bergeforsen on the coast is the last of the river's many power stations. There is an aquarium where Baltic fish such as salmon, sea trout and eel are raised.

🏯 **King Chulalongkorn Memorial**
Utanede. Road 86, 7 km (4 miles) south of Bispgården. **Tel** 0696-68 10 90. **Open** mid-May–mid-Sep: daily. 🅿️ 🎫 daily. 🚻 ♿ 🎁 ♿ some facilities. 🌐 **thaipaviljongen.se**

⑮ Östersund

Jämtland. 🏘 44,000. 🚉 🚌 🛫
🛈 Rådhusgatan 44, 063-14 40 01.
🎭 Storsjöyran Festival (last weekend in Jul), Arnljot Games (Jul).
🌐 **visitostersund.se**

Established on the shores of Storsjön lake in 1786, the county town of Östersund lies opposite Jämtland's ancient centre of Frösön. Before coming under Norwegian rule in 1178, the people of Jämtland had ruled themselves and would be happy to do so again if the Republic of Jämtland movement had its way. In a fairly lighthearted manner, the movement protects local culture – the highpoint is the Storsjöyran Festival in July.

The county museum, **Jamtli**, with its Historieland feature, offers an exciting picture of life around Storsjön. This time machine transports visitors to scenes from the 18th and 19th centuries, where history can be felt, heard and even tasted. The museum's showpiece are the oldest preserved Viking *Överhogdal* tapestries.

A short bridge leads to the rolling, green island of Frösön. Its eastern parts are more like a part of town, but the views across Storsjön to the peak of Oviksfjällen inspired the composer Wilhelm Peterson-Berger to create his distinctive home, **Sommarhagen**, in 1914. The house is now a museum and the rich interior with decorative paintings by Paul Jonze is something of a companion to Carl Larsson's Sundborn (*see p241*). Every summer *Arnljot*, Peterson-Berger's drama about

Old stone fireplace in Jamtli Museum, Östersund

the Viking from 11th-century Frösö, is performed in a field a short distance away.

The 12th-century **Frösö Kyrka** is one of Sweden's most popular churches in which to get married. **Frösö Zoo** has 700 animal species from around the world.

Environs

Storsjön lake is best explored on a steamer, such as the 1875 *S/S Thomeé*, Sweden's oldest steamer still in regular use. Many enthusiasts try to spot the elusive Storsjö Monster, the so-called sister of Scotland's Loch Ness monster.

Brunflo, 15 km (9 miles) south of Östersund, has an 18th-century church with a 12th-century lookout tower.

🏛 Jamtli

Museiplan. **Tel** 063-15 01 10.
Open mid-Jun–mid-Aug: daily; mid-Sep–mid-Jun: Tue–Sun. **Closed** 24, 25, 31 Dec. 🏞 🏢 summer. 🔲 🖉 🏠 🚻 🏧

🏠 Sommarhagen

Frösön, 9 km (6 miles from the centre). **Tel** 063-430 41. **Open** mid-Jun–mid-Aug: daily; other times by arrangement. 🏞 🏢 by appointment. 🔲 🏧

🦌 Frösö Zoo

3 km (2 miles) south of the centre. **Tel** 063-51 47 43. **Open** mid-Jun–mid-Aug: daily. 🏞 🔲 🖉 🏧 🚻

⑯ Åre

Jämtland. E14. 🏔 1,000. 🚌 🚍 🚆 Östersund. 🛈 St Olavs Väg, 0647-163 21. 🎿 Alpine World Cup (Mar), St Olavsloppet (end Jun), Åre Bike Festival (1st wk in Jul), Tour of Jamtland (early Aug). 🖥 are360.com

Åreskutan is Sweden's most visited mountain peak. The cable car lifts passengers from the village of Åre to within 150 m (490 ft) of the summit at 1,420 m (4,658 ft). At this altitude, the skiing season lasts into June. Facilities are plentiful in what has become Sweden's leading ski destination. There are 40 lifts and 100 pistes, some of which are the longest and steepest in the country. Hotels and

The 1,700-m (5,600-ft) high Syl, just over a day's walk south of Storlien

conference centres rise up into the sky. This is in contrast to how the resort looked at the end of the 19th century with hotels such as Åregården and the Grand. Still here is the Berg-banan run, which has attracted tobogganists of all ages. Prominent visitors have included Winston Churchill, who came for the excellent flyfishing and to hunt elk. Today's range of activities includes scooter safaris, dog sledding, paraskiing, ice-climbing, surfing rapids and mountain biking on Åreskutan.

Environs

The **Tännforsen** waterfall, 20 km (12 miles) west of Åre, is one of the most impressive in Jämtland, with a drop of 37 m (120 ft).

Njarka Sameläger, on an island on Häggsjön lake, has a Sami camp where visitors can learn how to lasso, or taste delicacies such as reindeer heart. On Åreskutan's eastern spur, 10 km (6 miles) from Åre, lies **Fröå Gruva**, where copper was mined from 1752 to 1916. The countryside is beautiful to wander through, with buildings from various eras. At **Huså Bruk**, another centre for copper mining further to the north, is Huså Herrgård, a manor built in 1838.

Skiers resting at a hut on Åreskutan, Sweden's top ski resort

⑰ Storlien

Jämtland. E14. 🚌 🚍 🚆 Östersund. 🛈 SP Livs & Bensin petrol station, Vintergatan 25, 0647-700 20. 🖥 storlienturistbyra.se

The arrival of the railway in Trondheim in the 1880s opened up new opportunities for Storlien, which is located near the border with Norway. It is only 60 km (37 miles) to the Trondheim Fjord, and the broad pass between Stenfjället and Skurdalshöjden allows mild Atlantic winds to sweep through. The healthy air attracted spa guests to a mountain sanatorium, and with the dawn of the 20th century tourists began arriving.

Today, Storlien is a classic ski resort for both cross-country and downhill. It is also a starting point for walks in the Jämtland mountains, such as via the STF stations of Blåhammaren, Storulvån, Sylarna and Vålådalen. The mountains can also be reached from Enafors on the E14 and by train.

Popular with birdwatchers, nearby **Ånnsjön** lake has a bird station and sanctuary. **Handöl**, on the western shore, has been a site for soapstone mining since the late Middle Ages. It was also where the surviving Carolean forces gathered in 1799 after Carl Gustaf Armfelt's catastrophic retreat from Norway. The Carolean monument on the waterfront is a memorial to the 3,700 men who froze to death in the mountains. Today accommodation and better equipment have prompted more and more people to take up the challenge of completing the 75-km (47-mile) long Carolean March.

⑱ The Härjedalen Mountains

The tree line in Härjedalen is at 900 m (2,950 ft) and even in the forested lowlands in the east there are mountains with bare summits such as Sånfjället and Vemdalsfjällen. But the mightiest mountains loom large in the west towards Norway and the province of Jämtland, with Helagsfjället the highest peak at 1,797 m (5,900 ft). Funäsdalen is the local hub, from where in summer Sweden's highest road runs via the Sami village of Mittådalen and the plateau of Flatruet to Ljungdalen. There are many opportunities for ski-touring and downhill skiing, fishing in summer and hiking along the southern part of the Kungsleden trail.

Helags
STF *(see p312)* has a mountain station at the base of Helagsfjället, Sweden's highest peak south of the Arctic Circle.

Ramundberget
In the summer, this popular winter sports venue, known for its early snowfalls, is a good starting point for mountain hikes to Helags, Ljungdalen and Fjällnäs.

Funäsdalen
This lively town in the Härjedalen mountains has the award-winning Härjedalens Fjällmuseum, which shows how the Sami and upland farmers survived the challenges of past times.

Røros (Norway)

Fjällnäs

Tänndalen

84

84

Bruksvallarna

Mittådalen

Ljungd

Tännäs

Högvalen

Idre

KEY

① **Visit a musk ox sanctuary** and see musk oxen in their natural habitat. Guided tours start at Tännäs Fishing Centre.

② **The road** over the Flatruet Plateau is only open in summer.

③ **Parts of the Sånfjället** mountain in the forest were declared a national park in 1909, partly to protect the bear population. Wolves, lynx and wolverine also live here.

Rogen
The nature reserve around Härjedalen's largest lake system has unusual flora and fauna. It is great for canoeing. The Sami village of Ruvhten offers ice-fishing for grayling and char.

Reindeer Pastures
The Sami villages of Mittådalen and Ruvhten (Tännäs) have summer pastures in the western mountains. The winter pastures stretch as far as the forests of Sveg and into Dalarna.

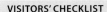

Vemdalsfjällen
This skiers' paradise has a joint lift system for the main resorts: Vemdalskalet, Björnrike, Klövsjö and Storhågna, as well as great facilities for cross-country skiing.

Klövsjö ☒

☒ Vemdalsskalet
  Storhågna
  Ånge
●Vemdalen
  ☒ Björnrike
Hede
  Sveg

ärsjövålen ☒
  (3)

84

☒ Lofsdalen
  Sveg

Key

■■■ Major road
■■■ Minor road
- - Walking trail

0 kilometres   20
0 miles   10

⑲ Sveg

Härjedalen. ▨ 2,700. ☐ Inlandsbanan (summer), or to Mora or Ljusdal then bus. ☐ ☒ **i** Ljusnegatan 1, 0680-125 05.

Härjedalen's central town is Sveg, the gateway to the mountains. The municipality of the same name covers an area larger than many counties, and with just 11,000 inhabitants it has a population density of less than one person per sq km. Forest stretches in every direction. Winding waterways provide opportunities for fishing, canoeing and beaver safaris. The nearest mountain for skiing is a 30-minute drive away.

Around Sveg, small villages such as Duvberg, Ytterberg, Överberg and Äggen are well-preserved, with 18th-century features. **Gammel-Remsgården**, 15 km (9 miles) north of Sveg, is a typical early-18th-century Härjedalen manor house with richly decorated interiors. About 15 km (9 miles) east of Sveg lies the village of **Älvros**, whose church has a beautifully painted bell tower.

Lillhärdal, 30 km (19 miles) south of Sveg, is said to have been founded in the 9th century by the Viking Härjulf Hornbrytare. Bildhöst has one of the last working crofts, complete with cattle and milkmaids, while Hamre Skans is a timbered fortification from the 18th century.

Älvros church near Sveg, with a free-standing, painted bell tower

For keys to symbols *see back flap*

NORTHERN NORRLAND

Stretching from the populated Baltic coast through wild forests and marshes to the open expanses of the mountains, Northern Norrland is a vast, almost untouched region. The biting chill and eternal darkness of the long northern winter are compensated for by summer's midnight sun, when nature seizes its short window of opportunity to flourish and the reindeer are moved to new pastures.

The three provinces of Västerbotten, Norrbotten and Lappland make up Sweden's most northerly region. Västerbotten, on the Gulf of Bothnia, is the most southerly. Its coast and river valleys had booming settlements for many centuries. But today commercial activity is concentrated in towns such as Umeå, with its university and youthful population, and Skellefteå, known as the "Town of Gold" because of its proximity to two of Europe's largest gold deposits. Inland, the wilderness takes hold with vast tracts of forest and marsh. After a journey between Lycksele and Sorsele, Carl von Linné wrote: "A priest could never make Hell sound worse than this." But with modern transport, today's traveller can look forward to outdoor adventures and wildlife in this unspoilt landscape.

North of Västerbotten, Norrbotten's coastline harbours features of rural culture such as the church village in Gammelstad, a UNESCO World Heritage Site. The Norrbotten archipelago is renowned for being the sunniest place in the country and its beach resorts lure holiday-makers. The border with Finland lies along the Torne river, and here the phrase "two countries, one people" is the most applicable.

Lappland borders Norway in the west and Finland in the northeast, but for the Sami (Lapp) people their land extends beyond official boundaries, across the mountains and forests and down to the coast, where their thriving culture of reindeer herding, hunting and fishing prevail. Known as Laponia, this area is also a UNESCO World Heritage Site. National parks such as Sarek protect the alpine landscape with its glaciers and waterfalls. The main towns of Kiruna and Gällivare in northern Lappland owe their existence to the mining industry.

Dog sledding in Jukkasjärvi, Lapland

◀ The amazing spectacle of the Northern Lights over the frozen forests near Kiruna

Exploring Northern Norrland

An area covering more than one-third of Sweden cannot be explored in a hurry. And things are not made easier by the large areas of wilderness north of the Arctic Circle without roads, in Europe's most sparsely populated region. Despite their northerly latitude, the coastal areas combine a captivating archipelago landscape with rich cultural sights. Spectacular roads lead up into the mountains with romantic names such as "Saga Vägen" (the Saga Highway) and "Blå Vägen" (the Blue Highway). Skiers are tempted by the record-length season, while for hikers, the northernmost section of the 440-km (275-mile) long Kungsleden trail *(see p278)* between Abisko and Hemavan crosses the mountainous UNESCO World Heritage Site of Laponia.

Lake Saggat seen from the Kvikkjokk road in northwestern Lappland

Getting Around

Flying is the most comfortable means of transport. Around a dozen airports offer scheduled flights. Only a few trains travel on the Vännäs–Luleå line and the Malmbanan line running Luleå–Kiruna–Riksgränsen. The Inlandsbanan line through Lappland from Gällivare provides a summer tourist route. The major roads E4, E10 and E12 (the Blue Highway) are of a high standard, but road conditions are variable elsewhere. Bus services between the main towns are usually good, but almost non-existent in the wilder areas. Ferries operate across some mountain lakes in summer, saving time for hikers.

Key

▬▬ Major road

═══ Minor road

▬▬▬ Main railway

──── Minor railway

▬▬▬ International border

For keys to symbols *see back flap*

Narvik

Riksgränsen

Kebnekaise
2111m

Stora Sjöfalle
National Par

Vakkotavere

Padjelanta
National
Park

Sarektjåkkå
2090m

Sarek
National
Park

18

Kvikkjokk

Bodø

Pieskehaure

Arctic Circle

Vaulajårro
1365m

Tjeggelvas

Mo i Rana

Jakkvik

95

Raker
1375m

Hornavan

THE KUNGSLEDEN TRAIL

ARJEPLOG **17**

E12

Ammarnäs

Udjaure

Hemavan

Tärnaby

363

Storavan

Storvindeln

Slagnäs

Ajaureforsen

Sorsele

Gardiken

LAPPLAND

45

Dikanäs

Sandsele

370

Klimpfjäll

Storuman

Storuman

E12

Björksele

Malgomaj

Vilhelmina

Lycksele

Umeälven

Ångermanälven

45

365

Dorotea

Ostersund

Åsele

92

Fredrika

90

0 kilometres   100

0 miles   50

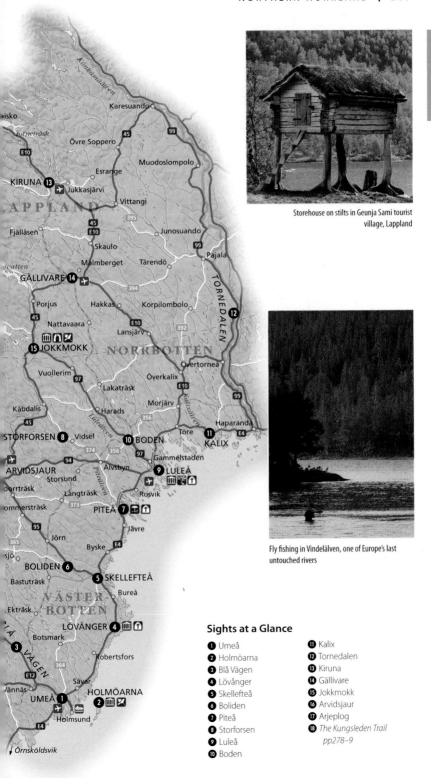

Storehouse on stilts in Geunja Sami tourist village, Lappland

Fly fishing in Vindelälven, one of Europe's last untouched rivers

Sights at a Glance

1. Umeå
2. Holmöarna
3. Blå Vägen
4. Lövånger
5. Skellefteå
6. Boliden
7. Piteå
8. Storforsen
9. Luleå
10. Boden
11. Kalix
12. Tornedalen
13. Kiruna
14. Gällivare
15. Jokkmokk
16. Arvidsjaur
17. Arjeplog
18. *The Kungsleden Trail* pp278–9

Late afternoon in Umeå city, on the banks of the Ume river

❶ Umeå

Västerbotten. 110,000. from Vasa, Finland. Renmarkstorget 15, 090-16 16 16. Jazzfestival (4th week in Oct), Film Festival (late Nov). visitumea.se

With 3,000 birch trees lining the streets, it is not surprising that Umeå is known as "The City of Birches". After a major fire in 1888, a new city was built with broad, tree-lined esplanades and parks to prevent fires spreading. Post-fire buildings of interest include the **Scharinska villa** on Storgatan, designed by Ragnar Östberg, and **Moritska Gården**, Umeå's grandest residence for a local timber baron. The city's Neo-Gothic church was completed in 1894.

Umeå dates back to the 16th century. An important trading and administrative centre, it became a county town in 1622. The opening of a university in 1965 prompted an expansion that transformed Umeå into a city – Norrland's only one. With 40,000 students and lecturers, it is very much a young persons' place

(average age 38). The splendid **Bildmuseet**, on the Arts Campus, is a great showcase for international contemporary art and design.

In Gammlia, a 10-minute walk from the centre, the **Västerbottens Museum** focuses on the history of Umeå and Västerbotten. It includes Svenska Skidmuseet, which covers the history of skiing, and the fishing and maritime museum Fiske- och Sjöfartsmuseet. In the summer, the open-air museum **Gammlia Friluftsmuseum** shows off its historic farm buildings, complete with pets, and there are activities for children.

🏛 Bildmuseet
Umeå Arts Campus, Östra Strandgatan 30. **Tel** 090-786 74 00. **Open** Tue–Sun. **Closed** Midsummer's Eve, 24 & 31 Dec. by appt. bildmuseet.umu.se

🏛 Västerbottens Museum
Gammlia. **Tel** 090-16 39 00. **Open** Tue–Sun (mid-May–mid-Aug: daily). **Closed** 24, 31 Dec. Gammlia Friluftsmuseum: **Open** mid-May–mid-Aug: daily. vbm.se

Sweden's 200-Year Peace

Infantryman, model, 1807

Sweden has enjoyed almost 200 years of peace. The last battles on Swedish soil took place in Sävar and Ratan north of Umeå in August 1809. Russian troops had been plundering the coast and a Swedish expeditionary force landed at the port of Ratan to attack the Russians from the rear. The troops marched south towards Sävar and clashed with the Russians on 19 August. The Swedes were defeated and withdrew to Ratan, where another battle was fought the next day. This time the Swedish troops stood their ground, but 1,000 men died in the conflict. A memorial in Sävar honours the fallen. As a result of the war, Finland was lost to Russia.

❷ Holmöarna

Västerbotten. 90. to Norrfjärden 30 km (19 miles) N of Umeå, then ferry. Umeå Tourist Office, 090-16 16 16. Sea Jazz Festival (2nd weekend in July).

A 45-minute free ferry trip from Norrfjärden leads to the Holmö archipelago. There are four main islands – Holmön, Grossgrundet, Angesön and Holmögadd – and several smaller ones. The majority of the group forms part of Sweden's largest archipelago nature reserve. It is an area of exciting geological formations and extensive fields of rubble stones. The forest and shorelines provide habitats for 130 species of birds and a variety of flora.

The islands have been inhabited since the 14th century and **Holmöns Båtmuseum** focuses on the lives of the local fishermen, seal hunters and farmers.

The archipelago is ideal for cycling, bathing and fishing.

🏛 Holmöns Båtmuseum
At the ferry quay. **Tel** 090-552 20 (summer). **Open** mid-Jun–mid-Aug: daily. holmons batmuseum.se

Encountering a reindeer on the Blue Highway

❸ Blå Vägen

Västerbotten, Lappland. E12. Renmarkstorget 15, Umeå, 090-16 16 16.

From Lake Onega in Russia to Träna on Norway's Atlantic coast, the Blå Vägen (Blue Highway, E12) stretches 1,700 km (1,050 miles). The Swedish section follows the Umeälven river from Umeå through the towns of Lycksele, Storuman and Hemavan.

Klabböle, near Umeå, is the site of the river's first power station, built in 1899. It now houses the museum of **Umeå Energicentrum**, which is well worth a visit. There is something for everyone here, and children enjoy the "Playing with Energy" exhibit and trying to balance on logs like a log driver.

At **Vännäs**, 26 km (16 miles) from Umeå, the unspoilt Vindelälven river joins the Umeälven, and a detour can be made to the mighty **Mårdsele falls** to ride the rapids or fish for salmon, salmon trout and grayling.

Lycksele, the only town in southern Lappland, lies 123 km (76 miles) from Umeå. The local zoo, **Lycksele Djurpark**, specializes in Nordic wildlife.

Umeå Energicentrum
10 km (6 miles) W of Umeå.
Tel 090-16 03 74 (090-16 00 00 in winter). **Open** 2nd week in Jun–3rd week in Aug: daily.

Lycksele Djurpark
Brännbergsvägen. **Tel** 0950-163 63.
Open 3rd week in May–Aug: daily.
w lyckseledjurpark.com

❹ Lövånger

Västerbotten. E4. 2,400.
Lövångers Kyrkstad, 0913-103 95.

The church village at Lövånger is one of the largest in the country with 117 cabins. It dates from the Middle Ages, although the oldest surviving cabin is from 1746. The village was built to accommodate churchgoers from remote outlying areas during church festivals. A number of cabins have been converted into hotel rooms. The 16th-century granite church of St Anne is decorated with medieval sculptures.

Sockenmuseet, just north of the church, illustrates how the people of Lövånger lived in the 19th century.

Sockenmuseet
Tel 0913-100 40. **Open** daily in summer (call for opening times).

The church village in Lövånger with accommodation for churchgoers

❺ Skellefteå

Västerbotten. E4. 35,000.
to Bastuträsk, then bus.
Nygatan 49, 0910-45 25 00.
Skellefteå Festival (4th weekend in Jun); Woodstock Music Festival (Jul).
w destinationskelleftea.se

Northern Västerbotten had to wait until 1845 for its first town, but there had long been a marketplace alongside Skellefteå church. In order to accommodate the large congregation, a Neo-Classical cruciform church was built in 1800 on the site of a 15th-century church. Worshippers came from far afield, staying in Bonnstan, Skellefteå's church village built in the mid-19th century.

It was with the boom in the mining industry in the 1920s that Skellefteå's development took off, fuelled by the huge smelting plant at the mouth of the Skellefteälven river.

The town's green lung is the Nordanå Centrum of Culture, a park on the northern bank of the river. It houses an art gallery, **Skellefteå Museum** and historic buildings.

Skellefteå Museum
1.5 km (1 mile) W of the centre.
Tel 0910-73 55 10. **Open** Tue–Sun.
Closed some public hols.
w skellefteamuseum.se

❻ Boliden

Västerbotten. E4/road 95.
Skellefteå, then bus. Skellefteå Tourist Office, 0910-45 25 00.

The Kingdom of Gold is the name given to Skellefteå's ore field which, with Boliden at its heart, stretches from Bottenviken through northern Västerbotten towards the mountains of Lappland. Europe's two largest gold deposits are mined here, in addition to zinc, copper, silver and tungsten.

Bergrum Boliden, in the old mining office, traces the history of the formation of the sulphide ores more than 4,600 million years ago to their extraction today.

In World War II, the world's longest cable car system was constructed to transport the ore 96 km (60 miles) from the mines in Kristineberg. It is possible to travel along a 13-km (8-mile) long stretch from Örträsk to Mensträsk, swinging over the beautiful countryside at a sedate 10 km/h (6 mph).

Bergrum Boliden
1 km (half a mile) NW of the centre.
Tel 0910-58 00 60. **Open** Jun–Aug: daily. **Closed** Midsummer.

The Kristineberg cable car system, once used to transport ore

Piteå's sandy beach, and Sweden's best chance of sun

❼ Piteå

Norrbotten. E4. 🅿 42,000. 🚉
✈ Luleå. 🚌 🛥 𝒊 Bryggargatan
14, 0911-933 90. 🎭 Piteå Summer
Games/International Midnight Sun
Football Tournament (late Jun/early
Jul), Piteå Dances and Smiles Festival
(Jul). 🆆 **visitpitea.se**

Originally located next to Öjebyn,
Piteå was moved after a fire to
the mouth of the Piteälven river.
The new town was burned by
the Russians in 1721 and rebuilt.
Picturesque wooden buildings
from the 19th century, such as
the town hall, can be found on
the square of Rådhustorget. But
it is the coast that is the main
draw. The **"Nordic Riviera"** offers
sandy beaches and Sweden's
best chance of sun. There's also
an indoor fun pool.
   Öjebyn has a well-preserved
15th-century church and village.

Environs
Jävre, off the E4 south of Piteå,
has traces of Norrbotten's first
settlers from the Bronze Age. The
archaeology trail takes in graves,
sacrificial stones and labyrinths.

❽ Storforsen

Norrbotten. 80 km (50 miles) NW of
Piteå, road 374. 🚌 𝒊 Älvsbyn Tourist
Office, 0929-108 60. **Open** Jun–Aug:
daily. 🅿 🆆 **alvsbyn.se/visit**

Europe's mightiest untamed
stretch of whitewater can be
found on the Piteälven river, 40
km (25 miles) north of Älvsbyn.
The rapids drop 82 m (270 ft)
over 5 km (3 miles), at speeds of
over 800 cubic metres (176,000
gallons) per second. Efforts to
channel the rapids into a single

course created Döda Fallet (Dead
Falls), where giant basins can be
seen. Log floating has ceased,
but a visit to the **Skogs- och
Flottningsmuseet** will reveal how
things looked when Storforsen's
huge log jams were formed.

🏛 Skogs- och Flottningsmuseet
Storforsen. **Tel** 070-296 68 88.
Open May–Aug: daily. 🅿 🎫
obligatory. 🖥 ✏

Storforsen in the Piteälven river, a vast
expanse of whitewater rapids

❾ Luleå

Norrbotten. E4. 🅿 45,000. ✈ 🚉 🚌
🛥 𝒊 Kulturens Hus, 0920-45 70 00.
🎭 Luleå Harbour Festival (mid-Jul).
🆆 **visitlulea.se**

The county town of Luleå is
surrounded by water as the
Luleälven river flows into
glittering bays with a lush
archipelago beyond. A good
harbour was the reason for
the town's location here in the
mid-17th century, when the
original site upstream became
too shallow.
   The church village, **Gammelstads Kyrkstad**, and its church,
Nederluleå Kyrka, form a unique
monument to the old trading

centre and are a designated
UNESCO World Heritage Site.
The 15th-century granite
building with its perimeter
wall is upper Norrland's largest
medieval church. The white
steeple towers over a group
of 408 small red cabins. This
is where churchgoers from
remote villages would
stay overnight and stable
their horses. The church's star
vaulting is decorated with
paintings from the Albert Pictor
school of the 1480s. The
magnificent altar-screen from
Antwerp dates from 1520.
   The cathedral in the new Luleå
was built in 1893. **Norrbottens
Museum** concentrates on the
history of Luleå and Norrbotten.
   The ore-loading harbour and
SSAB's steelworks are the
cornerstones of Luleå. They also
influence the science museum,
Teknikens Hus, where technical
experiments can be attempted,
such as drilling in a mine and
launching a space rocket.

Environs
Luleå archipelago, comprising
more than 1,300 islands and
islets, is a favourite place for
boat owners. Ferries provide
access to places of interest,
such as the fishing villages on
Kluntarna and Brändöskär.

🏠 Gammelstads Kyrkstad
10 km (6 miles) NW of the centre.
🚌 **Tel** 0920-45 70 10. **Open** 2nd
week in Jun–mid-Aug: daily; other
times: Tue–Thu. 🅿 🎫 🖥 ✏ 🏠 ♿

🏛 Norrbottens Museum
Storgatan 2. **Tel** 0920-24 35 02.
Open Tue–Sun (Jun–Aug: daily).
Closed some public holidays.
🖥 🏠 ♿

🏛 Teknikens Hus
University district, 5 km (3 miles)
N of the centre. **Tel** 0920-49 22 01.
Open Tue–Sun. 🅿 🖥 ✏ 🏠 ♿

Norrbottens Museum with a Sami summer
tent and hut

❿ Boden

Norrbotten. 35 km NW of Luleå, Road 97. 🚉 ➡ Kallax. 🚌 ℹ Kungsgatan 40, 0921-624 10. 🎭 Boden Alive Festival (weekend after Midsummer), Harvest Festival (Aug).
🌐 **experienceboden.nu**

Its strategic location on the Luleälven river, at the intersection of two main train lines, has made Boden a centre for Sweden's northerly defences. It became the country's largest garrison town at the beginning of the last century and countless young men from across the country have completed their military service here. Five artillery forts circled the town. The nuclear bunker deep in the rock was top secret until only a few years ago. Now **Rödbergsfortet** is a national monument open to the public who can experience life in the fort and even stay in rooms carved out of the rock.

The central Björknäs area is also worth a visit for its open-air heated swimming pool and to see historic Norrbotten farms.

About 3 km (2 miles) north of the centre, a Wild West ranch has been built which offers a taste of pioneering life in the 19th century.

Cannon from Boden fort

🏛 Rödbergsfortet

5 km (3 miles) W of the centre. **Tel** 0921-48 30 60. **Open** 3rd week in Jun–1st week in Aug; other times by appointment. 🎫 📷 💻 ♿ limited access.

⓫ Kalix

Norrbotten. E4, 50 km (31 miles) W of Haparanda. 🚉 🚌 ➡ Kallax. ⚓ ℹ Strandgatan 10, 0923-129 79. 🎭 Grayling Day (end Jul), National River Festival (mid-Aug). 🌐 **kalix.se**

The Kalix area to the north of the Gulf of Bothnia has been inhabited since Stone Age times. **Nederkalix** became a parish in the 15th century, but its church has had a turbulent history, with devastating fires and plundering by the Russians.

Kalixälven river, one of Europe's few entirely unregulated large rivers

During the 1809 war, it served as a stable for Russian horses. Englundsgården Cultural Heritage Centre is a good example of Norrland's beautiful wooden architecture.

Environs
The **Kalixälven** is one of Sweden's few unregulated rivers, ensuring good catches of salmon trout and salmon. The archipelago offers pike and whitefish and the opportunity for seine fishing. Of the islands which can be reached by tour boat, Malören has a timber chapel dating from 1769, an old lighthouse and a pilot station.

⓬ Tornedalen

Norrbotten. Road 99. 🚌 ℹ Haparanda-Tornio Tourist Office, 0922-120 10. 🎭 Pajala Market (end Jun), Whitefish Festival in Kukkola (last weekend in Jul).

The Torne river and its tributary, Muonio, form the border with Finland, but culturally the areas along both shores are united. Place names are in Finnish, and many of the inhabitants speak a local form of Finnish.

Haparanda, at the mouth of the river, was created as a border town when Torneå became part of Finland in the peace treaty of 1809. A bridge links the sister towns and they share a tourist office.

The disproportionately large train station, which has both normal and Russian wider gauge tracks, is a legacy from its time as a Russian border town.

Fishing is an important part of life on the Torne. Whitefish has been caught in the Kukkola rapids 15 km (9 miles) upstream since the 13th century, using large nets fixed to piers. The best fishing is to be had in late July, when the whitefish festival is held.

Övertorneå, 70 km (43 miles) north of Haparanda, is a fertile horticultural area. The long light summer nights help berries, fruit and vegetables to develop an exceptional flavour. There is a church dating from the 17th century and a good view from the top of the mountain, Luppioberget, where Father Christmas is said to live.

Pajala is the centre of northern Tornedalen. The area is popular for fishing and wilderness camps and it is possible to shoot the rapids on the Torne and Tärendö rivers. The latter is a 50-km (31-mile) long natural link between the Torne and Kalix rivers. **Laestadius Pörte** and museum attract Laestadian Lutherans on a pilgrimage to the simple cabin of the revivalist preacher and botanist Lars Levi Laestadius (1800–61).

🏛 Laestadius Pörte
Pajala. **Tel** 0981-202 05. **Open** May–Aug: Mon–Sat. 🎫 📷 💻

Octagonal church in Övertorneå, the Tornedalen valley's main town

Strikingly shaped church in Kiruna, inspired by a Sami hut

⓭ Kiruna

Lappland. E10. 🄼 19,000. 🚗 🚌 ✈
🛈 Kiruna Lapland Tourist Office, Folkets Hus, Lars Janssonsgatan 17, 0980-188 80. 🎿 Snow Festival (last week in Jan), Kiruna Festival (4th weekend in Jun). 🆆 kirunalapland.se

In terms of area, Kiruna is one of the world's largest municipalities. It is the site of Sweden's highest mountain, Kebnekaise, 2,014 m (6,607 ft), from where, on a clear day, one can see one-eleventh of the country. For 50 days in summer the sun never sets, and for 20 winter days it never rises. But even in the dark and cold, the people make the best of things. In January they hold a snow festival with exciting activities such as a scooter jump show, kick-sled racing and reindeer racing. Kiruna is also one of the best places in the world to see the Northern Lights.

Kiruna's development is due largely to the local iron ore deposits. In 1899 the first ore train rolled out from the mine on the newly laid railway line to Luleå. Ten years later, Kiruna had grown to a town of 7,000 inhabitants. Older buildings include the church, a gift of the mining company LKAB in 1912, whose shape was inspired by a Sami hut, and which is richly decorated by artists of the time, including Prince Eugen, Christian Eriksson and Ossian Elgström.

The Kirunavaara mine is open for guided tours. **LKAB Visitor Centre** lies 540 m (1,772 ft) below ground and paints a vivid picture of mining in the region. With work in the Kirunavaara

mine causing dangerous subsidence, both Kiruna and the town of Malmberget are gradually being moved to a safer location.

Environs
The space centre **Esrange**, 40 km (25 miles) east of Kiruna has, since the first rocket was launched in 1966, been a vital link in the European space programme.

The former Sami village of **Jukkasjärvi**, 17 km (11 miles) east of Kiruna, has Lappland's oldest church, dating from 1607. It houses Bror Hjorth's altar-screen in wood depicting the charismatic 19th-century preacher Lars Levi Laestadius' missionary work among the Sami and Swedish pioneers.

Jukkasjärvi is renowned for **ICEHOTEL**, first created in 1989. In mid-November each year, a team of builders constructs a hotel with ice blocks and snow. Drinks are served in the cool

Altar-screen by Bror Hjorth, Jukkasjärvi church

Icebar and guests sleep on ice beds, wrapped in furs, even though it is -40°C outside. As spring arrives, the structure slowly thaws. The ICEHOTEL has announced plans to build a hotel, with a bar, art gallery and suites, that will offer guests a permanent sub-zero ice experience year-round. This solar powered project is expected to open in December 2016.

ICEHOTEL also offers summer activities such as whitewater rafting, cross-country cycling, fishing and ice-sculpting.

Kiruna's vast mountain landscape is traversed by the **Kungsleden** trail (see p278).

🏛 **LKAB Visitor Centre**
Tel 0980-188 80 for bookings.
Open daily. 🎿 📷
🆆 kirunalapland.se

🏨 **ICEHOTEL Jukkasjärvi**
17 km (10 miles) E of Kiruna. 🚌 from Kiruna. **Tel** 0980-668 00. **Open** Dec–Apr & Jun–Aug. 🎿 📷 📷 📷
see also Where to Stay p289.

⓮ Gällivare

Lappland. E10. 🄼 8,500. 🚆 🚗 🚌
🛈 Storgatan 16, 0970-166 60.
🎿 Winter Market (mid-Mar), Laponia Festival (1st weekend in Jul).
🆆 gellivarelapland.se

The twin communities of Gällivare and Malmberget grew rapidly from the late-19th century as the mining industry developed. But there was a settlement here long before that time: a chapel was built for the Sami in the 17th century and the Sami church on the Vassaraälven river opened in 1751. The arrival of the railway in 1888 sparked an iron ore rush which can be relived at **Kåkstan** in Malmberget and experienced from 1,000 m (3,280 ft) down in the LKAB iron ore mine. **LKAB's Gruvmuseum** focuses on

Icebar in the ICEHOTEL, Jukkasjärvi, a creation of ice and snow

250 years of mining history. The Gällivare municipality stretches to the Norwegian border, covering parts of the Laponia UNESCO World Heritage Site *(see p279)*. The Dundret nature reserve offers a number of good cross-country skiing facilities.

ⓕ Jokkmokk

Lappland. Road 97 & 45. 🏠 3,500.
🚌 🚍 ℹ️ Stortorget 4, 0971-222 50.
🎿 Jokkmokk Market (1st Thu–Sat Feb), Folk Music Festival in Saltoluokta (end Jun). 🌐 **destinationjokkmokk.se**

The town of Jokkmokk is best-known for its winter market. For a few days in February, snow, darkness and cold give way to light, warmth and sparkling colours, when more than 30,000 people arrive to browse among the 500 market stalls and join in the festivities. The annual reindeer race through the town often causes chaos, but things are even faster at the reindeer race on the frozen Lake Talvatissjön.

The life of the Sami and the pioneering Swedish settlers is depicted in **Ájtte, Svenskt Fjäll- och Samemuseum**. Unfortunately in 1972 the Sami church built in 1753 burned down. The exterior of the new church replicates the original, but it has a modern interior.

Environs
The municipality includes the magnificent national parks of Padjelanta, Sarek, Stora Sjöfallet and a section of Muddus, which is part of the Laponia UNESCO World Heritage Site *(see p279)*.

Porjus, 40 km (25 miles) north of Jokkmokk, was Sweden's first major hydroelectric power station (1910–15). Its story is related in **Porjus Expo** which has a power station museum 50 m (164 ft) underground.

In Vuollerim, 43 km (26 miles) south of Jokkmokk, Stone Age settlements have been uncovered along the Stora Luleälv river. The museum **Vuollerim 6000 År** gives visitors the chance to experience Stone Age life.

Muddus National Park, part of the Laponia UNESCO World Heritage Site

🏛 **Ájtte, Svenskt Fjäll- och Samemuseum**
Kyrkogatan 3. **Tel** 0971-170 70.
Open Jun–Aug: daily; other times: Tue–Sat. 🏠 🏠 🏠 🏠 🌐 **ajtte.com**

🏛 **Porjus Expo**
Porjus. 40 km (25 miles) N of Jokkmokk, road 45. **Tel** 070-131 87 38.
Open mid-Jun–mid-Aug; daily; other times by appointment. 🏠 🏠

🏛 **Vuollerim 6000 År**
Vuollerim. 42 km (26 miles) SW of Jokkmokk, road 97. **Tel** 0976-101 65.
Open Jul–Aug: daily. 🏠 🏠 🏠 🏠 🌐 **vuollerim6000.se**

ⓠ Arvidsjaur

Lappland. Road 94 & 45. 🏠 4,700.
🚌 to Jörn, then bus. 🚍 🚍
ℹ️ Östra Skolgatan 18C, 0960-155 00.
🎿 A-smällen (1st weekend in Jul), Sami Festival (last weekend in Aug).
🌐 **arvidsjaur.se**

This community in central Lapland was founded in the early 17th century when King Karl IX set up a church here to bring Christianity to the Sami. **Arvidsjaur's Sami church village** contains 80 huts and cabins from the 18th century.

Located in Glommersträsk, a small village southeast of Arvidsjaur, is **Hängengården**, a homestead dating from the

Traditional huts and log cabins in Arvidsjaur's 18th-century Sami church village

1800s. It is now a museum with 12 old buildings and around 3,000 items of interest.

In the summer a steam train operates on the Inlandsbanan line to the **Rallarmuseet** in Moskosel, which tells of the pioneers who built the railway.

🏛 **Rallarmuseet**
Moskosel, 40 km (25 miles) N of Arvidsjaur, road Rv 45. **Tel** 0960-175 00. **Open** mid-Jun–mid-Aug: daily. 🚍 🏠 limited access.

🏛 **Hängengården**
Glommersträsk, 45 km (28 miles) SE of Arvidsjaur, road Rv 95. **Tel** 0960-202 91. **Open** early Jun–mid-Aug: call for opening times. 🚍

ⓡ Arjeplog

Lappland. Road 95. 🏠 3,100.
🚍 Arvidsjaur. 🚍 ℹ️ Torget 1, 0961-145 20. 🎿 Winter Market (1st week in Mar), Sami Culture Week (1st week in Oct). 🌐 **polcirkeln.nu**

On the "Silver Road" between Hornavan and Uddjaur lies Arjeplog, home to the **Silver-museet**. It was created by the "Lappland doctor" Einar Wallquist, whose home Doktorsgården is open to the public in July. In addition to 16th-century Sami silverwork, the museum looks at the life of the Sami and the pioneering incomers.

The area has much to offer hunting and fishing enthusiasts.

🏛 **Silvermuseeet**
Torget. **Tel** Tourist Office, 0961-145 20. **Open** Jun–mid-Aug: daily; other times: Mon–Sat. 🏠 🏠 🏠 🏠 limited access.

For hotels and restaurants in this area see p289 and p301

⑱ The Kungsleden Trail

The best way to experience the magnificence of the Swedish mountains is to hike along a few stages of the Kungsleden Trail. In 1900, the Swedish tourism organisation, Svenska Turistföreningen (STF), drew up plans for a network of marked walking trails and huts for overnight stays through the mountains from Lappland south to Grövelsjön lake in Dalarna. Today, the 440-km (275-mile) long stretch between Abisko mountain station on the Malmbanan railway line in the north and Hemavan in southern Lappland forms the Kungsleden Trail. The simple huts have given way to mountain stations and rest cabins which offer hikers shelter in bad weather and overnight accommodation. Some also have a ferry service to help people on their way.

Mountain walkers on the well-marked Kungsleden Trail

Sarek
Perhaps the most spectacular of Sweden's national parks, Sarek has 200 lofty peaks, more than 100 glaciers, wild waterfalls and valleys such as Rapadalen. It is home to elk, lynx and wolverine.

Ammarnäs
The village is located in the Vindelfjällen nature reserve, created in 1976 and known for its fauna. Its 200 inhabitants mostly live off tourism and reindeer herding.

Hemavan is the final point for the Kungsleden Trail's northern section. With the ski town of Tärnaby close by, it is a mecca for alpine skiers.

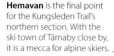

Key

- **·—·** Kungsleden Trail
- **·—·** Other walking trails
- ▨ Major road
- ▨ Minor road
- — Railway line
- ⛵ Mountain stations and cabins

Padjelanta
National Park

Vaisaluo

Kutjaure

Kisu

Låddejåkkå

Arasluokt

Stáloluokta

Tuottar

Sårjåsjaure   Staddajåkkå

Tarraluoppal

Sämmarlappa

Vaimok

Pieskehaure   Tarrekaise

Vuonatjviken

Jäkkv

Pieljekajse

Adolfström

Bäverholmen

Dalovardo   Sjnjultie

Vitnjul

Rayfallsstugan

Skidbäcksstugan

Tärnasjö
Viterskalet   Serve   Ammarnäs
Syter   Aigert

Hemavan

Tärnaby

0 kilometres		30
0 miles		20

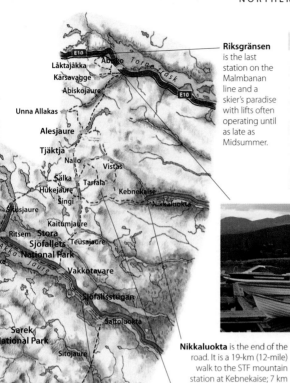

Riksgränsen
is the last
station on the
Malmbanan
line and a
skier's paradise
with lifts often
operating until
as late as
Midsummer.

VISITORS' CHECKLIST

Practical Information
Lappland. E12 to Hemavan, E10
to Kiruna and Abisko. 🛈 Kiruna
Tourist Office, 0980-188 80,
Abisko Tourist Station, 0980-402
00, Tärnaby Tourist Office, 0954-
104 50. 🚌 guided tours in some
parts. 🖳 **stfturist.se**

Transport
✈ Storuman or Kiruna, then bus.
🚆 to Kiruna and Abisko. 🚍

Nikkaluokta is the end of the
road. It is a 19-km (12-mile)
walk to the STF mountain
station at Kebnekaise; 7 km
(4 miles) can be cut by
catching the lake ferry.

Abisko
Thanks to the E10 and its own
train station, the STF tourist
facility at Torneträsk in Abisko
national park is a natural starting
point for mountain walkers.

Kebnekaise
Topping the Kebnekaise
massif is Sweden's highest
peak at 2,016 m (6,614 ft).
Below the summit, the STF
station in Ladtjodalen, 690 m
(2,264 ft), is a good starting
point for tackling the range.

Laponia World Heritage Site

The mountainous region of Lappland was designated a UNESCO World
Heritage Site in 1996. Laponia has been home to the Sami since
prehistoric times and provides the
ideal conditions for their traditional
nomadic reindeer herding, governed
by the seasons. It is also Europe's
largest single wilderness area,
home to brown bears and alpine
flora, as well as being geologically
important. These factors
contributed to its inclusion on
UNESCO's list. The region includes
the four national parks Padjelanta,
Sarek, Stora Sjöfallet and Muddus,
as well as the wetlands of Sjaunja
with their rich birdlife.

Sjaunja National Park's extensive wetlands

Stora Sjöfallet
This area is impressive for the
mountains and glaciers of
Akka and the primeval pine
forests, but the waterfall is dry
due to hydro-electric schemes.

TRAVELLERS' NEEDS

WHERE TO STAY

Sweden has a wide variety of hotels and guesthouses to suit all tastes and budgets – from small family-run establishments to historic manor houses and large luxury hotels. In addition, there are hundreds of youth hostels that offer great value, and impressive levels of comfort and cleanliness. There are also several bed-and-breakfast options, often advertised with a *RUM* (room) sign by the roadside. In the mountains, ski resorts offer both hotels and small huts to rent. Cottages are also plentiful elsewhere in Sweden, sometimes on or near camp sites. Pages 284–9 have details of places to stay throughout the country, covering everything from cosy B&Bs to designer hotels.

Outdoor sitting area at the pleasant Hotell St Clemes, Gotland *(see p286)*

Choosing a Hotel

Staying in well-appointed hotels in prime locations can be costly, but there are also plenty of budget options to choose from. Among the cheaper alternatives are youth hostels, or *vandrarhem*, most of which are of a high standard. Another good option is a self-catering cottage, ideal for families that want to stay outside busy tourist areas.

Several small, design-conscious hotels have begun catering to tourists in cities like Stockholm and Gothenburg. Larger hotels cater mainly to business travellers. Although often busy during the week, they usually offer discounted weekend rates.

It is advisable to book a room well in advance, particularly in cities during the week. Hotels in Stockholm tend to be busy in summer and when events or trade fairs are on. To find out when the busiest times are likely to be, check **Visit Stockholm**'s events calendar online.

It is very easy to make hotel reservations online. If you are looking for a room in Stockholm, Visit Stockholm offers a good booking service. Sites such as **Booking.com**, **Hotels.com** and **Visit Sweden** list a variety of options, and provide an online booking service. Most travel websites offer deals when you book your hotel and flight together.

Hotel Chains

International and Nordic hotel chains are well represented across Sweden. Some chains are renovating older hotels, keeping the classic features while modernizing the facilities.

The Swedish chain **Elite Hotels** has centrally located hotels in cities and towns across the country, often in classic buildings, and often with an attached English-style pub. Meanwhile, Nordic chain **First Hotels** has more than 60 different properties around the country. **Historic Hotels of Sweden** has 10 charming properties, including castles and manor houses, while **Nordic Choice Hotels** has a presence all across Sweden, with hotels in many northern towns and cities as well. **Radisson Blu** has a number of large hotels at the higher end of the price range in several Swedish cities, and **Best Western** has over 60 properties across the country. **Scandic Hotels** is the leading chain in the Nordic region, with more than 80 hotels across Sweden.

Prices and Payment

Prices in the hotel listings that follow are for a standard double room, including service and VAT. However, most hotels offer discounted rooms at weekends and in low season. For cheaper hotels this means a price reduction of 100–300 Kr per night, for medium-priced hotels around 500 Kr and for top hotels up to 1,000 Kr.

Most hotels accept credit cards, and many prefer it to cash. Larger hotels will change foreign currency, though the easiest and cheapest way of changing money is using a bureau de change *(see p322)*.

Youth Hostels

There are hundreds of youth hostels in Sweden; most are affiliated to the **Svenska Turistföreningen (STF)**, although there are an increasing number of independently run hostels. The flagship property is the *af Chapman* in Stockholm *(see p83)* – floating proof that a youth hostel can be just as spectacular as a top-class hostel. **Sveriges Vandrarhem i Förening (SVIF)** has around 180 youth hostels throughout the country. Both STF and SVIF are members of the International Youth Hostel Federation (IYHF). It is possible to book online on both the STF and SVIF websites.

The spectacular ICEBAR at ICEHOTEL in Jukkasjärvi *(see p289)*

Scandinavian design at its best in the lobby of the Sheraton Stockholm Hotel *(see p284)*

The standard of youth hostels in Sweden is generally high, and they are popular with people of all ages. Expect to pay around 300 Kr per person in a double room and between 200–250 Kr in a larger room or dormitory, with a discount of around 50 Kr for STF members. Prices usually exclude breakfast and bed-linen hire. Visitors can carry their own linen to avoid paying a daily surcharge. Be aware that many youth hostels close in winter.

Bed & Breakfasts

A B&B can be a good alternative to a hotel or youth hostel. There is usually a reasonable range of B&Bs in large towns and close to major roads. They offer a choice of single or double rooms or an apartment; breakfast, bed linen and towels are usually provided. Expect to pay 300–500 Kr per person per night at a town B&B; an apartment will cost from around 800 Kr per night. In the capital, rooms can be booked through **Airbnb**, **HomeAway**, or **HolidayLettings**, for a small fee.

The unmistakable Den Röda Båten, a hostel docked at Södermalm *(see p285)*

Camping

Exploring the countryside is one of the great pleasures of a trip to Sweden. *Allemansrätten* – right to roam – allows for the freedom to camp in forests and on open land, though not in view of houses on private land. Staying at a camp site will, however, ensure a more comfortable stay, with better facilities and often cottages to rent. Visit the **Sveriges Camping-och Stugföretagares Riksorganisation (SCR)** website for details. Camp sites are graded on a scale of one to five stars.

Recommended Hotels

The hotels in this book are among the best in the country and have been carefully selected to offer a variety of accommodation options. Boutique hotels are generally small with high design elements while budget includes superb value options, such as B&Bs. Business hotels feature contemporary rooms with business amenities, and family-friendly hotels have facilities suitable for children. Sweden's historic hotels are set in landmark surroundings, and the finest upscale hotels are listed as luxury. Finally, rural retreat includes cottages, cabins, mountain hotels and ski lodges.

Entries labelled as DK Choice draw attention to establishments that are exceptional in some way. They may be set in beautiful surroundings, in a historic building, or in an unusual location, such as on a boat, have stunning interiors, a superb on-site restaurant, or a great spa. Whatever the reason, you will have a memorable stay.

DIRECTORY

Central Booking

Booking.com
w booking.com

Hotels.com
w hotels.com

Visit Stockholm
Sergels Tog 5.
Tel 08-508 285 08.
w visitstockholm.com

Visit Sweden
w visitsweden.com

Hotel Chains

Best Western
Tel 020-792 752.
w bestwestern.se

Elite Hotels
Tel 0771-788 789.
w elite.se

First Hotels
w firsthotels.com

Historic Hotels of Sweden
Tel 0370-440 55.
w hhos.se

Nordic Choice Hotels
Tel 0047-22 33 42 00.
w nordicchoicehotels.se

Radisson Blu
Tel 020-238 238.
w radissonblu.com

Scandic Hotels
Tel 08-517 517 00.
w scandichotels.se

Youth Hostels

STF
Tel 08-463 21 00.
w svenskaturistforeningen.se

SVIF
Tel 031-828 800.
w svif.se

Bed & Breakfasts

Airbnb
w airbnb.co.in

HomeAway
w homeaway.com

HolidayLettings
w holidaylettings.co.uk

Camping

SCR
Tel 031-355 60 00.
w camping.se

Where to Stay

Stockholm

Gamla Stan

First Hotel Reisen Ⓚ Ⓚ
Historic **Map** 3 C3
Skeppsbron 12, 111 30
Tel *08-22 32 60*
Ⓦ firsthotels.com
Splendid location overlooking
Stockholm's waterfront. Some
rooms have saunas and Jacuzzis.

Hotel Sven Vintappare Ⓚ Ⓚ
Historic **Map** 3 B3
Sven Vintappares Gränd 3, 117 27
Tel *08-22 41 40*
Ⓦ hotelsvenvintappare.se
Located in a house built in 1607,
this hotel has seven rooms, all
decorated in Gustavian style.

Lord Nelson Hotel Ⓚ Ⓚ
Historic **Map** 3 B3
Västerlånggatan 22, 111 29
Tel *08-506 401 20*
Ⓦ thecollectorshotel.se
At just under 6-m (20-ft) wide,
Sweden's narrowest hotel is a
friendly, family-run affair.

Scandic Hotel Gamla Stan Ⓚ Ⓚ
Historic **Map** 3 B4
Lilla Nygatan 25, 111 28
Tel *08-723 72 50*
Ⓦ scandichotels.com
In a 17th-century building, this
hotel combines period decor
with modern amenities.

City

Clarion Hotel Sign Ⓚ Ⓚ
Business **Map** 1 B4
Östra Järnvägsgatan 35, 101 26
Tel *08-676 98 00*
Ⓦ clarionsign.com
One of Stockholm's largest hotels,
the Clarion has more than 500
rooms. Each floor's decor is
dedicated to a different
Scandinavian designer.

Comfort Hotel Stockholm Ⓚ Ⓚ
Family Friendly **Map** 1 B4
Kungsbron 1, 111 22
Tel *08-56 62 22 00*
Ⓦ nordicchoicehotels.com
Close to the World Trade Center,
this hotel is bursting with bright
colours, and has a pinball
machine in the lobby.

Hotel Rival Ⓚ Ⓚ
Boutique **Map** 3 A5
Mariatorget 3, 118 91
Tel *08-545 789 00*
Ⓦ rival.se
Owned by former ABBA member
Benny Andersson, this hotel has
comfortable rooms and suites,
along with a cocktail bar and bistro.

Nordic C Hotel Ⓚ Ⓚ
Luxury **Map** 1 B4
Vasaplan 4, 111 20
Tel *08-50 56 30 00*
Ⓦ nordicchotel.se
Nordic Light's sister hotel has
comfortable rooms, and is home
to the Stockholm Ice Bar.

Nordic Light Hotel Ⓚ Ⓚ
Luxury **Map** 1 B4
Vasaplan 7, 101 37
Tel *08-50 56 30 00*
Ⓦ nordiclighthotel.se
This hotel offers "Mood rooms" for
all the senses, a popular brunch
buffet and regular DJ sessions.

**Radisson Blu Royal
Viking Hotel** Ⓚ Ⓚ
Business **Map** 1 C5
Vasagatan 1, 101 24
Tel *08-50 65 40 00*
Ⓦ radissonblu.com
Enjoy all amenities, from a great
health centre and gym to a pool.
Good seafood restaurant.

Sheraton Stockholm Hotel Ⓚ Ⓚ
Business **Map** 1 C5
Tegelbacken 6, 101 23
Tel *08-412 34 00*
Ⓦ sheratonstockholm.com
Beautifully appointed rooms
and suites, many with views
across Gamla Stan.

Story Hotel Ⓚ Ⓚ
Boutique **Map** 2 D4
Riddargatan 6, 114 35
Tel *08-54 50 39 49*
Ⓦ storyhotels.com
Bohemian-chic with great art
and a graffiti decorated garden.
The hotel also has a lively bar.

The lounge and bar at Jumbo Stay, a unique
budget option at Arlanda airport

Blasieholmen & Skeppsholmen

af Chapman Ⓚ
Budget **Map** 4 E3
Flaggmansvägen 8, 111 49
Tel *08-463 22 66*
Ⓦ stfchapman.com
The *Af Chapman*, a well-known
city landmark, is now a hostel
with private rooms, disabled
access and on-site cafeteria.

Hotel Skeppsholmen Ⓚ Ⓚ
Luxury **Map** 4 E3
Gröna Gången 1, 111 86
Tel *08-407 23 00*
Ⓦ hotelskeppsholmen.com
Located in a historic building,
this upscale hotel is modern
and stylish on the inside.

Berns Hotel Ⓚ Ⓚ Ⓚ
Luxury **Map** 2 D4
Näckströmsgatan 8, 111 47
Tel *08-56 63 22 00*
Ⓦ berns.se
With modern interiors and a
majestic restaurant, this hotel
is located in the grand old
house of Berns.

Grand Hôtel Stockholm Ⓚ Ⓚ Ⓚ
Luxury **Map** 3 C1
Södra Blasieholmshamnen 8, 103 27
Tel *08-679 35 00*
Ⓦ grandhotel.se
Five-star hotel near the Royal
Palace. Fine-dining options and
the Nordic Spa & Fitness Centre.

Further Afield

ARLANDA: Jumbo Stay Ⓚ
Budget
Jumbovägen 4, 190 47
Tel *08-59 36 04 00*
Ⓦ jumbostay.se
A surprising airport hotel,
offering rooms inside a
decommissioned jumbo jet.

**DJURGÅRDEN: Scandic Hotel
Hasselbacken** Ⓚ Ⓚ
Family Friendly
Hazeliusbacken 20, 100 55
Tel *08-51 73 43 00*
Ⓦ scandichotels.com
Ideal for families, there is
a colourful playroom, kids'
activities and special rates
for family rooms.

Stately exterior of Djurgården's Scandic Hotel Hasselbacken

ÖSTERMALM:
Mornington Hotel ⓚⓚ
Boutique
Nybrogatan 53, 102 44
Tel *08-50 73 30 00*
🅦 mornington.se
This unique four-star hotel, located close to Östermalm Square, features a library, restaurant and health club.

SÖDERMALM: Den Röda
Båten ⓚ
Budget
Södermälarstrand 6, Kajplats 10, 118 20
Tel *08-644 43 85*
🅦 theredboat.com
A hotel and hostel spread over two colourful ships. There is also a café, and a common area with Wi-Fi and a TV.

DK Choice

SÖDERMALM: Långholmen Hotel & Vandrarhem ⓚ
Historic
Långholmsmuren 20, 117 33
Tel *08-720 85 00*
🅦 langholmen.com
A totally unique accommodation experience, this former prison has been converted into a three-star hotel and a youth hostel. The rooms, or cells, have been completely renovated but maintain features such as heavy secure doors. The establishment also has a bar and an inn; both serve food as well as drinks.

SÖDERMALM: Tre Små
Rum ⓚ
Budget
Högbergsgatan 81, 118 54
Tel *08-641 23 71*
🅦 tresmarum.se
This is a tranquil place to stay, with only seven rooms. Organic breakfasts are included in the price of the room.

Eastern Svealand

ESKILSTUNA:
Sundbyholms Slott ⓚⓚ
Luxury
Sundbyholms Slott, 635 08
Tel *016-42 84 00*
🅦 sundbyholms-slott.se
This romantic castle with lake views offers fabulous afternoon teas and murder mystery dinners.

KATRINEHOLM:
Dufweholms Herrgård ⓚⓚ
Historic
Herrgårdsvägen 16, 641 92
Tel *0150-754 00*
🅦 dufweholm.se
A carefully restored manor in Sörmland, with a spa, relaxation centre and library.

NORRTÄLJE:
Pensionat Granparken ⓚⓚ
Historic
Gjuterivägen 10, 761 40
Tel *0176-103 54*
🅦 granparken.com
A laid-back hotel in an early 19th-century villa, with 17 rooms and a beautiful garden.

SIGTUNA: Stadshotell ⓚⓚⓚ
Luxury
Stora Nygatan 3, 193 30
Tel *08-59 25 01 00*
🅦 sigtunastadshotell.se
Sweden's smallest five-star hotel opened in 1909, and is located in the heart of Sigtuna. King Gustav V stayed here once.

TROSA: Bomans Hotell ⓚⓚ
Boutique
Hamnen, 619 30
Tel *0156-525 00*
🅦 bomans.se
All the rooms are individually decorated, you can choose from a range of style such as Manolo Blahnik, La Dolce Vita and Carl Larsson.

UPPSALA: Clarion Hotel
Gillet ⓚⓚ
Business
Dragarbrunnsgatan 23, 753 20
Tel *018-68 18 00*
🅦 clarionhotelgillet.com
This pleasant hotel has well-appointed rooms and a popular restaurant and bar.

DK Choice

VÄSTERÅS: Utter Inn ⓚⓚ
Rooms with a View
Västeråsfjärden, Lake Mälaren, 721 87
Tel *021-39 01 00*
🅦 visitvasteras.se
One of the more unsuaul places to stay, this small, picturesque red hut on Lake Mälaren can be reached by boat from Östra Hamnen. Created by artist Mikael Genberg, there are great panoramic views from the platform the hut rests on. There is one bedroom, which is submerged in the lake, while the hut contains a small kitchen. Open Apr–Oct.

Eastern Götaland

BORGHOLM: Halltorps
Gästgiveri ⓚⓚ
Historic
Landsvägen Halltorp 105, 387 92
Tel *0485-850 00*
🅦 halltorpsgastgiveri.se
A 17th-century manor house with well-equipped rooms, a spa, open fires and wine tastings.

GRÄNNA: Hotel Amalias
Hus ⓚⓚ
Historic
Brahegatan 2, 563 32
Tel *0390-413 23*
🅦 amaliashus.se
This romantic 18th-century house features individually designed rooms, each with its own story.

JÖNKÖPING: Elite Stora
Hotellet ⓚⓚ
Historic
Hotellplan, 553 20
Tel *036-10 00 00*
🅦 elite.se
Scenically located on Lake Vättern. Comfortable rooms and an on-site English-style pub, The Bishop's Arms.

KALMAR: Calmar
Stadshotell ⓚⓚ
Historic
Stortorget 14, 392 32
Tel *0480-49 69 00*
🅦 profilhotels.se
A modern hotel in a historic building with a restaurant and pub. Buffet breakfast.

For more information on types of hotels *see page 283*

DK Choice

KOSTA: Kosta Boda Art Hotel Ⓚ Ⓚ
Boutique
Stora vägen 75, 360 52
Tel *0478-348 30*
🇼 kostabodaarthotel.com
This quirky hotel in the heart of the Kingdom of Crystal naturally has a strong emphasis on glass decorative touches, which can be seen throughout. Guests also enjoy spa facilities, a restaurant and a spectacular Glass Bar, which is worth a visit just for its gorgeous design.

NORRKÖPING: Elite Grand Hotel Ⓚ Ⓚ
Business
Tyska Torget 2, 600 41
Tel *011-36 41 00*
🇼 elite.se
A centrally located spa hotel, with modern rooms and suites, and a charming outdoor restaurant.

SKILLINGARYD: Villa Vilan Ⓚ
Budget
Galtås, 568 92
Tel *0370-741 31*
🇼 villa-vilan.com
This relaxed B&B offers guests a Jacuzzi and sauna, and is located close to nature.

SKRUV: Grimsnäs Herrgård Ⓚ
Rural Retreat
Grimsnäs Herrgård, 360 53
Tel *0709-141 456*
🇼 grimsnas.se
Environmentally friendly B&B/hostel in a pleasant manor house tucked away in a deep oak forest.

VADSTENA: Vadstena Klosterhotel Ⓚ Ⓚ
Historic
Lasarettsgatan 5, 592 30
Tel *0143-130 00*
🇼 klosterhotel.se
This former royal-palace-turned-monastery-turned-hotel features fabulous decor.

Entrance to Pensionat Warfsholm in Klintehamn

VÄXJÖ: Clarion Collection Hotel Cardinal Ⓚ Ⓚ
Business
Backgatan 10, 352 30
Tel *0470-72 28 00*
🇼 nordicchoicehotels.com
Built in 1929, this hotel has plenty of bright, modern touches, and offers its guests a sauna and complimentary organic breakfast.

VETLANDA: Best Western Vetlanda Stadshotell Ⓚ
Budget
Stortorget 5, 574 32
Tel *0383-120 90*
🇼 vetlandastadshotell.net
International chain hotel with comfortable rooms, good restaurant and a weekend disco.

VIMMERBY: Best Western Vimmerby Stadshotell Ⓚ Ⓚ
Historic
Stora Torget 9, 598 37
Tel *0492-121 00*
🇼 vimmerbystadshotell.se
A lovely hotel with modern rooms, spread across three buildings. The oldest dates back to the 1860s.

Gotland

BURGSVIK: Pensionat Holmhällar Ⓚ
Budget
Vamlingbo Austre 980, 623 31
Tel *0498-49 80 30*
🇼 holmhallar.se
Tranquil B&B near a 3-km (2-mile) stretch of beach. Breakfast buffet, lunch and dinner options.

KLINTEHAMN: Pensionat Warfsholm Ⓚ Ⓚ
Room With a View
Klinte Varvsholm 612, 623 76
Tel *0498-24 00 10*
🇼 warfsholm.se
This charming villa is scenically perched right by the sea. The top tower has been turned into a mini-suite.

LJUGARN: Kalkpatronsgården Borgvik Pensionat Ⓚ
Family Friendly
Katthammarsvik, 623 69
Tel *0498-520 87*
🇼 borgvik.com
Rooms and apartments, as well as cottages with sea views and a restaurant.

VISBY: Hotell St Clemens Ⓚ
Historic
Smedjegatan 3, 621 55
Tel *0498-21 90 00*
🇼 clemenshotell.se
This hotel offers bright rooms and suites across five buildings, connected via two picturesque gardens.

Southern Götaland

BÅSTAD: Hotel Skansen Ⓚ Ⓚ
Historic
Kyrkogatan 2, 269 33
Tel *0431-55 81 00*
🇼 hotelskansen.se
Built in 1877, this hotel was once a seed warehouse. Today, it has well-equipped rooms, a buffet breakfast, a bath house and a traditional spa.

DK Choice

GLUMSLÖV: Örenäs Slott Ⓚ Ⓚ
Luxury
Örenäs Slott, 261 63
Tel *0418-45 11 00*
🇼 orenasslott.com
Skåne is the heartland of Swedish fine dining and this hotel is known for its excellent food. A stay here guarantees a gastronomic experience amid luxurious surroundings. Rooms are individually decorated and a pool is available in summer. Golf and champagne weekend packages are available.

HELSINGBORG: Elite Hotel Mollberg Ⓚ Ⓚ
Historic
Stortorget 18, 251 14
Tel *042-37 37 00*
🇼 elite.se
One of Sweden's oldest hotels, dating to the 14th century, this period building has great views.

KARLSKRONA: Hotell Siesta Ⓚ Ⓚ
Design Hotel
Borgmästaregatan 5, 371 31
Tel *0455-801 80*
🇼 hotellsiesta.com
This Spanish-themed hotel has a sauna and outdoor spa, as well as a popular evening buffet.

KRISTIANSTAD: First Hotel Christian IV Ⓚ Ⓚ
Business
Västra Boulevarden 15, 291 31
Tel *044-20 38 50*
🇼 firsthotels.se
With its Renaissance-style architecture, this hotel was once a bank. The rooms are spacious with modern interiors. Guests can enjoy the complimentary breakfast buffet.

LANDSKRONA:
Hotel Öresund ⓀⓀ
Historic
Selma Lagerlöfs väg 4, 261 31
Tel *0418-47 40 00*
Ⓦ hoteloresund.se
The building dates from the 18th
century but the rooms are
modern and spacious.

LUND: Grand Hotel ⓀⓀⓀ
Luxury
Bantorget 1, 221 04
Tel *046-280 61 00*
Ⓦ grandilund.se
Rooms are decorated in Jugend
style at this hotel dating from
1899. Apart from its classy
interiors, the hotel boasts two
restaurants and a deli with
an excellent variety of dishes.

MALMÖ: Moment Hotel Ⓚ
Budget
Norra Vallgatan 54, 211 22
Tel *040-23 50 40*
Ⓦ momenthotels.com
Small but comfortable rooms
with Wi-Fi and flat-screen TVs.
Well-located, with a good café.

MALMÖ: Hotel Mäster
Johan ⓀⓀ
Modern
Mäster Johansgatan 13, 211 21
Tel *040-664 64 00*
Ⓦ masterjohan.com
Tastefully furnished business
rooms or suites, with a gym
and sauna on site. Bike
hire available.

SKANÖR: Hotell
Gässlingen ⓀⓀ
Historic
Rådhustorget 6, 239 30
Tel *040-45 91 00*
Ⓦ hotelgasslingen.com
A member of the Historic Hotels
of Sweden, the Gässlingen has a
Thai-Swedish spa, Jacuzzi, sauna
and outdoor pool.

YSTAD: Sekelgården ⓀⓀⓀ
Boutique
Långgatan 18, 271 23
Tel *0411-739 00*
Ⓦ sekelgarden.se
This romantic hotel is located in
an old townhouse. Family-run
and full of old-world charm.

Gothenburg

CENTRE: Barken Viking ⓀⓀ
Historic
Lilla Bommens Torg 10, 411 04
Tel *031-63 58 00*
Ⓦ barkenviking.com
Stay aboard a three-star ship in
Gothenburg's harbour. This unique

Beautifully lit and spacious sauna at Gothenburg's Scandic Opalen

hotel features nautical-style interiors, with a restaurant on the deck.

DK Choice

CENTRE: Clarion
Hotel Post ⓀⓀ
Design Hotel
Drottningtorget 10, 411 03
Tel *031-61 90 00*
Ⓦ clarionpost.com
Housed inside the former post
office building, this hotel
looks spectacular. Guests are
greeted by a dazzling crystal
reception desk, and the
public areas are equally
striking. Additional features
include a roof-top pool, bar
area and sun terrace, a spa and
two restaurants.

CENTRE: Elite Park
Avenue Hotel ⓀⓀ
Modern
Kungsportsavenyn 36–38, 400 15
Tel *031-727 10 00*
Ⓦ elite.se
Four-star hotel with a restaurant,
café and gym. Rooms have
TVs, Wi-Fi, and a range of CDs
and DVDs.

CENTRE: Scandic Opalen ⓀⓀ
Modern
Engelbrektsgatan 73, 412 52
Tel *031-751 53 00*
Ⓦ scandichotels.com
Sauna, gym, Jacuzzi, parking
and free Wi-Fi are available
at this hotel. Minimalist rooms
with parquet flooring and
flatscreen TVs.

FURTHER AFIELD: Radisson
Blu Riverside Hotel ⓀⓀ
Modern
Lindholmspiren 4, 417 56
Tel *031-383 40 00*
Ⓦ radissonblu.com/riverside
hotel-gothenburg
Elegant rooms and a fantastic
fitness complex with gorgeous
views of the harbour.

Western Götaland

DALS LÅNGED: Baldersnäs
Herrgård ⓀⓀ
Historic
Baldersnäs 22, 660 10
Tel *0531-412 13*
Ⓦ baldersnas.com
Classic Swedish mansion
set on a lakeside peninsula
in the middle of a nature
reserve. Great views.

FJÄLLBACKA: Stora Hotellet
Bryggan ⓀⓀ
Historic
Ingrid Bergmans Torg, 457 40
Tel *0525-310 60*
Ⓦ storahotellet-fjallbacka.se
Charming rooms, some with
a nautical theme, in this hotel
located on the pier.

HALMSTAD: Best Western Plus
Grand Hotel ⓀⓀ
Historic
Stationsgatan 44, 302 45
Tel *035-280 81 00*
Ⓦ grandhotel.nu
Opened in 1905, this
hotel has attractive, colourful
rooms with black-and-
white bathrooms.

LIDKÖPING: Stadt
Lidköping ⓀⓀ
Historic
Gamla Stadens Torg 1, 531 32
Tel *0510-220 85*
Ⓦ stadtlidkoping.se
A charming lakeside hotel with
a restaurant, pub and conference
rooms. Well-located, and
surrounded by natural beauty.

MARIESTAD: Hotell
Vänerport ⓀⓀ
Budget
Hamngatan 32, 542 30
Tel *0501-77 111*
Ⓦ vanerport.se
Individually decorated rooms
with great attention to detail.
Breakfast buffet.

For more information on types of hotels *see page 283*

**MARSTRAND: Marstrands
Havshotell** ⓚⓚ
Rooms with a View
Varvskajen 2, 442 66
Tel *0303-24 02 00*
W marstrands.se
Seaside hotel offering a variety of
spa and sports package deals.

**SMÖGEN: Hotell Smögens
Hafvsbad** ⓚ
Historic
Hotellgatan 26, 456 51
Tel *0523-66 84 50*
W smogenshafvsbad.se
Popular when it opened in 1900,
this spa hotel is now a year-
round resort.

STRÖMSTAD: Laholmen ⓚⓚ
Business
Laholmen, 452 30
Tel *0526-197 00*
W laholmen.se
Great for business and holiday
guests. Conference facilities, bar
and nightclub.

DK Choice

TJÖRN: Salt & Sill ⓚⓚ
Rooms with a View
471 51 Klädesholmen
Tel *0304-67 34 80*
W saltosill.se
This floating hotel is located in a
traditional herring fishing village.
The rooms have been designed
in modern Nordic style. A restaurant with outdoor seating in the
summer serves fine Swedish
cuisine. Also has the world's
fastest floating sauna boat!

TROLLHÄTTAN: Albert Hotell ⓚⓚ
Historic
Strömsbergsvägen 2, 461 57
Tel *0520-129 90*
W alberthotell.com
A four-star hotel housed in a villa
dating from 1857, complete with
a resident ghost. Great dining.

**VÄDERÖARNA:
Värdshus** ⓚⓚ
Rooms with Views
Ramnö, Norra Väderöarna, 457 40
Tel *0525-320 01*
W vaderoarna.com
This rustic hotel's prices include
accommodation, sauna and boat
transfer from Fjällbacka.

**VÄNERSBORG: Quality Hotel
Vänersborg** ⓚ
Business
Nabbensbergsvägen 2, 462 40
Tel *0521-57 57 20*
W qualityvanersborg.se
Facilities at this relaxed hotel
include conference rooms,
gym and spa treatments.

**VARBERG: Best Western Varbergs
Stadshotell & Asia Spa** ⓚⓚ
Luxury
Kungsgatan 24–26, 432 41
Tel *0340-69 01 00*
W varbergsstadshotell.com
Pleasant hotel in an old building
with an Asian-inspired spa.
The rooms offer spectacular
sea views.

Western Svealand

DK Choice

**ARVIKA: Spahotell
Scandic Arvika** ⓚⓚ
Historic
Torggatan 9, 671 31
Tel *0570-197 50*
W scandichotels.se
This elegant spa hotel is
housed in one of Arvika's oldest
buildings. Explore an excellent
variety of treatments at the spa,
which is adult's only – children
aged 15 or over are admitted
only with a parent or guardian.

**BORLÄNGE: First Hotel
Brage** ⓚⓚ
Business
Stationsgatan 1–3, 784 33
Tel *0243-21 76 60*
W firsthotels.se
Pleasant hotel with two
restaurants, a sauna and a
weekend nightclub.

**FALUN: Clarion Collection
Hotel Bergmästaren** ⓚⓚ
Business
Bergsskolegränd 7, 791 12
Tel *023-70 17 00*
W clarionhotel.com
This pet-friendly hotel offers
guests a sauna, hot tub and
organic breakfasts.

**KARLSTAD: Elite
Stadshotellet Karlstad** ⓚⓚ
Business
Kungsgatan 22, 651 08
Tel *054-29 30 00*
W elite.se
Stay in individually decorated
rooms at this beautiful riverside
hotel. There is a cosy pub and
restaurant on the premises.

**MORA: Best Western
Mora Hotell & Spa** ⓚⓚ
Rooms with a View
Strandgatan 12, 792 30
Tel *0250-59 26 50*
W morahotell.se
This 19th-century building
overlooks Lake Siljan. Steam
room, pool and sauna.

**ÖREBRO: Elite
Stora Hotellet** ⓚⓚ
Historic
Drottninggatan 1, 701 45
Tel *019-15 69 00*
W elite.se
Grand old building from the
1850s, set in a scenic riverside
location. Bar, sauna and parking.

**RÄTTVIK: Dala Wärdshus
Hotell Gärdebygården** ⓚ
Rural Retreat
*Hol Daniels väg, Hantverksbyn,
795 36*
Tel *0248-302 50*
W dalawardshus.se
A peaceful hotel with a private
beach, and views of the lake.
Open during summer.

TÄLLBERG: Åkerblads ⓚ
Historic
Sjögattu 2, 793 70
Tel *0247-508 00*
W akerblads.se
Beautifully furnished hotel with
a spa, restaurant and impressive
wine cellar. Some parts date back
to the 15th century.

Southern Norrland

DK Choice

ÅRE: Hotell Fjällgården ⓚⓚ
Rural Retreat
Fjällgårdsvägen 35, 830 13
Tel *0647-145 00*
W fjallgarden.se
Dating from 1910, this hotel
offers fantastic views, sauna,
spa and tasty cuisine right
on the slopes. There is also
a mountain funicular link to
the city. In summer there's
mountain biking, ziplining, elk
safaris and white-water rafting.

View from the slopes of the spectacular
Hotel Fjällgården in Åre

HIGH COAST: STF Vandrarhem Köpmanholmen Ⓚ
Budget
Köpmansholmsvägen 2, 893 40
Tel *0660-22 34 96*
W svenskaturistforeningen.se
This quayside hostel offers single, double and dormitory rooms. It also has an à la carte restaurant.

HIGH COAST: Hotell Höga Kusten ⓀⓀ
Rural Retreat
Hornöberget, 872 94 Sandöverken
Tel *0613-72 22 70*
W hotellhoga-kusten.se
Twenty-eight artistically decorated rooms at Sweden's first wind-powered hotel. Meditation path and pool.

HUDIKSVALL: Quality Hotel Statt ⓀⓀ
Business
Storgatan 36, 824 22
Tel *0650-150 60*
W nordicchoicehotels.com
Beautifully restored, this 19th-century building is now a conference hotel with a spa, gym and pool.

ÖRNSKÖLDSVIK: First Hotel Statt ⓀⓀ
Historic
Lasarettsgatan 2, 891 21
Tel *0660-26 55 90*
W firsthotels.com
The building dates from 1913, but the rooms are modern and functional. Breakfast is included.

ÖSTERSUND: Best Western Hotel Gamla Teatern ⓀⓀ
Historic
Thoméegränd 20, 831 34
Tel *063-51 16 00*
W gamlateatern.se
Housed in a converted theatre, this hotel offers guests all modern amenities. Stay includes complimentary breakfast.

STORLIEN: Storliens Högfjällshotell ⓀⓀ
Rural Retreat
Geijerbacken 10, 830 19
Tel *0647-701 70*
W storlienhogfjallshotell.se
One of Scandinavia's largest mountain hotels. Enjoy the roaring open fires, indoor pool and sauna.

SUNDSVALL: Gaffelbyn Ⓚ
Budget
Norra Stadsberget, 856 40
Tel *060-61 21 19*
W gaffelbyn.se
Good hostel with kitchen facilities. Some rooms have en-suite bathrooms. Free parking.

Comfortable seating in the lobby of the Scandic Ferrum, Kiruna

SVEG: Lilla Hotellet Ⓚ
Budget
Älvgatan 8, 842 32
Tel *0680-102 84*
W lillahotellet.se
Comfortable rooms, with discounts for longer stays. Buffet breakfast.

Northern Norrland

ABISKO: STF Abisko Turiststation Ⓚ
Rural Retreat
Abisko Turiststation, 981 07
Tel *0980-402 00*
W svenskaturistforeningen.se
Located above the Arctic Circle amid pristine scenery. Great for winter skiing and summer hiking.

HAPARANDA: Haparanda Stadshotell ⓀⓀ
Historic
Torget 7, 953 31
Tel *0922-614 90*
W haparandastadshotell.se
A quirky hotel with rooms dating back to 1900, conference facilities and a nightclub.

HARADS: Treehotel ⓀⓀⓀ
Boutique
Edeforsväg 2A, 960 24
Tel *0928-104 03*
W treehotel.se
Spectacularly designed tree rooms and a sauna in the forest near Harads. Fantastic views.

DK Choice
JUKKASJÄRVI: ICEHOTEL ⓀⓀⓀ
Luxury
Marknadsvägen 63, 981 91
Tel *0980-668 00*
W icehotel.com
ICEHOTEL is rebuilt every year with different room designs. Sample delicious Arctic cuisine here *(see p301)*. Northern Lights excursions can be arranged.

KIRUNA: Scandic Ferrum ⓀⓀ
Family Friendly
Lars Janssonsgatan 15, 981 31
Tel *0980-39 86 00*
W scandichotels.com
Child-friendly hotel with non-smoking rooms. Facilities include a sauna and gym. Complimentary breakfast.

LULEÅ: Elite Stadshotellet ⓀⓀ
Historic
Storgatan 15, 972 32
Tel *0920-27 40 00*
W elite.se
A unique and stylish hotel with a renowned restaurant and a pub on site.

PITEÅ: Piteå Stadshotell ⓀⓀ
Historic
Olof Palmes Gata 1, 941 33
Tel *0911-23 40 00*
W piteastadshotell.com
Four-star hotel with top dining and business facilities.

RIKSGRÄNSEN: Hotell Riksgränsen ⓀⓀ
Rural Retreat
Riksgränsvägen 15, 981 94
Tel *0980-641 00*
W riksgransen.se
Sweden's northernmost ski hotel. Excellent skiing and spa facilities.

SKELLEFTEÅ: Skellefteå Stadshotell ⓀⓀ
Business
Stationsgatan 8, 931 31
Tel *0910-71 10 60*
W skellefteastadshotell.se
Four-star city hotel dating to the middle of the 19th century. Comfortable rooms, with flat-screen TVs.

UMEÅ: Clarion Collection Hotel Uman ⓀⓀ
Historic
Storgatan 52, 903 26
Tel *090-12 72 20*
W clarionhotel.com
This pleasant old-fashioned hotel serves delicious organic breakfasts and afternoon tea.

For more information on types of hotels *see page 283*

WHERE TO EAT AND DRINK

Swedish cuisine is a serious contender on the world stage. The traditional *husmanskost* (home fare) in particular is enjoying a creative renaissance with a new generation of award-winning chefs. Several restaurants in the country have been awarded Michelin stars, and many of the top chefs run their own establishments. International influences are often combined to create innovative and delicious dishes often referred to as "crossover", or modern Swedish, cuisine. Traditional Swedish dishes are frequently served at lunchtime and are excellent value for money. There are also plenty of fast-food outlets, Chinese restaurants, pizzerias and kebab houses offering inexpensive food. Hot-dog stands, providing filling snacks, can be found practically everywhere.

Where to Eat

A wide range of restaurants can be found in Sweden's major cities. There are also a number of good places to eat in smaller towns and in the countryside, where many historic manor-house hotels have excellent restaurants. Larger department stores and shopping malls, as well as most museums, have decent restaurants or cafés. Open sandwiches with a variety of fillings can be bought at cafés and cake shops, which often serve inexpensive hot dishes at lunchtime as well. Larger towns often have market halls with excellent eateries, but they are not open in the evenings. Along the coast and inland there are many establishments that open only in the summer.

Many restaurants and cafés offer outdoor seating areas in the summer. In fine weather, eateries can also be spotted in parks and green areas, such as Djurgården in Stockholm and Kungsportsavenyn in Gothenburg.

Types of Restaurant

Popular restaurants can be very crowded, so if you are looking for somewhere quieter with a pleasant atmosphere, it may be best to choose an established restaurant. Sweden offers an excellent range of cuisines and there are many specialist eateries serving international dishes or modern Swedish cooking.

If you are looking for something cheaper, there are plenty of budget options. If you have a sweet tooth, you should visit one of the country's many cafés or traditional cake shops, with their delicious pastries, cakes, cinnamon buns and gateaux. An increasing number of bars have also opened up, often attached to restaurants in the cities and to hotels in the countryside.

The dress code is usually informal, even at the more elegant restaurants. Ties are very rarely required, though shorts are not acceptable. Many restaurants do not allow guests to take outdoor clothing into the dining room and charge a mandatory cloakroom fee on entry.

Smoking is banned in all bars and restaurants in Sweden.

Opening Times

The majority of restaurants open for lunch at 11:30am and close around 10pm. Dinner is served from 6pm or even earlier. Many establishments are closed on Sundays or Mondays. Smaller restaurants may close for their annual holiday in July or during the winter months. Prices for lunch are often reasonable, even at the more elegant establishments. *Dagens lunch* (lunch of the day) is generally not served after 2pm, even if the restaurant is open in the afternoon.

Restaurants with music, entertainment or a nightclub usually serve dinner until late. Hot-dog kiosks and pizzerias remain open till late, sometimes even round the clock.

Vegetarian Food

Vegetarian cuisine is served at most restaurants. There are also many completely vegetarian and vegan eateries in the major cities. Gluten-free options are easily available as well.

Booking a Table

Reservations are recommended for evening meals. However, many places do not accept bookings; if you want to be sure of a table at lunch it is best to arrive before 11:30am

The dimly lit and cosy dining space at Villa Sjötorp in Ljungskile *(see p299)*

The bright interiors of Sturehof, one of Stockholm's first seafood restaurants *(see p294)*

or after 1pm, by which time most of the lunchtime clientele will have left.

Children

Children are welcome in most restaurants, except those eateries that are open only in the evenings and have a nightclub. Kids will usually be offered a special children's menu or half-portions from the standard menu. Most restaurants provide highchairs.

Prices

Generally, hot dishes are priced from about 120 Kr; at expensive or award-winning restaurants, the average price of a main course is between 250–350 Kr.

Lunch prices are around 70–100 Kr, often including a non-alcoholic drink and coffee. However, the price of beer, wine and other alcoholic drinks varies considerably. The more expensive the restaurant, the higher the price of wine. The house wine is usually the cheapest, with a bottle costing 250–350 Kr. Beer is generally cheaper in pubs than it is in restaurants. Tap water is free of charge, and Sweden's drinking water is of excellent quality.

Tips are always included in the price, but if you want to reward particularly good service, you can round up the bill. Leaving your coat in a manned cloakroom costs about 20–30 Kr per item. Avoid using cash as most restaurants accept only credit cards.

Reading the Menu

Dinner at a Swedish restaurant usually includes a *förrätt* (starter), *varmrätt* (hot main course) and *efterrätt* (dessert). Most places offer one or more fixed-price meals, with a choice of two or three dishes at a lower price than the à la carte menu. It is perfectly acceptable to have just a starter or main course. At lunchtime most people order only one course. Some high-end restaurants may have dessert or cheese trolleys. Many restaurants have menus in English; if not, the waiters and waitresses are usually fluent in English and will be happy to explain the choices available.

Some restaurants serve a typical Swedish *smörgåsbord*, mostly on Sundays *(see p292)*. On the coast, they often specialize in fish or shellfish buffets. During December, a *Julbord* or a 'Christmas table' is usually available. This is similar to the usual *smörgåsbord*, but with a lavish buffet of traditional seasonal dishes. You can eat as much as you like at a fixed price, but drinks are not included.

What to Drink

Wine and beer are the normal accompaniments to a meal, as well as water. Beer is graded into three classes, with *lättöl* being the weakest. *Husmanskost* (traditional home-style cooking) is great when washed down with beer. For an authentic experience, end the meal with one of many different-flavoured snaps. Pubs and restaurants usually offer a wide selection of beers, including very good Swedish- and American-brewed craft beers.

Spirits and wines are more expensive in restaurants in Sweden than in most other countries; this is because of the high duty on alcohol and Systembolaget *(see p319)*, the state alcohol-monopoly chain.

Recommended Restaurants

The restaurants on the following pages have been carefully selected to give a cross-section of options in every region: you will find everything from fine dining and traditional restaurants to modern Swedish, international cuisine and bistro fare.

The fine-dining options include some of the best restaurants in Sweden, often located in historic, atmospheric and scenic places. Traditional restaurants have a strong emphasis on Swedish home cooking and classic ingredients, and are frequently found in rural locations. Modern Swedish cuisine combines local ingredients and international flavours. The international and bistro options serve mostly global favourites at reasonable prices. Many of the restaurants listed use organic local produce whenever possible.

The DK Choice entries highlight exceptional establishments that offer more than just excellent food.

A well-garnished dish at Frantzén, one of Stockholm's best restaurants *(see p294)*

The Flavours of Sweden

Thanks to strict regulations, Sweden is one of most unpolluted countries in Europe and produces some of the purest food. Salmon can be caught in the heart of Stockholm, zander and herring are fished from the nearby coastal waters and the lakes and rivers are full of crayfish and other delicacies. Fish is a staple, but other gastronomic treats are also on offer. Wild game, such as grouse, reindeer and elk, is abundant in autumn and winter. The forests are full of berries and mushrooms, and the rich pastures produce superlative dairy produce, including several fine cheeses.

Fresh dill

Fresh anchovies on offer at Östermalmshallen food market

The Smörgåsbord

The *smörgåsbord* made its first appearance on Swedish tables sometime in the 18th century, when it consisted of a spread of hot and cold hors d'oeuvres that would be served as a prelude to a grand lunch or dinner. All this was washed down with ice-cold "snaps" (vodka). Gradually, however, it has grown into a full-scale meal. A traditional *smörgåsbord* will start with a selection of different herring appetizers, followed by a variety of cold dishes such as hard-boiled eggs, meat pies and salads. Then a number of hot dishes are served, including such offerings as meatballs, fried potatoes and Jansson's Temptation (a gratin of potatoes, onions, anchovies and cream). Finally an array of desserts will be placed on the table. Diners help themselves, changing their plates between courses.

Some Swedes will prepare a *smörgåsbord* as a good way of using left-overs. Inventive cooks often improvise a very simple version when unexpected guests arrive, using larder staples, such as eggs, slices of

Beetroot & orange salad | Rye crispbread | Pickled herring
Cucumber salad | | Egg with lumpfish roe | Cheese
Lingonberry tartlets | Pork liver pâté | Cooked meat
Selection of items typically found on a cold *smörgåsbord*

Local Dishes and Specialities

A typical Swedish breakfast often includes yogurt or *filmjölk* (a type of soured milk yogurt) with cereal. Many Swedes, however, prefer a more savoury start to the day and cheese, ham and even liver pâté may be on offer. Bread spread with *kaviar* (a cod's roe paste) is also eaten at breakfast. For lunch, most people reach for something quick and simple to prepare. Salad, perhaps served with a seafood, ham or vegetable quiche, is common and pasta is popular too. As well as the main meals, a break for coffee and pastries, known as *fika*, is taken at any time of the day. This strong Swedish tradition is a sociable event as much as an occasion to eat. In the evening, families usually get together for the main meal of the day - dinner, a more elaborate, but still homely, affair.

Lingonberries

Gravad Lax, a salmon fillet, marinated for two days in sugar, salt and dill, is served with a creamy mustard sauce.

A colourful vegetable stall at Hötorget market

cheese and cooked meats, and tinned or pickled fish. During the Christmas season, many Stockholm restaurants serve a special *smörgåsbord*, known as *Julbord*, which could include everything from meatballs and sausages to smoked salmon.

Rustic Fare

The Swedes are very good at using cheap cuts to prepare delicious dishes. Seasoning is usually kept simple with salt, pepper and fresh dill. Such homely fare, known as *husmanskost*, is central to the Swedish diet and often features on the menus of many Stockholm restaurants. One favourite is yellow pea soup, traditionally served on Thursdays, accompanied by sausages or lightly salted meat and mustard. This is

generally followed by pancakes with jam, washed down with hot *punsch*. Other popular dishes include *pytt i panna* (a hash of meat, onions and potatoes) and meatballs served with lingonberry jam.

A selection of fine fish from Sweden's coastal waters

Sweden's Dining "Revolution"

The turn of the 21st century has witnessed a renaissance of gourmet cooking in Sweden, with people now visiting Stockholm for its food as well as its culture. Traditional dishes, made with the finest – usually organic – ingredients are being given an original, modern twist. Instead of simple meatballs with lingonberries, chefs are increasingly offering delights such as *foie gras* with a spiced mixed berry and apple chutney and turning cheap staples, such as pig's offal, into magnificent, melt-in-the-mouth mousses.

What to Drink

Beer Along with vodka, beer is the most popular drink to accompany a *smörgåsbord*. Until recently, little was on offer other than insipid lagers, but a recent beer-making revival has made styles from dark porters to pale ales available, including some interesting fruit beers.

Snaps About 60 types of "snaps", each flavoured with different herbs and spices, are made in Sweden.

Punsch This sweet arak spirit is traditionally taken with coffee or served hot with pea soup.

Wine A huge variety of fine wines are imported, but are usually very expensive.

Jansson's Temptation is a dish of layered potato, pickled sprats and onion with cream, baked until golden.

Meatballs made from beef or pork are drenched in a rich meaty sauce and served with lingonberries.

Apple cake is a delicious buttery dessert traditionally served piping hot with cold vanilla sauce.

Where to Eat and Drink

Stockholm

Gamla Stan

Hermitage ⓚ
Vegetarian   **Map** 3 B3
Stora Nygatan 11, 111 27
Tel *08-411 95 00*
A relaxed, cosy café serving an
excellent lunch buffet, with
fresh, organic ingredients.

Bistro & Grill Ruby ⓚⓚ
Bistro   **Map** 3 C3
Österlånggatan 14, 111 31
Tel *08-20 60 15*   **Closed** *Sun (bistro)*
This establishment in the
heart of Gamla Stan is the place
for charcoal-grilled beef, pork
and lamb. Weekend brunch
from noon.

Den Gyldene Freden ⓚⓚ
Traditional Swedish   **Map** 3 C4
Österlånggatan 51, 111 31
Tel *08-24 97 60*   **Closed** *Sun*
Serving typical Swedish dishes
since 1722. Enjoy pikeperch,
Swedish meatballs and other
classics in a beautiful setting.

Mr French ⓚⓚ
Fine Dining   **Map** 3 C3
Tullhus 2, Skeppsbron, 111 30
Tel *08-20 20 95*
The menu at this restaurant
is inspired by classic French
brasserie fare and features grills
and fresh seafood.

Frantzén ⓚⓚⓚ
Fine Dining   **Map** 3 B3
Lilla Nygatan 21, 111 28
Tel *08-20 85 80*   **Closed** *Sun & Mon*
An elegant addition to
Stockholm's culinary scene, this
establishment has appeared on
the World's 50 Best Restaurants
list. The 14-course taster menu
is highly recommended.

City

Grill ⓚⓚ
International   **Map** 1 B3
Drottninggatan 89, 113 60
Tel *08-31 45 30*
Housed in an old furniture shop,
this restaurant serves grilled
dishes from around the world.
The lunch buffet, on weekdays,
is popular with locals.

Nalen ⓚⓚ
Traditional Swedish   **Map** 2 D3
Regeringsgatan 74, 111 39
Tel *08-505 292 00*   **Closed** *Sun*
Located inside one of the best-
known nightspots in Sweden,
Nalen places the emphasis firmly

on simple, traditional Swedish
food. A bar, nightclub and concert
hall are also on the premises.

Sturehof ⓚⓚ
Modern Swedish   **Map** 2 D4
Sturegallerian 42, Stureplan 2, 114 46
Tel *08-440 57 30*
Boasting an illustrious history
as one of Stockholm's first
fish and seafood restaurants,
Sturehof now serves the
freshest daily catches and
other Swedish produce.

Ekstedt ⓚⓚⓚ
Modern Swedish   **Map** 2 D3
Humlegårdsgatan 17, 114 46
Tel *08-611 12 10*   **Closed** *Mon*
Run by Swedish celebrity chef
Niklas Ekstedt, this contemporary
Michelin-starred restaurant
serves rustic dishes cooked over
an open fire.

DK Choice

Operakällaren ⓚⓚⓚ
Fine Dining   **Map** 3 B1
Operahuset, Karl XII:s Torg, 111 86
Tel *08-676 58 00*   **Closed** *Sun &
Mon*
One of Sweden's historic culinary
institutions, Operakällaren
(meaning "Opera Cellar") got
its name as early as 1787,
when it was located in the
cellar underneath the Opera
House. The magnificent decor
of the restaurant complements
the exquisite dining experience.
Also on the premises are
Café Opera, the Opera Bar,
the Terrace and the tiny
Bakfickan bar.

Blasieholmen & Skeppsholmen

**Mathias Dahlgren
Matsalen** ⓚⓚⓚ
Fine Dining   **Map** 3 C1
Södra Blasieholmshamnen 6, 111 48
Tel *08-679 35 84*   **Closed** *Sun & Mon*
The restaurant of the Grand Hôtel
Stockholm is suitably impressive
and serves modern Swedish
gourmet food. The Matbaren
bistro is also in the hotel and
is open at lunchtime too.

Further Afield

**DJURGÅRDEN:
Rosendals Trädgårdscafe** ⓚ
Traditional Swedish
Rosendalsterrassen 12, 115 21
Tel *08-545 812 70*   **Closed** *Sun &
Mon in winter*
Set in a pleasant garden, this café
serves excellent seasonal lunches,
including sandwiches.

**DJURGÅRDEN: Wärdshuset
Ulla Winbladh** ⓚⓚ
Traditional Swedish
Rosendalsvägen 8, 115 21
Tel *08-534 897 01*
This former bakery dating from
1897 serves rustic Swedish home
cooking prepared with fresh,
seasonal ingredients. There is
indoor as well as terrace seating,
and a wide selection of fine wines.

Beautifully lit dining hall at Den Gyldene Freden, a traditional Swedish restaurant

GÄRDET: Dell'Attore ⓚ
Italian
Skeppargatan 60, 114 59
Tel *08-442 61 18*
Popular with locals, Dell'Attore is
a great place to enjoy authentic
Italian pizzas. Book ahead to
avoid waiting.

KUNGSHOLMEN:
La Famiglia ⓚⓚ
Italian
Alströmergatan 45, 112 47
Tel *08-650 63 10* **Closed** *Sun & Mon
in Jul*
Family-friendly restaurant serving
classic Italian pasta dishes, fish and
regional specialities cooked on a
wood-fire grill. Good desserts.

KUNGSHOLMEN:
Mäster Anders ⓚⓚ
Modern Swedish
Pipersgatan 1, 112 24
Tel *08-654 20 01*
The charcoal grill offers a mix
of meat and fish dishes. Try the
grilled Arctic char or the lobster
with Västerbotten cheese.

NORRTULL:
Stallmästaregården ⓚⓚ
Fine Dining
Norrtull, 113 47
Tel *08-610 13 00*
An old-fashioned inn in a scenic
location overlooking Brunnsviken
Bay. Classic Swedish dishes have
an emphasis on organic and local
produce. Delicious desserts.

DK Choice
ÖSTERMALM:
Östermalm Saluhall ⓚ
Traditional Swedish
Östermalms Torg, 114 39
Tel *08-553 404 40* **Closed** *Sun*
Stockholm's delightful indoor
food hall, housed in a beautiful
late 19th-century building, has
eight eateries to choose from,
including seafood restaurants,
sandwich bars, coffee shops
and bistros. Particularly popular
is Gerda's Fish and Seafood
Restaurant, serving up the latest
catch. There is also a market
that sells fresh produce. Open
only in the daytime.

ÖSTERMALM: Esperanto ⓚⓚ
Fusion
Kungstensgatan 2, 114 25
Tel *08-696 23 23* **Closed** *Sun–Tue*
This elegant restaurant offers
a menu that expertly mixes
Swedish-style dishes with
Japanese ingredients. The menu
changes seasonally but sample
dishes include wild river salmon
with chilled *dashi*.

Range of international wines on display
at the luxurious Gondolen in Södermalm

ÖSTERMALM: Teatergrillen ⓚⓚ
Modern Swedish
Nybrogatan 3, 114 34
Tel *08-545 035 65* **Closed** *Sun*
The menu at this fine restaurant
has an obvious French twist. Try
their famous *Biff Rydberg*, a
delicious beef and potato dish, or
the salt-baked sirloin served from
the *Silvervagnen* trolley.

SÖDERMALM: Café String ⓚ
Traditional Swedish
Nytorgsgatan 38, 116 40
Tel *08-714 85 14*
One of Södermalm's popular
eateries, Café String serves good
coffee as well as sandwiches and
pies. Unusually, some of the
furniture here is for sale.

SÖDERMALM: Kalf & Hansen ⓚ
Modern Swedish
Mariatorget 2, 118 49
Tel *08-551 531 51*
Enjoy seasonal, organic fast food
prepared with a distinct Nordic
twist. There are plenty of options
for vegetarians and vegans.

SÖDERMALM: Vurma ⓚ
Traditional Swedish
Bergsunds Strand 31, 117 38
Tel *08-669 09 60*
This bright, sunny café serves
good sandwiches and salads. It
also offers a selection of healthy
set meals for breakfast.

SÖDERMALM:
Koh Phangan ⓚⓚ
Thai
Skånegatan 57, 116 37
Tel *08-642 50 40*
In a playful setting, Koh Phangan
serves delicious soups, curries
and salads. The restaurant is close
to the Göta Lejon theatre and is
perfect for a pre-theatre dinner.

SÖDERMALM: Pelikan ⓚⓚ
Traditional Swedish
Blekingegatan 40, 116 62
Tel *08-556 090 90*
Swedish *husmanskost*, or home-
cooking, at its finest. Try the
meatballs, herring, crayfish and
local beers.

SÖDERMALM: Urban Deli ⓚⓚ
Modern Swedish
Nytorget 4, 116 40
Tel *08-425 500 30*
This popular place is a mix of
restaurant, food hall, deli and
bakery. Shop and eat all under
one roof.

SÖDERMALM: Gondolen ⓚⓚⓚ
Fine Dining
Stadsgården 6, 116 45
Tel *08-641 70 90*
Dangling 33-m (108-ft) above
water, Gondolen is one of the
city's most unique restaurants.
Enjoy spectacular views and
delicious gourmet food.

SOLNA: Ulriksdals
Wärdshus ⓚⓚ
Traditional Swedish
Ulriksdals Slottspark, 170 79 Solna
Tel *08-85 08 15*
This beautiful inn serves typical
rustic Swedish cuisine and is
particularly renowned for its
smörgåsbord and the Christmas
equivalent, *julbord*.

VASASTAN: Browallshof ⓚⓚ
Fine Dining
Surbrunnsgatan 20, 113 48
Tel *08-16 51 36* **Closed** *Sun*
Housed in a quaint inn that
first opened its doors in 1731,
this restaurant offers classic
Swedish dishes created with
international touches.

VASASTAN: Storstad ⓚⓚ
Fine Dining
Odengatan 41, 113 51
Tel *08-673 38 00* **Closed** *Sun*
This spacious family-run
restaurant located in a
traditional Vasastan building
serves creative Swedish cuisine.

Eastern Svealand

JÖNÅKER: Wreta
Gestgifveri ⓚⓚ
Modern Swedish
Wreta Gestgifveri, 611 90 Ålberga
Tel *0155-720 22*
A mix of Swedish and
international dishes, along
with great dessert options are
available. There is an outdoor
dining area in summer and a
pleasant garden.

For more information on types of restaurants *see page 291*

Lavish bar at the Asian-American restaurant Jay Fu in Uppsala

NYKÖPING: Mickes Skafferi ⓚⓚ
Modern Swedish
Västra Storgatan 29, 611 32
Tel *0155-26 99 50*   Closed *Sun*
"Micke's Pantry" offers plenty
of Swedish fare with interesting
Mediterranean influences, such
as the rack of lamb with
artichoke *aïoli.*

DK Choice

**TROSA: Bomans Hotel
& Restaurang**   ⓚⓚ
Traditional Swedish
Östra Hamnplan 1, 619 30
Tel *0156-525 00*   Closed *Sun*
This well-loved family-run
restaurant offers a small
but quality menu. You'll find
traditional Swedish cuisine
with an emphasis on food-
and-wine pairings. Try the
delicious loin of red deer
with spruce shoots. There is
an excellent selection of
international wines.

UPPSALA: Jay Fu   ⓚⓚ
Asian-American
Saluhallen, St Eriks Torg 8, 753 10
Tel *018-15 01 51*   Closed *Sun*
Known as an "Amasian
steakhouse", this restaurant
naturally serves fabulous steaks,
along with crispy tempura and
fresh burgers, all accompanied
by a wide selection of beers and
international wines.

**UPPSALA:
Restaurang Lingon**   ⓚⓚ
Fine Dining
Svartbäcksgatan 30, 753 32
Tel *018-10 12 24*
Old-fashioned food traditions
meet modern, creative culinary
styles at this classic Swedish
restaurant located inside a
wooden house. There is outdoor
seating in the summer.

UPPSALA: Villa Anna   ⓚⓚⓚ
Modern Swedish
Odinslund 3, 753 10
Tel *018-580 20 00*   Closed *Sun*
Award-winning chefs concoct
innovative culinary delights
based on traditional Swedish
recipes. The focus is on locally
sourced organic ingredients.

UTÖ: Utö Värdshus   ⓚⓚ
Fine Dining
Gruvbryggan, 130 56
Tel *08-504 20 300*
A former mining office has been
turned into a pleasant inn and
restaurant. There is à la carte
dining and alfresco seating in
the summer months.

VÄSTERÅS: Frank   ⓚⓚ
Bistro
Stora Torget 3, 722 15
Tel *021-13 65 00* Closed *Sun & Mon*
A busy and lively place where the
menu changes depending on the
seasons, the ingredients available
and even the chefs' moods. Try
the four-course "surprise menu".

Eastern Götaland

**JÖNKÖPING: Den
Småländska Kolonin**   ⓚⓚ
Modern Swedish
Kyrkogatan 4, 553 16
Tel *036-71 22 22*   Closed *Sun*
An exciting restaurant offering
some unusual dishes such as
deer with pumpkin and elder-
flower. The lunchtime menu
changes weekly, and there is a
bar upstairs.

KALMAR: Gröna Stugan   ⓚⓚ
Fine Dining
Larmgatan 1, 392 32
Tel *0480-158 58*
A former coffee house known as
the Green Barn in the 1920s, this

cosy green wooden cottage now
offers gourmet Swedish cuisine.
Daily fixed-price lunch menus,
as well as buffets for groups.

**LINKÖPING:
Stångs Magasin**   ⓚⓚ
Modern Swedish
Södra Stånggatan 1, 582 73
Tel *013-31 21 00*   Closed *Sun*
Located in an old warehouse.
There are à la carte and tasting
menus to choose from, as well as
a strong wine list. The emphasis
is on good-quality and locally
sourced organic produce.

MOTALA: Bomber Bar   ⓚ
Tex Mex
Prästgatan 3, 591 30
Tel *0141-23 39 13*   Closed *Sun–Tue*
Listen to live music while
enjoying delicious burgers and
chicken wings at this informal
bar. There is also a good selection
of beers and whiskeys.

**NORRKÖPING:
Pappa Grappa**   ⓚ
Italian
*Gamla Rådstugugatan 26–28,
602 24*
Tel *011-18 00 14*
Traditional Italian trattoria serving
quality *antipasti*, as well as pasta,
meat and fish dishes. A pizzeria
on the same premises offers
reasonably priced fare.

ÖLAND: Kvarn Krogen   ⓚ
Pizzeria
*Eketorpsvägen 1, 386 63,
Degerhamn*
Tel *0485-66 11 40*   Closed *Mon*
This restaurant, housed in a
quaint windmill, serves several
kinds of pizza and has an à la
carte menu. Family friendly.

DK Choice

**ÖLAND:
Guntorps Herrgård**   ⓚⓚ
Fine Dining
*Gunstorpsgatan, 387 36,
Borgholm*
Tel *0485-130 00*   Closed *Sun
in winter*
Housed in a traditional white-
painted manor house in a
pleasant setting, Guntorps
Herrgård offers some of Öland's
finest cuisine, made using
seasonal and locally sourced
ingredients. The menu changes
weekly according to produce
supply and has included baked
fallow deer fillet and smoked
pork belly salad. Choose
between the three- and five-
course dinners. There is also a
lovely spa and accommodation.

VÄSTERVIK: Saltmagasinet ⓀⓀ
Modern Swedish
Kulbacken, 593 38
Tel *0739-41 14 22*
This place is widely regarded as one of the country's best restaurants for its use of organic produce and strict environmental policies. There is an expert sommelier on hand, as well as a bakery and patisserie.

VIMMERBY: Brygghuset ⓀⓀ
International
Åbrovägen 13, 598 40
Tel *0492-753 80* **Closed** *Sun*
A gastropub serving fish and chips, burgers and more. There are lunch and dinner menus, a salad bar and a special children's menu. Good selection of drinks to choose from, including beers and whiskeys.

Gotland

VISBY: Bakfickan ⓀⓀ
Traditional Swedish
Stora Torget 1, 621 56
Tel *0498-27 18 07*
This picturesque Visby haunt features seasonal rustic cooking, including fresh fish and seafood. Signature dishes include smoked prawns and fish soup.

VISBY: Crêperie & Logi ⓀⓀ
French
Wallers Plats 3, 621 56
Tel *0498-284 622*
Housed in a charming iron-shaped building, inside the old city walls, Crêperie & Logi serves tasty French crêpes. There is also a single suite available to rent above the restaurant.

The unique iron-shaped exterior of Crêperie & Logi, Gotland

Beautiful interiors of Vimmerby's Brygghuset, featuring a fantastic bar

VISBY: Kitchen & Table ⓀⓀ
International
Strandgatan 6, 621 43
Tel *0498-25 75 00* **Closed** *Sun*
Part of a chain of hotel-restaurants headed by the Swedish celebrity chef Marcus Samuelsson, this Manhattan-inspired place serves burgers, steaks and hot dogs.

VISBY: Surfers ⓀⓀ
Chinese
Södra Kyrkogatan 1, 621 56
Tel *0498-21 18 00* **Closed** *Mon & Tue*
Flavourful Sichuan cuisine is served in stylish, atmospheric surroundings. There is a good selection of cocktails.

Southern Götaland

ÅHUS: Handelsbaren ⓀⓀ
Modern Swedish
Åvägen 4, 296 38
Tel *044-24 73 30* **Closed** *Winter*
Soak in some of the best views in Åhus from this charming restaurant in a red wooden villa by the sea. Great seafood.

BRÖSARP: Brösarps Gästgifveri ⓀⓀ
Modern Swedish
Albovägen 21, 273 50
Tel *0414-736 80*
Romantic inn painted a traditional red. On the menu are local delicacies, including wild boar. On Sundays, try the herring buffet.

GENARP: Häckeberga Slott ⓀⓀ
Traditional Swedish
Häckeberga Slott, 247 98
Tel *040-48 04 40* **Closed** *Sun*
Culinary delights in a castle setting. There is a breakfast buffet, as well as lunch and

dinner menus. Try the Swedish herring, goose and local cheeses.

HELSINGBORG: Fridas ⓀⓀⓀ
Fine Dining
Kullagatan 47, 252 20
Tel *042-122 612*
This upscale restaurant offers a diverse menu featuring small, sharable dishes ranging from mussels to elk sausages.

HELSINGBORG: Gastro ⓀⓀⓀ
Fine Dining
Järnvägsgatan 3, 252 24
Tel *042-24 34 70*
One of Skåne's finest restaurants, Gastro offers seasonal tasting menus as well as à la carte dishes made with the freshest, local ingredients.

KARLSKRONA: 2 Rum & Kök ⓀⓀ
Modern Swedish
Södra Smedjegatan 3, 371 31
Tel *0455-104 22* **Closed** *Sun*
"Two Rooms & Kitchen" serves modern and traditional dishes prepared with flair. Their "North to South" menu showcases food from all across Sweden.

KRISTIANSTAD: Bar-B-Ko ⓀⓀ
Bistro
Tivoligatan 4, 291 53
Tel *044-21 33 55* **Closed** *Sun*
As the name suggests, Bar-B-Ko specializes in all things grilled. Although the meat is first-rate, delicious fish and vegetarian options also appear on the menu.

KRISTIANSTAD: Tomarp Gårdshotell ⓀⓀ
Modern Swedish
Helmershusvägen 218, 291 94
Tel *044-931 18*
A pleasant country hotel and restaurant offering daily lunches, afternoon tea and tapas in the summer. Reserve in advance.

LANDSKRONA: Pumphuset ⓀⓀ
Traditional Swedish
Nedre Gatan 97, 261 61
Tel *0418-131 30* **Closed** *Mon & Sun evening*
A restored and redesigned old pumping station with fantastic views. Tasty traditional Swedish dishes include herring, Arctic char and sausages.

LUND: Gattostretto ⓀⓀ
Italian
Kattesund 6A, 222 23
Tel *046-32 07 77* **Closed** *Sun*
Spend all day here enjoying coffee and cake mid-morning, a pasta dish for lunch, delicious ice cream in the afternoon and an extensive dinner menu.

Beautifully lit dining space at Grand Öl & Mat in Malmö

MALMÖ: Bastard ⓚⓚ
Modern Swedish
Mäster Johansgatan 11, 211 21
Tel *040-12 13 18* **Closed** *Sun & Mon*
Arguably the trendiest place in Malmö, Bastard prepares meat-based dishes using organic and local produce whenever possible. Craft beers and organic wines.

MALMÖ: Grand Öl & Mat ⓚⓚ
Bistro
Monbijougatan 17, 211 53
Tel *040-12 63 13*
This is what you get when you combine a posh hotel with a noisy beer hall. Enjoy great food in a convivial atmosphere.

DK Choice

MALMÖ: Salt & Brygga ⓚⓚ
Traditional Swedish
Sundspromenaden 7, 211 16
Tel *040-611 59 40*
Considered one of the best organic restaurants in Sweden, Salt & Brygga relies on local produce and fish from sustainable sources, as well as Fairtrade coffee. Using the finest ingredients from Skåne, it re-creates traditional Swedish cuisine with exciting and innovative influences. Homemade bread and a large salad buffet are included in all lunchtime meals. Great sea views.

MALMÖ: Årstiderna ⓚⓚⓚ
Fine Dining
Kockska Huset,
Frans Suellsgatan 3, 211 22
Tel *040-23 09 10* **Closed** *Sun*
"The Seasons" combines the best of Swedish and international cuisines in an intimate setting. There is also a vegetarian menu and a good wine list.

MÖLLE: Grand Hôtel ⓚⓚ
Fine Dining
Bökebolsvägen 11, 263 77
Tel *042-36 22 30* **Closed** *Sun*
Feast on gourmet meals and enjoy lovely harbour views at this restaurant in the Grand Hôtel Mölle. Well-stocked wine cellar.

SIMRISHAMN:
En Gaffel Kort ⓚⓚ
Modern Swedish
Storgatan 3, 272 31
Tel *041-444 80 70*
The menu here features hearty meat, fish and vegetarian dishes, prepared with a Swedish twist. Try the local dishes such as wild boar with mustard and juniper broth.

SKANÖR: Skanörs
Fiskrögeri ⓚⓚ
Traditional Swedish
Skanörs hamn, 239 21
Tel *040-47 40 50* **Closed** *Mon (Apr,*
May & Sep); Oct–Mar
This old-fashioned rögeri (smokery) is located in an area that has a long fish-smoking history. Not surprisingly it specializes in smoked, marinated and grilled fish and seafood.

TRELLEBORG: Idala Gård ⓚⓚ
International
Idalavägen 335, 231 91
Tel *0410-33 13 13* **Closed** *Sun*
evening
Swedish cooking with a good dose of Italian cuisine thrown in. Great Italian cheeses, olives, cold cuts and salads, and delicious pizza on the last Thursday of every month.

DK Choice

VIKEN: Vikens
Hamnkrog ⓚⓚ
Fine Dining
Böösa Backen 6, 260 40
Tel *042-23 62 12*
The "Harbour Inn" is a pleasant restaurant in a serene village on the southern Swedish coast. Diners can choose from a great selection of seafood and fish, such as creamy fish soup with lemon *aïoli* and bread. The cosy bar does an "after-work" buffet, and self-catering accommodation is available.

YSTAD: Bryggeriet
Restaurant & Pub ⓚ
Modern Swedish
Långgatan 20, 271 43
Tel *0411-699 99* **Closed** *Sun & Mon*
Pleasant restaurant and pub with its own micro-brewery, in a rustic setting. Daily lunchtime specials, as well

as mains such as goose breast and Arctic char are popular.

Gothenburg

CENTRE: Ölrepubliken ⓚ
Traditional Swedish
Kronhusgatan 2B, 411 13
Tel *031-711 37 10*
With hundreds of unusual beers on offer, this relaxed place also serves pub food and exotic dishes like Vietnamese *Bãhn mì*.

CENTRE: Familjen ⓚⓚ
Traditional Swedish
Arkivgatan 7, 411 34
Tel *031-20 79 79* **Closed** *Sun*
A friendly and welcoming place, Familjen has an acclaimed bar with an excellent selection of wines. The menu features a wide range of small dishes with classic Swedish flavours and a set three-course menu.

CENTRE: Heaven 23 ⓚⓚ
International
Mässans gata 24, 412 51
Tel *031-750 88 05*
Located on the 23rd floor of the Hotel Gothia Towers and offering spectacular views over the city, this restaurant serves modern seasonal food. Its signature dish is the king-size shrimp sandwich. Good cocktails.

CENTRE: Restaurang
Gabriel ⓚⓚ
Fine Dining
Feskekôrka, Rosenlundsgatan, 411 20
Tel *031-13 90 51* **Closed** *Sun & Mon*
A gourmet seafood restaurant located inside Feskekôrka (Fish Church), the city's indoor fish market. The shellfish buffet is stocked with the freshest catch of the day. Open lunchtime only.

Modern seating arrangement at Malmö's Salt & Brygga

CENTRE: Restaurang Trädgår'n ⓀⓀ
International
Nya Allén 11, 411 38
Tel *031-10 20 80* **Closed** *Sun*
This popular, stylish restaurant is set in a lovely park. The à la carte menu offers a good range of dishes, from burgers to fish and salads. There's also a nightclub on the premises.

CENTRE: Smaka ⓀⓀ
Traditional Swedish
Vasaplatsen 3, 411 26
Tel *031-13 22 47*
Rustic Swedish home cooking in a pleasant red-brick building. Good selection of beers and outdoor seating in summer.

DK Choice

CENTRE: Fiskekrogen ⓀⓀⓀ
Fine Dining
Lilla Torget 1, 411 18
Tel *031-10 10 05* **Closed** *Sun*
One of the best fish and seafood restaurants in the country, Fiskekrogen has been serving up the tastiest catches since 1977. There are set menus, as well as a seafood buffet and a variety of fish dishes to choose from. The impressive setting makes it a perfect place for a romantic dinner. Extensive and impressive wine list.

CENTRE: Koka ⓀⓀⓀ
Fine Dining
Viktoriagatan 12, 411 25
Tel *031-701 79 79* **Closed** *Sun*
This Michelin-starred restaurant is the ideal spot to sample the flavours of West Sweden. Paired with different wines, the set meals focus on locally sourced fresh, seasonal ingredients.

FURTHER AFIELD: Sjömagasinet ⓀⓀⓀ
Fine Dining
Klippans Kulturreservat, Adolf Edelsvärds gata 5, 414 51
Tel *031-775 59 20* **Closed** *Sun*
Set within a red wooden house right by the sea. There is a special seafood menu and a lunch menu that changes daily. There are cookery classes inside the old smithy.

Western Götaland

HALMSTAD: Umai Sushi Bar Ⓚ
Japanese
Lars Montinsväg 29, 302 92
Tel *035-120 030* **Closed** *Mon*
This restaurant serves fantastic sushi and sashimi platters, plus

Beautiful white exterior of Villa Sjötorp, one of Ljungskile's best fine-dining places

grilled fish and meat on skewers. Vegetarian options are available.

KARLSBORG: Idas Brygga ⓀⓀ
Modern Swedish
Skepparegatan 9, 546 32
Tel *0505-131 11* **Closed** *Sun evening*
Historic hotel and restaurant by the Göta Canal. High-quality cooking with locally sourced ingredients and international influences. Lunchtime buffet.

LJUNGSKILE: Villa Sjötorp ⓀⓀ
Fine Dining
Sjötorpsvägen 5, 459 33
Tel *0522-201 74*
Set in a beautiful white villa by the sea, this restaurant has a large garden and outdoor terrace seating. The exceptional seasonal menus use local, organic produce. Extensive wine list.

MARIESTAD: Sill & Dynamit ⓀⓀ
Traditional Swedish
Gästhamnen, Hamngatan 19, 542 30
Tel *0501-141 80* **Closed** *Sun evening*
The menu at this restaurant reflects the lakes, forests and farmlands in the surrounding area. Great fish entrées and good food-and-wine pairings.

MARSTRAND: Restaurang Grand Tenan ⓀⓀⓀ
Fine Dining
Rådhusgatan 2, 442 67
Tel *0303-603 22*
The restaurant of the Grand Hotel offers elegant dining in a pretty setting. The signature dish, crayfish *au gratin*, is a must-try. Excellent Christmas buffet.

MELLBYSTRAND: Strandhotellet Mellbystrand Ⓚ
Traditional Swedish
Kustvägen 39, 312 60
Tel *0430-250 19*
Built in 1927, Strandhotellet used to be a favourite society hangout. Its restaurant, noted for its fine cuisine, offers delicious lunches. Dinner service only in the summer.

DK Choice

STRÖMSTAD: Rökeriet i Strömstad ⓀⓀ
Traditional Swedish
Torskholmen, 452 31
Tel *0526-148 60* **Closed** *Sun & Mon*
This family-run traditional smokery, located on the waterfront, sources most of its fresh produce and ingredients locally. Old-style wood-fired ovens are used to smoke the delicious fish and seafood dishes on the menu. There is also a fish and seafood shop on the premises.

SYDKOSTER: Kosters Trädgårdar ⓀⓀ
Fine Dining
Kosters Trädgårdar, 452 05
Tel *070-256 34 01* **Closed** *Sep–May*
Wonderful restaurant and garden using its own organic produce in many dishes. Try the summertime buffet, with lots of fresh greens.

VÄNERSBORG: Restaurang Teatergränd ⓀⓀ
Modern Swedish
Kungsgatan 13, 462 33
Tel *0521-644 60* **Closed** *Sun–Tue*
The à la carte menu here features seasonal, local ingredients. Early dinner specials and Friday buffet dinners are also offered.

Western Svealand

ARVIKA: Barbord ⓀⓀ
Modern Swedish
Hantverksmagasinet, Spårgatan 1, 671 30
Tel *0570-133 30* **Closed** *winter; Sun–Tue in summer*
Lovely harbour restaurant with a terrace on the lakefront. On the menu are tasty Swedish dishes with international touches. Great cocktails and weekend brunch.

For more information on types of restaurants *see page 291*

DK Choice

BOGEN:
Värdshuset Tvällen ⓀⓀ
Traditional Swedish
Tvällen, Bogen, 670 35
Gunnarskog
Tel *0570-77 30 24* **Closed** *Mon &*
Tue
This back-of-beyond rustic inn
by a lake in a deep forest is well
worth the trek. On the menu
is traditional Swedish home-
cooking, especially game
dishes – moose, reindeer, wild
boar – accompanied by wild
mushrooms or fresh berries.
A lovely treat for the palate.

The snow-covered ornate gate marking the entrance to Östersund's Take Mikado

FALUN: Kopparhatten
Café & Kök ⓀⓀ
Bistro
Stigaregatan 2–4, 791 60
Tel *023-191 69*
Guests can choose from an à la
carte menu and set lunchtime
meals at this Falun favourite.
Coffee and cake are served
all day.

KARLSTAD: Blå Kök & Bar ⓀⓀ
Modern Swedish
Kungsgatan 14, 652 24
Tel *054-10 18 15* **Closed** *Sun*
A trendy restaurant, Blå Kök &
Bar serves fine Swedish cuisine
with plenty of creative touches.
There are daily lunchtime and
dinner specials.

KRISTINEHAMN:
Mastmagasinet Ⓚ
Modern Swedish
Södra Hamngatan 5, 681 31
Tel *0550-803 40* **Closed** *Sun*
Housed in an old wooden
warehouse on Lake Vänern,
painted a traditional red. There
is plenty of variety on the menu,
including burgers, salads and
fish dishes.

ÖREBRO: Slottskällaren ⓀⓀ
Fine Dining
Drottninggatan 1, 701 45
Tel *019-15 69 60* **Closed** *Sun;*
Mon evening
Set in a rustic cellar dating back
to the 1300s, Slottskällaren offers
an extensive à la carte menu. In
summer, diners can eat on the
outdoor terrace overlooking the
river and the Örebro Castle.

RÄTTVIK: Bruntegården ⓀⓀ
Traditional Swedish
Vålsvedsvägen 51, 795 35
Tel *0248-79 87 70* **Closed** *Sun*
A charming, rustic restaurant,
Bruntegården serves the freshest
local and seasonal produce. Try
the Arctic char and herring.

SÄLEN: Gammelgården ⓀⓀ
Traditional Swedish
Sälfjället 1, 780 67
Tel *0280-877 00*
This ski lodge with cosy, intimate
surroundings and open fires
serves an à la carte menu of
traditional Swedish fare. It also
has a "waffle cottage" that uses
a 100-year-old waffle recipe.

TÖCKFORS: Waterside
Restaurant ⓀⓀ
Mediterranean
Bögatan 1, 670 10
Tel *0573-299 99* **Closed** *Mon;*
mid-Dec–mid-Feb
The Waterside enjoys a scenic
location along the Dalsland Canal.
There's a lunch menu and à la
carte options in the evening.

Southern Norrland

ÅRE: Villa Tottebo ⓀⓀ
Modern Swedish
Parkvägen 1, 830 13
Tel *0647-506 20*
This traditional hunting lodge
dating from 1897 serves rustic
dishes with a modern twist. Try
the local cheeses, Swedish air-
dried ham and game meatballs.

BJÄSTA: Näske Krog ⓀⓀ
Traditional Swedish
Norum, 893 91
Tel *0660-22 82 38*
Restaurant and café on the
picturesque High Coast. Along
with the traditional fare there
are some international dishes
on the menu too.

GÄVLE: Restaurang
Matildas ⓀⓀ
Fine Dining
Timmermansgatan 23, 802 52
Tel *026-62 53 49* **Closed** *Sun & Mon*
Family-run restaurant offering
fresh food of a high quality. A
classic Swedish menu includes

dishes made with locally sourced
seasonal and organic produce.

HIGH COAST: Fiskarfänget ⓀⓀ
Seafood
Norrfällsviken 870 31, Mjällom
Tel *0613-211 42*
At Fiskarfänget, diners can
choose from a wide selection of
seafood and fish. The à la carte
menu features everything from
fried herring to smoked salmon
and prawns.

ÖSTERSUND: Innefickan
Restaurant & bar ⓀⓀ
Fine Dining
Postgränd 11, 830 31
Tel *063-12 90 99* **Closed** *Sun & Mon*
Centrally located, the restaurant
serves fresh local produce and
unusual combinations. Try the
fillet of venison with a wild
mushroom sauce.

DK Choice

ÖSTERSUND:
Take Mikado ⓀⓀⓀ
Japanese
Infanterigatan 12, 831 32
Tel *063-209 08*
Closed *Sun & Mon*
Possibly the finest Japanese
restaurant in Sweden, Take
Mikado tempts with traditional
cuisine prepared by head chef
Tsukasa Takeuchi. There is fresh
tofu, *shabu-shabu*, sashimi,
tempura and miso soups on
the menu. Dishes and tables
need to be booked three days
in advance.

STORLIEN: Restaurang
Flamman Ⓚ
Modern Swedish
Vintergatan 46, 830 19
Tel *0647-700 10* **Closed** *Mon, Tue,*
Thu; Wed in winter
Housed in a wooden building
dating from the 1930s. The varied
menu ranges from modern

Swedish classics to wood-fired pizzas. A good budget option.

SUNDSVALL:
Restaurang 180 ⓚⓚ
Fine Dining
Södra Stadsberget 1, 852 38
Tel 060-67 10 00
This panoramic restaurant at Södra Berget Hotell & Resort serves well-presented food in fine surroundings. The restaurant also has an excellent selection of wines.

SUNDSVALL:
Udda Tapas Bar ⓚⓚ
International
Esplanaden 17, 852 31
Tel 073-098 66 07
A cosy bar and restaurant serving a menu of small, tasty tapas-style dishes. Some of the more unusual options include pig cheeks with apple and vinegar and soft-shell crab with mint and mango.

VEMHÅN: Vålkojan ⓚⓚ
Traditional Swedish
Vålkojan 615, 840 91
Tel 0684-320 41
Traditional restaurant, café and bar in a scenic riverside location. Choose between fine Swedish home-cooked dishes, open sandwiches and delicious waffles.

Northern Norrland

BODEN: Norrigården
Restaurang & Konferens ⓚⓚ
Traditional Swedish
Kyrkkläppen 3, 961 64
Tel 0921-103 51   **Closed** *Sat & Sun*
An 18th-century manor house with quaint wooden beams and a cosy atmosphere in a picturesque location. Open lunchtime only.

BORGAFJÄLL: Hotell Borgafjäll
& Spa ⓚⓚ
Fine Dining/Bistro
Hotell Borgafjäll, 917 04
Tel 0942-421 00   **Closed** *Oct, Nov, May & Jun*
This bistro-style place serves 'mountain cuisine', including lots of ingredients from across Norrland. Good wine list.

GAMMELSTAD:
Gammelstads Wärdshus ⓚⓚ
Traditional Swedish
Lulevägen 2, 954 33
Tel 072-578 67 35
An old-world inn with a strong focus on gastronomy, especially traditional Lapland cuisine. Cosy and convivial atmosphere. Hours vary, so call ahead.

JOKKMOKK: Hotell
Jokkmokk ⓚⓚ
Traditional Swedish
Solgatan 45, 962 31
Tel 0971-777 00
Guests can savour traditional Lapland cuisine while enjoying fantastic views of Lake Talvatis. Plenty of reindeer and elk dishes.

DK Choice

JUKKASJÄRVI: ICEHOTEL
Restaurant ⓚⓚⓚ
Modern Swedish
Marknadsvägen 63, 981 91
Tel 0980-668 00
Enjoy modern European cuisine with influences from Lapland at this award-winning restaurant. Food made with ingredients sourced from the lakes, rivers and mountains in the area are served on beautiful ice plates; the cocktails at the bar are also served in signature ice glasses made with water from the nearby Torne River.

KIRUNA: Restaurang Grapes ⓚ
International
Scandic Hotel Ferrum, Lars Janssonsgatan 15, 981 31
Tel 0980-39 86 00
Offers gorgeous views over Kebnekaise, Sweden's highest mountain. The menu features standard dishes, including pasta and hamburgers.

LULEÅ: Restaurang Ripan ⓚ
Modern Swedish
Varvsgatan 39, 972 32
Tel 0920-168 68
Classic Swedish fare, as well as international options such as a wide selection of pizzas. Popular with locals, the lunch buffet includes traditional food, home-made bread and a salad bar.

LULEÅ: Tallkotten
Restaurang ⓚⓚ
Italian
Storgatan 15, 972 32
Tel 0920-27 40 20   **Closed** *Sun*
High-quality classic food served in large, light and airy premises. Choose from a range of pizzas, pasta dishes, omelettes and other main courses.

SKELLEFTEÅ:
Nordanågården ⓚⓚ
Fine Dining
Nordanå, 931 21
Tel 0910-533 50
Charming old inn built in 1868. Inexpensive lunchtime buffet and popular Sunday buffet with cold cuts, salads and seafood.

TÄRNABY: Virisen ⓚⓚ
Traditional Swedish
Virisen 105, 920 64
Tel 070-274 41 88
The place to try Lapland cuisine, including ptarmigan, Arctic char, mushrooms and berries. Open for breakfast, lunch and dinner, but book in advance.

UMEÅ: Gotthards Krog ⓚⓚⓚ
Modern Swedish
Storgatan 46, 903 26
Tel 090-690 33 00
Housed inside the 19th-century hotel Stora Hotellet, this stylish New Nordic restaurant serves unique local dishes with an international twist.

VILHELMINA:
Hotell Wilhelmina ⓚⓚ
Bistro
Volgsjövägen 16, 912 34
Tel 0940-554 20
This restaurant in a pleasant mountain hotel offers Swedish and international cuisine. There is a children's menu available as well.

Spectacularly decorated interior of ICEHOTEL Restaurant, Jukkasjärvi

For more information on types of restaurants *see page 291*

SHOPPING IN SWEDEN

Sweden is worth visiting for the shopping alone. In all Swedish towns, and even in the big cities, the shops are within easy walking distance of each other. The city centres offer a good range of small, trendy boutiques for fashion and interiors, shops for antiques and curios, luxury international designer outlets and well-stocked department stores. Cameras, mobile phones, furs, children's clothing, toys and Swedish glass and designer goods are cheaper in Sweden than in many other countries. Those looking for a typical Swedish souvenir could buy a Dala horse or a proper Swedish snaps glass from one of the factories in the Kingdom of Crystal. Although Lapland is a long way north, Sami handicrafts can be bought in most craft shops, including knives with carved bone handles and silverwork. Leather and fur goods are also good value.

Opening Times

Most shops usually open at 10am and close at 6pm, although many in Stockholm city centre remain open until 7pm. Most shops are open until 2pm on Saturdays, while the major department stores stay open until 5pm. Large stores, shopping malls and some city-centre shops are open on Sundays. Market halls are closed on Sundays and public holidays. Many larger supermarkets are open daily until 8pm.

Payment

All the major credit cards are accepted at most Swedish shops. You may be asked for proof of identity. Some larger shops also accept euros *(see p322)*. Goods can be exchanged if you produce the receipt.

Purchases can be made on a sale-or-return basis if this is noted on the receipt.

Value Added Tax

Value added tax ("MOMS" in Swedish) is charged on all items except daily newspapers. The VAT rate is 25 per cent; but only 12 per cent on food and 6 per cent on books. VAT is always included in the total price.

Tax-Free Shopping

Residents of countries outside the European Union are entitled to a refund of the VAT paid on their purchases. Look for the "Tax-free shopping" sign in shop windows. Keep your receipts and on departure from the EU go to the Global Refund office at the airport or ferry terminal to obtain a 15–18 per cent refund.

Sale-time at an elegant shoe shop in Stockholm

Sales

Twice a year Sweden's shops and department stores have sales with reduced prices on clothing, shoes and other fashion goods. Sales are indicated by the *rea* sign. The year's first sales period starts after Christmas and continues throughout January. The second sales period lasts from late June to the end of July.

Shopping Centres and Department Stores

The best-known Swedish superstore internationally is **IKEA**, which has 18 outlets across the country from Haparanda in the north to Malmö in the south, and has become a popular tourist attraction in its own right. It sells not only furniture, but everything else for the home. The textiles section is particularly good, as well as the kitchenware and china departments.

NK, Stockholm's most exclusive department store

IKEA's home furnishings stores can be found in many parts of Sweden

Another well-known store is the fashion house **H&M** (Hennes & Mauritz), which has branches in many towns. It stocks the latest fashions at low prices. H&M has its own designers and makes clothing for women, men, teenagers and children. The shops also sell accessories, underwear, perfume and cosmetics.

NK (Nordiska Kompaniet) in Stockholm and Gothenburg is Sweden's leading department store, in which many well-known names in fashion and cosmetics have their own outlets. NK is a practical choice for those in a hurry. It stocks everything from Swedish-designed products, jewellery, handicrafts and souvenirs to cameras, films and books.

Åhléns, which has stores in many towns and cities, offers most items at good prices.

Opened in the 19th century, but thoroughly modern, **PUB** is a haven for fashionistas. Almost every large town has its own

Åfors glassworks store, Kingdom of Crystal, Småland *(see pp156–7)*

shopping centre or mall with a standard range of stores such as H&M, Lindex, Kappahl, Twilfit and Dressmann (clothing), Guldfynd (jewellery), Cervera (glass and china), Hemtex (textiles), Elgiganten (cameras, stereos, TVs) and Teknik-magasinet (electronics).

In Stockholm, **Gallerian** on Hamngatan is the largest mall and the prices are lower than in the elegant **Sturegallerian** near Stureplan with its many trendy boutiques.

Nordstan, off Brunnsparken in Gothenburg, is a mall with department stores such as Åhléns and specialist shops.

HansaCompagniet in central Malmö is a modern shopping centre.

A few examples of the larger shopping centres around the country include **Utopia** in Umeå, **Forumgallerian** in Uppsala, **Krämaren** in Örebro and **Emporia** in Malmö.

Most towns have local markets selling flowers, fruit, vegetables and sometimes also handicrafts. Smaller places only have an outdoor market once a week, but in Hötorget in Stockholm, trading carries on every day except Sundays.

Wines and Spirits

The only shops selling alcohol in Sweden are run by Systembolaget, the state mono-poly chain. They are open Mon–Fri 10am–6pm and Sat 10am–2pm (except public holiday weekends). The minimum age for buying alcohol at Systembolaget shops is 20 and staff are entitled to ask for proof of age *(see also p319)*.

DIRECTORY

Shopping Centres & Department Stores

Åhléns
Klarabergsgatan 50, Stockholm.
Map 1 C4. **Tel** 08-676 60 00.
W ahlens.se

Emporia
Hyllie Blvd. 19, Malmö.
Tel 040-36 36 00.

Forumgallerian
Bredgränd 6, Uppsala.
Map see p135.
W forumgallerian.se

Gallerian
Hamngatan 37, Stockholm.
Map 2 D4. **Tel** 073-531 94 96.
W gallerian.se

HansaCompagniet
Stora Nygatan, Malmö.
Map see p183. **Tel** 040-770 00.
W hansamalmo.se

H&M
Hamngatan 22, Stockholm.
Map 2 D4. **Tel** 08-524 635 30.
W hm.com/se

IKEA
Kungens Kurva, Stockholm.
Tel 0775-700 500.

Kompassen
Kungsgatan 58–60, Gothenburg.
Map see p196. W kompassen.se

Krämaren
Drottninggatan 29, Örebro.
Map see p243. **Tel** 019-760 92 40.
W kramaren.se

NK
Östra Hamngatan 42, Gothenburg.
Tel 031-710 10 00. W nk.se

NK
Hamngatan 18–20, Stockholm.
Map 2 D4. **Tel** 08-762 80 00.
W nk.se

Nordstan
Brunnsparken, Gothenburg.
Map see p196. **Tel** 031-700 86 60.
W nordstan.se

PUB
Drottninggatan 63, Stockholm.
Map 3 A1. **Tel** 020-75 27 52.

Sturegallerian
Grev Turegatan 9 A, Stockholm.
Map 2 D4. W sturegallerian.se

Utopia
Skolgatan 62, Umeå.
W utopiashopping.se

What to Buy in Sweden

The Dala wooden horse must be the most typical Swedish souvenir. But it is facing strong competition from the elk, which has become a symbol for a nation with vast tracts of unspoilt countryside. The Swedes love the great outdoors, so there are plenty of shops selling top-class sporting equipment. Swedish glass and crystal are renowned around the world. Orrefors and Kosta Boda are just two of several glassworks producing both classic and modern glassware. Educational toys in natural materials are a Swedish speciality and so are clogs, which can be found in most shoe shops.

Hand-painted clogs

Handicrafts & Design

Modern Swedish design is a familiar concept worldwide, even for simple everyday items (see pp30–31). Handicrafts have a long tradition in Sweden and contemporary designers often use old crafts such as wrought-iron work, weaving, pottery and woodcarving.

Dala Horse and Cockerel
Originally the brightly painted Dala horses and cockerels were toys carved from left-over fragments of wood. Later the horse became a national symbol, now sold in many variants.

Swedish Glass
Hand-blown sets are made in Småland's glassworks, as well as artistic crystal creations and objects for daily use.

Cheese slicer and knife by Michael Björnstierna

Nobel glass carafe from Orrefors by Gunnar Cyrén

Traditional snaps glasses

Tray with design by Josef Frank, Svenskt Tenn

Objects for the Home
The larger department stores often commission well-known designers for porcelain, glass, textiles and household items which make highly desirable gifts.

Mama, a humorous clothes hanger

Crux rug by Pia Wallén

Children's Toys
Colourful wooden toys from Brio are worldwide favourites. Educational picture books, games and puzzles are all excellent gifts for children.

Outdoor Gear

Many Swedes enjoy outdoor pursuits such as fishing, hunting, sailing, golf, camping and all types of winter sports, so there are plenty of well-equipped sports shops around. Unique items include Sami handicrafts beautifully made from reindeer horn or skin.

Hand Knits

Caps and gloves with attractive designs, known as *lovikka*, are made from a special wool which gives good protection in cold or wet conditions.

Drinking vessel in carved wood

Reindeer Skin Rucksack

Rucksacks have always been popular in Sweden. This exclusive leather model is made in Lapland.

Sami Handicrafts

A hunting knife with a sheath of reindeer horn, or a *kåsa*, a drinking vessel carved in birch, are not only attractive, but useful when out walking in the wild.

Spinning Reel and Lures

ABU-Garcia makes top-quality fishing tackle, perfect for Sweden's long coastline, countless lakes and rivers with their rich and varied fishing.

Swedish Delicacies

Among the many Swedish goodies are preserves made from wild berries, such as lingonberries (served with meatballs or pancakes) and cloudberries (delicious with whipped cream). Ginger biscuits are for Christmas while crispbread is great year-round, especially with herring.

Lingonberry preserve

Cloudberry jam

Pickled Herring

Pickled herring should be enjoyed with new potatoes cooked with dill, chopped chives and sour cream. Versions flavoured with mustard, dill or other herbs or spices are also available.

Swedish snaps gift-pack miniatures

"Raspberry boat" candy

Salt liquorice

Crispbread

Ginger biscuits

Where to Shop in Sweden

Clothing from all the well-known international fashion houses can be found in Stockholm, Malmö and Gothenburg. If you want something rather different, it is worth seeking out the creations of younger Swedish fashion designers. Swedish interior design is famous for its clean lines, functionalism and the use of pale wood, and the country is a paradise for anyone interested in design. Handicrafts are of a high quality. Leisurewear and sports goods offer excellent value for money.

Fashion

Stockholm's top places for fashion are in the "golden triangle" bounded by Stureplan, Nybroplan and Norrmalmstorg. Clothing at more moderate prices can be bought in department stores and shopping centres across the country. **GeKås** in Ullared and **Knalleland** in Borås have become popular attractions due to their low prices and large number of stores and factory outlets, not least in the "mail-order town" of Borås, with its weaving and textile traditions.

If you are looking for Swedish designers, **NK** in Stockholm and Gothenburg *(see p303)* has a good selection of clothing created by younger designers as well as mainstream Swedish brands. Classic men's clothing of high quality is designed by Oscar Jacobsson, while Stenström shirts are sold in department stores and the more elegant menswear boutiques. **Björn Borg** has his own shops selling men's and women's clothing and under-wear, perfume and accessories. The designer **Filippa K** produces smart clothing for fashionable women and men.

Design and Interior Decoration

Stockholm, Gothenburg and Malmö have a number of interior decoration shops selling the products of young designers and well-known artists. To see the latest on offer, it is worth visiting **DesignTorget**, which has stores in all three cities displaying designers' work. Stockholm's **R.O.O.M** in the PUB department store and **Asplund**

in Östermalm, and **Norrgavel** in Stockholm, Gothenburg, Malmö, Umeå, Uppsala and Lammhult are just a few of the shops with the most up-to-the-minute selection of products. **Svenskt Tenn** is Stockholm's oldest shop for interiors, with both new and classic designs. **Nordiska Galleriet** in Stockholm has exclusive modern furniture and decorative items, while **Blås & Knåda** on Hornsgatan displays and sells the largest selection of contemporary Swedish ceramics and glass, both objects of art and items for everyday use. **Nordiska Kristall** on Kungsgatan has a wide choice of Swedish glassware, which can also be found in department stores.

Music and Multimedia

Many Swedish pop bands now have an international reputation. Exciting new talents continue to find their way into the charts, and the latest products can often be bought in the large record shops before they become available outside Sweden. Apart from pop and rock, Sweden has a long folk-music tradition, as well as many jazz musicians and opera singers.

Sport and Leisure

The Swedes devote a lot of time to outdoor sports and activities. With shops all over the country, **Naturkompaniet** and **Peak Performance** have an exclusive selection of sportswear and equipment. **Stadium** and **Intersport** have a varied choice of sports clothing and equipment at attractive prices and are also nationwide. Good

equipment and exclusive clothing for hunting and fishing can be bought at **Walter Borg** in central Stockholm. **Löplabbet** countrywide specializes in running and jogging.

Souvenirs and Handicrafts

Snaps glasses, silver jewellery, hand-painted clogs, Sami crafts, hand-knitted garments, candles, Christmas decorations and wrought-iron products can all be bought in department stores and shops specialising in Swedish handicrafts.

At Skansen open-air museum in Stockholm, visitors can shop for handicrafts in attractive little houses.

Nusnäs in Dalarna is the place to buy the original Dala horse, which can be found at **Nils Olsson Hemslöjd AB**.

Yllet in Visby sells hand-spun wool, woollen garments and sheepskin goods.

Markets

Small local markets can be found almost everywhere, but a few have become so big that they have attracted international attention.

Jokkmokk's winter market (1st Thu–Sat in Feb) is a major Sami market. Skänninge market (1st Wed–Thu in Aug) is a classic affair dating back to the Middle Ages. The Kivik market (mid-Jul) is like an amusement park. Michaelmas markets are held in central Sweden in autumn.

The bustling flea market in Vårberg Centrum, Stockholm, is the place to find a bargain every day of the week. Entrance fee Sat–Sun, free after 3pm and on other days.

Glass and China

Most department stores and gift shops sell glass from Swedish manufacturers. Visitors to the Kingdom of Crystal in Småland have a choice of no fewer than 13 glassworks within a radius of a few miles *(see pp156–7)*. At **Orrefors Kosta Boda Glasbruk**, there are bargains to be had among the everyday glassware and the studio glass. **Reijmyre** in Östergötland is also popular among bargain-hunters. For porcelain, the factory shop at **Rörstrand** offers value for money.

Swedish Delicacies

The capital has three market halls – **Östermalmshallen, Hötorgshallen** and **Söderhallarna** – which are

a joy to just wander around. Salmon, bleak roe, smoked eel and smoked reindeer meat are all delicious culinary souvenirs. Lund's **Saluhall** and Gothenburg's **Briggen** are also pleasant market halls offering mouth-watering Swedish delicacies.

On the west coast, seafood is a must and whether you are after prawns, crab or autumn's black gold, lobster, it is best purchased at the harbourside when the boats come in.

In the north, game of various kinds is the big attraction and you can often find smoked reindeer and reindeer heart in grocery stores, along with fermented Baltic herring and Norrland cloudberry jam.

Swedish crispbread is another delicacy and the bakery in Leksand has a factory shop. Traditional red and white striped candy rock originates from Gränna, which has a large number of shops selling rock.

DIRECTORY

Fashion

Björn Borg
Sergelgatan 12,
Stockholm. **Map** 1 C4.
Tel 08-21 70 40.
W bjornborg.com

Charlotte Göteborg
Drottninggatan 28,
Gothenburg. **Map** see p196. **Tel** 031-701 75 40.
W charlottegoteborg.se

Dunderdon
Stuk, Södra Larmgatan 16,
Gothenburg.
Map see p196.

Filippa K
Grev Turegatan 18,
Stockholm. **Map** 2 D4.
W filippa-k.com

Ge-Kås i Ullared
Danska Vägen, Falkenberg.
Tel 0346-375 00.
W gekas.se

Knalleland
Sandgärdsg 12 -16, Borås.
Tel 033-14 03 35.

MQ
Södra Tullgatan 3, Malmö.
Tel 040-12 01 31.
Strömpilsplatsen 9–15,
Umeå. **Tel** 090-786 36 80.
W mq.se

Olsén Mode
Södergatan 21, Malmö.
Map see p183.
Tel 040-12 10 50.

Design and Interiors

Asplund
Sibyllegatan 31,
Stockholm. **Map** 2 E3.
Tel 08-662 52 84.
W asplund.org

Blås & Knåda

Blås & Knåda
Hornsgatan 26,
Stockholm. **Map** 3 A5.
Tel 08-642 77 67.
W blasknada.se

DesignTorget
Kulturhuset, Sergels Torg
3, Stockholm. **Map** 1 C4.
Tel 08–21 91 50.

Södra Förstadsgatan 3,
Malmö. **Tel** 040-30 70 82.

Vallgatan 14, Gothenburg.
Map see p196.
Tel 031-774 00 17.
W designtorget.se

Establish
Humlegårdsgatan 14,
Stockholm. **Map** 2 E3.
Tel 08-545 853 40.

Nordiska Galleriet
Nybrogatan 11,
Stockholm. **Map** 2 E4.
Tel 08-442 83 60.
W nordiskagalleriet.se

Nordiska Kristall
Kungsgatan 9,
Stockholm. **Map** 2 E4.
Tel 08-10 43 72.

Norrgavel
Birger Jarlsgatan 27,
Stockholm. **Map** 2 D3.
Tel 08-545 220 50.

Engelbrektsgatan 20,
Malmö. **Map** see p183.
Tel 040-12 22 46.
W norrgavel.se

R.O.O.M
PUB, Hötorget,
Stockholm. **Map** 1 C4.
Tel 08-692 50 00.

Svenskt Tenn
Strandvägen 5,
Stockholm. **Map** 2 E4.
Tel 08-670 16 00.
W svenskttenn.se

Music

Bengans Skivbutik
Stigbergstorget 1,
Gothenburg.
Tel 031-14 33 00.
W bengans.se

Sport and Leisure

Intersport
Björnvägen 1, Umeå.
Tel 090-70 63 50.

Löplabbet
Djäknegatan 2, Malmö.
Tel 040-12 35 70.

Naturkompaniet
Kungsgatan 4A,
Stockholm.
Map 2 D4.
Tel 08-723 15 81.

Peak Performance
Biblioteksgatan 18,
Stockholm.
Map 2 D4.
Tel 08-611 34 00.

Södergatan 9, Malmö.
Map see p183.
Tel 040-97 02 20.

Stadium
Fredsgatan 8, Gothenburg.
Map see p196.
Tel 031-711 06 09.
W stadium.se

Walter Borg
Kungsgatan 57B,
Stockholm. **Map** 1 C4.
Tel 08-14 38 65.
W walterborg.se

Souvenirs and Handicrafts

Nils Olsson Hemslöjd AB
Edåkersvägen 17, Nusnäs.
Tel 0250-372 00.

Svensk Hemslöjd
Norrlandsgatan 20,
Stockholm. **Map** 2 D4.
Tel 08-23 21 15.

Yllet
St Hansgatan 19, Visby.
Tel 0498-21 40 43.

Glass and China

Orrefors Kosta Boda Glasbruk
Kosta. **Tel** 0478-345 00.
Orrefors. **Tel** 0478-345 29.
W kostaboda.se
W orrefors.se

Reijmyre
Rejmyre. **Tel** 011-871 84.
W reijmyre.se

Rörstrand (Iittala)
Lidköping.
Tel 0510-250 80.

Gustavsberg.
Tel 08-570 356 55.
W rorstrand.se
W iittala.com

Swedish Delicacies

Briggen
Nordhemsgatan 28,
Gothenburg.

Hötorgshallen
Hötorget, Stockholm.
Map 1 C4.

Östermalmshallen
Östermalmstorg,
Stockholm. **Map** 2 E4.

Saluhall
Lund.
W lundssaluhall.se

Söderhallarna
Medborgarplatsen,
Södermalm, Stockholm.

ENTERTAINMENT IN SWEDEN

The range of cultural events and entertainment in Sweden is large and richly varied. The whole spectrum is covered from outdoor celebrations to mark local customs to top international acts performing in giant arenas. The seasons have an effect on what's on: large city theatres tend to close during the summer and launch their new programmes of plays, opera and dance in late August or early September. Meanwhile, summer reviews, popular comedies and local historical plays are staged across the country.

In parks, palace gardens and amusement parks, summer is a particularly eventful time, with artists of every imaginable kind putting on a performance. Added to that are the countless markets, festivals covering film, jazz, music, food, theatre, folklore, and much more besides. Winter brings ski races and skating, indoor fairs and Christmas markets. Nightlife continues all year. There are excellent nightclubs and casinos in the major cities. Jazz clubs and pubs offer a wide range of live music to suit all tastes.

Sources of Information

A reliable source of information is **Visit Sweden**'s official tourist and events guide on the Internet. This provides listings for everything from music and sport to seasonal events such as Medieval Week in Visby or the Vasaloppet ski race in Dalarna. The site has links to the websites of Stockholm, Gothenburg and Malmö, but also has details of events across the country.

Daily newspapers and free local papers are an excellent source for regional events such as concerts, theatre performances and nightclubs. The tourist information offices and most hotels also have listings and can often help with advice and booking tickets.

Booking Tickets

Tickets for most events can usually be bought at the box office of the theatre or sports arena in question, but to ensure admission it may be more practical to book in advance, with the help either of the hotel or a tourist information office. Another alternative is to use a booking agency, such as **ticnet.se**, which allows you to purchase tickets to stage shows, concerts and sports events online. At **Box-office** in Stockholm, tickets can be purchased over the counter for various events in Sweden and beyond, and tickets ordered via the event organizer can be collected. Many tickets are also sold via ticket service outlets across the country.

Major Arenas and Cultural Centres

In addition to the long-established, traditional theatres, many towns and cities have built multipurpose cultural complexes offering a wide

Dalhalla's music stage *(see p245)* in a dramatic quarry near Rättvik

spectrum of public events. Often such centres are home to the local theatre company and orchestra.

The major entertainment and event arenas, such as **Ericsson Globen**, **Tele2 Arena** and the **Friends Arena** in Stockholm, the **Malmö Arena** in Malmö and **Scandinavium** in Gothenburg, have a huge audience capacity. International rock and pop concerts, charity galas and major sporting events are usually held at these enormous venues.

In the summer, the large outdoor stages, for example at Skansen and Gröna Lund in Stockholm, Liseberg in Gothenburg and Dalhalla, between Rättvik and Mora, attract a wide range of jazz, folk and classical artists alike.

Theatre

Sweden has almost 500 theatres spread across the country. Many are town or county theatres, but there are also private theatres with long traditions and small park and amateur theatres.

Sea of people at the Philharmonic's annual outdoor concert, Stockholm

Sweden's national theatre is **Kungliga Dramatiska Teatern** *(see p77)*, which has six stages. It regularly mounts international and Swedish classics, including Shakespeare and Strindberg, as well as modern foreign and Swedish works.

Lighter plays and musicals are often performed at **ChinaTeatern** in Stockholm and **Lorensbergsteatern** in Gothenburg. Venues such as **Konsertteatern** in Sundsvall and **Göta Lejon** in Stockholm often stage performances suitable for children and families.

Classical Music, Dance and Opera

World-class music can be heard at **Berwaldhallen** in Stockholm, the home of Sveriges Radios Symfoniorkester and the Radiokören choir, considered one of the internationally leading a cappella ensembles. **Konserthuset** *(see p74)* is the base for the Royal Stockholm Philharmonic Orchestra. The season runs from August to May.

Konserthuset in Gothenburg is home to Göteborgs Symfoniker. Norrköping has the **Louis De Geer konsert & kongress** venue and Folkets Park in Sundsvall has **Tonhallen**, one of Sweden's best concert halls.

Classical opera and ballet of the highest quality can be seen at **Kungliga Operan** *(see p72)*. Every season at least three major ballets delight packed houses. This venue also stages traditional performances of most operas in their original language. During the summer, popular opera performances are held at **Drottningholms Slottsteater** *(see p115)*. All the

GöteborgsOperan, with a wide repertoire of opera and musicals

operas staged here are from the 18th century, with an orchestra of the period.

The spectacular modern **GöteborgsOperan** *(see p200)* is an exciting, internationally renowned venue for opera, ballet and musicals. Norrlandsoperan in Umeå and Malmö Opera och Musikteater are two of the country's other major venues for opera and ballet.

Dansens Hus in Stockholm, which has taken over the National Theatre's former venue, often hosts top-name dance companies from Sweden and abroad.

Folk Music

Swedish folk music is enjoying a resurgence in popularity. Skansen in Stockholm *(see p98)* is the prime venue, where musicians and folk dancing troupes perform regularly at traditional events. However, there are local folk groups and regional clubs covering practically every corner of the country. The easiest way of finding out where and how to enjoy Swedish folk music is to check at the local tourist information office or in the local press.

There are a few permanent venues for folk music: **Folkmusikhuset** in Stockholm, **Folkmusikkaféet** in Gothenburg and **Folkmusikens Hus** in Rättvik are just some of the places offering

a wide programme of performances and information about forthcoming events.

Church Music

Many churches in the cities hold organ recitals at lunchtime, for example Jacobs Kyrka in Stockholm *(see p72)*, where visitors can take a breather in a tranquil setting. Storkyrkan *(see p63)* also holds concerts on Saturday and Sunday afternoons in the spring and autumn. The cathedrals of Uppsala Domkyrka *(see p134)* and Västerås Domkyrka *(see p142)* stage organ recitals every Saturday. Many churches also have a concert programme, particularly in conjunction with major religious festivals.

Rock and Pop

The largest of the rock and pop venues are Ericsson Globen, Tele2 Arena and the Friends Arena in Stockholm, the Malmö Arena in Malmö and Scandinavium in Gothenburg. These attract top international artists, along with the many successful Swedish bands. **Cirkus** in Stockholm is a wellestablished venue for music and theatre in a beautiful old setting. More modern rock venues include **Münchenbryggeriet** in Stockholm, **Kulturbolaget** in Malmö and **Trädgår'n** in Gothenburg. Around the country there are smaller theatres, students' unions and clubs where groups and artists perform.

Sundsvalls Teater, an ambitious, go-ahead regional theatre

Concert in the ruins of Bohus Castle in Kungälv

Jazz Clubs

Jazz has enjoyed a renaissance in recent years and the range on offer increases annually. One venue of repute is **Fasching** in Stockholm, with performances almost daily. Another jazz haunt in the capital is **Stampen**, which attracts a rather more mature audience. Gothenburg has **Nefertiti** and across the country there are jazz clubs holding concerts once a month or so.

Jazz cruises have become popular in the summer. The Stockholm archipelago is plied by *S/S Blidösund*. Cruises are also organized elsewhere in the country, for instance across Lake Vättern and the Åland Sea, on the Dalälven river and out into the Gothenburg archipelago.

Music Pubs

Swedish pub culture has changed enormously and it is becoming increasingly common to follow the Continental pattern of slipping into a bar or pub for a while after work, having a beer and listening to music.

Many pubs have introduced live music – some have folk singers performing on a regular basis, while others have a DJ. The best way of being sure to hear live music is to scan the local press entertainment *(nöjen)* pages.

In Stockholm, the Irish pub **The Dubliner** offers live Irish music. The popular **Engelen** bar has live music several days a week. Gothenburg's finest pubs include **Sticky Fingers** and Jameson's pub, and Helsingborg has its own English pub, Charles Dickens, where the clientele can enjoy karaoke, live music, singers, bands and various other forms of entertainment.

There are a number of traditional English and Irish-style pubs spread across the country, usually offering a wide range of beer and spirits and serving a selection of bar snacks.

Nightclubs, Casinos and Shows

Generally speaking, nightclubs hold traditional disco nights on Friday and Saturday. During the rest of the week the venue is usually hired by various clubs focusing on different styles of music. Almost all the larger towns and cities have one or two nightclubs, but the quality varies, as does the music on offer. In Stockholm, the majority and the best of the capital's nightclubs are located around Stureplan. At the rear of the Opera House is **Café Opera**, Stockholm's longest-established nightclub, with an international style. The crowd is usually quite mixed – young, trendy types and older, smartly dressed folks. **Sturecompagniet** is a large club on several floors. At street level there is also a rock bar. Swedish celebrities and visiting foreign stars mingle at top celeb hangout **Spy Bar**, but it can be difficult to get in on certain nights. Other well-known nightclubs include **Crown** in Malmö and **Gutekällaren** in Visby.

A relative newcomer to the entertainment scene is the state-run casino chain **Casino Cosmopol**, which to date has opened branches in Stockholm, Gothenburg, Malmö and Sundsvall.

A combination of good food and top-flight entertainment is on offer at **Hamburger Börs** in Stockholm, with its shows featuring the best Swedish artists. **Wallmans Salonger**, which can be found in Stockholm and Helsingborg (summer) and Sälen and Åre (winter), offers musical entertainment with dinner served by waiters and waitresses who are, in fact, professional performers.

In Gothenburg, **Rondo** is a classic show venue.

Festivals

Countless festivals large and small are organized all across Sweden in the summer. Almost every town has its own festival, some with a specific focus, such as folk, jazz or rock.

Among the most renowned of the local festivals are Göteborgs kulturkalas in Gothenburg, Storsjöyran in Östersund and Gatufesten in Sundsvall.

There are numerous music festivals, often attracting huge audiences. Some famous music festivals include the

A traditional folk music festival in Tällberg on Lake Siljan in Dalarna

Sweden Rock Festival in Sölvesborg, the Gotland Chamber Music Festival in Visby, the Stockholm Jazz Festival and the Umeå International Jazz Festival.

The best-known film festivals in Sweden are the **Göteborg International Film Festival** (Jan/Feb) and the **Stockholm International Film Festival**

(Nov); however, several other cities and towns across the country hold their own film festivals with a different focus, such as Umeå (Sep).

DIRECTORY

Sources of Information

Visit Sweden
Tel 08- 789 10 00.
ⓦ visitsweden.com

Booking Tickets

Box-office
Kungsgatan 38, Stockholm.
Tel 08-10 88 00.
ⓦ boxoffice.se

Ticnet
Tel 077-170 70 70.
ⓦ ticnet.se

Arenas, Cultural Centres

Ericsson Globen
Globentorget 2, Stockholm.
Tel 077-131 00 00.

Friends Arena
169 79 Solna, Stockholm.
Tel 08-502 535 00.
ⓦ friendsarena.se

Malmö Arena
Arenagatan 15, Malmö.
Tel 0775-78 00 00.

Scandinavium
Valhallagatan 1, Gothenburg.
Tel 031-81 10 20.

Tele2 Arena
Arenaslingan 14, Stockholm.
Tel 077-131 00 00.

Theatre

China Teatern
Berzelii Park, Stockholm.
Tel 08-562 892 00.

Göta Lejon
Götgatan 55, Stockholm.
Tel 08-505 290 00.

Konsertteatern
Köpmangatan 11, Sundsvall. Tel 060-61 32 62.

Kungliga Dramatiska Teatern
Nybroplan, Stockholm.
Tel 08-667 06 80.

Lorensbergsteatern
Lorensbergsparken, Gothenburg.
Tel 031-708 62 00.

Classical Music, Dance, Opera

Berwaldhallen
Dag Hammarskjölds Väg 3, Stockholm.
Tel 08-784 18 00.

Dansens Hus
Barnhusgatan 12–14, Stockholm. Map 1 C3.
Tel 08-508 990 90.
ⓦ dansenshus.se

Drottningholms Slottsteater
Drottningholms Slott, Lovön, W of Stockholm.
Tel 08-556 931 00.

GöteborgsOperan
Christina Nilssons Gata, Gothenburg.
Tel 031-13 13 00.

Konserthuset
Götaplatsen, Gothenburg.
Tel 031-726 53 00.

Konserthuset
Hötorget, Stockholm.
Map 1 C4. Tel 08-786 02 00.

Kungliga Operan
Gustav Adolfs Torg, Stockholm. Map 2 D5.
Tel 08-791 43 00.

Louis De Geer konsert & kongress
Dalsgatan 15, Norrköping.
Tel 011-15 50 30.
ⓦ louisdegeer.com

Tonhallen
Universitetsallén 22, Sundsvall. Tel 060-19 88 00.

Folk Music

Folkmusikens Hus
Dalagatan 7, Rättvik.
Tel 0248-79 70 50.

Folkmusikhuset
Skeppsholmsgården, Stockholm. Map 2 E5.
Tel 076-930 99 80.

Folkmusikkaféet
Allégården, Gothenburg.
ⓦ folkmusikkafeet.net

Rock and Pop

Cirkus
Djurgårdsslätten, Stockholm. Tel 08-660 10 20.

Kulturbolaget
Bergsgatan 18, Malmö.
Tel 040-30 20 11.

Münchenbryggeriet
Torkel Knutssonsg 2, Stockholm. Tel 08-658 20 00.
ⓦ m-b.se

Trädgår'n
Nya Allén, Gothenburg.
Tel 031-10 20 80.

Jazz Clubs

Fasching
Kungsgatan 63, Stockholm. Map 1 B4.
Tel 08-534 829 60.

Nefertiti
Hvitfeldtsplatsen 6, Gothenburg.
Tel 031-711 15 33.

Stampen
Stora Nygatan 5, Stockholm. Map 3 B4.
Tel 08-20 57 93.

Music Pubs

The Dubliner
Holländargatan 1, Stockholm. Map 1 C3.
Tel 08-679 77 07.

Engelen
Kornhamnstorg 59 B, Stockholm. Map 3 B4.
Tel 0771-13 01 60.

Sticky Fingers
Kaserntorget 7, Gothenburg.
Tel 031-701 00 17.

Nightclubs, Casinos, Shows

Café Opera
Operahuset, Stockholm.
Map 3 B1. Tel 08-676 58 07.

Casino Cosmopol
Kungsgatan 65, Stockholm. Map 1 B4.
Tel 08-781 88 00.

Packhusplatsen 7, Gothenburg.
Tel 020-219 219.

Slottsgatan 33, Malmö.
Tel 040-664 18 00.

Casinoparken 1, Sundsvall.
Tel 020-219 219.

Crown
Amiralsgatan 23, Malmö.
Tel 040-611 80 88.

Gutekällaren
Stora Torget, Visby.
Tel 0498-21 00 43.

Hamburger Börs
Jakobsgatan 6, Stockholm. Map 2 D5.
Tel 08-787 85 00.

Rondo
Örgrytevägen 5, Gothenburg. Tel 031-40 01 00.

Spy Bar
Birger Jarlsgatan 20, Stockholm. Map 2 D3.
Tel 08-545 076 00.

Sturecompagniet
Sturegatan 4, Stockholm.
Map 2 D3. Tel 08-545 076 70.

Wallmans Salonger
Teatergatan 3, Stockholm.
Map 2 E5.
Tel 08-505 560 00.

Bollbrogatan 6, Helsingborg.
Tel 08-505 560 00.

Festivals

Göteborg International Film Festival
Tel 031-339 30 00.
ⓦ giff.se

Stockholm International Film Festival
Tel 08 677 50 00.
ⓦ stockholm filmfestival.se

SPORTS AND OUTDOOR ACTIVITIES

Sweden has countryside in abundance and the *"allemansrätt"* (Right of Public Access) makes it accessible in a way rarely found elsewhere in the world. An active outdoor life is a staple of the Swedish lifestyle. Constantly rising demand for outdoor activities has led to an increasing range of trails for hiking, canoeing and cycling, and the construction of hundreds of new ski lifts, golf courses and guest harbours. There has also been a boom in adventure sports – from challenging hikes in remote mountain regions and sea kayaking in the outer archipelagos to competing in the long-distance Vasaloppet skiing race, the Vansbrosimningen swimming race, the Lidingöloppet cross-country race and the Vätternrundan cycling race, which together make up what is known as the "Swedish Classic". More leisurely pursuits include horse riding and fishing.

General Information

In addition to the tourist information offices, there are a number of organizations to assist outdoors enthusiasts. The state-run **Naturvårdsverket** has an excellent website, which also provides useful information about Sweden's 28 national parks. **Friluftsfrämjandet** is a 100-year-old voluntary organization – the backbone of outdoor life for its many activities and operations.

Hiking Trails

Although it is possible to pitch a tent almost anywhere, it is often more practical to follow one of the many well-tended hiking trails. There are numerous lowland trails, such as the Skåneleden, which runs south to north through Skåne. Mountain trails proliferate, the best of which is the renowned Kungsleden stretching 450 km (280 miles) *(see pp278–9)*.

Maps of the trails usually provide information about stopping-off points, attractions, accommodation and services along the way.

The most popular mountain areas have marked trails for day trips and longer hikes with overnight accommodation in huts and at mountain stations. For more than 100 years, **Svenska Turistföreningen (STF)** has been the main provider of services in the mountains in summer and winter.

The mountain trails mainly run through road-free land. There are STF mountain stations at strategic locations from Abisko in Lapland to Grövelsjön in Dalarna. Although out in the wilds, these are relatively easy to access and make an excellent starting point for hiking tours in the mountains. The stations have hotel-standard accommodation, restaurants, self-catering kitchens, shops and equipment hire.

Walking with poles, a popular form of exercise

Along the trails, there are simple huts in which to stay, with a self-catering kitchen and in some cases provisions for sale. Space cannot be booked in advance, but everyone usually gets a roof over their head. In the summer, STF has special hosts to help with tips and advice.

The trails crossing the high mountains can be extremely demanding for the uninitiated. It is important not to be too ambitious and to have appropriate equipment.

Whatever the time of year, the weather changes quickly, so keep up to date with the forecast, which is usually posted at stations and huts. The summer season for mountain hiking is from about mid-June to mid-September.

Endurance Tests

Competitions for elite athletes and fitness enthusiasts alike have become increasingly popular in Sweden, attracting thousands of participants of

A hiker en route to the Sylarna mountain station, Jämtland

One of STF's many huts across the mountains

all levels. Some enter the "Swedish Classic", in which over one year competitors ski the Vasaloppet *(see p249)* or Engelbrektsloppet (60 km/37 miles), cycle the Vätternrundan (300 km/190 miles), swim the Vansbrosimningen (3 km/2 miles) and run the Lidingöloppet (30 km/19 miles). Other events include the Stockholm Marathon *(see p33)* and the O-ringen in orienteering.

Swimming

There are generally no restrictions for anyone wanting to take a dip in lakes, rivers and the sea. However, there is no need to take any risks as there are thousands of public bathing areas where the water quality is checked by the health authorities. Even in the north, there are plenty of opportunities to swim, for example at Pite Havsbad, where the sunny beaches are known as "The Nordic Riviera" *(see p272)*. In many places, the natural bathing spots are supplemented by water parks and fun pools offering all kinds of watery activities, such as at Skara Sommarland *(see p227)* and Sydpoolen in Södertälje.

Generally, water quality is high in Sweden and even in the cities it is sometimes possible to swim from rocks and beaches. Långholmen in central Stockholm is a favourite spot for a dip. In hot summers, however, poisonous algae sometimes blooms along the coast, so take advice locally on whether swimming is advisable.

Indoor pools are a popular choice. Stockholm has the historic Centralbadet and Sturebadet among others.

The spa and bathing culture has a long tradition in Sweden, particularly in places such as Loka Brunn *(see p143)*, with its modern facilities.

Cycling

Pedal power is a great way to experience towns and countryside alike. The bicycle has enjoyed something of a renaissance in Sweden and Stockholm in particular has invested heavily in cycle paths and special cycle routes.

Cycling holidays have long been popular on islands with little traffic such as Öland and Gotland. However, there are now cycle trails following minor roads and disused railway lines, often marked by green cycle-trail signs. A wide range of cycling packages is available and there are plenty of places to hire bicycles, tandems and trailers.

There are 30 or so regional cycle trails around the country, which require one or more stopovers to complete the distance. They can often be combined with the extensive Sverigeleden national trail which runs 2,590 km (1,600 miles) from Helsingborg in the south to Karesuando in the far north. The trail is well-signposted and special maps are available.

On the easier routes, 97 per cent of which are paved, those who have the time for a really long cycling holiday can experience Sweden's ever-changing landscape. Information about cycling trails is available from **Svenska Cykelsällskapet**.

Another option for those who fancy pedalling is to take a trolley trip on several railway tracks across the country where rail traffic has ceased.

A cycling trip on Visingsö in Lake Vättern, offering easy routes, fascinating sights and beautiful countryside

Trekkers heading for Storsylen in the Jämtland mountains

Winter Activities

It is no surprise that Swedish skiers have dominated the World Cup at times, both in downhill and cross-country skiing. In winter, much of the country is covered in snow and there is some great skiing to be had.

There is an extensive network of cross-country skiing trails, many of which are floodlit, a necessity during the long dark evenings. It is also possible to ski on snow-covered golf courses or on iced-over lakes and the frozen waters of the archipelagos. The ice is also ideal for skating, an enjoyable experience on a sunny winter's day. Check the safety information first, as things can quickly turn serious if the ice cracks.

Sweden has hundreds of lifts for downhill skiers, which are

Snowboarding and skiing are popular in the Swedish mountains

listed on the website for the skiing organization **SLAO**. **Skistar** deal with reservations for Sweden's two largest ski resorts: Åre, 600 km (370 miles) north of Stockholm, and Sälen, just over 400 km (250 miles) north of the capital. Most people on mountain holidays stay in self-catering cottages or apartments. Accommodation must be booked well in advance, particularly during the high season, and usually for complete weeks (Sun–Sun), weekends (Thu–Sun) or short weeks (Sun–Thu). It is easiest to buy lift passes and hire skis or snowboards at the resort.

Golf

Swedish golfers have achieved major successes in recent years, particularly in the ladies' events, with Anna Nordqvist leading the way. This golfing phenomenon is partly due to the ambitious junior programme supported by many of the country's golf clubs. Under the umbrella of the **Svenska Golfförbundet**, there are 450 golf courses, an extremely high figure in relation to the population size. Although the climate in parts of the country may be considered unsuitable for golf, the courses offer high quality during the summer. Almost all courses are open to guest players, but

demand is great and it can be difficult to find a suitable teeing-off time in high season at many clubs. Green fees vary from 300 Kr on basic courses to more than 500 Kr at exclusive city clubs. You must be a member of a golf club to play as a guest on a Swedish course.

Horse Riding

Horse riding is a popular sport in Sweden, and there are almost 1,000 riding clubs. There is a wide range of riding available, from trips for beginners on Icelandic ponies to mountain trekking for those with experience. The tourist offices can provide local contacts.

Trekking on Icelandic ponies

Boating, Canoeing, White-Water Rafting

The long coastline, inviting archipelagos and numerous lakes make exploring the country by water particularly rewarding. There are almost 500 classified guest harbours offering good facilities for sailors. The classification is administered by **Svenska Kryssarklubben**, which is also a good source of information about natural harbours and boating in general. All types of craft from simple rowing boats to large motor boats and yachts can be hired from marinas around the country. **Maringuiden** offers a wealth of useful information.

Although there are no specific requirements for sailing smaller boats, you will need basic knowledge of boating even for a day trip. As a rule, documented qualifications equivalent to the Swedish skipper's certificate *"förarintyg"* are required for taking out larger boats.

There are great opportunities for canoeing, with almost 20,000 km (12,500 miles) of trails on inland waters and around the archipelagos. The website for **Kanotleder i Sverige** lists 400 tours in Canadian canoes and kayaks, along with canoeing centres and rental sites across the country. For more advanced canoeists, there are plenty of opportunities to try sea kayaks in the outer archipelagos and white-water canoeing on the Norrland rivers. White-water rides are also possible, heading down the rapids in large rubber rafts or up on jetskis.

Hunting and Fishing

Sweden has more than 300,000 hunters and during the elk hunting season some forest villages are packed. Around 100,000 elks are shot every year. As a guest of land owners and hunting teams, foreign hunters can take part in small game and elk hunts. However, in the latter case, a special elk shooting test is required as well as a hunting permit. Taking your own weapon requires a great deal of bureaucracy, so hiring a weapon is recommended. Details about conditions, hunting times and hunt organizers are available from **Svenska Jägareförbundet**.

A third of all Swedes go fishing at least once a year, and no wonder with access to the

Rod fishing, often free along Sweden's lengthy coastline

most extensive fishing waters in Europe. There are more than 200 species of saltwater fish on the west coast, some of which also venture into the brackish water of the Baltic Sea. Added to this are around 40 species of freshwater fish in the lakes and rivers.

Rod fishing in coastal waters is often free. In other waters, the necessary fishing permit can be purchased locally. The **Sveafiskekortet** permit is a nationwide option offered by Sveaskog, which administers the national forests and land covering a fifth of the country. Sweden's leading and most traditional salmon fishing waters in Blekinge's Mörrum *(see p191)* are also state-owned. Salmon and sea trout can even be fished in the heart of Stockholm, where Strömmen has unusually clean water for a city of a million people.

Fishing trips by boat are offered widely. **Sportfiskarna** provides information about sport fishing.

DIRECTORY

General Information

Friluftsfrämjandet
Tel 08-447 44 40.
W friluftsframjandet.se

Naturvårdsverket
Tel 010-698 10 00.
W naturvardsverket.se

Svenska Turistföreningen (STF)
Tel 08-463 21 00.
W svenskaturistforeningen.se

Cycling

Svenska Cykelsällskapet
Sweden's cycle trails.
W svenska-cykelsallskapet.se

Winter Activities

Skistar
Central reservations for ski resorts of Sälen, Vemdalen and Åre.
W skistar.com

SLAO
Swedish ski lifts.
W slao.se

Golf

Svenska Golfförbundet
Tel 08-622 1500.
W sgf.golf.se

Boating, Canoeing

Kanotleder i Sverige
Canoe trails and canoe hire.
W kanot.com

Maringuiden
Tel 031-93 26 00.
W maringuiden.se

Svenska Kryssarklubben
Tel 08-448 2880.
W sxk.se

Hunting, Fishing

Sportfiskarna
Tel 08-410 806 00.
W sportfiskarna.se

Sveafiskekortet
info@sveaskog.se

Svenska Jägarförbundet
Tel 077-183 03 00.
W jagareforbundet.se

Experiencing the Swedish countryside by canoe

SURVIVAL
GUIDE

PRACTICAL INFORMATION

Sweden is a country of huge distances – it is as far from Malmö in the south to Treriksröset in the north as it is from Malmö to Rome. So, it is worth planning any trip in advance. The local tourist offices publish useful information on the Internet. All types of accommodation from luxury hotels to bed-and-breakfasts can be booked online. Once you have arrived in Sweden, there are more than 300 authorized tourist information offices nationwide which can provide help. The towns all have modern facilities for the traveller, including banking services and emergency medical care, and a top-ranking telecommunications service. Customs and border controls now apply mainly to travellers from countries outside the EU. For EU citizens and Norwegians, the entry procedure is relatively straightforward.

Tourist Information

Sweden has a number of tourist offices abroad, run by **Visit Sweden**. An overview of what's on offer for tourists and links to all the local tourist offices can be found at www.visitsweden.com.

Another general website is **Arrival Guides**, where visitors can find information on regional tourism organizations and obtain detailed information about accommodation, eating out, attractions and events. Brochures and travel tips can also be requested by email or phone.

In addition to the 300 official tourist information offices, information points open in summer, often attached to larger attractions. Offices with the blue and yellow "i" sign usually offer a broader service than those with the green and white "i".

The hub of Stockholm's tourist information is the **Stockholm Visitor Center**.

Visas and Customs

Citizens of virtually all countries can enter Sweden as tourists without a visa. Norwegians and visitors from European countries which have signed the Schengen agreement do not, in principle, need a passport. However, all airlines require passports for passengers flying from countries outside the Nordic region, so it is always wise to carry your passport. Always check the latest entry requirements with the Swedish embassy in your country before leaving.

Different customs regulations apply to travellers from the European Union (EU) and those from other countries. Citizens of EU countries can take an unlimited amount of alcohol and tobacco products into Sweden without having to pay tax, provided they are for personal use. Citizens from non-EU countries can take in 1 litre of spirits or 2 litres of fortified wine, including sparkling wine, 4 litres of wine, 16 litres of beer, 200 cigarettes, or 100 cigarillos, or 50 cigars or 250 g tobacco. But they can only take in goods up to a value of 3,000 Kr in addition to normal travel-related items. To import alcohol, you must be 20 years old, and for tobacco, 18.

Items such as milk, cheese, butter, eggs and potatoes may not be taken into Sweden by private individuals from non-EU countries. Norwegians and EU citizens may only take in a maximum of 15 kg (33 lb) of fish. Visitors from some other countries are permitted to bring in 1 kg (2.2 lb) of fish, but sometimes a certificate from a recognized exporter is required.

Dogs and cats from EU countries can be taken into Sweden, providing they have an identification marking, a veterinary certificate from the animal's home country, as well as an import permit issued by the Swedish Board of Agriculture (available at Swedish embassies).

Tax-free sales in Sweden are permitted only for travellers with a final destination outside the EU.

Tullverket provides up-to-date information in several languages by telephone and on its website.

Travel Safety Advice

Visitors can get up-to-date travel safety information from the **Foreign and Commonwealth Office** in the UK, the **State Department** in the US and the **Department of Foreign Affairs and Trade** in Australia.

Opening Hours and Admission Prices

Most museums and major sights are open between 10am and 6pm all year, and they often have longer opening hours in the summer. Many museums close on Mondays. Some have extended opening hours one evening in the week. Admission to a number of state-run museums is free of charge. Admission charges for other

Tourist information office, Stockholm

◀ Spectacular Northern Lights display in Lapland

museums can be as high as 150 Kr. Children, students and senior citizens usually get a discounted price. In many places, churches are only open for services, although some have opening hours for visitors.

Stockholm and other cities have special discount cards for tourists. They can be purchased from tourist information offices and many hotels and are valid for one or more days. A family card is usually also available. The card gives free travel on public transport, free or discounted admission to museums and other attractions and events, and may also offer discounts at restaurants and shops.

Discos and nightclubs generally charge an entrance fee of 60–200 Kr. Tickets for the theatre, concerts and sporting events can be bought locally, in the cities at special ticket offices, or online at Ticnet (www.ticnet.se).

Travellers with Special Needs

In Sweden, public areas have to be accessible for physically or visually disabled people, as well as those suffering from allergies. Sweden is a long away ahead of many other countries in this respect. All new buildings have wheelchair ramps and spacious toilets for disabled people.

Disabled car drivers with a disability permit from their home country can park in special areas.

In Stockholm, the Tunnelbana underground network and local trains are adapted for disabled passengers. Buses "kneel" at bus stops to give a reasonable height for passengers to get on or off. Visitors from abroad can obtain information in English before their stay from **DHR** by

The Göteborg City Card, giving free admission to museums

telephone or via the Internet. Brochures with information about facilities for disabled visitors at theatres, cinemas, museums and libraries are available from tourist information offices.

Etiquette

Bans on smoking are increasingly common throughout Sweden. Smoking is generally not permitted in public places, including all local transport and queues at bus stops and railway stations. Restaurants and bars are also smoke free.

The Swedes queue patiently, but guard their place jealously. They are usually friendly and pleased to help foreign tourists. The use of first names is the norm and a friendly *"Hej!"* is the common greeting.

Casual clothing is acceptable almost everywhere, including restaurants, particularly in the summer.

Service is always included in restaurant prices, but it is usual to round up the bill by up to 10 per cent for good service.

Alcohol

Swedish policy towards alcohol is restrictive. Wines and spirits can be bought only in the relatively few shops of the state monopoly **Systembolaget**. They are open Monday–Friday 10am–6pm, and Saturday 10am– 2pm. The minimum age for buying alcohol in these shops is 20, and young people may be asked to produce proof of their age. In restaurants, the minimum age for buying alcohol is 18. Most restaurants and pubs stop selling alcohol at 1am, but some bars stay open till 5am. With a maximum permitted blood alcohol level of only 0.2 per mil, drinking is effectively banned for car drivers.

The Swedish custom of *"skåling"* confounds many visitors. To *"skål"*, look the person in the eye, raise your glass, drink, then repeat the eye contact before putting down your glass. If the glasses are full of snaps, then Swedes like to sing their special snaps songs.

Personal Security and Health

Sweden is a safe destination compared with most countries in the world. You needn't worry about natural disasters such as earthquakes or hurricanes. Crime does occur, with some cities suffering more than others, but this is rarely a concern for tourists. However, it is important to lock the car and hide valuables when parked. Look out for pickpockets in the summer and avoid the empty, commercial parts of city centres late at night. Sweden has a well-developed network of emergency services which travellers can call on. Rescue services and hospital emergency clinics are highly efficient.

Policeman   Guard

Police car

Protecting Property

Although Sweden is a comparatively safe place, tourists can still run into trouble at times. Especially in the summer months, the many popular events attract bag-snatchers and pickpockets. In the cities and in crowded public areas visitors should be particularly careful to keep an eye on their property, especially handbags and cameras. Avoid using unmanned cloakrooms at restaurants and museums.

Valuables and personal documents should always be locked in the hotel safe. It is equally important not to leave any valuables in your car; ideally, choose a hotel with its own parking facilities.

There is no need to carry large amounts of cash. All major credit and debit cards are accepted in virtually all shops and restaurants, and cash machines are common, at least in larger places. When taking out cash, watch out for conmen who may

offer to help, but are actually after your money or card.

Personal Safety

The Swedish police are generally extremely helpful and speak good English. Police patrolling on foot or in cars are a routine sight in the cities, and mounted police are often in evidence at special events. In the suburbs, however, police can be thin on the ground. Not all towns have evening and night police patrols and even fewer have open police stations.

In many places, uniformed security guards have taken

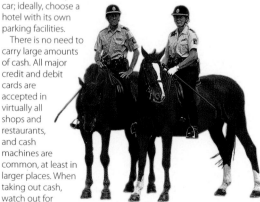

Mounted police

over the function of the police. They are a common feature in department stores, at train and Tunnelbana stations and as car patrols.

Stockholm, Gothenburg and Malmö are safe to stroll around on foot. Stockholm's Tunnelbana (underground railway) is efficient and comfortable, as well as being safe at most times. CCTV security systems are installed at some stations, squares, department stores and shops.

Beware the strict rules regarding alcohol, drugs and some medications when driving. A driver is guilty of drunk driving with a blood alcohol level of only 0.2 per mil and gross drunk driving (from 1.0 per mil) is punishable by imprisonment. The possession of drugs is illegal.

Breaking traffic rules, particularly speed limits, may lead to hefty fines.

For some years it has been illegal to buy sexual services in Sweden so it is the buyer, not the prostitute, who is prosecuted. Street prostitutes are now a very rare sight in the inner cities.

Lost Property

Lost or stolen property should be reported to the nearest police station. A police report will be needed for any insurance claim. In addition to the police lost property offices (Polisens Hittegodsexpedition), large towns and cities have lost property offices (Hittegodsavdelning) at railway stations, bus stations and airports. They are often only open during the day and not all of them will give information over the phone. There is usually a good chance of recovering lost goods.

Visitors from abroad should contact their embassy or consulate if they lose their passport.

Emergencies

The emergency telephone number for police, fire or ambulance is **112**. It can be dialled free of charge from all public telephones, but should be used only in emergencies.

Healthcare

No special vaccinations are needed to visit Sweden. Medical assistance is available across the country from doctors and district nurses at the local medical centres.

There are duty clinics in the evenings and at weekends, but you must make an appointment by phone. Many hospitals have accident and emergency departments, some of which are privately run. Patients should not report to emergency clinics with minor ailments. First, contact the healthcare information service **Sjukvårdsrådgivningen** for instructions in English. Its staff have up-to-date knowledge about the current situation in the city's hospitals and can assign patients to a suitable hospital or duty doctor. Particularly during the holiday period, it is always advisable to use this central information service, to avoid unnecessarily long waiting times. For severe toothache, patients can usually receive the help of a local

dentist and larger places have special duty dentists.

Citizens of other EU and EEA countries are entitled to emergency medical care at the same low rate as Swedes if they produce a European Health Insurance (EHIC) card and a valid passport or other form of identification. More extensive treatment costs extra so it is advisable to take out separate medical insurance covering specialist care, hospital expenses and repatriation before travelling.

Medicines

In Sweden, prescription medicines are sold only at *Apotek* (pharmacies). Medicines for minor ailments are available without a prescription, and these are also sold over the counter at supermarkets and petrol stations. However, many medicines which are available over the counter abroad require a prescription in Sweden. There is also a risk that the medication prescribed at home may not be approved in Sweden. It is best to ensure that you pack sufficient medication for the duration of your trip.

Pharmacy staff are well trained and can give good advice. Unfortunately, pharmacies can be hard to find in the countryside and they are not open on Sundays. A limited number of natural remedies are also sold in health food stores.

Pharmacy sign

Out and About

Sweden has a varied landscape and climate and it is important to respect the forces of nature. In the mountains, the weather can change very quickly from still

DIRECTORY

Emergencies

Ambulance, Police, Fire Brigade, Coastguard, Mountain Rescue
Tel 112.

Healthcare

Sjukvårdsrådgivningen
Tel 08-32 01 00 (24-hour) or 1177 (24-hour).

Embassies

British Embassy
Skarpögatan 6–8, Stockholm.
Tel 08-671 30 00.

Canadian Embassy
Klarabergsgatan 23, 6th Floor, Stockholm. **Map** 1 C4.
Tel 08-453 30 00.

US Embassy
Dag Hammarskjölds Väg 31, Stockholm.
Tel 08-783 53 00.

and sunny one moment to fog or a storm the next. If you have the right equipment and follow the rules, a trip in the mountains need not be dangerous. The STF mountain stations offer good advice about safe trails.

Along the coast, drowning accidents claim many lives every year. Avoid going out in flimsy craft and boats which are beyond your capabilities. Take advice from local people about the weather.

There is no need to worry about the forest predators – bears, wolves, lynxes and wolverines. They are shy creatures and prefer to avoid people. The same applies to Sweden's only poisonous snake, the adder. However, anyone bitten by a snake should seek medical advice.

Mosquitoes can be a nuisance from June to autumn, especially at dusk, along waterways and in the mountains. Pharmacies stock mosquito repellent. In the archipelagos, there is also a risk of being bitten by ticks, which carry a number of diseases. Ticks should be removed from the skin with tweezers as quickly as possible. If the redness around the bite area persists, consult a doctor.

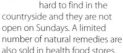

Ambulance

Banking and Local Currency

Sweden has retained its own currency, the Swedish krona, rather than adopting the euro. A number of shops in major tourist areas will accept euros, but goods are almost exclusively priced in kronor. As many banks are now cash-free or do not offer currency exchange, visitors are recommended to change currency at bureaux de change in the main towns, which have longer opening hours. Automatic cash machines can be found outside most banks and in shopping centres across the country. Credit and debit cards are accepted virtually everywhere, and the larger stores will take traveller's cheques.

Bankomat ATM

Banks and Bureaux de Change

There are plenty of banks in the towns, all providing a good service. Their opening times vary, but the normal hours are 9.30am–3pm. Some banks stay open until 6pm at least once a week. All banks are closed at weekends and on public holidays, as well as the day before a public holiday. **Svenska Kassaservice**, which handles the Swedish post office Posten's cash transactions, has almost 1,000 offices around the country. They are agents for certain banks and accept withdrawals on a debit card.

Various bureaux de change chains are represented in Sweden, including **Forex** and **X-Change**. In city centres there is always a bureau de change office close by. Changing money in your hotel is the most expensive option. It is worth checking exchange rates and commission charges, because the differences can be significant. Currency can be changed at international airports from 5.30am, and from 7am at city train stations seven days a week.

ATMs

There are nearly 3,000 automatic cash machines throughout the country. Foreign visitors can use all cash machines provided that they have a bank card with a PIN code that is linked to, for example, Visa or MasterCard. Machines usually have instructions in several languages. The charge for withdrawing cash varies according to the type of card.

The head office of Handelsbanken on Kungsträdgårdsgatan, Stockholm

Forex bureau de change, situated in large towns and at airports

Credit and Debit Cards

All the well-known credit cards, such as **Visa, Diners Club, Eurocard** and **MasterCard,** are accepted across Sweden, but not all places accept **American Express** because of opposition to the relatively high charges that the retailer has to pay.

Cards can be used not just at larger hotels and restaurants, but at nearly all shops and services. If you pay by credit card, you will need a PIN code, because all transactions are electronically processed, or

most shops will ask you to produce proof of identity. Some shops also offer a cash withdrawal service for small amounts in conjunction with purchases.

Cash machines can be used to make withdrawals using an internationally accepted credit card with a PIN code.

If your credit or debit card is lost or stolen, contact the company that isued the card immediately. In order to ensure your card works overseas, it is worth contacting your bank or credit card provider in advance of travelling.

Traveller's cheques are not accepted in all shops, but it is possible to exchange them for cash at banks.

Currency

Sweden's currency is the krona (plural kronor). The krona (abbreviated as SEK or Kr) is divided into 100 öre. In 2015 and 2016, a new series of banknotes and coins were introduced, including a new denomination, 200 kronor. The smallest coin is 1 Kr and the largest note is 1,000 kronor. If possible, it is advisable not to carry notes of more than 500 Kr.

Although Sweden has not adopted the euro, many shops in tourist areas and border towns accept payment in euros, but will usually give change in kronor.

20 Kr (Astrid Lindgren)

Notes

The new Swedish currency notes, issued in 2015 and 2016, are in denominations of 20, 50, 100, 200, 500 and 1,000 kronor. They depict Sweden's foremost cultural personalities of the 20th century.

50 Kr (Evert Taube)

100 Kr (Greta Garbo)

500 Kr (Birgit Nilsson)

1000 Kr (Dag Hammarskjöld)

Coins

Introduced in 2016, the new set of Swedish coins are in values of 1, 2, 5 and 10 kronor. The new coins are smaller and have a portrait of King Carl XVI Gustav on the obverse side.

1 krona

5 kronor

10 kronor

Communications and Media

Sweden has a top-ranking telecommunications industry and high living standards have placed the Swedes among the world's biggest users of telephones. Although the fixed telephone system is well developed, there are now nearly as many mobile phone users as there are people in the country. With the advent of the 3G and 4G systems allowing video telephony and advanced data services, only a very small percentage of the population does not have coverage. Internet use is widespread, with impressive investment in broadband.

A modern Swedish phone kiosk

Local and International Phone Calls

Sweden is divided into 250 dialling code areas. The prefix for international calls from Sweden is 00. Then dial the country code and the phone number without the initial zero of the area code. To dial Sweden from abroad, the country code is 46. For enquiries such as whether your phone will operate in the mountains, call **Telia customer services**.

Local numbers can be obtained by calling directory enquiries on 118 118, or online at Eniro (www.eniro.se) or Hitta (www.hitta.se). The number for directory enquiries also provides listings of mobile numbers. Computer-to-computer phone calls allow visitors to call free of charge using the Internet. Popular service providers include Skype and Google Talk.

Public Telephones

The number of public telephone kiosks has shown a marked decline, as most Swedes have a mobile phone. The remaining public phones are mainly card-operated and are usually found in public places such as hospitals, airports and public-transport locations. They are owned by Telia and are cheapest to use with a Swedish phonecard. These can be bought at news-paper kiosks (for example, Pressbyrån) and in supermarkets and shops, and are available for 50 or 120 units. Instructions on how to use public telephones are also shown in English. The emergency number is 112. Some 020 and 0200 numbers can be called free of charge. Coin-operated phones are very rare.

Mobile Phones

It is wise to contact your phone provider, prior to travelling, to clarify whether international roaming is activated on your mobile and discuss daily rates. A pre-paid SIM might be cheaper but talking to the relevant provider is advisable. Sweden's mobile network is based on GSM, and most foreign visitors will be able to use their GSM, 3G or 4G phones here. However, visitors from North America should check with their service providers to ensure their phones are GSM-compatible. The major network providers in Sweden include **Telia**, **Telenor**, Tele2/Comviq and 3 Sweden. Inexpensive GSM mobile phones can be purchased at a number of stores, including The Phone House (in Stockholm), Telia and Telenor, together with a prepaid SIM card for local phone calls.

Within the Stockholm area, mobile users must dial the area code 08 before a local number; the country code is not required.

The GSM network offers good service coverage outside the cities. Having a mobile phone is a good idea even out in the wilderness, although there is no guarantee that you will be able to call for help if you need it.

Internet

Although Internet access is offered in most hotels, you may be charged a daily fee. Hotels that focus on business travellers may have computers available for use. Public computers can be found at local libraries; users may be asked to present some form of identification.

Wireless Internet (Wi-Fi) is widely available, with many public places, hotels and cafés

Computer terminals at the Stockholm Public Library

offering Wi-Fi hot spots. Some are free of charge; others are inexpensive. Stockholm Visitor Center, Stockholm Arlanda Airport and Central Station Stockholm and Cityterminalen are just some of the places in Stockholm that offer free Wi-Fi.

Postal Services

The Swedish postal service has an almost 400-year history, but many Swedes think the service has deteriorated in recent years. Post offices have been closed and replaced by a few large postal centres, mainly for companies. For the general public, there are small service points, primarily in supermarkets and at petrol stations. They have the advantage of longer opening hours in the evenings and at weekends. The disadvantage is a frequent lack of space and services. Perhaps the best service is provided in remote areas by mobile postal workers. Stamps can be bought at post offices, shops, Pressbyrån kiosks and tourist information offices. The basic postage for a postcard or letter under 50 g within Sweden is 7 Kr; for abroad the postage is 4 Kr. Postboxes are painted blue for local letters and yellow for other domestic and international mail. Collection times are shown on the postbox and sometimes take place in the early afternoon. In large towns there are last-minute postboxes, which are emptied in the evenings.

Yellow postbox for national and international mail, blue for local mail

One of the country's many Pressbyrån kiosks

Most international courier services – such as **DHL**, **FedEx** and **TNT** – are represented in the cities, and special services are also operated by the Swedish post office, **Posten**.

TV and Radio

Most hotels provide a television in the room with both national and foreign channels. The most frequently used are the Swedish SVT1, SVT2, TV3, TV4 and Channel 5, as well as the international CNN, Sky News, BBC and Eurosport channels. SVT1 and 2 are state-run public-service channels. SVT2 and TV4 broadcast local programmes in the morning and evening, including weather forecasts.

Post office logo

There are also a number of local radio stations, broadcasting mainly international and Swedish music. P6, SR International broadcasts programmes in eight languages (including English) on 89.6 MHz.

Newspapers and Magazines

Major foreign newspapers and magazines can be bought in the cities, at airports and at other transport hubs. Pressbyrån kiosks, tobacconists, department stores and some tourist information offices stock a limited selection of foreign publications.

DIRECTORY

Local and International Phone Calls

Telia customer services
Tel 0771-99 02 00.
W telia.se

Mobile Phones

The Phone House
Gallerian,
Kungsgatan 29,
Stockholm.
Map 1 B4.
Tel 0771-99 10 00.

Telenor
W telenor.se

Telia
W telia.se

Postal Services

DHL
Tel 0771-345 345.
W dhl.se

FedEx
Tel 0200-252 252.
W fedex.com/se

Posten
Tel 020-23 22 21
(customer services).
W posten.se

TNT
Tel 020-960 960.
W tnt.com/se

TRAVEL INFORMATION

Stockholm Arlanda is the busiest of Sweden's international airports, although a number of other airports have international flights, notably Gothenburg's Landvetter and Sturup, near Malmö, in the south. Since summer 2000, Sweden has been linked with Continental Europe by a bridge over the Öresund Strait to Denmark for road and rail traffic. It is now possible to fly to Copenhagen and take a short train journey across the bridge to Malmö. There are still a number of car ferry services operating between Denmark and Sweden, as well as across the Baltic Sea from Finland and the Baltic States, and across the North Sea from Norway. In summer, an increasing number of cruise liners call into Swedish ports. Express buses operate services from cities across Europe.

Arrival by Air

Most major European cities have direct flights to one of Stockholm's three airports: Arlanda, Skavsta and Bromma. Landvetter near Gothenburg and Sturup outside Malmö also have international traffic. Arlanda is served by around 52 international airlines. It is also possible to fly via Copenhagen in Denmark. The leading Scandinavian airline **SAS** dominates. Other operators include **Lufthansa**, **British Airways** and **Finnair**. **Delta Air Lines** operates from the US to Europe with onward flights to Sweden via major airlines such as Air France or KLM; **American Airlines** flies to the UK with onward connections via British Airways.

Arlanda is 40 km (25 miles) north of central Stockholm and is also a hub for Swedish domestic flights and charter services. Bromma, situated 7 km (4 miles) from the city centre, may only be used by less environmentally damaging

Arlanda Express linking Arlanda Airport with central Stockholm

aircraft. Skavsta lies 100 km (60 miles) south of Stockholm, near Nyköping. Low-cost airline **Ryanair** flies routes to Skavsta, Gothenburg and Malmö from several UK airports and to other destinations in Sweden from other parts of Europe.

Getting from and to the Airport

All the international airports are served by airport buses to the city centre in conjunction with arrivals and departure times. Stockholm's Arlanda Airport has a **Flygbussarna** bus service, which operates every 10 minutes at peak times. Journey time is 45 minutes to the City Terminal at Central Station. An onward journey by taxi can be booked on the bus. The taxi ride into town from the airport is quicker, but more expensive. Most taxi firms have a fixed charge to the city centre. Avoid unauthorized taxis and check the fare before departure. The shortest journey time is by the pricier **Arlanda Express** train, a 20-minute trip to Central Station. Trains depart every 10 minutes at peak times from the two stations, Arlanda South (serving terminals 2, 3 and 4) and Arlanda North (for terminal 5).

Air Fares

Fare options are many and varied, particularly if you are flexible about departure and arrival dates, or can book well in advance.

Increased competition between the airlines has made it considerably cheaper to fly to Sweden from many European destinations, and now SAS offers low-cost tickets with a no-frills service to meet the competition. It is possible to find return flights from London, Paris or Frankfurt for less than £80. Tour operators often have packages with attractive air fares and accommodation included. Newspaper advertisements and travel companies' websites have details of last-minute deals.

Departure Hall, Terminal 5, at Stockholm's Arlanda Airport

Scandlines passenger ferries connect Helsingør to Helsingborg

Arrival by Ferry

There are a number of ferry companies operating direct services across the North Sea and the Baltic to Sweden. The large car ferries used on most routes offer plenty of passenger comforts, including good food, entertainment options and shopping facilities.

Although the Öresund Bridge has reduced ferry traffic from Denmark, the short Helsingør–Helsingborg hop still has several ferries an hour operated by **Scandlines**. **Stena Line** covers the routes Grenå–Varberg and Fredrikshavn–Gothenburg.

The busiest route in terms of passenger numbers is from Finland with regular crossings from Helsinki, Turku and Mariehamn to Stockholm and Kapellskär. Both **Viking Line** and **Tallink Silja Line** have terminals in Stockholm – at Stadsgården and Värtahamnen respectively. The crossing takes about 15.5 hours from Helsinki and 11 hours from Turku. **Vasabåtarna** operates ferries between Vaasa in Finland and Umeå in northern Sweden. From Estonia, Tallink Silja Line operates the routes between Tallinn and Stockholm

and between Riga in Latvia and Stockholm.

Polferries has the routes Świnoujście–Ystad and Gdansk–Nynäshamn. **Stena Line** operates the Gdynia–Karlskrona route.

Trelleborg is the major port for traffic from Germany. **TT-Line** goes from Rostock and Travemünde, while **Scandlines** goes from Rostock and Sassnitz, as does **Stena Line**, which also sails the Kiel–Gothenburg route.

Arrival by Train or Express Bus

There are excellent train links from continental Europe and Norway and a large network of express bus routes. To find out the best connections by coach or train to Sweden from Copenhagen, Oslo and Sassnitz (Germany), visit the **ResRobot** website.

Arrival by Car

Motorists arriving from Denmark can use the spectacular Öresund Bridge between Copenhagen and Malmö *(see p185)*. On the Swedish side, the toll bridge connects with the E6 motorway to the north. Alternatively, there are car ferries.

Car ferries are also the most practical option from Finland and the Baltic States, since driving around the Baltic Sea can take two days.

The borders with Finland and Norway have customs posts which are often unmanned. However, the entry regulations still apply *(see p318)*.

The Öresund Bridge, which connects Denmark and Sweden

DIRECTORY

Airlines

American Airlines
Tel 1-800-433 7300 (from USA);
0771-200 666.
W aa.com

British Airways
Tel 0770 11 00 20.
W britishairways.com

Delta Air Lines
Tel 08-519 922 16.
W delta.com

Finnair
Tel 0771-78 11 00.
W finnair.com

Lufthansa
Tel 0770-111 010.
W lufthansa.com

Ryanair
Tel 0900-100 0550.
W ryanair.com

SAS
Tel 0770-727 727.
W sas.se

Getting from and to the Airport

Arlanda Express
W arlandaexpress.se

Flygbussarna
W flygbussarna.se

Ferry Companies

Polferries
Tel 040-12 17 00.
W polferries.se

Scandlines
Tel 042-18 61 00.
W scandlines.se

Stena Line
Tel 0770-57 57 00.
W stenaline.se

Tallink Silja Line
Tel 08-22 21 40.
W tallinksilja.se

TT-Line
Tel 0410-562 00.
W ttline.se

Vasabåtarna
Tel 0207-71 68 10.
W wasaline.com

Viking Line
Tel 08-452 40 00.
W vikingline.se

Train or Express Bus

ResRobot
W resrobot.se

Getting Around Sweden

Flying within Sweden has its advantages considering the enormous distances between places, and in many cases the fares are reasonably priced. The high standard of overnight sleeper trains makes long journeys by train a comfortable option. The SJ high-speed train running between the major cities often competes well in terms of time and comfort with domestic flights. Elsewhere in the country, buses provide much of the public transport. Travelling by boat offers exciting opportunities to discover Sweden's magnificent archipelagos and waterways.

SAS, one of the companies offering domestic flights in Sweden

Domestic Flights

The vast length of Sweden makes domestic flights a convenient option, and deregulation and increased competition in recent years have made prices more reasonable. Of the 45 airports offering scheduled flights, 12 belong to and are operated by state-owned **Swedavia**. Visit the **Luftfartsverket** website for links to information on all of Sweden's airports, including flights and current arrivals and departures.

Stockholm/Arlanda dominates the domestic flight scene, but several companies have chosen to fly from the capital's more centrally located Bromma Airport. Landvetter, outside Gothenburg, and Sturup, outside Malmö, are other major airports.

Flight times are generally short: Stockholm–Gothenburg takes 55 minutes. The longest direct flight, Stockholm–Kiruna, takes 1 hr 50 mins.

SAS is still the leading airline in terms of passenger numbers. Other operators include **Malmö Aviation** and **Norwegian**. Tickets can be bought at travel agents or directly from the airlines. Tickets booked online can generally be paid for with a credit card, then printed out or saved on your smartphone. It is worth searching for the lowest prices, particularly if you book a long way in advance. Young people under 26 can buy cheap standby tickets.

Travellers to Malmö could consider flying to Kastrup in Copenhagen, as there is a fast train transfer to central Malmö across the Öresund Bridge.

Larger airports are served by airport buses, which operate in conjunction with arrivals and departures.

Train passing through the village of Storlien in Southern Norrland

Travelling by Train

There is a well-developed train network covering parts of Sweden from the Öresund Bridge in the south to Riksgränsen in the north. Stations and services are good by international standards. The trains are run by a number of competing companies. The state-run **SJ** operates most long-distance routes. Other major players include **Veolia Transport** and **Tågkompaniet**, which have parts of the lines in Norrland. At county level, train services are run by local train companies in partnership with bus services and in some cases ferry services.

Travel involving different companies and forms of transport is administered by **Samtrafiken**, which is part-owned by each of the transport companies. Resplus is a unique cooperative service offering travellers one ticket for all journeys and all transport operators in the country.

Since the 1990s, airlines have experienced tough competition from the SJ high-speed train (formerly known as the X2000 Express), which links the cities of Copenhagen/ Malmö, Gothenburg, Östersund and Falun to Stockholm. The journey time is around 5 hours from Malmö and 3 hours from Gothenburg. The trains offer a business class service similar to that of airlines.

InterCity is the main long-distance alternative to the SJ, offering first- and second-class seats. The overnight sleeper trains are recommended for longer journeys such as Gothenburg–Östersund and routes in northern Norrland. The standard is high, and you can often have your own compartment with shower, if you wish. Compartments contain between one and six beds.

SJ logo

Ticket prices vary considerably depending on the type of train. Discounts are worth searching for.

Tickets can be bought online and at larger stations. Buying tickets on the train attracts a fee of around 100 Kr. Note that seat/berth reservations are necessary for the SJ and night trains.

The **Inlandsbanan** line operates in summer, offering the opportunity to travel through the Swedish wilderness, forests and mountains. It runs 1,300 km (800 miles) from Kristinehamn on Lake Vänern north to Gällivare in northern Lapland.

Travelling by Bus

In many places buses are the only public transport available and although services are patchy in rural areas, it is possible to get about. Local timetables are on **Samtrafiken**'s website.

Express buses compete with trains and airlines on longer routes. Journey times are longer, but ticket prices are lower and the buses are modern. See Samtrafiken's website for routes and times. Some bus companies, such as **Swebus Express**, do not require pre-booking. If one bus is full, another one is laid on.

Many express bus companies arrange special excursions in the tourist season. Contact the tourist information offices for information. Trips are also arranged to the southern Fjällen where there is no train line. **Fjällexpressen** is one of the operators running ski buses from Stockholm and Gothenburg.

Abisko's modest station building on the Malmbanan line

Travelling by Boat

Sweden's long coastline, vast lakes and extensive archipelagos make for busy boat services. In addition to the scheduled services, sightseeing trips and tours are offered in summer, occasionally on classic old steamers.

The Dalsland, Strömsholm and Kinda canals attract some charming boats, but the best tourist trail is the Göta Canal (see pp150–51). Sweden's blue ribbon takes you 611 km (380 miles) in a relaxed three days, negotiating 65 locks, the country's three largest lakes and some of Sweden's most attractive scenery. Contact **Rederi AB Göta Kanal** for more information.

Boat services to the Baltic Sea's largest island, Gotland, are run by **Destination Gotland**; its high-speed ferries take less than 3 hours on either of the Nynäshamn–Visby or Oskarshamn–Visby routes. In peak summer season, there are up to eight departures a day. Although the ferries can take 500 cars per trip, it can be difficult to get a place for a car during holiday periods if you have not booked in advance.

Gotland's high-speed catamaran service approaching Visby

DIRECTORY

Domestic Flights

Luftfartsverket
Airports, timetables, information
W **lfv.se/en/About-us1/
Swedish-Airports**

Malmö Aviation
Tel 0771-55 00 10.
W **malmoaviation.se**

Norwegian
Tel 0770-45 77 00.
W **norwegian.com**

SAS
Tel 0770-727 727.
W **sas.se**

Swedavia
Tel 010-109 00 00.
W **swedavia.se**

Train, Bus, Boat

Samtrafiken
Tel 010 199 24 50
(general enquiries).
W **reseplanerare.resrobot.se**

Train Travel

Inlandsbanan
Tel 0771-53 53 53.
W **inlandsbanan.se**

SJ
Tel 0771-75 75 75.
W **sj.se**

Tågkompaniet
Tel 0771-444 111.
W **tagkompaniet.se**

Veolia Transport
Tel 0771-26 00 00.
W **transdev.se**

Bus Travel

Fjällexpressen
Tel 08-12 00 45 60.
W **fjallexpressen.com**

Swebus Express
Tel 0771-218 218.
W **swebus.se**

Boat Travel

Destination Gotland
Tel 0771-22 33 00.
W **destinationgotland.se**

Rederi AB Göta Kanal
Tel 031-80 63 15.
W **stromma.se/sv/Gota-Kanal**

Road Travel in Sweden

Distances within Sweden are huge, and in the rural areas travelling in your own or a rented car is often the only way of getting about. The well-developed road network varies in quality, but the major roads are generally of a good standard. State-run ferries operate a free service in the archipelagos. Although traffic can be heavy in the cities in rush hour, it is never on the same scale as in the UK and on the Continent, and Swedish motorists are generally good-natured. For advice on driving in Stockholm, *see p332.*

Elk on the road, a hazard for motorists in the forests

Road Standards

Sweden has an extensive road network, with more than 210,000 km (130,000 miles) open for public use. Almost the same again is not accessible, primarily forestry roads which are closed with a boom. The majority of the public roads are sealed and of a good standard. The exceptions can be found in the forested counties of the northwest, where ice and heavy traffic can make the roads difficult to negotiate.

The national road network comprises *europavägar* ("European motorways"), *riksvägar* (national roads) and *länsvägar* (county roads). Motorways such as the E4 and stretches of the E20 and E6 make up less than 1,200 km (700 miles). With the exception of the Öresund and Svinesund bridges, roads are toll-free.

The three-lane highways require some attention for the uninitiated. The traffic runs in opposite directions along one or two lanes with a wire barrier to separate the flow.

Traffic Rules

Generally, Swedish traffic is comparatively well organized and most motorists follow the rules of the road. Road safety is good, despite occasionally dense traffic and severe weather conditions. The number of road fatalities is around 500 a year, the same level as in the 1940s.

The most common breach of the rules relates to speed limits, despite the presence of speed cameras and radar patrols. The fines are high and there is a risk of losing your licence for serious speeding offences.

The maximum speed on motorways is 120 km/h (74 mph), but the limit is more often 110 km/h (68 mph), 90 km/h (55 mph) or 80 km/h (50 mph), depending on the road. On country roads the limit is usually 70–80 km/h (43–50 mph) and in built-up areas the limit is 40 or 50 km/h (25 or 31 mph). The limit is reduced to 30 km/h (19 mph) around all schools and nurseries. Residential areas often have traffic calming measures such as road narrowing and speed bumps. By law, the driver and all passengers must wear seatbelts. Children under a height of 135 cm (53 in) must use child seats.

Beware of the strict rules regarding alcohol and driving. A driver is guilty of drink-driving with a blood alcohol level of only 0.2 per mil and gross drink-driving (from 1.0 per mil) is punishable by imprisonment.

Motorists must give way to pedestrians at crossings not controlled by lights. Vehicles must stop at junctions onto major roads, even if there is no Stop sign. At roundabouts, vehicles already on the roundabout always have right of way. Traffic lights with a continuous amber light mean "stop" and there are hefty fines for driving through a red light. Side-lights or dipped headlights must be used even during daylight hours.

Winter tyres must be used from 1 Dec–31 Mar. Studded tyres may be used, but not during the period 1 May–30 Sep, unless the road conditions require them.

Car Ferries

State-run car ferries operate free of charge in the archipelagos and across some of the larger rivers. Some places also have private ferries, which do levy a charge. You rarely need to book, but check the timetable carefully as the ferries may not run late at night unless in emergencies. **Färjerederiet Trafikverket** can provide information.

Uddevallabron on the E6, one of Sweden's many road bridges

Road Signs

Swedish road signs mostly follow the European standard, but the country also has some signs of its own. Signs carrying the symbol for elk, reindeer or deer warn drivers that there is a major risk of colliding with wildlife. Thousands of accidents involving animals occur every year and a collision between a car and a full-grown elk is often fatal. The risk is particularly high in the summer around 5am–8am and 10pm–2am, when visibility is poor. Fences along the roadside are no guarantee that animals won't suddenly appear on the road.

As in the rest of Europe, brown signs with white symbols indicate recommended tourist routes, heritage sites, tourist areas and attractions along the road such as a national park or a historic building.

Individual attractions may be indicated by a sign with a white "pretzel" on a blue background.

Warning sign for elk

Parking

There is usually a charge for parking in towns and built-up areas, especially in the centre of towns and cities. City car parks and on-street parking are often expensive. Sometimes charges apply 24-hours a day and at weekends, too. Many ticket machines accept credit cards and petrol cards, but they may not always work, so it is best to keep a good number of 10 Kr coins to hand.

Diligent traffic wardens hunt out illegally parked cars and the fines can be high, particularly if you have parked illegally in a space reserved for disabled drivers.

Where parking is free during the night, there is sometimes a parking ban on certain days for cleaning, so it is always important to check the signs – otherwise your car may be towed away. Supermarkets and other

Traffic warden

large stores often have free parking for a few hours, but be aware that sometimes they require a special parking ticket for your windscreen showing your arrival time.

Fuel and Services

There are plenty of service stations along the major roads and in built-up areas, but they may be few and far between in rural areas. Although some stations are manned 24-hours a day, drivers are often directed to automatic pumps which take cards and notes. It is sensible to fill up before a night drive. In the event of technical problems, there are few places which can help outside working hours – garages are usually closed in the evenings and at weekends.

Assistancekåren and **Falck** offer emergency roadside assistance. They often have an agreement with motoring organizations and insurance companies abroad.

Renting a Car

In addition to the familiar international car hire chains, there are a number of local options, including the petrol companies' extensive rental service. Most places will have some form of car rental.

It is possible to pre-book cars at airports and major train stations, often for one-way rental where you leave the car at your destination. Bookings can be made from abroad via the Internet or by phone. You generally only need a valid driving licence to rent a car, but there may be an age limit of 20, or even 25 for exclusive vehicles. Prices vary considerably, so it is worth shopping around. Special weekend deals are common and considering Sweden's long distances, it is best to opt for offers which include unlimited mileage.

Winter Driving

Road conditions in the winter vary depending on the severity of the weather and the location. Studded tyres are permitted in Sweden and their use is recommended, at least from central Sweden northwards.

Anyone not used to winter driving should not venture out if there is a risk of snow and ice. The major roads are treated with salt, and ploughing is generally good, but even in Skåne in the far south, snow storms can cause traffic chaos and in some years military tracked vehicles have had to be called out.

Getting Around Stockholm

Stockholm is a perfect city for pedestrians. Distances between sights are short, and there is always something interesting to discover among the eye-catching vistas and waterfront scenes. Cycling is popular and there are many cycle lanes throughout the city, although for the visitor a green area such as Djurgården might be more relaxing for a cycle trip. Public transport on buses, trams, underground trains, local trains and ferries is efficient. Apart from Gamla Stan, and during the rush hours, driving a car in Stockholm is relatively easy, although parking can be difficult.

Taking a waterfront stroll along Djurgårdsbrunnsviken

Stockholm on Foot

In central Stockholm, walking is the best way to see the sights and get a feel for the place. Road users are more disciplined here than in many other cities. Pedestrians are not allowed to cross a road against a red light, but motorists must stop and give way to pedestrians at zebra crossings without traffic lights.

The clear street signs make it easy to find one's way around, and Stockholmers are always glad to help visitors. There are walking and cycling routes everywhere in the city. Take care not to step out in the cycle lane, which is often marked just with a white line to separate it from the walking lane.

Gamla Stan is a popular area for exploring on foot, and there

is always something to see around Kungsträdgården as well. In good weather, nothing beats Djurgården, with its host of attractions set in beautiful parkland only a short distance from the centre.

There are pleasant waterfront walks along the quays, for example from Stadshuset along Norr Mälarstrand and the Riddarfjärden bay.

Walks with multilingual guides are organized regularly, often with a special theme – history, architecture or parks, for example.

Cycling

The capital's network of cycle paths is increasing all the time, but you need to be an

experienced city cyclist if you want to explore the central area from the saddle. Otherwise Stockholm and its surrounding area are tailor-made for cycling. Djurgården is a lovely place to explore by bike. It is possible to hire bicycles from **Djurgårdscykeln**; they are free with an SL Access Card *(see Public Transport, opposite)*.

Driving in Stockholm

Anyone familiar with driving in large cities will have no problems in Stockholm. It is relatively easy to get about by car, except during the rush hours (7:30am–9:30am, 11:30am–1pm, and 3:30–6pm). Cars are not really necessary in the city centre because of the short distances between sights and excellent public transport. However, a car is an advantage if you want to explore further afield.

Congestion charges were introduced in 2007 to tackle busy traffic and to improve the environment.

The speed limit is usually 50 km/h (31 mph), but near schools it is 30 km/h (19 mph). Speeds up to 70 km/h (43 mph) are permitted only on the main roads in and out of the city.

It is often hard to find a parking space. There are 25 Park-and-Ride facilities just outside the inner city. In some areas, parking charges apply 24-hours a day, but usually parking is free in the evenings, at night and at weekends.

Stockholm's Tunnelbana

- T10 Kungsträdgården – Hjulsta
- T11 Kungsträdgården – Akalla
- T13 Norsborg – Ropsten
- T14 Fruängen – Mörby centrum
- T17 Åkeshov – Skarpnäck
- T18 Alvik – Farsta strand
- T19 Hässelby strand – Hagsätra

Check for street cleaning times when parking is prohibited. The city's traffic wardens are diligent. Being wrongly parked could cost you a fine of 550 Kr or more. Do not leave valuables in your car, particularly in a car park.

Taxis

Distances between places in the city centre are short and brief journeys by taxi start from around 300 Kr. There are usually plenty of taxis available, particularly at taxi ranks and major sights, with the exception of the rush hours. You can also hail an empty taxi, indicated by the illuminated sign on the car roof. The best method is to order a taxi by phone or book one in advance. It is always worth enquiring what the fare is likely to be, as many companies charge a fixed rate. Be careful about using unauthorized taxis without a taxi sign on the outside, or a taxi identity card on display inside, especially at night.

Public Transport

All public transport in the county of Stockholm is under the control of **Stockholms Lokaltrafik**, but the actual services are run by several companies. An extensive network of local trains, underground trains, buses and ferries carries hundreds of thousands of commuters in from the suburbs every day. In the city centre, the Tunnelbana (T-bana) underground system's green, red and blue lines are the mainstay, supplemented by city buses, a few tramlines and ferry routes.

On regular lines in the Stockholm area there is a choice of tickets: single-trip or

Ferry linking Gamla Stan and Djurgården

1-, 3-, 7- and 30-day travel cards. It is worth buying an SL Access Card, which can be topped up with credit and held to a card reader as you enter your chosen method of transport. The tickets are valid for one hour from the start of the journey. Single tickets can be bought on departure, while return tickets, SL Access Cards and travel cards are sold at Pressbyrån outlets and SL and T-bana stations.

The network of red city buses is built around a number of blue "feeder" routes. These run more frequently. Many streets in the city centre have special bus lanes which speed up the traffic. The best routes for sightseeing are 3, 4, 47, 62 and 69.

Run by **Waxholmsbolaget**, public transport in the archipelago is good all year round, with more frequent services from June to August. An excellent way to explore the archipelago is to take the ferries from Strömkajen, which stop off at countless picturesque jetties along the way.

Other recommended trips include Birka, Drottningholm and Mariefred/Gripsholm *(see pp116–17)* A popular way of getting to Djurgården is on the ferry from Slussen to Allmänna Gränd. SL's one-day and three-day cards are valid on the Djurgården ferry.

Sightseeing

A pleasant way of enjoying Stockholm from the water is to take an excursion run by Stockholm Sightseeing (**Strömma Kanalbolaget**).

Red city bus and blue "feeder" bus

DIRECTORY

Traffic Information

Stockholms Lokaltrafik
Tel 08-600 10 00.
w sl.se

Cycling

Djurgårdscykeln
Tel 031-227 227.
w djurgardscykeln.se

Taxis

Taxi Kurir
Tel 08-30 00 00.

Taxi Stockholm
Tel 08-15 00 00.

Taxi 020
Tel 020-20 20 20.

Archipelago and Sightseeing Boats

Open Top Tours
Tel 08-12 00 40 00.
w opentoptours.com

Strömma Kanalbolaget
Nybrokajen, Stadshusbron.
Tel 08-12 00 40 00.
w stromma.se

Waxholmsbolaget
Strömkajen, Vaxholm, Stavsnäs.
Tel 08-679 58 30.
w waxholmsbolaget.se

A "Round Kungsholmen" tour departs hourly from the quayside near the City Hall. The "Under Stockholm's Bridges" and "Round Djurgården" tours depart from Strömkajen near the Grand Hotel, and passengers are also picked up from Nybroplan. Tickets can be bought at both these points. A commentary is provided on headsets in several languages. The tours generally run once an hour. Most tours are only available in the summer, but some run until December.

Sightseeing tours by bus include the **Open Top Tours** double-deckers, which run between strategic stops close to attractions in central Stockholm. Passengers can hop on and off along the way.

General Index

Acknowledgments

Streiffert Förlag would like to thank the following staff at Dorling Kindersley:

Publisher
Douglas Amrine

Publishing Managers
Jane Ewart, Anna Streiffert

Senior Editor
Christine Stroyan

Map Co-ordinator
Casper Morris

DTP Manager
Jason Little

Production Controller
Linda Dare

Additional Picture Research
Rachel Barber

Additional Photography
Ian O'Leary

Dorling Kindersley would like to thank all those whose contributions and assistance have made the preparation of this book possible.

Main Contributors
ULF JOHANSSON has produced Swedish guidebooks such as *Sverigeboken* and *Sverigevägvisaren*. He has also been a publisher and year-book editor at the Swedish tourist association Svenska Turistföreningen.

MONA NEPPENSTROM is an editor and travel journalist and has written a large number of Swedish guidebooks, including *Sverigeboken, Sverigevägvisaren, Turisttoppen* and rail company SJ's travel guide series *Längs spåret.*

KAJ SANDELL wrote the *Eyewitness Stockholm* travel guide. He is a journalist and formerly wrote for Swedish publishers Åhlén & Åkerlunds Förlag and Swedish daily broadsheet *Dagens Nyheter.*

Factchecking
Lena Ahlgren

Proofreader
Stewart J Wild

Index
Helen Peters

Artwork Reference
Svenska Aerobilder AB

Revisions Team
Namrata Adhwaryu, Parnika Bagla, Kate Berens, Subhashree Bharti, Hilary Bird, Alannah Eames, Anna-Maria Espsater, Anna Freiberger, Amy Harrison, Yvette Holman, Shobhna Iyer, Bharti Karakoti, Leena Lane, Alison McGill, Sonal Modha, Vikki Nousiainen, Susie Peachey, Rada Radojicic, Lucy Richards, Ellen Root, Marta Bescos Sanchez, Kathleen Sauret, Sands Publishing Solutions, Kathleen Blankenship Sauret, Azeem Siddiqui, Rituraj Singh, Deepika Verma, Nikhil Verma, Steven Vickers, Alex Whittleton.

Photography Permissions
The publishers would like to thank all those who gave permission to photograph at museums, palaces, churches, restaurants, hotels, stores and other sights too numerous to list individually. Particular thanks go to the Guild of Museum Directors in Stockholm for permitting access to picture archives as well as making additional photographing of objects and exhibitions possible.

Picture Credits
a = above; b = below/bottom; c = centre; f = far; l = left; r = right; t = top. .

Works of art have been reproduced with the permission of the following copyright holders:

© ADAGP, Paris and DACS, London 2008: Paradise 1963 Jean Tinguely and Niki de sainte Phalle 53bl, 80clb; © DACS, London: Nils Ferlin KG Bejemark 239c; Concrete Jonas Bohlin 31tr; Noble Glass carafe Gunnar Cyren 304clb; The Dying Dandy Nils Dardel 86bl; The Child's Brain Giorgio De Chirico 85bl; The Dance Carl Eldh 107bl; Selma Lagerlof Carl Eldh 237bl; Einar Forseth 106tr; Simon Gate 157tr; statue of Evert Taube Gordon Willy Gordon 66clb; Hans Hedberg 30tr; Visby Wall Hanna Hirsch-Pauli 168tr; Altarpiece in Jukkasjärvi Church Bror Hjort 276c; Märta Måås-Fjetterström 30br; Orpheus Carl Milles 75tl; Poseidon Carl Milles 197cr, 204t; Sigurd Persson 31tl; Crux rug Pia Wallen 304bl; © DACS. London/VAGA, New York 2008: Monogram Robert Rauschenberg 86crb; © Succession Picasso/DACS, London 2008; Breakfast Outdoors Pablo Picasso 84tr.

Every effort has been made to trace the copyright holders. Dorling Kindersley apologizes for any unintentional omission and would be pleased, in such cases, to add an acknowledgment in future editions.

Commissioned by the publisher, the book's main photographers, Peter Hanneberg, Erik Svensson and Jeppe Wikström, produced the majority of the photographs reproduced in this book. They have also contributed archive pictures which have been listed among the other picture credits. The publisher would like to thank the photographers and all the other individuals, organizations and picture libraries for permission to reproduce their photographs and illustrations:

Alamy images: Annems 20; Arterra Picture Library 2-3; Marie-Louise Avery 292cl; blickwinkel 144; Matija Brumen 270tl; Frank Chmura 17b, 78; Peter Forsberg 293c; Hemis 324br; Niels Poulsen Kirke 188-9; Lphoto 211b; Nicholas Pitt 293tl; Prisma / Chmura Frank 210; Dirk Renckhoff 167tr; Rohan Van Twest 198bl. **Amarok AB**: Magnus Elander 24tr, 24clb. **Armémuseum**: 270bl. **Áttje Fjäll- och Samemuseum**: Jan Gustavsson 28tr.

Brygghuset Restaurant: 297tc.

Corbis: Bettmann 6-7; Bob Krist 162; Hans Strand 274-5; Heritage Images 8-9.

Creperiet & Logi: 297bl.

Dreamstime.com: Per Björkdahl 177clb; Alexander Bondarchiuk 14b; Gunold Brunbauer 25cb; Byggam79 206-7; Kim Carlson 13b; Hans Christiansson 33br, 59tl; Davthy 172br; Michael Elliott 25clb; Rose-marie Henriksson 11c; Inger Anne Hulbækdal 328b; Jensottoson 316-7; Stefan Johansson 146cl; Joyfull 65tr; Ingemar Magnusson 160bc; Mamahoohooba 327tl; Antony Mcaulay 13tl, 16bl; Sophie Mcaulay 10cl, 29tr; Rolf52 246-247, 327bl; Sasalan999 194, Stef22 23t; Victorianl 166tl.

Drottningholms Slottsteater: Bengt Wanselius 115tr, 115bc.

Fagersta Turism: 143cl. **Hotel Fjällgården:** 288b. **Fjärils & Fågelhuset:** 103cl. **Fotolia:** Mikhail Markovskly 14 cr; Philipp Weiss 219br.

Frantzén: Stefan van der Kwast Gissberg 291br.

Getty Images: AFP 249cla; Christian Aslund 14tr; David Clapp 266; Dan Wiklund 174. **Gondolen Restaurant:** 295t. **Gunnebo Slott:**229cla. **Göteborg & Co**: 319bl. **Göteborgs Konstmuseum:** *Karin and Kersti*, Carl Larsson 241br. **Grand Öl & Mat:** Martin Axén 298tl. **Den Gyldene Freden Restaurant:** 294b.

HSB Malmö 2006: Ole Jais 185lbr. **Peter Hanneberg:** 4-5tc, 24cla, 24cra, 25tc, 25tr, 25cl, 25br, 27cr, 28bl, 29cb, 129b, 165bl, 165br, 173tr; 251b, 252c, 262bl, 263tr, 267b, 272c, 273br, 278cla, 279crb, 279br, 310bc, 312b, 313tl, 313b. **Christer Hägg:** *East Indiaman Wasa*, Jacob Hägg 202bl. **Härjedalens Fjällmuseum:** Joakim Lagercrantz 264clb. **Hotell St. Clemens:** 282cla.

ICEHOTEL Sweden: 282b, 301bl, 382b. **IMS Bildbyrå:** 49tl.

Jay Fu Restaurant: 296tl. **Jönköpings Läns Museum:** *Bianca Maria in Among Elves and Trolls*, John Bauer 29bl; **Jumbo Stay Hotel:** 284b.

Kolmardens Djurpark: Rickard Monéus 148tl. **Kosta Boda:** Ann Wåhlström 31bl; Ulrika Hydman Vallien 156bc; Kjell Engman 157bc. **Kungliga Biblioteket:** 42br, 76bl. **Kungliga Husgerådskammaren:** Alexis Daflos 4br, 60tr, 60clb, 61tr, 113tc; 112cl, 112bl, 113bl, 114tr, 114clb; *The Triumph of Karl XI*, Jacques Foucquet 43tl; 52b; Håkan Lind 58cb; 59cr, 60cla, 113cr; 139cl. **Kungliga Myntka-binettet:** 57crb; Jan Eve Olsson 62cl, 75tr. **Kungliga Operan:** Mats Bäcker 70tr, 73tl, 73c. **Källemo AB:** 31c.

Livrustkammaren: 43bl, 47br; Göran Schmidt 47cla, 57tl; Nina Heins 62bl.

Malmö Turism: Mårten Swemark 183tl; **Medelhavsmuseet:** Ove Kaneberg 70cla. **Moderna Museet:** 84br, 84bl; Per Anders Allsten 84bc. **Museum tre Kronor:** 61br.

Nationalmuseum: 30clb; *Flowers on the Windowsill*, Carl Larsson 30–31c; *Gustav Vasa*, Cornelius Arendtz 36; *Ansgar Preaches Christianity*, Georg Pauli 38bl; *Stockholm Bloodbath*, Dionysius Padt-Brügge 39t; *The Entry of King Gustav Vasa of Sweden into Stockholm, 1523*, Carl Larsson 40t; *Portrait of Erik XIV*, Steven van der Meulen 40c; *The Fire at the Royal Palace 7th May 1697*, Johan Fredrik Höckert 41tr; *Portrait of Queen Kristina*, David Beck 41clb; *The Death of Gustav II Adolf of Sweden at the Battle of Lutzen*, Carl Wahlbom 42bl; *The Crossing of the Belt*, Johan Philip Lemke 42–43cr; *Karl X Gustav*, Sébastien Bourdon 43cr; *Bringing Home the Body of King Karl XII of Sweden*, Gustaf Cederström 43br; *King Gustav III of Sweden*, Lorens Pasch d.y. 44tl; *Portrait of the Bernadotte Family*, Fredrik Westin 44crb; *The Coronation of Gustav III*, Carl Gustav Pilo 46cla; *The Battle at Svensksund*, J T Schoultz 46clb; *A Noisy Dinner*, Johan Tobias Sergel 46bc; *Conversation at Drottningholm*, Pehr Hilleström 46–47c; *The Murder of Gustav III*, A W Küssner 47tr; *Bacchanal on Andros*, Peter Paul Rubens 53tl; 59br; *The Conspiracy of the Batavians under Claudius Civilis*, Rembrant 86cla; *Amor and Psyche* (1787) Johan Tobias Sergel 86clb; 86bc; *Lamino Chair*

(1955) Yngve Ekstrom photo Hans Thorwid 87clb;*The Love Lesson*, Antoine Watteau 86tr; *The Lady with the Veil*, Alexander Roslin 87tl; *Karl XIV Johan's Visit to Berga*, A C Wetterling 150tr; *Valdemar Atterdag Plunders Visby 1361*, Carl Gustaf Hellqvist 171br. **Naturhistoriska Riksmuseet:** Staffan Waerndt 102c. **Nordiska Museet:** Birgit Brånvall 94tr; Mats Landin 53tr; 94cl; Sören Hallgren 94bc; *Snowstorm at Sea*, August Strindberg 95cr; 95ca; *The Proposal*, Knut Ekwall 95tl. **Östasiatiska museet:** 80tl, Erik Cornelius 82bl; Karl Zetterstrom 80cla.

Parken Zoo I Eskilstuna AB: 139bc. **Pensionat Warfsholm:** Staffan Fritz 286bl. **Postmuseum:** 65crb. **Pressens Bild:** 5tr, 21b, 22tl; Hans T. Dahlskog 49br; 93tl; Jan Delden 74br; Gunnar Seijbold 77tl; Axel Malmström 105tr; 111br, 126tr, 302cr, 303tl, 308cr, 314tl.

Red Boat Hotel: 283b. **Rederi AB Göta Kanal:**151cra. **Laila Reppen:** 26–27c. **Riksbank:** 323cra, 323cl, 323cr, 323clb, 323crb, 323bl, 323bc, 323br. **The Royal Court (Kungliga Hovstaterna):** Alexis Daflos 58bc, 59c, Charlotte Gawell 76cr, Håkan Lind 58cl.

Salt & Brygga: 298b. **Scandic Hotels:** 285t, 287tr, 289t. **Sheraton Stockholm:** 283t; **Villa Sjötorp:** 290b, 299t. **Sjöhistoriska Museet:** 100c. **Skansen:** Marie Andersson 12br. **Skogskyrkogården:**111c. **Ingalill Snitt:** 26tr. **Statens Historiska Museum:** 90cla, 90clb, 90bl, 90br, 91tc, 91ca, 91cb, 91br, 91bl, 136br. **Steninge Slott:** 136t. **Stockholm Arlanda Airport:** 326bl. **Stockholm Marathon:** Martin Ekequist 33tl. **Stockholms Auktionsverk:** 47bl. **Stockholms Stadshus:** Jan Asplund 107br, 107tl. **Stockholms Stadsmuseum:** *Tre Kronor Palace*, Govert Camphuysen 42cl; *Newspaper Readers*, J A Cronstedt 45tl; *The Regicide Anckarström Punished in Front of the House of Nobility*, 47cr; 48clb, 49clb. **Strindbergsmuseet:** Per Bergström 75bc. **Sturehof:** Håkan Elofsson 291tl. **Superstock:** Age Fotostock 124-5; Anders Ekholm 35cr; Macduff Everton 50-1; Robert Harding Picture Library 128; Hemis.fr 35tc; Imagebroker.net 222-3, 264br; Image Source 68; Johner 250; Jonathan Larsen t; Nordic Photos 192, 263bl; Prisma 145b; Stock Connection 116cla, 152-3, 232. **Svenska Akademien:** Leif Jansson 46tr. **Rolf Sørensen:** 24bl, 25bl.

Thielska Galleriet: *Hornsgatan*, Eugène Jansson 99tl.

Vasaloppsmuseet: 249cra, 249br. **Vasamuseet:** Hans Hammarskiöld 53br, 96tc, 96cla, 96bl, 96br, 97tc, 97cra; 97br, 97bl. **Spritmuseum:** 93c. **Visit Karskrona:** Therese Hagstrom 193cr.

Claes Westlin: 30cla. **Jeppe Wikström:** 32br, 35bl, 62tr, 70bl, 71crb, 71bl, 74tl, 82br, 83ca, 92t, 103br, 105cla, 105br, 106br, 108t, 109t, 109bl, 116cr, 117tl, 117br, 308bl.

Front Endpapers: Alamy Images: blickwinkel Rbc, Prisma / Chmura Frank Lc. **Corbis:** Bob Krist Rc. **Dreamstime:** Sasalan999 Lcl.; **Getty Images:** David Clapp Lbl. **Superstock:** Johner Rcr, Robert Harding Picture Library Rbr, Stock Connection Ltr

Cover: Front - Alamy Images: Johner Images main. Spine - **Alamy Images:** Johner Images t.

Special Editions of DK Travel Guides

DK Travel Guides can be purchased in bulk quantities at discounted prices for use in promotions or as premiums. We are also able to offer special editions and personalized jackets, corporate imprints, and excerpts from all of our books, tailored specifically to meet your own needs.

To find out more, please contact:

in the US **specialsales@dk.com**

in the UK **travelguides@uk.dk.com**

in Canada **specialmarkets@dk.com**

in Australia **penguincorporatesales@penguin randomhouse.com.au**

Phrase Book

When reading the imitated pronunciation, stress the part which is underlined. Pronounce each syllable as if it formed part of an English word, and you will be understood sufficiently well. Remember the points below, and your pronunciation will be even closer to the correct Swedish.

ai:	as in 'fair' or 'stair'
ea:	as in 'ear' or 'hear'
ew:	like the sound in 'dew'
EW:	try to say 'ee' with your lips rounded
oo:	as in 'book' or 'soot'
OO:	as in 'spoon' or 'groom'
r:	should be strongly pronounced

Swedish Alphabetical Order
In the list below we have followed Swedish alphabetical order. The following letters are listed after z: å, ä, ö.

You
There are two words for 'you': 'du' and 'ni'. 'Ni' is the polite form; 'du' is the familiar form. It is not impolite to address a complete stranger with the familiar form.

In an Emergency

Help!	Hjälp!	yelp
Stop!	Stanna!	stanna!
Call a doctor!	Ring efter en doktor!	ring efter ehn doktor
Call an ambulance!	Ring efter en ambulans!	ring efter ehn ambewlgnss
Call the police!	Ring polisen!	ring poleesen
Call the fire brigade!	Ring efter brandkåren!	ring efter brandkawren
Where is the nearest telephone?	Var finns närmaste telefon?	vahr finnss ngirmasteh- telefgwn
Where is the nearest hospital?	Var finns närmaste sjukhus?	vahr finnss- ngirmasteh shewkhews

Communication Essentials

Yes	Ja	yah
No	Nej	nay
Please (offering)	Varsågod	vahrshawgOOd
Thank you	Tack	tack
Excuse me	Ursäkta	ewrshekta
Hello	Hej	hay
Goodbye	Hej då/adjö	haydaw/ahyur
Good night	God natt	goongtt
Morning	Morgon	morron
Afternoon	Eftermiddag	eftermiddahg
Evening	Kväll	kvell
Yesterday	Igår	ee gawr
Today	Idag	ee dahg
Tomorrow	I morgon	ee morron
Here	Här	hair
There	Där	dair
What?	Vad?	vah
When?	När?	nair
Why?	Varför?	vahrfurr
Where?	Var?	vahr

Useful Phrases

How are you?	Hur mår du?	hewr mawr dew
Very well, thank you.	Mycket bra, tack.	mewkeh brah, tack
Pleased to meet you.	Trevligt att träffas.	treavlit att trqffas
See you soon.	Vi ses snart.	vee seas snahrt
That's fine.	Det går bra.	dea gawr brgh
Where is/are …?	Var finns …?	vahr finnss….
How far is it to …?	Hur långt är det till …?	hewr lawngt ea dea till
Which way to …?	Hur kommer jag till …?	hewr kommer yah till …
Do you speak English?	Talar du/ni engelska?	tghlar dew/nee engelska
I don't understand	Jag förstår inte.	yah furshtgwr inteh
Could you speak more slowly, please?	Kan du/ni tala långsammare, tack.	kan dew/nee tghla lgwng- ssamareh tack
I'm sorry.	Förlåt.	furrlgwt

Useful Words

big	stor	stOOr
small	liten	leeten
hot	varm	varrm
cold	kall	kall
good	bra	brah
bad	dålig	dawleeg
enough	tillräcklig	tillraikleeg
open	öppen	urpen
closed	stängd	staingd
left	vänster	vainster
right	höger	hurger
straight on	rakt fram	rahkt fram
near	nära	ngira
far	långt	lawngt
up/over	upp/över	ewp/urver
down/under	ner/under	near/ewnder
early	tidig	teedee
late	sen	sehn
entrance	ingång	ingawng
exit	utgång	Ewtgawng
toilet	toalett	too-alett
more	mer	mehr
less	mindre	meendre

Shopping

How much is this?	Hur mycket kostar den här?	hewr mewkeh kostar dehn hair
I would like …	Jag skulle vilja …	yah skewleh vilya
Do you have?	Har du/ni …?	hahr dew/nee…
I'm just looking	Jag ser mig bara omkring	yah sear may bghra omkring
Do you take? credit cards	Tar du/ni kreditkort?	tahr dew/nee kredeetkoort
What time do you open	När öppnar ni?	nair urpnar nee
What time do you close?	När stänger ni?	nair stginger nee
This one.	den här	dehn hair
That one.	den där	dehn dair
expensive	dyr	dewr
cheap	billig	billig
size (clothes)	storlek	stOOrlek
white	vit	veet
black	svart	svart
red	röd	rurd
yellow	gul	gewl
green	grön	grurn
blue	blå	blaw
antique shop	antikaffär	anteek-affair
bakery	bageri	bahgeree
bank	bank	bank
book shop	bokhandel	bOOkhandel
butcher	slaktare	slgktareh
cake shop	konditori	konditoree
chemist	apotek	apotegk
fishmonger	fiskaffär	fisk-affair
grocer	mataffär	mght-affair
hairdresser	frisör	frissurr
market	marknad	mgrrknad
newsagent	tidningskiosk	teednings-cheeosk
post office	postkontor	posstkontOOr
shoe shop	skoaffär	skOO-affair
supermarket	snabbköp	sngbbchurp
tobacconist's	tobakshandel	tOObaks-handel
travel agency	resebyrå	reasseh-bewraw

Sightseeing

art gallery	konstgalleri	konnst-galleree
church	kyrka	chwrka
garden	trädgård	traidgawrd
house	hus	hews
library	bibliotek	beebleeotgk
museum	museum	mewseum
square	torg	tohrj
street	gata	gahta
tourist information office	turist- informations- kontor	tureest- informashOOns- kontOOr
town hall	stadshus	stgtshews
closed for holiday	stängt för semester	staingt furr semgster
bus station	busstation	bewss-stashOOn
railway station	järnvägsstation	yairnvaigs-stashOOn

Staying in a Hotel

Do you have any vacancies?	Har ni några lediga rum?	hahr nee nawgra legdiga rewm
double room with double bed	dubbelrum med dubbelsäng	doobelrewm med doobel- seng

alternatives for a female speaker are shown in brackets

twin room	dubbelrum	doobelrewm
	med två	med tvaw
	sängar	sengar
single room	enkelrum	enkelrewm
room with	rum med	rewm med
a bath	bad	bahd
shower	dusch	dewsh
key	nyckel	niwckel
I have a	Jag har	yah hahr
reservation	beställt rum	bestellt rewm

Eating Out

Have you got a	Har ni ett	hahr nee ett
table for…	bord för…?	bOOrd furr…
I would like	Jag skulle vilja	yah skewleh vilya
to reserve	boka ett	bOOka ett
a table.	bord.	bOOrd
The bill, please.	Notan, tack.	nOOtan, tack
I am a	Jag är	yah air
vegetarian	vegetarian	vegetariahn
waitress	servitris	sairvitreess
waiter	servitör	sairviturr
menu	meny/	menw/
	matsedel	mahtseadel
fixed-price	meny med	menw med
menu	fast pris	fast prees
wine list	vinlista	veenlista
glass of water	ett glas	ett glahss
	vatten	vatten
glass of wine	ett glas vin	ett glahss veen
bottle	flaska	flaska
knife	kniv	k-neev
fork	gaffel	gaffel
spoon	sked	shead
breakfast	frukost	frewkost
lunch	lunch	lewnch
dinner	middag	middahg
main course	huvudrätt	hewvewdrett
starter	förrätt	furrett
dish of the day	dagens rätt	dahgens rett
coffee	kaffe	kaffeh
rare	blodig	blOOdee
medium	medium	medium
well done	välstekt	vailstehkt

Menu Decoder

abborre	abborreh	perch
ansjovis	anshOOvees	anchovies
apelsin	appelseen	orange
bakelse	bahkelse	cake, pastry, tart
banan	banahn	banana
biff	biff	beef
bröd	brurd	bread
bullar	bewllar	buns
choklad	shooklahd	chocolate
citron	sitrOOn	lemon
dessert	dessair	dessert
fisk	fisk	fish
fläsk	flaisk	pork
forell	fooraill	trout
frukt	fruckt	fruit
glass	glass	ice cream
gurka	gewrka	cucumber
grönsaksgryta	grurnsahks-grewta	vegetable stew
hummer	humm-er	lobster
kallskuret	kall-skuret	cold meat
korv	koorv	sausages
kyckling	chwkling	chicken
kött	churtt	meat
lamm	lamm	lamb
lök	lurk	onion
mineralvatten	minerahl-vatten	mineral water
med/utan	mehd/ewtan	still/sparkling
kolsyra	kawlsewra	
mjölk	m-yurlk	milk
nötkött	nurtchurtt	beef
nötter	nurtter	nuts
ost	oost	cheese
olja	olya	oil
oliver	oleever	olives
paj/kaka	pa-y/kahka	pie/cake
potatis	potahtis	potatoes
peppar	peppar	pepper
ris	rees	rice
rostat bröd	rostat brurd	toast
räkor	raikoor	prawns
rökt skinka	rurkt sheenka	cured ham
rött vin	rurtt veen	red wine
saft	safft	lemonade
salt	sallt	salt
sill	seell	herring

skaldjur	skahl-yewr	seafood
smör	smurr	butter
stekt	stehkt	fried
strömming	strurmming	baltic herring
socker	socker	sugar
soppa	soppa	soup
sås	saws	sauce
te	tea	tea
torr	torr	dry
ungsstekt	ewngs-stehkt	baked, roast
vinäger	vinniger	vinegar
vispgrädde	veesp-graiddeh	whipped cream
vitlök	veet-lurk	garlic
vitt vin	veett veen	white wine
ägg	aigg	egg
älg	ail-y	elk
äpple	aippleh	apple
öl	url	beer

Numbers

0	noll	noll
1	ett	ett
2	två	tvaw
3	tre	trea
4	fyra	fewra
5	fem	fem
6	sex	sex
7	sju	shew
8	åtta	otta
9	nio	nee-oo
10	tio	tee-oo
11	elva	elva
12	tolv	tolv
13	tretton	tretton
14	fjorton	f-yoorton
15	femton	femton
16	sexton	sexton
17	sjutton	shewton
18	arton	ahrton
19	nitton	nitton
20	tjugo	chwgoo
21	tjugoett	chwgoo-ett
22	tjugotvå	chwgoo-tvaw
30	trettio	tretti
31	trettioett	tretti-ett
40	fyrtio	furrti
50	femtio	femti
60	sextio	sexti
70	sjuttio	shewti
80	åttio	otti
90	nittio	nitti
100	(ett) hundra	(ett) hewndra
101	etthundraett	ett-hewndra-ett
102	etthundratvå	ett-hewndra-tvaw
200	tvåhundra	tvawhewndra
300	trehundra	treahewndra
400	fyrahundra	fewrahewndra
500	femhundra	femhewndra
600	sexhundra	sexhewndra
700	sjuhundra	shewhewndra
800	åttahundra	ottahewndra
900	niohundra	nee-oohewndra
1,000	(ett) tusen	(ett) tewssen
1,001	etttusenett	ett-tewssen-ett
100,000	(ett) hundra-	(ett) hewndra
	tusen	tewssen
1,000,000	en miljon	ehn milyOOn

Time

one minute	en minut	ehn meenewt
one hour	en timme	ehn timmeh
half an hour	en halvtimme	ehn halvtimmeh
ten past one	tio över ett	teeoo urver ett
quarter past one	kvart över ett	kvahrt urver ett
half past one	halv två	halv tvaw
twenty to two	tjugo i två	chwgoo ee tvaw
quarter to two	kvart i två	kvahrt ee tvaw
two o'clock	klockan två	klockan tvaw
13.00	klockan tretton	klockan tretton
16.30	sexton och trettio	sexton ock tretti
noon	klockan tolv	klockan tolv
midnight	midnatt	meednatt
Monday	måndag	mawndahg
Tuesday	tisdag	teesdahg
Wednesday	onsdag	oonssdahg
Thursday	torsdag	toorsdahg
Friday	fredag	freadahg
Saturday	lördag	lurdahg
Sunday	söndag	surndahg

alternatives for a female speaker are shown in brackets

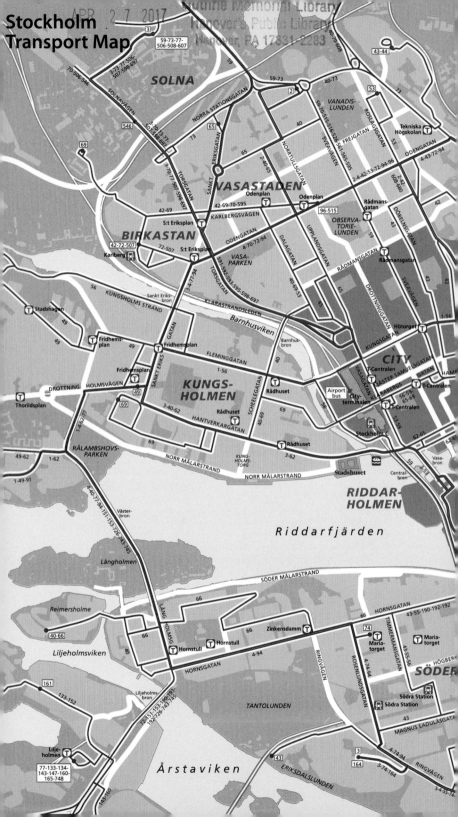